D1569787

The Mongol Conquests

The Military Operations of Genghis Khan and Sübe'etei

Carl Fredrik Sverdrup

 Helion & Company Limited

Helion & Company Limited
26 Willow Road
Solihull
West Midlands
B91 1UE
England
Tel. 0121 705 3393
Fax 0121 711 4075
Email: info@helion.co.uk
Website: www.helion.co.uk
Twitter: @helionbooks
Visit our blog http://blog.helion.co.uk/

Published by Helion & Company 2017
Designed and typeset by Serena Jones
Cover designed by Paul Hewitt, Battlefield Design (www.battlefield-design.co.uk)
Printed by Gutenberg Press Limited, Tarxien, Malta

Text © Carl Fredrik Sverdrup 2016
Maps drawn by George Anderson © Helion & Company 2016
Cover: Defeat of the Iranians at the Battle of Ladan. Book of Kings (per 114, f. 38a), Chester Beatty Library
(Dublin)

ISBN 978-1-910777-71-8

British Library Cataloguing-in-Publication Data.
A catalogue record for this book is available from the British Library.

For details of other military history titles published by Helion & Company
Limited contact the above address, or visit our website: http://www.helion.co.uk.

We always welcome receiving book proposals from prospective authors.

Contents

List of Maps

Preface

My study of the Mongols and their military operations has over the years gone through several stages. I started reading Western, mainly English, books on the subject. Dupuy & Dupuy's *Encyclopaedia of Military History* provided the first introduction. In their overview of the history of warfare from 3,500 BC to the present, they included a substantial section on the Mongols. They ranked Genghis Khan as one of 12 'Great Captains' of military history and lauded the Mongols for their military brilliance. The books of Liddell Hart, Harold Lamb, Michael Prawdin, James Chambers, Leo de Hartog, and Stephen Turnbull added to this beginning. With this base, the next level of my Mongol 'journey' was to understand the sources these authors had relied on. Most European and Near Eastern primary sources are readily available in English, German, or French and so is the Mongolian *Secret History*. The Chinese sources, notably the dynastic histories, presented a bigger challenge. De Mailla (1730), Gaubil (1739), and de Harlez (1887) made translations of the dynastic histories long ago. These are, however, condensed accounts and the translations of titles and names are often difficult to follow. Further, the translations are not supplemented with extensive commentary as is now standard in such works. Some limited parts of the *Yuanshi* and the first part of *Shengwujinzhenglu* have been properly translated. However, with these few exceptions, the rest of the Chinese source material is unavailable to Western readers. The task in the third and final stage of my Mongol research was to work my way through the 'raw' Chinese dynastic histories with the help of Abel Yu, an experienced Chinese translator. Supplemented by the scholarly articles as well as Desmond Martin's book *The Rise of Chingis Khan And His Conquest Of North China*, I was able to develop a better understanding of the Mongol military campaigns.

My Mongol studies were driven by a desire to know what really happened. It was only afterwards that I considered using the research for other purposes. I have published two articles on the Mongols in academic journals. The first looked at the numbers of the Mongol armies at different times, while the second, at the recommendation of Igor de Rachewiltz, dealt with Sübe'etei. This book is a more ambitious step, a full military history of the Mongols.

The eminent Norman Baynes wrote an article called *The Military Operations of the Emperor Heraclios* more than a century ago. I read this wanting to understand how Heraclios operated against the Sasanians from 622 to 628. The article was a brilliant start for the subject, even if the reconstruction of the campaigns I now consider correct is very different from the version of Baynes. The format and approach of his study was, however, very good and hoping to match his spirit I have given the book the subtitle *The Military Operations of Genghis Khan and Sübe'etei*. A specialised or selective study can look at the subject in depth, avoiding areas where the sources are weak. A broader narrative can avoid difficult areas by being vague. I have made a broad-based narrative without shying away from details. To construct a narrative, much guesswork and assumptions are needed at times. Hopefully, I explain the assumptions well and leave the ground open for others to improve on the narrative. Our understanding of the Mongol military campaigns is certain to improve with time. Hopefully this reconstruction, like that of Baynes for Heraclios, can contribute positively to this process. As rendered by the '36 Stratagems', I 'toss out a brick to attract the jade.'

I would like to thank publisher Duncan Rogers, editor Serena Jones, and map maker George Anderson for helping transform my script and drafts into this book.

Introduction

Seven hundred years ago a man almost conquered the earth. He made himself master of half the known world, and inspired mankind with a fear that lasted for generations.

– Harold Lamb[1]

Napoleon associated great military achievement closely with individual military genius, saying:

The Gauls were not conquered by the Roman legions, but by Caesar. It was not before the Carthaginian soldiers that Rome was made to tremble, but before Hannibal. It was not the Macedonian phalanx which reached India, but Alexander. It was not the French army that reached Weser and the Inn; it was Turenne. Prussia was not defended for seven years against the three most formidable European powers by the Prussian soldiers but by Frederick the Great.[2]

During the 13th century, the Mongols established the greatest land-based empire known to history, stretching at one point from the Adriatic Sea in the west to the China Sea in the east. Initially an insignificant tribal group, the Mongols united the Inner Asian tribes under their leadership and then proceeded to make territorial conquests unequalled in speed and extent. What genius, it may be asked, was the driving force behind this achievement?

Genghis Khan was the dominant personality of the early Mongol period. To Napoleon and his era, Genghis Khan was a bloodthirsty conqueror who overwhelmed his foes with innumerable forces. It was only during the first part of the 20th century that the Mongols came to be seen as masters of warfare who won by means of skill rather than numbers, and Genghis Khan was accepted as one of most outstanding military commanders known to history. Had Napoleon made his comment in, say, 1934 he might have included Genghis Khan amongst his Great Captains. American

---

1   Harold Lamb, Genghis Khan, *The Emperor of All Men* (New York: R. M. McBride and Co., 1927), p.1.
2   *Memoirs ecrits a Sainte-Helene*, Montholon, volume 2 (Paris, 1847), p.90. Napoleon also counted Gustav II Adolf and Eugene amongst his Great Captains, having in total seven.

general MacArthur was certainly impressed. He wrote during that year in his closing report as Chief of Staff:

> Were the accounts of all battles, save only those of Genghis Khan, effaced from the pages of history, and were the facts of his campaigns preserved in descriptive detail, the soldier would still possess a mine of untold wealth from which to extract nuggets of knowledge useful in moulding an army for future use. The successes of that amazing leader, beside which the triumphs of most other commanders in history pale into insignificance, are proof sufficient of his unerring instinct for the fundamental qualifications of an army.[3]

The Mongol Empire continued to expand after the death of Genghis Khan. The later conquests are closely associated with his general Sübe'etei. Not as widely known as Genghis Khan, Sübe'etei has gained a high reputation amongst military specialists. For example, famed military theorist Liddell Hart wrote: 'As a logistical strategist Napoleon is unrivalled in history – save possibly by the Mongol Subutai, from what we can pierce together from the scanty records of his campaigns.'[4]

Though many military historians and commentators regard Genghis Khan and Sübe'etei highly, the details of their actual operations are far from clear to them. One of the most well-known Mongol campaigns is the one Genghis Khan directed against Khwarezm in what is now Uzbekistan during 1220. It has been described in detail in many popular militarily-focussed accounts, for example by Liddell Hart, Trevor Dupuy, and James Chambers. Liddell Hart and Dupuy both have high reputations as military theorists and commentators and Chambers wrote a very influential account of the Mongols' campaigns in the Near East and Europe. However with regard to the Mongol operations against Khwarezm they fail to agree on basic details. According to Liddell Hart the Mongol left wing struck from Kashgar in the east, entering Ferghana to 'distract' the enemy (for locations see map 14). The Mongol main forces, in the west, struck through the Kyzylkum Desert to suddenly appear in front of Bokhara. Dupuy improved on this narrative, saying the Mongol left struck from Kashgar across the Pamir Mountains to the lower Amu Darya, an ambitious outflanking movement. Further, he proposed the main forces actually moved *around* Aral Lake to reach Bokhara from the north-west. Chambers adopted the version of Liddell Hart with regard to the movement of the main army, but made the left wing execute an outflanking movement as described by Dupuy. Adding his own twist, he says another Mongol column coming from Kashgar made hit and run attacks along the entire length of the Syr Darya – the enemy front. With such major differences it is fair to wonder 'who is right?' In fact, as will be seen later, none are.

Liddell Hart, Harold Lamb, and Michael Prawdin published articles and books during the years between the First and Second World Wars, helping to shape a new

---

3   Gavin Long, *MacArthur as Military Commander* (London: Batsford, 1969), pp.43–44.
4   B.H. Liddell Hart, *Scipio Africanus: Greater than Napoleon* (New York: Da Capo Press, 1994), p.257.

view of the Mongols. They saw the Mongols as military supermen.[5] The generals of the First World War were widely criticised for being unimaginative and ineffective, suffering great losses in dead and wounded that could have been avoided. The Mongols provided an example of how war should be waged; by means of brilliant strategy they were held to have won easy victories. Liddell Hart wrote: 'they had grasped the essentials of strategy, while their tactical mechanism was so perfect that the higher conceptions of tactics were unnecessary'.[6] Harold Lamb worried that Nazi Germany had unlocked Mongol secrets: 'There are other indications than these that readers in the Third Reich have made a close study of the Mongol campaigns and especially the Mongol technique of attack.'[7] The Western historiographical 'Mongol supermen school' has evolved and gained traction up until the present, sustained by a remarkable unwillingness to make use of primary and good-quality secondary sources. A whole host of later historians have added to the original narrative. Later authors include Trevor Dupuy, Leo de Hartog, James Chambers, Stephen Turnbull, Bevin Alexander, and Richard Gabriel to list a few. They all agree on the brilliance of the Mongols, but cannot agree on operational specifics. This holds true for the 1241 invasion of Central Europe, the 1220 campaign discussed above, and even more for operations in China. None of the cited authors had access to many primary sources. While most know the *Secret History* and some of the Muslim sources, the bulk of the Chinese sources have not been properly translated into any European language. Without these it is difficult to go into detail with regard to many military operations of the Mongols.

The military campaigns and operations of notable commanders such as Alexander III ('the Great'), Hannibal, Caesar, or Napoleon are dealt with in detail in many high-quality works. Authors describe events step by step and consider the decisions taken by the commanders at different points. They review alternatives and evaluate the performance of the key players. Alexander is often faulted for not pursuing the Persians after defeating them at Issus in 333 BC; Hannibal for not marching on Rome in 216 BC; and Caesar for dallying with Cleopatra in Egypt when his foes raised new forces in Africa and Iberia in 47–46 BC. In Belgium in 1815, misunderstandings left the corps of French officer Erlon marching between two battlefields without having an impact on either of them, perhaps denying Napoleon a decisive victory. Napoleon relied on certain strategic ploys he tended to repeat. When he defeated two enemy armies in detail in 1796 it was a novel idea. When he tried the same in 1815 his foes knew what he was up to and did what it took to defeat him. When Federal commander Grant struck into the Wilderness in 1864 he was severely mauled by Confederate commander Lee, but instead of accepting defeat and retreat, as his predecessors would have done, he pushed forward. Though losing more men than Lee, his army was larger and the Union able to replace losses. Lee on the other hand could ill afford to fight a war of attrition. These are samples of military considerations and

5   The earlier Leon Cahun influenced all three, *Introduction al'histoire de l'Asie; Turcs et Mongols, des origins a 1405* (Paris, 1896).
6   B. H. Liddell Hart, 'Two Great Captains: Jenghiz Khan and Sabutai', *Blackwood's Magazine*, vol. 215, p.646.
7   Harold Lamb, *The March of the Barbarians* (New York: Doubleday, Doran & Co., 1940), p.376.

different situations, be it lost opportunities, impact of friction of war, innovation and the enemy response, or trade-off between a quick victory and reliance on attrition. In the Mongol supermen school, no errors are seen in their conduct, no worn-out strategic ploys fail to surprise the enemy, and no unexpected event derails a plan. This is how Montgomery wanted the world to see the battle of Normandy in 1944, with everything unfolding in accordance with his master plan. It is also how Liddell Hart, Trevor Dupuy, and James Chambers see the Mongol conquest of Transoxiana in 1220 or of Hungary in 1241. Complex plans were implemented with ease, giving the Mongols cheap victories. This, however, does not fit the reality of war. There are always mistakes, misunderstandings, opportunities missed, and surprises. The aim here is to produce a more realistic narrative of the Mongol military campaigns, based on primary and good-quality secondary sources. No a priori assumptions will be taken about the Mongol military brilliance. They would have had to overcome the friction of war as much as Alexander, Hannibal, Napoleon, and other commanders.

War can be considered in many different ways. The historian John Keegan famously focussed on the experience of battle, how the soldiers actually fought.[8] This can be called a 'bottom up' approach. Strategic movement, numbers, and maps help look at the reality of war from a different angle. This is what will be the initial focus here. Combat is a social action, but statistical laws govern it. At heart, war works like a Lancaster model. One hundred men fighting against 50 in the open with similar weapons, training, and social context will have an advantage. If the 50 men hold a pass or a fortified position, it becomes a different matter. If one side have the advantage of surprise or more supplies, it can again change the context. Trevor Dupuy promoted this type of thinking and developed analytical tools.[9] Mongol victories and defeats must be understood in operational context, as the commanders of the period would have seen it. To track events, the focus needs to be on geography, time, and numbers. Numbers and geography are no easy matter, especially with regard to the early wars of the Mongols. What the numbers were is often a matter of guesswork and many locations are either uncertain or not known at all. In the interest of establishing a framework, estimates and guesses will be made. The timing of operations is generally well understood when the theatre of war is in central China, the Near East, or Europe, but much less so in the plains far from sedentary states.

There is much still to understand with regard to how Mongols and their foes fought, that is to say the face of battle as well as grand tactical details such as unit deployment, formations, and movement during battle. The sources are far from satisfactory. Certainly there is no description of the kind that, for example, Polybius offers on the battle of Cannae (216 BC) or Arrian offers for the battle of Gaugamela (331 BC). Even so, the sources offer some information. Although not the main emphasis here, the point will be pursued wherever the sources allow it.

The 'big man' theory of history is generally discredited today, though as seen above Napoleon does not agree with this. For sure, Genghis Khan, his general Sübe'etei, the other

---

8   John Keegan, *The Face of Battle* (Harmondsworth: Penguin, 1983).
9   Trevor Dupuy, *Numbers, Predictions, and War* (Indianapolis: Bobbs-Merrill, 1979).

Mongol commanders, and their foes operated with teams around them. It is difficult to say much about this. The reader should always consider that the commanders functioned in a team and operated in an organisational structure. A little is known about how Genghis Khan managed war as the people around him and his organisation is quite well described in near contemporary sources, but for other key players almost nothing is known.

This book is structured into two main sections with the focus being Genghis Khan in the first and Sübe'etei in the second. Before that an overview will be given of the world where Genghis Khan and Sübe'etei operated. Genghis Khan was active from before 1191, to 1227. What he did before 1191 is almost entirely lost to history. Sübe'etei had his first significant independent command in 1216 and retired only just before his death in 1248. They operated jointly in 1220, 1226, and 1227. The last two of these years will be covered in the Sübe'etei section only. The bulk of the narrative is focussed on the campaigns Genghis Khan and Sübe'etei directed in person, but in addition an overview is given of other Mongol campaigns in China (1216–1228 and 1235–1246), and Korea.

	Section I: Genghis Khan
Ally of To'oril	1191–1202
Master of Mongolia	1203–1208
The Chinese Campaigns I	1209–1215 Overview of China, 1215–1227
The Great Western Expedition	1220–1223
	Section II: Sübe'etei
Circling the Caspian Sea	1216–1224
The Chinese Campaigns II	1226–1234 Overview of Korea
The European Expedition	1236–1242 Overview of China, 1234–1245 1245–1246

The numbers given for armies are rounded and nominal. The effective totals were certainly lower, though by how much is hardly ever known. The nominal totals help give a magnitude even if effective totals could be much lower. This is especially true for infantry forces, the more so the larger they were.

The intention is to render Chinese names in Pinyin format. Quotes, however, will be given in the original format and can therefore be Wade-Giles. Modern names are used for the major cities, such as Beijing or Kaifeng, in China instead of whatever they were called at the time. Chinese administrative districts as well as the main city in them – where the administration was based – were called 'zhou', as, for example, Weizhou. 'Guan' means 'pass'. On the maps, places like Weizhou are simply labelled Wei to save space. The Chinese distance measure *li* is about half a kilometre. The Chinese standard is to list the family name first.

A Note on Sources

The details of Temüjin's ... rise to chief of the Mongol tribe are told in the Secret History of the Mongols, the Shengwu Qinzheng Lu, and in Rashid-ud-Din's COMPENDIUM OF CHRONICLES. While often sharing episodes, they also diverge on many points, particularly chronology, and it is difficult, if not impossible, to reconstruct a synoptic narrative of his political vicissitudes before 1201.'

– Christopher Atwood[1]

The important sources for the rise of the Mongols are the *Shengwujinzhenglu* (SWQZL), the *Yuanshi*, Rashid al-Din's *Compendium of Chronicles*, and the *Secret History*. Of these the *Secret History* is generally considered to be the earliest, with the other sources compiled somewhat later. They all appear to draw on common sources, with the SWQZL, *Yuanshi* and Rashid al-Din in particular being very closely related to each other. The two former, both Chinese chronicles, are shorter and crafted in the tradition of dynastic histories. This means having quite an economical account, leaving out non-essential information, and also to be respectful to the man with 'the Mandate of Heaven'. In some parts there is also a clear link between the *Secret History* and the other sources.

The Secret History: The most well known early source, at least in the West, is the *Secret History*. It is in the style of an epic, and draws on oral traditions. Many episodes are described in great detail, but it is a selective account which fails to cover all events. This is clear, for example, from its short treatment of the early Xia or Jin campaigns (between 1205 and 1215). It also seems that the *Secret History* sometimes modifies events to build dramatic tension. On the positive side, the author is quite ready to be honest, in several places clearly saying some negative things about Genghis Khan. Clearly the overall chronology has somehow been mixed up, perhaps in part due to careless editing. The work may have been updated as late as c.1252, but the bulk of the material seems to have been compiled much earlier. Igor de Rachewiltz translated and provided a detailed commentary of the *Secret History*.[2]

---

1   Christopher Atwood, *Encyclopedia of Mongolia and the Mongol Empire* (New York: Facts on File, 2004), p.98.
2   Igor de Rachewiltz, *The Secret History of the Mongols: A Mongolian Epic Chronicle of the Thirteenth Century* (Leiden: E. J. Brill, 2004); Francis W. Cleaves, *The Secret History of the Mongols* (Cambridge, Mass.: Harvard

Shengwujinzhenglu: The best overall early source is arguably the *Shengwujinzhenglu* (SWQZL). It is a more comprehensive source than the *Secret History* with regard to headline events covered and has a much more disciplined chronology. It is polite – it will not say that Genghis Khan was defeated – and does have some possible errors. The source loses quality once the focus shifts into China. The SWQZL places Samuqa's Henan raid in 1215, a year too early, and says the Jin emperor left Kaifeng in September 1231, three months too early. Almost nothing is said about the final Xia campaigns during which Temüjin died. The SWQZL has been translated and annotated by Pelliot and Hambis up to the year 1201 in *Histoire des campagnes de Gengis Khan – Chen-wou ts'in-tcheng lou*. John Emerson continued this work, adding 1202 and 1203. Erich Haenisch translated the years 1219–1227 in *Die letzen Feldzüge Cinggis Han's und sein Tod*.[3]

Yuanshi: *Yuanshi* is the official dynastic history of the Mongol ruling house in China, finalised around 1370 during the Ming dynasty. The *Yuanshi* base annals (*Yuanshi* 1) are close to the SWQZL, but are generally more condensed. It does have details on the campaigns against Xia not found in the SWQZL. The *Yuanshi* as a whole seems to be edited somewhat poorly (it has been said it is the worst edited of any of the 24 Chinese dynastic histories). For example, Sübe'etei has two biographies with different spellings of his name. Eight other non-Han Chinese also have two biographies. Temüjin's march against the Merkits in 1198 is misplaced, and names and places where fighting took place against the Jin in 1211, 1212, and 1213 are duplicated. A wealth of detail about the campaigns in China and the Western regions is found in the biographies.[4]

Collected Chronicles: The Persian historian Rashid al-Din used similar sources as the SWQZL and *Yuanshi*, but made a more extensive commentary. Rashid al-Din's understanding of geography outside the Middle East was poor. For events in China, where geographical understanding is important, his work is of less value. Thackston has made an excellent translation with a lot of effort to match names to those known from

---

University Press, 1982); Paul Pelliot, *Histoire Secrète des Mongols* (Paris: Libraire d'Amérique et d'Orient, 1949).

3   SWQZL in *Meng-ku shih liao ssu chung*, editor Wang Kuo-wei; *Histoire des campagnes de Gengis Khan – Cheng-wou ts'in-tcheng*, translated and commented by Paul Pelliot and Louis Hambis (Leiden: E. J. Brill, 1951); *Sheng Wu Jin Cheng Lu: Partial translation, comments and notes, translated by John Emerson*; and 'Die letzen Feldzüge Cinggis Han's und sein Tod', translated by Erich Haenisch, *Asia Minor* 9, pp.503–551. For a discussion of the source, see Christopher Atwood, *Commentary of Shenwu qinzhenglu*.

4   *Yuanshi*, editor Song Lian; *Yuanshi* 1, F. E. A. Krause, Cingis Han; *Die Geschichte seines Lebens nach den chinesischen Reichannalen* (Heidelberg: C. Winter, 1922); *Yuanshi* 2, Waltraut Abramowski, 'Die Chinesischen Annalen von Ögödei und Güyük', *Zentral Asiatische Studien* 10 (Wiesbaden, 1976); *Yuanshi* 98 and 99, Ch'i-ch'ing Hsiao, *The Military Establishment of the Yuan Dynasty* (Cambridge, Mass.: Harvard University Press, 1978). Antony Gaubil translated some of the material, *Histoire de Gentchiscan et toute la dynastie des Mongols … tirée de l'histoire chinoise* (Paris: Briasson, 1739). In the text, references are given to Krause and Abramowski for respectively *Yuanshi* 1 and *Yuanshi* 2. All others are to the Chinese text of Song Lian. Paul Buell has a translation of *Yuanshi* 121 in his Nomads of Eurasia syllabus (part B); A. Remusa, 'Souboutai', *Nouveaux melagnes asiatiques*, volume 2 (Paris, 1829), pp.89–97, offers an early translation of *Yuanshi* 121.

Mongolian and Chinese sources.[5] Before Thackston, the only European translation was in Russian.

For the later period, only the *Yuanshi* and Rashid al-Din's *Collected Chronicles* remain important. For Genghis Khan, the *Yuanshi* 1 is most important. For the later period, in addition to *Yuanshi* 2, much valuable information can be gained from the many biographies. Other important sources are the *Jinshi*, the *Songshi*, Juvaini, ibn al-Athir, Nasawi, Juzjani, and the Georgian, Rus, and Central European chronicles.

Jinshi: The dynastic history of the Jin dynasty (compiled 1268–1343, during the Mongol Yuan dynasty) is much better edited than the *Yuanshi*. The base annals are not very detailed, but a wealth of detail is provided in the many biographies of the various military men. Many events can be followed on a day-to-day basis. In particular *Jinshi* 112 is vital for the 1231–1232 campaign.[6]

Songshi: The dynastic history of the Song dynasty (written like the *Jinshi* during the later years of the Yuan dynasty) is not all as effectively edited, as the *Jinshi*, but it is vast in scope. The compilers had access to many diaries and other contemporary records. The *Songshi* is especially noted for the high quality of its biographies. Much other Song literature is preserved in addition to the *Songshi*. Other early Chinese sources include accounts of Song officials going to meet the Mongols as well as Mi Zhou's eyewitness description of the 1234 campaign.[7]

Wang Yun wrote a biography about Sübe'etei and his family. He was a contemporary of Sübe'etei's grandson Aju. This work is related to the two *Yuanshi* biographies.[8]

Juvaini: A Persian civil servant in Mongol Iran who wrote a history c.1260, Juvaini is especially well informed about events in and around Transoxiana and Khorasan. Rashid al-Din made use of his work.[9]

Ibn al-Athir: A contemporary (died in 1233) based in Mosul, Ibn al-Athir wrote a history of the world vast in scope. He is certainly well informed about events close to his hometown. For events further away he drew on Muslim traders and travellers as well as other people he met. The Mongol defeat of the Bulgars in 1224 is alluded to in the *Secret History*, but only Ibn al-Athir provides details on this. Rashid al-Din relied on Ibn al-Athir for some sections of his work.[10]

Nasawi: Shihab al-Din Muhammad al-Nasawi (died c.1250) was another contemporary who later wrote a history (around 1241). He was close to Jalal al-Din

---

5   Rashid al-Din, Rashiduddin Fazlullah's *Jam'u't-tawarikh* (*Compendium of Chronicles*), translated by W. M. Thackston (Cambridge, Mass.: Harvard University Press, 1998–99).

6   Tuotuo, *Jinshi*, and C. de Harlez, *Histoire de l'Empire de Kin; Ou, Empire d'Or Aisin Gurun-I Suduri Bithe* (Louvain: Typ. de C. Peeters, 1887), offer a summarised translation of the *Jinshi*.

7   Tuotuo, *Songshi*; Peter Olbricht and Elisabeth Pinks, *Meng-Ta Pei-Lu und Hei-ta Shih-Lüeh* (Wiesbaden: Harrassowitz, 1980); Mi Zhou, 周密, Qidong yeyu 齐东野语, pp.77–80.

8   Wang, Yun, *Wuliang shi xian miao bei ming* 兀良氏先庙碑铭, *Qiuqian xiansheng daquan wenji* 秋涧先生大全文集.

9   Juvaini, *The History of the World-Conqueror*, translated by John Andrew Boyle (Manchester: Manchester University Press, 1958).

10   Ibn al-Athir, *The Chronicle of Ibn al-Athir for the Crusading Period from al-Kamil fi'il-ta'rikh*, translated by D. S. Richards (Aldershot: Ashgate, 2008).

and hostile towards the Mongols. He wrote an account of the eventful life of Jalal al-Din.[11]

Juzjani: Minhaj al-Siraj Juzjani (born 1193) experienced the Mongol attack on Khwarezm first-hand and wrote what is at times a very detailed narrative of events. He is hostile towards the Mongols, providing balance to Juvaini and Rashid al-Din. He is best informed about events in what is now Afghanistan and Pakistan.[12]

The Georgian/Armenian Chronicles: Written some decades after the events, Grigor Aknerc'i, Kirakos Ganjakec'i, Vardan Arewelc'I, and *The History of Kart'li* still has much to offer on the Mongol invasion of Georgia in 1221.[13]

The Rus Chronicles: The early chronicles are *The Chronicle of Novgorod* and *The Hypatian Chronicle*, treating the northern and southern region best, respectively. *The Nikonian Chronicle* is a later work, merging the accounts of many chronicles into one continuous whole. It offers some information not found in the two earlier works.[14]

The Central European Chronicles and sources: Julian, Thomas of Spalato, Rogerius, *The Tartar Relation*, Carpini, and others wrote eyewitness accounts. There are also many preserved letters sent by kings and dignitaries. In addition there are various chroniclers.[15]

In general, the sources on Genghis Khan are weaker the earlier the period. For Sübe'etei the sources are weak when he operated far away from Han China, Persia, or Europe.

Many modern historians have helped to make great progress regarding use of these sources and in developing an improved understanding of the period. They face a serious challenge, having to master Mongolian, Chinese, and many other languages. Paul Pelliot, Louis Hambis, Erich Haenisch, Francis W. Cleaves, Paul Ratchnevsky, Igor de Rachewiltz, Thomas Allsen, Paul Buell, Ruth Dunnell, and Christopher

11 *Histoire du sultan Djelal ed-Din Mankobirti prince du Kharezm par Mohammed en-Nesawi*, translated by O. Houdas (Paris: E. Leroux, 1895).

12 *The Tabakat-i-Nasiri of Minhaj-i-Saraj, Abu-Umar-i-Usman: A general history of the Muhammadan dynasties of Asia, including Hindustan from A.H. 194 (810 A.D.) to A.H. 658 (1260 A.D.), and the irruption of the infidel Mughals into Islam.* Translator H. G. Raverty made an extensive commentary, including a summary of many other Persian sources that wrote about events (Calcutta: The Asiatic Society, 1895).

13 Robert P. Blake and R. N. Frye, 'Grigor Aknerc'i: History of the Nation of the Archers', *Harvard Journal of Asiatic Studies*, 3–4, pp.269–443; Kirakos Ganjaketets'i: *History of the Armenians*, Robert Bedrosian (1986), http://rbedrosian.com/kg1.htm; Vardan Arewelc'I: *Compilation of History*, Robert Bedrosian (2007), http://rbedrosian.com/vaint.htm.

14 *The Chronicle of Novgorod*, translated by R. Mitchell and N. Forbes (London: Camden Society, 1914); *The Hypatian Chronicle: The Galician–Volynian Chronicle*, translated by George A. Perfecky (München: W. Fink, 1973); *The Nikonian Chronicle*, translated by Serge A. Zenkovsky and Betty Jean Zenkovsky (Princeton: Kingston Press, vols. 2 and 3).

15 János M. Bak and Martin Rady, *Anonymus and Master Roger* (Budapest, 2010); Maurice Michael and Paul Smith, *The Annals of Jan Długosz: A History of Eastern Europe 965 to 1480* (Charlton, West Sussex: IM Publications, 1997); Giovanni da Pian del Carpini, *The story of the Mongols whom we call Tartars*, translated by Erik Hildinger (Boston: Branden Publishing Company, 1996); Christopher Dawson, *The Mongol Mission* (London: Sheed and Ward, 1955); R. A. Skelton, *The Vinland Map and the Tartar relation* (New Haven: Yale University Press, 1965); Shinobu Iwamura, 'Mongol invasion of Poland in the Thirteenth Century', *Memoirs of the Research Department of the Toyo Bunko* (Tokyo, 1938); Hansgerd Göckenjan and James Sweeney, *Der Mongolensturm: Berichte von Augenzeugen und Zeitgenossen, 1235–1250* (Graz: Styria, 1985); *Monumenta Germaniae Historica* (Hanover and Berlin, 1826+).

Atwood are some of the important historians. For the Near East and Europe important translators and historians consulted include H. G. Raverty, V. V. Barthold, J. A. Boyle, W. M. Thackston, D. S. Richards, T. Bedrosian, J. Fennell, Martin Dimnik, and G. Strakosch-Grassmann. The only militarily focussed broader narrative of value is that of Desmond Martin. Helped by Chinese scholars, he drew on a large base of Chinese sources and developed a very detailed description of Mongol operations in China from 1209 to 1227.

Geographical locations in Mongolia are often hard to place. The views of Pelliot and de Rachewiltz are almost always followed in this study. There are many opposing views. For these the readers are referred to the commentary of de Rachewiltz on the *Secret History*. For locations in China reliance has been put on *The Historical Atlas of China*, volume VI. The book *A Sino-Western calendar for two thousand years 1–2000 A.D.* by Zhongsan Xue and Yi Ouyang has been used to convert traditional Chinese dates to modern Western ones.

Translations used for primary key sources quoted in the text:

The *Secret History*	Igor de Rachewiltz (2004)
SWQZL	Paul Pelliot and Louis Hambis (1951)
	John Emerson (website)
Yuanshi 1	F. E. A. Krause (1922)
Yuanshi 2	Waltraut Abramowski (1978)
Yuan Shi 123/Sube'etei	Paul Buell (Nomads of Eurasia syllabus)
Rashid al-Din	W. M. Thackston (1998-1999)
Juvaini	John Andrew Boyle (1958)
Ibn al-Athir	D. S. Richards (2008)
Nasawi	O. Houdas (1895)
Juzjani	H. G. Raverty (1895)
The Chronicle of Novgorod	R. Mitchell and N. Forbes (1914)
The Galician–Volynian Chronicle	George A. Perfecky (1973)
Roger	J. M. Bak and M. Rady (2010)
Carpini	Erik Hildinger (1996)
The Tartar Relation	R. A. Skelton (1965)

The Environment: Nomads and Sedentary States

Infants could ride on a goat and draw a bow to shoot small birds and rats. As they grew up, they would shoot foxes and hares and these are what they used to eat. Their warriors were powerful archers, and all were armoured cavalrymen. Their custom when at peace was to follow their flocks, and thus archery and hunting formed part of their way of life. When war threatened, they practiced battles and attacks so that they could invade or make unexpected attacks. This was part of their very nature.

– Sima Qian on the Xiongnu, 1st century BC[1]

I have never run away from any man. I am wandering, as I always wander in time of peace. You ask me why I did not fight you at once. May I remind you that we have neither cities nor cultivated land of our own; since we are not afraid of our territory being ruined and plundered, we had no reason to fight you outright … Nor will we until we see fit.

– Scythian king Idanthyrsus to Persian king Darayaraush (c.513 BC)[2]

Since early times horse-mounted nomad tribes dominated the plains stretching from the north side of the Black Sea to Mongolia and Manchuria. They lived in tents and moved about in groups with their livestock. A tribe could cover 150 to 600 km in a year. Winter camps would usually be in the north and summer camps in the south. A tribe travelled with herds of animals, but hunting was critical for survival and children were taught to ride and use bow and arrow from an early age. Though the nomad population was far smaller than those of sedentary societies, their horse-mounted forces were quick, tactically potent, and highly motivated. In the face of attack they could retreat and fight an evasive war. They resorted to battle when and where they wanted. The nomads had no cities to defend and the land yielded limited food and forage for invading forces. Persia, Han, and many other powerful empires discovered this to their cost time and time again. In the engaging narrative of Herodotus the story is told of how the Persian king Darayaraush (Darius) led a large army across the Danube and into the plains beyond with the aim to crush the nomad Scythians

---

1   Stephen Selby, *Chinese Archery* (Hong Kong: Hong Kong University Press, 2000), p.174.
2   Herodotus, *The Histories* (London: Penguin, 1972), p.312.

(around 513 BC). The Scythians retreated, taking their people and livestock with them, and burned the country to deny the Persians food and forage. Darayaraush was finally forced to retreat. When the Han sent armies into the plains of Mongolia to crush the Xiongnu during the 2nd and 1st centuries BC, they encountered the same response from the nomads. Often after the Han armies turned around and moved homewards, weakened due to lack of supplies, the Xiongnu tribesmen would strike against them, winning complete victories.

The Mongolian plateau stretched from the Khingan Mountains along the border to Manchuria in the east to the Altai Mountains and the Erdis (Irtysh) River in the west. This region hosted a very sizeable nomad population. The people endured a harsh climate and at times had to live on meagre means. This environment produced tough and sturdy warriors. There were frequent conflicts between tribes and clans; at times an exceptional leader would impose strong rule over the various tribes. The first to do so was Modo (before 200 BC). Usually unity was brief with many ready to challenge a leader at the first sign of weakness. Modo himself was killed in an ambush, though his house ruled over the plains for two hundred years. However, by the late 12th century AD no local lord had ruled over the Inner Asian tribes for centuries.

The strongest tribes were the Naimans in the west, the Kereyits in the centre, and the Tatars in the east.[3] There were many smaller groups around them, notably the Merkits who lived north of the Kereyits. The powerful Inanca Bilge ruled over the Naimans, To'oril over the Kereyits, and Chinese sources speak of a Tatar lord called Zuxu. The Kereyits were not as numerous as the Naimans and To'oril was not a strong ruler. Relatives challenged his rule on several occasions. The Tatars were numerous, but were even more divided than the Kereyits. It is not clear how large a faction Zuxu headed, but he is perhaps unlikely to have dominated the whole tribe. Toqto'a was a dominant leader amongst the Merkits. Inanca Bilge, To'oril, Zuxu, or Toqto'a had no programme for conquest; they prospered in the divided world of Inner Asia, but did not attempt to change the status quo. Between the core territory of the Kereyits, Merkits, and Tatars, along the Onon and Kerulen Rivers, is where the story of the Mongols makes its beginning. The biggest tribe in this area were the Tayici'uts who like the Tatars did not have a strong centralised leadership. Other groups in this area were the Jadaran and Borjigen. The Mongols developed from the base of the latter.[4]

The various tribes and sub-tribes were fluid structures with frequent movements of people from one to the other. A tribal leader looked for new followers a little like a modern politician looks for votes. Inter-tribal wars were more like civil wars than conflicts between long established nation states.

To the south of Mongolia was the vast Chinese civilization. China, like the Inner Asian plains, could be divided or united under a single rule ('all under heaven'). The Qin were the first to unite all of China (in 221 BC), but their rule did not endure for

---

3   Rashid al-Din (57) says the Tatars had 70,000 tents. When the Naimans submitted to Jin in 1175 they were said to bring 30,000 households (*Jinshi* 121, 4a–5a, 7. 7b).
4   On the various tribes see Thomas Allsen, 'The rise of the Mongolian Empire and Mongolian rule in North China', *The Cambridge History of China*, vol. 6, pp.321–324.

long. Lio Bang then prevailed in a fresh round of wars, overcoming the formidable Xiong Yü, and set up the mighty Han dynasty (202 BC). The Han ruled China for almost two centuries (so-called West Han). After another round of civil wars a Han prince was able to restore the dynasty (now called East Han because the capital was in Luoyang rather than Xi'an). In AD 189 central authority collapsed again. Eventually the Sima family united China (though Cao Cao had done much of the hard work before them), setting up the Jin dynasty, but again unity was short lived. During the early years of the 4th century nomad groups settled in North China rose up and established their own kingdoms, conquering all the land north of the Yangtze River. The nomads quickly assimilated into the far larger Chinese population (like Germanic or Viking settlers in West Europe), but China remained fragmented until the Sui finally united the country in 589. This dynasty was, like the first Qin, short-lived. New civil wars followed before the Tang imposed their rule over all of China during the 620s. They also conquered the Inner Asian plains, a unique achievement. The second Tang ruler, Li Shimin, was Emperor of China as well as *Great Khan* of Inner Asia. The power of Tang was some generations later (in 756) effectively broken by the revolt of a northern border commander (who was a Sogdian). Afterwards, the power rested with the various governors; in time, some set up their own dynasties. The Song finally united the country again and reintroduced a strong centralised administration during the second half of the 10th century. Under Song rule China prospered, making great technological and social advances. The Song failed, however, to secure *all* of China and did not maintain their material powers for very long.

There was ongoing interaction between the Chinese and the nomads. The nomads raided into China looking for loot and glory. The Chinese provided incentives to keep them from making raids, giving tribute, presents, and titles, and attempted to keep the tribes divided and busy fighting against each other. The Chinese population was more than 20 times as numerous as the nomads, but they could not easily send large forces into the barren north, and lacked strong cavalry forces. The military threat of the nomads was much more than the relative population sizes would indicate.[5]

The area close to and beyond Liaodong, Manchuria (modern north-east China), had a sedentary as well as a nomad population.[6] In this mixed and somewhat protected environment emerged strong, well-organised armies. They were able to merge elements of the nomad and Chinese worlds and thus create a kind of hybrid army able to defeat nomads as well as sedentary forces. It was here that heavy cavalry with stirrups, fighting in formation, is first attested (c.350)[7] and here later emerged the very sophisticated Khitan war machine. The Khitans, a local tribe with a long history, established the Liao dynasty in Liaodong in the early 10th century. Their well-organised armies were too strong for the Song, whose leaders were forced to accept that the Beijing region,

5   Chinese–Inner Asian tribal relations are described by Thomas Barfield, *The Perilous Frontier: Nomadic Empires and China 221 B.C. to A.D. 1757* (Cambridge, Mass.: B. Blackwell, 1989).
6   Kenneth Douglas Klein, *The Contributions of the Fourth Century Xianbei States to the Reunification of the Chinese Empire* (Los Angeles: University of California, 1980), pp.24–29.
7   Albert E. Dien, 'The Stirrup and its effect on Chinese Military History', *Ars Orientalis*, 16 (Michigan, 1976), pp.185–201.

the so-called Sixteen Prefectures, remained in Liao hands in spite of frequent efforts to reconquer it. The Liao also gained control, or influence, over the Inner Asian plains, establishing some settlements there.

The Liao lost their military vigour after about two centuries (c.1100). The Jurchen, tribesmen living further east, crushed them and also conquered the northern part of China from the Song. The Jurchen established the so-called Jin (Gold) dynasty. The Jin was less interested in Inner Asia than early Liao, though they strove to keep the tribes divided. They did build new fortified lines to cover the borders, some deep inside Mongolia. The Jin also controlled the Önggüt tribes who lived along the south side of the Gobi Desert.

Pursued by the Jurchen/Jin, a Khitan/Liao nobleman, Yelü Daisi, fled westwards. He was able to establish the so-called West Liao dynasty in what is now Kazakhstan. His house dominated the territory between Transoxiana and the Erdis River. This was something unique. Before this, tribes had migrated eastwards across the Altai and the Chinese had at times controlled the Tarim by means of garrisons, but Yelü Daisi established a state in that area which was organised along Chinese lines. West Liao had a standing army, a bureaucracy, and tax collection.[8]

The Liao and later Jin were not the only foreign policy problem for the Song. The Tanguts, or West Xia, developed a strong state in the area of the upper Huang (Yellow) River. This was largely outside the traditional core Chinese Han territory, but the Song still fought plenty of wars against the Xia. The Song-Xia wars were protracted and costly, but indecisive.[9] After the Jin conquest of North China, the Xia no longer had a common frontier with Song. The Jin occasionally fought against Xia, but were never drawn into such large-scale conflicts as the Song had before them.

Jin and Song were engaged in drawn out wars, stretching from the 1120s to the early 1140s. The Jin were much more successful against the Song than Liao had been. The Jin did not have larger armies than Liao, and if anything Liao had better leadership, but by now the Song was much weaker. The Song were forced south of the Yangtze River, but held this line (the dynasty is afterwards called South Song). This was the era of the celebrated Song general Yue Fei. Eventually, the Song and Jin made peace. Later wars were more limited in nature. The Jin were left in control of a major part of central China.[10]

It was an established ideal in the Chinese world to have one ruler with 'the Mandate of Heaven.' However, none had managed to unite *all* the traditional Chinese territories since Tang times. *Xiaozong* (reigned 1163–1194) was the Song emperor at the start of

8   Michal Biran, *The Empire of the Qara Khitai in Eurasian History* (Cambridge: Cambridge University Press, 2005).

9   See Shi-lung Tsang, *War and peace in Northern Sung China: Violence and Strategy in Flux 960–1104* (Arizona: University of Arizona, 1997).

10 See Tao Jing-Shen, 'The Move to the South and the Reign of Kao-tsung (1127–1162)', Denis Twitchett and Paul Jakov Smith (eds.), *The Cambridge History of China*, vol. 5 part 1 (Cambridge: Cambridge University Press, 2009), pp.644–672; Edward Harold Kaplan, *Yueh Fei and the founding of the Southern Sung* (Ph. D. dissertion, University of Iowa, 1970); Xueliang Wang, *Ideal versus reality: Han Shizhong and the founding of the Southern Song 1127–1142* (The University of Arizona, 2000).

the period that will be covered in this book. He was a seventh generation descendant of the founding emperor of the dynasty, but only the second emperor to rule after the Song had fled south across the Yangtze. Apart from a limited confrontation with the Jin in 1164 his reign was peaceful.[11] *Shizong* (reigned 1161–1189) was the ruling Jin emperor. He was the grandson of the founding emperor. A key concern for him was to keep the Jurchen spirit and the material quality of his fighting men. However he was, like all tribal leaders living in China before him, unable to keep his people from gradually assimilating with the Han Chinese. A grandson, Wanyan Jing with the temple name *Zhangzong*, succeeded him as ruler (reigned 1189–1208). He hunted for recreation, not viewing it as a necessity for military training.[12] The Xia emperor *Renzong* (reigned 1139–1193) ruled for a long time. Under him the empire was prosperous, but after a failed coup he developed a mistrust of the army officers. *Renzong's* son succeeded him with the temple name *Huanzong* (reigned 1193–1206).[13] The West Liao emperor was Yelü Zhilugu (reigned 1178–1211). He became ruler during a confusing time, with soap opera style family plots.[14] The four dynasties, all founded by fighting men, were now ruled by people with no military experience. The rulers all lived a sheltered life inside the walls of the court; none of them could lead an army in person, and none of them could even dream about uniting the Chinese world under their rule.

This was the world into which Genghis Khan was born. The Mongols, if his followers can be called that at this early stage, were just a small band travelling up and down the Kerulen River. Surrounded by more powerful tribes and well-established sedentary states to the west, south, and south-east, there was no easy road open for a would-be world conqueror.

11   See Gong Wei Ai, 'The Reign of Hsiao-tsung (1162–1189)', *The Cambridge History of China*, vol. 5, part 1, pp.710–755.
12   Herbert Franke, 'The Chin Dynasty', Herbert Franke and Denis Twitchett (eds.), *The Cambridge History of China*, vol. 6. (Cambridge: Cambridge University Press, 1994), pp.226–258.
13   Ruth Dunnel, 'The Hsi Hsia', *The Cambridge History of China*, vol. 6, pp.197–204.
14   Biran, pp.57–58.

The Khitan War Machine

While avoiding engagements against superior numbers, they would frequently use the tactics of manoeuvre and ambush to harass and cut enemy supply lines. When the Khitan laid siege to a city, they forced the local Chinese populace to fill the surrounding moats and used Chinese-style catapults to break down the outer walls. Storming a city was particularly brutal, as the Khitan would drive Chinese captives ahead of their army into the face of stones and arrows fired by the prisoner's townspeople and relatives.

– William M. Caraway, *Korea in the Eye of the Tiger*

The Mongol military doctrine evolved from the base developed by the Khitans. It was much more a copy than an original development, and therefore it is important to understand the Khitan art of war. Khitan warlord Abaoji (872–926) set out on his path to power and dominance during the early years of the 10th century. He became khan of the Khitans and quickly subjected the neighbouring tribes. He was a remarkable military commander, but even more remarkable for his administration; he turned the Khitan realm into a Chinese-style organised state. His army became a mix of a traditional nomad force and a Chinese formation. He strove to combine and get the best out of what the nomad and sedentary worlds had to offer.

Like most successful nomad warriors, the Khitans were noted for their iron discipline. A Chinese general commented: 'Such discipline the Chinese can never attain.'[1] Hunting was a critical element for training. A Liao emperor said in 940: 'Our hunting is not simply a pursuit of pleasure. It means practising warfare'. It was Khitan custom to advance with three columns covered by many scouts: 'The 3 armies which invaded China proper employed an unbelievably large number of scouts ... who moved within a radius of 10 to 100 li'. They avoided battle until the enemy was weakened: 'Combat at close range was avoided until such moment when the enemy was exhausted or his massed force loosened.' They liked to operate against the enemy supply lines: 'To weaken morale and fighting power supply lines were cut, fires set at night, and annoying dust clouds were raised.' The Khitans made use of both heavy

---

1 Li Cunxi (885–926), one of the great generals of the 10th century. *History of Chinese Society: Liao 907–1125*, K. Wittfogel and C. S. Feng (Philadelphia: American Philosophical Society, 1949), pp.505–575. The following quotes are also from this work.

and light cavalry, probably having more of the former than had been usual in nomad armies before. In battle:

> The first regiment of troops galloped their horses and with a great uproar assaulted the enemy's formation. If an advantage was gained, all regiments advanced together. If no advantage was gained [the first] withdrew and a second regiment took over. Those who withdrew rested their horses and partook of water and dried food ... If the enemy's formation refused to budge ... [they] waited two or three days until the enemy became worn out.

The Khitans tended to avoid fortified points. If a siege was necessary they made effective use of civilian labour: 'The gruesome spectacle, the Chinese civilians were compelled to lead the way. They and not the Liao soldiers bore the brunt of the defending forces' missiles, arrows, stones and rolling logs.' Abaoji created a 2,000 man strong elite military force in 922. It later increased in size, reportedly counting more than 50,000 men total.

Abaoji raided with some success into China, but was by no means universally successful. He also imposed his authority on the Inner Asian tribes as far west as the Altai Mountains. Abaoji's son Yelü Deguang was also an able general. He dominated his Chinese rivals to a degree never achieved by his father. The Khitan military was still more successful under the general Yelü Xiuge some years later. He defeated the Song in many battles. His Liaoshi biography describes a victory gained in 980:

> The Liao emperor *Jingzhong* personally led his army in a military operation. They surrounded Waqiao Guan. A Song army came up to succour [the besieged city]. Zhang Shi, general of the garrison force, broke out [of the besieged city] ... Yelü Xiuge killed Zhang Shi. All the other Song forces retreated back into the city. The Song army [approaching the city] deployed for battle on the south bank of a river. Before the start of the battle, the emperor noticed that both Yelü Xiuge's horse and armour were yellow and worried the enemy might easily recognise him. So the emperor bestowed him black armour and a white horse to charge them. Yelü Xiuge led a force of picked troops to ferry across the river and defeated the enemy. They were chased to Mozhou. Corpses of the enemy covered the road, and they used up all their arrows. At last, Yelü Xiugo captured several of the Song generals and presented them to the emperor. The emperor was very happy, and bestowed him imperial horses and gold receptacles to reward him. "You are far braver than said" ... When the army returned, [Yelü Xiuge] was promoted to *Yuyue* [the highest honourable title for battle achievement].

The Song learned to fear him. His biography claims: 'At that time, Song people would stop crying babies by saying "Here *Yuyue* comes!"' At this stage the Khitan army had a clear quality advantage. The Khitans could not, however, translate tactical victories into strategic conquest. Finally, in 1004, the Song and Khitans, or Liao to use the chosen dynastic name, made peace. They learned to coexist. In the course of the next century both states gradually lost their material powers.

Part I

Genghis Khan

_____

1

Temüjin

Before I ascended the throne I was riding alone on one occasion. 6 men lay in ambush along the route, with evil intentions towards me. As I approached them I drew my sword and attacked. They, for their part, loosed arrows at me but these all flew past without one hitting me. I hacked the men down and rode on unscathed. On my return I passed close to their bodies. Their 6 geldings were roaming masterless in the area and could not be caught, but I drove them on before me.

– Rashid al-Din, 440

Temüjin (c.1162–1227),[1] the personal name of Genghis Khan, was at heart a simple nomad and his aim in life was simple. He told his men: 'The greatest pleasure is to vanquish your enemies, to chase them before you, to rob them of their wealth, to see their near and dear bathed in tears, to ride their horses and sleep on the white bellies of their wives and daughters.' He had no interest in the luxury that contact with the Chinese world brought him, preferring to continue the life of a simple nomad. He was an aristocrat who viewed the world much in the same way as Alexander the Great of Macedonia had done. With regard to Alexander, Fuller tells the story how 'some of his friends who knew he was fleet of foot urged him to run a race in the Olympic Games, his answer was that he would only do so if he might have kings run with him.'[2] Temüjin would probably have considered this to be a very proper response. For Alexander and Temüjin the World was divided into lords and followers, upstairs and downstairs.

Though born the son of a tribal leader, nothing was given to Temüjin for free. As a boy, after the early death of his father, he endured some desperate times and had to fight hard for everything he gained. The first rival, or perceived rival, he killed when aged about thirteen or fourteen, was his half-brother Bekter. Temüjin also spent time as a captive amongst the Tayici'uts. The loss of position, the hard daily life, and the time in captivity were humiliating to the young lord. Without this experience he

---

1   See Zhou Qingshu, 'A critical examination of the year of birth of Chinggis Khan', in Xin Luo, *Chinese Scholars on Inner Asia* (Bloomington, Indiana: Indiana University, 2012), pp.331–352.
2   Fuller is retelling a Plutarch anecdote.

might never had developed into to such a hard and focussed person. He was single-minded and stubborn. He told his sons: 'The merit of an action lies in finishing it to the end.' He was not content with victory. He wanted to destroy the enemy. This single-minded determination was not matched by any of his rivals in the contest for supremacy of the Inner Asian plains. Where rival lords were content with the added prestige a victory brought, Temüjin continued to press the attacks until the rival tribe was captured and their leaders killed.

Temüjin shared power with nobody, but generously rewarded those who served him well. He was charismatic and attracted able men into his service, and they prospered with him. Song visitor Zhao Hong said he 'had the gift to win over people.' One example is the Khitan Yelü Ahai. He met Temüjin as a Jin envoy. Impressed by him, Ahai defected and entered into his service. Temüjin actively sought out able men to join him. He told Taoist monk Yelü Chucai: 'In 7 years I have accomplished the task of conquering … the world, and my supremacy is acknowledged. I have few talents therefore I am fond of intelligent men, treating them as my brothers.' Still, he was careful to keep successful officers in place. In 1218 he told Jebe not to be too proud of himself after he had successfully overrun the West Liao state. Jebe tactfully offered Temüjin a present of many horses. Temüjin promoted people partly on merit and carefully assessed the capabilities of his men, deciding who was suitable for command and who was not. He said of one man:

> There is no greater warrior than Yisubei and no man who possesses his ability! But because he does not suffer from the hardships of a campaign, shrugs off hunger and thirst, he assumes that all others, officers and soldiers alike, who accompany him, are equally able to bear those hardships, whereas they cannot. For this reason he is not suitable to command an army.

When some Tayici'ut visited his camp they found he 'is a ruler who takes care of his subjects and knows how to command.' He established detailed rules, which were clearly communicated and strictly enforced. A courier on the road had the right to seize a fresh horse from any man, even high-ranking military commanders; a soldier in Temüjin's bodyguard had seniority over officers in other formations; and there were detailed regulations with regard to scouting, handling of plunder, etc. Temüjin always learned from mistakes and kept looking for better ways of doing things. He shared his lessons and ideas with others and made sure that they and the whole army learned from them also. In 1221 he returned to a battlefield where he carefully, though not politely, explained to the defeated officer the mistakes he had made. He wanted to make sure that he learned from the experience.

Temüjin demanded 100 percent loyalty, even from the men who served rival lords. He had nothing but contempt for those who defected, unless they did not first try to fight valiantly and fulfil their duties to their previous lord. He said: 'A man who is once faithless can never be trusted.' He was, however, happy to take into his service a brave enemy who *had* served his previous lord faithfully. He never had to deal with serious revolts by relatives or senior lords (though some defected early on). When he returned to Mongolia after a seven year campaign in the west there had been no unrest or any other problem at home. When Alexander returned to Babylon after a seven year campaign in the east (Sogdia and India), someone had run off with the treasury and started to hire mercenaries in Greece. After Temüjin died the succession measures he put in place worked smoothly. The comparison is often made to the Macedonian realm of Alexander, which fell apart after his death.

Temüjin was a skilled politician who was able to win over factions to his side. A trademark ploy was the use of misinformation and devious diplomacy to weaken the enemy's resolve even before a military attack was made. He famously sent messages to enemy leaders in 1203 detailing their unjust conduct, and he attempted to divide the family of Muhammad II in 1220. Before he attacked Jin in 1211 he had won over the border tribes, had Jin defectors in his service, and probably had contact with Khitan leaders ready to rebel in Manchuria.

Many commentators and historians have misunderstood the military style of Temüjin. He is often presented as conquering through 'pure' strategy without having to fight battles. Thomas Barfield is one of few historians who know better. He commented:

> In one important respect Chinggis Khan differed from all other nomadic leaders: he had a penchant for fighting decisive battles. The traditional nomadic approach, when confronted with a large well-organised force, was to withdraw and delay giving battle until the enemy was exhausted and had begun retreating. The campaigns of the Persians against the Scythians or Han Wu-ti against the Hsiung-nu demonstrated the effectiveness of this approach. Nomads traditionally advanced before weakness and retreated before strength. Chinggis Khan on the contrary, was willing to risk all on the effectiveness of his force and tactics in an open battle. Of course he was experienced at using the tactical retreat to lead an enemy into an ambush – the most common Mongol trap – but he never employed the strategic retreat of withdrawing long distances to avoid the enemy. Instead he sought the best tactical position and attacked.

The battle focus of Temüjin influenced his strategy. He was happy, like Hannibal before him, to let the enemy mass their forces so that they would be more likely to accept his challenge.

Very little is known about Temüjin's specific battlefield tactics. He could use both penetration and outflanking tactics and had reserves ready to exploit advantage gained. He defeated the Naimans at the Naqu in 1204 by first inducing them to deploy in an extended formation and secondly making a strike with a compact body against their centre. On this occasion he faced a relatively strong foe. In 1221 he attacked the much weaker army of Jalal al-Din along the Sindhu (Indus). Jalal al-Din's right rested on the river and his left on the mountains. Temüjin outflanked the enemy right, after it ventured forward, with his reserve and drove their whole army against the Sindhu. It was probably also an outflanking attack that helped secure victory against the Jin in 1213. The Mongols always held substantial forces in reserve. This is something all steppe people did.[3]

The one pre-battle strategy Temüjin used fairly often was to wrong-foot the enemy by means of a surprise march, either simply moving quickly or by moving along an unexpected path. He surprised his foes by a direct approach in 1206 and 1207. In 1208 and 1209 he attacked the same general areas, but then gained surprise by moving along a different path. He pursued defeated forces and especially the enemy leaders ruthlessly. He knew that a defeated leader could re-emerge as a threat if not eliminated. He explained in 1220, speaking about Muhammad II: 'It is necessary to make an end of him ... before men gather around him and nobles join him from every side.' Temüjin resorted to strategic manoeuvre and trickery if he had been defeated or if he faced a very strong enemy army/position. After a defeat in 1203 he retreated to a distant place and regrouped, waiting for the enemy coalition force to disperse, supporting this process by actively sending messages to various enemy leaders. Once that happened he made a surprise attack on the main group and eliminated it. Unable to storm a strong position in 1209 he was again able to regroup. He was later able to tempt the enemy into the open by means of a feigned retreat, and then ambushed and routed them. In 1213 he outflanked and encircled a strong position he could not assault directly.

The fortified cities of China and Persia presented a new challenge to Temüjin. He first encountered the problem in 1207 when he was at least 40 years old. He asked Ambughai some years later: 'In attacking cities and seizing territory what goes first, troops or weapons of war?' Ambughai replied: 'In attacking cities first employ stone catapult shot because they are strong, heavy and have great range.' Temüjin decided to form a corps of catapult operators. Temüjin himself never took much interest in siege operations, preferring to hand over the task to specialists.

Temüjin claimed to have overcome great odds in personal combat during his youth. He is likely to have overstated whatever might have been the original core, though he is unlikely to have been able to avoid getting into fighting in person. By the time it is possible to follow his campaigns, he no longer personally engaged in close combat. He was no 'heroic' leader like Alexander III, Xiang Yü, Heraclios, Gustav II Adolf, or Karl XII. Instead he directed operations from the rear, though he ventured forward enough to get wounded on occasion.

Temüjin assumed the title Genghis Khan in 1206.[4] In this section he will be called Temüjin – covering his own campaigns – and Genghis Khan in the second, where the focus is Sübe'etei. In Chinese annals he is referred to as emperor or specifically the first ruler. They view him as the founder of the Yuan dynasty, though it was only his grandson Kublai who set up court in Beijing.

---

3   See, for example, in the East Roman manual the *Strategikon* (written c.AD 620).
4   This title is perhaps best rendered into English as Genghis Khan. Genghis Khan is used in this book as this form has become the most recognised.

Sources: Zhao Hong, in P. Olbricht and E. Pinks, *Meng-Ta Pei-Lu und Hei-ta Shih-Lüeh* (Wiesbaden: Harrassowitz, 1980), p.12; Rashid al-Din, 437–440; Juvaini, p.143; George Dennis, *Maurice's Strategikon* (Pennsylvania: University of Pennsylvania Press, 1984) p.23; Harold Lamb, *The Earth Shakers* (Garden City, New York: Doubleday and Company Inc., 1949), p.67; Boyle, commentary on Juvaini, p.55; J. F. C. Fuller, *The Generalship of Alexander the Great* (New Brunswick: Rutgers University Press), p.58; James Chambers, *The Devil's Horsemen, The Mongol Invasion of Europe* (London: Cassell, 1988), p.15; Barfield, p.160; Ratchnevsky, *Genghis Khan: His Life and Legacy* (Oxford: Blackwell, 1991), pp.17–19; Trevor Royle, *A Dictionary of Military Quotations* (London: Routledge, 1990), p.55.

2

The Officers

Further, Činggis Qa'an said to Qubilai, 'For me you pressed down the necks of the mighty ones, the buttocks of the strong ones. You, Qubilai, Jelme, Jebe and Sübe'etei – these "four hounds" of mine – when I sent you off, directing you to the place I had in mind, when I said, "Reach there!", you crushed the stones to be there; when I said, "Attack!", you split up the rocks, you shattered the shining stones, you cleft the deep waters. When I sent you, Qubilai, Jelme, Jebe and Sübe'etei, my "four hounds", to the place I had designated, if Bo'orču, Muqali, Boroqul and Čila'un Ba'atur – these "four steeds" of mine – were at my side, and when the day of battle came and I had Jürčedei and Quyildar standing before me with their Uru'ut and Mangqut troops, then my mind was completely at rest. Qubilai, will you not be in charge of all military affairs?'

– the *Secret History*, 209

Temüjin relied on relatives to command his armies. Family members, mainly uncles and cousins, commanded nine of 13 units in the Dalan Bajut battle in 1194. By 1201 his brothers had gained a more prominent position. In the final stages of his career, after 1211, his sons started to command armies. Thus, while family members were always important in the command structure, those Temüjin actually relied on changed over the course of his career.

During the Dalan Bajud battle, his mother Hö'elün commanded a unit, as did Temüjin himself. Bültecu, Saca, Taicu, Daritai Otcigin and Qucar, Joci, Altan, Mönggetü Qiyan, and Bültecu, uncles, cousins, or other relatives, commanded other units. Temüjin fell out with Saca and Taicu in 1196 and with Daritai Otcigin, Qucar, and Altan in 1202. All except Daritai Otcigin were later killed. Some of the family leaders viewed their association with Temüjin as an alliance rather than a clear subject/ lord relationship, but this was not an attitude Temüjin was ready to accept.

Qasar, Otcigin, Belgutai, and Alcidai were the leading family commanders of the next generation. All except Alcidai were Temüjin's full or half-brothers. Alcidai was a nephew. For a long time, Qasar was the most significant of these. At times he marched separately from Temüjin and held senior command positions in battle. During the early years he was also a potential rival. According to Rashid al-Din,

Sorqan the Baya'ut said that Qasar 'has the same aim [as his brother] and counts on his strength and skill as an archer.' Temüjin later fell out with Qasar and would have killed him had their mother not arrived in time to stop him (if the *Secret History* can be trusted). Later Qasar's sons commanded only one unit of 1,000. Belgutai and Alcidai retained command, but dropped in relative seniority compared to the sons of the *Khan*. Belgutai, a half-brother, had seen Temüjin kill his older full brother when they were children and was well aware of the dangers of defying Temüjin. He was, however, unable to avoid trouble. He faced the wrath of Temüjin after leaking information from a military council he had attended.

Temüjin's sons – Joci, Ca'adai, Ögödei, and Tolui – had started to command armies by 1211.[1] By then Joci, the oldest, was probably more than 30 years old. Tolui, the youngest, was 21. They always operated with experienced officers and it may be questioned whether they had much talent. Temüjin never had any loyalty issues with his sons, though they could anger him by failing to give him a share of plunder gained or by failing to act with enough energy.

Unlike Frederick II ('the Great'), Temüjin had no Henry (brother), a close family member with real military talent. Temüjin needed family to help control the army, but hardly relied on their military skills. For that task, he built up a large pool of talented officers. In 1203 there were 65 senior officers, each with a unit of 1,000. By 1206 or a little later he had some 98 to 110 such officers. Of these, 12–16 were more senior than the others; the *four steeds* (*dorben külü'üd*), *four hounds* (*dorben noqas*), and several other officers commanded of several units of 1,000.

The *four steeds* were Bo'orcu, Boroqul, Cila'un Ba'atur, and Muqali. They are first mentioned as a group during the 1199 campaign when they led a detachment that helped the Kereyits fend off a Naiman attack. Bo'orcu was the most senior. He had been with Temüjin from the beginning, first helping him recover some stolen horses. Though rarely mentioned, he probably always held effective command over the right wing. Boroqul saved the life of Ögödei after a defeat in 1203. The Tumeds defeated and killed him in 1217. Cila'un Ba'atur and his family helped Temüjin escape after the Tayici'ut captivity. Cila'un was known to be incredibly brave, fighting effectively with the spear.

Muqali (1173–1223) has an extensive *Yuanshi* biography. He was a persistent and consistently successful general who was never defeated in the open; Temüjin came to trust and respect him like no other officer in his service, except perhaps Bo'orcu about whom little is said about in the sources. A close association already existed between Temüjin and Muqali's father Gu'uan. They once rode together with six other men; they were lacking food, and when they finally had food to prepare a large group of Naimans arrived. An arrow hit Temüjin's horse and incapacitated it. Gu'uan gave him his, remaining behind to hold off the Naimans, and fell fighting. Muqali later found himself in a difficult situation with Temüjin. They were riding with a small group of men, entering a wooded ravine where a group of bandits attempted to ambush

---

1   The younger Kölgen (c.1219–1238), born by a different wife, only emerged as a commander during the reign of Ögödei.

them. Muqali acted boldly, placing himself between himself between Temüjin and the bandits; the leader of the bandits asked who he was. He answered: 'I am Muqali.' The bandits fell back and Temüjin was saved. Muqali learned to make use of Chinese officers and soldiers and was able to conquer significant amounts of Chinese territory. He commanded the *left hand* for many years.

Muqali was clearly an effective commander. It is hard to say anything about the other three *steeds*: none of them are credited with victories like Muqali, and Boroqul is even associated with a serious defeat. Temüjin had political reasons for giving them prestige and power as they formed part of a new aristocracy, built up to replace the rival leaders Temüjin had eliminated. Muqali was, for example, important for just that reason. It is therefore wrong to think these officers were promoted solely on merit.

The *hounds* differed from the more senior *steeds* by having a more operational role. They led roving columns operating ahead and around the main army, like dogs sent ahead of a hunting party. These four officers were Jelme, Qubilai, Sübe'etei, and Jebe. They are first mentioned as a group in the *Secret History* in connection with the battle against the Naimans in 1204.

Old Jarci'udai of the Uriyangqai, a blacksmith, brought Jelme to serve Temüjin at an early age (c.1177, just before the Merkits kidnapped Temüjin's wife). Rashid al-Din says he was nicknamed Uha, meaning bandit. The *Secret History* details how Jelme saved the life of Temüjin during a battle against the Tayici'uts in 1200 (dated to 1201 in the *Secret History*). He probably retired or died soon after c.1206. Qubilai belonged to the Barulas, and came to Temüjin around the time of the first clash with Jamuqa (c.1193). Jebe and Qubilai were tasked to confiscate some plunder from officers who did not follow procedure during the Tatar campaign in 1202, and Qubilai was in 1210 sent across the Altai to receive the submission of Arslan. He later commanded a guard unit. Sübe'etei, also of the Uriyangqai, joined Temüjin at the same time as Qubilai; Jelme was his cousin. The *Yuanshi* has two Sübe'etei biographies. Like Muqali, Sübe'etei had descendants who were important men in China, hence he gets much interest from Chinese scribes. Much more will be said about Sübe'etei later.

Jebe is one of the most famous of all Mongol generals. Desmond Martin suggested that 'Had Jebe lived he might have surpassed any Mongol general of which we have a record, including Samuqa, but he died at the early age of 42 or 43.' He does not have a *Yuanshi* biography. This does necessarily mean that he was not considered a great general. Jebe, unlike Muqali and Sübe'etei, did not have descendants with a prominent position in Yuan China whom the chroniclers were eager to impress. Jebe's original name was Jiryo'adai; he probably joined the Mongols before 1196.[2] A Besüt of the Tayici'uts, he had ended up in a difficult situation. The SWQZL says he was 'without resources.' He got into trouble, says Rashid al-Din, when he 'stumbled into the middle of a Mongol hunting circle.' A Mongol challenged Jebe to single combat. He agreed, but asked to be given a horse, and once given one he rode off. He returned later to

---

2   In the SWQZL sequence he joined the Mongols after Dalan Baljut and before the Tatar campaign. The entry is, however, also including events that only happened in 1200; the *Secret History* (147) associates this event with Köyiten, but this must be too late.

submit to Temüjin who admired his courage and took him into his service. He was given the name Jebe, meaning weapon. Jebe is celebrated for making long range feigned retreats to draw the enemy forward. In the *Secret History* he explains his strategy before the Cabiyal Pass: 'When enticing them and making [them] to remove, I shall make [them] to come, then I shall try [them].'[3] The same source says that Temüjin held Jebe in high esteem, saying: 'Jebe, thou hadst the name Jiryo'adai, coming from the Tayiciud, thou art become Jebe.' Jebe as an officer is first mentioned in connection with the 1202 campaign against the Tatars. He had a brother called Monggadu Saru who served Tolui and a son called Suqursun who became a commander of 1,000. Some of his relatives ended up in Persia. Jebe directed only a few campaigns on this own, really only in 1212 and 1216–1218. From 1218 to 1224 he operated with Sübe'etei. Temüjin told Jebe and Sübe'etei to command 'a thousand over as many of those people that they themselves have acquired and constituted as their own patrimony.' The *Secret History* places this ruling in 1205–1206, but it may have been made later after the two generals found many willing recruits in the western regions (after 1216).

In addition to these eight senior officers, a number of other individuals were given command of more than one unit of 1,000. Mönglik Ecige, Qorci, Jürcedei, Qunan, Tolon, Önggur, and Quyildar were some of the important commanders who came to Temüjin before 1206 and are likely to have had several units. A number of other important commanders were those married to his daughters, more distant relatives, or adopted sons. These included Buqa, Qadai, Cigü, Alci, Butu, Olar, Asiq, Sigi Qutuqu, Caqan, Yeke Qutuqu, and Belgutai.

Temüjin mixed family alliances with promotions on merit. A position usually remained with the family, but the most able son or other relative would get the senior appointment. For example, Sübe'etei emerged as a key leader and not his older brother. It cannot be said that Temüjin promoted on merit as it is done, or should be done, in a 'modern' organisation. Rather it was a mix of a feudal family system and a meritocracy.

Appendix 1 lists the commanders in 1227 and compares them to the *Secret History* officer list of 1206. By 1227 Temüjin also had a number of Khitan and Han Chinese officers.

Sources: the SWQZL; Pelliot and Hambis, *Histoire des campagnes de Gengis Khan*, pp.148–149; Rashid al-Din, *The Successors of Genghis Khan*, 18, 160, 247; *Yuanshi* 120, 2962; the *Secret History*, 97, 99, 137, 146–147, 147, 202+, 209, 213, 247, 257, 276; Martin, *The Rise of Chingis Khan and his Conquest of North China* (Baltimore: John Hopkins Press, 1950), p.274; de Rachewiltz, 'Muqali', *In the Service of the Khan: eminent personalities of the early Mongol–Yüan period (1200–1300)* (Wiesbaden: Harrassowitz, 1993), pp.3–8.

---

3   The incident relates to the seizing of a city in Liaodong in 1212, rather than the taking of the Cabiyal Pass in 1211.

3

The Mongol Army

Their army consists of people over 15 years old. There are only horsemen with no foot troops. Each man has 2 to 3 horses, at times 6 to 7 horses ... The most courageous leaders and their strongest men flock together into groups and always remain close to the main leaders. One calls it the *bature* troop. At the time of the wars against the countries Hoxi and the Jurchen, [the Tatars] attacked their cities by letting these people [the *bature* troops] lead the attack.

– Peng Daya

They shoot with their arrows further than other nations do, and at the first onset of combat they do not shoot arrows, but, as one says, they are seen to 'rain' arrows: in combat with swords and lances they are said to be less skilled. The (conscripted) warriors are forced into battle ... Fortified cities they do not assault until first laying waste the district around them and plundering the people: and from the same land they gather people and they force them into fighting for the conquest of their very own castles.

– Julian

The 13th century Mongol army and its doctrine of war have acquired almost mythical status. In the view of James Chambers, 'its tactical principles and its structure of command would not have been unfamiliar to a soldier of the twentieth century.' French historian Rene Grousset offers a more grounded view:

Much has been written about Mongol tactics. Some have compared them with those of Frederick or Napoleon. Cahun sees them as the prodigious conceptions of genius, born at some war council of supermen. In fact, Mongol tactics were a perfected form of the old methods used by the Hsiung-nu and Tu-chueh, the eternal nomad tactics, evolved from continued raids on the fringe of civilization and of great hunting drives on the steppes.

To understand what the Mongol army really operated it is best to turn to the eyewitnesses. Zhao Hong (1221), Peng Daya (1233), Zhou Mi (1234), Su Ding (1237),

Julian (1238), and Carpini (1247) provide early eyewitness accounts of the Mongol army and its tactics. In addition, naturally, plenty of the material in the dynastic histories is supported by eyewitness accounts. The *Secret History*, the SWQZL, and Rashid al-Din provide some glimpses of the early army from the time before Genghis Khan became master over Mongolia.

The tactical unit of the Mongol army was the nominally 1,000 men strong *minghans*. The minghans were grouped together into larger units called *tümens*. Several tümens formed an army. For example, Sübe'etei, Jebe, and Toqucar set out with three tümens in 1220 with a total of about 10,000 men. The *Secret History* gives examples of tümen commanders with two, three or four minghans. A minghan was subdivided into units of 100 and these again were subdivided into units of 10. The minghans contained heavy as well as light cavalry. The Mongol attire has was described by eyewitness Carpini:

> They all have to possess the following arms at least: two or three bows, or at least one good one, three large quivers full of arrows, an axe and ropes for hauling engines of war. As for the wealthy, they had swords pointed at the end but sharp only on one side and somewhat curved, and they have a horse with armour; their legs also are covered and they have helmets and cuirasses. Some have cuirasses and protection for their horses, fashioned out of leather.

The level of armour was a matter of wealth and not something defined by organisation. This is the conclusion of Witold Swietoslawski in his study of Mongol equipment. He does not support the view that there was an organised split between heavy and light cavalry: 'there is no information that nomad cavalry included uniformly armed units which correspond to divisions of light and heavy cavalry.' The Mongols added more and more armour after they started to make inroads into sedentary states. Su Ding says that it was only after the Uighurs submitted in 1209 that the Mongols had access to blacksmiths who could make armour and weapons for them. By the time they fought the Jin they were reportedly better armoured than previous nomad attackers. This comparison must be with previous nomads coming from the Mongolian region as the Manchurian Khitans and Jurchen clearly were well-provided with armoured troops. When the Mongols in 1221 invaded Georgia, it was noted that their men were lightly armed. *The History of Kart'li* says: 'Chingiz-Khan sent princes Yamay and Salpian with 12,000 soldiers having no arms or food, no swords, and only [bows and] arrows.' Therefore, while better armed than earlier Mongolian tribes, it does not seem they were armed well enough to impress the Georgians.

The Jurchen Jin are known to have operated with two ranks of heavy cavalry in front and three ranks of light cavalry behind them. While the Mongols may not have had such clear organisational split between heavy and light cavalry, it is certainly likely that the heavily armed soldiers were deployed in the front ranks when fighting was at close quarters and in the rear when the army fought in skirmishing mode. Timothy May well summarises the Mongol hit-and-run tactics:

Approximately 80 men in each *jaghun* [unit of 100] participated, the remaining 20 acting as heavy cavalry. Each *jaghun* sent 20 men per wave. The waves fired several arrows as they charged, and then circled back to the Mongol lines after completing their charge, having loosed their final shot roughly 40–50m from the enemy line before wheeling around. This distance was close enough to pierce armour, but far enough from the enemy to evade a counter-charge. While circling back, the Mongols often used the 'Parthian shot.' Since each man was equipped with 60 arrows the Mongols could maintain this barrage for almost an hour.

Carpini, while not describing this detailed firing process, does write: 'when they come in sight of the enemy they attack at once, each one shooting three or four arrows at their adversaries.' The earliest source describing the Mongol tactics in detail is Peng Daya, a Song official who visited the Mongols in 1233. He said:

If it is necessary to overcome strong opposition and break through an enemy front, they rely completely on their assault vanguard. [That] The armoured [soldiers] go in front occurs usually in 3 cases out of 10. When they collide with the hostile line, they always hold themselves to [groups of] 3, 5, or 4 and 5 each. They never combine to [larger] groups in order not to allow the enemy to encircle them. As concerns their fast rider attacks – whether now from far or near, to few or to many, whether closed or scattered, when emerging or with the disappearance; they come, as if the sky collapsed, and they go, as if lightning struck.

When he says three to five men attacked it was probably out of a unit of 10, meaning five to seven remained behind to cover the rear. Clearly the Mongols were seen as having potent strike capabilities. However, according to Carpini 'the Tartars do not like to fight hand to hand', and the travelling European priest Julian observed that the Mongols were less noted for their close quarter fighting skills. His comment is of particular interest, as he may have drawn this information from the Volga Bulgars and the people living near them. Europe and the Near East had developed well-armed horsemen relying on shock tactics: quite possibly, against these the Mongols may have been at more disadvantage in close quarter fighting than against foes in China. Consequently, they may have been more reluctant to fight at close quarters in Europe and the Near East. Peng Daya says that the Mongol cavalry usually deployed in a dispersed formation, but that they formed into more compact units if the enemy did so. In Armenia, it was observed that they deployed in compact formation.[1] Here they faced heavy cavalry in dense order. Against the Rus, Hungarians, and Poles they are also likely to have deployed in compact order.

Actual battle accounts clearly show the Mongols capable of fighting at a distance as well as at close quarters. Zhou Mi says the Mongols made 'a sudden charge' on one occasion and on another they must have fought at a distance as the fighting lasted a

---

1   Noted by Hayhon of Armenia.

long time ('battle went on and not ended until noon'). The tactics the Mongols used at Yushan in 1232 are described in the *Jinshi* biography of Yila Pua:

> The cavalry of the Mongol Army marched forward suddenly so that the Jin troops had to go battle with them and even fight hilt to hilt. Two sides engaged each other three times before the Mongol Army withdrew slightly … The detachment of the Mongol Army in the west attacked three times after they found that Pua personally walked round the back of the cavalry, [but] were driven back by Pucha Dingzhu's all-out effort.

The account shows the Mongols fighting at close quarters, and though no mention is made of spears or swords they must have been used. When the Mongols defeated a combined Rus-Kipchak army the Kalka in 1223 they attacked with spears in the centre and bows on the flanks. *The Nikonian Chronicle* says that 'Vasilyok was pierced by a spear.' *The Galician–Volynian Chronicle* says on later events in the same battle 'other [Tatar] regiments engaged them', and from the side 'the [Tatar] bowmen were showering them relentlessly with arrows.' Clearly here the Mongols fought with both spears and bows.[2] The Mongols are known to have fought dismounted, for example in a battle against Khwarezm in 1219. This practice may seem strange, but dismounted knights and men-at-arms in medieval Europe often proved able to hold off mounted forces. It was fairly rare for the Mongols to dismount and when they did it usually involved defending or attacking a camp covered by wagons.

The Mongol grand tactical deployment is almost never described in any detail. Possibly, the standard deployment was a strong centre backed by a reserve and one or more detachments covering either flank. This is what Carpini claimed to be normal:

> The chiefs or princes of the army do not take part in the fighting but take up their stand some distance away facing the enemy … and they have beside them their children on horseback and their womenfolk and horses; and sometimes they make figures of men and set them on horses … They send a detachment of captives and men of other nationalities who are fighting with them to meet the enemy head-on, and some Tartars may perhaps accompany them. Other columns of stronger men they dispatch far off to the right and to the left so that they are not seen by the enemy and in this way they surround them and close in and so the fighting begins from all sides.

The Mongols are known to have deployed drafted forces in the front. The body of Turkmens serving with the Mongols when they fought the Georgians in 1221 was in front and at Liegnitz in 1241 the deserter running to the Poles may have come from a front line of newly drafted forces. The description of Carpini also fits with how the *Secret History* says the Mongols deployed against the Naimans in 1204, though there is no mention of captives or recently drafted forces deployed in front. In battle the

---

2   It is reported in the *Yuanshi* that 'Liu Hengan … charged forward levelling his spear and spurring his horse. The troops of the Song ran disorderly and jostled into the Luoshui' and that 'Liu Bin abandoned his horse and attacked the enemy with his spear. They defeated the Song forces.'

Mongol generals were able to have a good measure of battlefield control by means of flags. At Yushan in 1232, the *Jinshi* says '[a] Mongol commander came to inspect and two little flags were raised. [Then, the Mongol Army] stopped marching.' Later: 'The commander [of the Mongol Army] called up various generals with a flag and consulted each other for a good while.' The Mongols had exceptional control over their forces during that battle.

On the strategic level, the Mongols moved forward on a broad front with scouting detachments usually, says Peng Daya, moving 50 to 100 km ahead of the main forces. The reach of the Mongol scouting columns was astonishing. When in 1232 Sübe'etei moved north from Dengzhou to Hsuzhou, some scouting units approached Bozhou, 300 km off the Mongol line of advance. In Poland in 1241 the main forces moved past Cracow and Opole to Breslau, while scouting units made their way into Prussia in the north. The scouts provided the Mongol officers with detailed intelligence and gave them a clear picture of where they could expect to face serious opposition. According to Peng Daya typical questions of the Mongols to local people were: 'Which roads can we move along? What towns can we attack? In what area can we fight? In what places can we camp? In what direction stand enemy forces? In which places are there food and forage?' The various scout units and army detachments kept the central command informed by means of frequent messages.

Usually the camp was far off the rear and nowhere near the battlefield. The Mongol army travelled with many spare horses, two, three, or more per fighter, and needed to detach a considerable part of their forces to guard the horses as well as the camp. The *Jinshi* says: '*Liangsheng* consulted with his officers again and said: "The Mongol Army is known to have 30,000 soldiers, but their impedimenta take up one-third."' The third guarding the camp was normally left in the rear: the *Yuanshi* says at one point: 'Tolui had no more than 40,000 forces. On hearing the intelligence [of the approach of the Jin army], [Tolui] left all the supplies and gear at behind and sent light-packed cavalry ahead as vanguard.' The same happened in Georgia where local historian Kirakos Ganjakec'i says that the Mongols had 'secured their bags and baggage in the marshy, muddy place which lies between the cities of Bartaw and Belukan.' In Mongolia the tribal population remained behind when the army set out. A guard was left to guard family and livestock. The Mongols therefore had a 'strategic camp' (with families, horses, and other livestock) and a 'tactical camp' (mobile camp with spare horses) with the army.

The Mongol fighting style was initially much the same as any other Inner Asian tribe, but finally evolved into something very similar to the Liao Khitans. It is seems possible Temüjin copied the organisation and doctrine of the Kereyits, as he was initially a subject lord to them.[3] Harold Lamb thought Temüjin introduced more compact Khitan fighting tactics as early as the Dalan Baljut battle in marked contrast to his foe ('Temüjin was able to throw his heavy masses against the lighter squadrons of his foe'), but there is no evidence for this. It is clear, however, that the Mongols

3   Like To'oril, Temüjin initially had a 1,000-strong guard.

eventually learned to fight much like the Khitans. Did the Kereyits also do that, or did the Mongol tactics change later? The Naimans, previously West Liao subjects, could have adopted some of the Khitan tactics as well. Temüjin probably already had Khitan military men in his service in 1197. They could have helped to diffuse the Khitan doctrine of war.

In 1206 the previously 1,150 men strong personal guard of Temüjin was increased to 10,000. It later almost tripled in size with units attached not just to Temüjin, but also to his sons and other relatives. Nearly 30 percent of the Mongol army was then guards. The army started to change in a different way after 1211 when significant Liao, Jurchen, and Han Chinese contingents were gradually added. A key addition was siege specialists. By 1229, these non-Mongol units made up about 40 percent of the total. With the Mongols continuing to add Chinese units, this percentage increased year by year, and by 1241 the Mongols only accounted for 40 percent of the total. The non-Mongols would by then have provided significant infantry forces though even later Song observers continue to insist the Mongol army was 100 percent cavalry. By 1270, when the final conquest of Song China started in earnest, there were even relatively more Chinese forces. By then it was really a Chinese rather than a Mongol army.

Sources: Zhao Hong, Peng Daya, and Su Ding, in Olbricht and Pinks, *Meng-Ta Pei-Lu und Hei-ta Shih-Lüeh*; Zhou Mi, *Zhitongyeyu*, pp.77–80; Julian; Hansgerd Göckenjan and James Sweeney, *Der Mongolensturm: Berichte von Augenzeugen und Zeitgenossen, 1235–1250* (Graz: Styria, 1985), pp.101–109; Carpini, *The story of the Mongols whom we call Tartars*, chapters 15–16; *The Vinland Map and the Tartar Relation*, translated by R. A. Skelton and others (New Haven: Yale University Press, 1965), pp.98–100; *Yuanshi* 115, p.2885, 150, pp.3559–3560; *Jinshi* 112, pp.2470–2475; Perfecky, *The Hypatian Chronicle: The Galician–Volynian Chronicle*, p.25; Zenkovsky and Zenkovsky, *The Nikonian Chronicle*, p.287; Lamb, *Genghis Khan*, p.25; René Grousset, *Empire of the Steppes: a history of central Asia* (New Brunswick: Rutgers, 1988), pp.219–226; Martin, *The Rise of Chingis Khan*, pp.11–47; Chambers, *The Devil's Horsemen*, pp.62–84; Robert Bedrosian, *The Turco-Mongol Invasions and the Lords of Armenia in the 13–14th Centuries* (Ph. D., Columbia University, 1979), note 164; Witold Swietoslawski, *Arms and armour of the nomads of the Great Steppe in the times of the Mongol expansion* (Łódź: Oficyna Naukova MS, 1999), p.104; Timothy May, *The Mongol Art of War* (Barnsley: Pen & Sword Military, 2007), p.72.

Overview: Ally of To'oril, 1191 to 1202

Yisügei was leader of the Borjigen tribe. He was on bad terms with the Tatars, and some by chance recognised him when he was out travelling and fatally poisoned him (c.1175). Yisügei's wife Hö'elün was of Onggirad stock. Yisügei had originally intercepted her while she was on the way to marry a Merkit. According to Rashid al-Din she was 'highly intelligent and competent.' After Yisügei died, many people left; Hö'elün went after them with a banner and managed to get some of them to stay. According to later Muslim sources Yisügei had ruled over 40,000 families, but after his death only one third stayed loyal to the clan. Yisügei's heir and Hö'elün's eldest son, Temüjin, was at this time about 12 years old.[1] Little is known about events of this period, though at one point Temüjin spent time as a captive amongst some Tayici'uts. Shortly after he married Börte of the Onggirads (c.1177), Toqto'a and some 300 Merkit warriors made a sudden raid on his camp at the Burgi Escarpment along the Kerulen River. Temüjin managed to get away, but his wife was captured. To'oril, the Kereyit *khan*, helped Temüjin get her back. A Merkit may have fathered the child she soon afterwards gave birth to. Even so, Temüjin raised the son, whom he named Joci, as his own (Joci was born c.1178).

Years before, a rival had forced Kereyit ruler To'oril into exile. Yisügei had helped To'oril recover his position. Perhaps To'oril backed young Temüjin because of the debt he felt he owed to his father? Such support could have been vital for Temüjin. What is clear is that he emerged as a leader with a fairly significant following. Even if To'oril supported Temüjin, it did not deter other tribes from fighting him. Rashid al-Din says that Temüjin often fought against the Tayici'uts and their allies the Salji'uts and Qadagins and that result of these early military undertakings were mixed. He also says he had fought against the Tatars before the first recorded campaign in 1196. However, no real details are given. The early phase of Temüjin's military life – 1177 to 1191 – is largely lost to history. One episode given by Rashid al-Din and SWQZL seems to describe an early event. Ölug Bahadur and Taqai Dalu and the Je'üreyit followed Temüjin for a while, but finally left. The Tayici'ut Qadun Orchang later defeated Taqai

---

1 The *Secret History* says 9 (8). Rashid al-Din says he was 13 (12). Yisügei had named his son Temüjin because at the time of his birth he had captured a Tatar lord with that name. Temüjin means 'iron', like the Turkish name Temür.

Dalu and dispersed the Je'üreyit. At some later point Jamuqa became the Je'üreyit leader (these events could be placed during the 1180s).[2]

The *Secret History* says To'oril, Temüjin, and Jamuqa attacked the Merkits in order to get Börte back after she was kidnapped. As it seems more likely that To'oril helped Temüjin get Börte back without any military operations, then what to make of the campaign described by the *Secret History*? Pelliot suggests the account is a composite of pieces from later campaigns against the Merkits. Here it is assumed that it was an actual operation that happened around two years before the Dalan Baljut campaign, but that it had nothing to do with Börte.

The Dalan Baljut campaign is the first one known to all key sources. During it Temüjin fought a battle against Jamuqa. It is by a late source dated to early 1194, and in the narrative sequence of the *Secret History*, the Merkit campaign could be placed about two years before that, therefore dated to late 1191. From 1196 onwards the chronology is clearer, but not without issues. The sequence of the SWQZL is accepted as the best. The main problem is the events of the years 1200, 1201, and 1202: the SWQZL, Rashid al-Din and *Yuanshi* say there were battles against tribal coalitions in 1200 and 1201 and against Tatars in 1201 and 1202, whereas the *Secret History* has only one clash with a coalition and one Tatar battle. Possibly some events have been duplicated in the other sources. The sources are very brief in general and certainly much important information is left out. Sometimes it is not clear if Temüjin directed operations in person, and it is not always clear if he was on his own or operated with his ally To'oril.

The *Secret History* provides figures. At the start of the period covered in this section Temüjin made an attack with 10,000 men, but more would have been left behind to guard the base camp, and he had 30,000 when fighting against Jamuqa. When he had subjected all of Mongolia by 1206, he had a little more than 100,000 men. By then some people had been killed and some driven into exile, but even so the two early numbers look high. They are, however, the only figures given in the sources and will be used as a base to track his development and estimate numbers.

Mongolia experienced a period of drought from the 1180s onwards. This is likely to have put pressure on population and livestock and served as a trigger for increased conflict between tribes. The situation only improved by 1211 and finally from 1214 onwards.[3] The sources of the early period put the spotlight on Temüjin and offer no complete history of Mongolia. While it is possible the inter-tribal wars intensified from the 1180s onwards it is hard to see support for or against this contention in the written sources. Certainly from 1196 to 1208 there was constant warfare involving most tribes at some point. Possibly that was also the case from the 1180s to 1196, even if Temüjin only played a limited part in these.

2   The *Secret History*, 59–103; Rashid al-Din 53, 72, 202–203, 210, 223, 418–419; Ulug Big: *The Shajrat ul-Atrak of Muhammad Taragay ibn Sahruh*, translated by Col. Miles (London: W. H. Allen and Co., 1838), p.221; Raverty, *Tabakat-i-Nasiri*, p.938; Ratchnevsky, pp.17–48; Paul D. Buell, *Historical Dictionary of the Mongol World Empire* (Oxford: The Scarecrow Press, Inc., 2003), pp.1–11.
3   *Scientific American*, 12 March 2014, History of Science.

4

The First Raid on the Merkits

Starting from Botoqan Bo'orjin they arrived at the river Kilqo. They made rafts and crossed it … While Toqto'a was asleep, some fishermen, sable catchers, and wild animal hunters who happened to be by the river Kilqo, left it and, travelling all through the night, brought the news of the allies' approach saying, 'The enemies are coming, pushing forward at high speed.' When they received this news, Toqto'a and Dayir Usun … joined together, went downstream along the Selengge and entered the Barqujin territory … the Merkit people fled in disarray … during the night.

– the *Secret History*, 109–110

Jamuqa was the leader of the Jadaran tribe, who lived along the Onon. Temüjin and Jamuqa had known each other since childhood and were sworn blood brothers, so must have been about the same age. Rashid al-Din describes Jamuqa as 'very intelligent and crafty.' He had at one point been taken captive by Toqto'a and had only managed to get away after spending some time in the Merkit camp. It seems possible that Jamuqa afterwards persuaded To'oril to make a joint attack the Merkits in order to punish them. Temüjin also took part in the expedition in the capacity as a subject lord of To'oril. Though To'oril was the senior lord, it was Jamuqa who planned the operation (the expedition could be dated to late 1191). He guessed or knew where To'oril camped and planned to make a surprise rear attack on his position. He specified where and when the attacking coalition force should assemble, and knowing a river had to be crossed near the enemy camp, instructed all to bring many 'sedges'.

To'oril set out from the Qara Tun along the Tu'ula River. He marched eastwards in two columns led by himself and his brother Jaqa Gambo.[1] Temüjin joined him on the way, coming from his camp along the upper Kerulen and Jamuqa set out from the area around the upper Onon. They had agreed to meet at Botoqan Bo'orjin near the source of the Onon. Jamuqa arrived at the time agreed, but To'oril and Temüjin were three days late, and Jamuqa was upset: 'Jamuqa said: "Even if a snowstorm stands

---

1   Jaqa Gambo is a Xia title: his real name was Kerabetai. He was either To'oril's brother or uncle. One of his daughters later married Tolui, the mother of Möngke, Qubilai, and Hülegü.

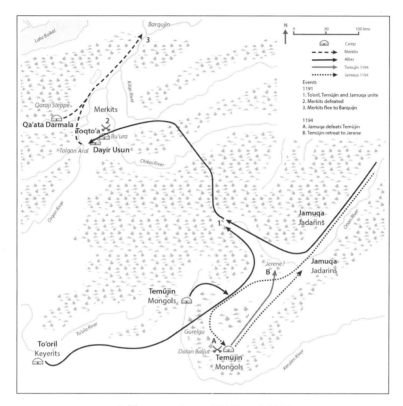

1. The operations of 1191 and 1194.

in the way of the appointment, even if rain hinders the meeting, we [should] not be late. Did we not so agree? [When] we Mongols say 'yes', are we not bound by oath?"' To'oril managed to calm him down, saying 'Because we are 3 days late at the rendezvous younger brother Jamuqa has the right to criticise and chastise us.' The allies are reported by the *Secret History* to have fielded a total of 40,000 men with To'oril having half and Temüjin and Jamuqa each 10,000.

There were three main Merkit groups, the Uduyit, U'as, and Qo'as. With regard to their respective camps, Jamuqa said 'Toqto'a … must be in the Bu'ura Steppe. Dayir … must be at Talqun Aral. Qa'atai Darmala … must be in the Qaraji Steppe.' The sources say nothing about how many fighting men the Merkits had; certainly the forces mobilised against them this year must have been much stronger than anything they could field. The allies planned to make a detour along an eastward arc to get in the rear of the Merkit camp at Bu'ura. To do so they twice had to cross the Chikoi – assuming the *Secret History* is wrong to say Kilqo. The allies crossed the river and moved towards the enemy camp from the north-east. Some fishermen saw them along the river and quickly rushed to warn Toqto'a, but in spite of this the Merkits failed to prepare for combat in time and were quickly dispersed, pursued by To'oril, Jamuqa, and Temüjin to Talqan Aral. Toqto'a and Dayir Usun of the U'as fled across the Selengge and hurried northward to Barqujin. The allied pursuit ended at Talqan Aral. No mention is made of the Qo'as Merkits who perhaps camped west of the Selengge.

Jamuqa seems to have conceived an imaginative campaign plan. He was angered by the late arrival of To'oril and Temüjin at the agreed meeting point: evidently the tribesmen could plan operations in some detail with intent to follow a plan with a time schedule. Jamuqa was known as an intelligent man and he may have planned operations in more detail and with more imagination than was normal. The Merkits were taken by surprise and did not offer effective resistance, but this was a raid and no permanent damage seems to have been inflicted on them.

Sources: The *Secret History*, 66, 108–109; Rashid al-Din 71–72; Pelliot and Hambis, *Histoire des campagnes de Gengis Khan*, pp.265–267; Ratchnevsky, *Genghis Khan: His Life and Legacy*, pp.17–48; Ruth Dunnell, 'The Fall of the Xia Empire', in G. Seaman and D. Marks, *Rulers from the Steppe: state formation on the Eurasian periphery* (Los Angeles: Ethnographics Press, 1991), pp.162–163; Denis Sinor, 'On Mongol Strategy', in Cheih-hsien Ch'en, *Proceedings of the fourth East Asian Altaistic Conference* (Tainan: National Ch'engkung University, 1975), p.240; de Rachewiltz, commentary on the *Secret History*, pp.421–422; Vito Pecchia, *Geography of 'the Secret History of the Mongols'* (paper, 2010).

5

The Victory of Jamuqa

They fought at Dalan Baljut: Činggis Qa'an was repulsed there by Jamuqa and sought refuge in the Jerene Gorge by the Onon River.

– the *Secret History*, 129

After the Merkit campaign Temüjin and Jamuqa decided to stay together, moving as one group with their followers. Together they were stronger, but two leaders in one camp was not likely to remain workable for long. The political history of this period is not known. At one point Jamuqa and Temüjin sent an embassy to the Qadagins and Salji'uts, perhaps to win them over in order to weaken the Tayici'uts who relied on the support of these two tribes. In early summer 1993, after travelling together for a year and a half, Temüjin decided to leave Jamuqa and marched away with his people during the night. The *Secret History* says that 'without pitching camp they set off, travelling at night. As they proceeded, they passed the Tayici'ut encampment along the way. The Tayici'ut, for their part, became frightened and that same night in great confusion actually moved to Jamuqa's side.' These people viewed Temüjin as a threat, but many others wanted to join him. According to the *Secret History*, 41 named tribal leaders left Jamuqa to join Temüjin after their break-up. The most significant leaders coming over at this point were Önggur, Cülgetei, Qorci, Ünjin, Qunan, Daritai Otcigin, Saca Beki, Taicu, Qucar Beki, and Altan Otcigin. These new followers may have helped Temüjin increase the size of his army from about 20,000 to 30,000 men. Jamuqa had 10,000 men in 1192, but this was probably not his full force and afterwards he may have gained more followers. Even so, a loss of 10,000 men would have been highly significant.

Sometime after the break with Jamuqa, Temüjin was elected *khan* by his followers. Already a leader, he now claimed a more formal title. To'oril was reportedly pleased with this. At a later point, angered by a cattle-raiding incident that had led to the death of a relative, Jamuqa set out to attack Temüjin. He made an alliance with the Tayici'ut, Ikires, Uru'ud, Noyakin, Barulas, and Ba'arin and was able to assemble 30,000 men along the upper Onon (late 1193 or early 1194). Temüjin camped at Dalan Baljut, probably just east of the upper 'bend' of the Kerulen River, while Jamuqa crossed through the Ala'ut Turqa'ut Mountains and reached the area south of the Gürelgü Mountains. It seems he moved in an arc to the north to outflank Temüjin's position, much like he had outflanked the Merkit camp two years before. The Merkits had been taken by surprise, but Temüjin was not: the tribes of Jamuqa and Temüjin were too closely related to make it possible for one to surprise the other, and there was always somebody ready to send a warning.[1] Furthermore Temüjin, unlike Toqto'a, acted quickly on intelligence. As he approached the Mongol camp, Jamuqa found Temüjin deployed in a battle line, ready to fight.

All sources credit Jamuqa with 30,000 men, and the *Secret History* says Temüjin had the same number. Temüjin deployed in 13 circles with non-combatants, camp items and animals in the middle of each. His men seem to have fought dismounted, presumably using carts at least in part to cover their positions. The 13 units were possibly:

1.   Mother Hö'elün
2.   Temüjin
3.   Bültecu of the Kereyits, Muqur Qa'uran of the Hadargins, and Ca'urqa of the Qorolas
4.   Dereng and Qoridai with the Nirun and Buda'at
5.   Saca Beki and the Jürkins
6.   Taicu and the Jalayirs[2]
7.   Qulan Ba'atur and Tödö'en Otcigin with the Kiyat[3]
8.   Mönggetü Qiyan with the Cangsi'ut and Önggur[4] with the Baya'ut
9.   Daritai Otcigin,[5] Qucar, and Dalu with the Doqolat, Saqayit, and Nünjin
10. Joci, son of Qutula, younger brother of Temüjin's grandfather
11. Altan Otcigin, brother of Joci
12. Daki Ba'atur with the Qonggiyat and the Sükeken
13. Gendü Cina and Olukcin Cina

Saca Beki (5), Taicu (6), Önggür (8), Daritai Otcigin and Qucar (9), and Altan Otcigin (11) had all left Jamuqa for Temüjin after their break-up. Possibly Temüjin placed the new followers in the centre, with his own person and long-serving leaders on the wings. Several commanders are not listed. Qunan, Önggur, Ünjin, and Qorci/Üsün/Kökö Cos should all have commanded a 'camp'; perhaps they camped separately and did not have time to join Temüjin.

How the battle unfolded is not known. Jamuqa may have overwhelmed the Cina unit, which could have been stationed on a flank, as amongst those killed was Caqa'an U'a of the Ne'us. Years later, says the *Secret History*, 'Genghis Khan said to Caqa'an U'a's son, Narin To'oril: "Your father, Caqa'an U'a, went to great lengths in fighting for me at Dalan Baljut. During the fighting, he was killed by Jamuqa."' Temüjin was finally, to use

---

1   Rashid al-Din says Näkun of the Ikires sent a warning 'because his son Butu was Genghis Khan's attendant'; Mülqa and Totaq of the Barulas were sent to deliver the warning, and according to the *Secret History* Boroldai and Mülketotaq of the Barulas also acted.
2   Saca Beki and Taicu were grandchildren of an older brother of Temüjin's grandfather.
3   Alternatively, Utuju and another lord were the leaders of this group.
4   Önggür was a son of Mönggetü Kiyan.
5   Younger brother of Temüjin's father.

the wording of the *Secret History*, 'repulsed.' He retreated some distance before taking up a defensive position in a pass called Jerene near the Onon River. This line of retreat was probably chosen because Jamuqa had approached from the west and therefore blocked the direct route to the upper Kerulen, the favoured Mongol territory. A later source, which says Temüjin won the battle, claims Jamuqa lost 5,000–6,000 men. According to the *Secret History*, Temüjin later blamed Jamuqa for having caused him 'to be afraid' at the Jerene Pass. However, Jamuqa did not pursue the defeated forces. After the battle captured Cinas lords were boiled alive, an act of cruelty that probably did not play well with many of his men. The *Secret History* also says Jamuqa 'cut off the head of Čaqa'an U'a of the Ne'üs' and 'dragged it away bound to the tail of his horse.' Jamuqa's weakness as a political leader was well understood. Sorqan the Baya'ut said: 'Jamuqa … constantly incites one person against the other and pursues his aims with flattery and guile.' Having won the battle, he actually lost followers to Temüjin. Jürcedei, Quyildar and Mönglik came to Temüjin with their people;[6] they may have brought 10,000 or more men.[7] Jamuqa and his allies must have returned to the eastern regions.

The various numbers given in the *Secret History* are as previously noted probably too high, but may correctly illustrate the Mongol growth in power. The *Secret History* says Temüjin had 10,000 men when he took part in the Merkit campaign; other forces guarded his camp. After the break with Jamuqa an additional 10,000 could have joined him with 10,000 more coming after the Dalan Baljut battle. If Jamuqa had had 30,000 men at Dal Baljut, he was with this count left with fewer than 20,000 men. Additional men probably guarded his camp also. Even so, he was perhaps no longer powerful enough to challenge Temüjin, who was now the dominant leader in the upper Kerulen and western Onon region. Jamuqa had tried without success to gain advantage by means of strategy, but probably could never hope to completely surprise Temüjin; the battle was a victory for Jamuqa, but not a decisive one. Evidently Temüjin was able to make his men resist effectively, though the tactical details are not clear. Many lords found Temüjin a more attractive leader even after having the worst of this battle. Unable to reach a decisive military decision, the leadership of Temüjin and Jamuqa became the key issue, and Jamuqa lost this contest much like a political leader can lose an election.

Sources: the SWQZL; Pelliot and Hambis, *Histoire des campagnes de Gengis Khan*, pp.35–141; Rashid al-Din, 159–160, 243–249, 273, 276; *Yuanshi* 1, p.12; the *Secret History*, 116–130, 201, 218; Aboul Ghazi Bahadour Khan, in *Histoire des Moguls et des Tatares*, translated by Le Baron Desmaisons (St Petersburg, 1874), pp.78–79 (specifies the year and losses of Jamuqa); Raverty, p.938; Grousset, *Empire of the Steppes*, pp.201–203; Allsen, 'The rise of the Mongolian empire', p.337; de Rachewiltz, commentary on the *Secret History*, pp.269, 474, 522; Christopher Atwood, *Commentary of Shenwu qinzhenglu*, http://cces.snu.ac.kr/com/18swqe.pdf, accessed 31 Dec. 2012, p.12.

---

6   Caraqai, the father of Mönglik, is by the SWQZL credited with remaining loyal to Temüjin after his father died. He fought against those wanting to defect and was mortally wounded. Mönglik initially remained loyal, but seems to have left later.

7   Jürcedei and Quyuldar later had 4,000 men each. Mönglik brought additional men.

6

The Defeat of the Tatars

Činggis Qa'an and To'oril ... together set out with their troops. As they approached, moving downstream along the Ulja to launch the attack in conjunction with Wanyan Xiang, and the Tatar Meüjin and the other Tatars built a stockade there, at Qusutu Sitü'en and Naratu Sitü'en by the Ulja.

– the *Secret History*, 133

The ruling house of the Manchurian Jurchen tribesmen had taken the dynastic name Jin. The Jin controlled large parts of Han Chinese territory, but remained in the Manchurian state with the core fighting men provided by Jurchens and Khitans. They were eager builders of fortified lines along the border, but could also make military strikes deep into Mongolia. It was when the Jin sent forces to operate against troublesome tribesmen that Temüjin saw a new chance to increase his power. The background was as follows. On 7 July 1195, Jin officer Jiagu Qingchen was tasked to deal with the unruly Onggirad tribe. He operated from Linhuang, a city located on the lower eastern side of the mountains separating the Mongolian plains from Manchuria; the Onggirads and Tatars lived further north along the western side of the same mountains. The Jin made an alliance with the Tatars and with their help defeated the Onggirads. Qingchen claimed to have seized 14 enemy camps and to have reached the Qalqa and Kulun. He sent a report to the Jin Court in Beijing, which was received 5 August.

Zuxu, a senior Tatar lord, quarrelled with Jin officers over the handling of loot (August–September 1195).[1] Jiagu Qingchen failed to get on top of the situation during the subsequent months, and on 25 December was finally replaced by the more senior Wanyan Xiang. In January 1196 Xiang set out to deal with Zuxu, and sent Wanyan Anguo forward with a detachment, following with the main forces on the left and right. The Jin moved north-westwards towards the Kerulen River, and Zuxu attacked the forward detachment, as Xiang probably expected. The Jin advance forces

---

1   Zuxu is the name as rendered in Chinese sources.

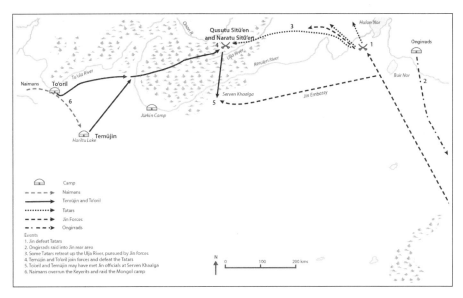

Legend on map:

- Camp
- Naimans
- Temüjin and To'oril
- Tatars
- Jin Forces
- Ongirrads

Events
1. Jin defeat Tatars
2. Ongirrads raid into Jin rear area
3. Some Tatars retreat up the Ulja River, pursued by Jin forces
4. Temüjin and To'oril join forces and defeat the Tatars
5. To'oril and Temüjin may have met Jin officials at Serven Khaalga
6. Naimans overrun the Keyerits and raid the Mongol camp

2. The operations against the Tatars in 1196.

held off the Tatars for three days before the main Jin forces arrived; the Tatars were defeated and driven off. Anguo set off in pursuit. The Wanyan Xiang biography claims the Tatars lost many men under difficult winter conditions. Evidently the Onggirads remained hostile: on 4 February 1196 they defeated a Jin detachment, killing Jin officer Yila Du at a place called the Great Salt Lake. Pelliot considers it likely that the lake in question is Dabsutu, east of Linhuang. If so, the Onggirads had struck deep into Jin territory.

Anguo chased some Tatars towards the Ulja River. Mägüdjin-säültü, a Tatar strongman and evidently a supporter of Zuxu, led a Tatar group westward along the Ulja with the Jin in pursuit. To'oril and Temüjin set out to intercept him, and Temüjin asked Saca Beki, and Taicu and the Jürkins to support him.[2] They had commanded two of the 13 units at Dalan Bajut. Temüjin waited for six days, but the Jürkins did not show up; he then set out with what Rashid al-Din calls a small force. If he disposed over 40,000 men or so in total, then a Jürkin no-show might reduce this total by at most 10,000. After leaving a third of his force to guard the camp, Temüjin could still set out with 20,000 or more men. To'oril may have led a similar-sized force, as during the earlier Merkit campaign. To'oril and Temüjin, marching up along the Ulja, came against the Tatars from the west and attacked them at Naratu Sitü'en and Qusutu Sitü'en – in a plain, according to the SWQZL – and successfully stormed a barricade the Tatars had constructed. It is seems likely that both sides fought dismounted. If

---

2   The *Secret History* says To'oril was there, though the SWQZL, Rashid al-Din, and *Yuanshi* 1 say Temüjin was alone. As To'oril was later given a Jin title it seems he could have been there. According to the *Secret History*, the Jin communicated with To'oril and asked him to move against the Tatars.

the Tatars opted to defend a position rather than fight in the open they were almost certainly much weaker than To'oril and Temüjin. The SWQZL says Temüjin 'captured all their wagons and horses, food and supplies; he killed Mägüdjin-säültü … [and] took a placket with pearls and a silver cut.'

To'oril and Temüjin reported their success to Wanyan Xiang; the *Secret History* says that they even met him. The Jin official was pleased with their achievement and titles were conferred on To'oril and Temüjin. To'oril was given the title *Ong* (Wang) *Khan*. Temüjin received a smaller title. There is an inscription on a rock at Serven Khaalga (Serban Qada);[3] not attested in the sources, this monument was perhaps erected where the Mongol, Kereyit, and Jin officials met. To'oril and Temüjin could have headed to this location after the victory over the Tatars. As the Jin emperor probably needed to grant the titles (by means of an edict), some time is likely to have passed before the process was finalised.[4]

Yelü Ahai and his brother Yelü Tuhua were ethnic Khitans in Jin service, based in the border town of Huanzhou. They defected and joined Temüjin along with some followers before 1203. Yelü Ahai had brought a Jin message to To'oril, perhaps now, after the Tatar campaign. Meeting Temüjin, he was immediately impressed and decided to follow him, but first returned to Huanzhou, bringing his brother Tukha with him the next time he returned to Mongolia. When the Jin understood they had defected, they seized their families. Temüjin was evidently a charismatic character, able to attract the followers of Jamuqa as well as Khitans in Jin service.

Soon after the victory over the Tatars To'oril was deposed by an uncle or a brother, Arka-Qara, who was backed by Inanca Bilge, the ruler of the strong Naiman tribe. A Naiman army entered Kereyit territory, perhaps before To'oril returned from the Tatar campaign; he fled to West Liao, and his brother Jaqa Gambo fled into Jin territory with his followers. A Naiman column attacked Temüjin's camp at Hariltu Lake, causing some damage: the SWQZL says the Naimans 'plundered' the people in the camp. The location of Hariltu Lake is not known, but it could have been in the open country south or south-west of the upper Kerulen River.[5]

The Tatar leader Zuxu submitted to the Jin, but quickly rebelled again in December 1196. Evidently the Jin successes were not decisive. The Jin campaigns in 1195 and 1196 were the last offensives into the Mongolian plains, and the operations were fairly successful. Why did they not return during the later years to check the expanding influence of first To'oril and Temüjin and later of Temüjin only (say in 1199, 1201, 1202, 1203 or even 1204)? They attacked the Tatars because they misbehaved, but the Jin did not have an active policy to keep the tribes divided. In 1211 they had to face Temüjin at the head of a united tribal empire and then found it impossible to challenge the Mongols in the open country.

---

3   Location 47.17°N 110.82°E.
4   Pelliot speculated that it could only happen after Wanyan Xiang returned to the capital in September. If
     To'oril did not take part in the battle, perhaps he came forward to take part in the meeting with Jin officials.
5   Chen Dezhi favours a location north of Mandalgobi; it could also be somewhere near Darkhan. A different
     solution is to place it near Gürelgu.

The Jin constructed new fieldworks to cover the outer border during the 1190s. The biography of Wanyan Xiang reports specifically that he constructed fieldworks after defeating the Tatars in 1196. These were constructed deep into the plains to cover new sedentary settlements in the north. Paul Buell says about the walls:

> Evidence from available population data for large scale penetration of marginal territories in Inner Mongolia by non-pastoral population elements in the 12th century is fully supported by archaeological findings. Inner Mongolia is dotted with ruins from the 11th and 12th centuries. Among these are remains of many small settlements, towns, and even small cities, contained within an area protected by the remains of several lines of outer frontier fortifications constructed by Chin government in the 12th century to protect the expanded agricultural cultural areas of its subjects from nomadic incursions.

The outer population may have been more than 800,000 men strong. A trench was created north of the Kerulen River, but that was probably an earlier Liao construction. The Jin would have worked on the trenches further south and also east.

Sources: the SWQZL; Pelliot and Hambis, *Histoire des campagnes de Gengis Khan*, pp.191–214; Rashid al-Din, 250; *Yuanshi* 1, p.15; the *Secret History*, 134; *Jinshi* 10, 11, 93, and 94, summarised by Pelliot and Hambis, pp.195–198, 402–403; Grousset, *Empire of the Steppes*, pp.203–204; Ratchnevsky, 'Sigi-Qutuqu, ein mongolischer Gefolgsman im 12–13 jahrhundert', *Central Asiatic Journal*, vol. 10, p.77; Paul D. Buell, *Tribe, Qan and Ulus in early Mongol China: some prolegomena to Yüan History* (Ph. D., University of Washington, 1977), pp.20–21; Paul D. Buell, 'Yeh-lu A-hai' and 'Yeh-lu T'u-hua', in de Rachewiltz, *In the Service of the Khan*, pp.113–114; Buell, *Historical Dictionary of the Mongol World Empire*, pp.19–20; de Rachewiltz, commentary on the *Secret History*, p.500; Bazargür Dambyn and Enkhbayar Dambyn, *Chinggis Khaan: A historic-geographic atlas* (Mongolia, 1996), pp.24–25.

7

Showdown with the Jürkins and the Restoration of To'oril

[The emperor] … therefore set off with the troops through the Big Valley and arrived at Dolon Boldau Mountain; he captured the majority of the Jürkin tribe. Only Saca Beki and Taicu, with their wives and their children and furthermore some men managed to escape.

[The emperor and Jaqa Gambo] … found the Merkits coming to do battle. In conjunction with Jaqa Gambo, the emperor marched against the enemy who were defeated and ran away … In the winter of the same year, he pursued Saca Beki and Taicu of the Jürkins who had previously escaped, and, reaching them in the Telegetü Pass, destroyed them.

– the SWQZL

The Naiman-backed overthrow of To'oril changed the power balance in Mongolia, with the Naimans extending their influence into the central regions. Temüjin operated on the fringes of their sphere of control, and wanted to punish them for the attack on his camp. Mobilising his forces, he sent 60 men to ask the Jürkins to join the expedition, but they killed 10 and stole 'the horses of 50 men, and stripped them of their clothing'; perhaps they had reached some kind of agreement with the enemy. Temüjin afterwards said: 'Now they have united with rebels and I am forced to deal with them.' The rebels in question could be the Naiman-backed Kereyit faction who had overthrown To'oril. Failing to deal with the Jürkins would have undermined Temüjin's authority amongst his followers. Temüjin had commanded 13 units at Dalan Baljut; he gained three after the Dalan Baljut battle, but lost two with the defection of the Jürkins. With 14 units against the Jürkins', Temüjin would have been by far the strongest even though the units must have varied in size. Surely the Jürkin units were larger than the average, otherwise how could they dare defy Temüjin?

In the autumn of 1196 Temüjin crossed a desert and defeated the Jürkins at Dolon Boldau.[1] Saca Beki and Taicu escaped with some followers, but the major part of the

---

1   Rashid al-Din says he 'marched through the sand-desert'; the SWQZL says he went 'through the Big Valley.' There are several such locations at Dolon Boldau in Mongolia. According to the *Secret History* this one is associated with 'Ködö'e Island in the Keluren River.'

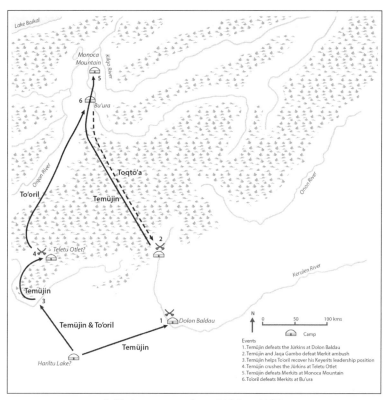

Lake Baikal

Monoca
Mountain

Kilgo River

5

6 Bu'ura

Toqto'a

Oroon River

To'oril

Temüjin

2

4 Teletü Otlet?

Kerulen River

Temüjin

3

Temüjin & To'oril

1 Dolon Baldau

Temüjin

Hariltu Lake?

N   0   50   100 kms

Camp

Events
1. Temüjin defeats the Jürkins at Dolon Baldau
2. Temüjin and Jaqa Gambo defeat Merkit ambush
3. Temüjin helps To'oril recover his Keyerits leadership position
4. Temüjin crushes the Jürkins at Teletu Otlet
5. Temüjin defeats Merkits at Monoca Mountain
6. To'oril defeats Merkits at Bu'ura

3. Various events from 1196 to 1199.

tribe was taken captive. Saca Beki and Taicu fled westwards, settling close to or inside Kereyit territory where the Naiman-supported leadership welcomed them. The Jürkin lord Telegetü submitted to Temüjin, bringing along his sons Gu'un U'a, Cila'un, and Jebke. Gu'un U'a's two sons Muqali and Buqa also came. Muqali was at this time about 23 years old. Temüjin must have been keen to find Jürkin lords he could rely on to replace Saca Beki and Taicu. Muqali very quickly became one of his most senior officers.[2]

Some time later, encouraged by Temüjin, Jaqa Gambo came back from Jin territory and set up camp next to Temüjin at unidentified Darasut. They later defeated Toqto'a and the Merkits somewhere along the uppermost part of the Kerulen.[3] According to the *Secret History*, Temüjin said later to To'oril: 'was it not at my call that your brother returned from his flight into distant lands? Did I not save him from the ambuscades of the Merkits…?' It therefore seems the Merkits moved forward to strike against Jaqa Gambo and that Temüjin and the Mongols helped drive them off. It was perhaps then

2   In the *Yuanshi* biography, Muqali on his deathbed claimed to have served Temüjin for 40 years. If correct, then he joined in 1183, long before Temüjin defeated the Jürkins.
3   Raverty says the battle was fought at Karas Muran near the Kerulen River.

that the Mongols killed Tusa, a son of Toqto'a.[4] Many Kereyit tribesmen, the Tümen Tübegen and the Olon Dongqayit, joined Temüjin and Jaqa Gambo after they had scored this success in early 1197. In his overview of the various tribes, Rashid al-Din lists five Kereyit sub-groups, including the 'core' Kereyits. Two of these five now left Arka-Qara, so it was a significant defection. He was losing support. To'oril had stayed a year in exile in the west; he returned along a southern route, encouraged by the successes Temüjin and Jaqa Gambo had achieved, and met them at the Hariltu Lake. Temüjin gave To'oril and his men food and shelter; this was autumn 1197. Backed by Jaqa Gambo and Temüjin, To'oril was able to re-establish himself as leader of the Kereyits.

Soon afterwards (winter 1197–1198), Temüjin and To'oril intercepted Saca Beki and Taicu, the Jürkin leaders, at the Telegetü Outlet. This place was probably north or north-east of the Tu'ula River. This victory was more complete than that gained over the Jürkins some months before. Perhaps Temüjin somehow cut off all escape routes, as the two rival leaders were captured and executed. By disposing of the exiled Jürkins Temüjin did To'oril a favour, helping him secure his pasture grounds. Temüjin's aim, naturally, was to eliminate rivals to his power.

Temüjin helped To'oril regain control over the Kereyit tribe. Politically he improved his position vis-à-vis To'oril: instead of a subject, he was now an ally. Temüjin directed three military operations between the end of 1196 and the end of 1197, dealing with the Jürkins twice and the Merkits once. No strategy is really evident here though he may have surprised his foes on at least two occasions. Before the first battle against the Jürkins, Temüjin had moved through the desert, perhaps a route considered difficult to an army to march through. He crushed the Jürkins, but despite needing to make two attacks he gained in the end a complete victory. Jamuqa had been content to defeat Temüjin a few years earlier, being happy with the enhanced prestige he secured, but Temüjin wanted total victory. The Jürkins were the first rival group he completely crushed. Many more would suffer the same fate during the next decade.

Sources: the SWQZL; Pelliot and Hambis, *Histoire des campagnes de Gengis Khan*, pp.214, 224, 230; Rashid al-Din, 72, 251, 266, 420-421; *Yuanshi* 1, p.15; the *Secret History*, 150–152, 177; Raverty, p.940; de Rachewiltz, 'Muqali', p.3; de Rachewiltz, commentary on the *Secret History*, p.503.

---

4   Rashid al-Din says he was killed in an ambush, perhaps fitting this battle better than that the year after.

8

Further Raids on the Merkits

The following year, during the autumn, the emperor sent troops to the Qara in order to attack Toqto'a, chief of the Merkits. They battled at Monoca Mountain, finally they plundered the Uduyit Merkit tribe and they dispersed their people; all of what they captured the emperor gave to *Wang Qan*. Soon afterwards his tribe was more or less assembled. He, without our army, attacked the Merkits in the Bu'ura Valley ... Toqto'a fled to the Barqujin Pass.

– the SWQZL

In the east, on 27 March 1198, the Tatar leader Zuxu finally submitted to the Jin, ending the unrest that had prevailed since 1195. Zuxu must have died soon afterwards for he is not heard of again.

In autumn 1198 Temüjin invaded Merkit territory, and defeated Toqto'a and the Uduyit Merkits at Mürüce Se'ul by the Qadiqliq Ridge. The Merkits retreated quickly northwards in the direction of the Barqujin lowland. Temüjin captured Qutuqtai, a daughter of Toqto'a, and she was given as a wife to his 13-year-old son Ögödei. Temüjin also secured much booty, the *Secret History* says 'their many herds of horses and palatial tents, their grain stores', which he gave to To'oril. This was a serious matter for Temüjin who was very sensitive about how plunder was handled. The next year To'oril launched his own expedition against the Merkits, defeating them at Bu'ura: Toqto'a Beki again retreated to the Barqujin area. Töguz, his eldest son, was killed. His other sons, Qudu and Cila'un, defected to To'oril and brought followers with them ('with their soldiers and folk').[1] To'oril gained a significant success and secured much booty, but gave none to Temüjin: Temüjin had reason to be upset, as it was his spies who had provided intelligence to To'oril before the attack was made. Temüjin had sent an embassy to Toqto'a, perhaps to negotiate a peace agreement after the attack made in 1197; he later told To'oril: 'we had sent a messenger to Toqto'a Beki to spy and

---

1   Qudu is sometimes held to be a brother rather than a son (although he could be both if he had a different mother).

gather information. When there was an opportunity, you did not stop and wait for me.' At the time, probably early 1199, he said nothing.

For the expeditions of Temüjin and To'oril the sources give no hint of any sophisticated strategy, such as that Jamuqa had employed before in the same area. It is interesting to learn that Temüjin sent an embassy to the Merkits to gather intelligence. The Mongols probably did this often, but it is rarely mentioned in the sources. It seems Temüjin had intended to attack as well, but To'oril moved too quickly.

Sources: the SWQZL, Pelliot and Hambis, *Histoire des campagnes de Gengis Khan*, pp.264–265; Rashid al-Din 72, 267–268, 285, 421; *Yuanshi* 1, p.16; the *Secret History*, 157, 177; *Jinshi* 10, pp.1117–1147; de Rachewiltz, commentary on the *Secret History*, pp.580–581.

9

War with the Naimans

Next the emperor and Ong Qan made a joint campaign against Buyiruq Qan; they reached the Kisil Bas Plain and captured his entire people. Buyiruq Qan had sent in advance Yadi-Tobluq, at the head of 100 cavalrymen, to form the advance guard; our troops pressed him, he fled; as he was on a high hill, the saddle on his horse turned; he fell, and was captured by us.

– the SWQZL

By 1197 the Naiman lord Inanca Bilge had probably died: had he been alive and in good heath, he would surely have reacted to the return of To'oril. He may have died of natural causes. Carpini says 'their leaders ... died of old age.' After his passing, the Naimans split into two factions led by his sons Bai Buqa and Buyiruq. Rashid al-Din says the two 'had an extremely bad relationship.' Bai Buqa, the older brother, is portrayed in the *Secret History* as a weak ruler who could not impose his will on his senior officers. Buyiruq was headstrong, and his father had known this well. He reportedly said: 'Buyiruq is like a camel that will not budge until a wolf has eaten half of its leg.' Bai Buqa at times lived along the Erdis and Buyiruq along the Urunggu. Both groups migrated back and forth across the Altai.

During the autumn of 1199, To'oril and Temüjin set out to attack Buyiruq. Jamuqa operated in conjunction with them, reappearing in the headline events of the chroniclers for the first time in five years. Later in 1201 he was leader of the north-eastern tribes of Mongolia, but he was already allied to them in 1194 and very likely was so now. To'oril must have been keen to punish the Naimans after they had supported his overthrow a few years before, but with many of the western tribes involved perhaps this was a bigger project. Seeing the Naimans weakened, did the eastern side of Mongolia want to inflict a blow on them? It could be a scheme devised by Jamuqa. To'oril left his son Ilaq Senggüm as well as Jaqa Gambo behind to guard his home territory, therefore perhaps only a smaller force set out. In 1192, when Jaqa Gambo was with him, To'oril was credited with bringing 20,000 men; perhaps he only took 10,000 this time? If Temüjin and Jamuqa had as many, they could set out with 30,000 men in total. Temüjin probably left his brother Qasar behind to guard the

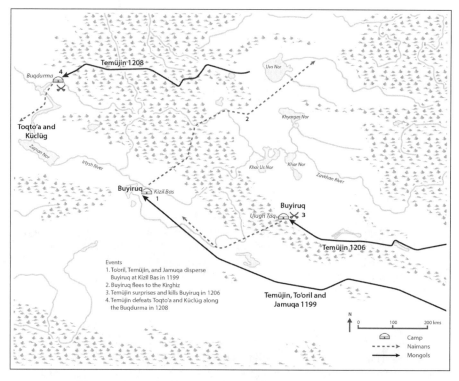

4. The attacks on the Naimans in 1199 (first part), 1206, and 1208.

Mongol base camp. The Naimans might have as many as 60,000 men, but Buyiruq had at most half of these and perhaps less.

The allies surprised Buyiruq close to Kizil Bas, west of the Altai Mountains. Rashid al-Din says 'they seized and plundered those people.' Buyiruq, presumably at that time further north, had sent Yadi-Tobluq with 100 men forward to scout. Chased by Mongol scouts, Yadi-Tobluq was driven up a hill, where he fell off his horse and was taken captive. Unable to challenge the attackers, perhaps because he could not concentrate his forces in time, Buyiruq fled to Kämkämchi'üt in the region of the Kirghiz – far up in the north. By moving south of the Altai Mountains, the eastern tribes may have chosen an unexpected line of advance: perhaps Jamuqa again demonstrated his talent for devising surprise strategic strikes. The Naiman group of Bai Buqa must have camped further north, perhaps east of the Altai Mountains. Avoiding Bai Buqa, the eastern tribes attacked the more distant Buyiruq.

Having made a successful raid, Temüjin, To'oril, and Jamuqa returned towards their own territory. Bai Buqa must have been alarmed by the success they had gained over his brother: perhaps it was he who sent Kökse'ü Sabraq with a sizeable force to intercept the eastern tribesmen. Rashid al-Din says Kökse'ü Sabraq served Buyiruq, but in the *Secret History* he is associated with Bai Buqa. At this time, Kökse'ü Sabraq could have drawn warriors from both Naiman factions. The *Secret History* says Kökse'ü was a

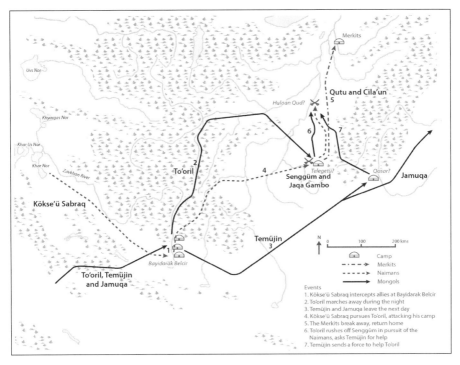

5. The second part of the 1199 campaign.

'great warrior' though nothing is known about his earlier achievements. During the winter of 1199–1200 Kökse'ü intercepted To'oril, Temüjin, and Jamuqa at Bayidarak Belcir, perhaps having taken up position east of the river. Evidently Kökse'ü had a large force, perhaps 30,000 men or more, but nightfall prevented a battle. Tohgrul, Temüjin, and Jamuqa spent the night in 'battle order', To'oril in one place and Temüjin and Jamuqa in another. To'oril relocated during the night: leaving the fires burning in his camp, he marched upriver to take up a new position some distance away. He might have expected Temüjin and Jamuqa to move as well. Perhaps there was some misunderstanding between the leaders? The next day all three retreated. To'oril headed northwards, 'upstream along the Qara Se'ül River', and then east towards the Tu'ula where he could link up with Senggüm and Jaqa Gambo. Temüjin set out for Sa'ari (the area between the Tu'ula and Kerulen), probably marching along a more southern route than To'oril. He crossed the Bayidarak at the unidentified Eder Altai Confluence. Jamuqa could also have headed eastwards along a separate route.

The resourceful Kökse'ü focussed on the Kereyits. He probably marched as fast as he could towards the Tu'ula River along a very direct route. Senggüm and Jaqa Gambo camped at Telegetü, and Kökse'ü Sabraq reached them before To'oril. His sudden assault surprised the Kereyits; Rashid al-Din says they were ambushed. The Naimans captured 'half the people and livestock of Ong Qan.' Senggüm and Jaqa Gambo escaped and made their way to To'oril and the approaching Kereyit army. It was perhaps during this moment of confusion that the Merkits of Qutu and Cila'un decided to defect. The *Secret History* says: 'Qutu and Cila'un, the two sons of Toqto'a of the Merkit who were also there, separated from Ong Khan and, taking their own people with them, moved downstream along the Selengge River to join their father.'

To'oril ordered Senggüm to pursue the Naimans, giving him all available forces. He also hurried off a messenger to Temüjin begging for assistance. The Naimans retreated up along the Orqon towards the point where it meets the Selengge; this choice of route is best explained by Kökse'ü's desire to avoid the Kereyit army now that he had secured a lot of loot. His intention was to return to his home territory by way of a northward detour. Temüjin sent a detachment commanded by Bo'orcu, Muqali, Boroqul and Cila'un Ba'atur to support the Kereyits. Kökse'ü turned on Senggüm at a place called Hulaan Qud and drove him back, but the Mongol force arrived before the battle was over and turned the balance in favour of the Kereyits. According to the accounts the Naimans were routed, much booty recovered, and the Kereyit captives freed. Bo'orcu was said to have saved Senggüm during the battle and was afterwards rewarded by To'oril. Meanwhile, Temüjin marched against Toqto'a whom he heard had advanced out of the Barqujin Pass and set up camp at Tunglak. Pelliot locates the latter place along a side river to the upper Kerulen. It was, however, a false alarm. Rashid al-Din writes: 'Genghis Khan, having consulted with Joci Qasar, recognised that this rumour was not well founded, and [both] did not pay attention to this news. And that is it!' Qudu and Cila'un had returned to Toqto'a and could have alerted him to the opportunity for making a raid on Qasar before Temüjin could return, but if Toqto'a made an advance at all it ended quite quickly. Temüjin reunited with To'oril at Burgi in the Sa'ari Steppe.

Before setting out to succour Senggüm, Bo'orcu said to Temüjin: 'I do not have a jä[bä]lägü (= armoured) horse.' He asked to borrow one of Temüjin's horses. If armoured horses were at this time so rare amongst the Mongols that even Bo'orcu did not have one then overall the forces were evidently lightly armed. The story is transmitted by Rashid al-Din.

The economical account of the SWQZL and the selective focus of the *Secret History* make it difficult to understand just why To'oril and Temüjin led their tribes eastwards during the following year, away from their traditional pastures. Where they forced or at least felt obliged to leave the central plains because of the Naiman threat? The 1199 campaign was perhaps in the end more a Naiman victory than a success for To'oril and Temüjin. Hulaan Qud was probably no real Naiman defeat. Possibly To'oril and Temüjin feared the two Naiman factions would come to terms after they had fought against both of them. To'oril, Temüjin, and Jamuqa had surprised and shattered Buyiruq's tribe. It was bold to go beyond the Altai and hit such a distant tribal group: they had to cover 1,500 km, needing probably two to three months to do this. They would therefore leave their camps with their guard to fend themselves for up to five or six months. Key to steppe warfare was to fall on the enemy base camp without exposing one's own camp to danger, and faced with an enemy counterattack, both Temüjin and To'oril hurried back to protect their home camps. Both leaders had failed to protect their camps in 1196 and To'oril evidently failed to do so this year again. It was stressful to live in the Kereyit camp.

Sources: the SWQZL, Pelliot and Hambis, *Histoire des campagnes de Gengis Khan*, pp.198, 293–296, 387–389; Rashid al-Din 82, 91, 95–98, 103, 268–272, 285–286, 421–422; *Yuanshi* 1, pp.16–17; the *Secret History* 158–165, 177, 189–190; Carpini, p.57; *The Tartar Relation*, p.58; Grousset, *Empire of the Steppes*, pp.204–206; Ratchnevsky, *Genghis Khan: His Life and Legacy*, pp.57–59; de Rachewiltz, commentary on the *Secret History*, pp.583–596.

10

Migrating to the Eastern Regions

He sent an army to attack the Tayici'uts ... he fought a great battle along the Onon
River, and he destroyed [them]. Tarqutai Kiriltuq and Qududar attacked by surprise, [as]
he arrived at the Ulangut-Turas Steppe and [he] captured the two ... Soon afterwards,
the Qadigins, Salji'uts, Dorbans, Tatars and Onggirads united at the source of the Alui
to make an alliance ... The emperor having received the news, immediately with Ong
Qan sent troops from the Qutu Marsh; they went to meet them in the Buyira Valley and
defeated the enemy completely.

– the SWQZL

In spring 1200, To'oril and Temüjin migrated eastwards, marching up along the Onon
River. They were moving into Tayici'ut territory. A'ucu Ba'atur, Quril and Qudu'udar
were the senior Tayici'ut leaders. At that time Toqto'a had sent his brother Qudu to
the Tayici'uts to ask for help. According to Rashid al-Din, A'ucu 'initiated hostilities
between Temüjin and the Tayichi'ut.' He does not elaborate; perhaps the Tayici'uts
and Merkits plotted to make a combined attack on Temüjin and To'oril. If so, Temüjin
moved against the Tayici'uts before the Merkits could join them. Rashid al-Din
says the Tayici'ut had assembled a large force so it does not seem they were taken by
surprise, but To'oril and Temüjin defeated them along the Onon River.

Separating from To'oril, Temüjin pursued Qudu'udar and Tarqutai Kiriltuq to a
place called Ulengüt Turas. This was perhaps where at least some of the Tayici'uts had
their base camp. The *Secret History*, at variance with the other sources, says the enemy
leader was A'ucu Ba'atur. Though this is probably incorrect, the other details given
sound credible: 'As soon as A'učů Ba'atur reached his own people, he had them moved
along with him in haste.' On the opposite side of the Onon, they 'arrayed their troops
at Ulengüt Turas on the other side.' The Tayici'uts attacked Temüjin just after he had
crossed the river, perhaps taking the Mongols by surprise. Presumably the Mongols
dismounted to fight. The two sides 'battled ... until evening', when nightfall ended
the fighting. Temüjin was wounded, and Jelme tended to him during the night, saving
his life. The parties slept on the field and continued the battle on the second day. The
Tayici'uts had 'set up a circular camp', which was finally overrun on the second day.

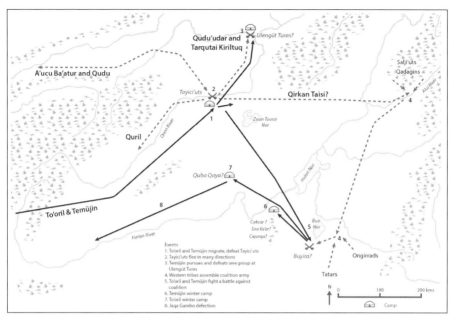

6. The operations against Tayici'ut in 1200.

The *Yuanshi* says 'countless' Tayici'uts were killed. The survivors were incorporated into the Mongol tribe. Qudu'udar and Tarqutai Kiriltuq were both killed;[1] the latter was a relatively minor lord, but it was he that had held young Temüjin captive years before. Quril fled to the Naimans and A'ucu Ba'atur and Qudu to the Merkits in the area of the Barqujin Pass. Many Tayici'uts fled eastwards to join the Salji'uts and Qadagins, their traditional allies. What To'oril did in the meantime is not clear, but he could have pursued one of the other Tayici'ut groups.

To'oril and Temüjin probably rested during the summer, remaining in the area south of the Onon. A threat emerged further east where the Qadagins and Salji'uts started to organise an alliance against them. Rashid al-Din writes: 'most of the Tayichi'ut tribes had gathered, and with the Dörbän, Tatar, and Onggirad tribes had also joined them.' They assembled with their forces along the upper Alui River. The SWQZL says 'they cut a white horse into two swearing an oath to attack our army as well as Ong Qan.' The leaders are not named, but perhaps the senior leaders were Cirgidai and Buq Coroqi, who are later said to lead respectively the Salji'uts and the Qadagins. According to Rashid al-Din the Salji'uts and the Qadagins were 'fanatically devoted' to Qirkan Taisi, who may have led the Tayici'uts who were with them. The Tatar leaders were possibly Alaq Udur and Caqun. Dai Sechon, an Onggirad lord who was Temüjin's father-in-law,

---

1   The SWQZL says Sirgätü-äbügän and his sons Naya'a and Alaq captured Tarqutai as well as A'ucu Ba'atur, intending to hand them over to Temüjin. They decided finally to release them, coming over to Temüjin without them. Temüjin viewed this as correct conduct, and anyway Taqutai fell into Mongol hands. The *Secret History* knows this story, but here there is no mention of A'ucu.

sent a person to warn Temüjin. Dai Sechon was leader of the Onggirad Bosqur sub-group; the more senior Terge Emel headed the Nirgin sub-group. Temüjin and To'oril camped apart, but quickly joined forces in the face of the new threat. They passed a place called Hulun Nor and fought a battle against the enemy coalition at Buyira, close to Buir Nor. It was a fiercely contested battle, and a case can be made for a scenario where To'oril and Temüjin in fact had the worst of the fighting.[2] After the battle, To'oril and Temüjin marched to the Kerulen, perhaps rejoining their base camps. Temüjin wintered at Cakcar Mountain, remaining in the general area, while To'oril wintered at Quba Qaya. Pelliot suggests this was somewhere near Cakcar, perhaps somewhat further westward. Jaqa Gambo deserted To'oril during the march to Quba Qaya, and led his followers – including four senior military leaders – to join the Naiman Bai Buqa.[3] Jaqa Gambo and his followers preferred to live in their old territory under Naiman overlordship than with To'oril. Here is probably additional confirmation that the 1199 campaign ended as a reverse for To'oril and Temüjin.

Jamuqa makes no appearance this year. The brief accounts may simple fail to mention him even if he was in fact the enemy lead commander, or was for some reason absent. He could, for example, have had a falling out with the other local leaders and lost influence. If so, he recovered his position by 1201.

Temüjin had fought protracted wars against the Tayici'uts for many years. No details are known, except for the Dalan Baljut battle where the Tayici'uts supported Jamuqa, but Temüjin was certainly not able to gain a decisive victory. Now, in 1200, he dispersed the Tayici'uts. He was able to do so because To'oril supported him, and the Tayici'uts had not been able to call in other tribes to support them. Temüjin and To'oril might have had more than 50,000 men and were probably stronger than the Tayici'uts. Many Tayici'uts got away, some of them joining forces with five other tribes in the east: presumably eastern tribes were able to field a force equal or superior to that of To'oril and Temüjin. Again it is clear that To'oril was a weaker political leader than Temüjin; he was somehow unable to impose his power on his people to the same degree. Temüjin had his own problems with his brother Qasar, but Qasar never betrayed him like Jaqa Gambo betrayed To'oril.

Sources: the SWQZL, Pelliot and Hambis, *Histoire des campagnes de Gengis Khan*, pp.389–393; Rashid al-Din 272–275; *Yuanshi* 1, p.17; the *Secret History*, pp.144–145, 152; Ratchnevsky, *Genghis Khan: His Life and Legacy*, pp.61–62; de Rachewiltz, commentary on the *Secret History*, pp.539, 559, 566; Isenbeke Togan, 'The Qongrat in History', *History and Historiography of Post-Mongol Central Asia and the Middle East* (Wiesbaden, 2006), pp.61–83.

---

2   Ratchnevsky: 'A victory for Temuchin is not easy to reconcile with the fact that Wang-khan spent the following winter in Kuba-kaya on the Manchurian border, east of Lake Kulun, while Temuchin was actually in China.'
3   Jaqa Gambo may have left with some of the core Kereyits and the Albats. The leaders following him were Il Qutur, Il Qongqur, Narin To'oril, and Alin Taishi.

11

Overcoming the Tribes in the East

Yet, oh, khan, father of mine, after that I flew, similar to a falcon, to Jurqa Mountain, through the Buir Naur and have caught cranes whose feet are bound and which are grey in colour. If you will ask: 'Who are they?' – these are tribes of Dörban and Tartars! I once again became a grey falcon, passed through Koka Naur, caught blue cranes with blue feet for you, and gave them to you. If you will ask: 'Who are they?' – they are tribes of Qatakin, Salji'uts and Onggirads. Now they are, those tribes, with whose help you now threaten me. This is another of the favours for which you are indebted to me!

– Temüjin's message to To'oril in 1203, Rashid al-Din, 286

If we defeat them chase them north. If you see abandoned goods scattered about, you must pay them no heed. When the military business is finished, the plunder will be divided fairly.

– Temüjin's instructions to his men before the second Tatar battle, the SWQZL

The defection of Jaqa Gambo is likely to have left To'oril incapacitated for some time. He did not take part in the subsequent campaign, staying perhaps at Quba Qaya Mountain. No mention is made of him until he rejoined Temüjin during the fall of 1202. For a year and a half he vanishes from the narrative. Temüjin later claimed to have protected To'oril by attacking their common foes when he was weak, counting it as a service for To'oril.

Temüjin fell on Tatars and, perhaps, Dörbens. The enemy leaders were two sons of Mägüdjin-säültü called Alaq Udur and Caqun. It seems therefore to be the same Tatar faction Temüjin and To'oril fought against in 1196. Gulltaur, another enemy lord, was perhaps another Tatar. The Tayici'ut Qirkan Taisi, listed by Rashid al-Din, was also present. Temüjin intercepted the Tatars in the Dalan Nemürges region, and at the same time sent his brother Qasar against the Onggirads along the Qalqa. Temüjin defeated and dispersed the Tatar army. The SWQZL says 'he destroyed them', but Rashid al-Din says 'some managed to escape and regroup.' Meanwhile, Qasar came upon and attacked the Onggirads. It was said they had planned to join Temüjin, but

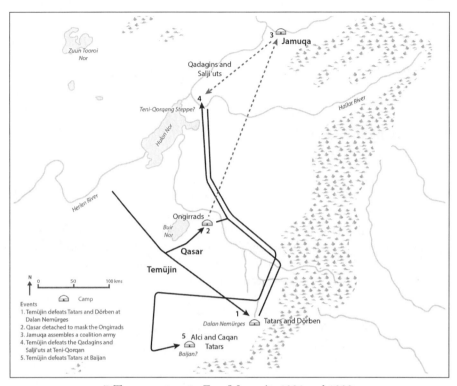

7. The operations in East Mongolia 1201 and 1202.

now joined his foes instead, and the sources fault Qasar for attacking them (early winter 1201?).

Reacting to the victory of Temüjin, the eastern tribes again – as in 1200 – united. The SWQZL says the Onggirads 'gathered with the Ikires, the Qorolas, the Dörben, the Tatar, the Qadagin, and the Selji'üt tribes at the Gan River. Together they named Jamuqa Gur Qan and plotted to attack us. They made a covenant at the Tülber River … they all lifted their feet to trample the bank, and swung their swords to cut down the trees.' A certain Taqaiqa served Jamuqa. Cha'ur was a follower of Temüjin and a relative of Taqaiqa, and happened to visit Taqaiqa who told him about the new alliance formed against Temüjin. Cha'ur hurried back to the Mongol camp and transmitted the news. Temüjin attacked and defeated his foes along the Hailar at a place called the Teni-Qorqan Steppe (after February 1201, perhaps autumn 1201). In one place Rashid al-Din says Temüjin defeated only the Qadagins, Salji'uts, and Onggirads: perhaps he was able to defeat these three tribes before the others could join them. Jamuqa could have decided to fall back after a part of his forces suffered this setback. Afterwards the Onggirads submitted to the Mongols, but are found fighting against Temüjin the next year. Possibly the Bosqur faction, under Dai Sechon, submitted at this point whereas the Nirgin remained hostile?

In spring 1202 Temüjin next turned southward, intent on attacking the Alci and Caqan Tatars. Jalin Buqa was perhaps the leader of the former. Temüjin assembled his forces along the Ulqui Šilügeljit River and defeated the Tatars at a place called Baijan. Unidentified, this could be some distance to the south. As Temüjin planned to drive the Tatars northwards, he may have moved around them, perhaps from the western side. The *Secret History* says: 'they forced them to rejoin their tribe (= base camp) on the Ulqui Šilügeljit River and thoroughly plundered them.' If the Mongols came from the Ulqui Šilügeljit River this is certainly not likely, but the Tatars may have fled northwards towards this river. The *Secret History* also says 'rain poured down incessantly day and night.' As this source only knows one Tatar battle one or both pieces of information might refer to the earlier battle.[1] Most of the Tatars were taken captive (summer 1202?).

Before the battle, Temüjin introduced new rules on how to handle plunder. He regulated the plunder gathering process, imposing rules on how it should be collected and shared. Otcigin, Qucar, and Altan failed to follow the new system, taking plunder as soon as they had a chance. They had commanded two of the 13 units Temüjin fielded against Jamuqa almost a decade before, and as senior family members they assumed they did not need to follow the rules. Temüjin sent some officers, Qubilai and Jebe, to seize what they had taken; the offenders then left with their followers. Very likely Temüjin lost a significant number of fighting men, perhaps 10,000 or more in total.

According to the *Secret History*, Temüjin decided to kill most of the Tatar captives. He said: 'We will measure them against a linchpin and kill off [those who are taller than the linchpin]', but to the fury of Temüjin, word leaked out: his half-brother Belgutai disclosed the planned action to Tatar lord Yeke Čeren. Warned, the prisoners broke away and barricaded themselves on a hill. The *Secret History* says:

> At these words of Belgütei, Yeke Čeren issued a proclamation to his Tatars, and they raised a barricade. As our soldiers tried to surround and attack the Tatars that had barricaded themselves in, they suffered great losses. After much trouble, when they forced the barricaded Tatars into submission and were about to slay them to the last man by measuring them against the linchpin of a cart, the Tatars said among themselves, 'Let everyone put a knife in his sleeve and let us die each taking an enemy with us as a death-companion!' And again we suffered great loss.

It is not reported how many Tatars fought against the Mongols, but as narrated in the *Secret History* it seems to have been a serious engagement. Temüjin took two Tatar sisters, daughters of Yeke Čeren, as wives. Their brother later became a senior commander. Already before, the adopted Tatar Sigi Qutuqu was attached to the household of Temüjin. He also emerged as senior commander and important official. Joci Qasar, Temüjin's brother, also had a Tatar wife. He attempted to hide a number of Tatars, in all about 500, who should have been killed; Temüjin only discovered this

---

1   Heavy rain is most likely between June and August, so it should refer to the second battle.

later, counting it as one of his brother's offences. Therefore it is clear that at least some Tatars were integrated into the Mongol establishment.

Temüjin dealt with the enemy forces in detail, defeating one group after the other. It seems his strategy was quite sophisticated. Qasar operated with a separate force, perhaps to distract the Onggirads at the same time as Temüjin struck against the Tatars. In 1200, To'oril and Temüjin had fought against five tribes in one battle. In 1201, Jamuqa formed an alliance with seven tribes, but Temüjin fought against only three in one battle, three in another, and a part of one in the third. Therefore he was probably in no battle confronted by enemy forces as large as in 1200. In 1202, Temüjin again exploited victory ruthlessly, effectively destroying the Tatars. The campaign is typical of Temüjin: he struck fast and hard, pursued to gain complete victory, and finally exterminated the opposition. He butchered the captured Tatars in an act of genocide. They were presumably singled out for punishment because they were traditional rivals of the Mongols, and because they had killed his father. No other tribe was punished in this way, though captured enemy leaders were routinely killed.

Sources: the SWQZL, John Emerson (*Sheng Wu Jin Cheng Lu: Partial translation, comments and notes*, http://www.johnjemerson.com/shengwu.htm/, accessed 31 Dec. 2012); Rashid al-Din 61–65, 276–279, 286, 422; *Yuanshi* 1, pp.17–19, 123, p.3022; the *Secret History* 141–144, 147, 204; Grousset, *Empire of the Steppes*, pp.206–207; de Rachewiltz, commentary on the *Secret History*, pp.515–528.

12

Confrontation at Köyiten

The emperor sent the baggage-carts to a different location. With Wang Qan he took cover under the Alan fortifications and built a wall.

– Yuanshi 1

A huge coalition army gathered to crush To'oril and Temüjin. The SWQZL says: 'In the fall the Naiman Buyiruq Qan joined with the Merkit chief Toqto'a Beki and the Dörben, Tatar, Qadagin, and Salji'ut tribes, together with A'ucu Ba'atur, Quduqa Beki, and others in order to attack ourselves and Ong Qan.' Bai Buqa did not support the venture. The politics are not clear. Bai Buqa had supported Buyiruq at least indirectly in 1199; perhaps this year they had some kind of agreement. At a minimum Bai Buqa remained neutral. Buyiruq may have harboured a desire to crush To'oril and Temüjin whereas Bai Buqa was content to leave them in eastern Mongolia. Toqto'a, Tayici'ut exiles, as well as Oyirats backed Buyiruq. Toqto'a and the Tayici'uts had good reasons to be hostile towards To'oril and Temüjin; A'ucu and Quril were eager to get revenge for the defeats handed them in 1200. Why the Oyirats joined the alliance is hard to say. They lived closer to Bai Buqa than Buyiruq, but Buyiruq had fled to their general region to get away from To'oril and Temüjin in 1199 and perhaps had some relationship with them. Quduqa Beki led this tribe. Furthermore, Jamuqa agreed to join the allies as well. The Naimans, Merkits, Oyrats and Tayici'uts moved as one group, and Jamuqa marched south with his allies to join them. With Jamuqa, if the Secret History can be trusted, were Buq Coroqi and the Qadagins, Cirgidai and the Salji'uts, Tuge Maqa and the Ikires, Terge Emel and the Onggirads, Conaq Caqalan and the Qorolas, as well as Jalin Buqa and the Alchi Tatars. Buyiruq, the Merkits, the Oyirats, and other tribes coming from the east might have fielded 40,000 men. Jamuqa with perhaps another 30,000 only arrived later. With these estimates Buyiruq had 40,000 men rising to 70,000. Temüjin and To'oril should have had about 70,000 before the defections of Jagumba, Otcigin, Qucar, and Altan, but now certainly had fewer men than Buyiruq and Jamuqa combined and perhaps not much more than Buyiruq on his own.

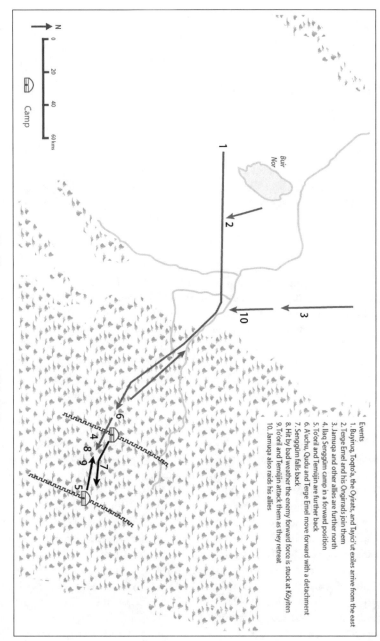

8. The Köyiten campaign in 1202–1203

Events
1. Buyiruq, Toqto'a, the Oyirats, and Tayici'ut exiles arrive from the east
2. Terge Emel and his Ongirads join them
3. Jamuqa and other allies are further north
4. Ilaq Senggüm camp in a forward position
5. To'oril and Temüjin are further back
6. A'uchu, Qudu and Terge Emel move forward with a detachment
7. Senggüm falls back
8. Hit by bad weather the enemy forward force is stuck at Köyiten
9. To'oril and Temüjin attack them as they retreat
10. Jamuqa also raids his allies

Buir
Nor

Camp

N

0   20   40   60 kms

Temüjin camped in the area east of Buir Nor, and To'oril joined him there. The SWQZL says Temüjin sent 'riders to climb up and keep watch from Mount Negen-Güiletu, Mount Cekcer, and Mount Chiqürqu. A rider came from Mount Chiqürqu reporting that the Naiman were approaching. From Ulqui-shireljin the emperor and Ong Qan moved their forces inside the Barrier.' The Barrier was presumably a part of the fortified lines the Jin had constructed in the area, probably along the waterways of the Sungari. This was some 150 km further south-east. The Naiman, the Merkits, Oyirats and the Tayici'uts came from the west, and Jamuqa and his allies gathered to the north, moving down along the Ergüne River. They were initially the closest to Temüjin, but arrived last. Ilaq Senggüm, the son of To'oril, camped further north than Temüjin and To'oril with a forward force. He was in wooded terrain. Threatened by the Naiman and Merkits he sought refuge on high ground behind the 'northern Barrier'. The Jin had two fortified lines in this area, one near modern Wuchagouzhen where Senggüm might have first taken up position and another 30 km south-east where Temüjin, To'oril, and the rest of the forces and people could have taken up station. Buyiruq was keen to defeat the enemy forces in detail, saying: 'Their army is scattered; we can roll them up.' He detached A'ucu, Qudu, and Terge Emel to attack Senggüm. The SWQZL continues: 'They were about to attack but they saw that Ilaq's army's position was strong, so they returned. Ilaq also tried to cross the barrier and join our troops to make ready for war. The baggage-wagons were moved to a different location. The emperor and Ong Qan relied on the Aral barrier as a bulwark.' Senggüm joined Temüjin and To'oril, and they remained inside their fortified position. The enemy army, not yet joined by Jamuqa, moved forward through a narrow valley with wooded hills on both sides. At this point the weather turned bad: it snowed and was windy. Buyiruq turned about. Rashid al-Din reports that he tried 'to get out of these mountains' only to get 'stuck at Köyiten.' This could be a little open area about 15 km south of Wuchagouzhen. Temüjin moved forward, aiming to inflict losses on the retreating enemy forces. The *Secret History* says: 'they pressed on each other downhill and uphill, and reformed their ranks.' Also: 'Genghis Khan said: "When we fought at Köyiten and, pressing on each other, were reforming our ranks"'. Though the Chinese sources say the Naiman forces suffered a big defeat, it seems there was no real battle. However, it was probably here Ca'urqai, Sübe'etei's brother, was credited with scoring a success: 'when they were south of the long wall [they] fought a battle against a Naiman lord. Ca'urqai threw them back with his archery. The [Naiman] army fled into the Kuochitan Mountains and dispersed.' The enemy army fell into confusion as they retreated under difficult conditions. Jamuqa, now close, added to his reputation as a somewhat feckless leader by plundering the baggage of some of his allies before retreating back up the Ergüne. He sent word to To'oril and Temüjin that he was ready to submit.

The distances involved are not certain, with the Alan Barrier as well Köyiten not firmly located, but perhaps Temüjin and To'oril moved backward and forward some 300–400 km and the winter campaign could have been decided in two or three months. Buyiruq had to cover 1,200 km or more to get to the eastern end of Mongolia from his home area. He needed two to three months to get there and join forces with his allies (if he set out in September 1202 the actual confrontation may have been in December 1202 or January 1203). Temüjin and To'oril afterwards camped at Abji'a Ködeger Mountain.[1] To'oril a little later moved away, camping separately in the Berke Elet and Jeje'er Heights area.

Faced with a strong enemy coalition, Temüjin and To'oril first retreated, seeking cover behind Jin fieldworks. This is a defensive ploy, which may seem surprising to find used in the plains of Inner Asia. However, even wagon-fortresses could be used for defence and the defensive ploy was well known to the nomad tribes even if weaker sides normally preferred to retreat quickly rather than to adopt it. On this occasion Temüjin used an attrition strategy, like Gustav II Adolf or Turenne did later when faced by a strong foe. A strong leader like Temüjin could hold his forces together under even difficult circumstances; weaker leaders and even more so alliances found it difficult to do so for a long time. Buyiruq and Jamuqa failed to even unite. Jamuqa failed to really impact events in 1201 and 1202. The sources do not explain why.

Sources: the SWQZL, John Emerson; Rashid al-Din 422–423; *Yuanshi* 1, pp.19–20, 121, p.2975; the *Secret History* 141–144, 147; Grousset, *Empire of the Steppes*, pp.207–208; de Rachewiltz, commentary on the *Secret History*, pp.536–538, 600.

---

1   Upper Qalqa River, east-south-east of Buir Lake.

Overview: Master of Mongolia, 1203 to 1208

By 1203 there only four major leaders left in Mongolia, namely To'oril, Temüjin, Bai Buqa, and Buyiruq. To'oril and Temüjin had been allies since before 1191, but the balance of power between them shifted. Gradually Temüjin grew stronger, while To'oril became weaker. Urged on by Jamuqa, Mongol defectors, and his son Senggüm, To'oril was finally ready to turn against Temüjin. The Mongol leader was probably stronger than To'oril, but the new allies increased the numbers of the latter to such an extent that the Kereyit leader became the strongest. Bai Buqa and Buyiruq were together probably stronger than both To'oril and Temüjin. When Jamuqa tried to incite Senggüm against Temüjin he claimed: 'My elder brother Genghis Khan is in cahoots with Tayang Khan [Bai Buqa].' In fact, neither To'oril nor Temüjin tried to involve the Naimans, though that would have made a lot of sense. Here was a chance for Jin diplomacy have an impact, but at this stage they showed no interest in Mongolian politics.

Temüjin and To'oril planned to cement their alliance with two weddings. Joci, the eldest son of Temüjin, was to marry Cha'ur Beki, a daughter of To'oril, and Tusaqa, a son of Senggüm, was to marry a daughter of Temüjin called Füjin Beki. In the face of Senggüm's determination to crush Temüjin, the initially unwilling To'oril relented. They planned to ambush Temüjin as he was on the way to the Kereyit camp to plan the wedding of Joci and Cha'ur Beki. A Kereyit called Yeke Chaqaran facilitated a timely warning to Temüjin, and with his few followers Temüjin hurried back to his own camp. The climactic confrontation between To'oril and Temüjin followed.

The locations of Berke Elet and Jeje'er Heights are an issue. According to most commentators they are in the area of the upper Kerulen. This is far to the west, and To'oril would need more than one month to get to and from there. A location along the Ergüne, which has been proposed by Bazargür Dambyn and Enkhbayar Dambyn, seems better from a timing point of view. With a location in the west, various parties, whole tribes, or messengers had to cover 8,700 km as the sequential events unfolded. This might require more at least 350–400 days, more than the time available for the events between winter 1202–1203 and the autumn of 1203. The closer location would reduce the travel distance to 2,700 km, a much better fit with the narrative.

The period 1203–1208 seems fairly straightforward in terms of the sequence and main events. The *Secret History* is again at variance with other sources, saying Temüjin inflicted the final defeat on Toqto'a in 1205 rather than 1208. Again the chronology of the SWQZL, Rashid al-Din, and the *Yuanshi* is preferred.

13

To'oril's Bid for Supremacy

One evening, Wang Khan took his forces to make a surprise raid. [The emperor] did not prepare quickly enough, all his forces scattered. The emperor fled hurriedly, followed only by 19 people ... Taking the order, Jürcedei rode on his horse and attacked the enemy array alone. He shot Xiangun dead, subdued his great general Silemün and other generals.

– Yuanshi 120

Jamuqa and many other tribal lords came to the Kereyits during the spring. Amongst them were Daritai Otcigin, Altan Je'ün, and Qucar Beki who had left Temüjin after the quarrel over the Tatar loot; also another relative, To'oril the Söge'en, a descendant of Noqta Bool, who probably had left with them. In addition, there was Muqur Qa'uran the Hadargin, who had been with Temüjin when he fought against Jamuqa in 1193, Taqai Qulaqai the Mangqut, and Qudu Temür (Dalu Qutuqut) the Tatar. The *Secret History* also lists Ebügejin and Noyakin of the Qarta'an (Qatdakin) as well as Qaci'un Beki of the Dörbens.[1] When it later came to battle, the *Secret History* has To'oril tell Jamuqa: 'Younger brother Jamuqa, you set our troops in battle array!' Surely he was effective commander from the start of the campaign. To'oril had been weakened by the defection of Jaqa Gambo three years before, but now, supported by those who fallen out with Temüjin, he was stronger than ever. No numbers are given in the sources, but the forces joining To'oril were clearly sizeable. To'oril may have had 20,000 men after Jaqa Gambo left. Jamuqa, the Mongol defectors, and other new allies probably raised his total to at least 35,000. Temüjin had perhaps 30,000 men, but Qasar camped separately, so his own force was somewhat weaker, maybe 20,000. Senggüm spent the summer the area of the Jeje'er Heights, To'oril was nearby at Berke Elet, and Temüjin remained near the Aral Barrier. Qasar and his followers camped further south near Qara'un Jidun, probably about 100 km south of the upper Qalqa and Temüjin's position.

---

1   The *Secret History* is in part supported by the SWQZL which names Qurqaila and Qadarkid.

76

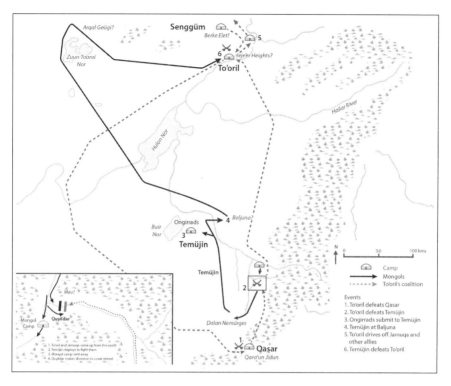

Arqal Getigi? Senggüm Berke Elet? 5 Zuun Tooroi Nor 6 Jejeïer Heights? To'oril Hailar River Hulan Nor Buir Nor Ongirrads 3 4 Baljuna? Temüjin Temüjin 2 Mau? Quyildar Mongol Camp Dalan Nemürges 1 Qasar Qara'un Jidun

N 0 50 100 kms

Camp Mongols To'oril's coalition

Events
1. To'oril defeats Qasar
2. To'oril defeats Temüjin
3. Ongirrads submit to Temüjin
4. Temüjin at Baljuna
5. To'oril drives off Jamuqa and other allies
6. Temüjin defeats To'oril

1. To'oril and Jamuqa come up from the south
2. Temüjin deploys to fight them
3. Mongol camp sent away
4. Quyildar makes diversion to cover retreat

9. The confrontation with To'oril in 1203.

To'oril and Jamuqa may first have attacked Qasar. Perhaps Jamuqa again made one of his trademark strategic outflanking strikes and was able to make a surprise assault on the enemy camp? Qasar escaped, but most of his family was captured. This was probably a real victory, even if the sources say almost nothing about it. Having defeated Qasar, To'oril and Jamuqa set out to deal with Temüjin; because they came from the south rather than the north or west, they were in a position to surprise him. Temüjin had been outmanoeuvred on the strategic level. Temüjin, says the SWQZL, 'stationed his troops at the Aral barrier and quickly shifted his baggage-wagons to the upper reach of the Shireljin River. He sent Jelme ahead as the advance guard along north side of Mount Mau-yundur. Ong Khan also sent troops along Mau-yundur's south side from Mount Hula'ut and Mount Buraqut.' To'oril and Jamuqa surprised Temüjin by coming from the south side of Mau Mountain. It is reported that it was only the warning given by some herdsmen that alerted Temüjin to the enemy approach. He prepared for battle in a place called Qalaqaljit Sands, and sent the Uru'uds and Mangquts forward. According to the traditional lore, they attacked and defeated in succession the Jirgin, the Tümen Tübegen, the Olon Dongqayit, To'oril's bodyguard – 1,000 men – as well as the forces led by Senggüm. It is certainly not likely that the Mongol attack was so successful, but they could have held off the enemy advance guard for a while. The battlefield was narrow, less than 1 km wide, so Jamuqa would struggle to quickly make his larger numbers have an impact. Senggüm was wounded during the fighting, throwing his own line into confusion. Temüjin retreated under the cover of a diversion, having sent a detachment under Quyildar to seize the Koyidan (Gupta) Hill on the flank of the Kereyits.[2] This was perhaps on the hills in the south or east. Quyildar occupied the hill and held off the Kereyits until nightfall, then slipped away under the cover of darkness and rejoined Temüjin. Though many sources do not say so, the battle was a Mongol defeat.[3] Ögödei, now aged about 17, was injured by an arrow in the neck and became separated from the rest of the army; Boroqul saved him. Quyildar was also wounded, and soon afterwards died. Temüjin retreated southwards to Dalan Nemürges while To'oril returned to Jeje'er Heights, failing to finish Temüjin off. It was a mistake Temüjin would never have made. Perhaps To'oril had left a minimal guard of the base camp and was eager to hurry back (June–July 1203?).

Temüjin later marched up along the Qalqa, reportedly with only 4,600 men. The number seems much too low, but perhaps his forces had dispersed and only gradually reassembled. Frederick II escaped from the defeat at Kunersdorf in 1759 with only 3,000 men, but eventually reassembled 25,000. Temüjin may have been in a similar situation. Rashid al-Din says 'most of his army deserted him.' If so, it certainly seems many returned during the next months as Temüjin evidently later fielded a large force. He also added new contingents. He sent Jürcedei with a detachment to the Nirgin Onggirads, still led by Terge Emel, just where the Qalqa runs into Buir Nor. They submitted to the Mongols. According to the SWQZL, Temüjin made a 'raid and captured them'. The *Secret History* says that Co'os Caqon (Co'oq Cala'an) and the Qorolas also came and submitted to Temüjin, but the other sources say that the Qorolas drove Butu out of their camp and that he joined Temüjin. In fact he had done so much earlier and was married to a sister of Temüjin called Temülün. He was certainly a Temüjin loyalist. Perhaps he tried to win the Qorolas over, and ended up splitting the tribe? Butu and Co'os Caqon might in such a scenario have left with some people and gone to Temüjin. Temüjin set up camp south of Buir Nor, at one point staying next to the Baljuna Lake.[4] Hasan, a Muslim trader, came from the Önggüts with 1,000 sheep. Another trader called Ja'far Khwaja also came to the camp. Sübe'etei's father Qaban also brought some livestock to Baljuna.[5]

Temüjin sent messengers to the various enemy leaders, aiming to weaken their resolve. He had verbal messages delivered to To'oril, Senggüm, the Mongol leaders who had left him, and to Jamuqa. For his part, To'oril faced new difficulties: Jamuqa, Otcigin, Altan Je'ün, Qucar Beki, To'oril, Muqur Qa'uran, Taqai Qulaqai, and Qutu

---

2   While Jürcedei temporised, Quyildar volunteered to lead this dangerous assignment.
3   *Yuanshi* 141, Jabar's biography, is in no doubt: 'The Emperor had a rift with Wang Qan of the Kereyit. One evening Wang Qan came, moving his troops surreptitiously. Taken by surprise and being [entirely] unprepared for [it], the army [of the Emperor] was completely routed. The Emperor straightaway fled.' *Yuanshi* 120, Jürcedei's biography, also says it was a defeat.
4   Cleaves suggests the Baljuna covenant should be placed before the Qalaqaljit battle: 'I am inclined to the belief not only that there is a displacement of the Baljuna episode in the account by Rashid al-Din, but also that there is a similar displacement of it in the *Secret History*, the Yuan shih and the Ch'in-cheng-lu.' This is hardly a significant issue for the military narrative.
5   Is there a mix up with Hasan? Perhaps they moved together?

Temür separated themselves from him and conspired against him. To'oril got wind of this, and attacked and dispersed them. Rashid al-Din says he 'mounted an attack to raid them', but no location is given. Jamuqa, Altan Je'ün, and Qutu Temür fled to Bai Buqa, but Otcigin, Muqur Qa'uran, Taqai Qulaqai, and the Kerayit Saqayid clan decided to go to Temüjin.[6] They may have joined him while still camping near Buir Nor. The *Secret History* says Temüjin wanted to execute Otcigin, but that he was finally persuaded to show leniency. From another direction Qasar also made his way to Temüjin's camp, as did perhaps many men who had been with him. If Temüjin had 20,000 men before the battle against To'oril, he was perhaps finally able to raise this to 40,000 or more. It was estimated before that To'oril had almost 40,000. After falling out with his allies, this could have been reduced to 20,000. By autumn, To'oril was no longer the strongest.

With Qasar's family still held by To'oril, Temüjin saw a chance to overcome his rival. He sent a messenger to To'oril bringing the news that Qasar wanted to join him; To'oril replied that Qasar was welcome. The messenger returned to Temüjin's camp, and was able to inform him that the Kereyits camped in the Jer Gorge at the Jeje'er Heights. Perhaps Temüjin already had a general idea about where they were, but now received more specific intelligence. He had marched from the Buir Nor region to Arqal Geügi near the sources of the Onon River, perhaps having the intent to approach To'oril from an unexpected direction. Informed where To'oril camped, Temüjin moved quickly towards him. Rashid al-Din writes: 'That night he did not dismount but kept riding until he caught up with Ong Khan.' Most likely a base camp was left behind with a guard. Jürcedei and Arqai led the Mongol forward forces. Approaching undetected, Temüjin surrounded the Kereyit camp; the Kereyits, led by Qadaq Ba'atur, defended themselves for three days before they surrendered. On the final day Muqali led the attack that penetrated the camp, ending the enemy will to resist.

To'oril escaped from the disaster, but did not survive for long: a Naiman lord called Qori Sübeci killed him at Nekun Usun near Didik Saqal, not believing To'oril when he told him who he was. Bai Buqa was angry with Qori Sübeci for having killed such a distinguished lord, and covered To'oril's head with silver and kept it as a mark of respect. To'oril's son Senggüm also got away, though separately from his father. He fled across the Gobi Desert into Xia. With regard to the Kereyit captives, Temüjin incorporated most of the warriors into his own army, perhaps 15,000 men or more. Qadaq Ba'atur was allowed to take service with Temüjin, having fought on loyally even after To'oril had fled, to give him time to get away. Temüjin again showed willingness to employ a man who had a proven record of loyalty and bravery. A follower of To'oril called Haira Beg got away with thousands of fighting men. He crossed the Altai and settled far away in Kangli territory, north of the Syr Darya River, where he secured a position of eminence. Much later, a descendent called Buhumu in Chinese sources would meet the Mongols again.

---

6   Rashid al-Din also lists Qujin of the Kilungqut.

During this campaign there were four battles; two Mongol defeats, a battle fought between the anti-Mongol foes, and a Mongol victory. This was a conflict decided by politics. Defeated, Temüjin was able to win over new allies. At the same time, To'oril lost allies. First weaker than To'oril, Temüjin became stronger. Initially, To'oril and Jamuqa had a clear strategic plan by means of which they defeated the Mongols in detail: this is perhaps the worst performance on record of Temüjin as a general. Did Temüjin expect To'oril to come from the west rather than swing to the south? Fortunately for Temüjin, To'oril and Jamuqa made no attempt to exploit the victory gained. Temüjin was ready to accept battle, even against a larger enemy army. Defeated, he retreated quickly (as in 1194). At the battle of Qalaqaljit Sands Temüjin made a diversionary outflanking move, presumably with the intent of providing cover for the retreat rather than with a hope to defeat the enemy army.

Sources: the SWQZL, Emerson, 35a–53a; Rashid al-Din, 95, 143, 147, 280–291, 423–424; *Yuanshi* 1, pp.23–25, 118, p.2921, 120, pp.2962–2963, 121, p.2975, 130, p.3163, 141, pp.3381–3384; the *Secret History*, 166–185, 188, 242; Aboul Ghazi Bahadour Khan, in *Histoire des Moguls et des Tatares*, pp.83–84; Raverty, pp.941–944; Lamb, *Genghis Khan*, pp.34–42; Grousset, *Empire of the Steppes*, pp.209–212; Francis W. Cleaves, 'The Historicity of The Baljuna Covenant', *Harvard Journal of Asiatic Studies*, vol. 18, no. 3/4 (1955), pp.357-421; Ratchnevsky, *Genghis Khan: His Life and Legacy*, pp.66–83; Isenbeke Togan, *Flexibility & Limitation in Steppe Formations, The Kerait Khanate & Chinggis Khan* (Leiden: Brill, 1998), pp.99–107; de Rachewiltz, commentary on the *Secret History*, pp.599–600, 614–615, 655, 660 (for a location of Jeje'er Heights near the Kerulen); Dambyn and Dambyn, *Chinggis Khaan: A historic-geographic atlas*, pp.32–33 (placing Jeje'er Heights in the east).

14

The Showdown with the Naimans

Soon afterwards, the emperor attacked the Naiman tribe with his younger brother Qasar; [they] arrived at Hulan-Jancai, [and] defeated them completely. They killed all the people of the tribe and assembled their bodies.

– the SWQZL

Naiman lord Bai Buqa – who styled himself *Taiyang*, a Jin title – was now ready to confront Temüjin. Jamuqa, Temüjin's refugee relatives, and Toqto'a supported him. It was perhaps this group of devious characters who stirred him into action. In addition, Alin Taishi the Kereyit and Quduqa Beki the Oyirat backed the Naimans. Bai Buqa attempted to win the Önggüts over to his side, suggesting they attack Temüjin from the east at the same time as the Naimans came from the west. Alaqus, the Önggüt leader, having no desire to fight Temüjin, informed him about the request. As a Jin client, the Önggüt leader may have been in no position to offer active support to any of the factions, even if he seems to have favoured Temüjin.

Temüjin wintered at Abji'a Ködeger and only mobilised his forces east of Buir Nor well into the spring. He reorganised the army, establishing a small guard and dividing the army into units of 1,000. At this point there were 65 *minghan* commanders so possibly he now, adding the guard, had a total of about 66,000 fighting men. He moved westwards with his people, spare horses, and livestock, unwilling to leave a significant body behind to guard a rear camp. The Naimans must have left their main camp near the Altai.

After setting out on 17 May 1204, Temüjin reached the Sa'ari Ke'er. Naiman scouts on Qangqarqan Mountain observed the Mongols, and reportedly were unimpressed with the quality of their forces. On the advice of Dodai Cerbi, one of the six bodyguard commanders, Temüjin ordered the Mongols to light extra campfires – each man lit five – and put dummies on the spare horses to make the army look bigger in the eyes of the enemy. The Mongols spread out occupying Sa'ari Steppe. The intent was to deter the Naimans from attacking, while the Mongols rested during the peak summer months. Informed that the Mongol army was very large, Bai Buqa considered falling back beyond the Altai, opting to fight a war of attrition ('fighting a dog's fight') against the

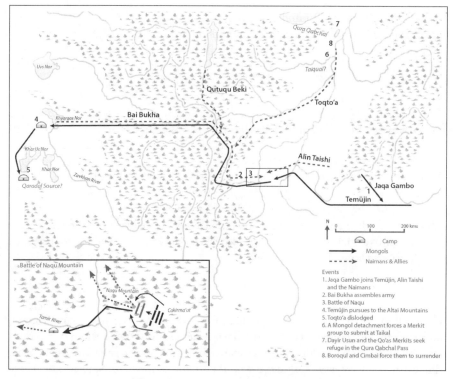

10. The defeat of the Naimans in 1204–1205.

Mongols, but he faced opposition from his son Küclüg as well as his senior officers. Qori Sübeci said:

> Your father Inanča Bilge Qan never showed a man's back or a gelding's rump to an enemy that was his match. Now you, how can you lose heart when it is still so early in the morning? Had we known that you would have lost courage in this manner, shouldn't we have brought your mother Gürbesü, even though she is only a woman, and given her command of the army? What a pity, alas, that Kökse'ü Sabraq should have become so old! The discipline in our army has grown lax!

Gürbesü was Bai Buqa's stepmother and wife. She gained notoriety for saying the Mongols smelled badly. In 1202, Temüjin and To'oril had waged a delaying war against a force they were not ready to fight, but this was not possible for Bai Buqa: lack of political power limited his options.

Jaqa Gambo submitted to Temüjin with some followers, perhaps at this time. Temüjin welcomed him and gave him a position of importance. Some of Jaqa Gambo's followers opted to remain with the Naimans, who were camped at Qacir Usun. Bai Buqa 'was joined by chieftain Toqto'a Beki from the Merkits, chieftain To'oril Alin Taishi from the Kereyits, chieftain Quduqa Beki from the Oyirats, and Jamuqa with the Dürbens, Tatars, Qatagins, and Seljiuts.' The Naimans were a powerful tribe and Bai Buqa probably controlled most of it. Perhaps he had as many 40,000 warriors. His five significant allied leaders possibly added another 25,000 men to this total, to equal the total of Temüjin. Both sides needed to detach some soldiers to guard their people and livestock.

The Naimans marched up along the Tamir, crossed the Orkhon, passed Naqu Mountain, and finally reached Cakirma'ut. Informed by his scouts that the enemy approached, Temüjin collected his army in the Sa'ari Steppe and moved forward. The Naimans fell back to the foot of Naqu Mountain. The *Secret History* provides more details on the tactics of Temüjin than usual: 'He rode against them and, having driven away their patrolmen, he arrayed his troops and together with the army leaders decided to advance in 'caragana" marching-order, to stand in "lake" battle-formation and fight a "chisel" combat.' The meaning is not clear. Perhaps Temüjin first deployed his men in a long, dispersed line as if intending to outflank both Naiman flanks (*lake array*), but really aimed to deliver a strike against the enemy centre (*chisel fight*). Having deceived the enemy about his numbers and intent, it is possible that the Naimans reacted by deploying in a long line as well: they were thus poorly placed to deal with a strike against the centre. The Naimans deployed on the south side of Naqu Mountain. According to the *Secret History*, Temüjin led the first line followed by Qasar and the main body. In a third line Temuge Ot'cigin guarded the camp and spare horses.[1] The Uru'ud and Mangqut covered the wings of the centre; Jebe, Qubilai, Jelme and Sübe'etei were perhaps out wide on each flank, and are reported as moving ahead, chasing the Naiman scouts. The Naimans were driven up the mountain, which was subsequently surrounded by the Mongols, and Bai Buqa died from a wound received during the battle. The next day a core of Naiman warriors charged the Mongols. They rejected Temüjin's offer of surrender and fought until they were all killed; Temüjin publicly praised their courage. Jamuqa had left with his men before the serious fighting started. Toqto'a was said to have fought well in the battle, but was able to get away.

Küclüg 'had been staying apart', probably guarding a rear camp, and was therefore not amongst the men surrounded on Naqu. When the Mongols moved against him, he tried to defend a circular barricaded camp along the Tamir. Defeated, he escaped with only a few followers. The Mongols pursued the Naimans towards the Altai, needing several weeks to get there. The *Secret History* says: 'Činggis Qa'an utterly defeated and conquered the people of the Naiman tribe on the southern slopes of the Altai. The Jadaran, Qatagin, Salji'ut, Dörben, Tayiči'ut, Onggirat and other people who had been with Jamuqa also submitted on that occasion.' They had 4,000 men.[2] Jamuqa was soon afterwards delivered to Temüjin who had him executed. Altan and Qucar were also caught and executed. Temüjin took Gürbesü as a wife.

---

1 Presumably there was another main camp further back, probably in the Sa'ari region, with the Mongol families.
2 Rashid al-Din and the SWQZL have them surrender just after the battle, but the narrative is short and the *Secret History* may be right to place these events at the foot of the Altai.

Toqto'a and his Merkits camped at the Qaradal Source, perhaps a plain south-west of Khovd;[3] Temüjin moved against him, and Toqto'a and his sons fled westwards with some followers. The *Secret History* says Temüjin 'dislodged' the Merkits from the position they held, but the other sources make no mention of a battle and it seems possible that if there was a confrontation it was a rearguard action rather than a battle. The Merkits were in no position to challenge Temüjin. They joined Buyiruq west of the Altai, and Küclüg also made his way there. Merkit leader Dayir Usun submitted with the U'as Merkits, offering Temüjin a daughter in marriage. Other Merkit groups, said to be half of the whole tribe, camped inside a naturally strong position called Taiqal.[4] Temüjin sent a detachment to secure their submission.[5] He considered the U'as Merkits weak and did not want to integrate them into his forces: they therefore felt unsafe and quickly rebelled, marching off with the supplies and gear they had been tasked to guard. The Mongols who moved with them quickly recovered the provisions, but Dayir Usun managed to get away with some followers. Meanwhile, at Taiqal, the Qo'as Merkits surrendered.[6] Dayir Usun led his men to Qura Qabchal Pass near the Selengge River, perhaps north of Kyakhta, where he constructed a fort. Temüjin sent Boroqul and Cimbai, Cila'un's brother, with the *right hand* to deal with Dair Usun. The Mongols overcame the Merkits and killed many of their men (winter 1204–1205).

Rashid al-Din relates that the captured wives of Qudu, Chibuq, and Cila'un were paraded before Ögödei and Ca'adai. Ögödei wanted to rape them, but Ca'adai did not consider it right to do so. Ögödei took the Naiman Döregene anyway. Temüjin heard of this and approved of the action, and gave the other two women to other people. Döregene was not known for her beauty, but she had a forceful personality. The story of Rashid al-Din may not be true, but she did marry Ögödei; after he died in 1241 she effectively ruled the Mongol Empire for three years until her son Güyük was finally elected *Great Khan*.

In April–May 1205, Temüjin made a raid into Xia territory.[7] Yelü Ahai, the Khitan who had left the Jin to take service with Temüjin years before, was with the advance guard. He served with an officer called Qiegulitu. Önggüt leader Alaqus Digit Quri provided guides for the Mongols; the main task of the raiders may have been to track down Naiman refugees. This was perhaps the time when Yelü Ahai looked for Senggüm, To'oril's son, and struck into the western provinces of Xia. Three of the 12 Xia armies were stationed in the west, one at Heishui and the others further back at Gua and Gan. It seems the Xia did not to challenge the invaders in the open. The Mongols, probably bypassing Heshui, took Lijili, according to Rashid al-Din 'an extremely impregnable place.' He writes, 'in a short while they took it and destroyed all

---

3   Alternatively located somewhere between the Selenga and Tes, following de Rachewiltz (assuming the 'Ter' of the texts is an error for 'Tes'). It could also be somewhere in or near the traditional Merkit pasture grounds.

4   The Kuru Khapchal Gorges or Taiqal Khorkha, probably on the Selenga close to Kyakhta.

5   This detachment could have come from the base camp.

6   The SWQZL and Rashid al-Din mention the Maigudan/Mudan and the Tolijin/Toadaqlin sub-groups.

7   Drawing on later a Xia source, Martin and Ratchnevsky consider it unlikely that Temüjin led the Mongol forces in person.

its ramparts and foundations.' The Mongols afterwards passed a fortress called Louso, took Jilingosa, and plundered the open country.[8] Rashid al-Din says the Mongols captured many camels. The advance guard reached the districts of Guazhou and Shazhou. After the Mongols left, Xia quickly rebuilt the places destroyed (May-June 1205). In December 1205 a Xia army assembled to make a counter-raid against the Mongols, but ultimately no attack was made.

Amongst the Tangut captives brought back to Mongolia was a boy they called Caqan.[9] He was adopted by Temüjin and emerges as a senior officer by 1211. Senggüm was at an unknown time killed during a raid on the districts around Kucha; it must have happened before the Mongols invaded West Liao in 1217, but perhaps only after this Mongol raid into Xia. The Mongols were never close to capturing him.

Getting to and from Xia required passing through 300 km of sand desert. The Inner Asian people were used to making this crossing, in small groups, with armed forces, or with a whole people. The sources do not throw light on what measures Temüjin took to facilitate the crossing in the best way.

In 1204, Temüjin made no use of pre-battle manoeuvring. The Naimans assembled a large force; Temüjin did the same and marched against them with the intent to do battle. He exploited the victory gained with energy, dealing successive blows to a separate Naiman force and the various Merkit groups. At Naqu Temüjin deployed with three echelons. The last line was probably tasked to guard the mobile camp, but even so this is a very deep deployment. The Mongols struck like a battering ram. Bai Buqa attempted to win over the Önggüts and make them serve his purposes, however the political position of Temüjin was too strong and the ploy failed. Though unsuccessful, Bai Buqa – or his advisors – clearly had a grand strategic vision of some kind. As events unfolded it is clear Bai Buqa should have supported Buyiruq in 1202 or To'oril in 1203. To'oril and his allies had defeated Temüjin and the Naimans clearly put up a stiff fight. Temüjin overcame them in detail, but united they could have crushed him. Bai Buqa was not a strong leader, and he was unable to opt for a strategy of attrition because his men preferred a straight fight. Temüjin had been able to implement such 'unmanly' strategy with success in 1202. As a political leader and as a leader of men in general, Bai Buqa was no match for him. Again the triumph of Temüjin had a lot to do with political power. If Temüjin ever fought a 'decisive battle' then a case can be made for Naqu being the one. The Naimans clearly dominated the old Kereyit territory and central Mongolia, and a defeat would have been a serious blow to Temüjin's political prestige. Though Bai Buqa was evidently no first class leader, he might have been better able to hold his allies in line than To'oril had done the year before.

Sources: the SWQZL, 53b–56b; Rashid al-Din, 72–74, 95, 103, 302–306, 412, 424–425, 444; *Yuanshi* 1, pp.25–26; the *Secret History*, 186–198, 200–201; Ulug Big, *The Shajrat ul Atrak*, pp.67–73; Raverty, p.946; Grousset, *Empire of the Steppes*, pp.213–216; Martin, *The Rise of Chingis Khan*, pp.93–95 (drawing on the *Xi Xia Ji* and *Xi*

---

8   Martin suggests the two fortresses are modern Dingxin and Jinta.
9   His Tangut name was Yide.

Xia Shu Shih amongst other sources); Ratchnevsky, *Genghis Khan: His Life and Legacy*, pp.83–88, 103; de Rachewiltz, commentary on the *Secret History*, pp.103, 729–730; Urgunge Onon, *The Secret History of the Mongols: The Life and Times of Chinggis Khan* (Richmond, Surrey: Curzon, 2001), p.179; Dambyn and Dambyn: *Chinggis Khaan: A historic-geographic atlas*, pp.34–35.

15

The Defeat of Buyiruq

The emperor ... raised an army and marched against the Naimans. At this time Buyiruq
Qan was hunting in the Wuluta Mountains. He captured him and returned.

– *Yuanshi* 1

Temüjin sent two ambassadors to the Kirghiz. The Kirghiz leaders Quduqa Beki
and Orus Inal, living in different places, both submitted to the Mongols. During the
summer, Temüjin held a large assembly at the source of the Onon River and was set
up as Genghis Khan – Genghis meaning 'fierce', according to Rashid al-Din. He
reorganised the army, refining the organisation established in 1203. The number of
the minghan commanders was increased from 65 to 90 plus another 10 in the now
expanded guard. In addition the Önggüts had 5,000 men with their own minghan
commanders. They are listed in the *Secret History* in the army of 1206, but while
sympathetic to the Mongols, they only openly came over to their side after 1207.

During the autumn Temüjin headed towards the Altai Mountains to deal with
Buyiruq, Küclüg, and Toqto'a. Buyiruq had fought against Temüjin in 1199 and 1202,
but failed to support his brother Bai Buqa in 1204. In winter 1206–1207 Temüjin
surprised the Naimans at Ulugh Taq (Suja'u). Rashid al-Din says 'he was ambushed in
his winter grounds.' Buyiruq was out hunting hawks when the Mongols struck; he was
killed and his party shattered. Küclüg and Toqto'a escaped with many followers and
fled up along the Erdis River. This time, as so many times before, Temüjin surprised
his foe and gained a quick victory. Buyiruq was surprised in 1199 and again in 1206,
and does not emerge as one of the impressive commanders of this period. Temüjin was
probably able to attack with 50,000 or more men; Buyiruq must have been weaker, but
had perhaps 30,000 to 40,000 men. Though Buyiruq was killed, Temüjin may have
failed to inflict significant losses on the enemy forces.

In China war broke out between the Jin and the Song, the so-called Gaixi War
(1205 to 1207). This war is of interest as it involves future foes of the Mongols, and
was fought on the same ground where the Mongols would later fight. The two powers
clashed in the plains between the Huang (Yellow) and Yangtze Rivers and around the
mountains in the east. The fighting evolved over a 2,000 km long front where separate

armies operated in the various local theatres of war. Initial Song attempts to reconquer some border territory, starting May 1206, were largely unsuccessful. Bi Caiyu did take Sizhou on 11 July, but another officer failed to secure Suzhou on 30 July. In the centre a Jin army defeated a Song detachment in Caizhou. In the west, Wu Xi could not take Yenquan (he was driven off by Wanyan Wangxi). The failure in the western sector was critical as the Song committed 90,000 men in that theatre compared to only 10,000 in the Xiangyang sector. The Jin concentrated 100,000 out of 145,000 men mobilised in the centre and east. Subsequent Song attacks in the west were also unsuccessful. Wu Xi attacked Qinzhou with 50,000 men, but was again repulsed. Zheng Song, the overall Song commander in Sichuan, led an army into the Fang Shan Plain south-east of Xi'an, but quickly fell back.

The Jin struck into Song territory later during that same year. They attacked at nine different points. In the east they besieged Chuzhou for three months; Bi Caiyu, holding a command in Xui, brought supplies into the city and raided the Jin supply depots. Afterwards, Jin commander Hosheli Zhizhong decided to retreat. Wanyan Guang was responsible for the attacks on Caoyang, Guanghua, De'an, and Xiangyang. The first two places fell to the Jin, but De'an and Xiangyang famously held out. Zhao Qun defended Xiangyang with 10,000 men armed with crossbows or spears, and in addition raised at least 6,000 militia tea-carriers, who proved to be very effective soldiers. He also built 98 catapults to mount on the walls in addition to the 16 already there. The defenders also had *thunderclap* bombs (grenades). The Jin were credited with having 200,000 soldiers in the Xiangyang sector, an impossible number, but they probably fielded a significant number of Henan militia forces. As the Jin approached, Zhao Qun brought the local rural population inside the city walls, and the whole of Fancheng was evacuated via the bridge over the Han River. The Jin first attempted to bring Xiangyang to the north side of the Han by diverting the river, but their engineering was not equal to the task. Evidently having crossed to the south side, they next attempted to break through the Song defences by means of a wooden ramp but the Song defenders destroyed it using incendiary fire. Throughout the siege, the Song made frequent sorties. At night small groups of 30 to 60 men ventured out, seeking to damage Jin siege equipment by means of fire attacks. The attacks were usually mounted on small boats. Less frequently the Song also made larger sorties involving more than 1,000 men armed with spears and crossbows. After 90 days (24 January to 27 April 1207) the Jin gave up and fell back.[1] De'an was small compared to Xiangyang: the Song commander, Wang Yunchu, had only 600 regulars and 5,400 militiamen at his disposal. Nonetheless the 10,000, or 'many', soldiers of Jin failed to break into De'an, and retired after a 108 day siege. In the easternmost theatre, however, the Jin held the initiative: Fura Zhen attacked the area around Tianshui, Xihezhou, Mianzhou, and the Hoshang Plain.

The Amdo region in the far west, beyond Kokonor Lake, had a mixed nomadic population. The Zhao family, credited with controlling 40,000 households, backed Jin.

---

1   The siege is described in a diary, A record of the defense of Xiangyang.

Qingyike in Diezhou backed Song. He was said to rule over 300,000 households. Jin turncoats killed the ruler of Zhao, and afterwards Qingyike suddenly switched sides, declaring for Jin. In the confusion that followed, Xia may have tried to gain influence in Amdo by using Ilaq Senggüm as a vehicle.

The Jin and Song both fielded about 150,000 men in several armies. When Temüjin fought the Naimans each side may have fielded somewhat more than 50,000 men. As the Chinese population was 20 or more times larger than the Mongolian population, it can be seen that the Jin–Song conflict was much more limited in scope compared to the overall size of their societies.

Sources: the SWQZL 57a; Rashid al-Din, 97, 306–308, 398, 425–426; *Yuanshi* 1, pp.27–28, 120, pp.2962–2963; the *Secret History*, 202; Martin, *The Rise of Chingis Khan*, p.95; Dunnell, 'The Fall of the Xia Empire', p.164; Ratchnevsky, *Genghis Khan: His Life and Legacy*, pp.101–102, 849–851.

Jin–Song War: Richard L. Davis, 'The Reigns of Kuang-tsung (1189–1194) and Ning-tsung (1194–1224)', Denis Twitchett and Frederick Mote (eds.), *The Cambridge History of China*, vol. 7, part 1 (Cambridge: Cambridge University Press, 2008), pp.789–796; Christopher Atwood, 'The first Mongol contacts with the Tibetans', *Revue d'Etudes Tibétaines* (2015), pp.27–29. On the sieges of Xiangyang and De'an see Herbert Franke, 'Siege and Defense of Towns in Medieval China', in Edward L. Dreyer, Frank A. Kierman and John K. Fairbank, *Chinese Ways in Warfare* (Cambridge, Mass.: Harvard University Press, 1974), pp.181–188. The siege of Xiangyang is also described by Ralph Sawyer, *Fire and Water = Huo zhan yu shui gong: The Art Of Incendiary And Aquatic Warfare in China* (Boulder, Colo.: Westview Press, 2004), pp.366–371.

16

The Conquest of Wulahai

In 1207, in autumn, a campaign was started against Xi-Xia. The town of Wulahai was destroyed ... In 1208, in spring, the emperor returned from Xi-Xia.

– *Yuanshi*, 1

The tribes living in the border region between Mongolia and Jin China declared for Temüjin. Chinese sources credit them with having 30,000 horsemen, but even if they did not have this many, they were a significant force. In 1206 they had been mobilised to take part in operations against the Song in the Wei River region. They were sent back home in 1207, but without fair rewards for their service. The growth of the sedentary populations in the north also caused unhappiness, and the tribesmen were also tasked to work on the defensive walls, hardly a popular task. The tribesmen the Jin called Juyin included Khitan, Tangut, Merkit, Tatar, and Jurchen elements. They lived in the region where the Jin, Xia and Önggüt borders meet. Aggravated, the Juyins marched off and joined the Mongols: Temüjin formed them into three units of 1,000 with Qoshaul and Jusuq as leaders.[1] Possibly the Jin blamed the Önggüts for the Juyin revolt. The Önggüts had the leader Alaqus assassinated at some later time. He had gained power in c.1190 after killing his older brother Sesui; the Jin let Alaqus retain power, but took Sesui's infant son Bayisbu (Shimgui) and assigned him to some Jin family. Bayisbu was after the death of Alaqus installed as leader of the Önggüts, but surprisingly he formally sided with the Mongols (and certainly by 1211).[2] Bayisbu married Alaqai Beki, a daughter of Temüjin.[3] When Temüjin later found a child of Alaqus called Boyauqa he made sure he was taken care of. The Önggüts added 5,000 men to the Mongol army, increasing the total to 105,000. The Mongol control over the border tribes and eventually the sedentary population provided a source of manpower that was critical for the later conquest of China. Paul Buell observes: 'So important

---

1   In one place Rashid al-Din says men from Mongolia were sent (two out of 10) to help form these units. Were these reinforcements?
2   It was said he was angered by the Jin refusal to let him marry a daughter of his foster parents.
3   She came to control the Önggüts, living until 1237.

were frontier zone allies in the Mongol conquest of China that it can almost be said that this conquest itself grew out of Mongol control over it.'

In September–October 1207 the Mongols again raided into Tangut territory, this time attacking in the east. Temüjin personally led this expedition, say the *Yuanshi* and Rashid al-Din. The Mongols plundered the western Ordus region and took and sacked Wulahai, probably the biggest city taken by them up to this point. It is not clear what kind of resistance the fortress offered. The brief statements in the sources can perhaps be taken to mean the city simply submitted. The Xia had an army stationed north-east of Wulahai, but it is not known what it did in the face of the Mongol attack. The SWQZL says the Mongols set out during the autumn and took Wulahai only during the winter, so the fortress might have been isolated for some time before it was taken or submitted. The Mongols left Tangut territory six months later, in March–April 1208, avoiding an army sent against them from the interior.

The Song–Jin war continued. Wu Xi, the Song commander in Xing, held back his forces, avoiding confrontation with the Jin. Then he suddenly rebelled, coming to terms with the Jin, who recognised him as Prince of Shu. His reign was brief: his own officers killed him 41 days later. Yang Zhuyuan and Li Haoyi were the ringleaders of the counter-coup; Li Haoyi took command of the army and marched against the Jin in May 1207. He recovered Xihezhou, Chengzhou, Jiezhou, Fengzhou, and the Dasan Pass, then struck into Jin territory, targeting Qinzhou. This place was perhaps beyond Song reach, but it was internal politics that brought ruin to the project: Wang Xi and Liu Zhangguo suddenly turned on Li Haoyi and killed him, and afterwards no more attacks were made. The central Song authority found it difficult to impose control on the western region. Local strongman An Bing was put in charge of Sichuan and dealt with the unruly officers, but was himself an independent-minded warlord. The Song and Jin came to terms, ending the war.

The Jin and Song had shared a common border for almost a century and their wars were now limited in nature. The violent wars of the first half of the 12th century gave way to more and more constrained conflicts. The situation can perhaps be compared to that seen in Europe where the relatively bloody Seven Years' War between Prussia and Austria and her allies was followed by the much more uneventful Bavarian Succession War. The French, driven by the social impetus of the Revolution, again injected drive and ambition into European wars two decades later. Mongols would do the same to war in China, as will be seen later.

Sources: the SWQZL, 57b; Rashid al-Din 155, 308, 426; *Yuanshi* 1, p.27; Martin, *The Rise of Chingis Khan*, pp.102–103; Ratchnevsky, *Genghis Khan: His Life and Legacy*, pp.13–14; Buell, *Tribe, Qan and Ulus in early Mongol China*, pp.50–54; Buell, 'Sübötei', in de Rachewiltz, *In the Service of the Khan*, pp.51–52; Buell, *Historical Dictionary of the Mongol World Empire*, pp.20, 23–24; de Rachewiltz, commentary on the *Secret History*, pp.856–857; Christopher Atwood, 'Historiography and transformation of ethnic identity in the Mongol Empire: the Öng'ut case', *Asian Ethnicity* (Indiana, 2014), pp.514–534.

17

Battle along the Buqdurma

In winter, he launched another attack against Toqto'a Beki and Küclüg Qan. By then chieftain Quduqa Beki from the Oirats surrendered without ever fighting when he met the Mongol vanguards. Therefore, he was taken as a guide to the Erdis River. The Merkit tribes were completed crushed. Toqto'a Beki was killed by a flying arrow. Küclüg Qan managed to escape with several followers to Gur Qan in West Liao.

– the SWQZL, 58b

Temüjin rested his forces during the summer before setting out again during the autumn. He now aimed to deal with Toqto'a, his oldest rival, and Küclüg. He marched towards the northern end of the Altai Mountains where he unexpectedly came upon the Oyirats. This tribe must have fled westwards after the defeat of the Naimans in 1204. Quduqa Beki, the Oyirat leader, submitted. He provided guides who showed the Mongols the way to the camp of Toqto'a and Küclüg, and the Mongols surprised and shattered the enemy forces along the Buqdurma River. Küclüg is later credited with assembling 8,000 men without the Merkits, who were then probably weaker. Perhaps there had been as many as 30,000 Naiman and Merkit fighting men before the Mongols struck. Certainly the Mongols were much stronger and they probably gained a quick victory. Many of the defeated men are said to have drowned in the Erdis as they tried to escape across the river. The battle was perhaps fought close to where the Buqdurma flows into the Erdis. Half of the enemy tribesmen were killed, including Toqto'a who was hit by an arrow. However Toqto'a's sons Qudu, Qaltoqan, Cila'un, and Majar, as well as Küclüg escaped with a substantial number of men. Qudu handled the retreat with skill. The *Secret History* says: 'The sons of Toqto'a having at their head Qudu, Qal and Čila'un left in fright and haste, then turned back, exchanged shots with us and went off like lassoed wild asses or stags with arrows in their bodies.' Unable to carry the body of Toqto'a with them, his sons cut off his head and carried it away. The Mongol army afterwards re-crossed the Altai and returned home (winter 1208–1209).

Temüjin again surprised and crushed a weaker foe, this time helped by guides who showed him a route through the mountains to where the enemy camped. Toqto'a had fought against Temüjin in 1197, 1198, 1202, 1204–1205, 1206, and 1208. During those years he was involved in at least five battles against the Mongols, all defeats.

Temüjin was now master of the country from the Altai to the Khingan. Inanca Bilge had been too powerful to challenge, but in To'oril, Jamuqa, Buyiruq, and Bai Buqa, Temüjin faced leaders lacking in political and leadership skills who were unable to form effective alliances or even to impose their wills on their own people. The Tayici'uts and Tatars were divided. The Tatar leader Zudu was perhaps able to keep many factions united under his leadership, but Temüjin never fought him. If the Naimans had retained strong leadership, and if the Tatars had not fragmented, it is hard to see Temüjin emerge victorious. For all the unique skills and single-minded determination of Temüjin, his rise to power depended on some outside factors as well.

The Oyirats added 4,000 men to the Mongol army, raising the total to 109,000.

Sources: the SWQZL, 58b; Rashid al-Din, 72–74, 308–309, 426–427; the *Yuanshi*, pp.28–29; the *Secret History*, 199; Raverty, p.950; Martin, *The Rise of Chingis Khan*, p.102; Ratchnevsky, *Genghis Khan: His Life and Legacy*, p.102.

Overview: The Chinese Campaigns I, 1209 to 1215

China was, like Caesar's Gaul, divided into three parts, with the Jin dynasty in the north, the Song in the south, and the much smaller Xia in the north-west. The Mongols had already raided into Xia in 1205 again in 1207, but it was only in 1209 that a full-scale assault was mounted. Next, in 1211, they attacked Jin. At this stage Temüjin fielded far stronger forces than his foes and won major battles. The real challenge, however, was not to win battles, but to conquer fortified cities. Attacking Han China had been something the founders of the Khitan Liao and Jurchen Jin dynasties had also been quick to do, but they came from Manchuria rather than Mongolia. Earlier warlords coming from the region of Mongolia, leading the Xiongnu, Turks, or Uighurs, had been content to raid into China. Temüjin was the first Mongolian-based warlord to adopt the Manchurian approach. The 4th and 5th century nomad warlords that carved out kingdoms for themselves in China did so after having been settled for a long time inside Chinese territory, therefore their situation was different. The initial objective of Temüjin was not conquest: he intended to humble the Jin emperor. The Khitans and Han Chinese in his service would have pushed for an agenda of conquest and probably influenced Temüjin to later expand his aims.

Many Western historians and commentators have assumed Temüjin attacked the equivalent of Ming China, with massive walls guarding the northern border and huge infantry armies coming up from the interior to deal with raiders able to get through the walls. This was the challenge faced by the Manchu during the first half of the 17th century, but not by the Mongols. The situation was different in two important respects. First, the walls were fieldworks rather than regular walls,[1] except for some locations like the Juyong Pass north of Beijing, and second, the Jin was itself a dynasty created by nomads fighting on horseback. The core of their army consisted of cavalry, just like the Mongols. However, with regard to cavalry they were probably outnumbered two or three times. The Jin also had infantry. Spear- and crossbow-armed infantry could hold off cavalry, but there is no real evidence that the Jin at this stage put effort into making effective use of infantry in open country. Jin had many fortified positions and could from there resist Mongol forces.

---

1   Similar to the fortified lines Marlborough had to break through in Flanders during the War of Spanish Succession (1701 to 1714), or those the Rus and Volga Bulgars constructed to provide cover against Kipchak raiders.

Most of the Jin population lived along or near the Huang River. Its lower course changed in 1194, when Just east of Kaifeng the river started to flow south-eastwards instead of north-eastwards. This was a social disaster for the country, with many communities suddenly finding themselves without the water needed to maintain their farming production. This helps explain why bandit leaders found many eager recruits, particularly in and near Shandong. The Huang River had changed course before; in the wake of such an event social unrest was a certain consequence.

The SWQZL and Rashid al-Din are no longer first-rate sources and the *Yuanshi* 1 entries for 1211 and 1212 are confused. The best source is the *Jinshi* base annals, though the various *Yuanshi* and *Jinshi* biographies add much information. The *Secret History* has almost nothing to offer. Amongst modern works, at least in English, the best account is that of Desmond Martin.

Assault on Xia

It is clear that the Tanguts cannot break through the border without fully mobilising their masses. Their current concentration of forces on the border of Huanjing shows that such a general mobilisation takes 40 to 50 days … It is exhausting and punishing for a state to mount such a campaign from summer to autumn with limited territory and people.

– Song official Qan Ze, evaluation of Xia military capabilities late 11th century

Having crushed all tribal foes, Temüjin was quick to decide on external conquest. His first target was the Tangut Xia state. It was the first time the Mongols struck against a sedentary state with such intent, and the campaign marks the real beginning of the Mongol run of conquests. With about three million inhabitants, Xia was a small state. It had a mixed population of Tanguts, Han Chinese, and Uighurs, as well as other ethnic groups. Used to fighting against Song and later Jin, Xia concentrated most of their forces along the southern border. Six out of the 12 permanent armies were stationed between Lanzhou and Yingzhou, while another two were placed close to the capital. Xia also stretched far westwards, with two armies guarding this end of the country. That left only two armies to guard the northern border, each with six divisions; these armies were called *Heishui Zhenyan* and *Heishan Weifu*, most likely headquartered respectively at Heishuijeng in the west, and in the Langshan, north or north-west of Wulahai. The Xia standing armies were skeleton structures which needed to call in a militia before being fully combat-ready. Song sources credit the Xia with having very large armies, but with a total population of three million, it is hard to see that the armed forces could ever be much more than 150,000 men in total. This, divided across 12 armies, gives each 12,500 men or so on average, though possibly with a higher number for the armies stationed in the more densely populated areas along the upper Huang River. Desmond Martin details the Xia military deployment during the 11th century, where only 7,000 men out of a total of 158,000 were stationed in the north. One hundred thousand were deployed along the border to Han China. Xia

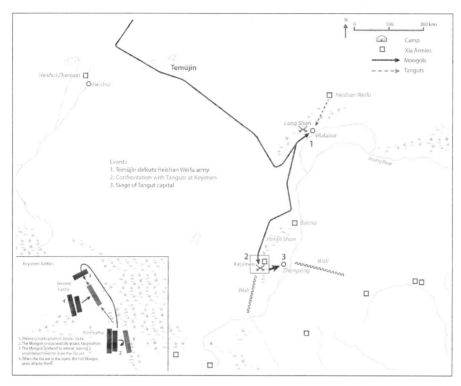

11. The invasion of Xia in 1209–1210.

ruler Li Anquan (reigned 1206–1211)[1] understood that a united Mongolia posed a potential threat, but it seems he did nothing of significance to strengthen and prepare the defences. He could, for example, have shifted more armies northward.

At this time, May 1209, Temüjin had more than 100,000 horsemen, and most could have taken part in the upcoming campaign. He led the army south along a route taking him towards Heishui before turning sharp left towards Wulahai. This line of approach first suggested to the Xia forces stationed at Heishui that he intended to attack them (as in 1205), but he finally outflanked the forces stationed near Wulahai by approaching them from the west rather than north (as in 1207). He moved through open terrain and avoided the Lang Mountains altogether. Li Cunxiang and the *Linggong* Gao commanded the *Heishan Weifu* army stationed north of Wulahai. They are credited with having 50,000 men, but a total of at most around 15,000 quality fighting men seems possible.[2] The proper line of action for the Xia was now to retreat or seek refuge inside a city; instead, the Xia commanders engaged the Mongols in battle and were overwhelmed. Gao was captured. The sources do not say how the

---

1   His temple name was *Xiangzong*. He overthrew a cousin to gain power.
2   In addition to regular soldiers, Xia had auxiliaries. This catgory was, according to Dunnell, a 'very low-class outfit.' They were servants, not fighting men, but could be included in army counts.

battle came about, nor how the Mongols won it. If the Xia accepted battle in open terrain they are likely to have severely underestimated the size of the Mongol army. In July the Mongols moved on Wulahai itself (defended by Xianbai Uda). They had to engage in street-to-street fighting before securing control of the city.

The Mongols rested in the area around Wulahai during the peak summer period. Xia therefore had plenty of time to mobilise a large force near the capital. They had permanent armies stationed at Keyimen ('Barbarian Vanquishing Pass') and Baima, guarding respectively the road through the Holan Mountains running due west from the capital, and the northern end of this mountain chain. Keyimen was seen as the weak point, and it was here Li Anquan ordered the *Linggong* Weiming to take up station with the main army. To the reported 70,000 men first assembled at Keyimen came another 50,000 from the capital, including perhaps forces from the armies deployed along the border to Jin as well as the 3,000 guard cavalry normally stationed in the capital. An effective total of around 40,000 seems possible, mostly spearmen and archers. The Holan Mountains covered the Xia right, and a wall (fieldworks) running due south covered the more open left. East of the capital, beyond the Huang River, there was another wall, this one running eastward. The capital was well protected on all sides.

In October, having waited for the peak of the summer to pass, Temüjin led the army up along the Huang River before skirting around the west side of the Holan Mountains. He was unwilling to push through the pass between the northern end of this mountain chain and the Huang River, the Baima route. The Mongols found the Keyimen pass strongly held by the enemy. Temüjin is likely to have outnumbered the Xia and in particular had an overwhelming superiority with regard to cavalry, but when the Mongols approached the Xia position, Weiming charged downhill and drove them back. Martin writes that the Xia commander 'launched a furious attack and forced the Mongols to retire.' It seems Temüjin was actually defeated even if the Xia certainly scored only a defensive success. For weeks the two armies camped opposite each other, waiting. Temüjin finally broke the stalemate by means of a favourite steppe trick, the feigned retreat. He left a small detachment to act as bait and fell back with his main forces. Weiming moved forward and attacked the detachment; possibly it retreated northward along what are now the S218 and S5 roads, with the main Mongol army in a hidden position further westward. In November, confronted by the full Mongol army in the open, Weiming was defeated and taken prisoner. After this victory the Mongols could advance to the Tangut capital Zhongxing (now Yinquan). In January 1210 they started to besiege the metropolis, but lacking means to break through the strong defences, Temüjin built a dam in order to flood the city. This feat of engineering must have surprised the Tanguts, but it was probably no high-quality effort: after just three months, the dam broke and water flooded into the Mongol camp, and Temüjin was forced to move his camp to higher ground. A later source says the dam broke as a result of a Tangut action. In spite of this setback, the siege – or blockade – continued. Eventually Li Anquan opened negotiations with the Mongols, and in April 1210 he accepted Temüjin as his overlord and gave him a daughter in marriage. Content with this, Temüjin led the army back home. Ruth Dunnell speculates the Mongols may have annexed Wuhalai, though no source directly says so.

The initial Mongol strategy against Xia was impressive, but the final approach to the Xia capital was not. Confronted by a large army in a strong position, the Mongols were stuck. The Xia eventually moved out of that strong position, which was fortunate for Temüjin. Xia should probably be faulted for not having taken more effective measures to prepare against an attack from the north, but seems to have secured the area around the capital well enough. Had the Xia commander not been tempted forward, the Mongols would probably have been forced to retreat. Even after the capital was surrounded the Xia continued to resist; they submitted on terms, and were not conquered.

Temüjin had established his authority in the west as far as the Erdis River, but made no attempt to extend his influence further westwards. West Liao was the dominant power west of that river; among their subjects were the Turfan Uighurs. In spring 1209, unhappy with West Liao rule, an angry crowd in Karakhocho killed a tax collector to trigger a general revolt. The Iduqut, the political leader of the Uighurs, was not strong enough to hold off a West Liao attack on his own, and when Temüjin sent an embassy offering protection he immediately accepted him as overlord. Küclüg and Qudu remained active with some followers in the western regions. The Merkits first moved southward towards Turfan. The SWQZL says about this: 'At that time Qudu, Cila'un, Majar and Qaltoqan, the four of them, the sons of the Merkit Tokta'a ... after fording the Erdis River were going to Uighur country. They first sent one Ebugen as an envoy to the Iduqut, who killed him. When the four arrived they fought a large battle with the Uighurs at the Djem River.' This was perhaps in 1209.[3] Defeated, the Merkits eventually made their way to the other side of West Liao, settling in the plains beyond the western border of this state.[4] For his part, Küclüg found refuge with Yelü Zhilugu, the ruler of West Liao. Zhilugu let him assemble an army along the Imil and Qobuq, and Küclüg quickly gathered together 8,000 men. Temüjin sent Qubilai and a small force across the Altai in 1210, and received the submission of Arslan of the Karluks, a West Liao subject tribe living south of Balkhash Lake. The Iduqut and Arslan soon afterwards went to Mongolia to pay their respects to Temüjin in person, and the Iduqut married a daughter of Temüjin. The Uighurs acquired importance out of proportion to the size of their country: the Mongols adopted Uighur script and administrative ways, and Uighur metal-making skills are credited with helping the Mongols improve their armour. The Uighurs, however, hardly had the capacity to quickly provide arms for more than 100,000 horsemen.

---

3   The river is called Cui, Cem, Cham or Techem. The battle was presumably fought close to the northern borders of the Uighurs, perhaps close to Jambalik; see V. V. Barthold, *Turkestan down to the Mongol invasion* (translated by H. A. R. Gibb; London: Luzac and Co, 1968), p.362, note 2.

4   Qudu may first have stayed with Küclüg, but if so left his company fairly quickly. *The Shajrat ul Atrak* says: 'At this time Tokatughan, the son of Toktabegi, the king of the tribe of Mukreet, left the service of Koshluk Khan, the son of Naimanuk Khan, and retired to the Khum Kuchuk.'

Nine months after submitting to the Mongols, Xia invaded Jin territory. In October–November they took and sacked Riazhou; perhaps this was a diversion made at the request of Temüjin to distract the Jin. It was certainly the formidable Jin whom the Mongol khan now planned to attack. In December 1209 Xia had asked Jin for help against the Mongols, but received none. The Jin emperor was simply not interested, saying: 'It is to our advantage when our enemies attack one another. Wherein lies the danger to us?' Though Xia attacked Jin, they still sent embassies to their court, and for a while at least tried to play it both ways.

Sources: *Yuanshi* 1, p.29, 60, pp.1423–1452; Wu Guangcheng, *Xi Xia Shu Shih* (XXSS), 40; Ulug Big, *The Shajrat ul Atrak*, p.106; Martin, *The Rise of Chingis Khan*, p.113–119; Ratchnevsky, *Genghis Khan: His Life and Legacy*, pp.104–105; Ruth Dunnell, *Tanguts and the Tangut State of Ta Hsia* (Ph. D., Princeton University, 1983), pp.239–252, 341–348; Dunnell, 'The Fall of the Xia Empire', pp.169–171; Dunnell, 'Locating the Tangut Military Establishment: Uraqai (Wulahai) and the Hesishui Zhenyan Army', *Monumenta Serica XL* (1992), pp.219–224; Dunnell, 'The Hsi Hsia', p.207; Shui-lung Tsang, *War and Peace in Northern Sung China*, p.469.

The events in the west: the SWQZL 58b; Rashid al-Din, 309–310, 320, 427; *Yuanshi* 1, p.29, 120, pp.2963–2964;[5] Martin, *The Rise of Chingis Khan*, pp.109–111; de Rachewiltz commentary on the *Secret History*, pp.842–846.

---

5   The *Yuanshi* biography of Cinqai refers to a campaign against Küclüg in 1212, which could be the expedition of Qubilai (assuming Cinqai was attached to Qubilai). According to his biography, Cinqai fought against the Naimans in 1210, clearly an error for 1208. It also says Cinqai in 1212 was in China (having him in two places during the same year). The first 1212 entry may therefore be wrong and should refer to the 1210 campaign of Qubilai (rather than the 1216 expedition of Jebe). Cinqai was a Kerei Önggüt who later became an important Mongol official. See Paul Buell, 'Cinqai', *In the Service of the Khan*, pp.122–123.

19

The Road to Beijing

The battle was of such a large scale and so renowned that the battle Genghis Khan did at Hunqgan Doba'an is [still] very well known amongst the Mongols.

– Rashid al-Din, 333

Ever since Temüjin was set up as Genghis Khan in 1206 he is likely to have intended to attack Jin. However, he was in no hurry, preferring first to deal with smaller targets and to build up his strength. Wanyan Yongji, uncle of the ruling Jin emperor, was sent to visit Temüjin in 1208. Temüjin did not show him much respect, and Yongji returned to the Jin Court urging action to be taken against the Mongols. No action was taken, however. When the emperor died the next year, Yongji succeeded him, and took the temple name *Weishaowang* (reigned 1209–1213). Temüjin refused to acknowledge him as overlord as he had the previous Jin ruler. People from Liaodong informed Temüjin about a revolt by prince Ai against Jin rule in 1206, and in 1208 Jin officers Li Zhao, Wu Fengchen, Bai Lun, and Tian Guangming fled to Temüjin. They had urged an attack to be made on the Mongols, but ran away after this proposal got them into trouble. They now urged Temüjin to attack Jin. Later, Jebe, Yelü Ahai, and Yelü Tuhua made forays into Jin territory, perhaps making one such raid in 1210.[1] They were presumably preparing the way for the major attack by gathering intelligence and by probing various points along the border. The defectors and the raids would have helped Temüjin gather much valuable information about his intended target. Finally, he was ready to make a fully-fledged attack in 1211.

Qubilai perhaps returned when Arslan the Karluk went to see Temüjin. Temüjin sent Toqucar into Karluk territory with 2,000 men, and tasked him with covering the western border against West Liao, the Merkits, and Naimans. Other forces were left to guard Mongolia. Temüjin could have led 70,000 or more men against the Jin. The Jin state boasted a population of 55.5 million, but the ethnic Jurchen, the ruling group, numbered less than 4.8 million. This lower total included the fellow

---

1   Unless *Yuanshi* 1 made a mistake.

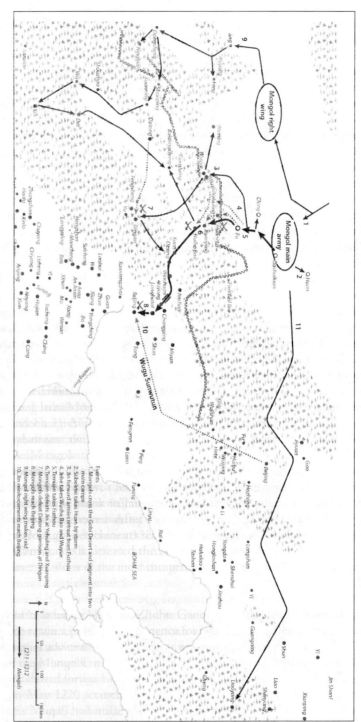

12. The first attack on the Jin in 1211–1212.

Events:
1. Mongols cross the Gobi Desert and segment into two main camps
2. Subedei takes Huan by storm
3. Jin forward armies retreat from Fuzhou
4. Jebe takes Wusha Bao and Wuque
5. Temujin takes Fuzhou
6. Temujin defeats Jin at Yehuling and Xuanping
7. Mongols defeat Datong garrison at Dingan
8. Mongols reach Beijing
9. Mongol right wing makes raid
10. Jin reinforcements reach Beijing

Manchurian Khitans and Bohai. A century earlier the Khitans and Bohai had an estimated population of respectively 0.5 and 0.75 million. The Jurchen, Khitans, and Bohai soldiers formed the backbone of the army. Though the overall population size of the three groups was much more than Temüjin ruled – the Mongolian population has been estimated at not more than 700,000 though it could have been at least twice that – it did not yield the same proportion of motivated, mounted fighting men.

The Jurchen tribal leader Aguda (reigned 1113–1123) founded the Jin dynasty. As a youth he was much impressed by the Khitan army. The *Jinshi* says:

> Aguda, during his uncle Yingge's chieftainship in 1102, was the first wild Jurchen ever to have commanded an army of more than a few hundred soldiers. Seeing the force of 1,000 mounted soldiers that his uncle, with Liao support and approval, had recruited from various tribes that year to pursue a fleeing traitor wanted by the Khitans, he said with great excitement, 'With armed troops of this number, where are the limits to what we can do?'[2]

He later raised his own army, overthrew the Liao, and easily conquered North China from the Song. The Jurchen adopted Khitan tactics. Ma Duanlin says they deployed for battle in squadrons of 50, '20 with heavy cuirasses and long lances in front and 30 with light cuirasses and bows behind.' They were said to deploy five men deep. Eyewitness Fan Zhongxiong wrote about the heavily armed troops: 'Both men and horses were fully armoured and at their waists they all carried a sword and bludgeon.' The spears were 3.7 metres long. The lightly-armed troops each carried 100 bows. They 'never shot at a range of more than 50 paces.'[3] Unlike Xia, Jin did not have regional permanent army structures: most of the cultivated land was in the hand of military colonists who had an obligation to serve when called on by the state, and would serve as horsemen. Herbert Franke says about the Jin military structure: 'The basic unit was the *mouko*. The number of households attached to the one unit varied. In theory it should have been 300 households but in reality was frequently smaller. Nor did the *mengan* have 1,000 households, as the name implies. Normally, a *mengan* was composed of 7 to 10 *mouko*.' The 1183 census counted 202 *mengans* and 1,878 moukos. In practice a *mouko* had 25 men.[4] Very likely the Jin did not have much more than 50,000 horsemen. The various units were spread out all over the country and could not quickly be concentrated in one place, and militias were called out to serve as foot soldiers. This is how Jin was able to field 150,000 men against the Song some years before, but it was easier to raise infantry militias in the more densely populated southern part of the country. The Jin initially never fielded more than 50,000 men close to the Mongols, and probably not all horsemen. There was a 3,000 man mounted guard unit in the capital, which after the war with the Mongols began was increased in size to 5,000. The early Jurchen had been famed for their ferocity. The *Sanchao Beimeng Huibian* says:

---

2   *Jinshi* 1, E. W. translated by Frederick Mote in *Imperial China 900–1800* (Cambridge, Mass.: Harvard University Press, 2003), p.214.
3   Selby, *Chinese Archery*, pp.236–237.
4   A unit included a flag bearer, a drummer, and 5 cooks(!) so they were not all fighting men.

They can bear cold, endure hunger and do not shrink back from hardships. They eat things raw. Brave and violent, they are not afraid to die. Their character is deceitful, covetous and cruel. They honour the strong and despise the old. They are excellent riders who go up and down steep cliffs as if they would fly. When they cross a river, they do not use boats but get across on their swimming horses. They are fine archers and hunters.

By now, a century later, this description is likely to fit the Mongols better than the Jurchen, who had gone soft after having gained riches in China.

In May–June 1211 Temüjin led his army across the Gobi Desert.[5] The defensive line constructed by the Jin along the edge of the desert is given no mention in the sources covering these campaigns, and therefore seems to have been of no significance. The Önggüts had declared for the Mongols, and Temüjin entered their territory without difficulty. At this stage he opted not to use their forces. It seems possible that Temüjin now detached the *right hand* to cover his western flank. The *right hand* could have pushed west along the south side of the outer Jin defensive line, but alternatively, it crossed the Gobi along a separate more westerly route.[6] Joci, Ca'adai, and Ögödei operated with this wing. The *right hand* seems for some time have remained inactive, as it is only later that this body is reported to have started to attack Jin cities.

The Jin had no forces stationed in the border districts and their general state of preparedness was poor. Their first action was to attempt to buy peace, and Nian Hoda was sent to open negotiations with the Mongols. No further mention is made of this Jin envoy; Temüjin was certainly not in the mood for peace and probably did not respond to the Jin at all.[7] At the same time, the court ordered Qian Jiannu (Zheng Shi) and Wanyan Husha (Cheng Yu), each with their own force, to fortify the border area. The latter came from Xuande.[8] In July Doji Si Zhong was tasked to construct defensive works at Wusha Bao. Huanzhou, Changzhou, Fuzhou, and Jingzhou formed the forward defences of the Jin border region. Behind these, the main city was the more important fortress of Datong (Xijing). The Juyong Pass guarded the road into the interior to Beijing (Zhongdu), the Jin capital where the emperor resided. The two Jin officers ordered to guard the border camped close to Fuzhou, covering the route to Juyong and Datong. Wusha Bao helped secure western side of Fuzhou, providing cover for Datong, which was located further south. Geshi Liezhong, whose real name was Hu Shahu, was stationed in Datong with 7,000 men. The size of the two forward Jin armies is not given, but they were perhaps about the same. In total therefore the Jin may have fielded 20,000 to 30,000 men. They did not call out local militia forces. Clearly the Mongols seriously outnumbered them.

5   Following the *Jinshi*. The *Yuanshi* says February. Martin held that the later date 'provide better marching conditions in the Gobi.'
6   Martin considered it likely the Mongols crossed the Gobi in two separate bodies.
7   Nian Hoda, commander in charge of the north border, had warned the Court about the impeding Mongol assault. For that reason he was thrown into prison. When the Mongols did attack, he was released and sent to them as an envoy.
8   Martin says they were joint commanders of Xuande.

Temüjin arrived in the area between Fuzhou and Huanzhou. Jebe and Güyigünek Ba'atur seized Dashui[9] and later Usha. The Mongols also took Lo(?) and Fengli (near Fu?). A Mongol detachment led by Sübe'etei, took Huanzhou by storm.[10] Huanzhou, the city and surrounding area, hosted a fairly large Khitan population; Huanzhou itself was small with 578 registered families. Temüjin rested his men during the summer months, which was not normal conduct for a steppe warlord entering into Chinese territory. Horse-mounted nomads tended to strike quickly, plunder the open country and seize weakly held places, only to fall back just before armies arrived from the interior, yet Temüjin waited, giving the Jin time to mobilise their forces and to bring them into position. However he did not usually undertake operations during the hot summer months, preferring to rest men and horses during this period, and this was probably the reason for the break in operations rather than a clever strategy to bait the Jin forward. Evidently he felt strong enough to deal with whatever the Jin threw against him.

If the timeline of the *Yuanshi* 1 can be trusted, in August 1211 Jebe made a forward move before the main Mongol army resumed operations. Jebe, leading a roving detachment, attacked and took Wusha Bao (Ulanqab) and Wuyue (Xinghe). Yelü Tuhua operated with him. According to the *Jinshi*, the Mongols were successful due to Jin 'lack of preparation'. The Jin Court faulted Doji Si Zhong for the loss of Wusha Bao and Wuyue and dismissed him. Wanyan Husha was given overall command on the border. Then in September Temüjin and the main Mongol forces set out towards Fuzhou. Changzhou was perhaps taken quickly. Qian Jiannu and Wanyan Husha fell back, not daring to face the Mongol army in the open; their forces remained divided, perhaps taking up position to guard the two roads leading to Xuanping. In this area a fortified line (or wall) of the Jin was there to take advantage of. Perhaps Wanyan Husha deployed to keep Jebe from moving eastwards towards Xuande, separating him from Qian Jiannu?

Meanwhile, the Mongol main army took Fuzhou by storm. Qian Jiannu camped to the south of this city at Yehu Ling ('Wild Fox Range').[11] Khitan officers urged him to attack the Mongols, saying: 'Since the capture of Fuzhou, the Mongols have become much occupied with their booty and their horses are grazing loose near the town, so if we now attack them with our cavalry they will be unprepared and we shall win a decisive victory.' However Qian Jiannu was not ready to move forward: he wanted to confront the Mongols from a prepared defensive position. His army cannot have been large. Perhaps apprehensive about having to fight the Mongols even from a prepared position, the Jin commander attempted to find a peaceful resolution, and Shimo Mingan was sent to see Temüjin. Temüjin listened to his message and then ordered the envoy held. Mingan later defected to the Mongols.

---

9 Dalinur Lake? The Stele of Laosuo says a battle was fought there.
10 When it was taken is not clear. *Yuanshi* 1 says 1211, *Yuanshi* 121 and 122 say 1212. Many biographies misdate events between 1211 and 1212. Martin thinks Huan was one of the first places taken in 1211, citing a later source. Wang Yun says the fortress was attacked 'first' and the stele of Laosuo also implies an early capture.
11 Qian Jiannu is known from *Jinshi* 13, but there is no mention of a battle at Yehu Ling. In *Yuanshi* 1 the Jin commander is Dingxie or Hoshilie Jjujin; the SWQZL 63a says Geshi Zhi Zhong; and the Stele of Laosuo offer Wanyan Jiujin and Wannu.

Temüjin sent Caqan forward to scout the Jin position. He 'reported that there was no need to fear the enemy, as they seemed unprepared.' The Mongols attacked and quickly gained a total victory. Muqali's biography records that: '[Muqali] led dare-to-die warriors, charging [with] levelled spears, loudly shouted [and] breached enemy lines, the emperor signalled to various armed forces to advance together, [they] routed the Jin army, pursued [them] to Huihe river, the corpses [laying over] hundred miles.' The SWQZL says: 'The Jin sustained a terrible reverse, men and horses trampling each other down in the rout and the dead being without number' (September 1211). With a smaller army, it seems most likely that Qian Jiannu deployed behind the fortified line running along the foot of the hills, but the entry in Muqali's biography seems to show the Mongols prevailing by means of a cavalry charge. The description is short and could be a simplification of events. The Mongols probably outnumbered the Jin three times or more, and with such superiority in numbers it certainly seems likely that the Mongols attempted to outflank the Jin on one side or even both flanks. Ten years later Chang Chun and his fellow travellers 'passed a defile called Yehu Ling ... We saw a field of battle covered with bleached human bones.' Evidence of a crushing Mongol victory was still there to see. No mention is made of Jebe in this battle. He may have remained in position further westward, but the Stele of Laosuo could be taken to show he had rejoined the main army.

Temüjin quickly turned on Wanyan Husha's forces. The SWQZL says: 'The emperor next advanced on Wanyan Husha, whom he crushed at Huiho Bao, thus destroying the best forces of the Jin.' A full account is given in Wanyan Husha's *Jinshi* biography:

When the Mongol main army reached Yehu Ling, Cheng Yu was disheartened, did not dare to resist in war, [so he] fell back to Xuanping. The local people asked him to use the local militia as a vanguard, [and] take the province soldiers as support, [but] Cheng Yu [was] timid [and] did not dare to use [the local forces]. He asked how to go to Xuande along side roads ... During night, Cheng Yu commanded the troops to move southward, the Great Yuan soldiers were at his heel and attacked it [the Jin army]. The next day, [the two sides] met along the Huihe Quan, [where] Cheng Yu's soldiers suffered a big defeat. Cheng Yu fled alone, [he] went to Xuande.

The *Yuanshi* says: 'The emperor come up and fought a battle against the Jin at the meeting of the rivers near Xuanping, [and] defeated them.' About 40 km south of the first battlefield, this engagement, in September, could have been fought the day after the first. Wanyan Husha retreated over Xuande and Dexing to Beijing. Temüjin pursued south-eastwards, taking Xuande as well as Dexing. Another Mongol column, associated with Caqan, may have secured Tiancheng and Baidengcheng. Wang Ji defended a position – the Zhuolu Pass – attacked by the Mongols. Holding out for three days, he finally surrendered, and entered into Mongol service. Jin officers Liu Bolin, Jiagu Changgo, and others also submitted to the Mongols. Liu Bolin helped them secure control over Weining, where he had been in command, as well as other places.

Hu Shahu led his detachment out of Datong, heading westwards, and collided with a Mongol force at Ding'an. Yelü Tuhua was with the Mongol detachment, but

Jebe was probably the senior commander. The Jin were again defeated. Hu Shahu eventually made his way to Beijing via a pass south or south-west of Ding'an with his remaining soldiers. Without a garrison, Datong should have been an easy target, but the Mongols did not try to take the fortress. Perhaps this was a missed opportunity? Jebe and his 3,000-strong detachment moved ahead of the main army, approaching the Juyong Pass, which he found unoccupied, more proof of the poor Jin level of preparedness. Jebe pushed through the pass and arrived in front of Beijing, the Jin capital. In October he had the worst of a skirmish fought against a 500-strong guard unit outside the city-walls, but the reverse had no strategic significance. In fact, Jebe may have been trying to bait the enemy force forward. Temüjin followed him with the main forces, setting up camp at Longhotai. He left forces behind north of the Juyong Pass to secure the various forts located in the immediate area. Temüjin had no intention of attacking the strongly defended enemy capital. According to the *Jinshi*, Mongol detachments took places to further south (Chingzhou and Cangzhou) and east (Miyun, Fengrun, Luanzhou, Pingzhou, Funing, and Linyu). Presumably these were scouting and plundering raids rather than any serious effort to make conquests.

Jin officer Liang Dang put Beijing in a state of defence. Gradually additional forces arrived there. Wugu Sunwutun led 20,000 men, probably largely cavalry, from Shangjing (Huining) in Manchuria to Beijing. In November Zhuhu Gaoqi, having assembled another army in Daizhou, also marched to Beijing. Somewhat later, in February 1212, two 5,000-strong detachments arrived from Shanxi. Finally, the Jin had concentrated more than 50,000 men in and around Beijing. Having left detachments to guard his rear, Temüjin probably had less than half of that. The Mongols fell back northwards perhaps hoping the Jin would follow them. Just when the Mongols retreated is not reported.

The Mongol *right hand* had initiated operations towards the end of the year. In this sector the Mongols first took Jingzhou. Afterwards, in December, Yelü Ahai afterwards made a raid up along the Huang River to overrun the Jin horse pastures around Yunnei. The Mongols also took Fengzhou and Dongsheng. Feng was the major city in this region. The Mongols continued past Shahukou to Xuanning, and a detachment secured Ningbian. They avoided strongly fortified Datong, instead raiding deeper into Shanxi. In February 1212 they marched over Shuoxian and Wu to Xin and Dai. From here they marched back north via the Yenmen Pass. They passed Datong to link up with the main army somewhere east of this city.

Temüjin, acting on intelligence provided by Chinese defectors, sent Jebe into Liaodong to seize Liaoyang. This town was 700 km east of Beijing with many other major fortresses in between. To make an attempt on this place was an extraordinary decision. Jebe reached the city, perhaps without any difficulties as no mention is made of trouble on the way. It seems likely that he moved along an inland route from the area around Huanzhou. Each man had one spare mount. Jebe camped in front of the city for some time before suddenly retreating, leaving his camp for the Jin to plunder. He then returned at night at the start of February and forced the gates on a completely surprised enemy. No attempt was made to hold the city, and Jebe left as quickly as he came.

The Mongols returned to the edge of the Jin territory where they had spent the previous summer, and set up camp in the area between Fu and Huan. Liu Bolin guarded Tiancheng and other former Jin officers in Mongol service guarded other places. Yila Nieer was a Khitan who came over to the Mongols with 100 fighting men. The *Yuanshi* biography of this lord says he defected even before Temüjin set out to attack the Jin in 1211. Temüjin ordered Yila Nieer and his men to guard Jizhou.

In the west, in April–May 1212, Xia unsuccessfully attacked Jiazhou. Jin forces from Yan'an held them off. This attack was entirely consistent with the usual pattern of Xia–Jin wars. The Xia and Mongols did not coordinate their efforts at an operational level: the Xia were some 300–400 km from where Mongol forces had operated a few months before so a coordinated effort could have been made.

Temüjin struck into Han Chinese territory, following the classic 'program' of any nomad warlord who had gained mastery of Inner Asia. He fielded a very large force. The Jin completely failed to act with energy, raising only small forces and failing to defend the key points. Temüjin was able to defeat the small Jin forces in detail, but this was due more to a divided enemy command than a clever central position ploy. Once confronted by large enemy forces, Temüjin retreated.

Herbert Franke saw the division of the Mongol forces, the right wing and main body, as proof of a clever strategy: 'On the western front the Mongols advanced into Shanxi and thereby prevented the Jin auxiliary troops in Shensi, where strong garrisons protected the border with Hsi Hsia, from coming to the rescue of the Jin armies on the eastern front.' The western column, however, struck later than the main column and was probably meant as a flank cover rather than a diversion. In any event the Jin had strong forces in Liaodong and not along the Jin–Xia border. In 1004 the Khitans (Liao), setting out from Liaodong, sent a column to make a diversionary attack towards the Song–Xia border region to tie down the forces stationed there. Unlike Jin, Song had strong forces stationed along the border to Xia. The main Khitan forces struck into Song territory south of Beijing, bypassed the frontier fortresses and headed towards the Huang River. The Song emperor famously took up position with an army at the Huangling Ferry point (where battles would be fought between the Mongols and the Jin in 1223 and 1233). The Khitans set up camp next to him, but did not attack the Song position, and the war ended with a negotiated settlement. The Khitan strategy was thus very close to the one Franke believed Temüjin used in 1211. It was a strategy similar in style to the one Sübe'etei used in Europe in 1241, but it is unlikely that Temüjin devised anything so elaborate in 1211. He may have split his forces to reduce the logistical burden on a single area and to be able to raid more widely.

Desmond Martin held the 1211 campaign to be Temüjin's 'greatest feat of arms', writing he would never again 'be opposed by such powerful armies.' This is a faulty estimate. It is clear from the *Jinshi* that the Jin only fielded border forces and that even in the border area they failed to raise militia forces. The *Yuanshi*, naturally, insisted that the Jin army was huge, but this cannot be accepted. Jin officer Tu Shanyi had a clear view of the situation, saying:

> Since the Mongolian army is on horseback, it goes into the plain in only one body; we
> defend ourselves divided, our defeat is certain. To bring together people of the small

boroughs in the large cities [is one measure], [but this] is not sufficient to make a common effort of defence. Changzhou, Hozhou, and Fuzhou are 3 strong and rich cities. Its inhabitants are brave and form the elite of our troops. While bringing them back to the centre they will increase considerably the force of our army and thus people, herds and goods will not be the prey of the enemy.

Temüjin's ability to attract able men from the enemy ranks into his service was remarkable. Yelü Ahai and Yelü Tuhua had served him for more than a decade. This year Liu Bolin, Wang Ji, and Shimo Mingan came over to his side and were quickly given senior responsibilities. He now had more people serving him who grew up living in cities than those who were raised in tents. Another fairly recent recruit was Laosuo, known from his funeral inscription. A Tangut, 'he was renowned for his courage.' Impressed by the success of Temüjin, he took service with the Mongols (perhaps in 1209 or even before). Temüjin 'had him join his bodyguard. Laosuo diligently [carried out his duties] from dawn to dusk. When it came to fighting the enemy he wore sturdy armour and carried a sharp blade, dodging arrows and missiles he led the troops from the front.' The inscription says he served Caqan, but the engagements he is credited with participating in suggest he served under Jebe in 1211.

Temüjin's 'hounds' moved with boldness at great distance from the main army. Jebe's conquest of Liaoyang 700 km distant from the main camp was an impressive achievement. Jebe also took Wusha Bao and Wuyue and defeated a Jin army east of Datong; Sübe'etei took Huan; and Qubilai marched across the Altai the year before in 1210. Possibly, the rowing commanders undertook other missions not captured in the sources between 1203 and 1210, but it is probably fair to assume they grew bolder and bolder and the willingness to attack fortified positions was certainly a new feature.

Sources: the SWQZL 61a–63a; Rashid al-Din, 320–327, *Yuanshi* 1, pp.29–30, 119, pp.2929–2936, 120, pp.2955–2957; 149, p.3532, 150, pp.3541–3543, 3548–3550; the *Secret History* 247–248, *Jinshi* 13, pp.285–391, 93, pp.2063–2067, 132, pp.2832–2840; De Harlez, *Histoire de l'Empire de Kin*, pp.208–209; Wittfogel and Feng, *History of Chinese Society*, pp.52–58; Martin, *The Rise of Chingis Khan*, pp.33, 121–154, 336–337; Ratchnevsky, *Genghis Khan: His Life and Legacy*, pp.105–112; Herbert Franke, 'The Military System of the Chin Dynasty', in Franke, *Krieg und Krieger im chinesischen Mittelalter (12. bis 14. Jahrhundert): drei studien* (Stuttgart: Steiner, 2003), pp.215–245; Franke, *The Chin Dynasty*, pp.252, 278–279; Buell, 'Yeh-lu A-hai' and 'Yeh-lu T'u-hua', in de Rachewiltz, *In the Service of the Khan*; C. A. Peterson, 'Wang Chi', in de Rachelwiltz, pp.113, 177–178; Da-Feng Qu, 'A study of Jebe's expedition to Tung Ching', *Acta Orientalia Academiae Scientiarum Hungaricae*, vol. 51, No. 1/2 (1998), pp.171–177; Andrew West, Babelstone, *Two Tangut Families*, http://babelstone. blogspot.ch/2015/01/two-tangut-families-part-1.html, parts 1 and 2, accessed 31 Dec 2015.

20

The Failed Siege of Datong

In Jenghiz Khan's conquest of China we can trace his use of Taitong-Fu to bait successive traps as Bonaparte later utilized the fortress of Mantua.

– Liddell Hart, *Strategy*

The Jin mobilised large forces, calling out cavalry as well as raising militia. In June 1212, 20,000 soldiers came to Beijing from Shanxi and another 10,000 came from elsewhere. Forces were sent into the northern border region where the Mongols had operated in 1211, reoccupying some places that had been lost. This was easy, with no Mongol garrisons left to hold most of them. Jin officer Hu Shahu took up position at Weichuan with 3,000 soldiers, guarding the route to Juyong. There were also garrisons in Datong, Dexing, Xuande, and other places. Aodun Xiang commanded a strong army of some 20,000 men, held back at Beijing. It was perhaps during the summer that the Jin mounted several attacks on Tiancheng, but Liu Bolin held them off. Without authorisation, He Shuhu later retreated southward from Weichuan to Nankou. For that reason he was eventually dismissed.

In Liaodong in April 1212, Yelü Liuge, a Khitan prince and officer in charge of 1,000 men, rebelled against the Jin. Liuge moved south from the Khingan region and operated in the area around Hanzhou and Lungzhou. Temüjin sent a column under Alci and Sigi Qutuqu to make contract with Liuge and to support him, and in May they met near Jin Mountain. Liuge made a ritual oath, accepting Temüjin as his overlord. Liuge may have been encouraged to rebel after the successful raid Jebe undertook into Liaodong earlier in the year.

In October, Temüjin resumed military operations and marched on Datong. This city could perhaps have been easily taken the year before, but was now strongly held. Temüjin started to besiege the fortress.[1] Aodun Xiang led the Jin army camping near Beijing towards Datong, most likely marching through the Juyong Pass. He could have increased the size of his army by calling in garrisons, but even so could hardly

1 Moran Jinzhong commanded the Jin garrison.

110

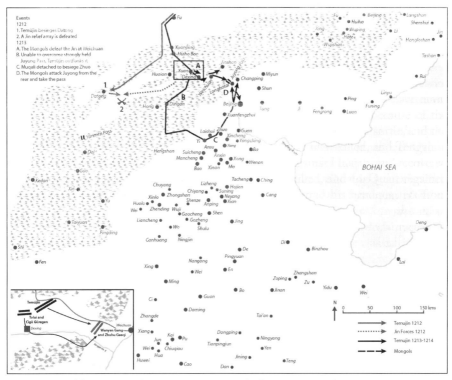

13. The continued operations against the Jin in 1212 and 1213–1214.

have had much more than 40,000 men, and only a part of these were horsemen. The Mongols probably had 50,000 or more men. Temüjin gave up the siege of Datong and deployed his forces in the Migukou Valley, perhaps east of the city; the Mongols ambushed and crushed the whole Jin army. The *Yuanshi* says the Mongols made a 'sudden attack'. The *Jinshi* biography of Aodun Xiang says 'all his forces were destroyed in the Migukou Valley. Only [Aodun Xiang] himself managed to escape'. This was late 1212. Temüjin afterwards resumed the siege of Datong, but fell back after being injured by an arrow. The *Yuanshi* says: 'A stray arrow hit the Emperor.'[2] The event is perhaps more a testament to the range of the Jin defensive weapons than Temüjin's eagerness to fight in the front line. The Mongols returned to the more northern districts where they had rested before.

Determined to improve his siege capabilities, Temüjin set up specialist siege corps, probably during the following summer. Ambughai, a Mongol officer, commanded it, but the 500-man unit consisted almost entirely of Khitan and Han Chinese experts. Gao Baoyu, who came over to the Mongols at Wusha Bao in 1211, is also associated with this unit. The creation of the engineering unit is a good example of how Temüjin

---

2   Martin says Temüjin was wounded 'while directing an assault which cost his troops heavy casualties.'

responded to a reverse. He learned and developed the army to handle the challenge it faced better next time.

There was unrest amongst the Önggüts; troublemakers killed Bayisbu. Alaqai Beki fled with her stepsons Zhenguo and Boyaoha to Temüjin who was then at Datong, so perhaps the event should be dated to the last quarter of 1212. Temüjin was only with difficulty persuaded not to wipe out the Önggüts. Evidently he easily regained control over the tribe. Alaqai Beki afterwards married Zhenguo. When he died fairly quickly, Alaqai Beki married the other stepson, Boyaoha. She was the de facto ruler of the Önggüts for many years.

The *Jinshi* base annals do not even mention the Mongols in the entries for this year. The 1212 campaign may appear to be the least successful of Temüjin's later campaigns; his aim was to take Datong and failed to do so. However, Temüjin defeated a large enemy army. Much more than in 1211, the tactical dominance of the Mongols was established this year and the victory gained in the field was decisive. The Jin fielded large forces and should have done better. If Aotun Xiang had operated from a strong defensive position and waged a delaying war, he surely could have achieved better results? The Khitan revolt was a major gain for the Mongols, threatening the Jin ancestral home and a key recruiting ground. As was often the case, Temüjin gained more through politics than military operations this year.

Sources: the SWQZL, 63b (assumed to duplicate events of 1213); *Yuanshi* 1, p.31, 149, pp.3511–3514, 3515–3516; *Jinshi* 13, pp.285–391, 103, p.2275; 132, pp.2832–2840; Martin, *The Rise of Chingis Khan*, pp.149–158; B. H. Liddell Hart, *Strategy* (New York: Praeger, 1967), p.61; Allsen, 'The Circulation of Military Technology in the Mongolian Empire', *Warfare in Inner Asian History* (Lieden, 2002), pp.274–275.

21

Into Central China

Within 100 years from now my work will be vindicated.

– Wanyan Nianhan, fortified Beijing during the first half of the 12th century

There were drafts in parts of Jin territory and in the north criminals were pardoned to create a bigger pool of military recruits. In April 1213 a small-scale revolt broke out in Daming. In July the Tanguts again invaded Jin territory, taking Bao'an and Qingyang, and killing the officials in charge of both places. On 5 November they attacked Huizhou. The Daming revolt and Xia offensives were, however, minor distractions. The Jin had to consider how best to deal with dual threats posed by the Mongols and Yelü Liuge. It was decided to try to first deal with the latter, and the Jin Court ordered Wanyan Husha, the officer defeated by the Mongols in 1211, to attack the rebel. He set out from Xianping, promising a big reward for killing Liuge. Temüjin sent 3,000 men under Alci, Butu (the leader of the Ikires), and Aluduhan(?), to support the Khitan rebels. In June, with the Mongol help Liuge was able to repel the Jin army, defeating it at Dijinawuer;[1] An early cavalry charge led by Yelü Annu helped secure victory. Some of the plunder from the Jin camp was sent to Temüjin, a sure way to earn his goodwill. Liuge set up his own government, appointing people to hold various administrative positions. Gedege later replaced Alci as the local Mongol representative amongst the Khitans. Puxian Wannu replaced Husha as the Jin commander in this theatre later the same year. Husha died soon afterwards.

Having rested during the summer, in August or early September 1213 Temüjin again struck deep into Jin territory. He easily took Xuande (again), but when he entered the next valley he found himself opposed by strong enemy forces – a reported 100,000 men. Wugu Sunwutun guarded Dexing with 16,000 men. Dexing was a small town with no space to accommodate such a force, so it is likely Sunwutun had established a bridgehead, fortifying a position around the town. He blocked the road south and could threaten the flank of the Mongols if they advanced along the main, more

---

1   Martin says 'probably a small lake located between the lower Liao and the northern reaches of the Lao-ha River.'

easterly road towards Beijing. Wanyan Gang and Zhuhu Gaoqi camped at Jinshan with the main Jin army, and from there moved forward to Weichuan. Here they could deploy with the mountains covering the right, and the Sangganho River that also ran past Dexing, the left. The deployment of the Jin may indicate quite an aggressive intent. Expecting the Mongols to move towards Weichuan, the force at Dexing was ready to fall on the Mongol flank and rear. Temüjin, however, understood the risk and first sent Tolui and Cigü to attack the Dexing position.[2] They overwhelmed the Jin garrison, and Sunwutun was killed. Temüjin then advanced on Wanyan Gang and the main Jin army. The *Secret History* offers rare operational specifics: 'Tolui and Cigü Gürigen then arrived and, charging at their flanks, forced back the Red Coats, repulsed and completely defeated Ile and Qada, and slew the Kitat until they were like heaps of rotten logs.' If this is correct then Tolui and Cigü may have moved in an arc from Dexing around the left flank of the Jin. Perhaps the Jin left wing contained ex rebel formations.[3] The Jin was completely routed, and the defeated forces pursued to Beikou. Gang and Gaoqi got away, as did probably the bulk of the Jin army, even if the SWQZL says the Jin dead were beyond number. The Jin retreated through the Juyong Pass, where the Mongol advance ended as the pass was held in force. The *Yuanshi* says: 'The Jin people relied much on the strategic pass of Juyong Pass. They had smelt metal to block the pass gate, distributed metal caltrops over 100 *li*, and guarded it with picked troops.' Temüjin set up camp north of the pass.

Temüjin remained in front of the Juyong Pass for about a month, but dared not make an assault. Ja'far Khwaja, a trader from the Near East who had previously been sent to act as an ambassador to the Jin Court, suggested a way around the pass. His biography relates:

> So he [= Temüjin] summoned Ja'far and asked for advice. Ja'far answered, 'From here northward there is a byroad in the dark forest. The space is only sufficient for one cavalry line. I have tried the road myself. If we make the troops march silently, then we may arrive at the destination before dawn.' Temüjin then ordered Ja'far act as guide and show the way. They entered the valley at sunset; at dawn, all the forces were already at the plain. Then they quickly approached the south part [of the pass]. The drumbeat and horn sound were like from the sky. Yet the Jin people were still asleep and unconscious of it. Whilst they were woken up, they couldn't resist any more. Wherever the Mongols went, the wild land was covered with blood. Once the pass was broken into, Zhongdu [= Beijing] was shocked.

Temüjin left Ketei and Buqa behind with a detachment, the 4,000 Uru'uds plus perhaps other forces, to mask Juyong. Jebe led the advance guard of the main forces,

---

2   Cigü was perhaps a son of Terge Emal. Terge Emal had been executed after refusing to marry an 'ugly' daughter of Temüjin; Cigü married her instead.

3   Overall the *Secret History* entry is confused, and may mix up events with this year that only happened much later. Ile and Qada should be Yila Pua and Wanyan Heda who fought against Tolui in 1232. Tolui also outflanked the Jin position that year. Either he did so twice or the 1213 entry is a duplication of 1232. The term 'Red Coats' only came into use a little later. The *Secret History* entry seems similar to Rashid al-Din 456.

passed Yuzhou and secured the Zijing Pass. In early November Temüjin quickly followed with the main forces. A Jin general (the *Yuanshi* says it was Wu Huiling) hurried west to intercept the Mongols, but he arrived too late. Temüjin had moved through inner pass and – perhaps – defeated the Jin army in the Wuhui Mountains. The Jin commander fell back, and Temüjin seized Yizhou and sent Jebe and Sübe'etei to attack the Juyong position from the rear. They marched quickly along a small track and managed to surprise and shatter the garrison stationed at the southern end of the long pass. The Khitan officer in charge of the northern section of the garrison opted afterwards to surrender. Jebe and Sübe'etei were free to join the detachment stationed at the other end of the pass. On 10 November Temüjin detached Muqali to mask Zhuozhou, while he himself set up camp at Longhutai, just north of Beijing. Ketei and Buqa were sent forward to mask the enemy capital with 5,000 men.

Hu Shahu was disgraced after his unauthorised retreat in 1212, but was suddenly restored to high office a little before the Mongol attack the following year, in June 1213. He was given command of 5,000 men stationed just outside Beijing. Elements in the Jin Court blamed him for the defeat suffered by Wanyan Gang:[4] unhappy, on 13 September Shuhu marched into the capital with his men, overwhelmed the 500 man palace guard, and seized power. He killed *Weishaowang* and set up a puppet emperor in his place, Wanyan Xun with the temple name *Xuanzong* (reigned 1213–1223). Shuhu also seized and executed Wanyan Gang. Zhuhu Gaoqi led 5,000 Jin cavalry from Zhenzhou to Beijing, and Shuhu also called in forces from other places, including Jizhou and Pingzhou. He felt strong enough to attempt to hold off the Mongols outside the city walls, and took up position at Gao Qiao along the Caohe River, north of the city. He may have clashed with the forces of Ketei and Buqa. Shuhu, who was sick and unable to mount a horse, personally directed the battle. He was successful on the first day, 28 November, even though Gaoqi failed to arrive with his forces as ordered. The Mongols, perhaps under Muqali, had intercepted Gaoqi at Liangxiang; he eventually made his way to the capital, but arrived much later than planned. Shuhu also held off the Mongols on the second day. On the third day, November 30, he remained inside the capital, leaving Gaoqi to command the forces deployed outside the city. The Jin force was on this day driven back, and Gaoqi, fearful of being punished by Shuhu, went to his house and killed him. Gaoqi took his head to the Emperor, ready to accept punishment, but the Emperor pardoned him. Hu Shahu's short career in the centre of high politics was over, having lasted for only 78 days; he did the Jin a service by getting rid of an incompetent emperor and militarily had acted with some energy. At around this time Zhuozhou fell after a 20 day siege. Xiao Bodia, Shi Tianni, and Shi Tianxiang submitted to Muqali, offering to enter into Mongol service. Bodia was sent to hold Bazhou, perhaps a responsibility he also held for Jin before.[5]

---

4   Either because of poorly done fortification work in 1212 or because he failed to reinforce Wanyan Gang in 1213?

5   Elsewhere in the *Yuanshi* it is said the Shi clan submitted later at Mizhou. Shi Pingji, leader of the Shi family, was unsure how to act. Frightened by the slaughter in Mizhou he considered going into hiding, but after hearing that the Mongols treated those who surrendered well, he decided to submit. On the different versions, see Martin pp.163–164, note 25.

On 26 December Temüjin sent an ambassador to Jin, seeking to work out a peace treaty, but the Jin were unresponsive. This is hardly surprising given the chaotic situation inside Beijing. With some pragmatic bargaining the Jin could probably have bought off the Mongols. Unable to get an agreement, Temüjin decided to make a raid deep into the interior with several columns. The sources say nothing about his motivation, but he must have intended to demonstrate his power by moving across the enemy land at will and thereby hopefully forcing the Jin to the negotiating table. The Mongols would also have aimed to gather loot. Temüjin and Muqali, the *left wing* commander, headed southward closest to the ocean. Joci, Ca'adai, and Ögödei commanded the forces in the west. Certainly Bo'orcu was the effective commander, the man in charge of the *right wing*. Joci Qasar commanded a force sent eastwards from Beijing. Five thousand Mongol soldiers were left outside Beijing, presumably a detachment of Ketei and Buqa. The *Yuanshi* and other sources list many cities as taken by the Mongols; most of these must have submitted nominally and got away with only a token payment. Only a few cities were actually taken by siege. Even so, the sweep of the Mongol forces was on a grand scale. Temüjin first secured places in the Xidinghu area, Xiong,[6] Ba, Mo, and An, before pushing on to secure Hojian, Xian, Shen, De, En, and Bo. Muqali may have led a separate group, which bypassed Chingzhou and moved via Cangzhou, Dizhou, Bin, Yidu, Ci, Wei, Lai to Dengzhou at the tip of the Shandong Peninsula where he could see the ocean. The Mongols did not make a move against Dongping or Daming. Martin suggests the columns of Temüjin and Muqali reunited at Jining south of Dongping (taking Muqali first past Jinan and Tai'an). Mongol columns approached Haizhou, Beizhou and Xuzhou. All these cities resisted them: located close to the Song border they were probably all in a good state of military preparedness. Muqali, however, besieged and took Mizhou. Joci, Ca'adai, and Ögödei moved south along the eastern side of Taihang Mountains. They passed Sui, Ansu, Baozhou, Zhongshan, Zhengding (certainly untaken), Xing, Ming (Yeming), Ci, and Zhangde. Close to the Huang River they operated in the area around Weihui, Huaiching, and Meng. They then marched back northwards through Ze, Lu'an, and Liao. The *Yuanshi* places Tolui with Temüjin and the western column. The SWQZL associates Tolui with an offensive up the Fen River valley. Perhaps Temüjin detached him at a later stage to make this attack? The SWQZL says he took Pingyang and Taiyuan. The *Yuanshi* lists these and many other places amongst those taken or passed by Joci, Ca'adai, and Ögödei. Based on this, it seems the Mongols struck down (northward) along the Fen, passing Fen, Taiyuan, Xin, and Dai, as well as along the Huang River, where they passed Xi, Shi, Lan, and Wu. Joci Qasar, Alci, and Jürcedei operated in the area east of Beijing; perhaps Caqan and Tolon Cerbi were also with them. They secured Jizhou, Luanzhou and Pingzhou. Shunzhou and Dongzhou defied the Mongols.[7]

---

6   Wang Ji induced local commander Sun Tzu to surrender, and later prevented him recovering the city for Jin.
7   SWQZL associates Qasar with places *Yuanshi* 1 says the central column took. It is assumed the SWQZL made an error here. *Yuanshi* 1 also says Qasar took Liaoxi.

In early February 1214, the Mongol forces reassembled just west and north-west of Beijing. With the Jin remaining defiant, Temüjin finally decided to assault the city, perhaps having gained confidence after seeing so many cities surrender or fall to his armies. Beijing was, however, nothing like the other cities the Mongols had passed. It was much larger, with some 226,000 households, and had been strongly fortified decades earlier. The capital was guarded by 36,000 soldiers. Of these 20,000 were in the city itself and 4,000 were in each of the four large forts constructed around the city, outside the walls. These forts had two gates, as well as an underground connection to the main city. Beijing's walls were 18 km long not counting the forts, 13 metres high, and reinforced by 900 towers. The walls were covered by a triple moat. In April, undeterred by the imposing fortifications, Temüjin ordered the Mongols to charge, and they struck at Nanxunmen. They got into the city, but possibly this was part of a deliberate Jin plan. Certainly, the Mongols were checked in the streets beyond the wall: Jin forces cut off their line of retreat and the isolated Mongol force found itself in a firetrap, suffering severe losses as it tried to get out again. The Mongols mounted a second assault, but it was aborted after forces from the four forts fell on the attackers' rear. Many Mongol officers wanted to attack again, but Temüjin decided against it. He had been effectively defeated, checked by an extremely well-fortified city.

Temüjin started to blockade the Jin capital. He was eager to come to an agreement with Jin after a plague broke out in his camp, but had to send an envoy twice before they agreed to come to terms. Temüjin's message was as follows: 'The whole of Shandong and Hubei are now in my possession while you retain only Yendu; God has made you so weak, that should I further molest you, I know not what Heaven would say; I am willing to withdraw my army, but what provision will you make to still the demands of my officers?' Zhuhu Gaoqi urged continued confrontation with the Mongols, saying: 'I have heard that both the men and horses of the Mongols are greatly fatigued and suffering from sickness; should we therefore not take this opportunity to fight a decisive battle?' The Jin Emperor accepted the advice of his commander Wanyan Fuxing who said:

> Our troops have been collected from every direction and at the last moment. Though they are in the capital, their families are scattered far and wide in the various districts from which they have come. Hence their loyalty is uncertain. If defeated they will fly like birds and animals; if victorious, they will want to return home and who then will guard the capital? … In my opinion the best policy is to send an envoy to seek peace.

The details of the peace treaty are not known, but the Mongols must have kept territory their Chinese followers could occupy. Certainly they must have retained plenty of territory beyond the Juyong Pass; perhaps Temüjin even kept the pass itself and some places south of the northern mountains. Yelü Ahai held Texing and Liu Bolin was in Weinei, and Xiao Bodia, Shi Tianni, and Shi Tianxiang must also have held territory. As part of the agreement the Jin gave the Mongols 3,000 horses, 10,000 *liang* of gold, and 10,000 bolts of silk. Further, Temüjin was given a daughter of the previous emperor as a bride, though according to Rashid al-Din it was generally said she was ugly. As part of the peace treaty the family of Yelü Ahai and Yelü Tuhua were returned to them. Temüjin had given Yelü Ahai a Mongolian noblewoman as a wife, so the reunion was perhaps awkward. On 9 May 1214 the Mongols took Lanxian in Shanxi. Evidently there was still a Mongol corps operating in the west. However, during the summer the Mongol forces did fall back, returning to the northern regions where they had spent the summer during the three preceding years. Some sources say Temüjin ordered the massacre of all prisoners before again moving north of the Juyong Pass. Others credit the Mongols with a similar action in Pakistan in early 1222, and after they left Hungary in 1242. Possibly it was standard practice, when operations were over, to dispose of all the people gathered together to support siege work and other labour.

The nine month campaign (August 1213 to May 1214) witnessed serious fighting at Weichuan and Beijing, in addition to several smaller engagements. The Jin clearly lacked cavalry to seriously challenge the Mongols in the open, and therefore very properly started to rely on defensive positions. Temüjin overcame the Jin at Weichuan, but was unable to make an impression on Beijing. The campaign has some of the hallmarks associated with the later Mongol style of war, with a wide outflanking movement and bold strikes in several columns deep into enemy territory. The *Yuanshi* credits the idea for the outflanking movement to Ja'far. Faced with a position impossible to attack, the idea to outflank it is a natural one. How the decision to divide into three and make raids deep into Central China was taken, is not discussed in the sources. It was, however, a clear message to the Jin that the Mongols were now too strong to challenge and is very much in line with how Temüjin behaved. Indeed, Jin dared not intercept the Mongol raiding columns even after the Mongols divided their forces. Never before had an Inner Asian warlord demonstrated such power deep inside Chinese territory. The Xiongnu, Turks, or Uighurs, never operated in Central China with such a huge army nor operated with such impunity. The Mongol assault on Beijing ended in what can only described as a military defeat. It was, however, not a decisive reverse. Perhaps the situation was comparable to Grant making two unsuccessful attacks on Vicksburg in 1863. The Mongols suffered tactical defeats, but they were not decisive and Beijing remained strategically isolated. The Jin had brought many soldiers into Beijing from the countryside, which was therefore left vulnerable when the Mongol columns suddenly struck into the interior. For this reason the Mongols had an easier time when they raided the interior, but now were opposed by large forces.

Temüjin accepted a peace treaty with the Jin, but with many Chinese followers now on his side and the Khitans rebelling, it is not clear how such a treaty could be expected to hold. His new subjects had no interest in peace.

Sources: the SWQZL, 63b, 64a; Rashid al-Din, 327–329; *Yuanshi* 1, pp.31–32, 120, p.2962; the *Secret History* 251; SWQZL, 64a; *Jinshi* 13, pp.285–391, 14, pp.301–327; 98, pp.2174–2182, 132, pp.2832–2840; Martin, *The Rise of Chingis Khan*, pp.158–171.

22

The Siege of Beijing

The Emperor ordered Samuqa and Shimo Mingan together with Jalar and others to besiege Beijing. The Emperor spent the summer in Yu'erpo.

– Yuanshi 1

In August 1214 *Xuanzong* decided to transfer the Jin capital from Beijing to the more secure Kaifeng south of the Huang River. Though now at peace with the Mongols, the Jin still feared an attack. Zhuhu Gaoqi marched out of Beijing with a major part of the garrison, but the transfer of forces to the south did not go smoothly. At Liangxiang the Jin wanted to disarm 2,000 Khitan soldiers, presumably temporarily to protect the local population. When the Khitans refused, their commander Xiang Gon was executed; enraged, Jalar and Bisier led the Khitan cavalry detachment away, heading back northwards. Desmond Martin says they 'met a contingent of Tatar tribesmen that were in the same area.' These also defected from Jin service and joined the rebel Khitans. Wanyan Fuxing, who commanded the rear section of the Jin forces, attempted to intercept them, taking up a position at the Lugou Bridge along the Yongding River. The Khitans and Tatars divided into two groups, one crossing the river further upstream (in all 1,000 men so perhaps the Tatars), while the other headed directly for the bridge. These parties attacked the Jin loyalists from two sides and defeated them. They then continued northwards, passing Beijing, to join the Mongols.

The Mongol main forces had not yet passed the Gobi desert – it was too hot during the summer – and still camped at Yu'erpo. Temüjin was furious when told the Jin was moving their capital: 'The Jin emperor made an agreement with me, but now he has moved his capital south, evidently he mistrusts my word and has used the peace to deceive me.' The *Khan* was not slow to take advantage of the situation. Taking the relocation of the capital as a breach of faith, he restarted the war. An army commanded by the Salji'ut Samuqa was sent to Beijing. Rashid al-Din says of him: '[Samuqa] was the one who used to get angry whenever the word goat was used. This was because when he was a child he copulated with a goat, and of course anyone who fornicates with a goat will be called one by people. He fought with Sigi Qutuqu Noyan over this, and there was very bad blood between them. Later they made up and decided that henceforth the word goat would not be said.' The Persian historian further says 'he was not a military leader.' Why he was given command is not explained, but possibly Temüjin initially committed no Mongol forces. The many Chinese and Khitan leaders in Mongol service went with Samuqa, including Shimo Mingan,[1] Yelü Ahai, Yelü Tuhua, Liu Bolin, Shensa, and Jalar. In September–October Samuqa started to blockade Beijing as well as Shunzhou and Tongzhou.

Temüjin also moved south, returning to Longhotai in February 1215. Tongzhou submitted soon afterwards. There Pucha Qijin, a Jin officer, surrendered to the Mongols with his whole army on 23 February. During May, Temüjin sent an envoy to the Jin Court to try to work out a new peace agreement, but precisely as the Mongol envoy arrived in Kaifeng, a messenger came from Beijing asking for help. Perhaps the drama of the situation clouded the Jin judgement: they decided to rebuff the Mongol peace offer and to give aid to Beijing, sending an army of reportedly 39,000 men, and a large supply convoy. The Jin forces were divided into two. On the eastern side, Li Ying led forces from Hojian, Cangzhou, and Chingzhou, and in the west forces from Zhending, Zhongshan and Daming formed a second column with Wugu Lunqingshou as one of the commanders. The former column marched past Yongqing towards the Yongding River, along which Mongol officer Shansa intercepted them. Shimo Mingan, coming from Jianzhungong, led a second Mongol detachment behind Shansa. He may have outflanked the Jin, and certainly used a feigned retreat to draw them forward. When they scattered to pursue him, he turned, charged, and defeated them. Li Ying, reportedly drunk at the time, was taken captive. Then 'Mingan issued a letter to summon [the Jin army at] Yongqing to surrender, yet they refused, then [Mingan] took over the city and sacked it'. Shortly afterwards, Wanyan Hezhu and Ahsing Songe appeared with the second Jin army. Mingan intercepted and defeated them at Xuanfengzhai. The *Yuanshi* first credits the two Mongol commanders with 900 horsemen and says Mingan had 3,000 men in the second battle. It says the Jin had 12,000 men in the second engagement so that would mean 27,000 were engaged in the first battle. The Mongol numbers may exclude Chinese and Khitan forces supporting them and the Jin numbers are probably paper totals that could be three or four times higher than effective totals. The Mongols subsequently secured various places around the Jin capital. From April onwards Mingan took Wanning Temple, Fengyi, Fuchang, and Guan. Two other forces took Hojian (where 1,000 soldiers joined the Mongols), Chingzhou, and Cangzhou.

The Jin command in charge of Beijing imploded. Wanyan Fuxing wanted to make a sortie with the full garrison to die sword in hand; however Moran Jinzhong, his colleague who had led the defence on a day-to-day basis, was not ready to do this. Fuxing then committed suicide. He blamed Zhuhu Gaoqi, whom he must have heard in Kaifeng advising the emperor not to try to break the Mongol siege again. Jinzhong then fled with his family through the Mongol lines to reach Kaifeng.[2] The officers left behind surrendered Beijing to Shimo Mingan. Thus the metropolis fell on 1 June 1215

---

1   Rashid al-Din says he 'had submitted and acquired importance.'
2   Initially welcomed and given an official position, he was finally executed.

after an eight month blockade. The Mongols sacked the city, one of the few times a large town was sacked by the Mongols in China. Desmond Martin says they 'sacked a great part of the capital and slew many thousands of the inhabitants.' As usual the management of the loot became an issue for Temüjin. He tasked Sigi Qutuqu, Önggur, and Arqai Qasar to collect the valuables of the conquered capital, but Önggur and Arqai Qasar helped themselves to some of it. Sigi Qutuqu, on the other hand, did not take anything for himself, scoring brownie points with his master. He held all to be the property of the *Khan* as soon as the Jin yielded. Delighted, Temüjin said: 'Qutuqu has recognised a great custom.' Önggur and Arqai Qasar were punished. Shunzhou fell to the Mongols at around the same time.

The fall of Beijing ended the phase of the Jin–Mongol war personally directed by Temüjin. He had remained camped north of the city for a long time and was not personally involved in the siege operations. An embassy arrived from Muhammad II of Khwarezm to pay respects to Temüjin just after Beijing was taken. The ambassador was impressed by the magnitude of the occasion: on the way to the Mongol camp he saw much devastation and many dead, and was told 60,000 young girls had preferred death to capture. When he reached Temüjin he saw senior Jin captives brought before the conqueror. Temüjin was friendly towards the ambassador, loaded him with gifts, and made it clear he desired to have friendly relations with Khwarezm.

At the same time Beijing was attacked, Temüjin sent substantial forces into Manchuria. Before these arrived, Puxian Wannu, the new Jin officer in Liaodong, fought against Yelü Liuge, who defeated him at Gaiyuan along the Beixi River and took nearby Xianping. The Jin retreated to Liaoyang.[3] In July 1214 Temüjin sent Muqali and Joci Qasar with two separate armies into Manchuria. Joci Qasar operated with Jürcedei, Alci, and Buqa, probably with more than 10,000 men. They occupied Linhuang (upper Liao) and Bianzhou before crossing the Sungari to appear in front of Ningjiang (Songyuan). One story has it that the Mongols asked for 10,000 swallows and 1,000 cats in return for not attacking the city. Once these were handed over, lighted wool was attached to their tails and the animals set free. In panic, the animals returned to the city, where fire quickly broke out in many places. Perhaps the story grew out of Mongol siege machinery setting off fires in the city. In any event the city was taken. Joci Qasar next marched to the Nonni and Daoer region where the Solon (Solangs) submitted. The Mongols continued up along the Daoer. In February 1215 they reached the Khingan and, having crossed the mountains, returned to the Kerulen River.[4]

It was not clear what forces Muqali commanded. He might, like Qasar, have had about 10,000 Mongolian horsemen, but in addition had substantial Han Chinese forces. Turning south, he first seized Gaozhou in November 1214. He then divided

---

3   According to Martin an unnamed Jin officer may have suffered another defeat against the Khitan rebels later the same year, but no location is given. With no details, this is either a duplication of the previous battle or an insignificant affair.

4   Martin cites the *Sanang Setsen* for the details of the Mongol movement.

his forces and started to reduce the minor places near a second Beijing.[5] Muqali moved east, taking Yizhou and Shunzhou. Other columns may have operated west and south of Beijing, and Jiyuan, Fushu, and Huiho, Hozhang, Lijian, and Lungshan fell into Mongol hands. Muqali, having secured the surrounding country, moved on Beijing from the south. The Beijing garrison, led by Ao Denxiang, boldly marched out of the city and fought Muqali at Hote. This was some 75 km south of the town. The Jin were defeated and driven back into the city. The Jin reportedly lost 80,000 out of 200,000 men. In March the Mongols then started to besiege the enemy fortress. Some Khitan soldiers inside the city revolted and opened a gate; Muqali attempted a storm, but could not penetrate the defences. Another officer later killed Ao Denxiang, but afterwards Wugulun Yindahu took command and the garrison continued to defy the Mongols. Muqali was finally, in May, able to take the city by a ruse: making use of an intercepted letter and seal sent by the Jin Court with an official to Beijing he managed to gain entry into the city.

Uyer's biography details subsequent events: 'Jin general Dalu occupied Yuhekou River mouth at Huizhou (Huiho) as a strategic position, gathering thousands of people.' Presumably the force mainly consisted of a surviving part of the army defeated at Hote. The Mongols won a reported 100 minor actions before engaging in a major battle. The Jin were defeated and Dalu fled; another senior officer was killed and 12,000 soldiers were reportedly captured. The Mongols entered the Lu'an Valley and approached Xingzhou at the mouth of the Ju River. They defeated another Jin army, led by Zhao Shouyu, near Xingzhou, which was taken after the battle. During July, Dalu reassembled some forces further east, and seized Lungshan. Uyer and Shi Tianxiang hurried after him, cornered him and forced him to accept battle. Dalu made a desperate charge, and in the subsequent melee Uyer was unhorsed and might have been killed had Shi Tianxiang not come to his rescue. Dalu and 1,000 of his men were killed, and 8,000 Jin soldiers captured. Muqali occupied Xingzhong. Soon afterwards Zhang Zhi, governor of Jinzhou, revolted and declared for the Mongols. Jin Liaodong was now cut off from China proper. The Mongols also secured control over Luanzhou and Pingzhou further south.

The Jin faced new complications in Manchuria where in April Puxian Wannu suddenly rebelled.[6] He established himself in the eastern parts and campaigned actively during the subsequent months. His forces made a successful attack upon Yelü Liuge's camp outside Xianping in May, but Xianping itself was not taken. He next led his forces to the south where he occupied Shenyang and Chengzhou, and the Mukri submitted to him. Puxian then turned against Posilu (committing 9,000 men), but was here repelled by Jin loyalist Geshilie Huanduan. The rebels plundered some districts, though no real progress was made. An attempt in July to seize Daningzhen failed. Huanduan now seized the initiative, defeated Puxian south of Liaoyang and won back the Mukri to the loyalist side. Puxian retreated eastwards. The Jin Court afterwards

---

5   Not to be confused with the capital Zhongdu, which today is called Beijing; this second Beijing is today's Ningcheng.
6   Setting up his own ruling house in November 1215.

ordered Huanduan to Shandong to deal with the Red Coat rebels at large there. In November, after he left Liaodong, Liuge was free to seize Liaoyang.

Muqali seemed to have conquered most of Liaodong, but soon found out that the job was not finished. The Mongols planned to send Zhang Jing with a force to support operations in central China, and Muqali ordered Shimo Yexian to go with him. Jing was not keen to go, so Yexian arrested him and took him to Muqali's headquarters. When he attempted to escape, Yexian overtook him and killed him. In June, Jing's brother Ji rebelled after hearing the news. He controlled Jinzhou, Pingzhou, Luanzhou, Ruizhou, Lizhou, Guangning, and the two Yizhous. In July one Mongol detachment, under Shi Tianxiang, took Lizhou, Dashan, Hungloshan and other places. Shi Jindao, operating with another Mongol detachment, recovered Guangning in September, and Shi Tianni took Pingzhou in October. Puxian Wannu submitted to the Mongols, bringing eastern Manchuria under their nominal control.

In the west the Xia–Jin border fighting continued. The Tanguts started to focus on the Hui, Lan, and Jishi regions. In December 1214 they supported rebels in Lanzhou, and unsuccessfully attacked the small town of Xining in Huizhou. Later a Tangut army (said to number 80,000 men) again invaded Jin territory, targeting Lintao. Lintao is deeper inside Jin territory and well beyond Xining. The Tanguts attempted to wrong-foot the Jin by bypassing the first line of defence, but the gambit was no more successful than the first one attempted. The same year, An Bing organised a 'bandit' attack on Qinzhou. An Bing was the Song official in charge of Sichuan, but he acted without sanction from the Song Court, and the participants in the expedition were given severe punishments. An Bing was recalled, but not really punished (he was promoted to another post away from Sichuan). On 8 March 1215 the Tanguts attacked Huanzhou, then in December besieged Bao'an and Yan'an. Further west, the Tanguts took Lintao and on 12 November defeated the Jin army guarding Guanzhong. In January–February 1216 the Jin sent another army into the area, which defeated the Tanguts near Lintao and recovered the city.

The Jin also had to deal with bandit activity in Shandong. Yang An'er and Zhang Ruji operated with some men around Tai'an (at the foot of Tai Mountain). An'er had once been a manufacturer of boots and other leather goods based in what is now Penglai. He had rebelled before, during the war against Song, but had afterwards been forgiven. He served in the Jin army with his own band of soldiers, but defected again in 1214 after the setbacks the Jin suffered against the Mongols. In April–May Pusan Anzhen drove off the rebels. An'er got away with his men and managed to gain entry into Dengzhou (now Penglai) further east, when the local official let him into the town. Now An'er declared himself to be emperor. Anzhen again attacked the rebels, overcoming them in November–December. When An'er tried to escape by sea, some sailors killed him for the reward on his head. This happened in early 1215, just three months after he had declared himself emperor.

At the same time, Liu Erzu rebelled in western Shandong, but in February–March 1215 the Jin forces also overcame and killed him. The Jin were quick to grant amnesty to win over the bulk of the rebel leaders and forces. Zhang Ruji, who had before operated with Yang An'er, submitted, but soon afterwards rebelled again. Ruji was some months later, in September, captured and executed. These victories did not stamp out unrest in Shandong. Leaders holding fortresses remained ready to take up arms against Jin, and in late 1215 or early 1216 started to adopt red coats as a common symbol even if there was no central leadership. One of the stronger leaders was Hao Ding, who also claimed to be emperor.[7] In June 1216 the Jin overcame his forces and drove him to flight. A key reason for the trouble in Shandong was that it was a 'failed state' environment, the impact of the changed course of the Huang River years before remaining unaddressed. The river again changed course in some places in 1217.

The uncle of An'er, Liu Quan, was in charge of the military forces of this faction. He gathered the surviving forces and handed over command to Yang Miaozhen, the younger sister of An'er. This was an incredible decision given the social conventions of the times. In the *Songshi* biography of Li Quan, Miaozhen is described as being 'crafty and assertive as well as skilful in horsemanship and archery.' Miaozhen met Li Quan soon after getting command over the rebel forces. Li Quan commanded a separate band. His biography says he was 'the son of a peasant family of Beihai in Weizhou. Crafty, violent, and deceitful, he was nevertheless good at winning people with his unassuming and easy manners. He was a skilful horseman and archer. He wielded an iron spear so well that he was nicknamed "Iron Spear Li."' Miaozhen and Quan met at Moqi Mountain when out searching for food. They married. Afterwards, Miaozhen retained authority on her own.

Beijing was the first major city taken by the Mongols. After previous failures in the face of strong fortresses, this was a great success. It was blockaded into submission, as would be the case for all major Chinese cities taken by the Mongols. Temüjin did not take a first-hand interest in the siege, and left the immediate theatre of war even before the city fell. Temüjin was probably satisfied, having proven himself stronger than the Jin emperor. He had shown he could march across China at will and he had won all battles. How should the performance and success of Temüjin in China be rated? He was able to mobilise the tribes of Mongolia like no other leader before him and faced a fairly ill-prepared foe. With close to 100,000 horsemen at his command, he was far stronger than Jin and was tactically dominant. Even so he did not secure as much territory as the Jin had done against the Liao and Song less a century before. The Jin quickly set up court in Han Chinese territory and took pains to act like a traditional Chinese dynasty. This was not anything Temüjin was interested in. Having humbled the Jin emperor he returned to Mongolia. Had Temüjin moved his court to Beijing in 1215 and aimed for more conquests, he could have crushed the Jin quickly. As it was, the Jin only finally fell in 1234.

The Jin were slow to prepare. They did badly in 1211 mainly because they committed few forces and had neglected the border defences. In 1212 they fielded stronger forces, but should probably have waged a delaying war rather than rush into battle. They did not pursue the right strategy. In 1213 they probably aimed to act

---

7   Françoise Aubin says his 'base was a mountain stronghold', but does not say where.

defensively, but should have kept the army south of the Juyong Pass and near Beijing instead of moving forward. Afterwards they were distracted by internal strife. The Jin commanders performed poorly, and those who were defeated retained command and went on to suffer new defeats. Temüjin was lucky to face such an ineffective foe.

Sources: the SWQZL, 66b, 71b; *Yuanshi* 1, pp.33–34; 120, pp.2962–2963, 147, p.3486; *Jinshi* 102, pp.2243–2245; Rashid al-Din 140–141, 327–331; Juzjani, pp.963–968; Martin, *The Rise of Chingis Khan*, pp.171–184, 199–200; 204–206, 211–212; Françoise Aubin, 'The Rebirth of Chinese Rule in Times of Trouble: North China in the Early Thirteenth Century', S. Schram (ed.), *Foundations and limits of State Power in China* (Hong Kong: Chinese University Press, 1987), pp.113–146; Dunnell, 'The Fall of the Xia Empire', p.172; Ratchnevsky, 'Sigi Qutuqu', pp.80–83; Franke, 'The Chin Dynasty', pp.214–215; Davis, 'The Reigns of Kuang-tsung … and Ning-tsung', p.822; Pei-Yi Wu, 'Yang Miaozhen: A woman warrior in thirteenth-century China', *NAN NÜ* vol. 4, #2, 2002, pp.139–140.

23

The Continued War Against Jin

I have reduced to submission all the country to the north of the Taihang Mountains, it is for you to subdue the country to the south.

– Temüjin to Muqali, *Yuanshi* 119

This chapter will provide an overview of the Mongol campaigns in China from 1216 to 1227, to cover the period from when Temüjin left China up to his death. Tolon and Samuqa were initially active in central China, while Muqali remained engaged in Manchuria. In October 1217, when Muqali returned to Mongolia after conquering Manchuria, Temüjin ordered him back into central China to finish off the Jin. From this time onwards Muqali campaigned continuously, directing five campaigns, until his death in 1223. His son Bol and later grandson Tas carried on the struggle, taking over his position.

Muqali was a strong personality who could keep control over large mixed forces and who was able to dominate the Jin, but he could not penetrate into their core territory south of the Huang River. His son Bol (1197–1228) was a less forceful commander and in 1225 the Jin were able to throw the Mongols on the defensive. Finally, Bol made major gains in Shandong in 1227, but died soon afterwards. Bol's son Tas (1212–1239) also failed to have the impact of Muqali.[1] It was only when the main Mongol army returned to central China in 1230 that decisive results were again achieved.

With Muqali were Alci and 3,000 Onggirads, Butu and 2,000 Ikires, Ketei Noyan and Buqa and 4,000 Uru'uds, Möngkö Qalja with 1,000 Mangquts, and Bayisbu with 10,000, or 'many', Önggüts. Muqali and his younger brother Tas are credited with having their own units. Other senior Mongol officers serving Muqali directly were, according to the *Yuanshi*, Se'inidei, Ancar, Kökö Buqa, Bolot, and Burqai. Perhaps they commanded sub-units of the personal forces of Muqali and Tas? Yelü Tuhua had large civilian and military responsibilities, though he did not campaign in person. The private bands of Liu Bolin, Shi Tianni, and Jalar were under his administrative

---

1   Tas is a Turkish name. The Mongol name was Cila'un. Both mean 'stone'.

responsibility. Liu Bolin died in 1221, and his son Heima inherited his position. When Shi Tianni died in 1225 his younger brother Tianzi (1202–1275) took over his position. He was a large and powerful man, famed for his material powers. Other members of the Shi clan served with Muqali in Liaodong and followed him back into central China in 1217, including Tianxiang and Tianying. The Khitan Uyer was as senior as Yelü Tuhua, and campaigned in person with his own contingent. Once Muqali penetrated deeper into China, he won over more and more local strongmen to his side. The most significant of these were Zhang Rou (1190–1268), Yan Shi (1182–1240), and Dong Run or Jun (1186–1233). Muqali initially fielded about 20,000 Mongol, 20,000 Khitan and Jurchen, and 20,000 Han Chinese soldiers. The Jin, who started to vigorously raise militias, had larger forces, but with few mounted men and a need to place substantial numbers along the border to Xia and the Song, they were in no position to challenge Muqali in the open.

The Jin found effective commanders in Wanyan Heda (died 1232), Meng Gugang (died 1223), and – in his own way – Wu Xian (died 1234). The Jin occupied a strong defensive position with many well-fortified cities, and the Huang River covering their core territory. They mobilised fresh forces during 1215, putting reliance on conscription. Twenty thousand soldiers, raised in Shanxi, guarded the western side of Kaifeng, and a 40,000-strong army guarded the eastern side. Garrisons were placed inside Yuanwu, Yenjin, Fengqiu, Chenliu, Qixian, and Tongxu to provide a protective ring around the capital north and south of the Huang River. Many people migrated from the north to the south, the families of the soldiers alone counting one million. There was a famine in Henan, perhaps in part due to the inflow of people, and the various local peasant revolts also had an impact, disrupting matters further. The ongoing war with Xia was another distraction and when war broke out with Song in 1217, the Jin found their rear actively threatened.

As a consequence of the Mongols' attacks and also perhaps the transfer of the capital to Kaifeng, centralised authority collapsed in North China. Local strongmen rose up and took charge over their districts, raising forces and constructing fortified positions. These local leaders could choose to serve the Jin, the Mongols, the Song, or themselves as rebels or bandits. In 1214 Wang Yi took charge of Ningjin near Zhending and organised its defences, and Zhao Lin organised the defences of Guanshi north-east of Daming, holding off bandits. In 1215 Wang Shan was elected leader of Gaocheng, south-east of Zhending. Di Shun and Di Chang, two brothers, organised the defences of Xingtang, 30 km north of Zhending. They constructed two forts. These leaders were all eventually formally recognised by the Jin. The Jin also granted titles to Tian Zhuo who controlled Ding'an (April–May 1214) and Zhang Fu who held Xin'an (April–May 1222). In spring 1216 He Shi raised 3,000 men from the area near Datong and offered his service to Muqali. He is an example of a leader who opted to side with the Mongols.

1216

In January 1216 Yelü Liuge went to see Temüjin in person; while he was away Yelü Sibu rebelled, taking control of Chengzhou. According to Françoise Aubin, many

Khitans were unhappy because Yelü Liuge refused to declare himself emperor. Liuge returned and, starting operations against the rebels, quickly gained ground.

Muqali needed to overcome Zhang Zhi in order to complete the job in Manchuria. Zhi had strong forces at his disposal and acted with energy: in spring 1216 he took and plundered Xingzhong. Muqali, at this stage perhaps near Guangning, made no immediate counter-move. Only months later, in July–August, did he sent a detachment to reclaim Xingzhong. Two months later he led his main forces from Guangning towards Jinzhou. He was about to demonstrate generalship of a high order. He stationed a detachment on the hill five kilometres east of Yongde, under Möngkö Qalja, from where enemy movements could be easily monitored. He sent another detachment under Uyer against Liushi Shan, perhaps an enemy depot. As he had expected, this move triggered an enemy reaction, and 8,000 cavalry and a large infantry force, a reported 30,000 men (really 7,500?), set out from Jinzhou under the command of Zhang Dongping, a nephew of Zhi. The detachment stationed at Yongde reported this to Muqali, who immediately pursued the enemy force with his main army. Near Shenshui the enemy was caught between Muqali's army and the detachment sent ahead to threaten Liushi Shan. Noticing that the enemy was poorly armed, Muqali dismounted many of his men and showered the Jin infantry with arrows before the rest of his men charged and broke the enemy forces completely. The Mongols claimed to have killed 12,600 Jin soldiers. Muqali took Kaiyi before he started to besiege Jinzhou; a sortie was driven back, and the defenders lost a reported 3,000 men killed. Jinzhou was surrendered to him soon afterwards following a split inside the enemy command. Amongst the captives was the entire 12,000 man Black Army (*Heizhun*). Shimo Yexian took command of this body. Finally Muqali turned against Yizhou and Guangning. They submitted, but nevertheless were sacked as punishment for their previous conduct. Guangning had rebelled again after Muqali turned against Jinzhou.

In November–December two Mongol forces crossed the Liao River, led by Shi Tianxiang and another officer. Yelü Liuge already operated east of the river, and had driven the rival Khitan faction out of Chengzhou. The Jin officer in charge of Daningzhen had previously checked these Khitans. Liuge joined forces with the Mongols, and afterwards the combined forces defeated the Jin at Daningzhen and secured it. The Mongols also occupied Fuzhou and Suzhou, and the Khitan rebels fled across the Yalu River into Korea.

Further west, the Mongols made a raid south into central China. Shi Tianni, coming from Manchuria, joined Tolon Cerbi at Zhending. The two officers took this city as well as Daming. Dongping, however, proved too strong for them: the vigorous Meng Gugang still defended this fortress. The Mongols 'stopped the water of the river from above, but the city did not surrender.' Some forces were left in Shandong, while the rest headed for Zhangde. This town was also taken, in December 1215 or early 1216. Tolon and Tianni again plundered Daming on 30 January 1216, and by 6 February had also secured Enzhou, Xingzhou, and Caozhou. They then returned northwards. In November 1215 a Jin probe on Zhending had been defeated and driven back by the garrison just one month after they had surrendered to the Mongols. The main Jin effort, however, was launched after the Mongols returned to the north. Setting out from Jingzhou, Jin forces first recovered Xianzhou, Hojian, and Cangzhou in March 1216. A little later, in May, Chingzhou was recovered. Pushing westwards the Jin also occupied Shenzhou, Huolo, and Weizhou, and finally reclaimed Zhangde, Daming, En, and Xing.

In March 1216 in Shandong, rebels ravaged the area around Tai'an, Dezhou, and Bozhou without taking the local capital cities. In May the rebels were more successful further south where they took and sacked Liwu, Xindai, Yenzhou, Yizhou, and Dengzhou. The Jin Court had transferred Geshilie Huanduan from Manchuria to Shandong (he must have come by sea). In July–August he defeated the Red Coat rebel army in the open, but the victory failed to put an end to the rebellions.

The Tanguts invaded the western part of Guanzhong, approaching Huizhou, but the Jin had left a strong garrison in the region and in July the Tanguts were repelled. Later the Jin counter-attacked into Xia territory (the offensive ended only in 1217).

Tolon left China; the next Mongol officer to raid into Jin territory was Samuqa, the man Temüjin had sent to lead the operations around Beijing when the war restarted in 1214. Samuqa crossed the Huang River, fairly high upriver, and in September joined forces with a Tangut army said to be 30,000 strong – all cavalry, so it must have been much smaller – near Yan'an. Samuqa is credited with having 60,000 soldiers in total. In addition to the Tanguts, this included more than 13,000 Han Chinese. Possibly he had 10,000 Mongol soldiers and at most 30,000 in total. Samuqa attacked Yan'an on 9 October 1216. Separately the Tanguts attacked Fangzhou on 14 October, but without success: the Jin made a sortie, driving the Tanguts off. The Tanguts reportedly lost 2,000 men killed. Samuqa pushed south, crossing the Wei (perhaps north of Hua).[2] Near Luzhou he defeated and killed the Jin officer, Nagehe Puladu, stationed in X'ian (Jingzhao), and marched east towards Tong Pass. He probed the defences of this strongly defended pass on 23 November, but found them too strong. Instead, he marched through the mountains south of this fortress and emerged in the plains further east at Yao Pass.[3] The Jin had several forces in the area, and these now converged on Samuqa. One force moved east from Tong, another came from Meng (5,000 men), and a third from Lung'an (10,000 men). There were also strong forces in Lushi. Two forces moved out of this place, and one headed for Shangzhou, very likely the place Samuqa had passed to get around Tong Pass. The other marched towards Lingbao. On 2 December Samuqa headed south, towards Ruzhou, and from there turned towards Kaifeng, reaching Xinghuaying just 10 km east of the Jin capital. The Jin Lushi detachment that had moved on Lingbao pursued Samuqa and was now approaching him, but he evaded action and returned eastwards. The Jin forces at Lung'an and Meng had marched to Tong Pass, but the forces that had first come from this direction intercepted Samuqa at Mianzhou. Samuqa attacked and defeated them, and took the place. At this point it so cold that the Huang River had frozen, and in January 1217 Samuqa was able to cross the river at the Sanmenji Ford near Shenzhou. The Jin thinking is not clear, but they seemed eager to close the border passes after the

2 Encountering, says Rashid al-Din, 'extremely warm' weather.
3 Martin says he moved via Jinkeng.

Mongols had managed to sneak through. If Samuqa had around 30,000 men then he must have been heavily outnumbered. The five Jin armies could have fielded 50,000 men in total, but by failing to unite they lost their advantage in numbers.

Samuqa continued active operations north of the Huang River, and started to besiege Pingyang on 24 January 1217. Xu Ding, the local Jin area commander, called together forces from Jiangzhou, Jiezhou, Xizhou, Jizhou and Mengzhou and moved towards the besieged fortress. At the same time he was able to win back Chinese defectors, offering amnesty to those who returned to the Jin: 13,000 men deserted Samuqa, and he gave up the siege of Pingyang after 10 days. The Tanguts marched back home, perhaps crossing the Huang at Hozhou, but Jin forces from Qinyang attacked them in Ningzhou and inflicted some losses on them. Meanwhile Jin forces guarding Houzhou and the Lingshi defile blocked Samuqa's route back north. Mongol forces stationed at Daizhou, Shenxian and Pingding converged on Taiyuan. Xu Ding ordered forces from Jiangzhou, Hezhong, Lu'an, Pingyang and Mengzhou to march there, covering it, but the westward shift of the Jin forces opened the way for Samuqa. He was free to return to friendly territory in the north.

Samuqa's raid was an extraordinary achievement. He moved about with skill and audacity matched only by Jebe or Sübe'etei. Muqali never managed to do anything like this when he afterwards campaigned in central China even if he did make much more extensive conquests. Samuqa is never heard of again: perhaps he passed away soon after this campaign. The sources dealing with these events are quite laconic. There is no information on how Samuqa's plans evolved or what he hoped to achieve. Perhaps Temüjin could have ended the war if he had committed his full forces instead of taking most of them home? It seems clear that the raid was an improvised affair, but it is not clear who ordered the Mongol advance on Taiyuan. Was it Samuqa, Caqan, or someone else?

Muqali conquered the Manchurian Beijing and Jinzhou, but needed to fight five battles before he was master of the region. The Jin were able to raise forces again and again. It seems they had regional popular support to a degree they did not have in central China.

1217

Manchuria had been a major theatre of operations for several years, but now the main focus shifted to central China. However there was still some fighting in the north-east. The Jin made a final attempt to overcome Puxian Wannu. A Jin force set out from Posilu in June, but Wannu defeated it. The Jin rebel still felt insecure, however, fearing perhaps a possible Jin–Korean alliance, therefore he moved northwards into Shangjing where he took Huining (this place was renamed Kaiyuan). Further south, during the summer, Han Chinese rebelled against the Mongols in the Luan River area. With popular support, the commander of Wuping, Ji Hoshang, suddenly seized Manchurian Beijing, and there was a second revolt in Xingzhou. Uyer and Shi Tianxiang dealt with the rebel groups in detail. They first defeated the Wuping rebels at Beijing and recovered that city, and afterwards finally defeated the other rebels along the Che River, claiming 10,000 rebels killed. The Mongols finally received the submission of Datong during May. The sources do not state when Datong first was put under blockade. It may have been shortly after the fall of the Jin capital Beijing. There was some minor fighting in the area south of Beijing; Jin forces, under Wu Xian, seized Zhending in April. Another Jin detachment, under Qiuhe, secured Bazhou. Caqan defeated the latter, took Xincheng on 30 April, and recovered Bazhou on 1 May.

The Jin declared war on the Song in May: Zhuhu Gaoqi had been pushing for war. Xu Ding argued against it, but failed to persuade the Court, and the Jin mounted many attacks along the entire border. In the central sector Caoyang and Suizhou were targeted, but Meng Congzheng and Hu Caixing, subordinates of Zhao Fang, ambushed the Jin near Xiangyang. At this time Meng Gong emerged as an officer of note, serving under Congzheng, his father. The Song scored additional successes at Caoyang, Guangshan, and Suizhou in June. The Jin also raided out from Fengxiang in the west.

Muqali took over command of the Mongol forces operating in central China, receiving the mandate from Temüjin in person in Mongolia during the summer. Operations started, as per usual practice, during the autumn. The Mongol commander operated with two main groups plus a third smaller one. He pushed south from Beijing with the main army, while Shi Tianni and Liu Bolin struck towards the east. The smaller force was sent into the Fen River valley in the west in October.

Shi Tianni and Liu Bolin first recovered Pingzhou, Chingzhou, and Cangzhou. The Jin concentrated an army at Dizhou (Lo'an), reinforced by forces coming from Yidu. The two Mongol officers defeated this army and then began to besiege Dizhou as well as Binzhou. Seeing there was no quick conquest to be made here, they detached blockading forces and pushed south. Zhangshan (12 November), Zouping (29 November) and Cizhou (21 November), small places west and north of Yidu, quickly submitted to them, but Yidu resisted. Again a detachment was left to besiege the city. Shi Tianni and Liu Bolin next divided their forces. In late December one section moved east to secure Weizhou, Laizhou and Dengzhou and the other marched south to secure Luzhou, Yizhou and Mizhou. Dizhou, Binzhou and Yizhou were the first of the besieged cities to submit (Yizhou fell on 15 January 1218). Reinforcements sent by Muqali arrived and within a month (i.e. by February) all the various besieged towns were in Mongols hands.

Muqali first took Suicheng and Lizhou (Licheng). During the assault on the north wall of the latter place, Shimo Yexian was hit by a stone and died. For that reason Muqali intended to massacre the population of Lizhou, but finally decided not to do so. In mid November he secured some places near Zhending, including Zhongshan and Xinlo), but probably did not attack Zhending itself. He pushed on towards Daming. This major stronghold was taken on 27 January 1218, and afterwards Wo, Xingzhou, Weizhou, Mingzhou and Cizhou also surrendered (December).[4] Muqali finally secured Bozhou. After that he sent forces to support Shi Tianni and Liu Bolin.

---

4   Martin says Muqali 'apparently' masked all these cities before taking Daming.

The smaller Mongol army in the Fen River valley secured some places around Taiyuan, namely Xizhou, Fenxi, Jinzhou, Jiaocheng, and Chingyang. On 23–25 October the Mongols besieged Taiyuan itself, but found the city too strong and quickly gave up. Muqali's intent was probably to create a diversion in this sector rather than making significant conquests.

1218

Early in 1218 Muqali's forces returned to the northern regions for the summer break. Immediately afterwards, the Jin moved forward and reclaimed the places lost. Desmond Martin says: 'all the conquests … in Shandong and … in the neighbouring province were lost to … the still vigorous Jin' (March 1218). Their strategy was very economical. They followed Mao Zedong's dictum: 'The enemy advance, we retreat; the enemy retreat, we advance.' The retreat of Muqali hardly does him credit as a general.

The Jin relied on various militia leaders to defend the country located north of the Huang River. Nine of these were given official titles in 1220. They had an ongoing internal rivalry, and Jia Yu, for whatever reason, killed Miao Daojun. Shimo Xiandebu led a Mongol force across the Hengshan with the aim of attacking Jin loyalist Wu Xian who held Zhonding, Zhengding, and other places nearby. Zhang Rou tried to intercept the Mongols in Langyaling, but was defeated and captured after falling off his horse. He had been a follower of Miao Daojun. Rou was persuaded to take service with the Mongols. He was able to keep many of the men he had commanded before and perhaps added other forces as well (either reinforcements from the Mongols or new recruits). He quickly secured Xiongzhou, Yizhou, Ansu and Baozhou. He also besieged and took Kungshantai in Hengshan, after cutting off the water supply, and forced the garrison to take service with the Mongols. Jia Yu was captured and executed: Rou thus avenged the death of his old master. Rou afterwards occupied Mancheng where he set up his headquarters. Wu Xian remained established in Zhending, able to field 500 horsemen and a lot ('10,000') infantry. He fell upon Rou at Mancheng when most of his men were out foraging. Rou acted with boldness: he moved out of the city, making his forces look stronger than they were (as had Cao Cao in 193). He was able to hold Xian off, and subsequently took Wanzhou to the south.

In spring 1218 Song forces attacked Chuzhou without securing the district. Jin forces again attacked Caoyang and Suizhou with a reported 100,000 men, but Song officer Meng Congzheng defended Suizhou effectively. An 80 day siege, from March to June, cost the Jin a reported 30,000 men. Before, during February the Song tried to gain ground in Shandong by giving bandit leader Li Quan an official title, and thus recognise him as one of their commanders. Li Quan and Yang Miaozhen were eager for the alliance with Song in order to secure a steady food supply, as chronic food shortage remained a major problem in Shandong. They could perhaps field 15,000 to 20,000 men, and had many more dependents in the various communities. In the west, An Bing, back as Song governor of Sichuan, planned a coordinated offensive with the Xia. However the Xia failed to show up and the Song advance on Qinzhou and Gongzhou was defeated. An Bing raised a reported 100,000 men and some months later made a renewed advance on Qinzhou. He pushed through the Dasan Pass, but was ordered to retreat by the Song Court before he reached the targeted district.

After the usual summer rest, the Mongols were ready to initiate operations again in the autumn. Muqali shifted his focus, striking up the Fen River valley with his main forces. Pushing across the Daiholing he first besieged and took Taiyuan. The Mongols broke a bastion on the north side, but the Jin defenders used wagons to block the gap in the wall and successfully held off three storms. The fourth assault, covered by archery fire, overwhelmed the defenders. Next Fenzhou was besieged and taken on 26 October. These were two major conquests, and Muqali probably detached forces to hold the two cities. Pushing southward, Muqali may have outflanked the Lingshi Pass, marching via Xizhou, to arrive at Huozhou. He took Lu'an and thus isolated Lingshi from the south. Gaoping and Cezhou also submitted. Finally, the Mongol commander took Pingyang on 5 November. Muqali left a detachment under the command of Ancar Noyan to guard the place.

Ba'arin Qorci Noyan – if he is Hazhen of the *Yuanshi* – and Jalar led 10,000 Mongol soldiers down across the east side of the Korean Peninsula to deal with the Khitan rebels who held some cities inside Korean territory in early winter 1218. Wan Buxian Wannu supported them with a reported 20,000 soldiers. Wanyan Zuyuan commanded this force. Yelü Liuge remained behind in Huangning. The Mongols took Hwaju, Maengju, Sunju, and Tokqu.

1219

After a period of indecision, Korea decided to actively support the Mongols. Senior Koryo official Zhuo Zhong sent Kim Ingyong with some soldiers and supplies to join the Mongols, which he did outside Daeju. The place was taken and the Mongols then marched on Gangdong, the main rebel Khitan fortress. Additional Korean forces joined the Mongols outside this city. It was taken, ending the Khitan revolt, and the Mongols left Korea in early 1219.

Zhang Rou continued to operate against the various Jin militia leaders on the east side of the Taihang Mountains. He again defeated Wu Xian at Mancheng in spring 1219, and afterwards struck into hostile territory, occupying Langshanzhai (in Yixian), Chiyang and Chuyang. He subsequently started to besiege Zhongshan, but from Xinlou, Xian detached Ge Tieqian to drive him off. Zhongshan surrendered after Rou defeated Tieqian. In the summer Xian again attacked Mancheng, this time in conjunction with Niu Xian, Zhang Fu and Zhunggo, but Rou held them off. In the autumn, Rou and Dong Run defeated Xian yet again at Chiyang. Jun was another Han Chinese strongman who had joined the Mongols in 1215. Rou exploited the advantage gained, taking Guzheng, Shenze, Ningjin, and Anping while detachments secured Pingji, Gaocheng, Wuji and Luanzheng. In the Taihang Mountains some forts offered their submission.[5] The pro-Mongol leaders had conquered much of Zhending, but not the city of Zhending itself. However, in the *Yuanshi* Run is credited

---

5   The forts are called Luer, Yeli, and Langshan.

with temporarily gaining entry: 'Dong Jun took his forces and entered Zhending at night, driving Wu Xian away. People from Dingzhou, Wucheng and other cities then defected and surrendered to Jun.'

This year the Jin again sent large armies into Song territory, and again besieged Caoyang. Song general Zhao Fang devised a bold plan: he left Meng Congzheng to hold Caoyang on his own, as he had done in 1218, while he sent two columns towards Tang and Deng to destroy Jin depots and ruin their line of supply. After three months Zhao Fang recalled his forces, in all some 60,000 men, and fell on the now weakened Jin army besieging Caoyang. The Jin suffered a total defeat, losing a reported 30,000 men killed. Fang conquered by means of brilliant strategy. Having defeated the Jin, he again marched into Tang and Deng. The regions were overrun, but the Song made no attempt to conquer the two provinces. Rather, Fang aimed to create a zone of devastation along the Jin side of the border. In February–March 1219 a Jin army attacked Xiangyuan in the western sector, but the Song held the attackers off, with Jin losing 3,000 men. However the Jin did secure Xihozhou, Qingzhou, and Fengzhou closer to the Wei River. In Shandong, the Jin attacked Chu, Hao, and Guang. Jia She held them off, backed by freelance warlords Ji Xian, Shi Gui, Li Quan, and Li Fu. Somewhat later Peng Yibin and Li Quan invaded the Jin controlled Shandong. During the spring Li Quan inflicted two defeats on the Jin, and Daming was taken. Jin officer Zhang Lin defected to the Song. Lin controlled Jinzhou and the surrounding territory.

Even within Mongol conquered territory, Jin or bandit bands operated between the main cities. Muqali detached 500 picked men from the main army to deal with such bands in the region around Beijing, but it took years to finally secure the countryside.

Muqali launched his third offensive against the Jin in the central China. Liu Bolin and Shi Tianxiang led a Mongol army out of Datong. They crossed the Taihang south of Shuoxian and on 21 August 1219 took Wu and Kelan. Afterwards they secured various other places on the way to Jiangzhou including Lanxian, Shizhou, Xizhou, and Jizhou. The Mongols thus gained control over territory just east of the Huang River. Muqali and Shi Tianni marched up along the Fen River, establishing more secure control over the valley; then two Mongol armies joined forces and moved on Jiangzhou, which they took in January 1220 after successfully mining the walls. The population was slaughtered. After this success the Jin evacuated 80 forts in the neighbourhood. Mongol detachments secured Hezhong and Wenxi.

Jin officer Wanyan Heda defeated the Xia at Ansai near Yen'an on 11 June 1219. Heda would emerge as one of the most competent and important Jin military leaders.

1220

Found guilty of murdering his wife, Zhuhu Gaoqi was executed in Kaifeng. Gaoqi had managed to retain a position of eminence for a long time. His push to start a war with Song was poor advice to the Jin emperor, and in the field he fought and lost three battles against the Mongols.

The Jin again moved forward after the Mongols had returned to the north. An early Jin offensive in May 1220 secured Hejing, Wenxi, and Jiangzhou, and some of the significant gains Muqali had made the year before were lost. Jin forces also attacked

Zhangde. Song loyalist Yan Shi attempted to organise a relief effort, but recent Song convert Zhang Lin sent no reinforcements. When Shi finally reached Zhangde, the Jin had already taken the city and captured Shan Zhong. Dongping remained firmly in Jin hands, defended by strong-willed Meng Gugang, and Li Quan and Zhang Lin moved against the city. In September Meng sneaked out some forces and attacked the Song from two sides when they approached the walls, and the Song army was completely defeated. However they were still able to seize Haizhou. Meanwhile, in August, the Jin recovered Kaizhou and Daming. Muqali marched out of Beijing a little later (late September) with the aim of conquering the central and south-eastern regions. He moved straight on Zhending. Wu Xian anticipated this and sent a detachment to make a diversionary strike against Taizhou in the east, but Muqali sent 3,000 men under Möngkö Qalja to ward them off. This officer surprised and shattered the Jin force besieging Taizhou and then rejoined Muqali. Zhending submitted on 10 October, and Xian was soon afterwards persuaded to come over to Mongols. However Dong Run reportedly warned Muqali: 'Wu Xian is cunning and cannot be mastered. He can never be relied on. Please keep an eye on him.' Muqali is said to have agreed with him, and Shi Tianni was put in charge of Zhending with Xian as his deputy. Wu Xian's brother Gui retreated in the mountains in the south-east, to Yaoshui Shan, near the town Xingxi. The *Yuanshi* credits him with having 10,000 men (meaning many).[6] He guarded the key passes to his position, but Shi Tianxiang, Wanyan Husu, and 100 Black Army soldiers climbed up the mountain along a 'bird path' and were able to enter the fort. The Jin surrendered. Gui said: 'You are like winged people. Otherwise how could you make it?' Muqali pushed south. Zuzhou surrendered, but Zhangde and Linzhou had to be taken by siege. A detachment secured Hojian.[7] In November the Mongols marched into Shandong, where Yan Shi submitted to the Mongols. It was said he controlled 300,000 households in Daming, Li, Ming, En, Bo, Jun, and other places. He was the most significant defection so far for the Mongols in terms of what he brought with him. Yan Shi had his family in Qingya; Li Xin, the commander of this place, defected to Song, handing over the city to them, and Shi's wife and brother were killed.

The Jin had mobilised a large army, commanded by Wugulun Shihu, which took up position at Huanglinggang. Muqali's advance into Shandong was hardly anticipated so presumably the army was assembled for an offensive against the Song and the various warlords of Shandong. With the Mongols approaching, the Jin focussed on them, and Shihu sent a detachment forward (a reported 20,000 men). Muqali fell upon it with 500 cavalry and cut it to pieces. The Mongol commander marshalled his full force and marched against the Jin, dismounting his men and storming the Jin position. Shihu was forced to retreat back to the south side of the Huang River.

---

6 In Chinese, saying '10,000' means 'many'.
7 Perhaps this was the time when Wang Ji helped Butu recover Hojian. They had 3,000 men. Butu was inclined to massacre the population ('10,000' people) because it had again welcomed the Jin. Wang Ji likened the population to sheep, saying they only needed to punish the leaders. Butu was persuaded not to kill the people, but Wang Ji had to provide a written promise that the people would not rebel again.

The Jin made no major attack on the Song this year, but engaged in some fighting against Xia on the eastern border. During September 1220, the Xia defeated a Jin army at Huizhou and took the city, and Guo Xia and his brother were captured. The brother was killed, but Guo Xia managed to escape. Soon afterwards a Song army pushed north from Sichuan to support the Xia. The combined operation was not successful. The Jin captured several Tangut officers and defeated the Song army. Guo Xia is credited with helping defend Gong and Lan. In October the Jin finally recovered Huizhou. In January 1221 Guo Xia was given command over the forces in Lan, Hui, Tao, and He. In Henan, Song raids into Dengzhou and Tangzhou were not successful.

1221

Muqali continued operations, splitting his forces into three. Möngkö Qalja was sent west along the Huang River (upriver) to secure Weihui, Huaiching, and Mengzhou; another officer moved on Dan, Jining, Yen, and Teng, and Muqali in person attacked Chuziu and Tianping. After a storm on the latter place was beaten back, Muqali left and in January turned against the smaller Chuziu, filling in the moat and taking the fortress by storm. He then returned to Dongping, the main Jin stronghold in the region. An assault on the city failed, and Muqali blamed Uyer. Shi Dianxiang, attempting to defend Uyer, requested to be given the task to attack instead. However he was also unable to break through the defences. Muqali left Yan Shi to starve Dongping into submission, and Heima and a son of Ancar Noyan, Jirwadai, with 3,000 horsemen, were left with Shi. Muqali instructed them: 'When food runs short, Meng Gugang will force his way out; as soon as this happens, enter the city, but treat inhabitants with clemency for in that way the place may be pacified.' Muqali led the remaining forces away. The city of Mingzhou had rebelled. Muqali had first sent a detachment under his brother Daisun to blockade it. When Muqali returned to the north with the bulk of his forces he made a short stop at Meng. He left Shi Tianying there and marched away with the rest of his forces. The Dongping garrison eventually ran out of food. As predicted by Muqali, on 22 June Meng broke out with 7,000 soldiers: Yan Shi and the others pursued him and harried him so effectively that Meng only had 700 men left when he arrived in Peizhou, 200 km to the south-west of Dongping. As Muqali had demanded, the Mongols did not sack Dongping, and the city became a key Mongol base. Mengzhou fell just before Dongping, on 13 May. Yan Shi recovered his old fortress in Qingya the same year, capturing and killing Li Xin. Two junior officers killed Meng in Peizhou two years later, reacting to the iron discipline he imposed.[8]

The Mongol drive into China was called into question after a total eclipse – probably 23 May 1221 – was taken as a sign from heaven that the attacks should stop. Muqali brushed aside such suggestions. There was some diplomatic activity. Song ambassador Gou Mengyu came to visit Muqali. In July Meng Hong, a member of the mission, wrote an account about the Mongols. During August 1221 a Jin envoy reached Temüjin somewhere south of the Amu Darya in what is now Afghanistan, but

---

8   He was killed on 29 August 1223. The Jin afterwards needed to send a detachment to restore order in Peizhou.

Temüjin was in no mood to come to terms with the Jin. He demanded all the territory north and east of the Huang River, something the Jin could not accept. They were also unwilling to yield the Wei River region. Temüjin's answer was probably in line with advice given by Muqali.

In July–September the Mongols gained ground in Shandong after Shi Gui, holding Lianshui, suddenly turned against the Song and sided with them. In October–November Zhang Lin, holding Jinan, also declared for the Mongols. Gui attacked Caozhou; Jin officer Wang Tingyu first reclaimed Huanglinggang and then defeated and killed Gui at Cao, ending his short career as a Mongol loyalist.

After a short summer break in north China, Muqali turned against the territory located west of the Huang River. He crossed the river at Dongsheng, moved south, and took Jiazhou. He left Shi Tianying with 5,000 men to hold the city and build a bridge over the river there. Muqali moved on, in October–November taking Suide as well as the forts of Matizhai and Kerongzhai. Tangut general Yebu Gambo preferred to operate on his own rather than with Muqali (with a reported 50,000 soldiers), having first linked up south of Suide. He marched towards Ansai. Wanyan Heda and Naho Maizhu, Jin generals based in Yan'an, intercepted the Xia. The Jin made a quick night-march and were able to surprise and quickly scatter the Xia army on 19 November.[9] A chastised Yebu Gambo joined Muqali with the remains of his forces, submitting to his authority. Muqali then marched towards Yan'an where he found Wanyan Heda camped north-east of the city with a reported 30,000 men. Acting on the advice of Möngkö Qalja, Muqali deployed his forces in two valleys east of Yan'an. Möngkö moved ahead with 3,000 horsemen to tempt the Jin out of the strong position they had occupied. The ploy worked: on 8 December Möngkö was able to draw the Jin forward, and caught in the open they were quickly defeated, losing it is said 7,000 dead. Heda fled back into Yan'an. Muqali started to besiege the city, but gave up after an assault ended in failure.

Zhang Rou operated against Jin pockets of resistance in the central sector. Wang Zuzhang and Zhang Fu held respectively Guan and Xinan, two places located fairly close to Beijing. Rou made a surprise attack on Zuzhang, capturing the Jin leader as well as his city. Afterwards Fu fled from Xinan, leaving Rou to temporarily occupy this city as well.

The Jin struck deep into Song territory (entering Huainan), taking Huanzhou and attacking Qizhou, 200 km from the border. Hu Caixing and Li Quan eventually drove the Jin off. Li Quan had come south from Shandong to support the Song effort and pursued the retreating Jin, inflicting a reverse upon them as they made their way back across the Huai River.

1222

Muqali gave up the siege of Yan'an, preferring to turn on easier prey. He detached a force to secure Bao'an, and pushed south with Uyer and Shi Tianxiang (no longer at

---

9   The second Jin–Tangut battle in that location.

Jiazhou) to secure Fuzhou, Danzhou, Lochuan and Fangzhou. Fuzhou and Fangzhou had to be taken by storm. In the former place Uyer captured a Jin champion known as Zhang 'of the Iron Spear'. Muqali apparently was inclined to spare him, but Mongol officers unwilling to forgive this foe killed him before Muqali made a formal decision (April–May 1222).

Jin forces, meanwhile, struck into Mongol held territory north of the Huang River. They came from the hills near Xizhou and seized it. Daizhou revolted afterwards. Muqali hurried westwards, marching from Fangzhou over Danzhou towards Xizhou; as it was still winter he may have crossed the Huang River by simply marching over the frozen ice. Xizhou was retaken in two days. Muqali left a detachment under Ancar between Xizhou and Shizhou and marched with the remainder of his forces on Daizhou, crossing broken ground. The place was quickly taken. Jin forces, still active, reclaimed Jiangzhou and Hezhong a little to the south of Muqali.

Muqali then went to Datong, where Shi Tianying rejoined him. Then followed the usual summer pause. With regard to continued operations, it was agreed that Muqali push up along the Fen River and take Hezhong, while Tianying moved on Jiangzhou from Jiazhou. In October Muqali sent Möngkö Qalja back to the western side the Huang River to guard the conquests made in that area. Muqali marched slowly, securing the various places along the Fen River not in Mongol hands. The places he took included Niuxinzhai, Hubi Bao, and Rongzhou. In November Tianying marched down along the Huang River: Hezhong surrendered on his approach with Hou Xiaoshu making a hurried escape, and Jiangzhou surrendered to Muqali in December. Tianying built a bridge across the Huang River near Hezhong, completing the task in January 1223.

In October a Song force attacked the Tang province, but the Jin defeated it. Soon afterwards, in November, another Song army invaded Jin territory further east; the Jin defeated it near Lingxian, capturing two enemy generals. During December a 3,000-man Song cavalry detachment crossed the Huai, cut down trees and placed them in the middle of fords to block the Jin supply lines. A 1,000 man Jin cavalry detachment drove the Song raiders off, and 700 Song soldiers were taken captive. In October the Song had also invaded Mongol Shandong, probably setting out from Huaian. They were led by Peng Yibin, the previous rebel, so this was a private army. He quickly seized territory from the Mongols, securing control over eastern Shandong.

A revolt broke out against Jin in Lintao. Xia supported the rebels.

1223

Leaving Shi Tianying to guard Hezhong, Muqali again shifted operations to the west side of the Huang River. He secured Tongzhou on 8 December 1222, and Pucheng, and probably left a detachment to mask Jingzhou. He started to blockade Xi'an; it was guarded by Wanyan Heda, who had relocated there from Yen'an and had a reported 200,000 men. Möngkö Qalja was ordered to move against Fengxiang further up along the Wei River. Anticipating an attack, the Jin started to burn the country around Fengxiang to deny the Mongols' food and forage, however Möngkö defeated the local Jin forces and drove them into Fenxiang. An Önggüt in Jin service called Sirgis was captured outside the town, but refusing to accept the surrender, he was killed.[10] Muqali found Xi'an impossible to take. He left 6,000 men there to mask the city and placed another 3,000 between the city and Tong Pass. In February, with the rest of his forces, he first secured Chingzhou and various other smaller places in the neighbourhood of Fengxiang before linking up with Möngkö in front of the city in March. He then began to besiege the fortress, however Fengxiang held off the attacks and the Tanguts quickly lost interest in the project and marched away. On 30 March Muqali decided to retreat.

Along the Huang River Jin officer Hou Xiaoshu attempted to recover Hezhong. He had planned to operate with two detachments, one with 5,000 men and another with 3,000, but finally only one moved forward. Shi Tianying was informed about the impending attack and detached a force to ambush the Jin as they approached. Unfortunately the officer in charge was drunk when the Jin arrived early on 4 February and he failed to intercept them as planned: the Jin broke into Hezhong over an unguarded section of the wall. Tianying, refusing to flee, was killed in the street fighting that followed. Muqali had left Ancar Noyan with a detachment in Pingyang, and he now raced south to succour Hezhong. The Jin felt unable to resist him, and retreated. Before doing so they destroyed the bridge over the Huang River. Muqali sent Shi Wake to take command of his father's detachment. His first task was to rebuild the bridge.

From Fengxiang Muqali sent Möngkö against Fengzhou just south of the Wei River to distract the Jin. Heima led his detachment to Jiangzhou, while Muqali fell back towards Hezhong with the rest of his forces. He had to wait at Dajing Guan for the repair work on the bridge to finish. In April, while waiting, he attacked and secured various small places in the area. Möngkö rejoined him, having taken and plundered Fengzhou. Once the bridge was ready, Muqali marched to Wenxi, possibly to take up station there in anticipation of a new Jin offensive. At this point, in May, he fell ill and died. The *Yuanshi* credits him with the following death speech: 'For nearly 40 years I have waged war for the Qan, and east and west I have vanquished his enemies that he might bring to completion his great work. But Kaifeng still remains untaken. This I greatly regret, so see to it that you do your best to take it.'

At the same time Muqali attacked in the west, Shi Tianni and Yan Shi mounted an assault on Weizhou. Yan Shi led the advance forces, but the Mongol assault failed and Yan Shi ended up a Jin captive. However he was freed during subsequent Mongol assaults. The attackers failed to make any impression on the Jin defences, and fell back after learning that Muqali had died.

As Muqali had expected, the Jin attacked again. In June they struck across the Huang River and seized Rongzhou, and in July followed up this success by taking Houzhou, Hongtong, and Fenxi.

The Song continued operations in Shandong. In February 1223 Li Quan took Yidu. Peng Yibin persuaded Jing Yaigu to surrender Jingyai, where Yan Shi's family

---

10 Sent as an embassy to the Mongol Court before the invasion of China in 1211, Sirgis had impressed Temüjin, who wanted to take him into Mongol service. Sirgis refused and remained loyal to the Jin.

lived. Zhang Lin defected from the Mongols, again accepting Song overlordship. Peng Yibin also occupied Daming and Jinan. Li Quan and Yang Miaozhen had Huaian as their main strongpoint, and Miaozhen guarded this location. Li Quan operated from Yidu, trying to gain territory in the north. Liu Quan was stationed with a force near Yangzhou to guard the link to the Song, still a vital source of food supply.

Learning that Muqali had died, Puxian Wannu rebelled in east Manchuria and either now or later established himself in Ningjiang.

Jin recovered Huizhou from Xia. The Mongols punished the Tanguts for their defection in front of Fengxiang. Shi Tianxiang moved against Jishizhou, probably setting out from Hezhong, but in December a Jin army threatening his rear forced him to leave the Jishizhou area 10 days after arriving there. The Mongols suffered some losses during the retreat.

1224

Jin emperor *Xuanzong* died on 14 January 1224. The designated heir, Wanyan Shouxu with the temple name *Aizong*, ascended the throne (reigned 1224–1234). He was destined to be the last real Jin emperor. Though hardly a notable emperor, he did decide to end the war against the Song.

In January–February the Tanguts attacked Lanzhou, but failed to seize a fort at Jigo Bao and quickly fell back. The Tanguts ordered the Shara Uighurs to raid into Mongol territory. They may have set out from Elsin Gol, and the raid lasted from March until June. The logic of the Xia is hard to understand: they attacked the Jin *and* the Mongols. In June the Mongols counterattacked into Tangut territory, besieging Shazhou, and the siege turned into a protracted affair. The Mongols tried to mine their way into the city, but the Tanguts built a counter-mine.

In March–April Puxian Wannu tried to get Korea to support him against the Mongols. Koryo refused help.

The Song Court, according to Desmond Martin 'ill informed concerning the tarrying military power of the Mongols', ordered Peng Yibin to drive further northwards. He struck into Hebei from Daming. No Song army had operated that far north for 100 years. It had been a dream of Yue Fei less than a century before to push north and drive the 'barbarians' out of China, but the Song Court did not back the idea. Instead, they made peace with Jin and executed Yue Fei. Now Yibin was encouraged to make an ambitious attack. Yibin, however, was no Yue Fei, and Shi Tianni defeated him at Enzhou. The victory was probably not decisive, as the Mongols certainly did not pursue. Tianni returned to Zhending and Yibin to Daming.

Bol, Muqali's only son (a low output given the large number of wives he had), had been with Temüjin in the western regions. Temüjin now sent him into China to take over his father's position. Bol was to strike against Xia with a part of the forces while Daisun, the younger brother of Muqali, operated with the rest of the forces in central China. Bol, Möngkö Qalja, Uyer, and Heima set out against Yinzhou during September-November 1224. Taga Gambo led a Xia army against them, but Bol defeated and captured him and afterwards took and sacked Yinzhou. He left a detachment under Möngkö Qalja to guard the district. The Tanguts sued for peace, terms were agreed, and by early 1225 Temüjin called home the force besieging Shazhou.

During November–December the Jin again attacked across the Huang River, temporarily occupying Zezhou and Lu'an.

1225

Bol returned to Mongolia to pay homage to Temüjin, who had now returned from the western regions. While he was away, the Mongol position in China deteriorated. After two garrisons of Wu Xian were seen to have acted disloyally, Shi Tianni cut them down: angered, Xian assassinated Tianni and seized Zhending. In March he again declared for the Jin. Ge Diaqiang, who held Zhongshan, sided with Xian, and Dong Run was left isolated inside Yongan with less than 1,000 men. Xian spent a long time trying to take Yongan, but without success, and started to burn the surrounding country. Run yelled at him: 'You want to win over the people, yet you rob their grain. Even unschooled thieves would not do that.' Xian, reportedly, felt ashamed and left the area. Run attacked the retreating forces.

Shi Tianni's brother Tianze was in Beijing when Wu Xian revolted. In April, being told what had happened, he hurried south and was able to gather 1,000 men and 700 horses. He arrived in Mancheng, where Zhang Rou was ready to support him. Rou gave Tianze another 3,000 men, led by Jiao Weizhong. Bol conferred Tianni's titles on Tianze and rushed Seunidei forward with 3,000 men to join him. The quickly-assembled army first marched on Zhongshan, and Ge hurried back to the fortress. Seunidei and Tianze broke off the siege and intercepted Ge, having the best of initial encounter. Ge attempted hold off the Mongols from a second position behind a river, but once it was dark, he retreated. The Mongols pursued and defeated the Jin again, and Ge was captured. The Mongols were afterwards able to recover Zhongshan, Wuji, and Zhaozhou. Xian fled from Zhending in June, but by no means crushed, established a new stronghold at Baotou in the Taihang Mountains.

In Shandong, Lu Quan feuded with Song official Xu Guo. Quan helped set off a mutiny in Chuzhou. In the unrest that followed, in early 1225, Guo was killed. The Song then prepared to deal seriously with Quan. Peng Yibin could have supported them, but instead became committed against the Mongols and in May moved on Dongping. In July Yan Shi, getting no help from the Mongols, surrendered and declared for the Song. It was said he did this out of necessity and that he planned to return to the Mongols as soon as it was possible. Wu Xian made an alliance with Peng Yibin, who set out from Dongping and Daming to support Xian. As part of this effort Yan Shi set out as well, evidently moving initially along a separate path. However, in August Shi declared for the Mongols again and joined their forces. Yibin was undeterred. He set out towards Zhengding with Wu Xian, but they collided with Bulqa or Seunidei as well as Shi Tianze at Canhuang near the Wuma Hills, south of Zhending. Daisun, Ancar, Liu Homa, and Zhang Rou were also with the Mongol army. Yibin unconventionally tried to prevent the Mongols from outflanking him by setting fire to the grass behind his battle-line, but it did not work. Mongols archers worked their way over the mountain into his rear, and gained a total victory. Yibin was captured and executed, but Xian escaped. The victors divided their forces into many groups and quickly recovered lost places in Hebei and western Shandong. The retaken towns included Bo, Pu, Daming, Zhangde, Jinan, Tai'an, and Dongping. Zhang Lin took Yidu. However, the man left by Yan Shi to guard Dongping afterwards handed the city over to the Jin, and killed Yan Shi's relatives.

Wu Xian continued to resist Shi Tianze. In December his forces gained entry into Zhengding at night and drove out the Mongols, and Tianze fled to Gaocheng. Backed by the forces there, he quickly marched back to Zhengding. Xian considered his army large enough to confront him in the open, but this was a mistake for he was defeated. Tianze recovered Zhengding and Xian returned to Baotou.

In October Jin and Xia made peace. The negotiations had started the year before.

1226

This year the Mongol main army struck into Xia from the north (Mongolia) and west. Möngkö Qalja supported these operations by attacking Xia from the east (see chapter 37).

The Jin again recovered Hezhong, though for the last time. In September–October they also took Chuwo and Jiangzhou. Shi Tianze took Baotou and the other places controlled by Wu Xian in the Taihang Mountains. Wu Xian fled to Kaifeng, and soon afterwards established himself in Weizhou from where he raided into Mongol controlled territory.

Yan Shi occupied Puzhou as well as Dongping. In April, for his part, Li Quan took Yidu. Tas and Shi Tianze, supported by Jiao Weizhong, marched into Shandong after having dealt with Wu Xian. They set out against Quan. Normal Mongol practice was to first reduce the various smaller places to isolate the enemy strongpoints. In October Tas and Tianze, however, marched directly against Yidu and started to besiege the city.

The Jin and Song clashed along their common border. The Song, reports the *Jinshi*, lost 400 men.

1227

In January–February 1227 Bol and Uyer joined Shi Tianze, and kept up the siege of Yidu. The Song had fallen out with Li Quan to the extent they did not try to help him: they sent a fleet up the Huai River keep a watch on the events, but did not attempt to challenge the Mongols. Some time later, in April–May, Quan made a sortie and Bol and the Mongols fell back to the Zi River, north-west of the city. Quan pursued and a battle followed, which ended as a Mongol victory. Quan lost a reported 7,000 men killed, but was able to make his way back into Yidu. Lack of food forced him to surrender one month later, in May-June. Yidu had been a large city, but the major part of the population died during the siege. Bol spared Quan, after a considerable discussion amongst the Mongols. With his surrender the whole region submitted to the Mongols. Quan was for the rest of his life a nominal Mongol subject, but he remained de facto independent.

While the Mongols besieged Yidu, the Song tried to secure control over Li Quan's southern territory. Liu Zhuo commanded the Song forces. He moved on Huaian, backed by bandit leader Xia Quan. However Yang Miaozhen seduced Xia Quan and was with his help able to drive off the Song forces; Zhuo fled to Chuzhou. Miaozhen then turned Quan away, and he marched off and joined Jin. Without Song support, Huaian lacked food and Miaozhen had to leave after the soldiers rebelled.

Bol and Shi Tianze turned against Tengzhou. Some officers did not consider it wise to attack such a strong city during the hot summer time. Bol objected: 'I have never heard that while in the west Genghis Khan deferred an expedition because of the heat, how can we his subjects, remain inactive?'[11] The garrison made a sortie, and the Mongols defeated it. The defenders lost a reported 3,000 men killed, and Tengzhou surrendered afterwards. In October Zhang Lin moved against Huaian, and recovered control over the city. However, in December he was killed, and Li Quan regained control over Huaian. Further north, Zhang Rou transferred his headquarters from Mancheng to the bigger Baozhou.

In February–March, in the western sector, Jin officer Hoshilie Yawudai recovered Pingyang. Yawudai was a dashing officer famous for his brutality. He was called 'Black Drumstick' because he had a habit of beating soldiers with a drumstick when he lost his temper. His son Alige had a similar habit, and was called 'Little Drumstick.'

1228

Bol returned to Mongolia in order to attend the funeral of the *Great Khan* in 1227, and only returned to China the year after. In July he fell ill and died before initiating new operations. This year Wang Ji restored order in the Beijing region, dealing with bandits.

The ongoing Mongol–Jin conflict was very much a contest between Han Chinese warlords with their own bands supporting one side or the other. Mongol regular forces played a fairly limited part, as did the Jin main forces, deployed at Tong Pass by 1228. The Jin had evidently decided to focus on defending their core territory, and the approaches to it, giving up any hope of recovering the north. The Mongols for their part only made limited progress after conquering Beijing and Liaodong. Muqali was forceful and energetic, but it seems he was not much of a strategist. His willingness to use Chinese warbands was a plus for the Mongols, but this was very much in conformity with the usual methods of Temüjin who always drafted locals into his military apparatus. The Chinese warlords who came over to the Mongols constituted Muqali's only real gains. He defeated Wanyan Heda in 1221, but this tactical success did not translate into strategic gains. Heda rose to take command of the Jin forces, and is likely to have played a major role in the Jin strategy formulation and overall management of the war effort during the end of the period covered here. Heda and the officers he had around him were capable, and learned how to operate against the Mongols. This was a big improvement on 1211 when the Mongols first struck into China. Muqali and his successors hardly troubled Heda seriously. The Jin held off

---

11   If Bol really said this he was evidently not well informed about how Temüjin operated.

attacks on Xi'an, Fengxiang, and Weizhou and counterattacked to recover cities lost when the core Mongol forces had returned to North China to rest during the summer. This deadlock would only be broken in the early 1230s when the Mongols again led their main forces into central China.

Sources: the SWQZL, 72a–79b; Rashid al-Din, 330–331; *Yuanshi* 1, pp.35–37; 119, pp.2929–2940, 120, pp.2964–2966, 147, pp.3471–3478, 3486, 148, pp.3491–3507, 3505–3507, 150, p.3541, 153, pp.3611–3613, 155, pp.3657–3663; *Jinshi* 15, pp.301–326, 16, pp.327–377, 17, pp.378–380, 108, p.2402, 110, pp.2421–2426, 122, p.2661, 118, pp.2577–2580; de Harlez, *Histoire de l'Empire de Kin*, pp.252–255; Martin, *The Rise of Chingis Khan*, pp.189–190, 212–218, 240–249, 261–286 (main source for this chapter); Aubin, 'The Rebirth of Chinese Rule in Times of Trouble', pp.113–146; Dunnell, 'The Fall of the Xia Empire', pp.172, 175–176; Hok-Lam Chan, *The Fall of the Jurchen Chin: Wang E's memoir on Ts'ai-chou under Mongol siege* (1233–1234) (Stuttgart: F. Steiner, 1973), p.121, note 16; de Rachewiltz, 'Muqali', C. C. Hsiao, 'Shih T'ien-Tse', 'Chang Jou', 'Yen Shih', Peterson, 'Wang Chi', in de Rachewiltz, *In the Service of the Khan*, pp.5–9, 29–30, 47–51, 61–65, 178; Richard L. Davis, 'The Reign of Li-tsung (1224–1264)', *The Cambridge History of China*, vol. 7, pp.827–830, 848–850; William Henthorn, *Korea: The Mongol Invasions* (Leiden: Brill, 1963), pp.16–23, 32–33; Franke, *Sung biographies*, vol.1, pp.54–57; Franke, 'The Chin Dynasty', p.215; Allsen, 'The rise of the Mongolian empire', p.827; Pei-Yi Wu, 'Yang Miaozhen', pp.137–169.

24

Incidents at Home

The mother was furious. As soon as she got there and dismounted from the cart, she herself untied and loosened Qasar's sleeves, the opening of which had been tied up, and gave back to Qasar his hat and belt. The mother was so angered that she was unable to contain her fury ... After Činggis Qan had at last calmed the mother, he said, 'I was afraid of mother getting so angry and really became frightened; and I felt shame and was really abashed.'

– the *Secret History*, 244

Having covered events in China down to the year 1228 it is time to return the focus on Temüjin. He led the main Mongol forces back from China to Mongolia during the spring of 1216. Keeping control over nomad tribes was notoriously difficult and even Temüjin was sometimes challenged, also close to home. At this time the Tumeds, a tribe living in the region west of Baikal Lake, openly defied his authority; the trouble starting, it seems, just before Temüjin returned from China. A woman called Botokui Tarkun ruled over this tribe. She was the widow of the previous ruler Daiduqul Soqort. The Tumeds imprisoned Mongol officer Qorci after he went to them looking for some women. In January–February 1216 Temüjin sent the Oyirat leader Quduqa Beki as an embassy to the Tumeds, and he was also seized. Temüjin then ordered Naya'a to deal with the Tumeds militarily, but this officer fell ill and could not go. Instead, Boroqul was selected and he led a force along the usual route into Tumed territory. Attempting to draw the Tumeds into an ambush somewhere along the Zima River, it was instead the Tumeds who ambushed and routed him. Tumed scouts captured and killed the old commander. The defeat and death of one of the most senior of all Mongol commanders was a great blow for Genghis Khan. Enraged, the khan wanted to personally deal with the Tumeds, but was at length dissuaded from doing so. He rushed off a second army to deal with the troublemakers, this time commanded by Dörbei Doqsin. According to the *Secret History*, 'Dörbei set the army in order and beforehand made a decoy manoeuvre along the paths, trails and passes where the army was expected to advance and which enemy patrols would keep under surveillance', but in fact, turned off the main road and marched along a small path through the woods.

He surprised the Tumeds in their camp and routed their forces, perhaps along the upper Oka and Zima. Dörbei wintered in the area and only returned to Genghis Khan the next year (1217).

A number of local revolts and incidents are described in the *Secret History* without a clear dating. In the narrative they are placed after the Tumed revolt in 1216 and before Temüjin set out against Muhammad II of Khwarezm in 1219, but all probably happened before the campaigns against Jin started. In one episode Temüjin fell out with his brother Qasar and would have killed him had not his mother – who must have been quite old, considering that Temüjin was at least 50 in 1217 – learned about what he was up to and hurried to the scene. Qasar retained his position, though Temüjin reportedly afterwards reduced the size of his command from 4,000 to 1,400 men. This does fit well with Rashid al-Din who says Qasar's descendants had only 1,000 guard soldiers. The second episode involves Mungling Echiga's son Kököcu. He had played a central role in the events leading to Genghis Khan's coronation in 1206. He later challenged Otcigin, Temüjin's brother, and Temüjin finally let Otcigin kill Kököcu. The third incident is the revolt, or the planned revolt, of Jaqa Gambo, the Kereyit prince. He was, however, eliminated before he could do anything. Jürcedei disposed of him and pacified his territory: 'Jürcedei applied stratagem to raid Zhaha Jianbu, killed him, and took over his territory.' This event should perhaps be placed fairly soon after 1204. Perhaps Genghis Khan disposed of him fairly quickly after the Naqa battle, no longer needing a leader he may have felt he had given too substantial concessions to.

Sources: the SWQZL, 73b, 74b, Rashid al-Din, 332–333; *Yuanshi* 1, p.35, 120, p.2962; the *Secret History* 208, 237, 240–241, 244–246.

Overview: The Great Western Expedition, 1219 to 1224

Temüjin was probably content with the success gained in China and may have seen no need for further military campaigns, but in face of the insulting behaviour of Muhammad II of Khwarezm he felt obliged to lead his army into the distant western regions in person. His target was more than 4,500 km away from his home. Liddell Hart singled out the campaign as a remarkable example of 'indirect' strategy, and it has subsequently been dealt with often in Western military literature. Khwarezm is presented as a homogeneous and powerful state with 400,000 soldiers, much like the France of Louis XIV. Muslim contemporary chroniclers lamented the brutal conduct of the Mongols which left many cities of the Near East ruined. It was, for example, claimed that 1.6 million people were massacred in Herat in 1222. In truth, Khwarezm was a weak state that had only recently gained control over most of the territory it tried to defend against the Mongols. Further, before the Mongols arrived the various regional powers had been engaged in endless warfare that could be very destructive. Nishapur, Herat, Samarkand, and Balasagun were all sacked during the years before the Mongols arrived.

Turkic nomads from Central Asia gained entry into the various Near Eastern Islamic states as fighting men during the 9th and 10th century. They were quick to take political control when an opportunity presented itself. Cavalry formed the core component of all the significant regional armies, having both shock capabilities and archery skills. The early Islamic empires had been well organised and capable of fielding very large armies. The early Abbasids had struck into East Roman territory with 100,000-strong armies, but their empire had imploded long ago. None of the successor regional states could match the military organisational level of the Abbasids, even on a smaller scale. As was the case in Europe at this time, a ruler found it difficult to field armies more than 10,000 men strong. Only exceptional leaders like Mahmud of Ghazni (971–1030) had the personality and skill to field larger armies. He was, however, unable to create anything of enduring significance, and his domain imploded soon after his death.

Shah 'Ala' al-Din Muhammad II (1169–1220) inherited the city-state of Urganj, called Khwarezm, from his father in 1200.[1] At that time the dominant powers in the

---

1   Urganj is the name the Mongols gave to the city. Before that the Arabs had called it Gurgandj. It is now called Kunya-Urgench.

region were Ghur (centred on Afghanistan) and West Liao (modern Kazakhstan). In the shadow of these two major powers were the city-states in and around Transoxiana and Khorasan, of which Urganj was one. In the course of the next two decades, Muhammad defeated Ghur, drove back West Liao, and became the dominant regional power. Muhammad directed at least thirteen campaigns between 1200 and 1218 and may have made another two against the Kipchaks. Fighting five or six battles, he was defeated once and two other battles were ties. He greatly expanded his territory, securing all of Khorasan, Transoxiana, Afghanistan, territory in India (mainly in what is now Pakistan), and Persian Iraq, and extended his influence into the plains to the north. The conquests were, however, cheaply earned. The battle per campaign ratio was low and so was the win ratio of the battles he did fight. West Liao helped him check Ghur, and it was the sudden collapse of Ghur in 1206 and West Liao in 1210 that made significant expansion possible for Muhammad. Clearly Muhammad was gradually able to increase the forces he could field, but there is nothing in the narratives of the Persian or Arab historians to suggest he took steps to organise his armed forces or state effectively. What is clear is that a substantial part of his forces consisted of Kangli and Kipchak tribesmen. The Kangli lived just north of his territory, north and north east of Aral Lake, and the Kipchaks beyond the Ural River.

The Mongol operations in the west are covered in Far Eastern sources, but more important are the more detailed Persian and Arab accounts. The key sources are Juvaini, Ibn al-Athir, Juzjani, Nasawi, and Rashid al-Din. Juvaini and Rashid al-Din were pro-Mongol, whereas Ibn al-Athir, Juzjani, and Nasawi were hostile. Rashid al-Din, writing much later, drew on Ibn al-Athir and Juvaini. It is evident from Pétis de la Croix and Raverty that much other useful information is provided by later Persian and Turkish historians. Only a few of these have been translated into any European language. Barthold and Walker have written good modern accounts of the Mongol conquest of Khwarezm.

Rashid al-Din says Muhammad had 400,000 soldiers. All authorities credit Muhammad with large forces, but often they do not agree on details. The following is said about the size of the forces guarding Otrar, Bokhara, and Samarkand:

	Otrar	Bokhara	Samarkand
Juvaini	50,000	20,000+?	110,000
Nasawi	30,000	30,000	40,000
Juzjani		13,000	60,000
Ibn al-Athir		20,000	50,000
Rashid al-Din	20,000	30,000	110,000
Other	15,000		

Without militia raised to guard cities, it is assumed these totals are at least 10 times too high. In total Muhammad could hardly have more than 40,000 horsemen in and around Transoxiana. Certainly, the Mongols fielded the largest force.

On the rise of Muhammad II see Ibn al-Athir, pp.56–59, 63–66, 72–75, 92–111, 115–120, 127–135, 161–162, 164–167, 171–173, 204–207; Juvaini, pp.44–48, 61–70, 74–80, 315–396; Nasawi, *Histoire du sultan Djelal ed-Din Mankobirti prince du Kharezm par Mohammed en-Nesawi*, translated by O. Houdas (Paris: E. Leroux, 1895), pp.10–60; Juzjani, pp.254–270; Rashid al-Din, 295–298, 309–316, 320, 331–332, 334–338; Julian, pp.101–109; Barthold, *Turkestan down to the Mongol invasion*, pp.348–380; Wittfogel and Feng, pp.650–655; Biran, *The Empire of the Qara Khitai in Eurasian History*, pp.67–86.

25

The Defeat of Muhammad II

It is too late to do anything about Transoxiana. We must strive not to lose Khorasan and Persia. We should recall the troops we have stationed in every city, spend whatever necessary and make the Jaxartes a moat,[1] otherwise we will have to take refuge in Hindustan.

– Jalal al-Din's advice to his father Muhammad II, Rashid al-Din, 347.

In 1219 Temüjin decided to attack Khwarezm even though it was far away. The build-up to war will be described in detail later, involving as it did Sübe'etei who ended up near Khwarezm with Joci and Jebe. Muqali and the *left hand* continued operations against the Jin in China and Otcigin was tasked to guard the home territory. Some units still operated in Korea. Temüjin was left with at most 60,000 men for the western expedition (May 1219). He spent the late summer resting along the Erdis before continuing the march. Arslan joined him at Qayaliq, as did Iduqut and Suqnaq Tegin of Almayak. Joci, Sübe'etei and Jebe probably joined him in the region of the Talas River. Finally, after a three month march from the Erdis, Temüjin arrived in the area north of the central Syr Darya River (around November 1219).

Muhammad is likely to have expected a 'normal' sized nomad raid. He decided, wisely, to remain on the defensive, keeping his soldiers inside the walled cities until the raiders returned home. With the benefit of hindsight it seems clear that Muhammad should have stationed his main forces further back and not have put such strong forces inside Samarkand and the other Transoxianian cities. Though he knew they had taken Beijing, evidently he did not expect the Mongols to bring an effective siege train, and he should have understood that his hold on Transoxiana was tedious, and that the country was economically weak and therefore offered a poor base from which to resist the invaders. That Temüjin led such a vast army across the Syr Darya was something unheard of and unexpected. The nomad Yuezhi, Turks, and Seljuks had struck across

1   An error for 'Oxus'.

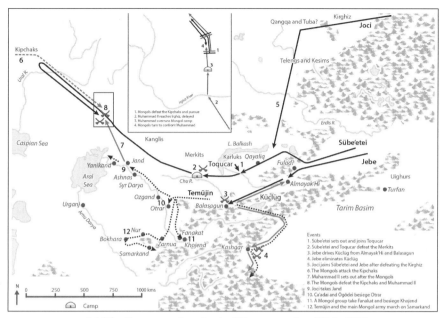

14. The first campaigns in the Western region 1216–1220

the river in earlier times, but none of them had been so numerous, well-organised, and well-equipped.

Muhammad left perhaps 2,000 soldiers to guard Otrar, and subsequently sent another 1,000 men under Qaracha Khass-Hajo into the town. One thousand men were placed in both Fanakat and Khojend. Further down river, 1,000 men guarded Jand and as many were in Yanikand (Shahrkent). Thus the Syr Darya River line was covered. Further back, perhaps 8,000 men were placed inside Samarkand and 2,000 guarded Bokhara. Perhaps 9,000 were stationed at the capital Urganj, including many Kanglis. There were additional forces in Khuttalan, Termez, Qunduz, Sarakhs, Wakhsh, and Balkh. Muhammad took station near Balkh with 'almost entirely … Tatar and Khitai troops.' He must have feared they could defect to the Mongols and therefore held them back. He had more than 7,000 men. There were also forces further away in Afghanistan and Persian Iraq, but these played no part in the initial phases of the war. In total Muhammad probably had about 40,000 horsemen in or near Transoxiana. By dispersing his forces so widely he was strong nowhere. He must have assumed each city could hold off the Mongols, but lacked a field force that could strike where an opportunity might present itself. His son Jalal al-Din questioned the strategy, favouring concentrating the forces further south, and was right to do so. The core strength of Muhammad was his cavalry, and the best use of horsemen was hardly to defend fortresses. Nasawi says Muhammad took measures to conscript soldiers from the general population, but that they were not ready in time.

Temüjin split his army into several divisions, each with its own mission: (1) Ca'adai and Ögödei began to besiege Otrar with at least 11,000 men, including the Uighurs and some Chinese auxiliaries; (2) Joci and at least 4,000 men was sent down the Syr Darya to secure that region and invade the territory of the Kanglis; (3) Alaq, Söyiketü, and Taqai with 5,000 men were sent to take Fanakat. Otrar was a strong fortress, guarding the border area where the Mongols entered the country, and it was a natural target for Temüjin. It is less obvious why Joci was sent upriver. The large part of the Khwarezmian field army consisted of Kangli tribesmen: by sending Joci upriver, Temüjin isolated Transoxiana from the Kangli home territories north of the Aral Lake. Joci's advance can therefore be viewed as a diversion and exploitation of a central position. Temüjin held back the bulk of his forces, perhaps 40,000 or more men. He only crossed the Syr Darya in person in January 1220, several months after arriving in the region. He therefore seems initially to have waited, resting his men after the long march from Mongolia. His intent may have been to attempt to draw Muhammad forward. This is the view of C. C. Walker, who says Alaq, Söyiketü, and Taqai were sent forward 'to present bait to Muhammad in the hope that it would draw him into the open.' If he took the bait, 'Jenghiz Khan and Tule could descend like a thunderbolt on the flank of Mahommed, in typical Mongol fashion.' According to Walker, Temüjin and Tolui camped north of the Kara Tau. If the enemy moved against one of the Mongol detachments, it could fall back and Temüjin could bring his main forces forward and catch the Khwarezmians in the open.

Nasawi relates that Badr al-Din al-Amid came before Temüjin. He was Muhammad's minister for 'the countries of the Turks.' Badr hated Muhammad because he had killed his father and other relatives, and provided the Mongols with detailed intelligence. He also drafted several letters, made out to have been written by Muhammad's senior officers and showing their eagerness to submit to Temüjin. Temüjin sent the letters to the mother of Muhammad, Terken Khatun, in Urganj. The idea was to show resistance was futile. Coming from Nasawi, the story with the fake letters could be true; if so, it was a remarkable scheme designed to weaken and divide the enemy command. Later from Bokhara or Samarkand Temüjin sent another message to Terken Khatun, saying he was making war on Muhammad, not her. Again he tried to divide the enemy. Terken Khatun, however, remained supportive of her son, but fled from Urganj.

Iletgu Malik and some Kangli Turks held Fanakat. That city fell after a three day siege, but Khojend, defended by the vigorous Temür Malik, held out much longer. Temür Malik had constructed a fort on a hill on an island in the middle of the Syr Darya, which the Mongols could not easily approach. Temür had 12 ships which Juvaini says were 'roofed over and sealed with felt polished with clay and vinegar' so that incendiary weapons could have no effect on them. The ships were used to good effect to fire on the Mongols from the riverside and keep them from getting to the island. Unable to mount an assault, the Mongols blockaded the enemy position.

After waiting for two or three months, and seeing that Muhammad remained on the defensive, Temüjin decided to move forward. The Mongol *Khan* crossed the Syr Darya and set out for Zarnuq, and the town submitted. The citadel was destroyed and a levy to handle siegework tasks was raised, but otherwise the population suffered no harm. Temüjin's line of march suggested that he was moving directly on Samarkand. Instead, perhaps at the urging of Sübe'etei, the Mongols turned to the right. Sübe'etei was near the advance forces and by now had been in the western region for more than three years, therefore had learned the geography quite well. Juvaini says 'one of the Turcomans of that region, who had a perfect knowledge of the roads and highways' acted as a guide and 'led them on by a little frequented road; which road has ever since been called the Khan's Road.' The Mongols passed Nur, which also submitted, and appeared suddenly in front of Bokhara. Local commander Inanch Khan, also called Badr ad-Din, attempted to break out three days later.[2] The Mongols, possibly under the direction of Sübe'etei if he was leading the advance forces, left open an escape route. The Muslims quickly fled instead of trying to continue the battle and the Mongols pursued them, driving them towards the Amu Darya.[3] Close to this river the Muslim force was intercepted and destroyed. Juvaini says: 'when the forces reached the banks of the Oxus, the patrols and advance parties of the Mongols army fell upon them and left no trace of them.' Inanch Khan, however, made his way across the river and managed to escape. Bokhara surrendered the next day, 16 February 1220. The citadel held out, defended by 400 horsemen. To create space needed for the siege operations, the Mongols cleared the houses close to the citadel: while so doing, a fire broke out, devastating the whole city. The citadel was taken 12 days later on 28 February 1220.

Temüjin was now centrally placed between Samarkand, Balkh and Urganj and divided the main forces of Muhammad in those three locations. Temüjin's army was far too strong for Muhammad to challenge. Had he concentrated all the nearby forces against the Mongols, including those in Urganj, he would probably still have been outnumbered by more than two to one. Temüjin marched on Samarkand, detaching forces en route to reduce Dabusiya and Sar-I-Pul. The Mongols encircled Samarkand, which was guarded by a large body of Turks and Iranians. They felt strong enough to venture outside the gates to challenge the Mongols, and 20 elephants were committed along with a strong body of horsemen. The Mongols ambushed the attackers and drove them back, and the Khwarezmians lost perhaps 1,000 men killed. A large part of the Samarkand garrison came out and surrendered on 16 March, and only the citadel had to be taken by siege. The citadel, defended perhaps by 2,000 soldiers, held out for one month. Finally, in April, the defenders made a sortie: some 1,000 soldiers, led by Alpär Khan, cut their way through the Mongol lines and made it across the Amu Darya. The garrison soldiers who had first surrendered, perhaps 3,000 men, were all executed. Temüjin had no time for traitors. He released the captive elephants into the countryside where they quickly died. Temüjin and Temür *Lenks* both encountered elephants late in their careers. Temür *Lenks* enthusiastically added captured elephants to his army, whereas Temüjin had no interest in such exotic things.

Meanwhile, Ca'adai and Ögödei took Otrar. In April Qaracha ventured out of a gate with his men, surrendering to the Mongols, who were able to enter through the

---

2   A title, also called Mongol Hajib. Juvaini also calls him Kök Khan. Barthold suggested it might be Jamuqa. Certainly he came from Mongolia. Juvaini writes: 'Kök Khan was said to be a Mongol and to have fled from Genghis Khan and joined the Sultan.' It cannot have been Jamuqa, but might have been another leader known from the earlier tribal wars.

3   Juzjani lists Arslan and Tolon. Juvaini lists Torbei, Yasa'ur, and Ghadaq. He also lists the Uighurs, which is perhaps a mistake. Probably Tolon should be Dörbei Doqsin.

gate he used. Judging Qaracha and his men to be faithless, they cut them down. The citadel held out longer, but was finally taken one month later. Perhaps the Mongols dug a tunnel in order to gain entry: Jia Talahun's biography says that he 'commanded his own tribe together with Khitan, Nuzhi, Tangut, and Chinese soldiers to attack Otrar ... He took the lead to enter through a tunnel they dug under the city wall, and took over the city.' Gayir Khan was captured and killed. Ca'adai and Ögödei then marched to Samarkand, rejoining their father.

Joci took Sighnaq, a small city, by storm after the people of that town had killed his envoy. The population was massacred as punishment. Joci next secured Ozgand and afterwards Ashnas – a place defended, says Juvaini, by 'a rabble and common soldiers' – en route to Jand. Qutlugh Khan did not attempt to hold Jand, but fled to Urganj before Joci even reached the fortress and on 21 April the Mongol prince quickly secured control over the city. There was no massacre. By taking Jand, Joci deviated from the objective given, for he had been ordered into the Qara-Cum. Joci next sent a detachment, Juvaini says 1 tümen, to secure Yanikant further upstream.

Temür Malik defended his position at Khojend stubbornly. Temüjin sent 'reinforcements from Otrar, Bokhara, Samarkand' and other places to help reduce it. Juvaini says 20,000 Mongol soldiers and 50,000 conscripted civilians were eventually involved. The fort fell, but Temür Malik, who was evidently an enterprising officer, escaped upriver with what was left of his garrison. Joci's men prepared to intercept him downriver, but Temür Malik eluded them by getting off the boats before reaching Joci's position and heading into the desert. He lost many men, but finally reached the capital Urganj during the summer of 1220. Temür subsequently made a raid on Yanikant, where he killed the Mongol official. He afterwards joined Muhammad and Jalal al-Din in Persia, and Rashid al-Din says that much later he ended up in Syria. Missing his homeland, he finally returned, and ended up in Mongol hands. A veteran Mongol soldier killed him.

Muhammad had moved forward from Balkh to Termez, aiming to get up-to-date intelligence. Understanding the Mongol army was too powerful, he decided to head for Persian Iraq, seeking to put distance between himself and the Mongols. Some of his men followed him and others retreated into the mountains in the south. Most, however, defected to the Mongols. A reported 7,000 Kipchaks and Kanglis headed for Samarkand under the command of Ala ad-Din, lord of Qunduz, and Djah Revi, a Balkh lord. They even attempted to assassinate Muhammad before leaving. The defectors provided the Mongols with valuable intelligence. In May, based on the information provided, Temüjin decided to send Jebe, Sübe'etei and Toqucar in pursuit of Muhammad. The Mongol officers crossed the Amu Darya and pushed into Khorasan. Toqucar was left behind in Balkh. Temüjin had now effectively split the enemy territory into three isolated parts, namely Urganj, Afghanistan and Persian Iraq, and the western regions. At the same time Temüjin ordered Dörbei Doqsin, with two other officers Juvaini calls Yasa'ur (Jalayirtai Yisa'ur?) and Ghadaq (Arqai Qasar?), in addition to Arslan, to secure the upper Amu Darya. The intent was probably for them to cover the west flank of Toqucar. Juvaini says they were tasked to take Wakhsh,

Kulab, and Talaqan. Temüjin marched into Nakhshab, a mountainous country south of Samarkand, where he rested his forces during the summer and early in the autumn.

Temüjin restarted operations during the autumn, and took Termez after an eleven day siege. Soldiers from Seistan defended the fortress.[4] The Mongols first had to clear some forts along the riverbank, using siege artillery. Guo Baoyu's biography says:

> Arriving at the Amu Darya, they were opposed by 10 or more forts of rammed earth and by boats deployed in the middle of the river ... Guo Baoyu ordered *huojian* to be directed against their ships. At once, all caught fire: seizing [the moment] they overcame [the opposition], advanced straight ahead and defeated 10,000 troops guarding [the opposite] bank.

All survivors were butchered. Temüjin afterwards marched towards the Amu Darya to spend the winter in the area between Hisar and Kulab.[5] The forces that had taken Khojend, or some of them, appear to have continued operations in Ferghana. Sübe'etei and Jebe, now deep inside Persian Iraq, informed the *Khan* that Muhammad died (on a small island in the Caspian Sea). The Uighur contingent was around this time, late 1220, allowed to return home.

Temüjin sent Ca'adai and Ögödei to take Urganj, the capital of Khwarezm. Joci was told to support them. He first sent a body consisting mainly of recently recruited Turks, in all 2,000 men. However the Turks revolted en route and the whole unit dispersed. Nasawi gives details on the composition of the Mongol army arriving in front of Urganj: along with Temüjin's sons served Dayir, Bo'orcu, Tolon, Qada'an, and a person called Usun (Yesun Toa Taraqi?). The army may have been almost 30,000 men strong.

In addition to Urganj, the Mongols turned their attention towards Khorasan. Ikhtiyar al-Din had left Amuya for Merv, where he won over many Turks and set up camp outside the city. Mujir-al-Mulk controlled the city. Toqucar marched from Balkh to Khorasan and attacked some positions near Herat, failing to respect the treaty Sübe'etei and Jebe had before made with local strongman Malik Khan. Temüjin had approved the treaty so Toqucar acted improperly. Toqucar did not, however, attack Herat itself: instead he continued towards Nishapur, and was killed in some skirmish near that place (November 1220). Yesu Buqa took command over his forces. Malik Khan had left Herat for Ghazni (passing Garmsir), probably fairly soon after the Mongols passed Herat for a second time. At the same time, Mongol detachments raided into Badakhshan and others were active further south. Initially the raiders may have come from Toqucar's forces, but later other Mongol forces crossed the Amu Darya. Sigi Qutuqu was probably the senior officer. He seems to have split his forces, leaving some to operate south of Balkh, while he led the rest towards Herat. He attempted without success to intercept Malik Khan as he made his way from Herat

4 Juzjani says Zangi-i-Abi-Hafs was the commander. Nasawi names Fakhr al-Din Habash, also called Inan al-Nasawi.
5 Juvaini says this was the region of Kangurt and Shuman.

to Ghazni; some detachments targeted Ghur and Ghazni. Other forces approached Tulak (under Sigi Qutuqu) and Firuzkoh (under Sutu). The latter place was attacked unsuccessfully over a 21 day period during the first months of 1221. The Mongols hovered around Tulak for eight months (presumably from May to December 1220, counting from when Sübe'etei and Jebe first passed the place). The Mongols took Garmsir, and the fortress of Astiash submitted on terms after being besieged for 11 days.

The march on Bokhara has captured the imagination of Western historians and commentators like no other Mongol military manoeuvre. Liddell Hart held: 'Rarely, if ever, in the history of war has the principle of surprise been so dramatically or completely fulfilled.' The manoeuvre quite likely surprised and unbalanced Muhammad as well as other enemy leaders, but it was hardly critical for victory: the Mongols were too strong. Had they marched directly on Samarkand they would surely also have prevailed easily. Temüjin gained a quick victory because his army was very large and because the enemy fortresses failed to hold out for very long. Muhammad was not a popular ruler: by 1210 he had only recently gained control over Transoxiana, and could not count of the cities to really support him. Transoxiana itself was economically weakened after the recent wars. The political and economic weakness of Muhammad probably explains better than the Mongol siege capabilities why the cities fell as quickly as they did. The cities fell to Temüjin as quickly as the German cities did to Gustav II Adolf in late 1631 and early 1632, or the cities of Belgium to Marlborough in 1706. The Stele of Laosuo marvelled at the ease with which the cities fell: 'The cities of Otrar, Bukhara and Samarkand all had strong walls, and it should not have been easy to take them quickly, but unexpectedly they were captured with a single roll of the drums.' It seems clear that Muhammad would have been better advised to attempt to hold the Amu Darya, leaving fewer forces to guard the various cities of Transoxiana.

Temüjin divided his forces upon reaching the Syr Darya, and left three detachments to clear the river, while he advanced on Samarkand. His superiority in numbers was such that his enemy could not hope to challenge this army even after it had sent off several detachments. He was therefore justified to divide his forces. Temüjin strove to reduce all the enemy territory, and dividing his forces he could attack several objectives at once, achieving the conquest faster. Even if Temüjin wanted to, he could hardly keep his full forces concentrated. It was logistically impossible, or at least very difficult, to collect food and forage for so many men and horses in one place. Presumably most of the spare horses were left in a camp north-east of the Syr Darya. Temüjin's decision to send off about 15 percent of his army to hunt down Muhammad was remarkable. He had the benefit of good intelligence provided by defectors, but it must still be seen as a very bold decision. This aspect of his art of war was not copied from the Khitans.

Temüjin's Transoxianian campaign can be compared to Napoleon's campaigns in 1805 or 1806. Napoleon assembled a large organised force, some 200,000 troops, and threw it against his foes – Austrians, Russians, and Prussians – whose armies were dispersed and not yet assembled. At Ulm in 1805 he had 180,000 soldiers against 70,000, and at Jena in 1806 he had 150,000 against 100,000. Temüjin had 70,000, or somewhat less, effectives against at most 40,000 (a rounded number) for Muhammad.

He took advantage of his superiority in numbers by encircling Samarkand moving over Bokhara with half of his forces. Napoleon, with numbers on his side, also worked his way around the enemy flank at both Ulm and Jena. Once advantage was gained, both commanders pursued ruthlessly to exploit the advantage gained.

Sources: the SWQZL, 75a; Rashid al-Din, 107, 356–362; *Yuanshi* 1, p.36, 149, pp.3520–3522; 151, p.3577; the *Secret History*, 257–258; Juvaini, pp.46, 81–109, 115–123, 128–130, 401; Nasawi, *Histoire du sultan Djelal ed-Din*, pp.62–63, 72–75, 100–103, 153–154; Juzjani, pp.274, 968–1008, 1023; B. H. Liddell Hart, *Great Captains Unveiled* (Salem: Ayer Co., 1928, reprinted 1984), p.15; Barthold, *Turkestan down to the Mongol invasion*, pp.403–428; C. C. Walker, *Jenghiz Khan* (London: Luzac, 1939), pp.71–121; Martin, *The Rise of Chingis Khan*, pp.326–334; Leo de Hartog, *Genghis Khan, Conqueror of the World* (London: L. B. Tauris & Co. Ltd 1989), p.98; Michel Hoàng, *Genghis Khan* (London: Saqi Books, 2001), p.224.

26

Khwarezm Crushed

You did not know the place of battle, and you were both at fault.

– Temüjin on the performance of Sigi Qutuqu and Jalal al-Din at Parwan, Rashid al-Din 375

Jalal al-Din, the son of Muhammad, was born in 1199. He had proved his bravery on the battlefield already in 1219, aged only about 20, when Muhammad fought against the Mongols along the Irghiz River (this battle will be dealt with later, in chapter 30). Not the designated heir, he emerged as the only man able to seriously challenge the Mongols. Since ancient times Persians valued a brave knight and Jalal al-Din was cast in the mould of the Persian heroes of earlier ages. After Muhammad died, Jalal al-Din headed from Mazandaran to Urganj. Though claiming to be the new shah, he found it impossible to impose his authority on the senior lords in Urganj and therefore decided to leave the city. Nasawi says Inanch Khan warned him about a plot against him. Jalal al-Din left with 300 men. They fought their way through the Mongol screen left by Sübe'etei and Jebe in Khorasan, encountering a reported 700-strong Mongol detachment at Shayaqan Hill near Ustuva and Nisa, to reach Nishapur. Two of his brothers, Ozlagh and Aq, followed in his tracks. They were less fortunate: the same Mongols intercepted and killed them. Jalal al-Din remained only a short time in Nishapur: Juvaini says he left one day before Tolui's army entered Khorasan. On 2 February 1221 he headed for Ghazni. Some Mongol forces, perhaps those he fought against before, pursued him past Zuzan to Barduya, but then stopped.

Earlier Malik Khan had gone from Herat to Seistan (after Mongol officer Toqucar attacked him; see chapter 33), which Nasawi says he 'vainly tried to conquer.' Muhammad b. Ali Khar Pust and other Ghur lords held Ghazni, Malik's next destination. Coming from Peshawar, the Ghur lord had taken Ghazni after Karbar Malik, who held the fortress before them, had gone to join Malik in Seistan. They were not ready to welcome Malik who therefore had to set up camp at nearby at Sura. Juvaini says Muhammad had

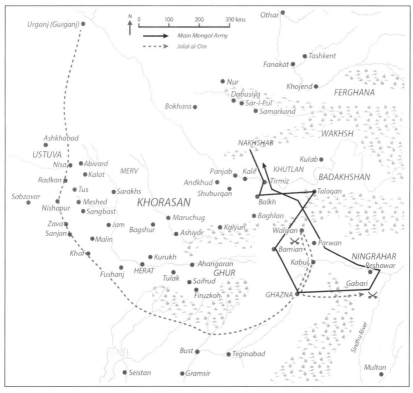

15. The advance to the Sindhu River 1221.

20,000 men;[1] soon afterwards, Sham al-Din and Salah al-Din killed him, seized the citadel of Ghazni and invited Malik Khan to join them. The hostile Ghurids left the city, and Malik Khan then dealt with some Mongol raiders. Juvaini says 2,000–3,000 horsemen went 'in search of Malik Khan'. The Mongol detachment fell back in the face of the larger Muslim force, passing Teginabad[2] and Bust.[3] Evidently the Mongols had followed the tracks of Malik Khan from Herat. Malik afterwards marched via Qusdar (Khuzdar) to Sivistan (Sibi) to the south-east, perhaps looking for food and forage and/or new recruits. Meanwhile, Razi-al-Mulk and Umdat-al-Mulk seized control of Ghazni. Sayf al-Din Ighraq Malik had led some Turks – according to Juvaini they were 'without number' – out of Transoxiana, and marched to Peshawar. Razi-al-Mulk marched against them, but was defeated and killed. A'zam Malik of Ningrahar and the Kabul governor Malik Shir marched against Ghazni, which was still held by Umdat-al-Mulk. They besieged and took the city in 40 days, using mangonels. They submitted to Jalal al-Din when he arrived there on 11 February 1221. Malik Khan also returned to

1   Juzjani offers 130,000 men.
2   Kandahar?
3   7 km south of modern Lashkargah.

Ghazni; Nasawi says he brought 10,000 Turks. Jalal al-Din was able to unite the various factions. Juvaini says 'Yamin Malik, who was in India, heard of the Sultan's arrival and hastened to his side. So too (Sayf al-Din) Ighraq Malik joined the Sultan from Peshawar with Khalaj and Turcoman troops.'

Ca'adai, Ögödei, and Joci began to besiege Urganj soon after Jalal al-Din had left the town (late January 1221?). Ca'adai and Ögödei arrived first, Joci somewhat later. Juvaini says 90,000 Kanglis defended Urganj, but the total regular garrison can only have been a fraction of that. The general population, however, was militant and many would have been prepared to join the fighting. A part of the garrison ventured outside the city walls to challenge the Mongol advance guard. The Mongols fell back, drawing the defenders into an ambush at Bagh-i-Khurram. The Mongols, says Juvaini, 'dispatched flying arrows' and were 'wielding sword and lance', and gained an easy victory. The defeated side lost 1,000 men.

Shaikh Khan and Inanch Khan escaped with 2,000 men, and headed for Nisa in Khorasan. The people of that town had refortified the citadel, and had become a rallying point for those unwilling to surrender to the Mongols. The Mongols in Khorasan set out to deal with the new arrivals. Juvaini says some of the Mongol forces besieged 'Qal'a-yi-Kalat and Qal'a-yi-Nau.' Other forces, said to be 800 strong, approached Nisa. The enemy commander 'fell on the rear of the Mongols.' An officer Nasawi calls Kush was killed and 20 Mongols taken captive. Yedu Buqa and Qush Temür may have deployed some 4,000 or more men in total, so this reverse was serious without being a great disaster. The unrest of Khorasan prompted Temüjin to order 7,000 men under Tolui into the province. Inanch Khan headed westwards where he managed to recruit additional forces. Sübe'etei and Jebe had by then marched into Azerbaijan and presented no threat to Inanch Khan. The Mongols afterwards took Nisa by siege, needing two weeks for the task.

In February 1221 Temüjin appeared in front of Balkh, and the city surrendered without a struggle. Even so the population was massacred, probably because Temüjin judged they had not behaved as loyal subjects after submitting to Sübe'etei and Jebe – perhaps by providing support to enemy forces passing by or/and disposing of the Mongol *shahna* official. Some 52,000 people were reportedly killed. It was afterwards that Temüjin sent Tolui into Khorasan to restore order; he set out from the Mongol camp at Pushtah-i-Nu'man.

Tolui had four tümens, in this case some 7,000 men,[4] plus what Juvaini call 'levies from subject territory.' He marched past Maruchuq and Bagshur (Qala-i-Mor) and secured (or re-secured) control over Sarakhs, Abivard, and other places before moving on Merv. He thus, like the Mongols had done before Samarkand, isolated the main target before turning against it. Ikhtiyar al-Din remained in camp at Dastajird outside Merv, where on 24 February the Mongol advance guard surprised and shattered his forces. The next day Tolui took and sacked Merv. Many people were killed, according to Ibn al-Athir in total 700,000. Tolui then turned southwards and attacked Nishapur,

---

4 Nasawi lists Thoulon (Tolon Cerbi), Qiqou, and Qeboqa as some of the commanders with this force. Thoulon is placed in two places at once as he is also said to have been at Khwarezm.

breaching the wall in just three days (8–10 April). The population was massacred. Herat submitted and was spared. Tolui had conquered Khorasan in about three months. During the time Tolui was in Khorasan, Toqucar's tümen and the other forces Sübe'etei and Jebe had left behind headed for Azerbaijan, to join those two Mongol commanders.

Urganj fell in April after a four month siege,[5] but the Mongols had to engage in house-to-house fighting before securing the city. Their operations were hampered because of a quarrel between Ca'adai and Joci. Reportedly the latter wanted to save as much of the city as possible, thinking it would become a part of his domain. Temüjin was informed about the problem, and ordered that Ögödei should take command over the combined forces. Urganj was completely destroyed and all the people captured were massacred. This was a true act of terror. The people of Urganj paid dearly for the conduct of their lord. Joci returned to the area north of the Aral Lake, while his brothers rejoined Temüjin. Joci's task was to subject the Kanglis and the Kipchaks. The Kanglis, or a part of them, seems to have fled across the Ural River. Joci remained close to Aral Lake. If he undertook active operations the sources fail to report it. Ca'adai and Ögödei got a frosty reception from their father. Temüjin was upset because his sons failed to give him a part of the booty taken at Urganj, and initially refused even to see them.

Temüjin started to besiege Talaqan in February 1221, soon after Tolui left him.[6] Tolui rejoined his father in May. Talaqan was taken in June, after a four month siege.[7] However, before the fortress fell, elements of the garrison broke through the Mongol lines and escaped. Dörbei Doqsin took Wakhsh after an eight month blockade.[8] The Mongols then marched on Fiwar (of Kadas), and started to blockade it.

Sigi Qutuqu operated in a forward position further south in central Afghanistan. In January officers Juzjani calls Mangutah, Karashah, and Utsuz, besieged Saifrud in Ghur. However the Mongols broke off the attempt after 50 days when in April a sudden rainfall again filled the cisterns of the fort. Jalal al-Din assembled a fairly large army. Malik Khan (credited with 10,000 or 30,000 men), Sayf al-Din Ighraq Malik (with 40,000) and Ghur strongmen A'zam Malik b. Imad ad-Din and the Kabul governor Malik Shir (with 50,000) contributed the main forces. They had perhaps 15,000 men in total.[9] Mongol officers Taqacaq and Mulgar (Muqur Qa'uran?), attempted to take Waliyan. Jalal al-Din moved to Parwan; making a quick move across the mountains to the north, he surprised and routed the Mongols at Waliyan, inflicting

5   According to Ibn al-Athir Urganj fell after a five month siege, which seems roughly right. Juvaini says the
     siege lasted seven months, and Nasawi that it started in January and ended in April, a span fitting well with
     the report that Temüjin sent his sons to attack the city during the autumn (Chinese annals).
6   The fortress should be located close to Nusrat-Kuh, perhaps a citadel of this city.
7   Ibn al-Athir says that Talaqan was taken in 10 months, but that Temüjin was only personally in charge
     during the last four. Rashid al-Din says the fortress was taken in seven months. The SWQZL 75a says that
     Temüjin spent the summer near Talaqan after taking the city. Mongol detachments had perhaps masked
     Talaqan since August 1220.
8   Nasawi says Balkhamurk Khan had been in charge of the fortress. Juzjani says the commander was the
     Pahlawan Arsiah.
9   Juvaini says 60,000–70,000 and Juzjani 45,000.

a reported 1,000 loss on them. The Mongols retreated across a river and destroyed a bridge to keep the enemy from following (spring 1221). Jalal al-Din had left his baggage behind at Parwan, and now returned there. Temüjin ordered Sigi Qutuqu to deal with Jalal al-Din. Rashid al-Din says that Taqacaq, Mulgar, and Iqar Qalja were with him as were Uqai Qalja and Qutur Qalja. Juzjani also lists Sutu (Uklan) and Söyiketü, perhaps a mix up with Uqar and Qutur. He may have commanded as many as 10,000 men. The two armies collided in a plain near Parwan. During the first day Malik Khan attacked on the right and drove back the Mongols. Jalal al-Din sent reinforcements from the centre and the left to progressively increase the strength of his right. Sigi Qutuqu called forward his reserve, which the Muslims at first took to be the approach of a new army. The next day Jalal al-Din dismounted his force and fought on foot, and was able to hold off the three Mongol tümens. The Mongols mounted dummies on their spare horses to form a second line: the idea was to make it look as if they had been reinforced, but Jalal al-Din was not fooled. Finally he mounted his men, counterattacked and routed the Mongols. He attacked the centre as well as both flanks, and Sigi Qutuqu was completely defeated (summer 1221). He fled northwards, returning to the Mongol main army. There Rashid al-Din writes that he 'complained of the negligent behaviour of the emirs Uqar Qalja and Qutur Qalja caused by their incessant joking and light-headedness.' Temüjin viewed the defeat as a useful lesson for Sigi Qutuqu, saying: 'Sigi Qutuqu has always been accustomed to victory and has never yet experienced fortune's cruelty; now that he has he will be more cautious.' He later returned to the battlefield with Sigi Qutuqu and explained the errors he had made. Uqar Qalja and Qutur Qalja remained in service and would play a positive role in the battle fought along the Sindhu later the same year.

After the battle, says Juvaini, 'a dispute arose between the Khalaj Turcomans and Ghurids on one hand and the Khwarzmians on the other over the sharing of the horses taken as booty',[10] with the result that a big part of the army, the section led by Sayf al-Din Ighraq and A'zam Malik, marched away and went to Ningranhar[11] and Peshawar. Jalal al-Din returned to Ghazni. Moving forward, perhaps after the peak of the summer had passed, Temüjin left his baggage at Baghlan, presumably with one third of the army to keep watch over it. Temüjin besieged and took Bamian, where Mo'atukan – a grandson, the second oldest son of Ca'adai – was killed during the operations. The city, including the castle, was for that reason destroyed. The siege lasted for one month (July 1221?). Ögödei and Ca'adai had rejoined their father just after Bamian was taken. Juvaini says Temüjin continued to advance southward after learning about Jalal al-Din's victory and 'the dispersal of the Sultan's forces.' He marched quickly. Close to Ghazni he learned that Jalal al-Din had set out towards to the Sindhu, having left two weeks before. Temüjin pursued, leaving Ghazni unconquered in this rear. Temüjin caught up with Jalal al-Din along the Sindhu, and the Mongols, says Juvaini, crushed the enemy rearguard: 'Orkhan, who was in the rearguard, took up a stand against the … [Mongol] … vanguard … but was defeated

10   Malik Khan 'struck Ighraq on the head with a whip.'
11   In modern Jalalabad.

and withdrew to join the Sultan.' Nasawi says Jalal al-Din personally inflicted a reverse on the Mongol advance forces: 'He threw back the Tatar advance guard at Djerdin.' There may have been more than one action. Djerdin is one-day march from Ghazni. The action of Orkhan should be placed near the Sindhu River.[12]

Jalal al-Din did not have enough time to get across the Sindhu and was forced to accept battle with his back to the river.[13] Temüjin had at least 30,000 effectives; Jalal al-Din had far fewer men, perhaps fewer than 10,000. The Muslim historians say that the Mongols deployed with their forces in several echelons. Juvaini writes, for example, that the Mongols lined up 'in several rings in the shape of a bow and made the Sindhu River like a bow string.' Jalal al-Din's right rested on the river and his left deployed on rising ground. Jalal al-Din thus covered his flanks, making it difficult for Temüjin to outflank his forces. The Khwarezm right wing, commanded by Malik Khan, charged the Mongol left and drove it back; Jalal al-Din attacked in the centre with his crack 700-man bodyguard. Temüjin had some units deployed beyond the enemy right. They fell on Malik and drove his forces against the centre. Malik tried to escape to Peshawar, but was intercepted and killed. The Mongols also overwhelmed the Muslim left. Pétis de la Croix says Jalal al-Din had weakened this wing by drawing units to reinforce his centre. Seeing this, Temüjin 'ordered Bela Nevian to go and attack it by some byways over the mountain, which a native of the country told him was possible. In effect, Bela conducted by this guide, marched without losing many soldiers, between rocks and dreadful precipices, and fell on the Sultan's left wing behind, which being much weakened, could not long resist.' Jalal al-Din held out in the centre, striking out in various directions. He finally cut his way through the Mongol lines and escaped in spectacular style, jumping on the horse off the cliffs into the Sindhu and making his way over that river to safety. Temüjin witnessed the feat and famously remarked: 'Fortunate should be the father of such a son.' He did not allow his men to shoot at the Khwarezmian prince. Only 700 of Jalal al-Din's men managed to get away (September 1221).[14] Jalal al-Din had thrown his gold and silver coins into the Sindhu: the Mongols used divers to try to recover some of it.

Temüjin marched upriver to winter in the area closer to the mountains of the north, taking Gabari. He spent the next few months hunting down the forces of Sayf al-Din Ighraq and Azam Malik, in all a reported 20,000–30,000 men. These had divided into two quarrelling groups based around Peshawar and Nangarhar respectively. Ighraq and Azam Malik had been killed, following a quarrel between the former and Nuh Jandar – a lord based in Nangarhar. Tekechuk and Sayyid Ala-al-Mulk, the latter commanding 'an infantry levy', led the active operations of the Mongols. Ca'adai was sent back south to hunt down Jalal al-Din who, reports given to Temüjin said, had re-crossed the Sindhu to bury his dead.

12 Caqan's biography reports of a victory over Jalal al-Din, but confusingly refers to the Iron Gates. Caqan is likely to have commanded the advance guard.
13 Boyle places the battle near Kalabagh. Further north in the area of Nizampur, Kabi, Kohat, and Attock is more likely. The distance from Ghazni is some 550 km. With a two week head start, Jalal al-Din evidently failed to move quickly. Perhaps he was slowed down by non-combatants.
14 Accepting the date of Juvaini, Nasawi says 24 November (seems late).

Meanwhile, there were new developments in Khorasan. First there was some unrest in Sarakhs; then in November 1221 Kush Tegin Pahlawan seized Merv, or what was left of it, killing Ziya al-Din. Nasawi says that from there he made a successful attack on Bokhara. Encouraged by the victory of Jalal al-Din at Perwan, the people in Herat rebelled, and disposed of the pro-Mongol leadership. There were still plenty of forts in enemy hands in Afghanistan. A certain Muhammad the Marghani twice attacked the base camp of Temüjin at Baghlan, and the raiders managed to get away with some loot. Perhaps this event triggered the decision of Temüjin to send a large part of the army under Ögödei back to Ghazni. Sigi Qutuqu, Söyiketü, and Alcidai served under him. They destroyed Ghazni, massacring the population, and then went to Pul-i-Ahangaran where they wintered.[15]

Temüjin had left Yelü Ahai behind to administer Samarkand and Bokhara and cover his rear. He was able to restore order in the cities, but not over all the surrounding countryside. He had this responsibility until his death in 1223. During the year Sübe'etei asked for and received permission to move around the Caspian Sea to fall on the rear of the Kipchaks. It was an extraordinary proposal. Almost equally remarkable is the approval Temüjin gave to the project. Sübe'etei was at this point in or near Azerbaijan.

The Mongols spent most of 1221 reducing Talaqan, Urganj and the cities of Khorasan in parallel operations. Jalal al-Din was in the meantime able to assemble an army at Ghazni. Temüjin could have masked Talaqan and pushed south to keep the enemy from uniting their forces around Ghazni, but did not, preferring first to clear the flanks. Once it was clear that Jalal al-Din was a force to be reckoned with, Temüjin moved against him with his full forces. He did not attempt to manoeuvre.

The Mongols earned a reputation for ruthlessness and brutality because of the way they operated in Transoxiana, Khorasan, Persian Iraq, and Afghanistan. The Mongols were less patient than in China, where they did not normally destroy cities recovered after falling into enemy hands. Balkh, Herat, Merv, Nishapur, Ghazni, Rayy, Qam, and Hamadan were left in ruins. However the region was hardly peaceful before the Mongol arrival. Samarkand was partially sacked in 1212 and rival factions brought ruin to Rayy and Qam in 1220 as much as the Mongols did. The Mongols only destroyed cities which rebelled after having submitted. The only exception was Urganj, the enemy capital. There was no 'terror' strategy to awe the enemy into submitting more quickly. The code of Temüjin was simple: if a city broke its word after submitting, it was destroyed and the people killed. The cities of this region had been used to rapidly changing conditions with empires rising and collapsing at high pace; it had been so since the effective collapse of the Abbasids during the 9th century. The city leaders therefore were ready to quickly shift allegiance according to which strongman appeared to be the strongest. This, however, was a grave error in face of a man like Temüjin who respected a determined foe but who was unforgiving when faced by betrayal.

15 Qal'a-yi-Ahangaran.

Sources: the SWQZL, 75a; Rashid al-Din, 137, 377; *Yuanshi* 1, p.37; 120, pp.2955–2957; Nasawi, pp.82–139 (dates Sindhu battle to November); Juvaini, pp.128–141, 147, 150–177, 396–411 (dates Sindhu battle to August–September, location of Sindhu battle, p.134, note 2); Ibn al-Athir, p.227; Juzjani, pp.1012–1038; Ulug Big, *The Shajrat ul Atrak*, pp.147–180; François Pétis de la Croix, *History of Genghizcan the Great* (London: J. Darby, 1722), p.317; Raverty, pp.1023, 1054–1055; Barthold, *Turkestan down to the Mongol invasion*, pp.429–446; Walker, *Jenghiz Khan*, pp.122–152; Ratchnevsky, 'Sigi Qutuqu', pp.83–86; Peter Jackson, 'Jalal al-Din, the Mongols, and the Khwarazmian conquest of the Panjab and Sind', *Journal of the British Institute of Persian Studies*, pp.45–54; Agha Hussain Hamadani, *The Frontier Policy of the Delhi Sultans*, pp.51–52; Johnny Torrens-Spence, *Historic battlefields of Pakistan* (Karachi: Oxford University Press, 2006), pp.20–23.

27

Mopping-Up Operations

The 14th of the fourth month [May 25] 1222, was fixed for explaining the doctrine of the Tao to the emperor; but just as the time arrived, news was received that the Mohammedan rebels in the mountains were about to renew hostilities. The emperor decided himself to attack the enemy.

– *The Travels of Ch'ang Ch'un to the West, 1220–1223*; by Li Ji Zhang

After the defeat of Jalal al-Din there was no army in the field able to challenge the Mongols. There remained, however, many mountain strongholds unwilling to submit and capable of offering stubborn resistance. The operations of the Mongol main army can be quickly described. Temüjin remained along the upper Sindhu River during the early winter; Juvaini says he considered 'returning home by a route through India to the land of the Tangut.' The Mongols never actually attempted to do this, but the notion shows that Temüjin, like Sübe'etei, had a fertile imagination with regard to geography and possible routes. However, the report in Muslim sources that Temüjin wanted to attack the Tanguts cannot be correct, as the Tanguts were at this point his allies, supporting Muqali against Jin (they only defected late in 1222). Before setting out again, Juvaini says Temüjin ordered all captives with the army killed. The hostile Juzjani, however, makes no mention of this. Temüjin returned to Transoxiana by way of Kabul, probably around February 1222. He picked up the baggage left at Baghlan and in April set up camp south of the Amu Darya, close to Balkh. Juvaini says the Mongols camped at Buya Katur in Ashtaqar. Local lord Salar Ahmad worked to provide the Mongols with 'victuals.'

Rebel bands and bandits were active in Transoxiana. One band of bandits (perhaps coming from Zarafshan), reported to be 2,000 men strong, hovered around Samarkand. Mongols had detachments operating along their lines of communications. In May one such detachment, 1,000 men, set out to hunt bandits after escorting the Taoist Chang Chun to Temüjin's camp. Temüjin delayed the second meeting with Chang Chun on the pretext that he needed to direct his attention against the rebels and bandits. Chang Chun, meanwhile, returned to Samarkand, only coming back to Temüjin's camp months later, in October. Temüjin by then had set up camp east of Balkh. The

Mongols crossed the Amu Darya on 6 October, settling in a place located 15 km east of Samarkand. Temüjin stayed around Samarkand for some time before crossing the Syr Darya and setting up camp north of that river in January 1223. He then awaited the return of his various detachments. On 10 March he fell off his horse and was nearly killed by a wild boar. He was later informed that the Tanguts had deserted his forces in China (perhaps June 1223). He decided that he needed to punish them and started the homeward march, but moved slowly, only returning to Mongolia in 1225.

While Temüjin did little from a military point of view in 1222, his detachments remained active elsewhere. In the north, Dörbei Doqsin finally took Fiwar in January, then crossed the Amu Darya and took up station on the other side of the river. Ca'adai reached Tez, an Indian Ocean port, but was never anywhere near Jalal al-Din. He then marched back northwards, eventually rejoining his father in central Afghanistan. Ögödei, while still in central Afghanistan, had wanted to take Seistan, but Temüjin would not allow it. The SWQZL says he told Ögödei: 'The heat is now too high, it is better to send another general.' Ögödei sent detachments to reduce Firuzkoh, Ashiyar, Seistan, as well as Herat. The Mongol advance on Firuzkoh was unexpected, and the city was quickly taken and completely destroyed (first part of 1222). The band holding the citadel above the town fled; they had been at odds with the people of the city. That was the end of the Ghur capital. Guo Baoyu (Abkah) was sent to reduce Ashiyar, the stronghold of Muhammad the Marghani. He held out for a long time: 15 months. During the siege of Ashiyar, Mongol forces reduced various other forts in Gharjistan. Alcidai and Söyiketü were ordered to reduce Herat and Seistan, and spent one month preparing before setting out for Herat in January; the city held out for six and a half months. Finally, says The Shajrat ul Atrak, in late June under 'the force' of the Mongol siege engines '100 feet of wall gave way and at once fell down and 400 Mongols posted and entrenched themselves in the breach.' The defenders held off the Mongols for another three days before they were overwhelmed, and all captives were killed. A reported 1.6 million – or 'many' – people were killed. Söyiketü then turned against Seistan. Alcidai remained in Khorasan where he began to blockade Kalyun, a fortress located between Herat and Balkh. The people of Tulak expelled its Mongol-friendly leader and adopted a hostile stance, perhaps around the same time that Herat rebelled. The Mongols, however, did not mount a major assault on this place. Ögödei returned north via Garmsir and the unlocated Buya Katur and rejoined his father near Balkh, probably in early spring 1222.

Sigi Qutuqu had left behind by Ögödei in Ghazni, and later set out to deal with Kush Tegin Pahlawan in Khorasan. Nasawi says he had 6,000 men. The Khwarezmian leader retreated with 1,000 men, but Sigi Qutuqu pursued, intercepted, and defeated him at Sangbast. Kush Tegin made his way with his remaining forces to Jurjan where he linked up with Inanch Khan.[1] A 200-strong Mongol detachment belonging to Sigi Qutuqu reached Merv. Half remained there, while the other half out set to rejoin Sigi Qutuqu. The unit remaining at Merv afterwards requested support from Dörbei

1   He had evidently left Urganj before the Mongols surrounded the city. He preferred to remain in the western regions instead of following Jalal al-Din to Afghanistan.

Doqsin and Qada'an (Qaban).[2] Dörbei left Nakhshab and arrived at Merv five days later and the city, or what was left of it, was taken and plundered. Dörbei returned to Nakhshab (January–February 1222?).

Khorasan was an endless source of problems. A certain Turkoman called Taj al-Din Umar b. Masud established himself in Merv. He came from the direction of Nisa. From Merv he made raids on the Mongols in all directions. Perhaps one such raid threatened Samarkand as mentioned above? Taj al-Din Umar remained in Merv for several months (Juvaini says half a year). Taj al-Din Umar finally attacked Nisa, but was driven off by a certain Yazir. Then in July Sigi Qutuqu returned to Merv from Talaqan to drive Taj al-Din away.

In July Söyiketü took Seistan and then returned to Alcadai who was still outside Kalyun. The fort held out for another four months. By then time it fell, in November, the garrison was reportedly reduced to 50 men. Guo Baoyu finally took Ashiyar (middle 1222).[3]

East of the Sindhu River Jalal al-Din remained at large, and defeated two local forces close to Lahore. He was reportedly able to build up his forces to as many as 10,000 men. After summer had passed, Temüjin sent Dörbei Doqsin and Bala back across the Sindhu to hunt down the refugee prince. The latter retreated towards Delhi. Dörbei and Bala did not remain for long east of the Sindhu, and Dörbei returned to Temüjin near Samarkand. Temüjin was furious that he had failed to hunt down Jalal al-Din, and sent him back to India.

In January 1223 Mongol forces coming from Khorasan, Seistan, and Ghazni converged on Saifrud, and after two months made an all-out assault. Beaten off in March, they gave up and retreated. A little later, on 14 May, they had the worst of some fighting outside Tulak. Finally, Mongol forces under a certain Kazil Manjuk (Mangqal Türkän?) made a renewed advance on the strongholds defying the Mongols in Khorasan and Ghur. He passed Herat and approached Tulak and Saifrud, and found both places deserted. He set out in pursuit of the Saifrud, garrison intercepting it along the Argehand River. The enemy group dispersed and fled into the mountains.

Dörbei Doqsin crossed the Sindhu for a second time. The Mongols first took Nandana and then began to besiege the larger Multan. With no stones in the immediate area, the Mongols quarried elsewhere and shipped the stones by boat to Multan. They breached the wall, but due to the heat decided to fall back due before the city was finally taken. The siege had lasted for 42 days (March–April 1224). They returned to the north via Ghazni.

Mongol forces remaining in Khorasan made a raid towards Rayy and Tabriz, and overcame some Khwarezmian forces. Ibn al-Athir says 3,000 Mongols fought against 6,000 Khwarezmians on this occasion. Perhaps it was the band of Inanch Khan? Nasawi places a battle involving this leader in Jurjan, in February 1224. Inanch Khan fled, but was soon afterwards poisoned by a lord in Persia after asking for this lord's

---

2   Probably the officers whom, Nasawi will have it, led the Mongol forces in Khorasan in 1221.
3   The siege is said to have lasted 15 and a half months, presumably taking a starting point from when the Mongols first arrived in the region.

mother in marriage. It was perhaps also at this time that the Mongols besieged and took Ustunavand (or perhaps Firuzkoh) near Rayy, an effort Juvaini says took five or six months. Rukn al-Din was in that place captured and killed. The Mongols again took Rayy and approached Qum and Qushan. Pursuing Khwarezmian forces, the Mongols defeated them near Rayy and Tabriz. Juvaini makes reference to an advance by Dörbei towards central Persia. Perhaps the forces of Dörbei made the foray towards Rayy before returning to Mongolia (though late rather than early 1224)?

For Temüjin the main operations were over. He was obviously keen to capture Jalal al-Din, but the Mongol detachment did not push deep into India as Sübe'etei and Jebe did into Iran. The Mongols later found the Delhi Sultanate able to offer very effective resistance, but at this point it seems the climate was the main challenge. Jalal al-Din appeared at Isfahan towards the end of 1225, having moved along a southern route. He later established himself in Tabriz, the westernmost 'tip' of the old Khwarezmian realm. As predicted by Temüjin he was still a force. His second career from 1225 to 1231 was remarkable, but he never became more than a minor player and never came close to his father's old core territory. Temüjin had crushed Khwarezm for good. In 1230, Mongol officer Chormaqan Noyan led a new army to the Near East and quickly dispersed the forces of Jalal al-Din. The refugee prince was killed in 1231. Brave and energetic, Jalal al-Din finally outlived Genghis Khan by about four years.

The sustained effort of the Mongols against so many different fortresses during 1222 and 1223 is really remarkable. Also remarkable is the continued resistance offered by the locals. The weak leadership of Khwarezm imploded quickly, but an endless line of Turkish and other leaders continued to resist, either from fortresses or even in the open. Ibn al-Athir reflected on the Mongol invasions some years later. He wrote: 'Nothing like this has ever been heard of before. Alexander, who is agreed by historians to have conquered the world, did not conquer it with this rapidity. He only conquered it in about ten years and did not kill anyone. He merely accepted the allegiance of people. In about a year these men conquered most of the known earth, its fairest part and the most civilized and populated and of its inhabitants the most equitable in manners and conduct.' He was unable to recognise the true state of affairs in Transoxiana, Khorasan, and Afghanistan. The Mongols operated in a 'failed-state' environment.

Temüjin attacked Xia in 1226. During the summer of 1227 he fell ill and died. Before dealing with these campaigns in detail, the focus is shifted to Sübe'etei.

Sources: the *Secret History*, 265; the SWZQL, 76a–78a; Rashid al-Din, 377; *Yuanshi* 1, pp.37–38; Juvaini pp.137–138, 141, 165–166; 474–476; Nasawi, *Histoire du sultan Djelal ed-Din*, pp.117–121, 140–163; Juzjani, pp.992, 1042–1079; Ibn al-Athir, p.203; Ulug Big, *The Shajrat ul Atrak*, pp.147–162, 186–191; Raverty, pp.1054–1055, 1080; Emil Bretschneider, 'Si You Ki, Travels to the West of Kiu Ch'ang Ch'un' in *Medieval Researches from Eastern Asiatic Sources; fragments towards the knowledge of the geography and history of central and western Asia from the 13th to the 17th century* (Ludgate, 1888); Barthold, *Turkestan down to the Mongol invasion*, pp.447–458; Hamadani, *The Frontier Policy of the Delhi Sultans*, pp.55–56.

Part II

Sübe'etei

28

Sübe'etei

Sübe'etei Ba'adur spoke: 'I shall be a rat, and with the others I shall hoard up goods for you; I shall be a black crow, and with the others I shall gather for you all that is found outside; I shall be a felt covering, and with the others I shall try to make a cover for you; I shall be a felt windbreak, and with the others I shall try to shelter you from the wind on your tent!'

– the *Secret History*, 124

Wanyan Heda emerged as the senior Jin commander. For years he held off the Mongols. When he was finally defeated and captured in 1232, he was taken before the senior Mongol leaders. Amongst them was Ögödei, who had succeeded Genghis Khan, and Tolui. It was not, however, the sons of Genghis Khan who interested Heda. He asked to have Sübe'etei pointed out to him before facing his executioner. Sübe'etei stepped forward, asking: 'You have not a moment to live. What do you wish of me?' The captive answered: 'It is not chance but destiny that makes conquerors such as you. Having seen you, I am ready to die.' This is not how the meeting between Napoleon and captured Austrian general Mack played out in 1805! Heda was executed. Though not the formal commander of the Mongol forces, Heda appreciated who had been his real opponent.

Wang Yun was an important official of the Yuan (Mongol) dynasty in China, receiving his first appointment in 1268. He wrote a biography about Sübe'etei's family, covering in addition to Sübe'etei his son Uriangqadai and grandson Aju.[1] Aju was born in 1234 and was a near contemporary of Wang Yun. Wang Yun must have known Aju and may have got information for the biography from him and other family members. Wang Yun is the only source to say something about Sübe'etei as a person. He says:

---

1 Wang Yun, Wuliang shi xian miao beiming 兀良氏先庙碑铭, Qiuqian xiansheng daquan wenji 秋涧先生大全文集 (Sibu congkan ed.), j.50.

Sübe'etei, who could always hide his real feeling, was very experienced and full of tactics. He was good at commanding troops. He was brave and always courageous. He was also decisive coming across big issues.

Sübe'etei held senior command for more than 40 years. As a commander, he was imaginative and calculating, aiming to manoeuvre the enemy into a position of weakness before contemplating offering battle. He liked to operate with several widely-dispersed columns, but coordinated the movement of each closely. If the enemy forces were stronger, he aimed to divide them and defeat them in detail. If his forces were stronger, he attacked at the same point from several directions. He must have collected a lot of intelligence before initiating operations, especially with regard to geography and the political situation, and he is likely to have learned how to use maps. Sübe'etei had his own ideas about military objectives, having a clear urge to lead the army into unknown territory. How Sübe'etei developed into such a sophisticated strategist and why he had such a longing for conquest and travel is not explained in any source. Jamuqa was known as an intelligent and crafty man, and he also had a liking for strategic manoeuvre to catch the enemy at disadvantage. Perhaps Sübe'etei learned from Jamuqa? How much Sübe'etei may later have taken from the Chinese civilization is unknown. He is unlikely to have learned to read or write, but could have started to use maps after contact with the Chinese civilization and must have developed at least some understanding of the Chinese military tradition.

The relationship between Genghis Khan and Sübe'etei was that of a master and servant. Wang Yun says that 'Genghis Khan appreciated him very much.' He rewarded Sübe'etei generously for his various achievements, but it seems clear that Muqali was regarded as the most senior officer in his service. Sübe'etei, however, was more closely involved in the operations directed by Genghis Khan himself. It seems possible, even likely, that Sübe'etei actually planned the campaigns in 1220, 1226, and 1227. It is not clear how Sübe'etei could have grown into this role, but then very little is known about the inner workings of the Mongol high command.

Sübe'etei showed no talent for administrating the places he conquered. He often left conquered territory unguarded by garrisons, made no known attempt to appoint administrators or to re-establish proper food production. His solution to the food shortage in Kaifeng after the fall of the Jin was to let the people leave the city. He was as a civilian administrator far inferior to Alexander, Caesar, Gustav II Adolf, Napoleon, or Chinese warlords such as Cao Cao, Li Jing, and the contemporary Meng Gong. Genghis Khan also took much greater interest in administrative affairs. Sübe'etei conquered for the sake of conquest. He had no higher purpose.

29

The Early Life of Sübe'etei

He was sent to serve [Genghis Khan] as a hostage at first, and eventually became a senior military officer.

– Wang Yun

Sübe'etei (1176–1248) was from the Uriangqai tribe. According to Rashid al-Din there were two tribes with this name, a 'Mongol' and a 'Forest' tribe. The latter was more 'backward' (herding reindeer etc.). Sübe'etei belonged to the former of these tribes, which lived next to the Mongols in the area just west of the upper Kerulen. His biographies claim his family had an association with that of Genghis Khan stretching back generations. According to the *Secret History*, Sübe'etei first served Jamuqa. If the family of Sübe'etei had really followed that of Genghis Khan, did they leave after Yisügei, the father of Genghis Khan, was killed? Sübe'etei was born in 1176, around the time of Yisügei's death. Sübe'etei's grandfather was Qaci'un Badur. He had two sons called Qaban and Qabul. Qaban in turn had two sons, the older Ca'urqan and the younger Sübe'etei. The *Yuanshi* says they were both 'strong and daring, and good at riding and archery.' They both joined Genghis Khan just after he had broken up with Jamuqa. Sübe'etei was then about 17 years old. Years before, Jelme had come to Genghis Khan. He was a relative of Sübe'etei, a cousin. Old Jarci'udai, the father of Jelme, was a blacksmith.[1]

When Sübe'etei was first married is not known. His oldest son Uriangqadai was born in about 1201, but Sübe'etei might have fathered daughters or non-surviving sons before that. He had a second son called Kököcü. Genghis Khan urged Sübe'etei take leave and return to Mongolia and see his family in 1226; Sübe'etei refused and only finally returned in 1228. He had left Mongolia in 1216 so had been away for 12 years. He departed for another extended campaign in 1230, only returning in 1234. He then set out for Europe in 1236, only returning in 1243. He therefore did not spend much time at home. As Genghis Khan had urged him to return to his family, it seems he did

---

1   Are the *Secret History*'s Jarci'udai and Wang Yun's Qabul the same person?

not bring it along during his campaigns. Uriangqadai is first mentioned as serving with Güyük in Manchuria in 1233, and later took part in the European expedition.

No mention is made of Sübe'etei during the first 10 years in the service of Genghis Khan. When To'oril defeated Genghis Khan in 1203 and the Mongols retreated with a few followers to Baljuna Lake, Qaban brought a food convoy to his camp. En route he was attacked and captured by bandits. Ca'urqan and Sübe'etei came to their father's rescue, and drove off the robbers. Wang Yun writes:

> At the time when the emperor was at Baljuna Lake their father Qaban once took a flock of sheep to feed the emperor. Midway he encountered robbers and was seized [by them]. Ca'urqan and his younger brother arrived straightaway and stuck the robbers with [their] spears and killed them. The rest of the band escaped and fled. And so they extricated [their] father from danger and the food convoy finally reached the emperor. From this [time on] the reputation for filiality and righteousness of the elder brother and the younger brother was [often] heard among the northern tribes.

Sübe'etei was at this time about 27 years old. Ca'urqan and Sübe'etei both became commanders of minghans. The long Sübe'etei biography places this promotion after the Baljuna event, but does not date it. The *Secret History* says Sübe'etei was one of the four roving (hounds) commanders of the whole Mongol army by 1204. Another of these four officers was Jelme. In 1206 the *Secret History* lists both Sübe'etei and Ca'urqan as commanders of a minghan. Not much is known about the career of Ca'urqan. He fought a battle against a Naiman group, throwing them back with a counterattack and pursuing them. The affair is not dated, but could refer to an event during the 1202 campaign. This is the only specific information preserved about Ca'urqan in the field. He may later have ended up in the guard of Alcidai. Certainly the younger Sübe'etei had a much illustrious career.

Sübe'etei re-emerges in the sources under entries for 1211 when the Mongols attacked the Jin. Sübe'etei took Huan. Wang Yun writes:

> The emperor planned to take over Zhongxia.[2] The first attack targeted Huanzhou, a small yet well-secured city, which could not be easily occupied. Sübe'etei bellied forward and took the lead to climb up the wall. The emperor awarded him with a cart of gold coins to show appreciation of his valour.

Huan was one the key outer fortresses guarding the Jin border. Genghis Khan had probably detached Sübe'etei and ordered him to take this place. Sübe'etei also receives mention for a role during the 1213 operations. After the Mongols had made their way around the Juyong Pass, Genghis Khan sent Jebe and Sübe'etei to attack the position from behind. They surprised the defenders and easily secured the position.

---

2   Part of moden Hebei, Shanxi and Inner Mongolia.

This is all that can be said about the early life of Sübe'etei; his career development cannot be followed in any detail. Since at least 1204 he commanded one of the forward units, and it is probable that he played a role in all the campaigns from before 1204 to 1214. The sources are generally brief and leave out minor events. The conquest of Huan must have been considered the most important early achievement, as it is what the biographies chose to mention. The Chinese sources are generally weak with regards to events in Mongolia, but the *Secret History* makes no mention of any episode involving Sübe'etei during those years.

Sübe'etei operated with Jebe in 1213 and again from 1218 onwards. Jebe is often held to be a more senior officer than Sübe'etei, but there is no direct evidence to support this. If anything the Sübe'etei biography suggests that Sübe'etei was more senior. In the biography it is Sübe'etei who commanded the main forces, with Jebe leading the advance guard and it was, as we will see later, Sübe'etei who set key strategic objectives: so possibly he was formally or informally the senior of the two. The Sübe'etei biography may downplay the role of Jebe, and Jebe has no biographer to promote him.

Sources: Wang Yun, p.4; *Yuanshi* 120, pp.2955–2957; 121, p.2976, 122, p.3008; the SWQZL, 64; the *Secret History*, 97, 120; Zhao Hong, p.35; Rashid al-Din, 119; Martin, *The Rise of Chingis Khan*, p.160; Cleaves, 'The Historicity of the Baljuna covenant', pp.406–407; Buell, 'Sübötei', in de Rachewiltz, *In the Service of the Khan*, p.13–14, 17.

Overview: Circling the Caspian Sea, 1216 to 1224

When Sübe'etei set out with his army from Mongolia in 1216 he probably did not know much about the Caspian Sea and the world around it. Muslim traders travelling along the Silk Road could have provided him with some information, but when he started he had the relatively limited objective of eliminating Qudu and the Merkits who had escaped from the Mongols last in 1208. However, the military aim kept expanding. Some of the Merkits fled to the Kipchaks living beyond the Volga River. Sübe'etei therefore attacked the Kipchaks. This took the Mongols westwards along the northern border of Khwarezm. Unwilling to accept this intrusion, Khwarezm attacked the Mongols. Genghis Khan led his full forces against Khwarezm in 1219. Muhammad II, the ruler, fled into what is now central Iran with Sübe'etei and Jebe in pursuit. Jebe had operated with Sübe'etei since late 1218. After they had hunted Muhammad down, Sübe'etei and Jebe headed for Azerbaijan. From there they raided into Georgia before moving north with the aim of falling on the rear of the Kipchaks. In time they moved against the Kipchaks of the Volga region as well as some Kanglis, but first they fought against the Alans, Circassians, Don Kipchaks, Rus, and Volga Bulgars. The Mongol detached force finally rejoined Genghis Khan and the main army somewhere north-east of the Syr Darya in 1224. Gibbon wrote in his 18th century opus *The Decline and Fall of the Roman Empire* that Genghis Khan: 'was joined by two generals, whom he had detached with 30,000 horse, to subdue the western provinces of Persia. They had trampled on the nations which opposed their passage, penetrated through the gates of Derbent, traversed the Volga and the desert, and accomplished the circuit of the Caspian Sea, by an expedition which had never been attempted, and has never been repeated.'[1] James Chambers summarises: 'In two years they had ridden over 5,500 thousand miles, won more than a dozen battles against superior numbers, and returned overloaded with plunder.'[2]

Paul Buell has argued the first part of the campaigns, here dated 1216 to 1219, should be pushed forward to 1208 to 1210, thus splitting events into two discrete sections a decade apart.[3] The campaigns against the Merkits and later Kipchaks–

1 Edward Gibbon, *The history of the decline and fall of the Roman Empire* (London, 1829), vol. 4, p.252.
2 Chambers, p.37.
3 Paul Buell, 'Early Mongol Expansion in Western Siberia and Turkestan', *Central Asiatic Journal*, 36 (1992), pp.1–32.

Merkits are dated between 1215 and 1219 in Chinese as well as Muslim sources, and there is no reason to accept the chronology of Buell.[4] The wide range of years is explained by the fact that Sübe'etei defeated the Merkits on the Chu River in 1216–1217 and only defeated the combined Kipchak–Merkit army in 1218–1219. The *Secret History* says 1205, but clearly 1217 is meant (a 12 year cycle later).

The victory over the Russians in 1223 is one of the best known of all Mongol operations. However, the subsequent raid against the Volga Bulgars is a different matter. Apart from small references in the *Secret History* and the accounts of European travellers, the only source is Ibn al-Athir who clearly says the Mongols were defeated. Many modern historians follow D'Ohsson in saying the Mongols defeated the Bulgars, but the eminent nineteenth-century historian made an error on this point.[5]

Very little information is given about the operations of the Mongols against the Alan, Kipchak, and other tribes in 1222 and 1224. Ibn al-Athir is a key source, but Pétis de la Croix offers much more detail. Presumably he draws on later Turkish or other Near Eastern historians. With regard to the 1224 campaign he is corroborated by Raverty. Understanding what later Muslim sources might add to the narrative of Ibn al-Athir and the Rus Chronicles, is a subject worthy of further study.

---

4   See de Rachewiltz commentary on the *Secret History*, pp.1045–1050.
5   C. A. Macartney, *The Magyars in the Ninth Century*, p.160, note 3. Buell, making no error, says the Mongols were 'roughly treated', *Sübötei*, p.19.

30

Defeat of Qudu's Merkits

When he sent him on his mission, Činggis Qan had the following verbal message conveyed to Sübe'etei: 'And again, I send you to cross high mountain passes, to ford wide rivers; mindful of the long distance you have to cover, you must spare the army mounts before they become too lean and you must save your provisions before they come to an end. If a gelding is already completely exhausted it will be of no use to spare it then; if your provisions have already completely run out, how can you save them then? There will be many wild animals on your way: when you go, thinking ahead, do not allow your soldiers to gallop after and hunt down wild animals, nor let them make circular battues without limit. If you make a battue in order to give additional provisions to your troops, hunt with moderation. Except on limited battues, do not allow the soldiers to fix the crupper to the saddle and put on the bridle, but let the horses go with their mouths free. If they so discipline themselves, the soldiers will not be able to gallop on the way. Thus, making this a matter of law, whoever then transgresses it shall be seized and beaten. Send to us those who transgress our order if it looks that they are personally known to Us; as for the many who are not known to us, just cut them down on the spot.

– the *Secret History*, 199

Küclüg and Qudu fled across the Erdis River with the remains of their forces back in 1208. At that time Genghis Khan made no attempt to hunt them down. In a twist suitable for a dubious soap opera, Küclüg subsequently seized the throne of West Liao (reigned 1211–1217). Qudu led the Merkits further westwards, settling along the Chu River on the other side of West Liao. His motives for remaining apart from Küclüg are not known, but he was perhaps not on friendly terms with his former ally.[1] Genghis Khan sent Toqucar with 2,000 men to Karluk territory in 1211, tasked to keep watch on the western border. Toqucar had probably taken over Jelme's position as a roving commander. In Muslim lore, Toqucar is held to have married a daughter of Genghis Khan. Possibly, he was the Onggirad Aqutai, a son of Alci. Alci was married to a

---

1   Khwandamir says 'Toqtoqan … also joined Gushülüg', but later left him 'and went to Qam Kämchik.' He says Genghis Khan decided to deal with Qudu after learning that he had left Küclüg.

daughter of Genghis Khan. Yedu Buqa Taishi, the son of Jelme, may have commanded the second minghan.[2] There is no record of any confrontation between Toqucar and Küclüg. Together with the Karluks and Uighurs, Toqucar was perhaps strong enough to deter attack. Küclüg for his part engaged in a small war against Muhammad II of Khwarezm, his south-western neighbour, when instead he should have been looking for allies to back him in the inevitable future confrontation with the Mongols. Küclüg also had to deal with revolts in the Tarim region.

On his return from China, Genghis Khan held an assembly along the Tu'ula River. He was now determined to deal with Küclüg and Qudu. Sübe'etei volunteered to lead the expeditionary force tasked to hunt down the Merkits. Jebe was ordered to deal with Küclüg.[3] Küclüg had quarrelled with the Almayak leadership, who in summer 1216 asked the Mongols to support them. This was quite likely the trigger for the Mongol actions and the primary objective. At this stage, Genghis Khan was perhaps a little unsure about Sübe'etei's ability to handle bigger responsibilities. This may explain why he felt obliged to give Sübe'etei very detailed instructions. He told him how to manage horses, collect supplies, and deal with offenders of the law.

In January 1216 Yelü Liuge, the Khitan pro-Mongol leader in Liaodong, came to pay his respects to Genghis Khan in person. He brought his eldest son Yelü Xuedu, who took service in the Mongol army. He commanded a minghan, perhaps serving under Sübe'etei, and is the officer called *Taisi* in Persian and European sources.[4] It is not clear who were the other commanders with Sübe'etei.[5] Jebe may have commanded the units of Megetü and Kökö in addition to his own.[6]

West Liao had been a powerful state. Credited at its peak with 84,500 households, it could raise large forces. To a core consisting of Khitan and other exiles, perhaps 10,000 men, West Liao had added auxiliaries from the regional nomad tribes. They were able to operate with great tactical skill. Michal Biran says 'the greatest victory, at Qatwan, was achieved after their separate contingents managed, acting together, to encircle the enemy troops, squeeze them into a narrow wadi and then defeat them.' West Liao at times made use of elephants in war. In 1210 West Liao was crippled after first losing a battle against Khwarezm and subsequently seeing the capital sacked. A portion of the West Liao forces ended up in Khwarezm service. The state was further weakened when the Uighurs and Karluks broke away and accepted Mongol authority.

Küclüg and Qudu led Naiman and Merkit tribesmen respectively, bolstered presumably by any tribesmen not able or willing to accept Mongol rule. Küclüg is reported to have had 8,000 men before he became ruler of West Liao. He could

2   Later when Toqucar died, Borgei took command of his forces. Nasawi mentions an officer called Yerka. Even the Taisi whom Juvaini says went to Merv in early 1221 could be him.

3   It is not certain that Jebe set out at the same time as Sübe'etei. The SWQZL says he set out one year later, but the chronology of this source is less secure for this period.

4   'Taisi' means 'crown prince' in Uighur script. See Boyle's note in Juvaini pp.144, 163, and 172 (though the second of these may be a mix up with the son of Jelme).

5   Later Qush Temür was left to guard a rear camp in Khorasan in 1220, and at Kalka in 1223 an officer called Cugur is mentioned.

6   Guo Dehai served under Jebe and was later with Kökö in China.

afterwards add more forces to this total, but probably commanded a nomad-type army rather than the more sophisticated force the earlier West Liao are credited with.

Sübe'etei set out during the autumn. He first headed for the territory of Arslan Khan where he linked up with the 2,000 horsemen of Toqucar. Pushing westwards, Sübe'etei finally reached the Chu River.[7] With 5,000 or more men, the Mongols probably outnumbered the Merkits. He needed to find a way to get close to the Merkits without being detected, and so resorted to guile. He sent Toqucar ahead with a detachment.[8] The plan was for him to drive the Merkits into flight. The Merkits left their families behind to move quicker, but Sübe'etei intercepted them anyway: perhaps he had outflanked the Merkits with his main body. The Mongols overcame the Merkits after some hard fighting. Most of the Merkits finally surrendered, but Qudu got away (early 1217?). The Merkit lord fled to the Kipchaks in the land beyond the Ural River. Putting more than 1,000 km between himself and the battlefield, he is likely to have vanished from the radar of Sübe'etei for a while. The captured sons of Toqto'a, Cila'un and Chibuq,[9] were executed, but other captured Merkits were drafted into the Mongol army.

The Kangli Ouyas Ozar was master of Almayak and Fulad. Having seen the Uighurs and Karluks successfully declare against West Liao and seek protection from the Mongols, it must have been tempting for Ozar to do the same. He finally did rebel, and Genghis Khan sent Jebe to support him, also calling on the Karluks and Uighurs to provide help. The Uighurs sent 3,000 men and the Karluks were capable of fielding even greater forces. Jebe could in total have fielded more than 10,000 men. With the revolts of the Karluks, the Uighurs, and now Almayak, the entire West Liao eastern frontier was crumbling. Trying to reverse the situation, Küclüg marched on Almayak. The somewhat careless Ozar was captured while out on a hunt, and killed. His son Siqnaq Tegin was safely inside Almayak and was in no mood to come to terms with Küclüg. When Jebe approached Almayak, Küclüg retreated. The Mongols continued from Almayak towards Balasagun, the West Liao capital. Possibly, Küclüg unsuccessfully tried to hold them off in a pass just east of the capital. Carpini speaks of a battle fought in a 'narrow valley between two mountains.' The sister account, *The Tartar Relation*, adds details, saying the Naimans held a pass. Some Mongols 'crossed the mountains at a lower point a long way from the army' and 'others climbed the precipices where only mountain goats find a way.' The Naiman army was surrounded and 'assailed from every side.' Küclüg is said to have had 30,000 men, but that seems much too high.[10] Sübe'etei could at the same time have approached Balasagun from the western side though the sources say nothing about any such coordinated movement

---

7   Location given by the SWQZL as 堊河. Wang Yun and the *Yuanshi* offer 蟾河, a mix up with the 1209 battle between the Merkits and Uighurs. The SWQZL is the only source to differentiate between the 1209 and the 1217 battle locations.
8   Assuming he is Aliju of *Yuanshi* 121 and Wang Yun.
9   Buell suggests he might be the same as Majar.
10   Even if he had more men than Jebe, he might have worried that some of the non-Naiman forces were ready to defect.

between the two Mongol armies.[11] What is known is that Küclüg fled into the Tarim Basin where he still controlled a number of cities. Ismail held authority over the more westerly Kosan and Bazehan.[12] He submitted to Jebe and afterwards persuaded many other cities to surrender to the Mongols.

Küclüg lost his kingdom, or most of it, as easily as he had gained it. With small forces and little effort, Genghis Khan pushed his western border all the way to the Syr Darya River. Consider Genghis Khan at this time. He stays in Mongolia, having Samuqa circling Kaifeng, Muqali conquering Liaodong, Dörbei Doqsin dealing with the Tumeds, Jebe romping into West Liang, and Sübe'etei on the Chu River in a thrust that will eventually lead him to the Ural River. Five officers operated at distances of between 500 and 2,000 km from his person. No central command managed such widely spread out forces until after the Industrial Revolution.

Sübe'etei masked his advance by a deceptive scheme in order to surprise the Merkits in their camp. It is possible he moved some months before Jebe so his advance could serve as a cover, keeping the Merkits from giving support to Küclüg. It cannot be read out of the brief accounts in the sources if this was indeed the Mongol strategy, but Sübe'etei is said to have gone out first and he certainly later used such a strategy.

Sources: Wang Yun, pp.4–5; *Yuanshi* 120, pp.2970–2971, 121, p.2976, 122, p.3008; the SWQZL, 72a; the *Secret History* 199; Juvaini, pp.67, 74–77, 174–175; Nasawi, *Histoire du sultan Djelal ed-Din*, p.87; Rashid al-Din, 72, 107, 158, 310, 331–333, 337–338; Khwandamir, *Habibu's-Siyar Tome Three: The Reign of the Mongol and the Turk*, translated by W. M. Thackston (Cambridge, Mass.: Harvard University, 1994), p.14; Carpini, p.57; *The Tartar Relation*, p.58–60; Christopher Dawson, *The Mongol Mission: Narratives and letters of the Franciscan missionaries in Mongolia and China in the thirteenth and fourteenth centuries. Transl. by a nun of Stanbrook Abbey* (London: Sheed and Ward, 1955), pp.19–20; Barthold, *Turkestan down to the Mongol invasion*, pp.402–403; Martin, *The Rise of Chingis Khan*, pp.220–225; Paul D. Buell, 'Early Mongol Expansion in Western Siberia and Turkestan', *Central Asiatic Journal*, 36 (1992), p.11, note 30; Biran, *The Empire of the Qara Khitai in Eurasian History*, pp.79–86, 146–160.

---

11   On many other occasions the Mongols organised such converging attacks, for example, in the westernmost Jin provinces in 1227 or Transylvania in 1241. It could be his forces that crossed the mountains 'a long way from the army'.
12   Kasan and Akhisikath?

31

The Hunt for Küclüg

Genghis Khan ordered Ismail to be a vanguard under command of Jebe to attack Naimans. They won and killed … Küchlüg. Jebe ordered Ismail to take Küchlüg's head and show around the region. All other cities like Kashgar, Yarkand, [and] Woduan[1] surrendered.

– *Yuanshi*, 120

Sübe'etei and Jebe probably rested during the summer of 1217. Küclüg remained at large in the Tarim region. Sübe'etei was perhaps during this period been able to inform his master that Qudu had fled to the Kipchaks, and Genghis Khan sent a messenger to them demanding that they hand Qudu over. The Ölbari clan took their name from a mountain located somewhere between the Volga and Ural Rivers. The Ölbari was the dominant house of the Kipchak tribes living in the plains between these two rivers, but the extent of their power is not known. They had migrated out of Inner Asia (Mongolia) less than a century before. Yinasi, an Ölbari leader,[2] received the Mongol embassy, who gave the following message from Genghis Khan (as transcribed by Chinese annalists): 'Why do you hide my stag who carries my arrow in his back? Give him back immediately, least disaster befall you!' Yinasi replied: 'A bush can save the life of a finch who has fled from the hawk. In my opinion, it is better for me to be the bush.' He evidently assumed that Genghis Khan was in no position to enforce his demand. This was a major miscalculation. Yinasi, like Muhammad II, assumed that the Mongols were too far away to present a serious threat.[3]

The main focus of the Mongols at this point was to finally eliminate Küclüg. This was the task of Jebe. In early 1218 Genghis Khan also sent an embassy and a caravan to Khwarezm. The *Secret History* and the SWQZL make mention of iron used to strengthen the wheels. Possibly, Sübe'etei added this cover to the caravan cart

---

1   South Tarim Basin.
2   Yanasi could be the same as Ikran/Kadr, the Kipchak lord who was the father of Terken Khatun, mother of Muhammad II of Khwarezm. This might also be the Euthet of Julian.
3   It is here assumed the ambassador to the Ölbari was sent in 1218. It could also be that the ambassador went with the Mongol army when it set out against the Kipchaks late in 1218 and that this exchange happened just before the Mongols attacked (say, December 1218).

wheels to make them stronger. Genghis Khan's objective was presumably to win over Muhammad as an ally or at least to keep him quiet while the Mongols dealt with Küclüg and the Kipchaks.

Küclüg was in Kashgar. Genghis Khan tasked Ismail to command the advance guard of Jebe, a prestigious assignment; he could have commanded a unit of 1,000 men raised locally. The Mongols set out late in 1217. The population in the Tarim did not support Küclüg, due at least in part to his hostile policy towards Islam. Jebe exploited the situation, treating well those who surrendered and by declaring religious freedom for all. Ismail and Jebe chased Küclüg out of Kashgar, and in February 1218 inflicted a defeat on him at a place called Salihuan or Sariq Qun. According to a later source they actually fought two battles: most of Küclüg's men and his family were captured and massacred in the first. A few days later there was a second battle, after which the Mongols tracked down and killed the Naiman prince in the Pamir Mountains. Kashgar, Yarkand, Khedan, and other cities surrendered to them. Most of these were cities on the famous Silk Road which for centuries had linked Europe with China.

The Mongol conquest of West Liao was complete. The kingdom had imploded and the Mongols were hardly challenged from a military point of view. Jebe is usually held to have conquered West Liao in a single blitzkrieg strike, but it seems clear from the *Yuanshi* that there was a pause between the first and second phase of this campaign. The pause may reflect Genghis Khan's determination to control each stage of the operations, even though he was far away. Surely the Mongols could have finished off Küclüg in early 1217 had they immediately struck into the Tarim? Küclüg had emerged as an independent leader after his father was killed in 1204. He had been involved in battles against the Mongols in 1204, 1206, 1208, 1217, and twice in 1218. All six battles were defeats. He ruled over West Liao for seven to eight years. It is unlikely he had any idea how to manage a state with a significant sedentary population, but surely he could have spent this time finding allies. As it was he did nothing to challenge the 2,000 Mongol horsemen stationed with the Karluks from 1211 onwards and could do nothing against the army of Jebe, hardly much more than 10,000 men. Perhaps Küclüg should have accepted the overlordship of Muhammad II in 1211 in return for aid against the Mongols.

The Tumed revolt described in chapter 24 had some repercussions. Temüjin had asked the Kirghiz tribe to help deal with the rebel tribe. Not only was the request refused, but the Kirghiz afterwards rebelled as well. Temüjin sent an army under the command of his son Joci to deal with them in late 1217: Oyirat leader Quduqa Beki submitted first, leading the Mongols to the camp of his people along the Delger and Kaa Kem Rivers. The so-called Forest Tribes all submitted. The SWQZL lists the Kirghiz, the Ursut, Qabqanas, Telengs, and Kesdims. The Ursut lived north of the Kem and the Qabqanas should be placed east of the Ursut; these tribes may have submitted first. The Kirghiz lived five post stations north of the Oyirat, perhaps about 100 km. Buqa commanded the Mongol advance guard: the SWQZL says he 'chased the Kirghiz to the Yimar River.' The Telengs and Kesdims could be placed in the region of modern Gorno-Altai, near the Kirghiz. They could have submitted at around the same time as the Kirghiz. The *Secret History* says the Kirghiz leaders were Yedi Inal, Aldi Er and Örebek Digin. This source also lists the Qangqa and Tuba amongst the tribes subjected. They may have lived even further north or west.[4] The Mongols gained an easy victory over foes that like the Tumeds lived in difficult terrain, but it seems the Forest Tribes were not really willing to fight. By summer 1218 Joci probably moved south-west to link up with Sübe'etei and Jebe in the western region.

Sources: *Yuanshi* 120, pp.2970–2971, 128, p.3131; the SWQZL, 73b, 74b; the *Secret History* 199, 239; Juvaini, p.66; Rashid al-Din, 158, 335–336; Aboul Ghazi Buhadur Khan, p.102; *The Tartar Relation*, p.72; Barthold, *Turkestan down to the Mongol invasion* pp.402–403; Allsen, 'Prelude to the Western Campaigns', *Archivum Eurasiae Medii Aevi*, 3 (Wiesbaden: Harrassowitz, 1983), pp.5–24; Peter Golden, 'Cumanica II, The Ölberli', *Archivum Eurasiae Medii Aevi*, 6 (Wiesbaden: Harrassowitz, 1986), pp.5–29; Buell, *Early Mongol Expansion in Western Siberia and Turkestan*, pp.4–7; D. S. Benson, *Six Emperors, Mongolian aggression in the thirteenth century* (Chicago, 1995), pp.169–170; Rulin Han, 'The Kirghiz and neighboring tribes in the Yuan Dynasty', in Luo, Xin, *Chinese Scholars on Inner Asia* (Bloomington, 2012), pp.353–410; Yaroslav Pylypchuk, Монгольское завоевание владений восточных кыпчаков и Волжской Булгарии, *Военное дело Золотой Орды: проблемы и перспективы изучения – Казань*, 2011 –С, pp.143–156; Z. M. Buniyatov, *A History of the Khorezmian state under the Anushteginids 1097–1231* (Samarkand: IICAS, 2015), p.108; Dambyn and Dambyn, *Chinggis Khaan: A historic-geographic atlas*, pp.38–39.

---

4   The Buriyat and Barqun, also listed in the *Secret History*, should be placed east of Baikal Lake and can hardly have been near Joci.

32

Rendezvous on the Irghiz River

[Sübe'etei] fought with the Kipchaks in the Yu Valley, and defeated them.

– Wang Yun

Genghis Khan ordered Sübe'etei to attack the Ölbari Kipchaks and finally to dispose of Qudu and the remaining Merkits. Jebe and Joci operated with him, bringing the Mongol forces up to at least 14,000 men.[1] The minghan commanders should have included Sübe'etei, Jebe, Toqucar, Yedu Buqa Taishi, Yelü Xuedu (Taisi), Ismail, Qunan, Möngke'ür , Kete, Bodai, and perhaps Megetü and Kökö.

The Mongol embassy reached Khwarezm in the second quarter of 1218, delivering the message that Genghis Khan would like to establish good relations with them. Juvaini says Sultan Muhammad II 'summoned one of Genghis' envoys, a Khwarezmian, appealed to his patriotism and demanded to know whether Genghis had indeed conquered North China. The envoy's confirmation of this fact led Muhammad to accept Genghis Khan's peace offer.'[2] In the summer the Mongol trade caravan arrived at the border town Otrar. The governor of Otrar, Gayir Khan,[3] seized the goods and killed the merchants.[4] Juvaini says a 'camel-driver ... who had gone to one of the (public) baths' was able to escape and (in time) make his way back to Mongolia to give Genghis Khan the dreadful news. Around September Genghis Khan sent an embassy to Muhammad to demand compensation, showing considerable restraint considering

---

1   Sübe'etei, Jebe, and Toqucar had 10,000 men in 1220 and Joci had a 4,000-strong personal guard.
2   The ambassador was Mahmad Yalavac. He could be the Mahmud Bay who was West Liao chief-vizir before 1211, though this is only speculation. Mahmad Yalavac later became an important Mongol official.
3   Juvaini says he 'was a kinsman of the Sultan's mother.' He was perhaps her brother or half-brother. He is also called Inalchik, Alp Derek, and Kadr Khan.
4   The caravan episode is not clearly dated in the texts. The *Yuanshi* says June–July 1219, which cannot be right. It dates many of the later events in the west a year too late. Summer 1218 seems most likely. No date is given in the Muslim sources, though the event is generally placed before Genghis Khan sent Sübe'etei and Jebe across the Altai.

what had happened. Muhammad seems likely to have sanctioned the act of Gayir Khan or at least sanctioned it after the fact. The thinking is not clear.[5]

Sübe'etei, Jebe, and Joci marched westward along the northern border of Muhammad's domain, through Kangli territory – perhaps November 1218. The Kangli lived along the Chu and Talas Rivers and are credited with having 10,000 tents. To get to Kipchak territory the Mongols needed to cross the Ural River.[6] The battle that eventually followed was fought somewhere near the Irghiz River,[7] well east of the Kipchaks, so it seems likely the Mongols first entered Kipchak territory and then fell back trying to tempt the Kipchaks into following them. The aim of the Mongols would have been to draw them forward and not to accept battle until they had a favourable opportunity. This is what Sübe'etei and Jebe later did in Georgia in 1221 and against the Rus in 1223. Sübe'etei defeated the Ölbari Kipchaks and the remaining Merkits; Qudu was killed during the battle or just afterwards. The Mongols captured the youngest son of Qudu, called Qaltoqan, an expert archer. Joci wanted to spare him, but his father later insisted that he was killed. The Mongols set out in pursuit of the defeated forces. A part of their forces remained behind to guard the camp and the spare horses.

The Kanglis were closely aligned with Muhammad, in whose army Abdul Ghazi Bahadur Khan says 50,000 to 60,000 of their fighting men served. The Kanglis are likely to have complained to Shah Muhammad when the Mongols crashed through their territory, as Muhammad left Samarkand for Jand in order to find out what was going on. Getting additional intelligence, he judged the army he had at hand too small to challenge the Mongols and therefore returned to Samarkand and Bokhara to gather more men. He was ready to leave Bokhara with the army just when the second embassy of Genghis Khan arrived around December 1218. The embassy was dismissed without any offer of compensation: Muhammad had decided on war. As the embassy needed several months to get back to Mongolia, Genghis Khan would only know this later.

Returning to Jand, Muhammad marched boldly into the plains, reaching the Irghiz River around April 1219. Breaking ice made it impossible to cross, so Muhammad had to wait on the riverbank for some time. After leaving Jand he had marched for four months and covered about 1,200 km, and his sudden appearance clearly surprised the Mongols. After crossing the river he was able to overrun their rear camp – Ibn al-Athir says 'woman, children and baggage train' – and immediately afterwards passed the battlefield where the Mongols had some days earlier, or perhaps even just a day

---

5   Juvaini says Inalchik was insulted by an Indian in the caravan and then acted. He sent a message to Muhammad, but there is no mention of an approval for his action before the act. Ibn al-Athir says Muhammad gave the order to kill the traders and seize the goods.

6   Benedict the Pole says: 'a river named Yaralk where the land of the Kangites begin.' Yaralk is the Ural, so to get into Kipchak territory the Mongols needed to approach or even cross that river.

7   The battle against the Kipchaks and the subsequent battle against Muhammad were fought very close to each other. Nasawi places these battles near the Irghiz. Juvaini speaks of the Qaili and Qaimich. Boyle, citing Minorsky, speculates this could be the Irghiz and the Turghai.

before, crushed the Kipchaks. Informed about the new threat, Sübe'etei, Jebe, and Joci quickly turned back to confront Muhammad.

The Mongols leaders did not see any need to fight the Khwarezmian army. They sent an envoy to assure Muhammad that they had no hostile intent and offered to hand over captives and booty in their possession. Muhammad rejected this offer: he was determined to fight. The Mongolians probably had at probably at least 10,000 effectives; Muhammad is credited with having 60,000 men. In reality his total was probably similar to that of the Mongols. Both armies were probably 100 percent mounted. It is possible that Muhammad had relatively more heavy cavalry than the Mongols, though the Kanglis serving with him should be armed much like the Mongols. Joci was on the right and Jebe on the left; Sübe'etei and Toqucar were probably in the centre or in a second line. Muhammad was in the centre with his 20-year-old son Jalal al-Din on his right. There was a small river between the two armies. Joci attacked and crushed the Muslim left. Juvaini writes: 'Joci personally charged the Sultan's left wing, cut it to pieces and forced it to flee in all directions.' Jalal al-Din struck on the other flank, driving Jebe back. Juzjani says about this: 'But an attack by the Sultan's right wing against the cursed's left restored the balance.' *Yuanshi* 121 says 'Jebe fought an unsuccessful engagement' so he is assumed to have been on the left. Most of the Muslim right pursued the Mongols, but Jalal al-Din remained behind, perhaps with his bodyguard, 300 or 700 elite horsemen. Joci, controlling his men better than Jalal al-Din, struck against the Muslim centre, putting Muhammad under pressure. Juvaini writes: 'The whole of the Mongol army attacked the centre where the Sultan had taken his stand. It gave way and had almost been put to flight when Sultan Jalal al-Din came to the rescue from the right wing, where he was stationed with a few horsemen.' In a later conversation Genghis Khan seems to offer relevant details: 'the Muslims … surrounded my first son [= Joci] at Kimach, but Yelü Xieshe took 1,000 men and brought him out in safety, though he himself was wounded by a lance.' Yelü Xieshe could have been with Sübe'etei who could have committed fresh forces to support Joci. The Muslims were checked, but the fighting continued. Ibn al-Athir from his sources adds: 'Some even dismounted from their horses and fought their opponents on foot.' Nightfall ended the fighting.

The *Yuanshi* says Sübe'etei afterwards 'stationed his forces to the east of the river. In order to protect his army from the numerous forces of his counterpart, he ordered each of his men to light 3 torches to make false show of strength. The king fled at night as expected.' The Guo Dehai biography has a somewhat different take on this: 'Because their clothes and flags were identical to that of the enemies, he (= Dehai) decided to burn wormwood as a signal. Smoke and flames spread, the enemy forces fell back. Then they took advantage (of the situation) and beheaded 30,000 (men).' Juzjani and Juvaini say it was the Mongols who retreated first. Ibn al-Athir will have it that Muhammad lost one third of his army. Losses could have been heavy and it is possible that as reported the affair left a deep impression on the Shah. Here was a foe of a far greater quality and determination than he had ever encountered before. Muhammad 'realized his weakness since he had been unable to win a victory over a part of Chingiz Khan's army. How would it be if they all came with their ruler?'

When the ambassador returned around March 1219 to tell Genghis Khan that no compensation was offered, the *Khan* decided on war. Sübe'etei and the other Mongol leaders may have returned to the former West Liao territory by the summer, and by then Genghis Khan should have informed them about his decision to lead a large army against Khwarezm. They are therefore likely to have remained in the west, waiting for the arrival of the main Mongol army. It set out from the Erdis during the autumn, perhaps uniting with the forward Mongol army along the Talas River some two to three months later (around November). Muhammad returned to Bokhara after the Irghiz battle, reaching Bokhara by September). Muhammad completely failed to understand what kind of man he was dealing with. Had he not ordered the caravan to be seized, or had he offered compensation, he could quite possibly have avoided coming under attack. If Genghis Khan intended from the beginning to attack Khwarezm, he would not have sent the second embassy. As it was, he felt compelled to punish Muhammad. The folly of Muhammad brought the Mongols into the Muslim world.

Sübe'etei operated far away from friendly territory, overcoming the Kipchaks and holding off the Khwarezmians. He offered the latter plunder in return for free passage, a ploy he would use again later. He also made use of a fire-deception ploy, a trick well liked by iconic military commanders Sun Bin and Hannibal. The battle against the Kipchaks is known only from one line in the Sübe'etei biographies, so it is hard to say anything about it, whereas the battle against Muhammad can be reconstructed in considerable detail. No other Mongol battle is covered by so many different sources. Even so, much is uncertain and needs to be inferred.

Sources: Wang Yun, 4–5; *Yuanshi* 121, p.2976, 122, p.3008, 149, pp.3511–3514, 3522–3523; Juvaini, p.80; Nasawi, *Histoire du sultan Djelal ed-Din*, p.17; Juzjani, p.272; Ibn al-Athir, pp.206–207; Rashid al-Din, 72–73, 331–332, 346; Dawson, *The Mongol Mission*, pp.58, 81; Abdul Ghazi Bahadur Khan, p.38; Barthold, *Turkestan down to the Mongol invasion*, pp.370–372; Allsen, 'Prelude to the Western Campaigns', pp.5–24; Allsen, 'Mahmud Yalacac', in de Rachewiltz, *In the Service of the Khan*, pp.122–128; Ratchnevsky, *Genghis Khan: His Life and Legacy*, p.122; Golden, 'Cumanica II, The Ölberli', pp.5–29; Pylypchuk, Монгольское завоевание владений восточных кыпчаков и Волжской Булгарии, pp.143–156.

33

The Hunt for Muhammad II and Raid into Georgia

These Tatars had done something unheard of in ancient or modern times. A people emerges from the borders of China and before a year passes some of these reached the lands of Armenia.

– Ibn al-Athir

The name of their leader was Sabada Bahatur.

– Kirakos Ganjakec'i, *History of the Armenians*, 167

The Mongols invaded Transoxiana with vast forces as described in chapter 25. Muhammad II could not possibly dare to challenge them to battle, and key fortresses fell in quick succession. Muhammad was in Balkh with only a small army. Juvaini says he sent 'a patrol from hence to Panjab to obtain news ... When he came to the bank of the river at Termez the patrol came up to report that Bokhara had been taken, and following upon this came the news of the capture of Samarkand.' Muhammad decided to fall back. He set out for Nishapur in Khorasan where he arrived some days later, on 18 April 1220. At the start of May, Genghis Khan, having learned from defectors that Muhammad had fled, detached Jebe, Sübe'etei and Toqucar to hunt down him down. He told them: 'It is necessary to make an end of him ... before men gather around him and nobles join him from every side.' Jebe led a 1,000-strong advance guard, Sübe'etei followed with the main body, and Toqucar brought up the rear. The combined forces were according to the *Yuanshi* some 10,000 men strong. The Mongols crossed the Amu Darya at Kelfit (Panjab), well west of enemy-held Termez. European observer Carpini knew how the Mongols crossed a river:

When they come to any rivers, the chief men of the company have a round and light piece of leather. They put a rope through the many loops on the edge of this, draw it together like a purse, and so bring it into the round form of a ball, which leather they fill with their garments and other necessaries, trussing it up most strongly. But upon the midst of the upper part thereof, they lay their saddles and other hard things; there also

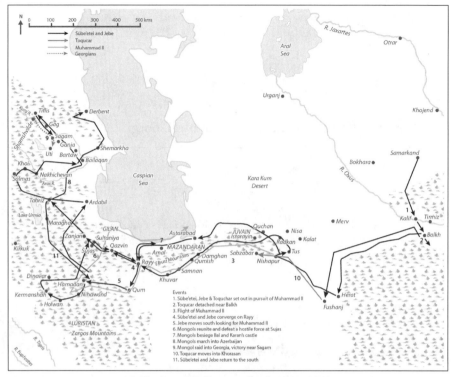

16. Circling the Caspian Sea I, 1220–1222.

do the men themselves sit. This, their boat, they tie to a horse's tail, causing a man to swim before, to guide over the horse, or sometimes they have two oars to row themselves over. The first horse, therefore, being driven into the water, all the others' horses of the company follow him, and so they pass through the river. But the common soldiers have each his leather bag or satchel well sewn together, wherein he packs up all his trinkets, and strongly trussing it up hangs it at his horse's tail, and so he crosses the river.

Ibn al-Athir, drawing directly or indirectly on an eyewitness, seems to confirm that this was precisely how the Mongols crossed the Amu Darya, around 10 May. In Balkh nobody attempted to resist the Mongols: the leadership submitted. Following in the tracks of Muhammad, Sübe'etei and Jebe continued into Khorasan, but Toqucar was left behind at Balkh, almost certainly in line with instructions given by Genghis Khan. Sübe'etei and Jebe extracted a contribution from Herat, making an agreement with local strongman Malik Khan. Genghis Khan accepted his submission. The two Mongol officers also demanded a contribution from Zava (Turbat-I-Haidar), but the official in charge of this place refused to pay up. Juvaini says the Mongols, who at this point lacked supplies, attacked using 'scaling-ladders'. Zava's three citadels fell after a three day siege, and the place was sacked. Muhammad had already left Nishapur on 12 May, probably after learning that the Mongols had crossed the Amu Darya. He went to Rayy by way of Isfarayin. Sübe'etei and Jebe reached Nishapur; outside the city the Mongols destroyed the local governor's bodyguard on 24 May, just after it had left the city.[1] Nishapur refused to admit the Mongols, but was willing to provide supplies in return for their departure (early June 1220). Sübe'etei remained in Khorasan, while Jebe marched via Juvain into Mazandaran with the advance guard. The mother of Muhammad, Turken Khatun, was in a castle near Amul called Ilal; she had arrived there from Urganj, somehow getting through or around the Kara Kum Desert (setting out no later than March 1220). Other family members were inside nearby Karan's Castle. Jebe ravaged the area around Astarabad and Amul; Juvaini says he ordered a 'general massacre' at the latter place. He did not at this point try to attack any of the forts. Sübe'etei, meanwhile, with the main part of the army continued operations in Khorasan. He arrived at Tus having circled to the east, reaching Jam. This detour is best explained by a need to find food and forage. The Mongols occupied Tus: the eastern districts submitted and were according to Juvaini 'at once saved', but in Tus and the country close to the city there was 'slaughter'. They also occupied Radkan, which suffered 'no harm', and Khabushan, where there was 'great slaughter'. Sübe'etei, says Rashid al-Din, 'liked ... [Radkan] ... and did not harass the inhabitants but stationed a *shahna* there.' Presumably he left behind a detachment to guard the camp and the spare horses. Sübe'etei next occupied Isfarayin and Adkan: in both places there was a 'great massacre'.[2] Jebe and Sübe'etei appear to have advanced in line with a fairly tight schedule, approaching Rayy simultaneously from different directions. Sübe'etei must have considered it likely that Muhammad was in Rayy, and his plan was for Jebe to move around Rayy to cut off his line of retreat, while he advanced on the city from the east.[3] Sübe'etei marched along the main road to Rayy, while Jebe crossed the Elbruz Mountains to approach from the north. Sübe'etei passed and occupied Qumish, Damghan, Samnan (Simnan), and Khuvar – in the two last places the Mongols 'slew many people.' People in Damghan fled to the better fortified Girdkuh in the mountains, leaving the Mongols to skirmish with some 'bandits' remaining in the city, where 'some few were slain on either side'. Jebe was the first to approach Rayy, and Sübe'etei arrived soon afterwards. The city was plagued by civil strife with two religious factions fighting against each other. Jebe supported one faction (the Shafi'is) against the other (the Hanifis), gaining entry into the city, and Rayy was partially sacked as the Mongols and their allies attacked the positions held by the other faction. It is reported that 70,000 people were killed, certainly a grossly inflated number.

Muhammad left Rayy well before the Mongols arrived, and headed for the Farrazin and Karaj area where his son Rukn al-Din camped with an army. The governor of Lursitan, Nasrat al-Din Hazarasp, joined Muhammad. It is reported that the army was

---

1   Newly appointed governor Sharaf al-Din, coming from Urganj, had died just before reaching Nishapur. Juvaini says 1,000 fighting men escorted him.
2   Adkan should be the Ardahan of Barthold where Muhammad had sent Taj ad-Din Omar Bistami with 'two chests of precious stones.' Boyle says Adkan is unidentified.
3   Ibn al-Athir reports that the Mongol arrival in front of Rayy was unexpected, evidence perhaps that Sübe'etei aimed to surprise and capture Muhammad inside this city.

20,000 or 30,000 men strong, but in reality it was hardly more than a few thousand men. The news of the sack of Rayy triggered a panic in the Khwarezmian camp and the army quickly dispersed; Rukn al-Din fled to Kerman. In Rayy, Sübe'etei and Jebe divided their forces again. Heading south, Jebe took and sacked Qum: religious factions brought ruin to Qum as before to Rayy. Again Jebe made an alliance with one group, the Shias, attacking the other group, the Sunnis. The Mongol general then continued towards Hamadan. This place submitted and was not plundered. Sübe'etei, meanwhile, approached Qazvin. When Muhammad headed for Qarun, a castle near Hamadan, he encountered some of Jebe's advance scouts, and with the aim of getting away from them fled westwards towards the Zargos Mountains. Behind him the Mongols attacked Qarun, thinking the Shah was still there. When they learned from a guide who had left Muhammad just before, that their prey was heading towards Baghdad, the Mongols broke off the siege and set out in pursuit. Muhammad, however, turned about and headed northwards before they got close to him. Jebe's forces collided with elements of Rukn al-Din's army in the area south of Hamadan. The Mongols overcame all forces encountered and occupied Nihawand, Kirmanshah, Hulwan, and Dinavar (Khurramabad). Muhammad stayed in Serdehan near Sultaniya for a full week; he was now north of Jebe, having successfully eluded his columns, and continued north into Gilan, making his way past Sübe'etei and onwards into Mazandaran. He reached Da-nu-i near Amul and from here sailed to an island, Abi-i-Sugun, off the bay of Astarabad. Jebe marched back northwards. Beg Tegin Silahdar and Kuch-Bugha Khan camped with an army at Sijus: Sübe'etei and Jebe united, and attacked and shattered this force. The Mongols subsequently took and sacked Zanjan, where it was said that they killed twice as many people as in any of the other cities recently taken. The Mongols then turned about and stormed Qazvin. They fought, says Rashid al-Din, 'a pitched battle with the Qazwinis.' The people 'fought with knives', and 50,000 were reportedly killed. This number is impossible, but may be taken to show that it was a bloody affair. A local lord, hostile to Muhammad, told the Mongols where the Shah was hiding. They returned to Rayy, and from here sent forces into Mazandaran. Juvaini says in one place that Sübe'etei personally entered the province; Wang Yun that he blocked the various passes to isolate it. The Mongols began to besiege Karan's Castle and Ilal in August 1220, and Karan's Castle was first taken. Ilal was forced to surrender after running out of water. The region was famous having frequent rainfalls, yet at this time there was no rain for several weeks.[4] The Mongols captured Muhammad's mother, harem, and treasure. Muhammad relocated to another island, remaining outside the Mongol reach, but fell ill and died soon afterwards (at the latest December 1220).

The news that Muhammad had died quickly reached the Mongols, and Sübe'etei and Jebe in turn informed Genghis Khan. Sübe'etei sent the captured valuables as well as Turken Khatun to his master. The *Khan* was highly appreciative. He said: 'Sübe'etei has slept on his shield, he has prevailed in bloody battles and has exposed himself

---

4   Juvaini says after '10 to 15 days no water was left', and that the defenders surrendered soon after. Nasawi says the siege lasted for four months, counting as the start the Mongols first passing the city.

for our house and we are deeply gratified.' He gave him a large pearl and a silver cup. Turken Khatun was later brought back to Mongolia where she died more than 10 years later. Meanwhile, Sübe'etei and Jebe took and sacked Senoravende (Sarchanan) and then rested for a while in that area. Rashid al-Din says that 'the vicinity of the city of Rayy, in the [district] of Kheil-I Buzurg' they experienced 'incredible severe icy weather.' They decided to look for a more agreeable place to rest, heading westwards. The distance to the Mongol main army near Samarkand increased, but 'they were still sending messengers with different current questions [to Genghis Khan]. Because in the [captured] areas the calmness was not yet established, a messenger was guarded by 300–400 horsemen.'

Georgia in the Caucasus and the Seljuks in Anatolia were the dominant powers in the wider region where the Mongols now headed. The Seljuks were nomad Turks, having migrated from the regions north of the Aral Lake and Syr Darya centuries before. They fielded large cavalry forces and were noted for their effective archery fire. Georgia was a Christian state. It was able to field strong cavalry forces, adding to its own forces Kipchak and other nomad auxiliary forces. The Georgian heavy cavalry was well armed and fought with lances; the Georgian horsemen were noted for their shock capabilities and were later able to drive back even the well-armed and well-trained Mamluk horsemen of Egypt. The Kipchaks and other tribesmen would have provided archery fire to support the Georgian heavy cavalry, which the Georgians usually deployed in several lines. Georgia was a well-organised state able to raise and maintain a sizeable army in the field. Under Queen Tamar (reigned 1184–1213) it became stronger, defeating the Seljuks at Basian in 1202 and making a raid past Tabriz to reach Qazvin in 1209. George IV, Tamar's son (reigned 1213–1223), succeeded her. Tamar had appointed the Kurdish brothers Zak'are and Iwvane Zak'arean commanders of the army. Zak'arean still had this responsibility in 1221. There were two weaker Muslim states to the east and south of Georgia: Shirvan and Tabriz. Gushtasb I (reigned 1204–1225) ruled over Shirvan, and the Eldiguzids ruled over Tabriz. The current ruler was Uzbeg b. Pahlawan (reigned 1210–1225). He had submitted to Muhammad II of Khwarezm in 1217.

When Sübe'etei and Jebe reached Tabriz, Uzbeg submitted to the Mongols, paying a ransom, money, and cattle, to avoid an attack on his city. Tabriz marked the westernmost point of Khwarezm. The Mongols continued into the Mugan Steppe where they set up camp. A certain Acouch, a *mamluk* who had served Uzbeg, raised a force of Kurds and Turkomans and took service with Sübe'etei and Jebe. Acouch is reported to have raised 6,000 men, though this seems high. At this point the two Mongol officers may have had over 6,000. An Armenian source credits them with 12,000, supporting the contention that Acouch brought a significant force.[5] The Mongols had headed to the Mugan Plain because they had learned it was a suitable place to rest with horses. Soon after coming there they set out again, marching up the Kura River. Sübe'etei and Jebe headed into Georgia, a state which the Mongols had

5   *The History of Kart'li* credits the Mongols with 12,000 men. Vardan Arewelc'i says that the Mongol army was 20,000 strong.

no reason to attack. The two Mongol commanders were now explorers with an army. Kirakos Ganjakec'i says they 'secured their bags and baggage in the marshy, muddy place which lies between the cities of Bartaw and Belukan' and set out towards Tiflis, the Georgian capital. Ibn al-Athir says they took a fort on the way, but does not name it. The Mongols finally reached Kotman, the plain located in the area just south of the Georgian capital. Atabak Iwvane and King Georgi III Lasha gathered an army in Tiflis. A local chronicler, the author of the *History of Kart'li*, observed that the Mongol army was very lightly armed, presumably in contrast to the Georgians who fielded a strong contingent of heavily-armed cavalry. They are credited with having 60,000 men, but could only have actually fielded a fraction of that. As it was winter, the army is likely to have been relatively small. Perhaps the Mongols had 8,000 men – having left one third behind to guard the camp – against 6,000 for the Georgians, including the contingent of Vardan?

Sübe'etei retreated to the Sagan River, in line with his usual practice of trying to draw the enemy forward. In this case he was playing into the hands of the Georgians, who must have been keen to link with up with the force assembled by Varham in Gag before fighting against the Mongols. The Mongols retreated some 100 km, perhaps over a four to five day period. Iwvane and Varham united and continued pursuit, and encountered them just west of the Sagan River. Grigor Aknerc'i says that 'Varham took the right wing and Iwvane the left.' Sübe'etei detached Acouch to mask Varham. Meanwhile he continued to fall back, making Iwvane believe he was winning the battle; the body sent against Varham aimed only to slow him down. Meanwhile, Sübe'etei drew Iwvane into an ambush. Jebe was in a hidden position with some forces, and once the Georgians passed him, Sübe'etei turned about and Jebe charged their rear. Kirakos Ganjakec'i wrote: 'the enemy had made an ambush, they fell upon the Georgian troops from behind and began to destroy them.' Rashid al-Din says it was Jebe who commanded the hidden Mongol force. Caught between two pincers, the Georgians were quickly routed. Varham had reached deep into the Sagan Plain when he learned about the defeat of his colleagues. Presumably the full Mongol forces were now turning against him. He retreated to seek sanctuary inside K'arherj in Uti (Gardman). Kirakos Ganjakec'i says the Mongols 'gathered booty from the troops and took it to their camp.' They then moved westward again, and reached Shamshvilde just south of Tiflis. They did not try to take the Georgian capital, instead returning to the Mugan Plain. These events can be dated to February 1221.

The Georgians communicated with Uzbeg, proposing that they make common cause against the Mongols. Joint action was agreed upon, but the parties decided to wait for spring before acting. Sübe'etei and Jebe, however, set out again before anything was done. They marched back into Persian Iraq, leaving a detachment to guard their train in the Mugan Plain.[6] Tabriz again provided a contribution: Ibn al-Athir says 'money,

---

6   The Georgians may have made a raid into the Mugan Plain, though if so with small forces (to explain lack of any mention in their own chronicles). Pétis de la Croix says the Georgians attacked after Sübe'etei and Jebe had returned to Persia: 'They entered in the mist of winter into Azerbaijan, to go in search of the Mongols whom the two generals had left there; but they found more troops than expected, for all the garrisons had

clothes and horses'. The Mongols took and sacked Maragha, using the ploy of driving forward Muslim captives during the siege operations to cover their own men. The city was taken in a few days, on 30 March.[7] Ibn al-Athir says the Mongols had planned to cross over the Zargos Mountains into the plains beyond (via the Mosul route, the home town of Ibn al-Athir). Muzaffar al-Din Kukburi of Irbil and Badr al-Din of Mosul assembled a force in the face of the Mongol menace, and the Abbasids sent 800 cavalrymen from Baghdad to reinforce them. The army, in total 6,000-strong, took up position at Daquqa near Kirkuk. It is unlikely that the Mongols intended to cross the Zargos Mountains. Rather they rested in the foothills of the mountains during the summer months, and remained close to the mountain passes for quite some time. It must have been a nervous period for the people of Mosul and the surrounding area. It is quite possible that the Mongols, as Ibn al-Athir writes, retreated to see if they could tempt the Muslim force forward (April 1221).

Muslim strongman Siraj al-Din killed the Mongol official left in Tus and assembled an army, reportedly 3,000 men. Qush Temür was in the area with 300 Mongol soldiers; he was 'in charge of animals.' Coming from Quchan, he 'surprised' and crushed the force raised by Siraj al-Din. Toqucar entered Khorasan with the intent to restore order in the province. He plundered the country around Herat, breaking the treaty Sübe'etei and Jebe had made with Malik Khan. The Mongols attacked and took a place called Fushanj (Ghurian). Toqucar subsequently approached Nisa: the forces inside this fortress made a sortie, killing and officer called Il-Kouch. Even so full Mongol forces afterwards took the citadel in 15 days. Nishapur, however, offered vigorous resistance, making frequent sorties. During one of these, in November 1220, Toqucar was killed, and Yedu Buqa Taishi (Borgei) took command of the tümen. He gave up the siege of Nishapur and instead turned on smaller cities in the region. He also detached some forces to support Qush Temür. Qush Temür took some strongholds near Tus (Juvaini mentions Nuqan and Qar). Yedu Buqa, meanwhile, took Sabzavar after a three day siege from 24 to 26 November. Eventually, Sübe'etei and Jebe called forward the forces left behind in Khorasan including the tümen of Toqucar.[8] This happened at the same time as Tolui approached Nishapur with fresh forces, in March–April 1221.

In 1806, Napoleon's *Grande Armee* defeated the Prussians at Jena and Auerstadt. He followed up these victories with a 'classic' pursuit, overrunning all of Prussia (East Prussia excepted) in three weeks.[9] Sübe'etei and Jebe needed seven months to hunt down Muhammad. However, they secured Central Persia in less than two months after moving over longer distances than Napoleon. Muhammad eluded them and a long time passed with no significant action; it took several weeks to reduce the fortresses in Mazandaran. Napoleon had the advantage of having far larger forces which could spread out to quickly secure the entire enemy territory. He had 30 times

---

joined: and the Georgians, after having been worsted in two encounters, returned to Tifles.' This sounds quite realistic.

7   Raverty says the city was taken in three days. He also says a woman was the ruler and that her base was a fort called Ru-in-dujz, located south of Maragha.

8   *The History of Khorezm*: 'and his troops joined with those of Jebe Noyan and Subedey Bahadur.'

9   David Chandler, *Atlas of Military Strategy* (London: Arms & Armour Press, 1980), p.105.

as many men and needed to secure a territory 10 times smaller. Even so, if the King of Prussia had wanted to elude capture he could have gone into hiding on an island in the Baltic Sea.

Sübe'etei's strategy is a matter of conjuncture, but it does seem that he attempted to trap Muhammad inside Rayy, that the country around Qazvin was secured before the city itself was attacked, and that he spread out his forces to secure the passes into Manzadaran. The Mongols covered their lines of communication, having at one point one detachment in Balkh, one near Nishapur, one near Rayy and one near Hamadan. Thus Genghis Khan had put in place a strategic barrage, splitting Urganj and the western districts from Afghanistan and the eastern regions. Genghis Khan was a master of this kind of strategic deployment, which Napoleon later excelled at. The pursuit of Muhammad was no wild raid, no gamble à la Lee or Rommel. Sübe'etei entered Georgia for unknown reasons, but perhaps aimed to secure his rear before returning to the south. It is one of the better examples of Sübe'etei having the urge of Alexander III to conquer anything close to his line of advance.

Sources: Wang Yun, p.5; the *Yuanshi* 121, p.2976 and 122, p.3008; Ibn al-Athir, pp.210–218; Juvaini, pp.143–147; Nasawi, *Histoire du sultan Djelal ed-Din*, pp.66, 87; Rashid al-Din, 158, 227–228, 380–381; Kirakos Ganjakec'i, *History of the Armenians*, transl. Robert Bedrosian (1986), http://rbedrosian.com/kg1.htm, accessed 31 Dec. 2015, p.167; Vardan Arewelc'I, *Compilation of History*, transl. Robert Bedrosian (2007), http://rbedrosian.com/vaint.htm, accessed 31 Dec. 2015, p.84; Grigor Aknerc'i, 'History of the Nation of the Archers', translated by Robert P. Blake and R. N. Frye, *Harvard Journal of Asiatic Studies*, 3-4 (1949), p.291; Munis, Munis, and Muhammad Riza Mirab Agahi, *The History of Khorezm*, translated by Yuri Bregel (Leiden: Brill, 1999) p.84; Carpini, p.74; Pétis de la Croix, pp.277–279, 287, 323–224; Raverty commentary, pp.990–997; Barthold, *Turkestan down to the Mongol invasion*, pp.420–427; Bedrosian, *The Turco-Mongol Invasions*, note 164; Ryan James McDaniel, *The Mongol invasions of the Near East* (dissertation; San Jose, 2005) pp.52–86; Mamuka Tsurtsumia, 'Couched Lance and Mounted Shock Combat in the East: The Georgian Experience', *Journal of Medieval Military History*, XII, 2014.

34

Across the Caucasus Mountains

Sübe'etei volunteered to start a punitive expedition against the Kipchaks. [Genghis Khan] approved [the proposal]. So he made a far outflanking move around Guanji Sea [= Caspian Sea], and arrived at Taihe Mountain. Then they paved the way by chiselling the rocks, and appeared unexpectedly [on the other side of the mountains]. Upon their arrival, the emirates [= local tribes] were just having a get-together at Buzu River. Sübe'etei used all his forces to fight. His counterpart simply could not resist, all the territory was afterwards occupied.

– Wang Yun

Sübe'etei asked Genghis Khan for permission to circle the Caspian Sea with his army. His idea was to fall on the rear of the Ölbari Kipchaks. At the same time Joci was moving against the Kipchaks from the eastern side. Genghis Khan accepted the plan (perhaps during the summer of 1221), giving him three years for the mission. The whole idea to strike north from Azerbaijan is one of the most singular found in the annals of war. Imagine Napoleon in 1799 returning from Egypt over Istanbul to fall on the rear of the Austrians! Even this does not capture what Sübe'etei and Jebe did, for they were operating in what for them was an unknown world. Sübe'etei had grown up knowing the geography of the country along the Onon and Kerulen, not the wider world. Presumably he had been able to absorb a lot of information about the western regions and his obviously fertile mind came up with the stunning idea to move around the Caspian Sea. He may have inspired his master, for a few months later Genghis Khan wanted to return home from the Sindhu River by making his way through the Himalayan Mountains. This idea, however, was not practical and no attempt was made to implement it.

Having rested along the foothills of the Zargos during the height of the summer, the Mongols were again ready to restart active operations. They divided their forces with Jebe moving against Hamadan, while Sübe'etei masked Tabriz. Factions hostile to the Mongols, led by Jamal-ud-Din, had taken control of Hamadan. The rebels ventured outside Hamadan to challenge Jebe, but after three days of fighting were defeated. The Mongols found a secret passage into the city, took it, and sacked it

(September 1221). Jebe then marched back north to rejoin Sübe'etei. The Mongols took Ardabil, where Ibn al-Athir says there was 'great slaughter', and passed Sarab on the way to Tabriz. Uzbek – whom Ibn al-Athir says generally 'was lost night and day in wine-drinking' – fled with his family to Khoy, and presumably onwards, leaving al-Tughrai to look after Tabriz. Al-Tughrai told the Mongols that he was prepared to fight if their demands were too high; the Mongols took what they could get and moved on. In the area north of Urmia Lake they took and sacked Selmas and Khoy and extracted a payment from Nakhichevan. They next marched back to Mugan, then moving on, they sacked Bailaqan (November 1221), bypassed the strong Ganja, and again raided across the border into Georgia. Kirakos Ganjakec'i says: 'Once again the king of the Georgians mustered his troops this time more than before, and wanted to battle with the enemy. But [the Mongols] collected their wives, children, and all their bags and baggage, and wanted to pass through the Derbent Gate to their own land' (also November 1221).[1] The Mongols turned their attention northwards and departed from the region.

Sübe'etei and Jebe aimed to cross through the Caucasus Mountains, even though it was winter. Shemakha was stormed and sacked on the way, the Mongols filling the moat with whatever material they could find before launching the assault. Garshasb, the Shah of Shirvan, had fled from Shermakha to Derbent. The fortress of Derbent guarded the route to the north and completely blocked the pass along the coast. Sübe'etei sent a message to Garshasb, telling him that he wanted to negotiate. It is unlikely that Garshasb at this point can have known that the Mongols intended to march north, and he sent ten notables from the city to meet Sübe'etei. The Mongol general selected one of them and had him killed to show the other nine what would happen if they did not do what he wanted. He then told them to lead his army through an inland pass in order to get around Derbent. The Mongols crossed the mountains, perhaps over the Bab al-Abwab Pass, with considerably difficulty; in Chinese lore they cut a road through the snow-filled mountains.[2] When they reached the coast, the Mongols turned south to arrive unexpectedly north of Derbent. According to Rashid al-Din the city submitted, offering them food. Nothing like that had never happened before. Sübe'etei prevailed by a combination of cunning and his traditional outflanking manoeuvre. In unknown territory he found a way to get around a position he did not want to attack frontally. Perhaps the spare horses were left behind, and only brought forward after Derbent was taken.

The only source for the following events is Ibn al-Athir, and there must be some element of hearsay in his information. The Mongols attacked the Lesghians as they pushed westwards, in fact they may have already clashed with these people when they moved around the Derbent Pass. No mention is made of the Qaitaq, Avars

---

1   Drawing on Ibn al-Athir and Rashid al-Din, historians usually hold that the Mongols fought two major battles against the Georgians, but it seems clear that the accounts describe the same battle. Ibn al-Athir, presumably drawing on different sources – speaking to travellers and other visitors coming to Mosul – turned one battle into two or three different ones.
2   According to Pétis de la Croix they needed 15 days to cross the mountains.

(Sarir), Ghumigs or Veinakhs so it seems possible that the Mongols kept close to the mountains, moving perhaps along the Samur River. They headed into Alan territory, the area between the Upper Terek and the Bolshoi Zelenchuk. The contemporary Riccardus wrote about the Alans some years later: 'There are as many counts as villages, and no count accept the authority of another. There is continuous conflict between the counts and villages. During the time of cultivation and harvesting all the men come out armed of the villages in a group.' How many local leaders were involved in the war against the Mongols at this stage is not reported. The Alans assembled an army of unknown size and joined forces with a Kipchak contingent. If correct, the Kipchaks involved must have been the sub-group that lived near the Derbent Pass. These allies then fought the Mongols. Ibn al-Athir says neither 'of the two sides could gain victory'. Sübe'etei may have held his forces back, unwilling to engage in a potentially costly battle. The two sides afterwards remained camped close to each other, and wily Sübe'etei sent an embassy to the Kipchaks. He said, again as rendered by Ibn al-Athir: 'We and you are a single race, whereas these Alans are different from you, to such a degree that they are Christians, and your religion is not like theirs'. He offered the Kipchaks a part of the Mongol booty and spare horses in return for their departure. The Kipchaks accepted the Mongol offer and marched away, and the Mongols were free to deal with the Alans: 'The Tatars fell upon the Alans, killed them, committed excesses, looted, took prisoners.' The Alans are likely to have fled into their many cities and forts, and the Mongols were certainly in no position to reduce many of them at this stage. Ibn al-Athir's short account gives no clues as to the timeline. He says the Kipchaks 'heard no word of the Tatars, not until they had come upon them and entered their lands, where they destroyed them one by one and seized back many times more than they had provided. Those Kipchaks that dwelt far away heard the news and fled a long distance without putting up any fight.' Therefore the Kipchaks first attacked were those nearby, that is, the Derbent Kipchaks. The defeated Kipchaks, or some of them, fled southwards and managed to get past Derbent, getting involved in some fighting with the Georgians later the same year. The 'Kipchaks that dwelt far away' would be the next target.[3]

In *The Art of War*, Sun Tzu held that the second best method for overcoming the enemy 'is to disrupt his alliances.'[4] This is what Sübe'etei did. Niccolo Machiavelli observed: 'Though fraud in other activities be detestable, in the management of war it is laudable and glorious, and he who overcomes an enemy by fraud is as much to be praised as he who does so by force.'[5] Sübe'etei used underhand diplomacy to divide the Alans and Kipchaks and thereby be able to defeat them in detail. To Sübe'etei, like Lenin and Mao Zedong, diplomacy was simply a military tool. He was fortunate

3   Pétis de la Croix has a longer and somewhat different account than Ibn al-Athir: he says the Alans and Circassians both fought against the Mongols. It is not clear what sources Pétis de la Croix used, but probably later Ottoman historians. What he says seems very credible, but the place names given are impossible.
4   Sun Tzu, *The Art of War*, translated by Samuel B. Griffith (New York: Oxford University Press, 1963), p.78.
5   Discourses III, 1517.

to fight foes that were far apart as it would be difficult to repeat the trick many times once people understood his method.

Sources: Wang Yun, p.5; *Yuanshi* 121, p.2976 and 122, p.3008; Julian; Ibn al-Athir pp.215–218; Rashid al-Din, 227–228, 380–381; Kirakos Ganjakec'i, *History of the Armenians*, 167; Riccardus, in Göckenjan, Hansgerd and Sweeney, *Der Mongolensturm*, p.76; *The Galician–Volynian Chronicle*, p.25; *The Chronicle of Novgorod*, p.285; *The Nikonian Chronicle*, p.285; Pétis de la Croix, pp.287, 323–324; J. Fennell, *The Crisis of Medieval Russia*, 1200–1304 (New York: Longman, 1983), p.91; Bedrosian, *The Turco-Mongol Invasions*, note 164; Allsen, 'Prelude to the Western Campaigns', pp.5–24; Peter Golden, 'Cumanica I: The Qipcaqs in Georgia', *Archivum Eurosiae Medii Aevi*, 4 (Wiesbaden: Harrassowitz, 1984), pp.45–87; Allsen, 'The Mongols and North Caucasia', *Archivum Eurosiae Medii Aevi*, 7 (Wiesbaden: Harrassowitz, 1991), pp.5–40; Benson, *Six Emperors*, p.104 ; Ryan James McDaniel, *The Mongol invasions of the Near East*, pp.87–99; Yaroslav Pylypchuk, *Первое вторжение монголов в Восточную Европу* (1222 г.), Степи Европы в эпоху средневековья. – Т. 10. Половецкое время. (Донецк, 2012), pp.325–336.

35

And Quiet Flows the Don

Coming upon them unawares, he encountered their chiefs Yurgii and Tatahaer just as they were meeting on the Buzu River. Their host was caught between a determined pincer movement. In the rout, the son of Yuliji was wounded by an arrow. He took refuge in a forest, but was betrayed by a slave and captured. The remainder of the host surrendered and the country was taken. Reaching the Aliji River, the greater and lesser Michisilao [Mistislav] or the Wolosi [Orus, Russians] were encountered. In one battle, he caused them to surrender. Having plundered the Asut tribe, he returned.

– *Yuanshi*, 121[1]

Kipchak tribes dominated the plains from the lower Danube in the west to the Volga in the east. This was a vast area with various tribal sub-groups dominating different regions. There were, perhaps, four major eastern and four western tribes. The Tuqsuba and Kokobici lived along the Volga, and the Terter-oba and Jetebici lived along the Donetz. These four were the so-called *Wild* Kipchaks. The four other tribes were Itoyli and Urusoba, and the Burcevyci and Ulasevici. The first two lived to the west of the Dnieper River and the other two to the east of it. The dominant leader was Jurij Koncakovic (son of Köncäk), perhaps of the Ölbari. He was perhaps the leader of the Terter-oba. Daniilo Kobiakovich (son of Kobjak) was perhaps of the Qay family. Kötän was another Kipchak lord, linked with the Durut tribe, perhaps a subgroup of the Terter-oba. The Mongols had already fought against the Kipchaks of the Volga region in 1219 and those living north of Derbent in early 1222. Now the Mongols targeted the Don and the central region of the Kipchak territory. Culturally aligned, the Kipchaks did not have strong centralised leadership that could respond quickly to Mongol attacks.

Sübe'etei and Jebe may have spent the summer in the region just north of Derbent, again moving forward only during the autumn. Possibly Jebe marched into Circassian territory. He may have marched to the Black Sea coast and headed

1   Paul Buell's translation.

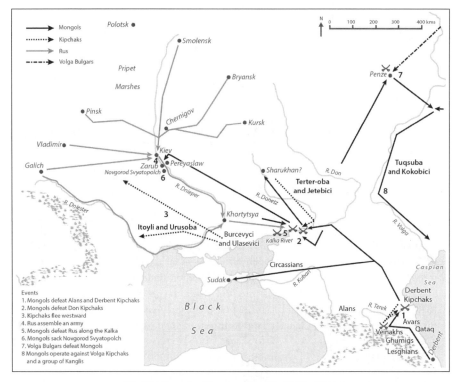

17. Circling the Caspian Sea II, 1222–1224.

northward along the shoreline for the Rus Chronicles record that the Abkbez were also attacked. Meanwhile, Sübe'etei struck against the Kipchaks in the Don River region. The Mongols collided with the Kipchaks close to the Don – probably the Buzu of Chinese sources – defeating them in one or more battles. According to the *Yuanshi* the Mongols struck from two directions: 'Their host was caught between a determined pincer movement.' Perhaps Jebe and Sübe'etei converged on the enemy force as they had done before in Persia. Alternatively, and perhaps more likely, the mission of Jebe was to distract the Circassians and keep them from supporting the Kipchaks. *The Nikonian Chronicle* reports that the Kipchaks were 'unable to resist them and fled – some were being massacred, some driven down the river Don to the bay of the sea where they died, and other being driven to the river Dnieper.' It is also said here that Iurii Konchakovich and Daniilo Kobiakovich were killed (it seems Yuliji and Tatahaer in the *Yuanshi*). *The Galician–Volynian Chronicle* states that: 'When the Polovcians went forth to meet them in battle, Jurij Koncakovic, the senior [prince] of all Polovcians, could not oppose them and fled. And many [Polovcians] were slaughtered, [fleeing] to the river Dnieper.' Amongst those fleeing across the river was Kötän. The Mongols are likely to have plundered the Kipchak settlements at Sarukan, Balin, and Sugrov. Sübe'etei was now master of the region between the lower Dnieper and the Don. A Mongol column, says Ibn al-Athir, marched into Crimeria where Sudaq was taken and sacked (in January 1223).[2] Perhaps Jebe crossed over the Kerch when the water was frozen? The Brodniki, whose leader was Polskinia, submitted to the Mongols and reportedly provided 5,000 men for their army. The Brodniki might have come from the western regions, and they can be described as freelance rowing mercenaries.

Viking settlers known as the Rus had developed cities along the larger rivers in Russia. The major city was Kiev, from where a king had once ruled over all the land. However, the Rus world had long since fragmented into a large number of independent realms. The Vikings quickly assimilated with the local Slav population and by the 11th century Scandinavia was no longer a source for new recruits. The Rus princes maintained small standing armies called *Druzhina*. These were typically well-armed mounted forces. In addition militia infantry could be called out, armed with spears and axes. However, it became increasingly difficult to call out militia and the cost of armour also made it difficult to raise large cavalry forces. Displaced nomads provided a new source of fighting men: these units were called *Chernye Klobuki*. In China, the infantry increased in significance further to the south; in Russia it was the opposite. In the south, armies were mobile and relied on largely cavalry, whereas in the north infantry retained some importance. The Rus cities could be fairly large. Kiev had perhaps more than 30,000 inhabitants and Chernigov did not have much less. It has been estimated that the Rus population had a total as high as 7 million. The cities were fortified, but extensive use of timber made them vulnerable to fire-attacks. A singular feature of the Rus defences was the construction of long trenches, the so-called Snake Ramparts, 1,000 km long, facing mainly south, to guard the borders. There was still construction work ongoing during the 12th century, but the fragmented nature of Rus affairs surely meant that the trenches were now in a poor condition and perhaps not manned at all.

Iurii and Daniilo had been the first and second leader amongst the Kipchaks. Afterwards, Bastyj was the first, Kötän second or third, and Nortz fourth. Bastyj and Kötän sought refuge with the Rus, and sent a message and presents to Mstislav Mstislavich of Galich. The Kipchaks and Rus had historically been bitter rivals, but they had enjoyed different relations in recent times with the Kipchaks supporting one or other of the Rus factions as they fought each other. Kötän was the father-in-law of Mstislav, and the Kipchaks argued to the Rus princes that it was in their own interest to help him. They said: 'Today the Tatars have seized our land. Tomorrow they will take yours.' Remarkably, the Rus princes united in face of the Mongol threat: Mstislav Romanovich of Kiev, Mstislav Mstislavich of Galich, Danilo Romanovich of Volyn, and Mstislav Svyatoslavich of Chernigov, meeting in Kiev, agreed to join forces.[3] The Rus princes and the Kipchaks planned to assemble on the island off Khortitsa, located

2   According to Ibn al-Athir, in 1221 a Seljuk army was shipped from Sinope to Crimeria where Sudaq was taken. A Rus lord led a 10,000 man army, including a Kipchak contigent, against the Seljuks, but was defeated. The two parties made a treaty soon afterwards. Sudaq was subjected to attacks from all sides during this period.

3   The *Lavrent'evskaja Chronicle* reports that Vladimir–Suzdal also sent an army under the command of Vasilko Konstantinovich, the Prince of Rostov, but that it arrived too late to take part in the battle. No mention is made of this in the other sources and it is unlikely to be true. In 1223 Vasily was just 14 years old. He was

on the middle-lower Dnieper, and then move eastward to look for the Mongols. This was a very aggressive response to the Mongol arrival in the Kipchak plains, which after all was far from the various Rus cities. In April 1223 a part of the Rus forces set out from Kiev, while the infantry coming from Galich sailed down river to the Black Sea and then up the Dnieper. The contingent joined the rest of the army at Ochelie, it seems in total 2,000 infantry. The Rus are said to have fielded 30,000 or 80,000 men, but 8,000 in total seems more likely. In addition there were many Kipchaks, though no number is given. *The Galician–Volynian Chronicle* says the Rus were 'joined by the entire Polovcian nation.' Sübe'etei and Jebe sent ambassadors to Kiev and Chernigov to assure the Rus that they had no hostile intent, however the Rus executed the ambassadors at Zarub, before they reached Ochelie. A second embassy arrived, saying that the Mongols took this to be a declaration of war: this embassy was allowed to return unmolested. At this point the Mongol army reportedly numbered 23,000, including the 5,000 Brodniki, but about 15,000 nominal seems more likely (that is, the original 10,000 plus some new units).

A Mongol detachment guarded some cattle near the Dnieper. *The Chronicle of Novgorod* calls the leader of this force Gemya. On 16 May 1223 Mstislav of Galich, leading 1,000 men, defeated, captured, and executed Gemya. The Rus archers were reportedly used to good effect, but possibly it was the Kipchaks who provided the archery fire support. The Rus captured a large amount of cattle. The Mongol context of this engagement is unclear. Was this a rearguard action or an isolated unit caught unprepared? It is reported that the Mongol survivors retreated towards the Cuman Hill (which could be Mount Mohila Bel'mak), perhaps the place where Sübe'etei and Jebe had set up camp. The Rus crossed the Dnieper with their full forces and set out in pursuit. The leaders of the Kiev detachment were most careful, building a fortified camp on the east bank before setting out after the Mongols. Jebe and Sübe'etei retreated eastwards until they reached the Kalka River,[4] where they deployed for battle. Sübe'etei commanded the centre, Jebe the right wing and Yedu Buqa Taisi the left.[5] An advance guard was left on the western side of the Kalka.

On 31 May 1223 the Rus advance detachment clashed with this Mongol advance guard, and there was a short fight during which three Rus lords were killed. The Mongols then fell back across the Kalka; Mstislav Mstislavich decided to cross the river also, and set up camp there, sending forward a Kipchak force – commanded by Yarun – to look for the Mongols. The Rus forces were at this point spread widely. Mstislav and Danilo were on the east side of the Kalka, other forces had not yet crossed the river and Mstislav Romanovich was still a long way from it. Sübe'etei was now ready to strike. It seems likely that he committed his heavy cavalry immediately, and the Kipchak advance force was quickly routed, fleeing towards the Kalka with the Mongols in close pursuit. The units of Danilo, Semjun Oljujevich and Vasilyok Gavrilovich were

---

later captured and executed when the Mongols returned early in 1238. It is not clear if Mstislav Yaroslavich Nenow of Lutsk took part.

4   Probably a side river, the Kal'chik, to the Kal'mius.

5   *The Chronicle of Novgorod* mentions Chigir/Chigyz and Teshi/Teshiu. Yedu could be the latter.

able to deploy, and charged the Mongols, but were checked and forced backwards. *The Nikonian Chronicle* says 'Vasilyok was pierced by a spear.' Mstislav re-crossed the Kalka and ordered the units on the other side to hurry forward. He did not, however, send any message to Mstislav Romanovich. Having rushed units forward, Mstislav hurried back to his camp and attempted to support Danilo, as did Oleg of Kursk. The Rus were able to drive back the Mongols, who may have committed reserve forces at this point. *The Galician–Volynian Chronicle* says that 'other [Tartar] regiments engaged them.' The Mongol archers worked against the Rus flanks: 'the [Tartar] bowmen were showering them relentlessly with arrows.' The Rus forces were overwhelmed. Danilo was wounded, but he managed to escape, and the forces of Chernigov and Smolensk were carried away in the rout. Ibn al-Athir was evidently well informed about this battle. He says: 'Many of the Rus were not prepared for the battle, but a great number of Tatars had come upon them.' The Rus resisted manfully, as attested by their own chroniclers as well as Ibn al-Athir, but the fact that they failed to deploy properly clearly put them in an impossible situation. When he came up, Mstislav Romanovich witnessed the disaster unfolding on the east side of the Kalka and deployed his force in a circle on a hill, covering himself with wagons. Sübe'etei left Yedu Buqa Taisi to mask Mstislav's position, while the rest of the forces pursued the Rus fugitives.

Mstislav Mstislavich and Danilo made it back across the Dnieper. They destroyed the boats they did not use to keep the Mongols following them across the river. Mstislav Svyatoslavich and the contingent from Chernigov retreated northwards, but the Mongols pursued them and destroyed the whole force. Mstislav was killed. The Smolensk detachment, said to be 1,000 men strong, also retreated northwards; it was able to evade the Mongols and reach safety. Yedu Buqa Taisi harried Mstislav Romanovich's camp for three days. On 2 June, during negotiations for the surrender of the Rus – who lacked water – the Mongols successfully stormed the camp and massacred most of them. According to *The Chronicle of Novgorod*, only 1 in 10 Rus got away from these encounters with the Mongols.

Jebe and Sübe'etei crossed the Dnieper in the wake of this victory and sacked Novgorod Svyatopolch, just 20 km south of Kiev on the west side of the river. One of the captured Rus princes, presumably Mstislav Romanovich of Kiev, was sent to Joci. During 1223 Joci had left the plains north of Aral and marched towards Transoxiana, bringing game for his father to hunt. He was perhaps close to the Syr Darya when the Rus captive sent by Sübe'etei and Jebe arrived (perhaps by July or August 1223).

The Mongols gained an easy victory over the Rus by means of the by now well-tested feigned retreat ploy. It is odd not more mention is made of the Kipchaks who only seem to have supported the Rus with modest forces. Substantial Kipchak forces may have remained behind to guard their families, but perhaps other forces crossed the Dnieper without managing to make an appearance on the battlefield.

Sources: Wang Yun, pp.5–6; *Yuanshi* 121, p.2976 and 122, p.3008; Ibn al-Athir, pp.223–225; Julian, pp.101–109; *The Tartar Relation*, p.72; *The Galician–Volynian Chronicle*, p.25; *The Chronicle of Novgorod*, pp.285–290; *The Nikonian Chronicle*, p.287; Buell, 'Sübötei', in de Rachewiltz, *In the Service of the Khan*, p.20; Fennell, *The Crisis of Medieval Russia*, pp.64–66; Dimnik, *The Dynasty of Chernigov, 1146–1246*, pp.292–298; David Nicolle and Viacheslav Shpakovsky, *Kalka River 1223: Genghiz Khan's Mongols Invade Russia* (Oxford: Osprey, 2001), pp.61, 70–75; I. Golijenkov, *Battle on Kalka*, 31 May 1223 (Moscow: 1994); O. Pritsak, 'The Polovcians and Rus', *Archivum Eurosiae Medii Aevi*, 2 (Wiesbaden: Harrassowitz, 1982), pp.320–380; Allsen, 'Prelude to the Western Campaigns', pp.5–24; Allsen, 'The Mongols and North Caucasia', pp.5–40; Golden, 'Cumanica II, The Ölberli', pp.5–29; Benson, *Six Emperors*, pp.104–108; Szilvia Kovacs, 'Brotz, a Cuman chief in the 13th century', *Acta Orientalia Academiae Scientiarum Hungaricae* (vol. 58 #3, 2005), pp.255–266; Pylypchuk, *Монгольское завоевание владений восточных кыпчаков и Волжской Булгарии*, pp.143–156; Pylypchuk, *Первое вторжение монголов в Восточную Европу* (1222 г.), pp.325–336.

36

Conflict Along the Volga

Sübe'etai Ba'atur had been put in a difficult situation by these peoples.

– Allusion to the defeat against Bulgars, the *Secret History*, 270

A Kipchak slave came to betray his master. Subutai freed him but reported to the emperor as follows: 'If a slave is unwilling to be loyal to his lord, will he be willing to be loyal to some other person?' Consequently, he executed him. In addition, he [Subutai] proposed forming an army by equal conscription of the thousands of the Mieliji, Naiman, Qieli [Käler, Hungarians], Hangjin [Qanglin], and Qincha under his command. Subutai plundered the Yemili [Armenian?] and Huozhi [Georgian] tribes. 10,000 horses were captured in order to present them to the court.

– *Yuanshi* 121

The Volga Bulgars were originally nomads, but they had settled in the region of Kazan along the middle Volga centuries before, and had long since given up the nomad lifestyle. Nothing substantial is known about their history, though accounts developed on oral traditions and forgeries have been used to fill the gap.[1] Viacheslav Shpakovsky and David Nicolle estimate the Bulgars could field 7,000 to 10,000 well-equipped horsemen. Allied or mercenary Mari or Mordvins could add to that total, and infantry was also fielded. Viacheslav and Nicolle say of their tactics: 'Volga Bulgar tactics were initially the same as those common to all steppe nomads. According to eyewitnesses, in battle they normally adopted a formation consisting of ranks, in which the archers moved around harassing the enemy while Bulgar light and heavy cavalry either charged directly forwards or tried to attack the enemy's flanks … At the centre of a Volga Bulgar army would be the commander's banner, while signals would be given by means of trumpeters.' The Bulgars fortified their cities, but like the Rus made much use of timber. Bilyar, the main city, is said to have had as many as 100,000 inhabitants.

1   On this see Allen J. Frank, *Islamic Historiography and 'Bulghar' identity among the Tatars and Bashkirs of Russia* (Leiden: Brill, 1998).

Sübe'etei and Jebe probably rested their men and horses during the rest of the summer. It seems likely that before and after the Kalka battle Sübe'etei busied himself with learning more about the regional geography and political situation. Told perhaps of the wealthy Bulgar kingdom located further up the Volga, he decided to enter it. The Mongols set out towards the end of the year. Ibn al-Athir is the only source for the following events. He writes:

> After the Tatars had treated the Rus as we have described and plundered their country, they withdrew and went to the Bulgars in the year 620.[2] When the Bulgars heard of their approach, they laid ambushes for them in several places. They then marched out to engage them and drew them on until they came to the place of ambushes, they attacked them from the rear, so that they (Tatars) remained in the middle; pulled their sword from all sides. Most of them were killed and only a few escaped. There is another version, however, they number about 4,000 and they set out for Saqsin on the way back.[3]

After the defeats in 1222, some Kipchaks could have fled to seek refuge with the Bulgars, warning them of the new danger. The Bulgars may have fought the Mongols in the area of modern Penze, which is well west of Bulgar territory. It seems the Bulgars were alert and moved forward to intercept the Mongols.[4]

The Mongols headed south, and crossed the Volga River with the remains of their forces; some of the non-Mongol forces might have defected. Raverty says:

> Having passed the Atil, with the consent of the Kipchak tribes, the season being far advanced the Mongols had to winter in the Dasht-I-Kipchak. They appropriated the lands and pastures of the Kipchak tribes, in consequence of which hostilities arose between them and the Mongols; but the latter, being unable to cope with the former, had to act on the defensive, and sent for aid to Joci, who … had retired into the Dasht-I-Kipchak … Joci sent them aid, the Kipchak tribes were now forced to submit.

The Kipchaks reportedly attempted to intercept the reinforcements, but failed to keep the two Mongol groups from uniting. Faced with the stronger united Mongol force, the Kipchaks submitted. Raverty is not clear on what source he used and the quality of the information is uncertain. Certainly Yinusi survived the Mongol attack, but perhaps with his authority reduced. The Ölbari Hoshang, a Chinese rendering of his name, afterwards served with Sübe'etei in China, so some sections of the ruling Kipchak family must have submitted to the Mongols. Joci ordered Sübe'etei and Jebe to deal with another tribal group located perhaps somewhere along the lower Volga. They defeated the tribesmen and took Bozebali, the main settlement. Khotosy, the

---

2   This year ended in January 1224.

3   Ibn al-Athir is the only substantive source. Traders coming from Bulgar may have been his source. The *Secret History* confirms that Sübe'etei suffered a reverse, as does Riccardus.

4   The Annals of Ghazi-Baradj offer a detailed description of the campaign and battle. Unfortunately they seem to be a 20th century forgery. In this account, Gabdulla Chelbir commanded the Bulgarian forces.

khan, was slain. Later sources say the Mongols defeated the Nogays, who later lived along the lower Volga and descended from some Kanglis. Some Kangli could have left their traditional home ground to get away from the Mongols.

The Mongols rested from the summer to the autumn before setting out to rejoin the main Mongol army. Around that time the Bashkirs, who lived in the region of the upper Ural River, may have submitted to the Mongols.[5] Jebe died before the roving army rejoined Genghis Khan,[6] leaving Sübe'etei to enjoy all the glory. Sübe'etei requested to be allowed to organise a new unit from Merkit, Naiman, Kipchak and Kangli captives. Genghis Khan allowed him to do this, leaving him in the west.

The Mongols invaded Kipchak and Kangli territory from opposite directions. It does not seem that they gained any specific advantage out of this; any benefit out of the unexpected arrival of Sübe'etei and Jebe from the west must have been ruined by the detour into Rus and Bulgar territory. Why did Sübe'etei consider it necessary to attack the Rus and next the Bulgars? If the aim was to crush the Ölbari Kipchaks, he should have moved straight against them after defeating the Don Kipchaks. It seems clear that Sübe'etei was exploring the western regions. He was in no particular hurry to move against the Ölbari Kipchaks.

Sübe'etei left the main army in May 1220 and rejoined it during the late summer of 1224. During those four years he covered some 6,500 km and fought more than ten battles. He operated far, far away from friendly territory without a secure line of retreat. Hannibal earned fame for leading an army from his base in Spain into Roman territory in Italy where he established himself: the challenges the two commanders faced were in some ways similar. Sübe'etei was separated from a friendly base for longer, four compared to two years, moved over much longer distances, and was further away from his base – at times more than 3,000 km compared to at most 2,000 km for Hannibal). He was probably opposed with relatively larger hostile forces, about five times his own forces compared to less than three times for Hannibal). On the other hand Hannibal faced a single foe able to control and coordinate the actions of the forces raised, and had the challenge of facing the large enemy forces in more constrained terrain. The losses the Mongols suffered during the expedition have not been recorded, but they were probably high. Of the three senior officers sent away by Genghis Khan, two died. Minghan commander Borkat also died. It can therefore be said that at least 30 percent of the senior commanders died. If 4,000 men were left after the Bulgar battle and 10,000 had set out on the longer expedition, then 60 percent of the total army was lost. However, neither of these numbers are secure.

Joci was assigned to rule over the western regions. There is a story in Egyptian sources about a war between Kipchak tribes dated to 1229: it involves the Tuqsuba and

5   The Bashkirs told the visiting European monk Julian in 1236 that they had defeated the Mongols in an early engagement ('In the first battle they were defeated'), but subsequently became allied to them and helped them conquer 15 kingdoms. The battle referred to might have been in 1224, if the Bashkirs supported the Bulgars, or a later clash with the forces of Joci or his son Batu. *The Tartar Relation* suggests they were conquered around the year 1224.

6   The cause of death is not known. Did he die because of a wound, or due to illness?

Durut(?).[7] Aq Kubak from the former tribe killed Manghush from the latter: Kötän, the leader of the Durut:

> Summoned his people and his tribe and prepared to destroy him (= Aq Kubak). [Great] discords took place; and both tribes clashed; and the tribe of Tuqsuba was broken; and Aq Kubak was wounded and his army was scattered. Then Aq Kubak sent his brother called Anas to Dūshī Khān (Joci), son of Jingiz khān, tell [him] and appeal for assistance. [Anas] complained to him (Dūshī khān) about what befell him, and about the people from the Kýpçak tribe of Dūrut, and what Kötän and his army did to his brother and his tribe. And he informed him that their (Mongols') purpose would not meet any hindrance, and no resistance would turn them away [in the Dasht-I-Kipchak]. And he (Dūshī khān) went against them (the Kýpçaks) with his army, and fell on them with stronger blows, and scattered them to many places, and annihilated most of them by killing, seizing, taking prisoner and stripping [them from all goods].

Joci died in 1227. If he was involved the campaign must be placed in 1225 or 1226. It could also be referring to the campaign of Sübe'etei or a later campaign of Batu, the son of Joci.

Sources: Wang Yun, pp.5–6; *Yuanshi* 120, pp.2269–2270; 123, pp.3039–3040, 128, p.3131, 134, p.3256; the *Secret History*, 270; Ibn al-Athir, pp.223–225; Juvaini, p.149; Riccardus; Göckenjan and Sweeney, *Der Mongolensturm*, p.79; *The Tartar Relation*, p.72; Pétis de la Croix, pp.349–350; Raverty commentary, p.1000; Howorth, *History of the Mongols from the 9th to the 19th Century* (New York: Cosimo, 2008), part 1, p.18 (on the Nogay tribe); Golden, 'Cumanica I: The Qipcaqs in Georgia', pp.10–11; Istvan Zimonyi, 'The First Mongol Raid Against the Volga-Bulgars', *Altaistic studies*, pp.197–203; Allsen, *The Mongols and North Caucasia*, pp.5–40; Buell, 'Sübötei', in de Rachewiltz, *In the Service of the Khan*, pp.19–20; Benson, *Six Emperors*, p.170; Dimitri Korobeinikov, 'A broken mirror: the Kýpçak world in the thirteenth century', Florin Curta and Roman Kovalev, *The Other Europe in the Middle Ages: Avars, Bulgars, Khazars, and Cumans* (Leiden: Brill, 2008) p.403–404; Pylypchuk, *Монгольское завоевание владений восточных кыпчаков и Волжской Булгарии*, pp.143–156; David Nicolle and Viacheslav Shpakovsky, *Armies of the Volga Bulgars & Khanate of Kazan* (Oxford: Osprey, 2013), pp.22–23.

---

7   Rukn al-Din Baybars al-Mansuri.

Overview: The Chinese Campaigns II, 1226 to 1234

Napoleon took pride in the victory he won over the Austrians and Russians at Austerlitz in 1805 and the battle is widely recognised as his greatest victory. The victory Sübe'etei achieved at Sanfeng in 1232 is arguably the high point of his military career, his Austerlitz. The Sanfeng defeat doomed the Jin. The fall of the Jin dynasty was a momentous event which contemporary scholars were determined to record in detail, and the movement of many different armies can be followed on a day-by-day basis. The Sanfeng campaign is amongst the best documented of all Mongol campaigns, arguably surpassed only by the final campaigns against the Song during the 1270s.

The victory over the Jin at Sanfeng was the culmination of a series of campaigns which started with the second Mongol attack on Xia in 1226. Xia had submitted to the Mongols in 1209 without having been truly conquered. Initially supporting the Mongols against the Jin, in 1225 Xia changed sides and formally made peace with Jin. Genghis Khan led his full forces against Xia the next year and Xia was quickly crushed and obliviated. Already in 1227 Genghis Khan had struck into the extreme western end of Jin territory: he was keen to finally crush Jin as well, but would play no real part in that project as he fell ill and died the same year. Though the succession was never in doubt, the death of Genghis Khan still caused a delay to Mongol military expansion projects, and it was only in 1230 that the Mongol main forces returned to China. By 1234 Jin was finally destroyed. The same year Song decided to attack the Mongols, initiating a new war in China. It only ended half a century later when Song, like Xia and Jin, were wiped out.

Sübe'etei was closely involved in the campaigns against Xia and Jin, and the initial year of the Song war. With Muqali and the other senior officers dead or retired, Sübe'etei emerged as the senior strategist and war leader. Having risen to high command as leader of the roving columns that often operated against the enemy flanks, it was perhaps a natural evolution for Sübe'etei to turn flank attacks into a standard feature of Mongol strategic plans. It was by means of a decisive outflanking attack that both Xia and Jin were defeated. Sübe'etei operated like Jamuqa against the Merkits in 1191, or against the Mongols in 1194, but on a much bigger scale. The geographic distances were longer and the forces involved much bigger.

Desmond Martin dealt with the Xia campaign in detail. His reconstruction is perfectly logical, but crucial points are the location of Hunchui Mountain and the role of the Amdo region. Here later contributions of Ruth Dunnell (1991) and Christopher

Atwood (2015) by implication challenge the narrative of Martin. Ruth Dunnell is probably right to place Hunchui Mountain in the north and Atwood to highlight how Sübe'etei struck into Amdo. Therefore, Genghis Khan and Sübe'etei are unlikely to have struck towards the Xia capital via Suzhou and Ganzhou as Martin will have it.

The *Yuanshi* and *Jinshi* are at variance with regard to events in the wider Xi'an region from 1228 to 1231. It is likely that the *Jinshi* is the better source and has been preferred.

The *Jinshi* is an excellent source – especially *Jinshi* 112 – for events in Henan from 1231 onwards, while the *Yuanshi* remains fairly unhelpful with regard to specifics. Various *Songshi* biographies add much detail with regard to the fighting in Hanzhong as does, oddly, *Jinshi* chapter 111. The 1231–1232 campaign is poorly dealt with in Western works. Even serious historians make basic errors.

Eyewitness Zhou Mi penned an account of the 1234 Song effort to secure Kaifeng and Luoyang. This campaign is also given significant attention in the *Songshi*. The *Yuanshi* offers almost nothing.

37

The Destruction of the Xia State

The emperor wanted to attack Hexi [Tanguts] … Sübe'etei memorialised that he wished to attack from the west.

– *Yuanshi* 121

In 1226 Xia prepared to deal with a Mongol attack, 17 years after the previous major assault. In between Xia fought continuously against the Jin, sometimes supporting Mongol forces directly. Xia must have been able to improve their military capabilities, gaining more experience and perhaps by making reforms. The sources say nothing about any changes, but Xia would surely have tried to increase the size and quality of their cavalry forces. Xia would also have a much better understanding of the Mongol army. It is not clear how they hoped to hold off the Mongols. Perhaps they intended, like the Jin, to defend their core territory and then counterattack when the Mongols retreated? Surely they looked back to 1209 and concluded they could have done better if they not left their prepared position, tempted forward by a fake Mongol retreat?

When Xia made peace with the Jin in October 1225 they lost any remaining chance of coming to terms with the Mongols. Genghis Khan, as he always did in these situations, acted with restraint. An ambassador was dispatched to the Xia capital to demand an explanation. Asha Gambo, the leader of the Xia war faction, confronted the ambassador, telling him according to the *Secret History*: 'As for now, if you Mongols, who are used to fighting, say, "Let us fight!", then turn towards the Alašai (Holan Shan) and come to me, for I have an encampment in the Alašai … Let us fight there!' With this insult the hand of Genghis Khan was forced. The *Secret History* relates that he had set out for Xia with his army even before sending the ambassador and how he fell off his horse while hunting and injured himself. Upon receiving the answer of Asha Gambo, Genghis Khan refused to return to Mongolia: he was determined to punish Xia. He said: 'If we retreat, the Xi-Xia will be bound to claim that we are faint-hearts.' It is quite possible that Genghis Khan had mobilised the army and that there was an exchange of ambassadors before the fighting started, but there is in this account a mix up with events in 1223 when Genghis Khan certainly fell off a horse. He hardly did so again. As for the Xia, it is hard to understand how they could expect to hold off

215

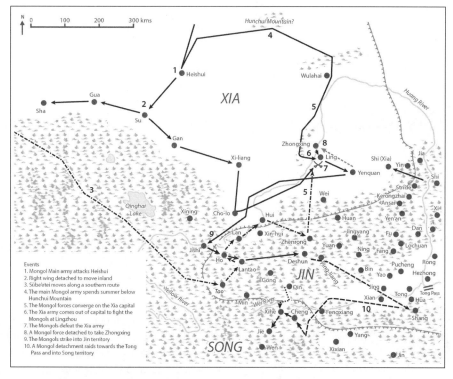

18. The final confrontation with Xia 1226–1228.

the Mongols. In 1209 they might not have understood how strong the Mongols were, but by 1225 they knew much better.

Wang Yun says:

> Sübe'etei volunteered to follow when Genghis Khan prepared a punitive expedition against Xi Xia. However, Genghis Khan told him to 'stay at home and take care of your family' and 'it will not be too late to serve me later.' Yet Sübe'etei made a second plea, 'There would never was such a rule that the master fights here and there, while his servants sit at ease. Genghis Khan appreciated him very much.'

The long *Yuanshi* biography says:

> The emperor wanted to attack Hexi [Xia]. He was afraid that Sübe'etei's parents were longing for him since he had been away year after year, and sent an order requiring Sübe'etei to return and pay his respects to them. Sübe'etei memorialised that he wished

to attack from the west. The emperor ordered [him] to cross over the 'Great Tidal Pools' and proceed [eastwards].[1]

Guo Dehai, who served in the army of Sübe'etei, dealt with some unrest in Turfan in 1225. The army can therefore be placed west of Xia. There is a second confirmation that Sübe'etei was still far away from Mongolia. The Khitan lord Yelü Liuge had passed away, and his widow asked Genghis Khan to send their son Yelü Xieshe back to Liaodong to take his place as ruler. Genghis Khan refused, saying he needed to remain with the army. The reason was probably that Yelü Xieshe remained with Sübe'etei and was thus still far away from Genghis Khan and the main army. The Uighurs sent a detachment to support the Mongols against Xia.[2] They may also have served with Sübe'etei.

The Amdo region west of Kokonor Lake had a mixed nomad population that could support Xia or Jin. The tribes included the Barigh-Bash Uighurs, the Caotou Tatars, the Chong'ul Turks, and Tsong-kha Tibetans. The Sübe'etei biographies say it was Amdo that was the first target in 1226. Such a strike took him south of Xia. According to Guo Baoyu biography, Genghis Khan had asked 'for a strategy on how to conquer the Central Plains (= the Jin core territory).' Baoyu answered: 'The power of the Central Plain is great and it cannot be taken in a sudden attack. The various Fan (specific western tribes) of the south-west are brave and can be brought into service. If you first take them over and use them for your plans against the Jin, you will certainly achieve your ambition.' Baoyu was from Huizhou and therefore well informed about the western region. Elsewhere in the biography there is more on a conversation between the two:

> The emperor was about to launch an expedition against the Western Fan, but worried that most of their walled towns were protected by rugged mountains. He asked Baoyu for a strategy to attack them, and he replied, 'If their walled towns are in heaven, then they really cannot be conquered, but if they are under heaven, then, yes, they can be conquered.' The emperor was impressed and authorised him to raid their horses and command their suppression.[3]

Perhaps Guo Baoyu played a role in the development of the strategy to attack in the south? It was, however, Sübe'etei who led the operation.

Genghis Khan left his son 'Ca'adai ... with a contingent to guard the rear of the *ordus* (home territory).' With Ca'adai and presumably the contingent of Genghis Khan's mother, there were at least 7,000 soldiers guarding Mongolia. The 4,000 men with Joci were in the west, as were other units, and the forces detached with Muqali were still in China. A part of these, perhaps 3,000 men under Möngkö Qalja, were stationed along the eastern border of Xia, and Alci and Butu now served with Genghis Khan, so they must have left China with their 5,000 men to join the main army. Bol

---

1   Paul Buell's translation.
2   Rashid al-Din says the Uighurs 'came out of Beshbaliq.'
3   Christopher Atwood's translation.

was left with a little more than 10,000 Mongolian horsemen plus Khitan and Chinese forces. He continued operations against the Jin in the east. Sübe'etei came from Turfan with the forces which had circled the Caspian Sea. Kipchak, Kangli, Merkit, and Naiman recruits had been drafted, though no numbers are given. He is likely to have fielded more than 10,000 men. That would leave more than 50,000 that could be with Genghis Khan north of Xia. A screen of Mongol scouts was placed along the frontiers of the Tangut kingdom, cutting communication.

Asha Gambo probably expected to face off with the Mongols from a strong position in the Holan Shan as in 1209. The Mongols intended to outflank this position, by first invading the western side of the country and by having Sübe'etei come up in their rear. In February 1226 Genghis Khan and the main army moved on Hei-Shui. As in 1205 it was the very western districts of Xia that were threatened. When the Mongols attacked Xia in 1209 most of the Xia forces were deployed along the border to Jin; now, surely, Asha Gambo had concentrated most of the Xia forces near the capital. He was, however, far away from where the Mongols struck, leaving the few armies stationed in the western provinces hopelessly outmatched. The advance forces of Genghis Khan repaired a bridge over the Shaji River near Jinjuan which the Tanguts had tried to destroy. The *Yuanshi* says:

> [Wang Ji] was in the army attacking West Xia. At the time when they arrived at Qinzhou, the Xia people had completely broken down the bridge for purpose of defence. The Yuan Army was blocked and could not move forward. The emperor consulted with all the generals, but none knew what to do. Wang Ji supervised the soldiers to carry woods and rocks overnight. A new bridge was built when dawn came. The army was able to move on.

The Mongols approached Hei-Shui, defeated the Tangut army stationed there and in March took the fortress.[4] Possibly Genghis Khan detached a wing to move south, holding his main forces back. The Mongols moved on Suzhou and Ganzhou. They sent Xili Qianbu, a recent Tangut defector, to attempt to win over Suzhou where his brother had held command: he was not successful, but Suzhou anyway fell quickly, in June–July, and the Mongols butchered all except 106 families Qianbu managed to save. Genghis Khan sent Caqan to induce Ganzhou to surrender. This was Caqan's native region. His father was actually stationed in Ganzhou, but was quickly killed and the garrison was determined to hold out. It did so for five months, guarded as it was by a Xia army. In August, after the city finally fell, Caqan managed to spare the population, and only the 36 officers associated with killing his father were executed. The Mongols afterwards divided, moving westward and eastward.

In the Shulo area in the west, Guazhou may have submitted, but Shazhou (Dunhuang) resisted. The Xia army guarding the west was based on Gua. There is no mention of any battle with the Mongols. Perhaps at least part of this army ended up inside Shazhou? Qudu Temür and Xili Qianbu were tasked to reduce the fortress.

---

4   Martin, citing the Mengwuershi and the Xixiashushi says that Sübe'etei led the Mongol forces.

They put it under blockade, but faced some difficulties. The grave epitaph inscription of Xiaoli Qianbu says:

> He assisted the horse official Qudu Temür to take Shazhou. They (the enemy) relied on their great numbers to staunchly defend [the city], and there were several battles. One time Qutu's horse was exhausted and unable to go forward, so [Qianbu] carried him on his own horse, and escaped. [Qianbu] alone attacked and dispelled the enemy, and thereby avoided disaster. Later the emperor enquired of him: 'Previously in battle when you used your horse to help someone in danger, how come you did not worry about yourself?' [Qianbu] prostrated himself, and replied to the emperor: 'He had already done great deeds for the kingdom, and had long held a trusted position; but I, on the other hand, had only recently defected, and had never yet done anything of merit, thus I acted as I did.

The emperor thought this remarkable. In spite of this setback, the Mongols kept up the blockade of Shazhou.

The Jurchen Niange Zhongshan led the eastward advance from Ganzhou, reaching Xiliang. Xiliang, one of the major cities of Xia, submitted immediately in September 1226. Other places were also taken in the area, including Cho-lo. Cho-lo was the base for one of the Xia armies, but what happened to it is not known. Sübe'etei might by then have passed Kokonor Lake, appearing in the Xia rear; before entering Xia territory, he struck through the western districts of Jin, passing Tao, Hui, Lan, He, Deshun, and Zhenrong. The sudden appearance of Sübe'etei on this side must have surprised the Xia, though the sources say nothing about this. Genghis Khan went to the Hunchui Mountain to spend the summer resting along the foothills of this mountain: the location of this mountain is unknown, but it was clearly somewhere close to Wulahai and Genghis Khan only left it towards the close of the year. The *Secret History* records: 'Genghis Khan moved away from Casutu Mountain and set up camp at the city of Uraqai.' It seems he led the main army into the Tangut territory along broadly the same route he followed in 1209. The Mongols may have held Wulalai since that year.

Niange Zhongshan and the Mongol forces coming from Xiliang and Cho-lo besieged Yingli. Martin says the city offered 'obstinate' resistance and a detachment may have been left to continue operations while the main forces moved on (the city fell during December 1226 or January 1227). Continuing down along the Huang River, these forces could have linked up with Sübe'etei, perhaps near Lingzhou. The approach of strong forces from the south made it impossible for the Tanguts to attempt to hold Holan Shan. The Xia forces very likely retreated to the capital. Genghis Khan and the main forces crossed the mountains. On 30 November 1226 Lingzhou was put under siege.

Weiming *Linggong* had assembled a large Tangut army. Rashid al-Din says it was 50 tümens, say 50,000 men, strong. Perhaps the armies stationed at Cho-lo, Lan, Wei, and Yen had retreated to the capital? Along with the two armies stationed near the capital, they could have made up such a total even allowing for some parts of the armies to garrison the various cities. The Xia army set out from the capital to succour

Lingzhou; Genghis Khan crossed the Huang River and defeated the Tangut army. Of the usual sources, only Rashid al-Din offers some details, though it is hard to make sense of what he says: 'Genghis Khan came out towards him for battle. In those places there were numerous lakes … and all [were] covered with ice. Genghis Khan, standing on this ice, ordered to shot arrows on the legs of the [enemies], that they have not passed on the surface of the ice, and in this way do not make mistakes' (6 December 1226). Genghis Khan evidently considered the victory decisive, concluding: 'After such a reverse Li Xian cannot recover.' Li Xian was then Xia ruler. Li Tewang, his older brother, had passed away just before.

Lingzhou fell soon after the battle, and in December Genghis Khan set out for Yenquanzhou.[5] This city was also taken. It was while camped there that he ordered the Tangut people to be exterminated. The Mongol army was hit by a plague, perhaps typhus, and the brutal order is likely to have been made in reaction to that: in barren country there would be fewer carriers of the disease. It may have been a local initiative and does not seem to have been continued for very long. In the east the Mongols took Xiazhou in December 1226. Xiazhou was probably taken by the Mongol detachment of Möngkö Qalja, which had some years earlier been stationed at Yinzhou. If the Xia armies stationed in Shi and Yin remained in the border region, Möngkö could have been confronted by a sizeable force.

The Xia were broken after the Liangzhou battle, though the capital Zhongxing and some other cities still held out. On 24 January 1227, from Yenquanzhou, Genghis Khan detached a force (sent 'back') to reduce the now completely isolated Zhongxing. The *Khan*, meanwhile, turned against the region west of the Liupan Mountains and south of the Huang River. Sübe'etei had raided through this region, but made no conquests, and the Mongols now returned to the region with the intent to conquer. The region had been important to Jin as it was from here that the trade routes to the Near East started ('the Silk Road') and it was from the trading posts in this area that the Jin purchased most of their horses. It was also in this region where centuries earlier the legendary Zhuge Liang had faced off against the capable Sima Yi. As it was the Jin border area facing Xia, it was well fortified and well guarded. Jin and Xia armies had raided and counter-raided across the border between 1210 and 1224, but after they made peace in 1225 the Jin could have shifted forces eastwards. Even if they did not, their border defences had never had to contend with such vast and well-equipped forces as Genghis Khan now brought forward.

Genghis Khan, crossing the Huang River twice, appeared in front of Jishizhou and the fortress was taken by storm. Anjur was reportedly the first to scale the wall. Genghis Khan then marched to Lantao, which was besieged and taken in late March to 8 May 1227. Detachments took Hozhou in early April, Tao in late March or early April, and Xining. Alci was tasked to reduce Xinhuizhou and Anjur sent against Gongchang and Qinzhou. The Mongol main force set up camp for the summer at Liupan near Deshun, having conquered the 10 westernmost Jin prefectures. However

---

5   Weimingxian.

the conquests were incomplete, with Guo Xia remaining established in Huizhou. He had been in charge of Lan, Hui, Tao, and He, but had evidently lacked the means to offer serious resistance. Shazhou finally fell in the distant west, in April-May.

When the Mongol operations in 1226–1227 are compared with those of 1209–1210, it is clear that the Mongols had learned much. They were now much more effective at siege warfare and were able to coordinate the movement of widely dispersed forces. In 1209 Genghis Khan had been stopped for some time in the mountains west of the Xia capital. In 1226 he struck first in the west, effectively outflanking the enemy defences, and major cities were taken in fairly quick succession. The Mongols had completely conquered Xia, a task beyond what the Song, Jin, or Liao could have contemplated in their prime. The Jin made no attempt to seriously challenge the Mongols, keeping their main forces inside Tong Pass. The Jin were probably surprised by the sudden Mongol assault on this sector, but did not commit major forces to defend the outer districts.

Sources: Wang Yun, p.8; *Yuanshi* 1, p.40, 120, pp.2955–2957, 2976, 121, 2982–2986, 122, pp.3011–3012, 146, pp.3465–3466, 149, pp.3511–3515, 3520–3523; the *Secret History* 267; Rashid al-Din, 107, 385; Pétis de la Croix, p.268; Martin, *The Rise of Chingis Khan*, p.283–308 (does not take Sübe'etei into Amdo); Peterson, 'Wang Chi', in de Rachewiltz, *In the Service of the Khan*, p.180; Christopher Atwood, *The first Mongol contacts with the Tibetans*, pp.29–31; Andrew Stone, Babelstone, *Two Tangut Families*, part 1 and 2.

38

Testing the Border Defences of Jin and Song

During the very year Genghis Khan died, the princes and amirs who remained in Genghis Khan's camp had held a council and sent Genghis Khan's nephew Eljigidai Noyan and the Qan's son Güyük Khan to the frontier of Qunqan territory in order for them to take it. They pillaged and conquered that territory and left a Tangut officer named Ba'atur to guard the area. Everybody had something to say about this action, but when the Qa'an [Ögödei] acceded the throne he silenced all those who were speaking against the action with the ordinance mentioned above [an amnesty].

– Rashid al-Din, 455

There were diplomatic contacts between the Mongols and Jin during the summer months. Genghis Khan first sent an embassy to the Jin Court in May–June 1227, demanding tribute. The Jin, who hoped they could buy peace as in 1214, sent Wanyan Hozhou and Aotun Ahu to negotiate with the Mongols. Genghis Khan clearly had no intention of ending the war and very likely initiated the contact in order to get information. The Mongols were at this point trying to understand the overall geography and the Jin deployment better, and wanted to know which routes could be used to reach the Henan plains. The *Jinshi* vividly describes what happened:

When Aotun Ahu … was dispatched to the north as an imperial envoy, one of the ministers in the Mongol Court fingered a map to ask: 'How many troops garrison in Shangzhou at present?' and also to Xingyuan: 'We may pass by Xingyuan to get into your territory even if we do not pass by Shangzhou.' After Aotun Ahu returned and reported [what had happened], the emperor was very worried.

Possibly Aotun Ahu was dealing with Sübe'etei, directly or indirectly.

Soon afterwards, c.26 August 1227, Genghis fell ill and died. The long-serving Ikires commander Butu died around the same time, and the Xia capital Zhongxing surrendered just afterwards. The city was destroyed and the people killed, though Caqan again managed to save some. This marked the end of the war against the Tanguts, and the Mongol main forces marched back to Mongolia with the body of their beloved ruler. Some forces remained behind and continued active operations: the leaders were Alcidai and Güyük, though Sübe'etei was perhaps the effective commander. The *Jinshi* says they 'marched towards Xi'an via Fengxiang. People in Guanzhong area were very frightened' (August–September 1227). This offensive may have started before Genghis Khan passed away, but Shangzhou was only taken some months later, in January 1228. Xi'an remained unconquered. The *Jinshi* Wanyan Zhongde biography provides more details. It says this officer:

> Was dispatched to the south of Tong Pass and Shanzhou … to protect Xiaoguan and Shanjuhuo. Right at that time, the Mongol army came and attacked Xiaoguan, while Zhongde was drinking with the former Yuanshui Aotun Alibu and organising the transfer of authority. The Mongol army came abruptly, so they were driven eastwards. Alibu had made no defensive arrangements, and he was impeached … [and given] death punishment to atone his fault. However, Zhongde submitted a plea and took the blame, saying, 'At the time when the Mongol army crossed the border, [his] Yuanshui official seal was already handed over. How could we incriminate a former Yuanshui? I beg your Majesty for the death sentence.' The emperor considered him very loyal to his friends, eventually only gave Alibu whip punishment and suspended his death sentence.

Yila Pua retreated with the Jin forces to Lingbao (Guozhou), and the Mongols took Juyang and Lushi.[1] Yila Pua had an encounter with a 10 man Mongol scouting group, an event he turned into a major victory in a report to the court. He was richly rewarded, but lost respect amongst his fellow officers. Yang Woyan and his subordinate Liu Xingge are also credited with offering effective resistance in Binxian ('winning every battle'). Mongol columns were active elsewhere. Guo Dehai, leading 500 horsemen, killed 300 Jin soldiers and seized Fenglingdu, a fort located on the north-eastern side of the 'bend' of the Huang River. However he was not reinforced and had to retreat.[2]

The Mongols did not attempt to push further eastwards. Their intent was presumably to scout and probe rather than to make conquests. Having investigated the area around Tong Pass, they turned southwards across the mountains into Song territory. The Mongols and Song had already previously collided in Shandong and were thus 'at war'. Anjur was last mentioned having taken up position at Qinzhou: from here he may have joined the Mongol raid into Song territory. The Mongols besieged Xihezhou. Some forces advanced on Jiezhou, and defeated the garrison. The Anjur *Yuanshi* biography gives details:

> Then he continued to divide up his forces to attack Xihezhou where Qiang Jun, a general of Song, had led thousands of people to strengthen the defences and clear the fields in order to defend from the Yuan Army. Anjur took his suicide squad down the city walls, challenging [the Song]. Qiang Jun was angry, and took out all his forces [to fight the

---

1   This entry is not without problems as it is very similar to the description of the Mongols attack in the same area in 1229–1230.
2   Guo Dehai served under Kökö, perhaps the same officer Rashid al-Din grouped together with Mogatu. They could have taken command over the tümen of Jebe.

Mongols]. However, Anjur feigned to retreat. Qiang Jun chased. Soon afterwards the city was taken over [by Anjur] using a prearranged squad. Then [Anjur] ambushed his forces to intercept [Song Army] on their return trip. They travelled and fought around about 10s of *li*. Thousands of soldiers were beheaded, and Qiang Jun was captured. The rest [of the] Song soldiers withdrew and defended Qiuchi. [Anjur] attacked and took it over.

Song sources, making no mention of a person called Qiang Jun, report that Zheng Xin advanced from Xiaren to confront the Mongols. He wrongly believed the Mongols had lost the first fight. His forces were defeated near the He Marsh; Ma Zhong, Ma Yi, and Wang Ping fell in this battle. It also seems clear that Xihe, unlike Jie, was not taken. He Jin defended the city. Another Mongol detachment made its way to Wuxiu. Faced with Mongol forces on both sides, the Song forces in Mianzhou panicked. The *Songshi* says: 'Zheng Sun abandoned Mianzhou and fled when the Great Mongol Army came to Wuxiu and Jiezhou.' The Mongols did not continue the offensive, distracted perhaps by affairs in Shaanxi.

Sübe'etei left 8,000 cavalry behind in the Wei River valley, perhaps under the officer Tangut Ba'atur.[3] He was probably tasked to mask the Jin Tong Pass position and to guard the Mongol interests in Shanxi. Heda and Pua decided to make an attack on this detachment. Wanyan Chen Heshang volunteered to lead it with 400 select cavalry, plus, presumably, other units, and defeated the Mongols at Dachangyuan near Qingyang. This was the first clear Jin victory over the Mongols. Ögödei seems to have been quickly informed about the event, and ordered Sübe'etei to hurry north to support the exposed Mongol detachment.[4] Sübe'etei broke off the reconnaissance into Hanzhong and returned to the Wei River region. The Jin retreated inside the Tong position.

Sübe'etei remained in the field for at least six months after Genghis Khan had died; the campaign was controversial. According to Rashid al-Din: 'Everybody had something to say about this action.' The problem was perhaps that the operations had continued after Genghis Khan died, which should be a time for mourning and not action. Ögödei, once enthroned, silenced people who spoke on this matter. This reconnaissance was perhaps much like the one Sübe'etei made into Azerbaijan in 1221. It was here he devised the plan to fall on the rear of the Wild Kipchaks. His operations in 1227–1228 seem to have persuaded him that the best line of attack into Jin territory was through Shangzhou, though he must have understood that the way through Hanzhong and the Han River Valley was a possible alternative.

Sources: *Yuanshi* 1, pp.40–41, 2, p.127; 120, pp.2955–2957; 121, pp.2982–2986, 149, pp.3522–3523; *Jinshi* 17, p.378; 112, p.2470, 119, pp.2604–2612; *Songshi* 449, pp.13230–13233; Rashid al-Din, 455, 542, 558, the *Secret History*, 267.

---

3   The *Yuanshi* 2 offers Duohulu (朵忽魯), but this probably was the commander that operated in the area in 1229–1230. Buell (Sübötei) equates Duohulu with Doqolqu Cerbi. Rashid al-Din mentions a Tangut Buhadur. In September 1235 a Tangut Buhadur led Mongol forces in Korea. In 1228 it might have been Taghai Gambo.
4   *Yuanshi* 2, dated to 1230: 'Then he [Ögödei] sent troops to besiege Jingzhao. The ruler of Jin hurried with an army to bring support to the city, but he was defeated and the city was taken. Douhulu fought against the Jin troops, but was defeated. [Thereafter] Sübe'etei received the order to bring aid to him.'

39

The Caspian Sea

So [Ögödei] dispatched Chormaqan Noyan and a group of officers with 30,000 horsemen to deal with him [= Jalal al-Din]. He sent Koktai and Sübe'etei Ba'atur with an equal number of soldiers in the direction of the Kipchak Steppe, Saksin, and Bulgar.

– Rashid al-Din, 455

Ögödei Qa'an in consultation with his elder brother Ca'adai sends reinforcements in support of Canmaqan and Sübe'etei who are fighting in the west.

– the *Secret History*, Summary

In that year, Ögödei's decree dispatched *Zhuwang* Batu to start the Western Expedition. Regarding Sübe'etei as brave and able to grasp opportunities for combat, Ögödei nominated Sübe'etei as the van [commander]. Finally, he captured Bachman's wife and children at the Kuanji Sea [= Caspian Sea].

– Wang Yun

Genghis Khan had decreed that Ögödei should succeed him and the succession was never disputed. Even after he died, the authority of Genghis Khan could not be questioned. However the formal transition was not quick. For more than two years Tolui ruled on an interim basis before Ögödei was finally formally elected *Great Khan* on 11 or 13 September 1229. In the meantime Mongol expansion was in standby mode. Ögödei reaffirmed Sübe'etei's importance by giving him a princess, Tümegen, as a wife.

In the west, in the Volga region, Batu struggled to keep Bachman and the Wild Kipchaks under control. Ögödei ordered Sübe'etei to crush the troublemakers. Rashid al-Din credits him with 30,000 soldiers, but 10,000 seems more likely. To these should be added the 4,000 men of Batu and his brothers plus whatever they had recruited locally, surely some thousands more. It was perhaps by early 1230 that Sübe'etei fell on Bachman's camp close to the Caspian Sea shoreline, presumably somewhere between the Ural and Volga Rivers. The Mongols somehow surprised the Kipchaks and Bachman's family was captured, but the Kipchak leader managed to escape. The Rus Chronicles say the Mongols 'defeated the people of Saqsin', and the Kipchaks, who 'fled to the Bulgars.' Saqsin should be located somewhere in the Volga Delta, and the As people of that town probably fought with Bachman. Pursuing Kipchak refugees, the Mongols entered Bulgar territory, but made no serious attack. This was perhaps the time when Hulusaman the son of Yinasi, offered his submission to the Mongols.[1] Sübe'etei then returned to Mongolia. He covered some extraordinary distances, clocking 4,000 km just to reach Bachman's camp. The army could have been sent ahead even before the coronation of Ögödei. When Karl XII went from Pitesti to Stralsund in 1714 on horseback, he covered 2,400 km in 15 days. Sübe'etei would have needed to move fast as well.

Ögödei also sent an army into Persia to deal with Jalal al-Din. The Sönit Canmaqan was put in command of the expeditionary force. Rashid al-Din says he had three tümens, some 10,000 men. One tümen was recruited from the people living west of the Altai, and Malik Khan commanded this unit. Baiju, a relative of Jebe, commanded another, and Yeke Yisa'ur of the Qorolas the third. Dayir may have commanded another tümen already in the Near East. None of these commanders figures in the 1227 army list of Rashid al-Din. Canmaqan moved quickly to Tabriz and dealt with Jalal al-Din who in the meantime had established himself in that area. Jalal al-Din was killed near Amida on 15 August 1231, and his forces dispersed.

Cila'un was sent with a force to the Qingyang area with the task to attack Jin positions in Hoshuo. Boroqul and Muqali were dead and Bo'orcu was perhaps no longer active. Cila'un was the last of the four most senior commanders of Genghis Khan. Perhaps he was given a more prestigious assignment than Sübe'etei this year, because of Ögödei's unhappiness with his conduct in the months following the death of his father? The Mongols began to besiege Jingyang in October–November 1229. The Jin, keeping their main forces in Tong Pass, sent gifts to the Mongols, attempting to initiate negotiations. Cila'un responded by sending an envoy to Wanyan Heda and Yila Pua, but the negotiations led nowhere. The Mongols left a detachment to mask Qingyang and pushed forwards with the main forces. Heda decided to seize the initiative, and sent a force forward under Pua to attack the Mongols in December 1229 or January 1230. Faced with a strong Jin army, the Mongols retreated, giving up the siege of Qingyang. In January–February the Jin stationed forces at Bin and Xi'an. Pua sent the Mongol ambassador, Wokuto, back only after the Mongols had retreated and the siege of Qingyang had ended. Pua told Wokuto that 'we have arranged for soldiers and horses, please come to battle.' This was reported to Ögödei who reacted with fury. The Jin had now, after years of constant failures on the battlefield, bested the Mongols in 1228 and in 1229.

In Shandong, Li Quan prepared to attack the Song city Yangzhou. He made a raid on Lin-an, destroying a depot in March–April 1230. This was not part of an overall

---

1   Hulusaman is the Kipchak name as rendered by the Chinese.

Mongol plan. Li Quan followed his own agenda even if the Mongols hardly objected to attacks on Song territory.

Sources: Wang Yun, p.6; *Yuanshi* 2, p.125; 121, p.2978, 122, p.3009, 128, p.3131; *Jinshi* 17, pp.380–382, 111, pp.2445–2448, 2456–2561, 112, p.2470; 114, pp.2503–2506; Rashid al-Din, 455; J. Fennell, *The Crisis of Medieval Russia*, p.76; Allsen, *The Mongols and North Caucasia*, pp.18–20 (places Sübe'etei's battle with Bachman in 1236), Buell, 'Sübötei', in de Rachewiltz, *In the Service of the Khan*, p.20 (here Sübe'etei did not defeat Bachman at all).

40

Defeat in Daohui Valley

Sübe'etei, the commander of the Mongol Army, broke through Xiao Pass, destroyed Lushi and Juyang and reached everywhere within more than 100 *li*.

– *Jinshi* 112

The Jin had been given a respite following the passing of Genghis Khan. Apart from the relatively minor affairs west of Tong Pass, they had only had to deal with the Chinese bands supporting the Mongols, and the few Mongol forces stationed permanently in central China. A major Mongol attack was, however, expected. Court officer Bai Hua proposed to increase the field army to 970,000 men, a three- or four-fold increase. Bai Hua argued that by recruiting all available men, recruits would be denied to the Mongols, but the proposal was hardly considered seriously.

Ögödei led the main Mongol army into central China in autumn 1230. It was the first time main Mongol forces had set out to conquer land located south of the Huang River. Genghis Khan and Muqali had always kept the focus on the regions north of that river. Samuqa had entered Henan and operated south of the river, but he made a raid with modest forces. This year the intent was to enter Henan with the main forces and make permanent conquests. The key to the Jin position remained Tong Pass where the main army was stationed. Rashid al-Din said that the Jin generals 'had built a stockade on the plain and at the foot of the mountains on the far side of the army and, having made their dispositions, stood in ordered ranks and waiting for battle.' Sübe'etei planned first to make a diversionary attack on Weizhou. The idea was possibly to draw the main Jin forces eastwards from Tong so that Sübe'etei with the advance forces were free to seize the passes south-east of Xi'an, outflanking Tong Pass from the south. Ögödei was to follow with the main forces. Under the cover of a diversion Sübe'etei planned to do what Samuqa had done in 1216, breaking into Henan through the mountains on the western side.

The Mongols initiated operations in the Datong area where Dianjin and other places were taken. They had controlled the region for many years, but as of August 1230 some isolated forts still held out. Meanwhile, Wu Xian advanced from Weizhou to Luzhou, a place held by Tas. In October 1230 Tas set out to intercept the Jin, but unwilling to confront him straight away, Wu Xian fell back to a position five kilometres to the south. Tas scouted the new Jin position, but as it was evening he decided to wait until the next day before attacking. He failed, however, to take adequate security precautions. Attacked at night by a unit commanded by Jin officer Ho Shilie, the Mongols were defeated and driven into the Fen River Valley. Wu Xian again attacked Luzhou, taking the city. Garrison commander Ren Cun was killed.

Ögödei, having completed the mopping-up operations in the north, led the main army south along the Fen River, passing Jüehjünai, Juan, Guanshan, Diemengguan and Pingyang. He ordered Tas and senior officer Eljigidei (Yinzhijitai), the commander of the guard, to deal with Wu Xian. Shi Tianze was certainly also involved in this operation and perhaps Doqolqu as well. Wu Xian retreated from Luzhou under the cover of darkness, but the Mongols pursued, intercepted, and dispersed his forces. Reportedly 7,000 men were killed, and many were captured. Xian fled to Weizhou, pursued by the Mongols who began to besiege the fortress. On 2 November the Jin Court ordered Heda and Pua to lead a part of their forces from Wenxiang to Weizhou to help Wu Xian. Once close to Weizhou, Heda sent Wanyan Chen Heshang forward with 3,000 cavalry. The Jin officer drove back Mongol forces and reopened to road to Weizhou, but after extracting Wu Xian was forced to retreat. The *Yuanshi* says:

> Wu Xian again stationed his army in Weizhou. Tianze summoned all the forces to surround them. Jin general Wanyan Heda brought forward 100,000 reinforcements, but the battle was disadvantageous for him. All the generals fled. Tianze used 1,000 men to go around and turned up in his back. Tianze defeated a contingent led by a lower ranked officer, and next joined the main forces in an attack on Wanyan Heda. Wu Xian escaped. Afterwards Weizhou was occupied.

The Jin evacuated Weizhou, and built a fort on the north side of the river close to it where they placed a garrison. Both sides could therefore view the affair as a success: the Jin because they saved the encircled army of Wu Xian and the Mongols because they actually secured Weizhou itself. The army of Wu Xian was transferred to southern Henan. After years in the front line, the soldiers of Xian must have been happy to move to a quiet sector, even if near the Song border. Their period of rest was, however, fairly short. One year later Xian and his men quite unexpectedly found themselves in the main combat zone again.

At the same time as Mongol and Jin forces squared off outside Wei, the main Mongol army crossed the Huang River just north of the great bend. They took Tiansheng(?), Hancheng, Pucheng, and some 84 forts in the area west of Tong Pass. Sübe'etei pushed ahead with the advance guard crossing the Wei River and moving into the mountains in the area south-east of Xi'an in January 1231. The *Jinshi* says: 'Sübe'etei, the commander of the Mongol Army, broke through Xiao Pass, destroyed Lushi and Zhuyang and reached everywhere within more than 100 *li*.' He was south-east of Tong Pass: he seems to have moved north of Shangzhou, bypassing this place, which had been taken in 1228. The Jin responded with energy:

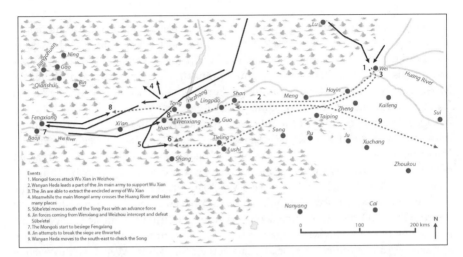

19. The operations in central China 1230–1231.

Naho Maizhu, the general commander of the Tong position, sent Jiagu Dilie and Gaoying … to fight [against the Mongol Army] and asked *Liangsheng* for assistance. *Liangsheng* ordered Chen Heshang with 1,000 *Jungxiaojun* soldiers and Jia Guze (Fanze) … with 10,000 soldiers should act in co-ordination [with Naho Maizhu]. The Mongol Army withdrew and was chased to the end of the valley [by the Jin troops] before they returned.

Sübe'etei found two or more columns converging upon him in the mountains, and retreated quickly towards the main Mongol army. The battle was fought at Daohui Valley, a name probably referring to some location south-east of Lantian. The Mongols seem likely to first have retreated through Luonan. In the narrow valley the engagement, on 7 February 1231, may have been a rearguard action.[1] The pursuing Jin retreated once they came near the main Mongol forces. The *Yuanshi* words it as follows: 'The [Mongol] forces were unsuccessful. After Ögödei reinforced them, Heda retreated.'

The Jin won a victory, but it was a probably a relatively minor one. Heda and Pua had been able to come back quickly to Tong Pass from Weizhou and, in addition, had clearly left substantial forces to keep guard at the pass. Sübe'etei's strategy had come to nothing. He had suffered his first defeat since 1223. It was also his last defeat. Less serious tactically than the first, it was a more serious strategic reverse, as now the whole Mongol army was unable to move forward. The Mongols turned against Fengxiang, a smaller objective. The Jin still controlled many cities along the Wei and its tributaries. Fengxiang was along with Xi'an the most significant of these cities, and Liu Xingge defended it against the Mongols.[2] Wang Ji, who was from the Fengxiang area, induced

1   This is long after the Weizhou battle. The sources give few dates, making it difficult to track the movement of the main forces. Sübe'etei might have spent some time in the area beyond Shanzhou and relied on the main Mongol army to keep the Jin main army in position at Tong Pass.
2   This officer is known as a deputy of Yang Woyan.

some local leaders to join the Mongols. Tas and the other commanders were called across the Huang River from Weizhou to support the main army, and tasked to mask Tong Pass.

Heda and Pua were not willing to challenge the Mongol army and remained within the secure position at Tong. The Jin Court did not accept this passive stance. After receiving repeated orders to move forward, the two Jin generals finally agreed to do so. First they attempted to distract the Mongols by means of manoeuvre. Yila Pua set out with a mobile force, crossing the Wei and marching north-westwards to threaten the Mongol line of communication. If the Mongols moved against him with their main forces, Heda would strike from Tong forwards to Fengxiang and defeat the Mongol forces left at that city. The Mongols, however, scouted well and moved faster than the Jin. They immediately detected Pua's advance and quickly advanced with a large force to intercept him. Ögödei and Tolui led the army in person; presumably Sübe'etei was with them. Faced with a strong army, Pua quickly retreated to Tong and the Mongols returned to Fengxiang before Heda was able to do anything. The Jin initiative achieved nothing. Heda and Pua then led the main part of their troops went out the pass,[3] and fought with the Mongol Army close to Huazhou (very near Tong Pass). They could not defeat them. The *Yuanshi* 2 says: 'and in a battle lasting a full day, the Jin were repulsed.' Pua Hua's biography says the Jin generals reported a defeat, but implies that they really had not fought against the Mongols. While it is quite likely that Huta and Pua did not make a strong attack, the Pua Hua biography is here a biased source. The Jin commanders retreated under the cover of darkness, and Heda decided to evacuate Xi'an, moving the people living there inside the pass. He left a military garrison to hold the citadel. Fengxiang fell a few days after the Huazhou battle: Peng Daya says the Mongols had concentrated the fire of 400 catapults against 'a corner of the city wall.' Anjur is credited with leading the 'suicide squad' which first gained entry into the city. Liu Xingge was killed, c.5 May 1231.

During the siege of Fengxiang, Mongol forces raided into Song territory and plundered the area around Jie, Feng, Cheng, and Tianshui. Song official Gui Ruyuan bought back many captives, trading food in return for their release. Anjur moved against the cities in the area around Fenxiang, and Pingliang, Qingyang, Binzhou, Yuanzhou, and Ningzhou all surrendered to him. In July 1231 Ögödei marched back north with the main forces to the area north of the walls to spend the rest of the summer there. For their part, Heda and Pua were not able to rest their forces, but were ordered to Chuzhou. In that area Li Quan continued his private war against the Song. In an ambitious effort, he raised 30,000 men and took Taizhou before attacking Yangzhou in force. The Song, led by Zhao Guai and Zhao Fan, defeated and killed him on 18 February 1231. Yang Miaozhen, Li Quan's wife, took command of his army. The *Jinshi* says:

---

3   They first camped at Mianji, having previously retreated from Wenxiang.

Yang Miaozhen, wife of Li Quan, constructed a float bridge at the north of Chuzhou in order to get revenge against the Song because her husband was trapped and destroyed by them. [The Jin emperor] … sent Heda and Pua to take up station at the Aohe river mouth along the border of Daoyuan to protect [it from] attacks [by the Great Mongol Army]. Yet the villagers in Balizhuang of Song refused to allow their commander to host Heda and Pua … [later] … the Song general burnt the floating bridge.

Heda and Pua returned to Wenxiang by July 1231. Yang Miaozhen maintained control over her husband's fief. The Song, however, raised large land and naval forces and attacked Huaian. Miaozhen managed to get away, relocating further north in June 1231. She remained in charge of the territory not lost to the Song, ruling as a Mongol governor. In time the son of Li Quan and Miaozhen, Li Tan, inherited the position. Much later, in 1262, he would rebel against the Mongols, or Yuan as the Mongols styled themselves by then. Yangzhou only fell to the Mongols half a century later, on 24 August 1276. Aju, a grandson of Sübe'etei, took the fortress.

This year Sübe'etei had a clear strategic plan, aiming to draw the Jin forces eastwards to Weizhou before he struck in the west south of Tong Pass. He failed, perhaps because he could not eliminate the Jin forces remaining in the Tong sector before the main Jin army came back from Weizhou. Heda and Pua undertook four separate military operations within a seven month period (November 1230 to May 1231). As for US civil war confederate commander Lee in Virginia, over a slightly longer period (he fought seven battles between June 1862 and May 1863), their successes looked better at first glance than they were in reality. They exploited a central position well, but were not able to inflict punishing defeats on their foes. The Jin gained time, but time was not on their side.

Sources: *Yuanshi* 2, pp.125–126; 115, p.2885, 119, pp.2599–2600, 121, p.2982–2986, 122, pp.3006–3007; 123, pp.3022; 153, p.3613, 155, pp.3657–3663; *Jinshi* 14, pp.2503–2506, 17, pp.382–383, 110, pp.2421–2426, 112, p.2470, 123, pp.2680–2686; Rashid al-Din, 456–457; Davis, 'The Reign of Li-tsung (1224–1264)', p.850; Pei-Yi Wu, 'Yang Miaozhen: A woman warrior in thirteenth-century China', pp.137–169.

41

The Battle of Sanfeng

Tolui … encountered the Jin general Heda with numerous infantry and cavalry under his command. Tolui asked Sübe'etei for advice. Sübe'etei said: 'City people easily get tired and frightened when faced with labour and pain. We can challenge them and make probing attacks to wear down their spirit first. Then victory can come easily.' It was after [doing] this [that] Heda was greatly defeated at Sanfeng Mountain.

– Wang Yun

In spite of a tradition of victory stretching back decades, Ögödei and the other Mongol leaders are likely to have felt apprehensive about the upcoming campaign. The Jin occupied a strong position from where they had held off all Mongols attacks for years, repelling even the main army during the previous campaigning season. Perhaps the Mongols could not prevail without Genghis Khan? Sübe'etei in particular must have felt some pressure. He had, possibly, guided Genghis Khan to victory in 1220 as well as in 1226, but perhaps his ploys did not work without the towering presence of his old master to support the implementation? He had led a campaign that was controversial in 1227–1228 and lost a battle in 1230–1231. In spite of years of success as a military commander, his reputation now might rest on the outcome of a single campaign. Though the stakes were high, Sübe'etei had no intention of operating with caution. What followed was a campaign without previous parallel in China or the rest of the world. This, more than the Khwarezmian campaigns or the later raid into Central Europe, is the ultimate military achievement of the Mongols; this was a campaign where they overcame a strong foe by means of imaginative strategy and all but secured victory before it came to battle.

The Mongol army
Right wing commander Tolui had seven senior officers serving under him. Sübe'etei and Sigi Qutuqu were certainly with him. Anjur, also with Tolui, and may have been counted amongst the senior officers. Perhaps two other were Jadai and Bala, the commanders Genghis Khan tasked to guard Tolui. There were also some senior non-Mongol officers. Yelü Tuhua led the forces under his command from North

China to join Tolui. He marched with Heima (Liu Ni) and Jalar. Yelü Tuhua passed away during the march (in Xiho in Gansu), but Heima and Jalar joined Tolui. Zhang Rou, who later emerged as a key Chinese commander in Mongol service, was also with Tului. Alci commanded the Mongol left wing.[1] He had been in China since the beginning of the war against Jin; Yan Shi served under him. According to the Song official Zhao Hong, the forces of Alci were noted for their good discipline. Ögödei commanded the forces of the centre. Cahen, Kuwen Butu, Alcidai, and Tas were with him. Doqolqu Cerbi was fairly near Ögödei, but camped separately near Weizhou. Shi Tianze operated with him.

Ögödei had sent forces into the Near East and also sent a smaller army into Korea. Further, as always, forces were left behind to guard Mongolia.[2] After making allowance for the other commitments Ögödei could have fielded more than 100,000 men in central China, although some of these would have been tied down guarding various fortresses and districts in the northern regions. Tolui and Sübe'etei on the right had 30,000 men,[3] split at least 2/1 between Mongol and Khitan/Chinese forces. The left wing probably had a smaller Mongol contingent with relatively more Chinese forces. Perhaps it was not more than 10,000 men strong in total. Ögödei commanded the largest body in the centre with more than 50,000 men including the detachments of Doqolqu and Shi Tianze.

The late Jin army

The Jin army had evolved significantly since the start of the Mongol war. The key reforms are described in the biography of Chizan Hexi:

> Ever since the days when [the emperor] was still the crown prince in Donggong,[4] he started to set up 13 *duweis*, each *wei* having up to 10,000 soldiers. All were strong and agile, very proficient. Each of the footmen can march about 200 *li* in one day and one night carrying his armaments and over 6 to 7 *dou*[5] of grain. The *Zhongxiao* forces had about 18,000 soldiers, all were Huihe people[6] or those escaped robbers from the west of the Huang River and central states. All of them had horses. They were recruited through testing of their riding and shooting skills. Bodyguards, cavalries, armed guards, guards, and forces stationed elsewhere made up to 200,000.

1   *Yuanshi* 2 says Wozhen Nayen commanded the eastern wing. In other places in the same work there is mention of an old Mongol officer called Ashulu who led the Shandong forces towards Xuzhou. Both must be different renderings of Alci Noyan.
2   For more detail on the Mongol army at this time see Appendix 1
3   They are credited in the sources with 10,000 (Juvaini), 20,000 (*Yuanshi* 2), 30,000 (*Jinshi* 112) or 40,000 (*Yuanshi* 115) men.
4   The palace where the crown prince lived.
5   About 35–40 kg.
6   Minority nationalities.

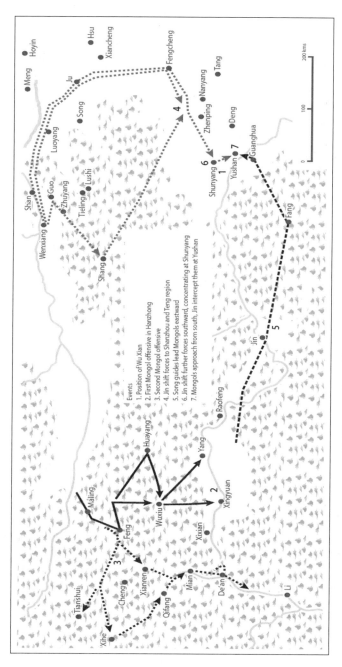

20. The assault on Song Hanzhong 1231–1232.

The Jin army therefore had a nominal total of 348,000 men. Foreigners rather than Jurchen tribesmen made up the core of the cavalry and serious efforts were put into developing a good-quality infantry force.

Wanyan Heda and Yila Pua commanded the best part of the Jin army. Late in 1231, after marching to southern Henan, they had 20,000 horsemen and 17 *duweis*, the 13 special units, plus another four, presumably those following Wu Xian. The army of Wu Xian had been stationed in the south following the fighting around Wezhou in late 1230. The nominal total was therefore 190,000. Rashid al-Din says they had 100,000 men, Wang E that they led several hundreds of thousands of men, and the *Yuanshi* offers 200,000 or 300,000. The *Jinshi* Pua biography says they had 20,000 horsemen and 100,000 infantry. This is likely to be the best number given in the sources, even if the infantry total seems high. Wu Xian is credited with having 10,000 men, and Yang Woyan with 8,000. They probably had respectively four and three *duweis* plus some cavalry. This means the infantry units had about 2,500 men rather than 10,000. It therefore seems possible the army had some 60,000 men in total with 1/3 being cavalry. Using this number as a reference point, it can be estimated that initially 80,000 men were stationed at Tongguan. Smaller armies 10,000–20,000 men strong guarded Xi'an, Luoyang, and Weizhou. The remaining garrison forces may have been numerous, but they were tied to the cities. Even without these, the Jin field army was possibly somewhat larger than the combined total of the Mongols. The Jin, however, were much weaker with regard to cavalry and had no chance in an open set-piece action against the main Mongol army.

The main army had 20,000 horsemen in south Henan 1232. There remained another 5,000 at Tong Pass and there would have been more in Kaifeng and other places, but in total there cannot have been more than 35,000 horsemen. The *Zhongxiao*, foreign drafts, were the best. Having lost the ancestral Jurchen country, Jin had lost a key source of motivated mounted fighting men. Nevertheless the Jin horsemen generally had a good quality and they were more than capable of defeating the Mongols if the odds were at least even.

The plan

The Jin adhered to the system of defence they had used since 1216. They held the Huang River line, backed as it was by major fortresses and covered by Tong Pass and Qinling Mountains in the east. In the east the Huang River bent southward and provided cover. Outside this 'core' area, the Jin still held places along the Wei River in the west and north of the Huang River, particularly in Shandong. Apart from the raid of Samuqa in 1216–1217, the Mongols only targeted the outer Jin territory. Towns were usually easily taken, but quickly lost again. The Jin avoided contact with the Mongol field armies in the open: they knew the Mongols always withdrew to spend the summer resting in the plains in the north and therefore launched their own attacks during this period. It was an easy way to recover cities lost or to take new places. This system was well conceived and had worked well enough for a long time. Less logical was the extremely poor relationship the Jin had with the Song, even if it had improved somewhat after 1223. Arguably, it was in Jin as well as Song interest to unite against the Mongols, but their relations were such that an alliance was impossible.

Ögödei was angry with Sübe'etei because of the defeat he had suffered during the previous winter. According to his biography, Tolui stepped forward to defend the veteran general: 'He held that victory or failure is commonplace in military operations. So he asked that Ögödei to decree Sübe'etei to exert himself through meritorious services. Ögödei Khan decreed that Sübe'etei should lead his troop and follow Tolui to conquer Henan.' When the Mongol commanders later gathered in Guanshan to discuss strategy, in summer 1231, Sübe'etei presented a complex plan with three widely separated forces invading Henan from different sides to converge on the Jin capital Kaifeng. Ögödei was to command the centre, Tolui and Sübe'etei the right wing, and Alci Noyan the left (Jinan). The SWQZL summarises:

> Ögödei took the middle troops to go south … cross the Huang River, and attack Luoyang; Wozhen Nayen took the left troops to attack [from] Jinan; while Tolui commanded the right troops to cross Wei River from Fengxiang, pass Baoji, enter Xiao Tongkuan, take the route in Song territory and march downwards along Han River. It was expected to join forces with each other at Kaifeng during the next spring.

The task of the right wing was to draw the Jin main army away from the Huang River line to make it easier for Ögödei to get over the river with the main forces. There was no easy way into the Jin rear areas. Tolui and Sübe'etei had to cross the Qinling Mountains south of the Wei River, march up the Han River, and then finally enter Henan from the south: no army had ever done that before. In addition to the geographic challenge, the Mongols had to work their way through hostile Song territory. In a similar way, the Germans struck into France through neutral Belgium in 1914 and 1940, but Belgium was a small country with mostly flat open plains. The Mongol plan could be likened to the Germans trying to enter France through mountainous Switzerland. Sübe'etei had known it was possible to enter Henan via Hanzhong since at least 1227. A Chinese man called Li Jangguo had been taken captive in Fengxiang in early 1231, and had provided detailed information on the route the Mongols needed to follow. Attacks had already been mounted into Song territory before the conference, in part perhaps to test the viability of the option of striking through Hanzhong.

On his deathbed in 1227, Genghis Khan is in *Yuanshi* 1 credited with devising the plan of outflanking the Tongguan position by going through Hanzhong. Walker summarises the *Yuanshi* account as follows:

> He pointed out that the strength of Tong Pass would make any attempt to try and force it far too expensive in men. The towering mountains on one side and the Huang River on the other would not give his armies room for manoeuvre, so he suggested that as the Song were now enemies of the Jin a request should be made to them for permission to march through Song territory. Then if the army moved rapidly down the Han River valley, it would debouch on the plains of Henan before the Jin could move their troops from Tong

Pass. As they would undoubtedly commence their army by forced marches as soon as they heard the Mongols were approaching from the south, the troops would be tired by the time they got into action, and the Mongol commander would have no difficulty in destroying them.

Possibly Tolui claimed it was a plan developed by his father in order to win acceptance for a risky plan amongst sceptical officers. Certainly the overall plan fits more the style of Sübe'etei than that of Genghis Khan. If Genghis Khan had indeed outlined such a detailed plan in 1227 it is hard to see why Ögödei should not have followed it the year before.

Sübe'etei and Tolui had to execute a long outflanking manoeuvre. It was measured in distance shorter than the previous plan to fall on the rear of the Kipchaks from Azerbaijan, but was now more tightly timed with the movements of other armies and entailed a march through the territory of a large centralised state with powerful forces. It was quite similar to the Mongol plan against Xia in 1226, except this time they faced a much stronger foe. In 1230–1231, Wanyan Heda had defeated the Mongols in detail. He now had the chance to do so again. Tolui and Sübe'etei, however, knew that they would face the best forces of the Jin, and Sübe'etei had definite ideas about what to do. He planned to harass the enemy, rather than challenge them to set-piece action. Though Tolui was the commander it is likely Sübe'etei had effective command. Buell says the command of Tolui was 'largely pro forma.'

In addition to the two main Mongol forces, a third column – that of Alci – threatened Xuzhou and fourth, perhaps a smaller detachment, masked the Tong Pass position. Haluhanzhi may have commanded the latter force. Doqolqu Cerbi camped close to the Weizhou fortress with his forces. The Jin were threatened from five different points.

Into Song territory

The Mongols had fought against the Song in and around Shandong, but had faced locally-raised forces supporting the Song. Now for the first time the Mongols fought against regular Song formations. The Song fielded largely infantry forces, armed with crossbows, spears, halberds, or/and swords. In total they had 400,000 regular soldiers on the payroll, either provincial (*xiangbing*) or palace (*jinbing*) troops. Not all were combat forces and, as always, effective totals would be lower. When the situation required it, militia was called out. The Song forces fought in units of 50, perhaps deployed five deep. Most of the infantry were armed with crossbows. These fought in specialised units, not mixed with spearmen or swordsmen. The favoured deployment was probably three units wide and three echelons deep. The crossbowmen should be deployed in the two rear echelons. In the open, the Song would try to occupy a hill from where the crossbowmen could shoot downwards. The Song had cavalry forces, but fewer than the Jin.

The command along the northern Song border was segmented into three with one official in charge of Hanzhong and Sichuan in the west, another in charge of the sector around of the Han River region in the centre, and a third in and south of Shandong in the east. In the western sector they had 100,000 soldiers, a nominal total, and the Song forces were probably substantially larger than the Mongol right wing. The Mongols fought on horseback and naturally preferred open terrain. They had operated with success in the mountains of Afghanistan, but there the valleys are wide and they mainly fought against foes that also favoured fighting on horseback. Hanzhong and the surrounding territory offered more constrained mountainous terrain. The immediate land around Xingyuan and Yang was flat and open, but all around this plain there were mountains with narrow valleys between them. To increase their defensive power, Song constructed forts and fortified lines. Gao Jia, recently appointed commander of Mianzhou, had taken steps to improve the defences:

> [He] set up 84 stockades and recruited 5,000 volunteer forces. [He] made an agreement with the civilians, 'Once the enemies come, the official army will garrison their original forts, the militias will guard the blockades, and the volunteer forces adopt guerrilla warfare. In this way, we may take back what the enemies have robbed on one hand, and they will not be able to stay here for long on the other.'

The Mongol plan of operations in Hanzhong is not known. Unusually, they attacked during the summer. The intent of the initial offensive may have aimed to try to secure the Raofeng Pass by surprise. The Mongols crossed the Wei River at Baoji and moved up the Baoye Road. The border fortress Maling was guarded by 1,400 drafted civilians: the Mongols overwhelmed the Song position after the defenders had used up their arrows (19 to 21 April 1231). The Mongols took Fengzhou some weeks later, on 30 May. Gui Ruyuan had ordered Gao Jia from Mianzhou to Yang already before Fengzhou had fallen. Very likely Mongol forces moved on the Wuxia Pass in parallel to the advance on Feng, threatening Xingyuan and Yang. Jia wanted to bring 1,000 forward from Jinzhou to reinforce Yang, but the transfer was delayed by Song bureaucracy and did not happen in time. A Mongol detachment outflanked the Wuxia Pass, passing Huyang (the *Jinshi* says: 'They paved their way through cutting into the mountains and bridging cliffs'). The Song garrison holding the pass tried to get away before being cut off, but lost all order during the retreat and was easily dispersed by the pursuing Mongols. The Mongols pushed forward in two directions, targeting Yangzhou (Lianpozhou) as well as Xingyuan, which the Song did not attempt to hold. The garrison and people fled southwards towards the Micang Mountains. The Mongols again pursued, defeating the Song in three encounters. Song official Guo Zhengsun fell during the fighting, on 9 June 1231. Confronted at Yang by strong Mongol forces, Jia retreated towards Hou and Jinzhou, and the civilians fled in the same direction. The Song held Raofeng Pass, blocking the eastward route for the Mongols. Jia regrouped at Huangjindu and communicated with Zhen Yu, who commanded the forces at Ankang (east of Yang). Yu had assembled a fairly large force, some of the men coming from Qingzuo and Huayang (bypassed by the Mongols). He led 3,000 soldiers to join Gao Jia. If the Mongols had hoped to take Raofeng Pass by a *coup de main* it did not succeed. There was then a pause in the operations. Tolui and Sübe'etei went to North

China for the meeting with Ögödei. It seems likely the Mongols did not try to hold Yangzhou and Xingyuan.

There was continued skirmishing between Mongol and Song forces along the border further west. The Cao Youwan biography says about this period: 'Cao Youwan used up all his wealth and properties to recruit loyal and brave civilians. He raised 5,000 troops. Li Huang … ordered him to guard Xianren Pass. He fought against the Mongols and marched forward. Then he came to the gorge mouth and occupied the natural barrier. Qu Xin took his forces [forward] to challenge the Mongols, and recovered the captured civilians and animals taken by the Mongols from the 4 States. At Qintian, [Youwan] sent Du Wu … to counterattack [the Mongols], irresistible. Youwan ordered all other forces to occupy high positions and natural barriers. He took the lead to challenge the enemies without caring [about] the flying arrows and rocks. Qu Xin and Zhang Anguo took their forces to follow. The Mongols retreated.' The Song defences were strong in this central sector.

The Mongol offensive operations resumed after Tolui and Sübe'etei returned to Shaanxi, in September 1231. The Mongols first stuck into the westernmost districts. The *Jinshi* says that '[Toli] separated another army to march westward.' The area around Tianshui was plundered, but the main fortress held off the Mongols. They then turned against Xihezhou, and began to besiege the city. At some point after this siege of Xihe started, Tianshui was taken. Cao Youwan retreated to Xianren Pass. The offensive in this sector outflanked the strong Song positions in Xianren from the west.

Gao Jia urged Gui Ruyuan to led a large force from Mianzhou to Fangzhou. Ruyuan, after first having 'hesitated', assembled 10,000 – or 'many' – men and set out for Xihe. He found the passes blocked by the Mongols ('because of the blockage of the roads') and gave up the attempt. Meanwhile, Cao Youwan claimed to have defeated Mongol units north of the Xianren Pass, and was afterwards sent to guard the Qifang Pass instead. Xihe held out for some time, but was finally taken on 11 October 1231. Tolui was probably at this point at Xihe: he sent an embassy to talk to the Song in Jiezhou, but the ambassador was executed. Furious, Tolui reacted by killing the captives taken in Xihe. The Mongols next turned against Xianren and Qifeng. The Song positions were probably attacked from many sides, and the garrison retreated into the mountains. The passes were open to the Mongols, but they had to detach forces to mask the forces holding out in the mountains. The *Songshi* Cao Youwan biography preserves a memory of a victory over the Mongols. He defended Tongqing:

Youwan secretly sent Wang Hanzhen and Zhang Xiang … to challenge the Mongols, and told them the tactics to be used. The Mongols approached the city walls. Yet Youwan distributed his forces and made each sub-general defend one gate. He had all the forces lower their flags and silence their drums, warned them to wait patiently until the enemies came nearer, and then beat the drums and wave the flags, shoot arrows and throw rocks. Moreover, he ordered Wang Hanzhen to challenge the Mongols by taking byroads, whereas he himself took the main forces to tail behind the enemies. The battle was a great victory.

This can only have been a local success involving a small force.

On 12 November 1231 Tolui again sent an envoy to the Song, a certain Subuhan, this time going to Mianzhou. The envoy was again executed. Tolui was further enraged, and the Mongols attacked and took Mianzhou on 15 November. The Song retreated. He Jin led forces forward from Lizhou and took up position at Da'an; when the Mongols approached Da'an on 19 November the Song fell on their advance guard and crushed it, and the Mongols reportedly lost 700 men killed.[7] Now the Mongol main forces turned against the Song, and a detachment outflanked them and fell on their rear, making successive charges. The Song army was crushed. He Jin, Wang Hao, and Wang Kan were killed. Cao Youwan's biography summarises:

> The Great Mongol Army broke into Wuxiu Pass in the east, and Qifang Pass shortly after.[8] Then they entered Jinniu of Mianzhou, and approached Da'an. Later, they divided a separate force to penetrate from Mupikou Ferry at the Jialingjiang River deep behind He Jin Forces. He Jin was defeated and killed. So the Mongols pushed deep into Jianmen Pass.

The *Jinshi* adds colour to the story: 'They broke down houses and made rafts to ferry across Jialingjiang River.' As this was an action fought by the main Mongol forces it seems likely Sübe'etei was involved. The ploy of outflanking the Song is similar to what he later did against the Hungarians at Mohi. From Da'an, some Mongol forces pursued towards Sichuan. The forward forces reached Jiange, and made their way through the mountains to the country south of Jiameng, where they plundered Xishui and Nanbu. Gui Ruyuan had to run for his life.

Gui Ruyuan had ordered Gui Jia to hold the Micang sector. Jia pointed out that this was no strategic area, preferring to move closer to Mianzhou. His proposal was accepted. He took up position at Xixian, near Mianzhou. The Song held other points in the area. The Mongols started to besiege a number of these positions, and took Tongqin on 15 December. On 17 December the Mongols crushed a Song group at Shajinping (near Xianren), where Song officer Liu Zhang was killed. Cao Youwan retreated from Qifang Pass to safety via byroads through the mountains. He reached Qinghaoju, claiming to have scored a success against the Mongols along the Baishijiang River. He took station with his men in Langzhou, in Sichuan just north of Napi. Gui Jia retreated to Ba Mountain.

The Song court was informed about the Mongol attack, but Zhen Gui considered the passes into Sichuan well held and only sent 3,000 soldiers to reinforce Jinzhou. Tolui sent yet another ambassador to Gui Ruyuan, demanding a guide to take the Mongol army around the Raofeng Pass. Ruyuan, by now keen to get the Mongols out of Song territory, decided to comply and Song guides led the Mongols around the Raofeng position. It seems Ruyuan did not have control over the Song forces guarding the pass. The Mongols continued via Jinzhou and Fangzhou towards the southern

---

7   The biography of Anjur says he commanded the advance guard, but naturally says nothing about a defeat.
8   In fact four months later.

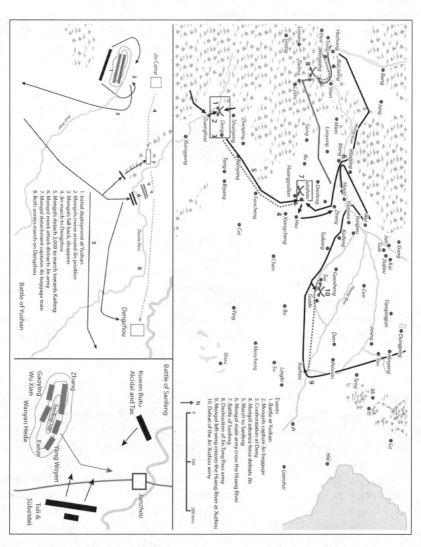

21. The Sanfeng Campaign 1232.

Battle of Yushan

1. Initial deployment at Yushan
2. Mongols move around Jin position
3. Mongols fall back, disappear
4. Jin march to Dengzhou
5. Mongols detach 3,000 to march towards Kaifeng
6. Mongol mock attack distracts Jin army
7. Mongol detachment captures Jin baggage train
8. Both armies march on Dengzhou

Battle of Sanfeng

Events
1. Battle at Yushan
2. Mongols capture Jin baggage
3. Confrontation at Deng
4. Mongol advance force defeats Jin
5. March to Sanfeng
6. Mongol main army cross the Huang River
7. Battle of Sanfeng
8. Destruction of Jin Tong Pass army
9. Mongol left wing crosses the Huang River at Xuzhou
10. Defeat of the Jin Xuzhou army

Jin border: the Song force stationed at Jinzhou was defeated, and Fangzhou as well as Zhushan were taken and sacked. Song officer Meng Gong led 20,000 soldiers westwards from Zaoyang and took up position somewhere near Xiangyang. The Mongols ignored him, instead turning northwards. It would be several years before Meng Gong got a chance to fight them. Perhaps luckily for him, this was the closest he ever got to a hostile Mongol army under the direction of Sübe'etei.

The Song court afterwards dismissed Gui Ruyuan, although Gao Jia remained in active service. He died in 1235 defending Mianzhou against the Mongols. Tolui sent another ambassador, Li Bangrui, to the Song. After some difficulties he was able to open discussions with Song officials, but Bangrui only met with the Song long after the Mongol army had passed through Song territory. Eventually, the two states formed an alliance.

Hanzhong was left completely devastated. The Mongol operations against the Song were extensive and hardly kept at a minimum. They gradually stepped up the extent of their operations and the level of violence until Gui Ruyuan agreed to guide them to the Xiangyang area. The Mongols seemed unwilling to attack the Raofeng position directly. Almost nothing is recorded in the *Yuanshi*, making it difficult to know which Mongol officers were involved where. Sübe'etei, who must have directed the overall operations, again showed his ability to manage widely dispersed columns and to use geography to his advantage.

The Jin redeployment

Ögödei led the main Mongol army into central China, marching up the Fen River in October 1231. Passing Taiyuan and Pingyang, the Mongols headed towards Hezhong, the fortress guarding the Huang River just north of the great 'bend'. The Jin had insufficient forces in the city and decided to defend only half of the citadel. After the Mongols initiated siege operations on 29 October, Wanyan Heda and Yila Pua were called from Tong Pass to the capital Kaifeng to discuss strategy. At this point it was not yet clear to the Jin what Tolui and Sübe'etei were up to, though the Jin knew they were attacking Song positions in Hanzhong. Heda was not prepared to challenge Ögödei's army directly, but agreed to send 10,000 (or many) soldiers forward to reinforce Hezhong. In November Heda and Yila Pua returned to Wenxiang and sent Wang Gan with the agreed number of men upriver to reinforce the besieged fortress.

The Jin evacuated Xi'an, and Wanyan Qing Shannu led his men from there to Xuzhou on the other side of Henan. Other Jin forces west of Tong Pass were less fortunate: Wang Yen (Big) Lushi, in charge of Yingyang, was intercepted, defeated and killed in the Bailu Plain.

Some weeks later it was clear to the Jin that Tolui and Sübe'etei were approaching Henan from the south-west. Even after Qing Shannu had departed, the Jin had more than 100,000 soldiers in the Tong Pass sector. Ögödei had more than 60,000 men north of the Huang River. This number included the separate force, probably about 10 percent of the total, deployed at Weizhou. Now Tolui and Sübe'etei and 30,000 Mongol soldiers appeared 200 km to the south in the general area where Wu Xian camped with some 10,000 Jin soldiers. The Jin needed to decide on the best strategy to follow. Court officer Bai Hua favoured sending the main Jin forces across the Huang River and moving directly against the army of Ögödei. Yila Pua was at this time in Luoyang, keeping watch on the Mongol army deployed near Weizhou. He was called to Kaifeng, but there offered no opinion on what to do. It was then decided again to call Wanyan Heda to Kaifeng (the second time in two months that both Jin commanders went to the capital). After he arrived it was finally decided to transfer the best forces from the Tong sector to Deng to intercept Tolui and Sübe'etei. Bai Hua felt Heda and Yila Pua lacked backbone because they were unwilling to confront Ögödei and the main Mongol army directly. Transferring 60,000 soldiers 200 km south (with a longer marching route) during the winter was, however, no low risk option. Meanwhile, the forces left in Tong and other places along the Huang River had to keep Ögödei from getting across to the south side of the river. Tushan Wudian was ordered to take command of the forces remaining at Wenxiang and Tushan Baijia took command of the forces remaining in Shaanxi (Guanshan).

Heda knew Tolui and Sübe'etei threatened Henan from the south-west, but did not know if they moved along a northern route via Shang, a middle route via Shunyang, or a southern route via the Guanghua/Xiangyang region. All these routes, however, would take the Mongols into Dengzhou. Heda rushed an official ahead to set up a supply depot in Deng itself.[9] Wu Xian camped near Shunyang, west of Deng, with his 10,000 man private army. Heda led a part of the main forces from Wenxiang to Deng, setting out on 21 December. He must have marched along a route taking him close to Luoyang before heading southwards. Next, Yang Woyan to lead a part of forces remaining at Tong and Wenxiang into Shangzhou (Muguaping). Woyan took up position at Fengyang south of Shang with 8,000 soldiers. He was seen to form 'a horn' in conjunction with the forces of Wu Xian, and they guarded the northern and middle routes into Henan. Wanyan Chen Heshang commanded a reserve remaining in Wenxiang. He could move either to Shang or follow Heda to Deng: once it was clear no Mongol force approached Shang, Heda decided to concentrate all his main forces close to Deng. Chen Heshang left Wenxiang, following in the footsteps of Heda, and Yang Woyan hurried from Shangzhou to join Heda as well. They all joined forces at Zhenping just north of Dengzhou. From there they marched to Shunyang and the foot of Wuduo Mountain where Wu Xian joined them from Hulingguan, c.28 December 1231. Heda now guarded the middle road with 20,000 cavalry and more than 50,000 infantry.

The transfer of such large forces so quickly during the winter was a major logistical feat, but Sübe'etei had dictated their movements. He could be said to have followed the advice of Sun Tzu in *The Art of War*: 'Appear at places to which he must hasten, move swiftly where he does not expect you.'[10] Heda and Pua were ready to ambush the Mongols at Shunyang. The *Yuanshi* says: 'After Tolui had crossed Han River, Jin general Heda laid an ambush of over 200,000 forces [in a position] west of Dengzhou.'

9   Wanyan Yaoshi. Wang E did not have a favourable view of him. He later found refuge in Cai where he 'died of sexual exhaustion' having 'married several women.'

10 Griffith The Art of War, p.96.

Finally, the Jin found out they were in the wrong place. Informed that the Mongols in fact approached the Han River well south of Shunyang, the Jin generals were not sure what to do. The *Jinshi* describes their discussion in rich detail:

> While discussing by which route the Mongol Army came from, [generals] put forward [proposals] that it was beneficial either to intercept them on the [Han] river at Guanghua or to wait for them to cross over the river. Zhang Hui said: 'It is best to intercept them on the river. If [we] let them cross over the river, it is possible for us to be defeated by them, considering our inland is empty.' Pua said: 'You only know the affairs of the south and do not know the ones of the north. I received the order from the Jin emperor at Yuzhou in the past, which reads: "If they were in the desert [of the north], [you] should manage to look for them", even less they came at present. Do not let them go away as they did at Dachangyuan, Jiu Weizhou, or Shanchehui.' Pucha Dingzhu, Gaoying, and Fan Ze thought that Pua's sayings were reasonable. However, then Heda consulted with Andemu, [and] he did not regard it as right. Andemu was well known a figure from the north in the Jin troops and was familiar with the conditions of the Mongol army. His sayings were reasonable, but Pua's sayings could not be rejected.

With the Jin commanders unable to decide on what to do, the army remained where it was. Tolui and Sübe'etei, meanwhile, crossed the Han River at Guanghua on 11 January 1232. They sent Güyigünek (assuming he is the *Yuanshi*'s Guiyunai) and 1,000 men back along the route they had come by to report to Ögödei that they now reached Henan. It probably took him about two weeks; he had return through Song territory, but no report is made of any effort made to stop him there. The two Mongol leaders left a third of their force on the north bank of the Han to guard the camp and spare horses and moved forward with the rest. Heda and Pua, informed that the Mongols had crossed the Han, marched to Yushan where they deployed on a hill. On 16 January the Mongols approached this position, and the next day both sides prepared for battle. Heda and Pua positioned their infantry on the hill, with the cavalry in a second line behind the infantry. The camp must have been some distance in the rear, perhaps towards the west. The Mongols first deployed in front of the hill. Then a 'Mongol commander came to inspect [the Jin deployment] along with two guides with small flags.' The Mongols probably had about 20,000 horsemen, but no infantry. Soon afterwards the Mongols 'scattered like the open wings of a wild goose and moved around the hill to the rear of the Jin cavalry.' Heda and Pua ordered their forces to turn about. The cavalry was now in the first line. The Mongols deployed in three bodies – two wings and a centre – and moved towards the Jin. They advanced and retreated three times, probably showering the enemy with missile fire without coming to close quarters. Then: 'The commander [of the Mongol army] called up various generals with a flag and [they] consulted each other for a good while.' They agreed to retreat as if afraid of the Jin. Tolui's biography says: '[Tolui] pretended to be beaten to seduce the

Jin army.' Heda was not fooled.[11] He ordered his men to remain in position, but Gao Yang failed to comply with this instruction, and pursued the Mongols with his cavalry unit. They quickly surrounded him, though Yang and his men were with some effort able to break free and fall back to the main line. The Mongols followed, attacking Yang and the units next to him. Yang held them off. Fan Ze's detachment next to him was also heavily engaged. Heda executed on the spot another officer whose unit failed to offer effective resistance: the unit held firm afterwards.[12] Sübe'etei decided to fall back. The Mongols again moved around the hill and marched back southwards, but Heda remained in position, not daring to follow. He had been able to hold off the Mongols, but could hardly count the affair as a victory.

The Mongols, and nomads in general, often drew enemies into their ruin by means of mock retreats, but Heda was experienced enough to understand what was going on. Muqali had defeated Heda at Yen'an in 1221 by means of that tactic. Seeing that no cheap victory could be gained, Sübe'etei fell back. Genghis Khan would perhaps not have left such a battlefield, but Sübe'etei had no qualms about it. He planned to ruin the Jin by way of a different method than a set-piece battle.

The Jin scouts failed to keep track of the Mongol army, and it vanished from sight. Heda, Pua and the other Jin generals were again unsure what to do. They remained static, while scouts looked for the Mongols. A messenger, a certain Er Xiang, was sent to the capital. He 'reported that a great victory had been gained ... At that time, all officials made their presentations in writing and praised [the Jin emperor]. Various districts held banquets.' All over Henan people who had fled into the cities returned to the countryside. Two Mongol soldiers entered the Jin camp by mistake just after the Yushan battle. They could not tell the Jin where the Mongols had gone, but did say Tolui had seven commanders serving under him. 10 other horsemen came to the Jin, claiming to be deserters. Heda believed them. They were given new horses and fresh clothes. When the 10 horsemen later disappeared, Heda understood they were really spies.[13]

Finally, four days after the Yushan battle the Mongol army was located: 'patrolling horsemen found the Mongol Army encamped at the date woods on the riverbank opposite Guanghua. They prepared food during the day and mounted at night. It could be seen that they came and went in the woods, but the noise made by them could not be heard beyond 50 or 60 steps'. The Jin did not attempt to force another battle. Instead, Heda 'decided to take the army back to Dengzhou to get food.' Sübe'etei was now ready to move forward, and on 23 January or earlier sent 3,000 men towards Kaifeng, while he led the rest of his forces towards the Jin army. When the Jin army 'arrived behind a wood ... [during the morning hours] ... the Mongol Army attacked them suddenly. The troops of [Heda] repulsed the attack. While the two sides were

---

11   *Jinshi* 112: 'Heda understood the intention of the Mongol Army.' *Yuanshi* 115: 'The Jin army was not tricked'.

12   This is a traditional Chinese literary device. At least it can be taken to mean that Heda was close to the front line of a section under pressure.

13   The SWQZL year 29 (1232) reports: 'After Tolui crossed over the Han River, a person, who originated from Kipchak country, reported to him that Heda ... prepared an ambush at Xiai in Deng and waited [for the arrival of the Mongol Army].' Is this obscure entry related to the story with the fake deserters?

fighting each other, 100 (= a smaller body) cavalry of the Mongol Army took away the baggage train. The Jin troops retreated, reaching the city [of Dengzhou] after nightfall. [Heda] ... feared that the soldiers would get lost and called them up by bell ringing. Fanze encamped the west of the city and Gaoying camped on the other side.' Pretending to offer battle, the real aim of Sübe'etei had been to capture the enemy baggage train.

The Mongols arrived in front of Deng two days later. Tolui's biography says: 'Tolui [and his forces] made a night march with bright torches. On hearing that the Mongol army was approaching, Heda retreated to defend Dengzhou.' The next morning, 25 January, the Jin army moved out of the camp and deployed for battle. Tolui and Sübe'etei sent an envoy to the Jin commander, demanding liquor. Heda sent them 20 bottles, opting for the friendly response instead of sending urine, a well-known Chinese ploy. The next day, or perhaps during the night, the Mongols marched northwards in several columns. The Jin army quickly followed.

Having marched to the south end of Henan some weeks before, the Jin soldiers now headed back in the opposite direction. This was the sort of back and forth movement Napoleon warned against: 'It should not be believed that a march of 3 to 4 days in the wrong direction can be corrected by a counter-march. As a rule, this is to make two mistakes instead of one.'[14] Heda did not appreciate the danger of the situation. Thinking a real victory had been gained at Yushan, he said: 'Even though we have won, the Mongol army is now dispersed and heading for the capital.' His officer Yang Woyan was less impressed, telling Heda and Pua: 'You two have been greatly favoured by the country with the great power of commanding the army. Yet you missed the opportunities for combat, failed to defend, and consequentially allowed the Mongol army to move inland.'

Ögödei crosses the Huang River

Having followed events in the south it is now time to return to the northern sector of the war theatre. Ögödei, after undermining the north-western wall, took Hezhong on 2 January 1232, less than two weeks after Heda left Wenxiang for the south. The fortress had held out for 66 days and a little more half a month after the Jin reinforcements arrived. Hezhong had exchanged hands many times over the years, but this time the conquest was permanent. Wanyan Oko fled down river with 3,000 soldiers loaded on a number of boats. The *Jinshi* records:

> The Mongols pursued ... [the Jin] ... along the north (= east) bank with clamour and uproar of drums, while arrows and stones fell like rain. Now several *li* away a Mongolian fleet came out and intercepted them, so that they could not get through. But the Jin ships had on board a supply of those firebombs called *thunder-crash* missiles, and they hurled these at the enemy. The flashes and flames could be seen clearly. The Northerners had not many troops on their barges, so eventually the Jin fleet broke through, and safely

---

14   Note made in 1808; James R. Arnold, *Crisis on the Danube: Napoleon's Austrian Campaign of 1809* (New York: Paragon 1990), p.78.

reached Tong Pass … [The] thunder-crash bomb … consisted of gunpowder put into an iron container; then when the fuse was lit (and the projectile shot off) there was a great explosion the noise whereof was like thunder, audible for more than a 100 *li* (50 km) … When hit even iron armour was quite pierced through.

The Mongols would see much more of this weapon some months later outside Kaifeng. Jin officer Wanyan Huo Liao also attempted to escape from Hezhong, but was less successful: Tas pursued and captured him. The Mongol use of a fleet was a first. The Mongol army was now also supported by sophisticated logistical arrangements. It is reported in Shi Tianxiang's biography that he moved up and down a canal, transporting and distributing food to the army. With naval forces and logistical arrangements, the Mongol army had clearly evolved since first entering Jin territory in 1211.

Ögödei remained in the area close to Hezhong after the capture of the city, waiting to receive word from Tolui. The message sent by Tolui can only have arrived in late January 1232, three or four weeks after Hezhong was taken. Afterwards, Ögödei again moved forward. The Tangut Sugo reported that the Huang River could be crossed at Meng (Baipo). The Jin knew this was an important location, and forces from Luoyang guarded the crossing point each winter. This winter the water was so low that people could wade across the river. On 28 January Jin officer Saho was sent out of Kaifeng with a reported 30,000 soldiers, tasked with keeping Ögödei from crossing the Huang River. Ögödei, however, got across long before Saho could get to Meng, and the local Jin forces lost many men trying to defend the river line. The Mongols captured 700 boats and quickly brought their full army across on 29 January 1232. The *Yuanshi* says Ögödei was concerned because 'Tolui had been confronting the Jin army for so long … he dispatched a messenger to set an agreed date for the forces to join and march together. He decreed that all forces should march on Junzhou.' Ögödei was, however, unable to move quickly. He spent several days at the crossing point. Perhaps the Mongol organisation was not perfect?

As part of the Jin redeployment some months before, Wulinda Hutu had been ordered to Tong Pass. He was now ordered to Yanshi with his forces. Seeing that the Mongols had crossed the Huang River, he marched to Denfeng where he sought refuge inside a fort called Daiping. Hutu later came to Cai where Wang E got to know him. His view was not favourable. He noted that Hutu had been 'defeated several times' and that he was 'a stubborn and self-willed officer.' He was destined to play a significant part in the events that followed over the next many months.

Doqolqu Cerbi and his detachment crossed the Huang River at Hoyin, east of Meng, and marched on Zhengzhou where the local commander surrendered the city to him.[15] Shi Tianze remained in position near Weizhou, or rather the Jin position near the city on the north bank of the Huang River. On 4 February Wanyan Xia Nian decided to evacuate this position after the Mongol main army crossed the

---

15   Wang Shan knew the commander and negotiated the surrender. He remained in command of the city under Mongol authority.

Huang River. Shi Tianze then crossed the river as well, at Meng, some days later (after 9 February). Ögödei marched eastwards along the south side of the Huang River and reached Zhengzhou on 6 February, joining forces with Doqolqu. The Jin army coming out of Kaifeng had marched only a short distance northwards; it now turned around and hurried back into Kaifeng. A Jin officer argued for an attack the Mongols while they were dispersed, but Neizu Baisa would not consider this. Mongol scouting detachments reached the outskirts of Kaifeng a day later, on 7 February. It is likely that it was Doqolqu who led this advance. On 25 January Wanyan Ma Jinju had taken many labourers out of Kaifeng to break down the dykes to flood the area around the capital, but the Mongols scattered the workforce (they had been at work for less than two weeks). The Jin started to prepare the city's defences. In the east, Alci assembled the Mongol forces in Shandong. He was probably ordered to move forward on Xuzhou at the same time as the main army set out to cross the Huang River.

The Jin leadership had decided to concentrate large forces against the Mongols in the south, but at the same time they needed to hold off Ögödei. It seems, however, that without Heda and Pua there was no functioning command structure. Heda should have put an officer in charge of holding the Huang River in his absence.

The road to Sanfeng
Even before the Mongol right wing departed from Dengzhou, on 25 January 1232, a Mongol advance detachment defeated a Jin unit near Xiancheng, half way between Deng and Kaifeng. Wanyan Lou Shi and Wanyan Lou Shi – two men with the same name – and their officers had been drinking all night and were completely unprepared for battle. The Mongols gained an easy victory. The defeated soldiers fled to Hsuzhou.[16] The main forces of the right wing advanced from Dengzhou towards Kaifeng along several different roads, passing Miyang, Nanyang, and Jia. Many people were caught in the open, having left the shelter of the fortified cities after being told the Jin had defeated the Mongols at Yushan. The Mongols burned towns and villages.

Jalar was detached with 3,000 Mongol cavalry to keep an eye on the Jin army. He may still have commanded the Khitans who had defected to the Mongols in 1214. When the Jin army set out after the Mongol main army, Jalar followed in its tracks. Yang Woyan commanded the Jin rearguard. He could report that Fangcheng (Shenzhou and Yuzhou) had fallen to the Mongols on 31 January. Heda and his fellow officers attempted to deal a blow to Jalar's shadowing force. They prepared an ambush during the night, placing a small body of horsemen in a hidden position, and deployed half of their cavalry, 10,000 men, for battle. The Mongols approached the Jin position the next day, 1 February, but retreated quickly after the hidden ambush force emerged to threaten their rear. The Jin cavalry set out in pursuit, but Heda called them back after a fog suddenly appeared; it was found afterwards that the cavalry would have ridden into a ravine had they not stopped. According to Rashid al-Din the Mongols lost 40 men killed, though this seems low. Tolui replaced Jalar with Yeli Zhijidai

16 This town (许州) is here spelled Hsuzhou, rather than Xuzhou, to differentiate from the Xuzhou (徐州) in the east.

who operated with more care. Having served the Mongols well for 19 years, it seems Jalar's career ended in disgrace. The Jin victory was probably of some importance as afterwards they were able to move much quicker. They had marched with a rate of about 15 km a day from Deng to Nanyang, but after the battle the distance covered each day more than doubled.

On 2 February, the day after the battle, the Jin passed Angao. The next day refugees from Fancheng crowded onto the road the Jin were moving along; the Jin soldiers took food from them to help met their own needs. When the Jin army reached the Shahe River near Wangjunzhou they found 5,000 Mongols camped on the north side of the river. Tolui's biography says: 'Tolui well hid his forces and only sent his general Huduhu [= Sigi Qutuqu] to tempt them [forward].' The Jin advance forces seized a bridge and began to cross the river and the Mongols retreated westwards, pursued by Jin cavalry. Sigi Qutuqu finally crossed to the south side of the river; Heda and Pua had set up camp just north of the Shahe with their main forces, and Sigi Qutuqu re-crossed the river and again harried the Jin. The Jin soldiers therefore got little rest. The Tolui biography records: 'Once it was dark, [Tolui] ordered his troops, "Do not ever let them take a rest. You should beat the drums to interrupt them."'[17] It started to rain at dusk; the next morning, 5 February, it started to snow. The Mongol forward force was reinforced to 10,000 men. The Jin marched 12 km to Huangyutian where they set up camp. The snow continued to fall, making movement difficult for both armies. The two sides remained in camp for three days.

The Battle of Sanfeng

The Jin Court sent a messenger to Heda, ordering him to hasten the march to the capital. It was only now that Heda and Pua learned that Ögödei had crossed the Huang River – 11 days after the event. They understood that the game was over. Pua in particular despaired. Even so, on 8 February the Jin army again pushed forward in spite of the snow. The Mongols had 'blocked roads with the trunks of big trees.' Yang Woyan led the Jin advance guard. He made his way through the Mongol barriers, though the route was probably more westerly than the Jin would have liked: otherwise they would surely have marched to Hsuzhou. The Jin army reached a bamboo wood located 5 kilometres from Junzhou, and Heda sent Wanyan Chen Heshang forward to occupy Sanfeng Mountain. It was a hill, or three connected hills, rather than a mountain. The Mongols fell back, one group to the south-west of Sanfeng and the other to the north-east. Yang Woyan and Fanze followed the former group, while Wu Xian and Gao Yang followed the latter. Zhang Hui and Antemu – under the overall command of Chen Heshang – pushed in between, making their way up Sanfeng with 10,000 cavalrymen. From the top they could see the Mongol army, deployed in an extended formation stretching a reported 10 km from one wing to the other. Zhang Hui and Andemu charged down the hill and the Mongols fell back, concentrating their forces in the east. Perhaps the Jin officers charged towards the western Mongol

---

17   Robert the Bruce would have approved: he used the same ploy against the English when they invaded Scotland.

group as it made its way eastward along the north side of Sanfeng. At this point it started to snow heavily again and the Jin cavalry halted. The various Jin units set up camp next to Sanfeng, probably along the north-eastern slope. Ögödei had sent forces forward under the command of Kuwen Butu (Belgutai's son), Alcidai, and Tas, some 10,000 men, to reinforce Tolui and Sübe'etei. They arrived on the same day.

The Mongol reinforcements brought food for Tolui and Sübe'etei's men and the Mongol forces spread out, seeking refuge with their horses inside the houses of the various villages in the area. It was at that time exceptionally cold, but the impact was worse for the Jin who camped in the open. Mongol detachments may have remained south and east of the Jin camp; Kuwen Butu, Alcidai, and Tas occupied a hidden position to the north-west of the Jin. Between them and Tolui and Sübe'etei ran the road to Jun. It was left open to the Jin. Heda was familiar with the Mongol feigned retreat, but may not have known what Sübe'etei was up to now. Carpini understood the ploy perfectly from his conversations with the Mongols and people familiar with the Mongols: 'If it happens that the enemy fights well, the Tatars make a way of escape for them; then as soon as they begin to take flight and are separated from each other they fall upon them and more are slaughtered in flight than could be killed in battle.'[18] It is possible the Jin soldiers at this point was impossible to control, lacking food and being fatigued after long marches under difficult conditions.[19] As they advanced along the road on the morning of 9 February, they must have been prepared for an attack by Tolui and Sübe'etei, but probably not for an attack on the other side.

Some Mongol officers advised Tolui to await instructions from Ögödei. He would not listen: 'It is now or never! If they escape and enter the cities, it would not be easy to destroy them. Moreover, the enemies are just in front of us, how can we simply hand over the issue to the emperor?'[20] Therefore the Mongols fell upon the Jin. The attack coming from the western side took them by surprise: 'Fleeing forces rushed to Huizhou. A hidden Mongol detachment appeared and defeated them again. Heda fled to Junzhou with only several hundreds of cavalrymen left.' The Jin lost all order. Juvaini says that they reassembled like a 'flock of sheep.' Once the three leading Jin army detachments, Yang Woyan, Fanze and Zhang Hui, were well on the way, the Mongols struck from both sides. The ground was covered with one metre-deep snow and initially the visibility was poor, but during the day the sky suddenly cleared and a brilliant sunshine lit the murderous battlefield. Zhang Hui fought bravely with his spear until he was killed. Other forces commanded by Gaoying were overwhelmed south of Shilincun. Pua attempted to make his way to Kaifeng, but was captured by a Mongol patrol close to the capital. Wu Xian turned about and reached the bamboo

---

18 The trick of leaving an open escape route for the enemy had been known in China since ancient times. Sun Tzu said in *The Art of War*: 'The king of Wu also asked: "What if we surround the enemy?" Sun Tzu replied: "The method for attacking them is to set our troops in ambush in dark and concealed places. Open a road for [the enemy] to depart. Show them a path for flight. When they are seeking life and escaping [from death] they certainly won't have any will to fight. Then we can strike them; even if they are numerous they will certainly be destroyed.' Ralph D. Sawyer, *The Art of War* (Boulder, Colo.: Westview Press, 1994), p.243.

19 Tolui's biography says 'the Jin soldiers were all frozen to utterly pale. They could hardly move.'

20 This is a traditional Chinese literary theme and may be an invention by the author.

wood with 30 men.[21] Shattered Jin forces found refuge in different cities around Henan. Close to the battlefield soldiers had gathered inside Junzhou and Xiangshan. Heda, Chen Heshang, and Yang Woyan had all made their way into Junzhou, with 5,000 men if Rashid al-Din can be trusted. The Mongols gained a complete victory, destroying the elite forces of the Jin. Ögödei and the main army reached Xincheng on the day of the battle and only joined Tolui the next day, when Ögödei was quick to praise his brother for the victory gained.

The Mongols captured two junior officers who served Yang Woyan. The captives suggested to an unnamed Mongol commander they should be allowed to go into Junzhou in order to try to get Woyan to surrender. The Mongol commander agreed, sending one of the two into Junzhou. Woyan killed the officer, saying: 'I came from a poor and low family background, yet have been greatly favoured by the country. How dare you to suggest surrender to humiliate me!' He then faced towards the capital on his knees and killed himself. His servants afterwards burned the house he was inside.

The Mongols enclosed Junzhou with a trench, and Guo Dehai began to undermine the walls. The city did not hold out for long, though the Mongols had to engage in some house-to-house fighting in order to finally break enemy resistance on 14 February. Heda and Chen Heshang stayed out of the fighting; Heda was found hiding in a basement. Chen Heshang surrendered after the fighting was over. The captive Heda asked to have Sübe'etei pointed out to him, having a desire to see the man who had conquered him. Heda was afterwards executed, but the Mongols tried to win over Chen Heshang. The Jin officer told a Mongol commander: 'I am Chen Heshang … I am the victor of Daizhangyuan and also of Weizhou and Daohuigu. If I had died during the confused fighting [street fighting], people would say that I failed in obligation to [my] state. Now, I die for all to see so that people will know about me under the heaven.' He was tortured to death, remaining defiant until the end. The Mongol commander was impressed: 'What an excellent man. If he is born again someday, let me have him.'

The Mongols also took Xiangshan, and next turned against Hsuzhou. The garrison of this place revolted and handed over the city on 22 February. Much of Henan submitted to the Mongols. The pro-Mongol sources say that Songzhou, Caozhou, Shanzhou, Luoyang, Wuzhou, Yizhou, Dengzhou, Yingzhou, Shouzhou, Suizhou, and other places submitted. Many cities later changed their mind, a fairly open choice, as the Mongols did not attempt to garrison the cities.

Battle of Yangyi

The operations in the east Henan sector started only after the battle of Sanfeng. Jin officer Wanyan Qing Shannu assembled a 15,000-strong army in Xuzhou and set out towards Kaifeng. Hou Jin, Zhang Xing and Du Zhen deserted before the army reached Yongzhou, crossed the Huang River and joined the Mongols. On 12 February 1232 Qing Shannu continued towards Suizhou with his remaining forces, probably

21   Or 500?

arriving there some 10 days later (c.21 February). At this point Doqolqu Cerbi camped close to Kaifeng where Shi Tianze joined him. Alci approached Xuzhou from the east: he had to get across the Huang River. The three Jin defectors would have been able to give the Mongols plenty of useful intelligence. Zhang Rong, perhaps an officer serving Yan Shi, is credited with playing a key role in the operations that followed: 'When the army came to Heshang, Rong led his suicide squad to the ferry point at night. The defending [Jin] forces were defeated. The next morning a Jin army came in battle array. Rong mounted his horse and fought them. He swept away all Jin officers and soldiers in his way and grabbed about 50 boats.'[22] Jin officer Tudan Yidu had taken command of the forces in Xuzhou just three days before. He sent forward a detachment – a reported 1,000 soldiers – to drive off the Mongols, but the undisciplined Jin soldiers were ambushed and defeated on 12–13 February. This was perhaps the action described in the Zhang Rong biography. The full Mongol army was quickly shipped across the river on the captured boats. Xuzhou was in danger, having only a small garrison. The Mongols seized two forts and captured 10,000 (= many) people in the surrounding country. Alci wanted to kill the captives, probably motivated by the usual Mongol security concerns, but Zhang Rong tried his best to stop him. On 17 February the Mongols made a probing attack on the south side of Xu, but did not make a serious effort to break into the city. Hou Jin requested to be given 1,000 men to attack the fortress, and the Mongols accepted his proposal. Houjin struck at night. Yidu had only 300 regular soldiers in the city, but even so prevailed after some confused fighting. The Jin afterwards recovered many places in the region. The three defectors were discouraged after this reverse and again returned to the Jin. Yidu welcomed them. Houjian remained in Xuzhou, while on 3 March Duzhan was sent to guard Pizhou.

Doqolqu and Shi Tianze left the Kaifeng area and turned eastward. They took Taikang in three days. Liu Bin is credited with playing an important role in the conquest of this place; he served with Alci who therefore seems to have moved westwards to join the two other commanders near Taikang. Liu Bin made a raid towards Chenzhou near where he routed some Jin forces. He camped at Xingdui, 70 *li* from Chenzhou. When he was informed that Chenzhou was preparing its troops at the outskirts, Liu Bin led his forces delivered a night raid and defeated them.' The Jin forces in Bozhou, which had taken station along the road west of the city, retreated after seeing the country around Taikang burning. Zhao Luyi attempted to keep a force in the field, but could not get enough support for this plan. A Mongol detachment subsequently approached Bozhou. On 19 February Jing Shan prepared to defend the city with 400 soldiers, but the Mongols made no attack. Having a different objective, Doqolqu, Shi Tianze, and Alci marched on Sui.

Qing Shannu decided to retreat – that is, go back to Xuzhou – just three days after reaching Suizhou. Doqolqu, Shi Tianze, and Alci intercepted and defeated him at Yangyi on 24 February. The Jin are credited with somewhat less than 15,000 men,

---

22   Yang Jiezhige is also credited being involved with this operation, though his biography is short on details.

but only a small number were mounted and the effective total must have been much lower. Seunidei commanded the Mongol detachment that caught up with the Jin. Shi Tianlu is also associated with this battle. His biography says: 'he arrived at the city wall of Guide at night. He attacked Jin camp and killed over 300 Jin soldiers. Jin general Zhen Fangyu sent his forces to chase and surround Tianlu. Tianlu broke the encirclement and fought back again. Jin army retreated.' The text is not clear and there is little help elsewhere. Perhaps the small Mongol force baited the Jin forward so they were drawn into an ambush? Qing Shannu fell off a horse and was captured, and only 300 Jin soldiers managed to escape into Guide.

Refusing to help the Mongols, Qing Shannu was executed:

> The Great Mongol Army transported Shannu on a horse and forced him to go with them. They met … [a Mongol officer] on the way … [Shannu] asked, 'May I know who you are?' … [he] answered, 'I am *Zhendingwulushi Wanhuhou*.' [Shannu] further asked, 'Are you Tianze?' [He] answered, 'Yes.' Then [Shannu] said, 'My country is broken. Please can you consider helping save the lives of our people.' Later when he met the great general Temutai [Doqolqu], he was asked to summon the defence forces in the capital city [Kaifeng] to surrender. [Shannu] refused, and he showed great arrogance not to give in. He did not give in even after the attendants cut off his feet. He was eventually killed.

The Mongols took Suizhou on 1 March, a few days after the battle. Zhang Wenshou, the officer in charge of the city, had fled, leaving the defenders demoralised. The Mongols then set up camp close to Guide.

The fall of Tong Pass
With the Mongol army established on the south side of the lower Huang River, Tong Pass lost its importance. Tushan Baijia decided to evacuate Shaanxi. According to the *Jinshi*,[23] he issued the following proclamation: 'The Mongol Army has invaded Huainan. We will not be able to defend [here] in consideration that they will come around Tong Pass. Therefore, [people of the region] … should move into big cities and grain or military supplies should be centralised to [the city of] Shanzhou. The people near mountains should enter fortified mountain villages.' Baijia fell back to Denfeng on 31 January 1232. The Jin Court ordered Tushan Wudian to lead the army from Wenxiang towards the capital, and they assembled 5,000 horsemen and many militia foot ('110,000 soldiers'), 'withdrawing from all of the passes in Qinlan. They came into Shanxi from Guo and prepared more than 200 boats to send several hundred thousand *hu* military food from Tongzhou, Huazhou and Wenxiang sailing with the current eastwards.' A Mongol detachment seems to have watched the Tong position from the western side. The Mongol officer named is called Huluhanzhi.[24] After the Mongols learned that Tong 'was burnt down and given up', they started to advance. Li

23 The quotes in this section are all from Tudan Wudian's *Jinshi* biography, which offers a very detailed narrative.
24 Uludai, son of Butu of the Ikires?

Pingyi had been left to guard the fortress with inadequate forces, and surrendered on 13 February. The Mongols pushed eastwards. Their sudden appearance caused a panic and in the confusion many boats were sent down the river before the supplies had been loaded on them. The people sought refuge inside Zhou and the Lingbao and Xiashi storehouses. Many were, however, were caught in the open and killed. Monian Suye sailed downriver with 80 boats on which grain had been loaded (from Tong Pass and Wenxiang). He reached Beihojiadan of Lingbao. Here Zhang Xin and Hou San had assembled 300 men and guarded a group of civilians in a position along the riverbank. Huluhanzhi attempted to break into the Jin position, but was not able to do so. When 'Monian Suye with the boats arrived, they surrendered to the Mongol Army. Thus, the Mongol Army got the boats to attack Zhang Xin and Hou San and killed all of them.'

Meanwhile, Tan Chun assembled 800 men close to Shanzhou, and Zhao Wei raised another 800 men on the north side of the Huang River. Both acted on the orders of Tushan Wudian. Wei led 300 men to encamp at Jinjibao, while Wudian kept his main forces inside Shanzhou. When the Mongols arrived in front of the city, an officer called Ho Duxi went out from the city to repulse them without waiting for orders. His horse slipped and he was nearly captured by the Mongols. Wudian sent a new horse for him and ordered that nobody was allowed to go out to fight. The Mongol Army withdrew, but by now all the boats and rafts had been lost, so Wei had no boats to ferry his men across the river. A scholar, whose surname was Li, told Wudian: 'The entire Mongol Army is concentrated in Henan, leaving Hopei vacant. You can take Weizhou quickly before the Mongol Army can do anything. When the Mongol Army learns that our troops are in the north, they must divide forces and send some across the Huang River. So our capital will find some relief from its straits at once.' Wudian did not like this advice and executed Li.

On 21 February Wudian led his army out of Shanzhou, moving out of the eastern and southern gates. He intended to march south to seek refuge from the Mongol cavalry in the mountains. The mountains are described as 'frozen and snow-covered.' Many civilians travelled with the army: refugees from Guanzhong, Hezhong, and the nearby districts as well as the families of the soldiers. The Mongols shadowed the Jin army. The *Jinshi* says they had only a few hundred horsemen, far less than the 5,000 cavalry of the Jin, therefore the Mongols kept a certain distance away. The Jin army, however, self-destructed. Liu and Zhao (commander of Jiazhou) deserted during the first day. During the next day, the detachment of Zhang Yi deserted, heading for Zhuyang. After it passed through the pass of Lulu, the Mongol army caught it up and forced the Jin soldiers to surrender. The rest of the Jin column struggled on. The *Jinshi* describes in vivid detail how the non-combatants suffered: 'The women following the troops abandoned their babies on the mountain track full of piled snow, which was dissolved by daylight and was frozen at night so that mire stifled shanks [of people]. The distressed wail of the women could be heard along the way.' The Mongols had secretly called in their main forces to come by Lushi from 'three Xian' in the west (i.e., Luoyang and beyond). The arriving forces seized Tieling, blocking the Jin from the south. Cut off and isolated, having covered some 100 km through difficult terrain in the middle of winter, the Jin collapsed. Wanyan Zhong Xi was captured and immediately executed, presumably to discourage the other Jin soldiers. Zheng Ti killed Miao Ying – who did not want to surrender – and went over to the Mongols. After this the Jin army dispersed. Wudian and Hojun led less than 100 horsemen into the mountains, intending to go to Dengzhou, but were tracked down and dispersed. Wudian and Hojun were both killed. Only one or two percent of the Jin soldiers are reported to have been able to escape (c.25 February–1 March 1232). Wanyan Sulan made his way back to Shanzhou. Qiang Shen was captured, but he was able to escape and to make his way to Luoyang. Shang Heng was also captured. He refused to help the Mongols by asking the defenders of Luoyang to surrender. He was somehow able to kill himself. Tushan Baijia remained in Shanzhou; he was able to assemble many soldiers who had deserted the Jin army before they collided with the Mongols (reportedly 10,000 men, meaning 'many').

In parallel with these events, as related before, Li Shouxian subjected Ruicheng on the other side of the Huang River (February–March 1232). Liu Qianhu led some forces from Sanfeng to Ruzhou. The Mongols came soon after he had arrived, and attacked, took, and sacked the town.

Sübe'etei seems to have planned for Mongol forces to converge on the Tong Pass position. A part of the Mongol main army formed the eastern pincer. It had to cover 300 km to get from Xuchang to Lushi. The narrative of the Tong Pass campaign comes exclusively from Jin sources; there is no mention in Mongol sources, so probably no officer with a *Yuanshi* biography was seriously involved.

Observations on the Sanfeng campaign

The Mongols had 2–3 times more cavalry than the Jin, but hardly had a general quality advantage. The Jin held off Tolui and Sübe'etei at Yushan on 17 January 1232, and won minor victories along the Yalu (1 February) and at Xuzhou (3 March). While the Jin clearly had the weaker army, they occupied a strong position and had many strong fortresses. The defeat of Jin was by no means a foregone conclusion. Rashid al-Din recognised that the Mongols overcame long odds. He wrote that Tolui 'by excellent strategy … defeated all that great army, which was twice the size of his own.' Sübe'etei had focussed first on the main enemy army, crushing it at Sanfeng (9 February), before turning against the secondary forces, defeating them at Yangyi (24 February) and Tieling (1 March). The Mongols first faced the Jin main enemy army at Yushan (17 January), holding it off for 24 days before finally closing in for the kill. Ögödei was able to make his way across the Huang River close to Luoyang on 29 January; his lead elements joined Tolui and Sübe'etei 11 days later. The Jin were outmanoeuvred and put into an impossible position even before the various battles were fought. Sübe'etei was able to coordinate the movement of several widely separated columns with great effectiveness. Napoleon said:

> It may be laid down as a principle that in invading a country with two or three armies, each of which has its own distinct line of operations extending towards a fixed point at which all are to unite, the union of the different corps should never be ordered to take

place in the vicinity of the enemy, as by concentrating his forces he may not only prevent their junction but also defeat them one by one.[25]

Sübe'etei broke this maxim, but avoided defeat in detail by being able to hold off the larger enemy army until reinforced. The superior Mongol scouting and mobility as well as ability to send messengers back and forth between their armies were critical for their success. They were able to improvise and had a strategic flexibility greater than what Napoleon considered possible in his day. Sübe'etei weakened the Jin army by fighting battles, by the seizure of their supply train (under the cover of a diversion), by continuous skirmishing, by burning the country around them to deny them food and forage, and even by making noise at night to disturb their sleep. The Jin army was close to collapse before the battle of Sanfeng was fought. Sanfeng was not a 'pure' strategic triumph like Ilirida in 49 BC for Caesar, or Ulm in 1805 for Napoleon, but it was pretty close.

It seems clear that the Jin would have been well advised to keep their main forces in place along the Huang River, based on the fortresses between Tong Pass and Kaifeng, and to order the people of the interior to take refuge inside the fortresses. The ruin of the Jin was perhaps that Heda and Pua were the only commanders able to act with energy. None of the officers stationed along the Huang River seem to have taken any effective steps to keep the other Mongol forces from getting across, and the Jin Court failed to appoint a single officer to be in command of the Huang River defensive line. Heda and Pua also made a mistake by following the Mongols from Deng towards Kaifeng. The best option would probably have been to march into east Henan. They could not know that the main Mongol army would get across the Huang River, but even without considering this, they put themselves in a difficult position by following Tolui and Sübe'etei. Even if the Mongols reached Kaifeng, it was well fortified and could not be taken quickly. If the Jin had crossed the Huang River and struck Ögödei at Hezhong instead of sending the main forces against Tolui they would hardly be better off. The Jin could have fielded a large army, but did not have much more than 25,000 cavalry (and this is a rounded number, the effective total must have been lower). Ögödei had at least twice as many horsemen. It could have been a good idea for the remaining Jin forces at Tong Pass to cross the Huang River and move on Weizhou, after Ögödei had crossed to the south side, as it might have at least temporarily have wrong-footed the Mongols, but with only 5,000 horsemen they might have failed to make much of an impression.

Sources: *Yuanshi* 1, pp.40–41, 2, pp.125–128; 115, pp.2889–2890, 119, pp.2537–2540, 121, pp.121, pp.2975–2782, 2553–2554, 122, pp.3006–3007, 3008–3009, 3013–3014, 147, p.3486, 148, pp.3505–3507, 149, pp.3511–3514, 3518–3519, 3520–3522, 150, pp.3546–3548, 151, pp.3563, 3572–3573, 153, pp.3614, 3620–3622, 155, pp.3657–3663; *Jinshi* 17, pp.384–387, 111, pp.2445–2449, 2451–2454, 112, pp.2463–2475,

---

25   J. Akerly, *Military Maxims of Napoleon* (New York: Wiley and Putnam, 1845), p.8.

113, pp.2484–2502, 114, pp.2503–2506, 115, pp.2523–2526, 116, pp.2537–2541, 2550–2551, 118, pp.2577–2581, 119, pp.2537–2540, 2599–2600, 123, pp.2680–2683, 2683–2686, 2689–2691; the SWQZL, 81b; *Songshi* 449, pp.13230–13233; Juvaini, pp.191–196; Rashid al-Din 456–460; Wang E, entry 23, 47, pp.75–76, 92; Su Ding (citing Wang Zi), in P. Olbricht and E. Pinks, *Meng-Ta Pei-Lu und Hei-ta Shih-Lüeh*, p.210; Joseph Needham, *Science and Civilization in China*, vol. 5 (Cambridge: Cambridge University Press, 1959), p.171; Buell, 'Yeh-lu A-hai', 'Yeh-lu T'u-hua', in de Rachewiltz, *In the Service of the Khan*, p.120; Chen Shisong, Guang Yuzhe, and Zhu Qingze, in *Chen, Shisong, and others*; 宋元战争史 (Song War History) (Inner Mongolia People's Publishing House 2010), pp.23–26.

42

The Siege of Kaifeng

Tolui returned [northwards] and took up station in Guanshan, leaving Sübe'etei to command all the other forces to surround and attack Kaifeng. [Later] the Jin emperor escaped north across the Huang River. Sübe'etei chased and defeated them [his forces] at Huanglinggang, killing 10,000 soldiers ... Kaifeng surrendered. Sübe'etei presented the captured wives and concubines of the Jin emperor along with all treasures to the throne.

– Wang Yun

The Mongols had within a brief three week period crushed the Jin field forces, but the Jin still held many strongpoints in Henan and were by no means destroyed. It was, however, no high priority for Ögödei to complete the defeat of Jin. Content with the victories gained, he led the main Mongol forces back home during the spring and left behind Sübe'etei to finish the job. The main strongholds of the enemy were Kaifeng, Luoyang, Guide, Xuzhou, and the various places near the Song border. Kaifeng, the Jin capital, was a huge metropolis. It hosted 1.7 million households in the metropolitan area and with a household at more than six members on average there were more than 10 million people. This compares to 226,000 households for Beijing at its peak. Strong walls and a moat covered Kaifeng and a network of canals made movement around the outside of the city difficult. Taking the Jin capital and the other fortresses still held by Jin was a huge challenge for Sübe'etei. Having showed his mastery of mobile warfare, he now had to show his ability to attack stationary positions.

The sieges of Luoyang and Guide
The main Mongol army remained near Zhengzhou. Three thousand Jin soldiers, including 100 *zhongxiao* horsemen, had escaped from the Sanfeng battle and made their way to Luoyang. The Mongols only moved against the city weeks later, on 18 March 1232. Perhaps the Mongol forces advancing on the fortress included those that before had defeated the Jin in the Tong region? The Luoyang defenders held four forts outside the walls covering the main gates. The Mongols took up position around the northern, eastern, and southern sides of the city and deployed their artillery. Luoyang was a strong fortress, but the Jin command was in a chaotic state: Do Jishi, the Jin official in charge

260   THE MONGOL CONQUESTS

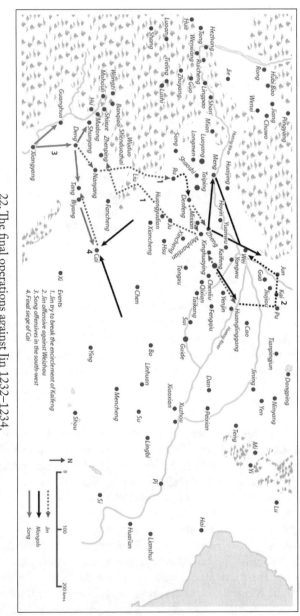

22. The final operations against Jin 1232–1234.

of the city, despaired and made no effort to prepare the defences. Sahe Nian killed him and took command. However, he was sickly and unable to provide active leadership. At odds with the soldiers, at one point some his men actually chased him outside the inner defences though he was able to get back in quickly (21 March 1232). Soon afterwards, on 28 March, his second in command fled, adding to the confusion. The next day the Mongols made a breach in the north-east, and Nian rushed out of the southern gate and was killed. Even so, the Mongols failed to secure the city and retreated (29 or 30 March). Luoyang remained defiant in spite of the poor leadership.

In the east, on 8 March, Doqolqu Cerbi encircled Guide. Wang E says that 'the city walls of Guide are surrounded by water.' Water would play a significant role during the siege. The *Jinshi* provides details:

> Temutai [= Doqolqu Cerbi], senior general of the Great Mongol Army, attacked [Guide] with all the forces from Zhending, Xinan, Daming, Dongping and Yidu. One day it thundered yet there was a clear sky. Someone [in Guide] made a divination using *Secret Stratagems of Military Operations*.[1] The result showed 'no harm to the city.' The people calmed down. Right at that time, the defeated troops of Qing Shannu came back to the city. With this reinforcement, [the people] of the city gained courage. The Great Mongol Army attacked the city day and night. They camped outside the southern suburb of the city, a place with a higher ground … When the Great Mongol Army surrounded the city, [Nu Luhuan] decided to breach the river at Fengji Bridge in order to encircle the city with water. Yet the *Dushuiguan*[2] said that he happened to have measured the water level when the river burst at Aoyougu the year before. That place was at the same level with the Longxing Pagoda inside the city. If it was breached then the whole city would be submerged. When the Great Mongol Army arrived, [Nu Luhuan] had sent Zhen Gui … to go and breach the river. Yet Zhen Gui was attacked just when he came out of the city, and not a single one returned [12 March 1232]. Somebody in the Great Mongol Army advised them to breach the river, and the commander accepted the idea. Once the river was breached, the water flew downwards from the north-west to the south-west of the city and then entered the original watercourse of Suishui River. The city, however, became more secure because of the water. [The Mongol commander] tried to find the adviser and kill him, but they could find him nowhere [25 March].

The Mongols have a great reputation for being skilled at taking places by siege, but their engineering was evidently not of high order on this occasion. Guide remained under blockade for some weeks more before the Mongols decided to give up: by May 1232 the people could go out of the city again.

Sübe'etei's attempts to secure Luoyang and Guide both ended in failure. He lost momentum.

---

1 A book about military stratagems compiled by Renzong of Song.
2 The officer in charge of irrigation works.

The siege of Kaifeng

The main Mongol army, or elements of it, approached Kaifeng. Sigi Qutuqu led the forward forces. This happened at the time when Doqolqu Cerbi left Kaifeng for Suizhou and Guide. On 6 April an envoy was sent to Kaifeng from the Mongol camp close to Zheng demanding that hostages, specifying who was wanted, were handed over. Ögödei offered to make *Aizong* governor of Henan under the Mongol administrative apparatus. He would have to give up his title as emperor. *Aizong* could not bring himself to accept this proposal, but hoped even so to secure a ceasefire. On 14 April he sent hostages, including his nephew prince Cao, to the Mongols.

Ögödei and Tolui led the bulk of the Mongol forces back north. This happened around the time when Jin dispatched the hostages to the Mongols. Ögödei must have been satisfied with the victory he had gained. He was probably unwilling to keep his main army away from grassland during the summer months, keeping to the seasonal campaigning schedule adhered to by his father. He left Sübe'etei with a reported 30,000 men to complete the conquest of Henan. It is quite likely that the Jin had larger forces than those left with Sübe'etei, but they were not concentrated in one place: strong forces defended Kaifeng and other forces assembled in Dengzhou, and there were also forces around Shangzhou, in Shaoshi, in Luoyang and around Xuzhou. To make matters more difficult, the Jin now lacked a strong overall military command. Nobody replaced Heda and Pua. The Jin were unable to take advantage of their numerical superiority.

Sübe'etei mastered the countryside around Kaifeng, assembled labourers for manual work, and filled out sections of the moats. Eyewitness Liu Qi says: 'The Mongols used prisoners, woman, and children to build paths to the walls with dirt and firewood.' He adds that they had also 'flooded the area around the city.' Sübe'etei finally enclosed the enemy capital with a line of entrenchments reportedly 30 km long. The Mongols had a vast array of large trebuchets, capable of throwing huge stones over long distances. The Jin on their side prepared their defences, backed by more advanced weapons.

With the Mongol preparations progressing, it became obvious that Sübe'etei intended to attack. He finally unleashed his forces the same day *Aizong* sent the hostages. The Mongols concentrated their attacks in the south-eastern and north-eastern sides, although there were also some along the northern side. There were none on the southern or western sides. Liu Qi, who was at this time inside the metropolis, wrote:

> The army of the Northerners then attacked the city with their trebuchets … The assault became more and more fierce, so that the trebuchet stones flew through the air like rain. People said they were like half-millstones or half-sledgehammers. The Jin defenders could not face them. But in the city there were the kind of fire-missiles called *heaven-shaking thunder-crash bombs* and these were at last used in reply, so that the Northern troops suffered many casualties, and when not wounded by the explosions were burnt to death by the fires they caused … All the people of the city were conscripted into a home guard … An order was issued to the effect that any man who remained at home would be summarily executed.

The Mongols attempted to cover their approach to the walls with cowhides, but this did not work well:

> The Mongol soldiers made cowhide sheets to cover their approach trenches and end beneath the walls, and dug as it were niches each with enough to contain a man, hoping that in this way the [Jin] troops above would not be able to do anything about it. But someone [up there] suggested the technique of lowering the thunder-crash bombs on iron chains. When these reached the trenches where the Mongols were making their dug-outs, the bombs were set off, with the result that the cowhide and the attacking soldiers were all blown to bits, not even a trace left behind.

The Mongol assaults were repelled. The Jin made sorties along the waterways: 'In between our soldiers made sudden sorties through the canal exits, whereby many enemies were killed or wounded.' A major sortie was made in the section of the front at the Nanxunmen Gate, the most western of the four northern gates, where Tacar commanded the Mongol forces. On 15 April Tacar gained a clear victory. After 16 days Sübe'etei stopped the assaults. The Jin artillery had inflicted great losses on the Mongols, and Sübe'etei was evidently not prepared to go through a drawn out siege, heeding the warning of Sun Tzu: 'If troops lay siege to a walled city, their strength will be exhausted.' On 29 April *Aizong* sent an envoy with gold and silk to beg for peace. This was the end of the famous siege of Kaifeng. For little more than two weeks the Mongols attempted without success to break through the Jin defences.

Intermission

Sübe'etei retreated to the area between the Huang River and the Luo River, just west of Luoyang, and started to draft more Han Chinese into his army in order to increase its size. At the same time he kept Kaifeng under blockade. One detachment was stationed at Huanglinggang, north-east of the city. Presumably Luoyang was also blockaded. At the same time Sübe'etei continued negotiations with the Jin Court.

Along the Luoshui River there was some skirmishing between the Mongols and the Luoyang garrison. Two engagements are described in the *Jinshi*. A Jin officer who had defected to the Mongols urged Qiang Shen to surrender: when he failed to do so, the Mongols charged across a bridge 'with hundreds of footmen'. Qiang drove them back. Later 500 Mongol cavalry attacked one of the four forts erected outside Luoyang's gates. Qiang made a sortie with 200 soldiers and drove them off (May 1232).

Ji Ruzuo re-established a Jin position in Ruzhou. The Mongols attacked the town, but could not take it.

Jing Shan was somehow not able to keep Bozhou under control. People and soldiers fled out of the city, and reinforcements sent from Guide were actually attacked and destroyed by the soldiers remaining in Bozhou. Finally, Jing Shan also fled, and on 4 June Yang Chun seized control of Bozhou. He surrendered the city to the Mongols on 16 June.

In the first week of June a plague broke out in Kaifeng, claiming a reported 900,000 lives in a matter of weeks (28 days). Densely populated Henan had a sophisticated infrastructure, which by now was damaged, leaving people in Kaifeng and other places short on food. It was an environment ripe for epidemics.

The negotiations between the Mongols and the Jin continued until derailed by an incident inside Kaifeng. On 25 July two Jin officers assembled a band that cut the Mongol ambassador and his entourage of 30 to pieces, after which no truce was possible. It was an act of madness by Jin partisans to dispose of the Mongol mission, but Sübe'etei is unlikely to have been negotiating in good faith anyway.

Confusion in the east
In Xu, Zhang Xing, the Jin officer who had deserted and then returned, fell ill. Wang You plotted against him and for that reason Feng Xian ordered him to be killed. Confusion followed. On 28 June the military commander Tudan Yidu fled, he and his wife descending from the wall using a rope, and some soldiers followed him. Guo Yongan, a Red Coat rebel who had submitted to the Mongols, marched from Shandong to Xu. He gained entry into Xu, securing control over the city on 3 July. Meanwhile, Yidu had gone to Suzhou where Geshi Lihahu refused him entry. Yidu set up camp near the city. Some officers inside, including Wang Dezhuan, then killed Lihahu and his son. Yidu refused to support them and led those under his command westwards. This group was intercepted by the Mongols and destroyed on 15 July. The Mongols may have belonged to the command of Alci.

Guo Yongan was able to secure control additional cities, including Su and Pei. Alci was not impressed, saying: 'I should take over these three cities. What kind of person is An Yong? A man who makes frequent surrenders!' He sent Xin An and Zhang Jin to seize Xuzhou. He thereby forced the hand of Guo Yongan, who decided to fight, and Wang Dezhuan backed him. They intercepted and defeated Zhang Jin, Tian Fu (the commander of Haizhou), and several hundreds of horsemen. Zhang Jin was killed.

Many garrison commanders in and around Xuzhou and Shandong met and decided again to accept Jin authority. Guo Yongan was left in a difficult position, being at odds with the Mongols as well as Yang Miaozhen. He opened a dialogue with the Jin Court, finally accepting to serve Jin again. His still commanded a sizeable army. He marched against Haizhou with 10,000 men; some of the soldiers defected during the march, but Yang Miaozhen still dared not oppose him, and retreated to Yidu.

Guo Yongan now had a Jin title and the nearby garrison commanders had also accepted Jin authority. Even so, the various officers remained at odds. Wang Dezhuan and Liu Guian held Xuzhou, but unhappy with not getting enough reward, they turned against Yongan. Yongan ordered Du Zhen to move towards Xu and Su with 3,000 men. He attempted to break into the city, but Dezhuan was alert and was even able to capture Zhen. Yongan led his full army against Xuzhou, but was also not able to enter the city. Liu Anguo and Zhong Sengnu set out from Suzhou to support Dezhuan, so Yongan dispatched some men who were able to kill them in Linhuan. Yongan remained outside Xizhou for some time before marching to Lianshui, where he set up camp.

Yin Shiying, with the forces under his command, marched to the area west of Suzhou where a Mongol detachment intercepted, defeated, and killed him on 30

December 1232. Shiying was a Jin officer earlier sent to give Yongan his official Jin titles. As during the summer, it seems clear that the Mongols kept forces in the area west of Su.

The Jin relief attempt
Substantial Jin forces remained at large in the western and southern part of Henan. Wu Xian and Neizu Silie, based on Nanyang and Teng respectively, marched towards Kaifeng with the intent to drive off the Mongols. They joined forces at Ruzhou. Here Wanyan Hu Xie also joined them with a small detachment, on 16 August 1232. Chi Zhan Hexi led 10,000 soldiers out of Kaifeng to support them. Wulinda Hutu, however, was not keen to support Neizu Silie: 'Wu Xian … and Silie … led their two forces … to camp at the woods to the south of Dengfeng city. They sent their representative to make an appointment [with Hutu] to go to Luoyang together. Hutu tried every excuse not to come down. At last, he had to detach 4,000 of his forces to follow Silie eastwards'.

The SWQZL credits the Jin with 200,000 men, but three main forces of 10,000 to 15,000 men each would be a more realistic estimate. Nobody, however, was clearly in command. The most extensive description of what happened, on 20 August 1232, is given in Wu Xian's biography:

> Silie arrived at the east of Mixian and met the troops under the command of Sübe'etei, a general-in-chief of the Great Mongol State, who were passing by there. Wu Xian took up station at Meishantian and sent off a message to Silie, telling him: 'Encamp near the gully that hinders [the Mongol Army] and wait for me to march forward together or you will be defeated.' Silie urgently attempted to reach Kaifeng and did not follow [the tactics proposed by his fellow officer]. When he marched to Jingshui, the Mongol Army took the chance to attack [his troops] so that they disorderly retreated without fighting.

The forces of Silie were dispersed and he reached Taipingding with only 20 or 30 soldiers and not a single senior officer. Hexi had led his army out of Kaifeng, taking up position at Zhongmou where he waited for the other two armies to join him (19 August 1232). Told on the third day that Silie had been defeated, Hexi retreated. His biography says:

> So he discarded all the supplies and gear [and] fled back [to Kaifeng] in high speed at night. [He and his forces] arrived at Zheng Gate at dawn … People commented, 'In the very beginning, Hexi disobeyed the order not to leave [the capital city], then the middle, [he] wandered not to march forward, and finally he fled without taking his soldiers. The left behind military supplies and gear were countless. There would be no other option to pacify the general public than beheading him.'

Xian also fell back. Splitting up his army into detachments, he ordered his officers to rejoin at Liu Shan (halfway back to Dengzhou). Xian was in Liu Shan able to rally the Jin forces. Xian got a message from *Aizong*:

Silie does not understand military operations. If he had followed your tactics about the encampment near the gully that hinders the Mongol Army, how could he have been defeated? All of military affairs are entrusted to you now. You should not only stand ready day and night but also pull together with spare no effort to prepare for future action.

The *Yuanshi* says about this period: 'The Mongols defeated all these armies in several encounters because they failed to unite.' The crucial Jin weakness was that no general had clear authority over his colleagues. Silie, a member of the royal family, refused to take orders from the more experienced Wu Xian. Wanyan Hu Xie later made his way to Shanzhou where he assumed command.

Jin officer Huang Guisanhe guarded Wuduo Mountain. He was later transferred to Biyang, a smaller appointment (some time after Wu Xian retreated back to Liushan), but was unhappy and defected to the Mongols with his men. Sübe'etei ordered him to guard Yuzhou. Guisanhe wrote to Wu Xian before the latter knew that he had defected, suggesting they made a common assault on Yuzhou. Xian agreed to this and moved forward: close to Liuhe, Guisanhe attacked him from two sides and defeated him. Xian retreated to Shenduozhai (probably c.15 January 1233). Wei Fan had been sent from the Jin Court to get Xian again to operate actively against the Mongols. He rallied thousands of dispersed Jin soldiers, but afterwards fell out with Xian. Angered by his criticism, Xian threw Fan into prison. This battle is given little attention in the sources. Possibly, Mongol forces supported Huang Guisanhe. Sübe'etei could have been involved in person.

The second siege of Luoyang

Sahe Nian was killed in or around Zheng during the failed Jin attempt to break the blockade of Kaifeng. In Luoyang, the officers elected Qiang Shen to take charge. There were now 2,500 soldiers left, but half were injured, sick, very young, or very old. The Mongols returned:

On the third day the Mongols surrounded the city on three sides. Qiang Shen tore in pieces all his silk garments and had them made into banners, which were placed on the ramparts, after which he led his men to fight stripped to the waist. Some hundred of them ran to and fro under orders from him shouting insults at the enemy, and calling them fools and madmen, to such good effect that one would have thought them as many as 10,000 … Qiang Shen furthermore invented a trebuchet called the arresting trebuchet, which was used to prevent [the enemy] from overrunning [his positions]. Only a few men were needed to work it, yet [with this engine] great stones could be hurled more than 100 paces, and there was no target which it did not hit right in the middle.

In September–October 1232 the Mongols continued active siege operations for a couple of weeks, but finally retreated and set up camp some distance away. They returned soon afterwards, in October–November, renewing siege operations; their force was now much larger. in December Silie was sent to Luoyang to assume command. He called on Hutu to join him:

Silie was *Liushanxingsheng* of Luoyang. He recruited soldiers to protect Luoyang. [Hutu] once again deferred to go. Silie sent him an official declaration, saying, 'If you still defer like before, there would be the imperial rules and I shall not coexist with you.' Hutu was scared, and then took his wife, children and soldiers to go to Luoyang, leaving half of his men at Daipingding for a base camp.

Silie's biography says of his last days: 'Ren Shouzhen was killed. When Jin emperor was informed, he repositioned Silie of Xingsheng and tasked him to defend Luoyang. Soon afterwards, the Mongol army surrounded Luoyang but could not break into it. Cui Li sent people with Silie's son to Luoyang Gate to make him surrender. Silie did not care and ordered his soldiers to shoot. Soon [afterwards] he learned that Cui Li had surrendered Kaifeng to the Mongols. He became ill and died several days later' (March 1233). Cui Li will be introduced later: he was a Jin turncoat. Silie appointed Hutu to take over his command.

The situation in the west

The earlier Tong Pass operations ended in March 1232 with Tushan Baijia, Wanyan Sulan, and the remaining Jin forces inside Shanzhou. Baijia and some of the forces were called to the central Henan some months later, in July. Further forces were called away three months later. Zhongde's biography says:

> [Wanyan Zhongde] was offered official post ... to administer ... affairs in Shanzhou. At that time, Wanyan Wudian had just been defeated and Shanzhou was heavily weakened. Zhongde renovated the fort and pacified the soldiers and civilians. Just then Jin emperor used waxed letter[3] to call the forces in all the routes for reinforcement. Other forces of Xingsheng, Yuan or Shuaifu either drifted or scattered once they met the Mongol army on the way. Only Zhongde took an isolated force of 1,000 soldiers and fought hard to break through passes and arrived at Kaifeng [in September] ... They marched through Qinzhou, Lanzhou, Shangzhou and Dengzhou by eating wild fruits and vegetables.

Some months afterwards, Mongol officer Li Shouxian moved against Jin held Taiping: Wanyan Yanshou defended the fortress. Shouxian sent a select force, 3,000 men, into the fortress at an unguarded point above a steep cliff face. They quickly secured the stronghold, on 25 January 1233. During the next 20 days Shouxian mastered the various fortresses in the region, including Liantian, Jiaoya, Lanruo and Xianglu.

In Ruzhou, Ji Ruzuo fell out with Hu Yanshi, an officer commanding forces nearby. He favoured leaving Ruzhou itself and only holding positions in the mountains. They split, and retained their respective positions. Ji Ruzuo, however, gained more prestige after defeating some Mongol forces at Xiangyang and Jia (Jiaxian). He is credited with capturing 100 horses, so it was evidently a small-scale affair. The Jin hold over

---

3   A kneaded letter coated with wax.

Ruzhou proved of some value as they could 'ship out produce to supply the people in other three directions [Deng, Luoyang, and Kaifeng] and send and receive messages.'

The Weizhou diversion

The supply situation inside Kaifeng continued to deteriorate. Finally, towards the end of the year, *Aizong* decided to leave the capital with a significant part of the garrison. The SWQZL says that he led 60,000 men out of the city, but such a total seems too high, and he took perhaps half as many men. Wanyan Zhongde was convinced that the best solution for the Jin was to move westwards into Hanzhong and Sichuan (a Zhuge Liang scheme), but *Aizong* was by others sold on the idea to make a breakout in the opposite direction. He therefore headed eastwards, setting out on 6 February 1232. Supplies were brought to his army from Guide on 300 boats moving along the canals.

The Jin crossed the Huang River at Huanglinggang with the intent to seize Weizhou. They first attacked and defeated Yan Shi's detachment, storming two forts on 10 February 1233.[4] Many Jin soldiers were ferried across the river, but 10,000 (or many) soldiers remained on the south bank by the time the Mongols arrived from the direction of Kaifeng. Sübe'etei had sent a 4,000-strong force in pursuit of *Aizong*, (the *Jinshi* says, under an officer called Huigunai). The Mongols attacked the Jin soldiers remaining behind, but failed to secure a quick victory. The close proximity of the Mongols made it difficult for the Jin to ferry men over the river and when the wind suddenly turned it was impossible. The Mongols attacked again the next day, 13 February, crushing the Jin force. In the Baisa biography it is said:

> He Duxi directed the battle with a yellow banner. He was hit by 17 arrows. [The Jin] army fought desperately and killed over 10 [Mongol] soldiers. Mongol army retreated a little. The emperor [of Jin] sent 100 pots of wine to cheer up his soldiers. In a very short time, there was a sudden burst of north wind, and all the boats were pushed to the south bank. The Mongol forces attacked them again. Nearly 1,000 men drowned … Zhu Er … Geshi Lie Elun and some others were killed … Wanyan Wulunju surrendered to the Great Mongol [Army]. Watching from the north bank [of the Huang River], the emperor was greatly shocked and filled with fear.

Aizong sent the bulk of his remaining forces to attack Weizhou. With at least six officers involved the Jin may have had more than 20,000 men. They were given more than 10 days' worth of grain. Baksan led this army past Pucheng (crossing a canal and the old main course of the Huang River) to reach Weizhou. The Jin advance triggered a panic in Dongping where people assumed the Jin were heading towards their city. The Jin hoped that people in Kai, Daming, and Dongping would rise up against the Mongols, but this did not happen. *Aizong* remained behind in a camp set up close to the Huang River. He had 3,000 guard soldiers, 1,000 Zhangxio horsemen, and the *duwai* of Gai Xian: in total perhaps 7,000 men. Baksan's advance elements quickly

---

4   Hsiao says of the defeat: 'Yen Shih's army suffered a serious defeat and more than 1,000 of his men are said to have been captured by the Chin army.'

reached Weizhou. They attempted to bribe their way into the city, but without success. Mongol cavalry approached the city, but the Jin soldiers were able to drive them off. Even so, Mongol officer Shi Tianze got close enough to the city to be able to tell the garrison that help was on the way:

> Tianze led light cavalries to come at a very fast speed. At the time when they arrived, Jin forces had already completed the encirclement. Tianze fought fiercely with his dagger-axe and reached the city wall. He shouted to the garrison: 'Do your best! The enforcement is coming soon!' He then fell back. All the guarding forces became excited and invincible.

At this point the Jin offensive lost momentum. It took Baisa eight days to move the main forces from Pucheng to reach Weizhou after crossing the Huang and in addition he had failed to prepare siege materials, even ladders. Starting on 17 February the Jin attacked for three days without being able to break into Weizhou. The forces of Doqolqu Cerbi, Shi Tianze, and Yan Shi crossed the Huang River at Henan and Zhangjiadu further west on 21 February. With the approach of the Mongol relief force, Baisa retreated towards Pucheng. The Mongols intercepted and defeated him at Baigong Temple near Zhixian or Oumagang Mountain near Changyuan:

> The people in Weizhou knew that they were not able to attack, and then strengthened the defending measures. The attack lasted for 3 days and yet failed. On hearing that the Great Mongol Army to the south of the Huang River had taken ferries across at Zhangjiadu and reached the south-west of Weizhou, they retreated. The Great Mongol army pursued and fought them at Baigong Temple. Baisa was defeated, and he fled discarding his men. Civilians killed Liu Yi and Zhang Kai. The chariots (here it refers to the forces) retreated and stationed 30 miles east at Pucheng.

In the *Yuanshi* mention is made of a converging attack: '[The Mongols] … started converging to attack the Jin army. Baisa was defeated and led his forces to Pucheng. Tianze followed them, beheaded and captured nearly all of his 80,000 forces.'

The *Jinshi* says of the closing stages of the Weizhou operation:

> Baisa presented a confidential memorandum to the Emperor saying that Liu Yi's force betrayed [them]. At the time … Mo Nian Wu Dian and … Wen Dun Zhang Sun were serving [the emperor of Jin] in the travel tent. They asked the Emperor to get aboard a boat. The Emperor said, 'It is a decisive battle. Why retreat in such a hurry?' After a short while, Baisa came. He reported in panic to the Emperor: 'The forces are defeated and the Great Mongol Army is nearby along the river bank. Your Majesty, please move to Guide.' The Emperor then went aboard. His bodyguards knew nothing and patrolled as usual. It was already the fourth watch, so [the Emperor of Jin] entered Guide like a drowned mouse. Aizong with a few followers crossed the Huang River (25 February 1233) and reached Guide (27 February 1233). Baisa collected about 20,000 routed troops at Daqiao. He was frightened not to dare to enter [Guide]. When the Emperor was told this, he sent

two housecarls … with a rowboat to bring Baisa back. When Baisa came, [the Emperor] did not see and listen to him. [The Emperor] put Baisa and his son into prison.

The Jin soldiers north of the Huang River ran out of supplies and took what they could find in the countryside: however they failed to pay for what they took and the local people turned against them. The effort of Baisa to reassemble an army north of the Huang River was only a temporary success and the force dispersed after a short while on 26 February, perhaps in part due to lack of food. Only 1,000 soldiers were able to escape across the Huang River. The Jin offensive ended as a complete failure.

It was perhaps at the same time that Jin forces, coming from the general Shanzhou area, attacked Huaizhou. Ismail, the officer who had served under Jebe during the sweep around the Caspian Sea, was responsible for guarding Huaizhou and Mengzhou. Backed by Xilijisi and Sulahai, he drove back the Jin. The *Yuanshi* says Wang You commanded the Jin army. Ismail sent Pucha Hannu and Qishi Liezhalu to pursue the defeated forces: they intercepted the Jin and captured an officer called Fan Zhen as well as many soldiers. Wang You soon afterwards surrendered with his forces to Li Shouxian. He was then at Nanshan.

Xuzhou
The Jin lost control over most of the territory east of the Huang River. Zhuo Yi, Sun Bi Chong and other officers in Peixian defected to Guo Yongan who renamed the city Yuanzhou (an administrative upgrade). Yongan was still a nominal Jin subject, but really operated as an independent warlord. The Jin Court sent Wanyan Zhongde to take charge of military affairs in the Xuzhou region, and he was able to win back Zhuo Yi, Sun Bi Chong, and the other rebel officers to the Jin side. Wang Dezhuan viewed Zhongde with suspicion. Remaining a Jin loyalist, Dequan also kept in touch with Yongan. When Zhang Xian killed Wanyan Hutu and plotted to hand over Bao'an (or Yushan) to the Mongols, Dezhuan did not want to support Zhongde in an attack on the new rebel threat. During March Zhongde marched to Bao'an with only 10 soldiers and 300 locally raised men (militia). Some officers, including Yan Lu, killed Zhang Xian, and Zhongde regained Jin control over the forces and Bao'an. Zhongde brought grain back to Xu; he also collected grain from Su, Xu itself, and Zhen.

Zhang Xian was probably in communication with the Mongols before he was killed, for Alci arrived soon afterwards at Bao'an with a Mongol army. Yan Lu fled, taking refuge with Guo Yongan in Lianshui. Min Xiu, another officer, fled to Xuzhou. Alci occupied Bao'an and pushed on towards Xiaoxian. Zhongde was at this point in Su. In April Dequan sent 800 cavalry out of Xu to drive the Mongols off, commanded by Zhang Yuange and Miao Xiuchang. Encountering the Mongols – who were led by Wang Zhen – Yuange was faulted for retreating before the fighting had even started. The Mongols overwhelmed the Jin and took Xiaoxian.[5]

5   The *Yuanshi* says: 'Then [Wang Zhen] participated in the pacification of Henan, under the command of Sübe'etei. He defeated Jin general Wu Xian at Zhengzhou, and then fought with Jin army at Xiaoxian

Zhongde pretended to be organising a food convoy for Pizhou. Dechuan was somehow tempted to come out of Xuzhou, and on 19 May Zhongde seized and killed him as well as his son. Soon afterwards, in June, Zhongde was recalled to the Jin Court, and on 4 August the aged Wanyan Saibu was sent to take charge of affairs in Xuzhou. The Jin tried to regain ground in Shou. Having lost Shouzhou itself, on 16 September they selected Mengcheng as the main city.

The fall of Kaifeng

Sübe'etei again encircled Kaifeng. Inside Kaifeng, Cui Li and some other officers staged a coup, overthrowing the leadership Wanyan Nuchen was killed (5 March 1233). Li was an officer who had been in charge of the western section of the wall, and he immediately opened negotiations with Sübe'etei. Sübe'etei had set up his camp at Qingcheng, where Li went to meet him on 30 March; Sübe'etei gave Li wine and accepted him as his son. Li declared himself willing to surrender Kaifeng to the Mongols, and handed over 500 royal consort woman and children to them. Sübe'etei sent them all to Ögödei, asking for permission to sack and destroy Kaifeng: 'This city has resisted for a long time, and many officers and men have been harmed. I request to be allowed to destroy the city.' Ögödei, advised by Yelü Chucai[6] – and perhaps to the surprise of Sübe'etei – refused. Li also tried to help Sübe'etei secure Luoyang (as related above). Li Shuner seized power in Chenzhou on 25 May, exploiting soldier discontent due to rationing of food, and on 27 May accepted the authority of Cui Li. Mongols entered Kaifeng some days later, on 29 May. Sübe'etei's men lightly plundered the metropolis. The citizens bartered valuables for food; the whole of Henan suffered from food shortages at this point. Chen surrendered at the same time as Kaifeng.

Sübe'etei had managed operations in his usual economical style. He continuously kept up negotiations with the Jin, obviously having no intent of actually making peace. He fielded a huge artillery park and attempted to take Kaifeng by means of a kind of blitz attack – a unique idea – but reverted to a blockade once it was clear this approach was proving too costly. 12 months later the city fell into his hands peacefully. Sübe'etei would probably have been better advised to turn against Kaifeng in March 1233 instead of first wasting a month attempting to secure Luoyang and Guide, as he gave the Kaifeng defenders an extra month to prepare their defences.

The Mongols attempted to take Kaifeng, Luoyang (twice) and Guide by siege, failing in all cases. Conventional lore praises the Mongols for their ability to reduce strong places by siege, however the fact is that although they could field a strong artillery park, they were even at this stage weak with regard to deeper siege engineering expertise, even if these well-fortified cities were simply hard to take.

Sübe'etei dealt with the forces of Wu Xian and his colleagues in detail. He probably operated with skill, but the Jin must be blamed for having a fragmented command. Wu

County, beheaded its general.' It therefore seems that at least elements of Ashulu's army had previously served with the main forces in central Henan.
6   He was a Khitan who had taken service with the Mongols after the fall of Beijing. Genghis Khan gave him great civilian responsibility about 10 years later.

Xian well understood the need to deploy the army in a strong defensive position. With this strategy he might have been able to hold off the Mongols. Wu Xian followed his own agenda and was perhaps not a true Jin loyalist. Even so, it seems he cannot be blamed for his conduct on this occasion. Knowing how to conduct operations near the Mongols, he was the only officer to get away from the debacle without damage to his reputation.

In strict military terms, the 12 month period from April 1232 to March 1233 was not very successful for Sübe'etei, mainly because of his inability to take strongly fortified cities. He remained dominant in open terrain, but the Jin generally stayed inside their cities. Time, however, worked to his advantage as the Jin economy was ruined. The Jin grew weaker and weaker.

Sources: *Yuanshi* 2, p.127, 119, 2945–2947, 120, pp.2969–2974, 121, p.2977, 122, pp.3009, 3013–3014, 123, 3031–3032, 146, pp.3455–3464, 150, pp.3546–3548, 155, pp.3657–3663; SWQZL, 81b; *Jinshi* 17, pp.384–387, 18, pp.393–403, 111, pp.2448–2455, 113, pp.2476–2482, pp.2484–2492, pp.2492–2501; 115, pp.2526–2531, 2524–2526, 116, pp.2542–2543, 117, pp.2555–2559, 2561–2565, 118, pp.2577–2581, 119, pp.2604–2612, 123, pp.2689–2691; SWQZL, 84a (Kaifeng exit dated three months too early); Wang E, entry 2, 17, 36, pp.61–62, 72–73, 83–84; Erich Haneish, *Die Ehreninschrift für den Rebellengeneral Ts'ui Lih* (Berlin: Verlag der Akademie der Wissenschaften, 1944); Erich Haenisch, *Zum Untergang zweier Reiche; Berichte von Augenzeugen sus den Jahren 1232–33 und 1360–1370* (Wiesbaden: F. Steiner, 1969); Needham, *Science and Civilization in China*, vol. 5, pp.146, 171–173, 218; Franke, 'The Chin Dynasty', p.257; Hok-Lam Chan, *The Fall of the Jurchen Chin*, p.126, note 72 (citing *Jinshi* 44); Hsiao, 'Shih T'ein-Tse', 'Chang Jou', 'Yen Shih', *In the Service of the Khan*, pp.30, 51, 65.

43

The End of Jin

In the winter following the fall of the city [= Kaifeng], Sübe'etei surrounded the Jin emperor in Caizhou ... Jin was destroyed.

– Wang Yun

The Jin retained control over only a few strongpoints in Henan. *Aizong* was inside Guide. Luoyang, Cai, and Deng also remained under Jin control and Jin loyalists also controlled some cities in Shandong. The Mongols dominated the countryside, but their level of activity was low. Sübe'etei camped close to Ruzhou in the western part of Henan. Probably, in line with Genghis Khan's normal practice, Sübe'etei was reluctant to campaign actively during the summer months. During these final operations Tacar emerges as Sübe'etei's key lieutenant, replacing his relative Doqolqu Cerbi.

The Song enter the fray

Wu Xian retained command over large forces in south-western Henan. He had evidently been able to draft many available men into his forces. His men were segmented into three different groups, namely his own, those of Wu Tianxi, and those of Yila Yuan. Meng Gong's biography says that they 'deployed their forces like deer horns so that they were able to support each other.' Wu Tianxi, who used to be a farmer, entered the area around Guanghua where the Mongols had crossed the Han, commanding no more than an armed rabble. The main preoccupation of this group was to find food. Yila Yuan was in Deng and Wu Xian was back in his old camp at Shunyang. Meng Gong still commanded the Song army in Xiangyang. Turning against the nearest foe, he attacked and crushed Wu Tianxi in early May 1233: 'Meng Gong approached his stockade, and took it over at first attempt.' The biography optimistically records 5,000 enemy soldiers killed, including Wu Tianxi. Four hundred, a more realistic number, were taken captive.

Meng Gong had garrisons holding Muzha, Dengyun, and Luyan, covering the approaches to Xiangyang. The men of Yila Yuan engaged in a small war against the Song. A Song detachment scored a success against the Jin at Xiajiaqiao, and later a larger Jin force commanded by Liu Quan and Lei Quwei attacked Luyan. Meng

Gong moved forward quickly with 8,000 men to ward them off. He 'took advantage of natural barriers provided by mountains and made strategic deployment of all the forces in different stockades.' Fifty-two armoured Jin soldiers were captured. Yila Yuan surrendered Dengzhou to the Song soon after these events, on 10 June. According to the *Songshi*, Yila Yuan had 1,500 horsemen and 14,000 foot soldiers.[1]

Yila Yuan told Song officer Shi Songji that Wu Xian's forces were in a poor state, and he dispatched Meng Gong with 5,000 soldiers to attack the Jin general. Xian had his men out collecting wheat when the Song arrived. Most of his men were one kilometre distant from the camp, but Xian boldly led the 100 or so guards remaining in the camp out to meet the attack. Gong's soldiers did not dare to advance, and Xian after assembling 500 or 600 soldiers moved forward to assault them. Gong and hundreds of soldiers ran away, and many Song officers were captured. Xian executed Zhu Gai and Liu Quo and some of his own officers after learning that they planned to surrender to the Song. This embarrassing affair was passed over in the biography of Gong.

With Deng in Song hands, Wu Xian was left somewhat isolated in Shunyang. Looking for a stronger position in the face of the Song threat, he fell back to the mountains to the north. Shunyang and Shenzhou submitted to the Song, who used Deng as a springboard for an attack on Tang, but in spite of persistent efforts they were not able to secure that city until much later. Xian is credited with having 70,000 troops. Such a total is not possible, but he may still have had substantial forces at his disposal, say 10,000–20,000 men. A core of these had served him for a long time and were probably veteran fighters. *Aizong* sent messengers to him, ordering him to lead his forces to Caizhou, but Xian refused, possibly considering it impossible to move his forces out of the area he controlled. Liu Yi, the favourite officer of Xian, defected to Meng Gong with 200 men. Gong, armed with intelligence provided by Yi, set out to finally deal with Xian. It is not reported how many men he had, but he is certainly likely to have had a larger force than Xian.

By now Wu Xian had been in the Madeng area for some time and had constructed nine fortified camps. The main position was the Shixue camp. Unable to place all his soldiers there, he constructed three other camps west and south of the rivers, at Hu (south-west), Shawo, and Madeng (south). Further camps were established inside the 'V' of the rivers. Meng Gong approached the enemy position undetected, perhaps through the mountains towards the south-west,[2] and first seized the smaller camps at Lijin and Wangzi in the north-west. Having thus placed himself between the main camp and the three covering camps further south – in the V between the rivers – he next attacked Madeng, positioning a detachment to cut off the camp and make sure nobody escaped. The Song overwhelmed Xian's soldiers. A sortie from the camp at Shawo was driven off, and the Song prevailed in three encounters in a single day. Later some Song forces overran the camp at Mohouli. Sending a captured officer to the fort, Gong was able to induce the Banqiao garrison to surrender. He anticipated that Xian

---

1   Yila Yuan was given a Chinese name and a new position. Reportedly dispondant, he died of illness during April 1234. Bai Hua submitted to Song along with Yila Yuan.
2   An approach through the plains in the south or south-east would surely be difficult to mask?

would go to the hill at Hu to better see what was happening and had prepared an ambush there: it was very successful. Xian escaped, but 730 of his men were captured. Finally, Gong mounted a dawn assault on the Shixue position and nearby Jiuzhai. It was a rainy day with limited visibility, which Gong considered to be an advantage, and the Jin position was overwhelmed. Xian fled to Nianyuzhai, hotly pursued by the Song, who caught up with him at Yinhulu Mountain where he was again defeated. The Jin commander escaped with only five or six horsemen: his army was ruined (16 to 23 August 1233). Gong returned to Xiangyang.

Mongol–Jin confrontations

Doqolqu Cerbi and Shi Tianze shadowed *Aizong* as he made his way south to Guide. Doqolqu, with 3,500 Mongol soldiers, set up camp north of Guide at a place called Wangjiasi. He had waterways in front, on both flanks, and in the rear. Shi Tianze camped nearby, but south of the large canal. According to his biography, he warned Doqolqu: 'Can here be a camp for forces? If the enemy attacks, you would then have no base to depend on.' The biographer may have added the comment to make Tainze look good, but it seems clear the position of Doqolqu was exposed and dangerous.

The Jin forces assembling in Guide were too large for the city to sustain, and units were sent to Su, Chen and Xu to relieve the logistical pressure. The emperor kept 450 soldiers under Pucha Guannu and 280 under Ma Yong to guard Guide itself. The various Jin officers and officials at the Court were not united and competed for influence: Guannu disposed of a rival and many of his followers, gaining control over the court on 5 May 1233.

Sübe'etei kept his main forces west of Kaifeng. With Doqolqu and Tianze close to Guide, Bozhou in Mongol hands, and Alci close to Xuzhou, he effectively encircled the Jin Court. This ring, however, was quickly broken. Yang Jun sent the forces of Bo out of the city to support the Mongol forces masking Guide. Wang Jin then made his way into Bo where he, together with Wang Bin, established himself. The two Wangs were recognised by *Aizong* as officials in charge of this city (May–June 1233). Mongol officer Tacar – if he is Taiji of the *Yuanshi* – surrounded Bozhou with many soldiers on 9 June. Xi Zhu, coming from Guide, managed to get into Bozhou with three men to support Wang Jin. The Mongols gave up the siege and retreated after eight days, on 18 June. It is not clear how serious this Mongol initiative was. Perhaps Sübe'etei aimed to again tighten the blockade of Guide?

On 9 June Tacar sent an envoy to *Aizong*, urging him to surrender. *Aizong* naturally refused to entertain the idea. Pucha Guannu and Aliho Yawutai marched out to Guide to Bo, and from there headed south-westwards. They left the baggage at Cai and from there went westwards, finally setting up camp at Shengduo close to Wu Xian, on 25 June. They considered Guanzhong as a potential point of refuge for the Court. At this point *Aizong* called him back to Guide. After receiving a second message, Guannu complied. He left half of his men in Bo and marched with the rest to Guide on 29 June.

Doqolqu opened a dialogue with the Jin: perhaps he did not think they had any fight left in them. Pucha Guannu, however, decided on military action. He prepared special fire weapons and moved out of Guide's south gate at night with a small force, comprising his own contingent of 450 men plus some other units. He secretly shipped his men along the canal on boats, moving east and then north, disposing of the Mongol patrols he encountered as he moved forward. He then began to attack the main position of Doqolqu, but after an initial advance fell back slightly. Perhaps he aimed to draw the Mongols forward to this sector of their camp? He then divided his force into detachments of 50–70 men, each in their own boat, deploying to attack the Mongol camp from all sides. The Jin attacked with 'flying fire lances' and the Mongol army was wiped out, 'caught between hammer and the anvil,' on 12 July 1233. At this time Shi Tianze was back in Kaifeng: as in 1225, he knew how to stay away when a disaster happened. Guannu won a remarkable victory. Doqolqu was at fault for setting up camp in an exposed position and probably for lax security. Guannu's use of boats and fire-weapons was novel, least in this part of China, and he boldly encircled the Mongol camp to attack from all sides. This was a 20th-century style of attack. Arguably, this was the most impressive victory ever gained by the Jin over the Mongols. Considering that Sübe'etei had fairly limited forces at hand and only part of them were Mongols, this defeat and destruction of a Mongol crack detachment must have been a fairly serious setback. Even so, the Jin did not afterwards attempt to seize the initiative. According to Rashid al-Din, Ögödei commented: 'From the time of Genghis Khan on, battle has been done so many times with the armies of Cathay, and we have continually defeated them and taken most of their territory. Now that they have struck our troops, it is a sign of their impending doom, like a lamp that flickers and burns brightest just before going out.' The Jin could have made better use of these weapons. Envision the Jin defending the Huang River in force with soldiers on boats armed with the advanced weapons against Ögödei in 1232. They could perhaps even have used such a force to break the siege of Hezhong in 1232. Like Nazi Germany the Jin had innovative weapons, for example thundercrash bombs, which they managed to make only limited use of. Doqolqu escaped the disaster but was later executed: poisoned by Ögödei under unclear circumstances. Looking back, Ögödei listed the 'injury' of Doqolqu as one of his errors. Pucha Guannu was executed in Guide just two weeks after gaining the stunning victory over the Mongols, the victim of some court intrigue. Aliho Yawutai, the son of Heshilie Yawutai, was amongst others executed at the same time, on 26 July. Thus both the winning and losing commanders were executed.

At this time the brave Qiang Shen who had defended Luoyang so well was finally overcome. After the fall of Kaifeng, Wulinda Hutu lost courage and left Luoyang, taking with him some light cavalry as well as his family. He headed for Cai, arriving there before 28 August 1233. A very small force was left to guard Luoyang, and a perhaps discouraged Jin officer opened the west gate to the Mongols. Qiang Shen and some soldiers fled out of the east gate. He fought his way to Yanshi, where he and his men were finally overwhelmed, and the Mongol soldiers took him to Tacar. Qiang Shen kept insulting his captors who then killed him on 18 July, before he reached the Mongol general. It is said that the Mongols had made 150 assaults on Luoyang: it only fell 15–16 months after the first attacks had been made. Sübe'etei may at this point have shifted his focus from east to west, wanting finally to secure Luoyang. Such a shift would leave the road open for the Jin to evacuate Guide. Pucha

Guannu had visited Caizhou and considered it folly to relocate the Court to this place, but with him out of the way, the idea to move to Caizhou was accepted by all. Little planning was involved. The Jin Court wrote to Wugo Lungao in Xi. In addition to Xi, Wang E says this officer was also responsible for Cai, Chen, and Ying and 'each [town had] to send cavalry to met [at the rendezvous]. They were informed of [His Majesty's] dates and routes of travel as agreed upon.' Wugo Lunpu Xian was ordered to prepare logistics. He surveyed tax collection in and around Cai and made plans for the collection of fodder and grain. *Aizong* left Guide, initially sailing along a canal. He stopped at Bozhou, 27–28 July, reaching Caizhou five days later on 2 August 1233. Wugo Lungao and Naizu Loso, coming from Xi, arrived in Cai before *Aizong*, bringing some cavalry forces (an order for them to go to Caizhou was sent from Guide on 14 July). *Aizong* and his advisers knew that Sübe'etei camped at Ruzhou and did not want to get near this place.

Cai had been the capital of a rebel Tang governor during the early years of the 9th century. The revolt collapsed after Tang general Li Su made a successful surprise attack on the city under the cover of a snowstorm. At that time the area around Cai was littered with forts guarded by dedicated soldiers, but no such network of forts existed now. Further, Cai itself was poorly prepared to withstand a siege. Some years before, it had a registered population of 36,913. Later scribes strongly held the view that it was a mistake to go to Cai. On 6 October soon after arriving in Cai, *Aizong* received a message from Guo Yongan urging him to either go back to Guide or come to Shandong. It seems clear that Cai was a poor choice, but at this point the final fall of the Jin was only a matter of time, no matter where the Court went. *Aizong* understood that Guannu had been right.

Bozhou remained with Jin, though Cui Hui fell out with Wang Jin after his men made an unauthorised raid. Zhang Tiangang killed Wang Jin and then on 31 July took steps to reduce the conscription of labour, which evidently before had increased resentment amongst the people.[3] The Mongols started to blockade Guide in September: the city held out for three months before surrendering in December. Luoyang, Guide, and Kaifeng, the cities that held off the Mongols in 1232, were now all lost.

With the Mongols in Ruzhou and the Jin at Caizhou, the main theatre of operations shifted from northern to southern Henan. Availabilty of food and forage forced this shift. Supplies had been exhausted in the northern parts of the province after a year and a half of protracted conflict. The various forces relocated to better-supplied regions, much like the mobile armies of the Thirty Years' War later did.

The Mongol–Song alliance

The Mongols negotiated an agreement with Song, seeking their aid to finish off the Jin. Wang Ji was sent to Xiangyang to work out an agreement. Song officials Shi Songji and Meng Hong, eager to secure a part of Henan, favoured the idea of supporting the Mongols. A deal was worked out, but the details are not known. Clearly the Song were

---

3   Wang Jin and Wang Bin did not impress Wang E: he wrote that they 'had committed many acts of wrongdoing, losing the loyalty of the soldiers.'

promised south Henan. A Song envoy was later sent north to hold further discussions with the Mongol leadership, in July 1233, but he only reached the Mongol Court much later. Sübe'etei may have considered his available forces and logistical resources too limited to be able to achieve an easy victory. Perhaps he simply preferred using allies to fight, conserving his own forces. The only Mongol commander mentioned during the final stages of the war is Tacar. The longer *Yuanshi* Sübe'etei biography implies that he took part in the siege of Cai. Certainly it is likely he continued to supervise operations, even if Tacar was the frontline commander. In Caizhou, the Jin knew that the Mongols and Song exchanged messengers, reason for them to worry, though with their foreign policy over the last decades this should not be a surprise.

Song officer Meng Gong took Tang. A Jin force, led by Wulinda Hutu and others, was sent from Caizhou to check the Song. Wang E recorded:

> [The Jin emperor] then ordered Hutu to lead about 100 of *Zhongxiao* soldiers together with … [other] … forces … to reinforce [the Jin in Tang]. Hutu led the forces and came to Tangzhou. The Song army … let half of his forces inside the city, then started converging attack. Hutu suffered a great defeat. Only 30 cavalrymen returned; Huan Zhu was killed … only a 1,000-odd braves [survived].

This happened some days after 28 August 1233. The Tang citadel only surrendered weeks later, on 18 September. *Aizong* was not happy to see the Song winning battles, commenting: 'The fact that the Tatars unleash their forces and often win battles is because they rely on their northern style and use the tricks of the Chinese. It is difficult to fight against them. As for the Song, they are really not our match. They are weak and not material, just like women.'

From Tang, Song forces turned towards Xi. A Jin detachment, some 3,300 soldiers under the command of Monian Wudian, was rushed from Cai to reinforce Xi on 19 September. On 25 September a Jin unit, 100 men, scored a success against the Song at Zhongdu; the next day Wudian raided across the Huai and collected grain from Song territory. It seems Song forces in Xi subsequently increased in strength, as these were the last Jin successes. *Aizong* ordered 5,000 men from Ying and Chen – presumably the parts of this general district still in his hands – to Xi, to look for food. Boqulu Loshi and Pucha Heda commanded the forces. They were ordered to turn back once it became clear that the Song forces camping near Xi where too strong. On 30 September Song forces pursued them as far as Gaohuangbei. Wang Canger, of the Anping command, led 1,000 soldiers and their dependents from Cai to Xi in order to reduce the food burden in Cai. When Wang Canger reached Pingyu on 1 October, he heard 'that there were roving enemy cavalry' nearby and therefore decided to retreat. The Jin tried again some days later, this time taking 3,000 soldiers and their dependents; Pucha Heda was in command with Canger as his deputy. They collided with Song forces at Maxindian about 30 km south of Cao. After 'fighting vigorously all day' the Jin soldiers were crushed, Canger killed, and Heda taken captive. An Guang led more than 100 survivors, all 'with war wounds', back to Cai on 4 October.[4]

Wang E reported under a later entry (6 October 1233) that '[the Song people] have seized our Shou and Si prefectures, induced Deng Prefecture [to submit] and raided Tang Prefecture.' It was, however, the Mongols who occupied Shouzhou. The people of Shouzhou surrendered the city to Kökö Buqa, and the Mongols subsequently handed the city over to the Song. The Jin afterwards used Mengcheng as their local administration point in the Shou district.

The end in Shanzhou and Xuzhou

Zhao Wei, camping with his men at Jinjibao, depended on food supplied from Shanzhou. This arrangement ended in May 1233 when the harvest was ripe and Zhao Wei was told to find his own supplies, then readily available in the countryside. By winter, Zhao Wei again needed supplies and started to look for food sources. During October forces were sent from Shanzhou to guard the food stored in Yuancun Fort. The Mongols took this fort before the end of the month. Wei attempted to take Jiezhou, but was not successful. He was, however, able to secure control over Shanzhou. In late Noveber an elite unit gained entry into the city, after which Wei crossed the Huang River with his full force. Zhao Wei then stayed in Shanzhou, but by the end of the winter the supplies had been used up in this town also. During March–April 1234 he surrendered to the Mongols with his forces. Guo Dehai was one of the Mongol officers masking Zhao Wei's position.

In Shandong, Guo Yongan started to communicate with the Song, offering to serve them with his private army in return for supplies. The Song, however, sent no supplies, and Yongan's army was decimated due to lack of food. Wanyan Saibu, the new – and final – Jin official in charge of Xuzhou was according to Wang E 'stocky and impressive looking; he was quiet, serious, and possessed great wisdom.' By now he was, however, old and sickly. Lacking food, in July–August 1233 he sent Guo En to attack Bao'an with forces raised in Xu, Su, and Lingbi. The effort was a failure. However an officer, Zhou Yi, was able to secure Fengxian in September–October.

Liu Shun and Yang Chun led a Mongol force in an attack on Bozhou, but the defenders held them off and the Mongols resorted to guile. They retreated back across the Huang River, but soon afterwards doubled back and quickly took Bozhou (August–September 1233).

A Mongol detachment force-marched out of Dongping, passing Lianshui en route for Cai. Jala commanded this force. Guo Yongan submitted to him when he approached his camp, but as soon as Jala marched away Guo Yongan was able regain control over his private army, and he again talked to the Song.

Jin officer Guo En communicated with Macong in Bao'an, the place he had failed to take three months before. Some Bao'an forces approached Xuzhou, gaining entry into the city. On 16 November Wanyan Saibu committed suicide after it was clear the

4   Meng Gong's biography mention of a defeat of Jin forces coming from Zhenyang and Hengshan, claiming 1,200 enemy soldiers killed.

city was lost.[5] Yi, Lai, Hai and Wei (Shandong districts) surrendered around the time the Mongols and the Song began to besiege Caizhou.

Zhang Rong and some Mongol forces attacked Pei. Jin general Suo E attempted to make a night attack on the Mongols, but Rong was alert and ready so E quickly decided to retreat. Rong followed, attacked, and killed him. Pei surrendered soon afterwards.

Guo Yongan, still stationed near the Lianshui, set out to drive the Mongols off. They defeated him, presumably some time before Suo E attempted to assault the Mongol camp, and Yongan retreated towards Xuzhou. The Mongol forces later followed him, and Zhang Rong defeated and killed Yongan outside Xuzhou. Yang Jiezhige outflanked the Jin line with 100 cavalry and fell on their rear. Yongan's men dispersed (February 1234).

In June, at the same time Luoyang fell, Mongol forces raided Ruzhou and made it impossible to farm there. The Jin therefore started to run out of food. In August, Liang Gao and other locals conspired against Ji Ruzuo and killed him. The Jin Court tried to punish Liang Gao, ordering a bodyguard called Zhang Tianci to go to Ruzhou. *Aizong* further ordered Hu Yanshi and Fan Zhen to provide support. Hu Yanshi was based on Xianshan, one kilometre south-west of Xiangyang, and some forts along the Hanshui River to the east. Fan Zhen was based on Deng, and sent a subordinate to go with Zhang Tianci. They went to Ruzhou, but instead of attacking they tried to negotiate. Liang Gao poisoned Zhang Tianci and managed to sustain his position for his while. The Mongols later killed Liang Gao.

The siege of Cai
On 20 November 1233 the Jin Court called on Guo Yongan (Shandong), Wu Xian (Nanyang), Wanyan Saibu (Xu), Niango Nuzhan (Shanxi), and Monian Wudian (Xi) to march to Cai with their forces. None of the officers attempted to do this, and the leaders of the remaining garrisons in Chen, Ying, Xiu, Shou, and Si, also ordered to march on Cai, also ignored the order. It was given in much the same circumstances as when Hitler ordered units to succour him inside Berlin even after the Red Army had encircled the city. By now the game had been over for some time. The only reinforcement that came was Yuan Zhi from Lushan with 1,000 men. He had been 'fighting the enemy all the way.' However, only half of his men made it into Cai, on 11 October 1233. The Mongols concentrated their forces around Caizhou. Wang E noted: 'the main force of the enemy forces had already penetrated beyond Jun and Xu prefectures' (reported 28 September 1233). It seems Sübe'etei gave Tacar the task of taking Caizhou, coming from Ruzhou (August 1233). Other forces approached Cai from the east. One column, having secured Lianshui in Shandong, moved across the Huang River south of Xuzhou and headed towards Cai. The Mongols first deployed along the east side of Cai, then the south, and finally enclosed the whole city. On 22 October the garrison deployed along the walls to defend the city. It is reported in the *Jinshi* that the lines of encirclement were built in eight days (15–23 October). The

5   Or 11 November? Hok-lam Chan says that Guo Yelü communicated with Lu Cung, Song official in charge of Pei, and that it was Song forces that took Xuzhou. Wang E in Cai received the news by 28 December.

stockade was not very tight, as evidenced by the conduct of Wendun Zhangsun, who sneaked out on the west side to 'a stagnant river called Lianjiang' where he caught fish for the emperor. Finally, on 27 November, 'the enemy had been spying and a trap was set to ambush him on his return trip. Our army was defeated and vanquished, but Zhangsun stayed and fought. He was thus killed.'

On 4 December Meng Gong joined Tacar in front of Caizhou, bringing 10,000 troops and 300,000 sacks of rice.[6] Without the food the Mongols would probably have been forced to retreat. Guo Yongan had in a letter to the Jin Court predicted this risk months before: 'should [the Song] supply the enemy with soldiers and grain, catastrophe will not be avoided.' Meng Gong took station on the south side of Cai, and the Mongols covered the other sides. A separate Song force remained at Xizhou, which surrendered to the Song some weeks later, on 28 December. Jin officer Monian Wudian was taken captive, but soon afterwards was able to commit suicide.

Jin lacked soldiers in Cai and reportedly equipped women and stationed them along the wall to increase the numbers. An official, Shimo Huer, came up with the idea of making a mask 'looking like a lion but very fierce' for the horses. He wanted to make a sortie with soldiers on horses wearing these masks, thinking it would scare off the Mongol horses. *Aizong* listened to the proposal, but turned it down after military men advised him that the Mongols and Song were too numerous and that clever men would laugh at them if they attempted to do this. Tian Dan in his day was able to make a successful sortie, but he used bulls rather than painted masks and backed up the bulls with 5,000 men ready to fight to the death. When the Jin made a sortie out of a southern gate, Meng Gong cut off their retreat and captured many soldiers. He learned from the captives taken that the Jin lacked men and supplies.

Wang E offers rare eyewitness account of a Mongol siege. Active siege operations started on 4 January 1234, 74 days after the Mongols had sealed off the city and 31 days after the Song arrived. The deep Ju River covered Cai on the northern and eastern sides and a moat covered the other two sides. A fortified tower out of which the Jin directed effective incendiary fire was the key to their position on the southern side. Mongol and Song forces targeted this sector, first attacking a forward redoubt close to the south-western corner. Zhang Rou's advance guard was defeated and he was himself wounded by an arrow. Meng Gong committed some forces and drove the Jin off. The Song and the Mongols, having secured the area outside the wall, dug a canal to divert the water from the Zhai Tarn Lake into the Ju River. Wang E says that 'the enemy burst [the embankment of] the Lian River [= the moat]. The Song people also inundated the Chai Tarn, flooding the Ju River.' This uncovered the southern and western sections of the city walls, flooding the other sides on 8 January. Subsequent attempts to breach the west walls failed, and on 12 January Tacar decided to switch the attention to the southern side. On 14 January Meng Gong assaulted and took the tower on that side, capturing 537 enemy soldiers. Soon afterwards on 20 January, Tacar broke through the western wall and found that the Jin had erected a new line

6   Meng Gong's biography says 20,000 men, a number that could include non-combatants.

of defences behind it. Wang E says he 'ordered his men not to rush the attack, hoping for an uprising among the Cai people as a superior tactic.' Tacar, like Sübe'etei, did not want to engage in combat under conditions where he was likely to lose many men, even if ultimate victory was quite certain. Caizhou finally fell 20 days later, on 9 February. *Aizong* committed suicide by means of hanging, and 500 Jin loyalist officers drowned themselves in a pond, following the ritual of loyal servants in the dying moments of a great dynasty.

After the fall of Caizhou, Zhang Rou saw 10 captured Jin officials about to be hanged. One of these looked distinguished. Told it was the noted literati Wang E, Rou secured his release and subsequently sponsored his efforts to publish a history of the Jin dynasty. Wang E lived with the guilt of having changed allegience to a new dynasty and was eager to produce an objective history.

In January a 1,000-strong Song force defeated Wu Xian at Zhezhuan, and he fled with a few horsemen. Later, in June–July, he was killed by one of his own officers. Wu Xian's remaining followers dispersed, many going to the Taiyuan and Zhending region. They set up camp in Damingquan and from there raided the surrounding territory in order to collect supplies. They held off several Mongol attacks. Finally, Yang Weizhong won over several of the leaders and dispersed the rest. Wang You gathered some soldiers in Nanyang: Shou Xian opened a dialogue with him and was able to induce him into surrendering. Wu Xian's army was no more.

Sun Tzu said: 'Thus, those skilled in war subdue the enemy's army without battle. They capture his cities without battle. They capture his cities without assaulting them and overthrow his state without protracted operations.'[7] The Mongols tried after the Sanfeng victory to take some places by siege without success and needed two years to finally crush the Jin – a fairly protracted end to the war – but in the main Sübe'etei did what Sun Tzu advised. Since he first entered Henan in January 1232, Sübe'etei had attempted to take eight places by means of active siege operations. Five of those failed, a 63 percent failure rate. Of the three that succeeded, one owed a good part to support provided by Song engineers. Sübe'etei did not lose any battles, but plenty of his officers did: in all, the Mongols lost four. It can be said that they were tactically strong, but not invincible. With a more organised defence, with emphasis on holding fortresses and forts, the Jin might have held them off. However the Jin leadership was divided and weak, and this was the reason for their fairly quick ruin. That said, even better leadership would have found the deteriorating logistical situation a serious challenge.

The Mongols did not put a high priority on securing the places that surrendered. Sübe'etei was content to leave a local leader in charge of a place with his own forces. Many cities surrendered, only to later turn against the Mongols. If Sübe'etei had taken better measures to secure places when the opportunity was there he could surely have defeated the Jin quicker. Sübe'etei finally crushed them with the help of the Song, yet again finding a way not to use his precious Mongol soldiers for serious fighting.

7   Griffith, *The Art of War*, p.79.

Even the fighting that was done with Mongol forces is likely to have involved largely involved Chinese soldiers rather than Mongolian tribesmen.

The Jin Dynasty was finally been destroyed 23 years after Genghis Khan first struck across their border. Most Chinese dynasties fade away without much of a struggle. The Jurchen Jin, however, resisted fiercely, served loyally by many able Han Chinese, and fought to the end.

Sources: *Yuanshi* 2, p.128, 122, pp.3013–3014, 123, pp.3022–3023, 149, pp.3522–3523, 150, pp.3557–3559, 152, pp.3603–3604, 155, pp.3657–3663; the *Secret History* 281; Rashid al-Din 460; *Jinshi* 18, pp.393–403, 111, pp.2450–2454, 113, pp.2476–2482, 114, 2503–2513, 116, pp.2537–2541, 2545–2550, 117, pp.2559–2565, 118, pp.2577–2581, 119, pp.2604–2611; *Songshi* 412, pp.12369–12380; Wang E, entry 1, 2, 3, 5, 6, 7, 8, 9, 23, 31, 33, 34, 37, 38, 43, 44, 55, 59, 62, 65, 68, 72, 73, 74, 75, 76, 77, pp.61–67, 75–76, 80–82, 84–85, 90–91, 93, 96–102, 105–109; Hok-Lam Chan, *The Fall of the Jurchen Chin*, pp.6–16, 134 (note 158); de Rachewiltz, *In the Service of the Khan*, p.186.; Charles A. Peterson, 'Old Illusions and New Realities: Song Foreign Policy, 1217–1234', in *Morris Rossabi, China Among Equals: the Middle Kingdom and its Neighbours, 10th–14th Centuries* (Berkeley: University of California Press, 1983), pp.223–224.

44

Recovering Luoyang in the Year of Duanping

Yang Yi arrived at Longmen, 30 *li* east of Luoyang. They sat down and were just about to eat a meal when then they were greatly scared at the sight of yellow and red umbrellas among the wild prickly ashes about 100 steps away – the ambushing Mongol army made abrupt charge from the thick wormwoods. The volunteer forces [of Yang Yi] stepped off the deep end, so they were scattered, a great number of them drowned in the Luoshui River. Only Yang Yi himself managed to escape.

– Zhou Mi, *Qi Dong Ye Yu*

The Mongol–Song alliance was short lived: the Song decided they wanted all of Henan, something the Mongols are unlikely to have promised them. The Song leaders were divided on the wisdom of attacking the Mongols. Zhao Kui, the commander in the Huai and lower Yangtze sector, was in favour of confrontation. He had never fought against a large Mongol army and was in a sector were the Song enjoyed a solid numerical advantage: therefore he may not have appreciated the Mongols' power. Further, in Shandong the Song were well backed by local warlords. Kui may have assumed they would find similar support in Henan. A mission had been sent to make sacrifices at the tombs of the founding Song emperors inside Mongol controlled territory near Kaifeng. The ceremony was done, but the people that went there could report that the tombs were in a state of disrepair. This helped serve as an emotional trigger for the decision to go to war.

The Song mobilised armies in Hefei and Yangzhou: in total 60,000 men were raised. As the bulk of the forces consisted of drafted low-status units, it is unlikely that the actual total was ever close to the nominal one. In addition, once the campaign started the effective total would fall quickly. Even so, this was most likely in total a larger force than the Mongols had available. The Mongols had only a small number of their own forces at hand and while the Chinese in Mongol service were numerous, they needed time to mobilise. It was fair for the Song to assume they fielded the largest battalions. Weary of challenging the Song directly, Sübe'etei ordered his forces to fall back. He left scouts to mask the enemy forces and keep him informed about developments, while he figured out the easiest way to deal with the invaders.

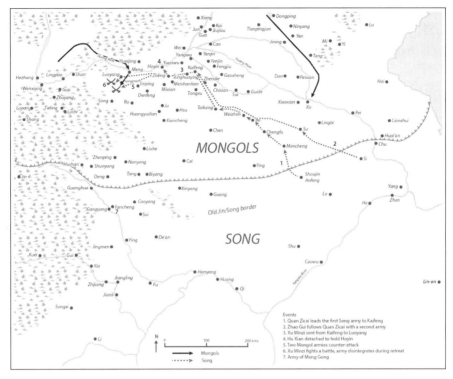

23. The Song attempt to recover Kaifeng and Luoyang in 1234.

On 9 July 1234 Song officer Quan Zicai led 10,000 men out of Hefei, and on 15 July crossed the Huai River at Shouzhou. Fan Wuzhong made a northward diversion from a position further east – between Guangzhou and Huanzhou – to distract the Mongols. Mongol forces guarded Guide, Kaifeng, and Luoyang, but the southern part of Henan was left largely unoccupied. Quan Zicai headed north via Mencheng (18 July), Chengfu (19 July), Bozhou (21 July), Weizhen, and Chengyi to reach Taikang. The Song found the countryside devastated, ruined after two years of protracted fighting. The Mongols evacuated Guide, Kaifeng, and Luoyang. As they fell back they broke the dykes at the Cunjin Lake to flood the roads south of Kaifeng. Sübe'etei hoped in this way to delay the enemy advance and make it more difficult for them to bring supplies forward. He assembled two forces north of the Huang River. Tacar assembled one army near Shangzhou and Alci assembled another in Shandong.

Quan Zicai and his men had to make their way along the flooded Kaifeng road. Zhou Mi says that 'the water reached people's waist and even neck. The journey was laborious and miserable. Luckily, there were no enemies in front.' Kaifeng had a huge population a few years before, but was now almost a ghost town with only 1,000 households. After the Mongols recalled their forces, only 600 local militias remained in the city. Cui Li, who had betrayed Kaifeng to the Mongols, was still command of the city: on 26 June he was killed by Li Boyuan, for his own reasons rather than love for the Song. He surrendered Kaifeng to Zicai who entered into the city some days later on 1 August, achieving the unrealised dream of Han Chinese heroes such as Tan Daoji and Yue Fei. The Song army had covered 600 km in 24 days, a fairly quick rate of advance. A detachment, led by Fan Xin, was sent westwards to seize Zhengzhou. This, however, marked the end of the Song advance. Zicai did nothing more. The devastated and ruined countryside could not sustain the Song and flooding made it impossible for supply carts to move along the roads to Kaifeng from the cities along the Yangtze. They were not able to quickly improvise rafts, somewhat odd given the Song mastery of river warfare. Shi Songji was in charge of logistics. He was later accused of deliberately holding supplies back in order to undermine an offensive he had opposed from the beginning. The logistical problems certainly worried Zicai.

Zhao Gui led a reported 50,000 soldiers past Sizhou and Bozhou to arrive at Kaifeng on 16 August, two weeks after the first Song army reached the city. Like the first army, the second had to make its way through the water. Quan Zicai remained unwilling to send forces forward to seize Luoyang and Tong Pass. Gui was upset, saying: 'In the beginning we together discussed about taking over strategic passes and making defence along the Huang River. Now you have arrived at Kaifeng and stayed here for half a month. Why did you not make immediate operation on Luoyang and Tong Pass, and what are you waiting for?' Zicai considered it impossible to continue the advance due lack of supplies, but in face of Gui's persistence he agreed to send forces westwards. The Song moved in two groups. Xu Minzi moved first with 13,000 soldiers, and Yang Yi was tasked to follow with 15,000. The second body was from Luzhou and the soldiers were armed mainly with crossbows.[1] Minzi set out for Zhengzhou on 17 August, provided with food for five days, which he rationed to make it last for seven. He had been told more supplies would follow after five days, but was concerned that this would not happen. Therefore after reaching Zhongmou, he sent Dai Yinglong back to Kaifeng to urge for resupply. At the same time Minzi found it difficult to control his own officers. Hu Xian did not favour a quick advance on Luoyang. On 22 August Minzi detached him with 2,000 militia from Xiangguan to guard Heyin; Zheng Di was sent ahead with 200 men to seize Luoyang. They scaled the wall at night and gained entry into the largely deserted city. Three hundred civilian households were all that was left inside the walls. Luoyang, like Kaifeng, was left ruined after the Mongol–Jin war without having been seriously sacked. Minzi arrived two days later with the main forces. That day, 24 August, the last rations were consumed. At this point, however, the Song had other matters than food to worry about.

Yang Yi followed in the tracks of Xu Minzi, and stopped at Longmen, 15 km south of Luoyang, to have a meal. Informed by scouts, the Mongols closely followed the Song movements. Tacar was sent across the Huang River at Meng, and Alci was probably ordered towards Xuzhou at the same time. Minzi had very properly detached Hu Xian to guard Heyin, but left Meng unguarded. Tacar crossed the river secretly, passed Luoyang without being detected, and fell on the Song at Longmen on 25 August. The

1   These two detachments were drawn from Zhao Wenzhong's army.

Song soldiers were having lunch when the Mongols struck. The *Yuanshi* biography of Liu Hengan says he charged the Song with levelled spears, and the surprised Song forces were quickly dispersed. Many were killed, though Yi managed to escape. Tacar praised Hengan, saying: 'This is a real brave general.' Yi's scouting was obviously inadequate, as were his general security arrangements. The advance unit of his army made its way to Luoyang, and the rest of the Song soldiers fled in all directions. Dai Yinglong was on his way to rejoin Xu Minzi from Kaifeng: meeting fleeing Song soldiers he returned to Kaifeng where he could bring the bad news to Quan Zicai and Zhao Gui. In Xiangyang, Meng Gong quickly understood the Mongols approached Luoyang and Kaifeng from two directions, but he did not do anything to support his colleagues. If the Song really wanted to secure the Huang River line they should have ordered Meng Gong forward. They could also have established a second line of supply running north from Xiangyang. As it was, Xu Minzi was now isolated in Luoyang without supplies, and his men mixed wild grass with flour to make pancakes. In the evening of the day of the battle, they learned that Yang Yi had been crushed. The Mongol Army arrived outside Luoyang soon afterwards. On 30 August Minzi sent detachments to hold the forts outside the eastern and western gate and marched out of the south gate with his main forces. He crossed the Luoshui River and deployed in battle-line. The Mongols deployed to intercept him. Zhou Mi says:

> At last, [Minzi] sent two separate forces to take over both the east and the west forts, and he ferried his main force across Luoshui River and deployed for battle. He ordered his forces to stay quiet and silent when the Mongol army charged. On the dawn of the 2nd day, the Mongols charged with round shields, dividing the Song army into three parts. The battle went on and did not end until noon. The Song army killed about 400 Mongol soldiers and captured about 300 shields.

Presumably the Song formed three squares or circles to hold off the Mongol cavalry. The Song army must have consisted of largely infantry, many of which were armed with crossbows. The battle was indecisive. Guo Dehai had served with Sübe'etei and Jebe in 1216 and remained with Sübe'etei after Jebe died; during the operations against the Song he was wounded in the foot by a missile, and subsequently fell ill and died. Perhaps he was wounded during this battle? Sübe'etei is likely to have ordered Tacar to avoid protracted fighting, expecting to wear down the Song before closing in for the kill.

Minzi was in trouble: his men had now been without organised supplies for 7 days. He attempted to retreat southwards with his army, but the Mongols followed and quickly shattered the Song army, killing 80–90 percent of the men. Minzi was wounded and lost his horse, but managed to get away. Fan Xin and Zhang Di were killed. Minzi found, as Napoleon knew well, that in battle combat losses tend to be about equal, but an army forced to retreat will suffer great loss without inflicting comparable losses on the pursuing army. Zhao Wenzhong and Quan Zicai also lacked food inside Kaifeng. With the Mongols approaching them from both the west and east the Song generals decided to retreat. The offensive ended as a total failure.

The Song attacked without having logistical measures in place to support their forces, and by moving *along* the Huang River they made matters worse, as it left them with a long front to defend and exposed their lines of communication. If they wanted to make additional attacks after taking Kaifeng, they should have struck *across* the Huang River and/or into Shandong. Meanwhile, Meng Gong did nothing in Xiangyang.[2] The Song wanted to secure all of Henan, but instead of trying to seize famous cities, they should have aimed to secure as good a position as possible before the inevitable Mongol counterattack materialised. The officers failed to scout and take security measures and they lacked strong cavalry to hold off enemy surprise attacks. In a defensive position, the Song foot soldiers could clearly hold the Mongols off. Under the right circumstances the Song could defeat the Mongols, which would be proven in the near future. Sübe'etei gained, as he almost always did, an easy victory. He was able to deal with the enemy forces in detail. One was surprised and another fell apart as it retreated due to lack of food. His ploys of flooding the roads to Kaifeng and of evacuating the cities to tempt the Song forward were quite in compliance with Chinese military tradition.

Mongol and Song forces skirmished in the Hanzhong area. A Mongol detachment moved over Feng and Heji to Tongqing. The Tongqing garrison held them off. A detachment was secretly sent forward to fall on the Mongols from the outside, and Cao Youwan and Shi Dangke later claimed to have fought with success against some Mongol forces. Another Mongol force raided past Xie towards Jie.

Sources: Zhou Mi, *Qidong yeyu*, pp.77–80; *Yuanshi* 121, p.2977; 149, pp.3532–3533; 150, pp.3559–3560; *Songshi* 41, p.803, 405, p.12234, 412, p.12374, 417, pp.12492–12494, 418, pp.12516–12517; Gaubil, *Histoire de Gentchiscan et toute la dynastie des Mongous*, p.73; Davis, 'The Reign of Li-tsung (1224–1264)', pp.859–863.

2   Like half the French army at Oudenarde in 1708, Meng Gong watched the committed Song forces being crushed without getting involved.

45

The Mongol Invasions of Korea

I have followed the army since I bound my hair [into plaits of youth] and so I am accustomed to seeing the cities of the earth attacked and fought over. Still I have never seen [a city] undergo an attack like this which did not, in the end, submit.

– A 70-year-old Mongol veteran comments on the Korean defence of Kuju in 1231

The Mongols struck into Korea at the same time, as the main forces were committed against Jin in Central China. Clearly a secondary theatre of war, it is still of interest as the sources cover it well and it allows further understanding how the Mongols actually operated. Initially Koryo, the kingdom in Korea, had no standing army. The paramilitary police division *Sambyolch'o* ('Three Elite Patrols') formed to deal with violent youth gangs was used as a core to form an army. Unable to confront the Mongols in open battle, the Koreans focussed on holding fortified positions and fighting a small war.

1231
On 26 August Satai (Sartaq) led a Mongol army across the Yalu into Korea, and Hamsin-chin submitted. The Mongols divided: one column struck eastwards towards the Sakchu region, while the second moved down along the Yalu and occupied Chongju and Inju. Ch'olchu was taken by siege, and the defenders killed themselves instead of surrendering. Korean forces from Chong-ju, Sakchu, Wiju and Taeju gathered at Kuju. The Mongols probed the defences of Kuju. Finding the place ready to resist, the Mongols moved on and secured control over Yongju, Sonju and Kwakchu.

The main Mongol forces remained in the region of the Yalu, but a detachment was sent south towards the Chabi Pass. It bypassed Chaju and Pyongyang, occupying Hwangju and Pongju. The Koreans assembled a large army in the south, commanded by Yi Chasong. Bandit, or freelance, bands ready to support the Court against the Mongols reinforced the army, most notably 5,000 men from Masan led by Yu Gexia. In October the Korean army marched to Tongson, where the Mongol advance force made an assault on the Korean camp. The Koreans rallied and held them off. During the fighting Korean officers were killed by both arrows and lances. The Mongols persevered and attempted to break the Korean right, but this attack was also defeated, and the Mongols fell back. The Koreans advanced to Anbuk. Here, in November, they were attacked and routed by the main Mongol army.

Satai pushed south, and left a Mongol detachment in the north. This was probably the column which had operated in the east after the Mongols had crossed the Yalu (upriver). In December Satai occupied P'yongju and Kaegyong and approached the Korean capital, leaving detachments to mask unconquered cities while he pushed on towards Kaesong. An improvised force attempted to hold the Ch'ungju Pass: the Mongols overcame the determined defenders and pushed on towards the Korean capital. The Korean Court opened negotiations with them in January 1232. Mongol columns continued operations while these negotiations were going on, attacking Kwangju and Chongju.

Kuju stubbornly resisted in the north. Pak So and his men held the city, but engaged in some furious fighting with the Mongols, breaching the walls 50 times. The Mongols attacked at different points with a variety of different methods, but all failed to break through the Korean defences. Pak So commanded fewer than 300 men and certainly faced a stronger Mongol force. Choju, defended by Choe Chun Myong, also continued to defy the Mongols. Both he and Oak So refused to surrender, even when ordered to do so by the Korean Court, but were eventually persuaded. The Korean officials wanted to punish them, but the Mongols would not allow it: they admired a determined foe.

1232

The Mongol army left Korea, and marched against Puxian Wannu.

The Koreans quelled a slave army revolt which broke out in Chungju, and the army was sent against the rebels. The revolt ended peacefully. In July the Korean Court was transferred to Ganghwa Island, where it was to remain for a long time. The island was gradually fortified. When a revolt broke out in Kaegyong, the army moved back to the old capital to deal with the rebels: the rebels, however, defeated the loyalists at Sungch'on-pu. The loyalists then sent a column around the rebel position and took control of Kaegyong. Afterwards, the rebels submitted.

The Koreans attacked Mongol officials and collaborators. In August–September 1232 Satai returned to the Korean interior. Hong Pogwon assembled a large Korean force to support the Mongols, took Kaesong, and took control of the entire country north of the Han River. After a stray arrow killed Satai outside Cho'in-song, the Mongols decided to retreat. Tiege-huo Erzhi took over command, but evidently did not feel he was able to continue offensive operations. In December Hong Pogwon was left behind to hold Pyongyang with some local forces.

1233

In May the Koreans attempted to recover Pyongyang, but without success. In June a revolt broke out in Kyongju: the main army was sent to deal with the rebels, and the revolt was suppressed. Korean leader Zhou U next sent 3,000 household troops to make a second attempt to recover Pyongyang, and this time was successful. Hong

Pogwon and part of the garrison fled into Liaodong. The Mongols established a large Korean settlement north of the Yalu.

The forces of the centre, led by Güyük and Alcidai, were sent into Manchuria to deal with Puxian Wannu. Tas served with Güyük as did Uriangqadai, the oldest son of Sübe'etei. He was now about 34 years old. In September the Mongols took Ningjiang by storm and captured Puxian Wannu.

1235

Tangut Ba'atur and Hong Pogwon led a Mongol army across the Yalu River. They occupied Yonggang, Hamjong, and Samdung in Sohae. Somewhat later East Jurchen forces, Mongol allies, entered Korea in the east and advanced as far as Haep'yong (Sangju). More Mongol forces crossed the Yalu in preparation for a new offensive. The Mongols and East Jurchen wintered inside Korean territory, in 17 different camps.

1236

The Mongols marched deeper into Korea, and in April occupied Hwangju, Sinju and Anju. Later, in September, Kaeju was reached, and in October other forces operated along the Han River at P'yongt'aek, Aju, and Hayang-chang. Koryo did not try to challenge the Mongols with a regular army. Various garrisons held out and smaller detachments clashed with the Mongols. Some protracted fighting followed. Roger Tennant summarises in *A History of Korea*:

> By 1235 the Mongols had completed their conquest of North China and over the next few years they would regularly send raiding parties … [into Korea]. The cavalry section of Ch'oe's Special Forces became hardened fighters who in local engagements could challenge the Mongol horsemen on their own terms, and in combination with guerilla bands and the courage and resourcefulness of those in the hill forts and walled towns, they would resist them probably for longer, and with more success than any other nation, though at a heavy cost to the common people who, even if they could find shelter in a hilltop fort, had to watch their houses and crops burning below them.

The Mongols made no attempt to secure Ganghwa Island.

1238

Mongol raiders sacked Kyongju, and the Korean Court again offered to submit. A 10 year lull in the fighting followed.

As in China, the Mongols drafted local men into their forces. Further, the neighbouring Khitans and Jurchens provided fighting men. Hilly and well-fortified Korea was not easy to conquer, but tactically the Koreans were remarkably ineffective, at least where it was not a question of defending a fortress. This was in part due to the confused state of Korea: it was a difficult place to equip and train an effective army, and to put effective logistical arrangements in place. The Korean Court developed a curious alternative response to armed resistance. Whenever the Mongols mounted a sustained offensive, they submitted to Mongol demands. Afterwards, they failed to follow through on the terms agreed. On Ganghwa Island the Court was safe as long as the Mongols did not have a strong navy. The frequent revolts show the Court only partially controlled the country. Even if the Court had submitted for real, the Mongols would hardly gain control over all of Korea.

Sources: *Yuanshi* 119, pp.2537–2540, 121, p.2978; Henthorn, *Korea: The Mongol Invasions*, pp.102–103 (main source); Roger Tennant, *A History of Korea* (London: Kegan Paul International, 1996), p.106; Samuel Bieler, 'Private Armies in the Early Korean Military Tradition (850–1598)', *Penn History Review*: Vol. 19: Iss. 1, Article 4, p.55.

Overview: The European Campaigns, 1236 to 1246

The series of campaigns that took Sübe'etei from the Ural River to the Danube represent something unique in the annals of war; no army moving by land ever covered such long distances or overran such vast tracks of territory in a continuous sequence of campaigns. Before, coming from Asia, the Huns, Avars, and Magyars had all ended up in Hungary, but did so as migrating tribes. The Huns may like the Mongols have come from Inner Asia, but if so they needed centuries to reach Europe. The Mongols set out from their homeland and reached Budapest 8,000 km to the west within five years. The next year most of the forces returned to Mongolia. The only comparable feats in the annals of war are the expeditions of Alexander the Great into Persia and beyond, the Western Expedition of Genghis Khan, and the later campaigns of Temür *Lenks*. By the time Alexander reached India he was some 5,000 km from his native Macedonia; when Genghis Khan reached the Sindhu River in 1221 he was almost 4,000 km from central Mongolia, and when Temür reached Smyrna he was 4,500 km from Samarkand. Sübe'etei went much further.

The Mongolian invasion of Europe has, as might be expected, been given much attention by Western historians and commentators. Charles Oman covered it in *A History of the Art of War in the Middle Ages* (1885) and the Mongol invasion of Europe forms the core of Liddell Hart's chapter on the Mongols in *Great Captains Unveiled* (1928). Trevor Dupuy, James Chambers, Stephen Turnbull, Bevin Alexander, Hugh Kennedy, and Richard Gabriel all dealt with the campaigns in some detail. According to Stephen Turnbull: 'There is no better way of illustrating the various facets of Mongol warfare than to study the classic expedition against Russia and Eastern Europe.' He associates the expedition closely with Sübe'etei: 'Subadai probably had overall command, as many of the bold strategic decisions bear his hallmark.'[1]

The *Secret History*, *Yuanshi*, and Rashid al-Din all continue to provide valuable information even for events in the western regions. The relevant sections have long since been translated in European languages and extensively analysed.[2] *Yuanshi* 3,

---

1 Stephen Turnbull, *The Mongols* (Oxford: Osprey Publishing, 1980), p.31
2 E. Bretschneider, *Medieval Researches from Eastern Asiatic Sources* (Ludgate, 1888); Paul Pelliot, *Notes sur l'histoire de la Horde d'Or* (Paris: Adrien-Maisonneuve, 1950) p.130; V. Minorsky, 'Caucasica III: The Alan Capital Megas and the Mongol Campaigns', *Bulletin of the School of Oriental and African Studies* 14/2 (1952), pp.221–238.

121, and 122; Juvaini, and Rashid al-Din describe the defeat of Bachman. What is uncertain is when and how Sübe'etei was involved. It is here assumed that he defeated Bachman in 1229–1230 (as described in chapter 49) and that Möngke finally crushed him in 1237. Thomas Allsen dates the involvement of Sübe'etei to 1236–1237 only.

The local sources claiming to describe Volga Bulgar history are likely either fake or elaborations of Rashid al-Din and oral traditions. Taking information from the Sübe'etei biographies (though they say the event involved the Russians rather than the Bulgars), *The Tartar Relation*, and archaeological findings, an outline of events can be proposed.

With regard to the conquest of Russia, the local chronicles describe events in great detail, though the traveller Julian adds some important missing information. Fennell and Martin Dimnik made good modern accounts. The Mongol assaults on Central Europe in 1241 get plenty of attention in local sources. The accounts of Roger, Thomas of Spalato, and *Annales Frisacenses* are important for events in Hungary. For Poland, the later account of Jan Długosz is important though there are some troubling differences with the shorter but earlier account of Boguchwala. Preserved letters by emperor Frederick II, Bela IV, and other leading figures add details here and there. Strakosch-Grassmann wrote a good modern account of the Mongol operations in Poland and Hungary. Kosztolnyik dealt with the invasion of Hungary, and Benson quoted at length from original Western sources.

46

Destruction of the Bulgar State

[Batu] attacked the Tulige city, yet failed. Then he presented a memorandum to the throne asking for Sübe'etei to superintend the campaign. [Sübe'etei] then captured Ye Lie Ban, king of the Wulusi tribe.[1] Sübe'etei started to attack the Tulige city, and took it over in 3 days.

– Wang Yun

Thereafter, in the winter, the princes and emirs gathered together on the Jaman River and sent the emir Subedei with an army into the country of the As and the region of Bulgar. They [themselves] went as far as the town of KRYK. The emirs [of that town], Bayan and Chiqu, came and paid homage to the princes. They were received with honour, but upon their return [Bayan and Chiqu] again rose in revolt, and Sübe'etei was sent [against them] for the second time in order to take them prisoner.

– Rashid al-Din (475)

The same year the godless Tartars having come, they captured all of the Bulgar land and took their great city, and they slew all, both wives and children.

– *The Chronicle of Novgorod*, entry for 1236

Batu, the second son of Joci, had his hands full imposing his authority on the people in the western region. He had increased his forces from the 4,000 men Temüjin first gave his father to perhaps as many as 10,000 by drafting local tribesmen, but was still not strong enough to extend his influence eastwards. Bachman remained at large along the lower Volga in spite of the defeat Sübe'etei had inflicted on him in 1230. He waged a guerrilla war against the Mongols. Juvaini says:

---

1   = Russian.

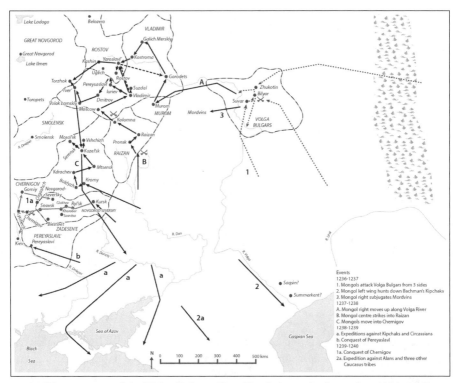

24. The conquest of the Volga Bulgars, Rus, Kipchaks, and other tribes 1236–1240.

Having no lair or hiding-place to serve as base, he betook himself every day and night to a different spot. And because of his dog-like nature he would strike wolf-like on every side and make off with something. Gradually his evil grew worse and he wrought greater mischief; and wherever the [Mongol] army sought him they could not find him, since he had departed elsewhere. Most of his refuges and hiding places were on the banks of the Etil. Here he would lie concealed in the forests, from which he would spring out like a jackal, seize hold of something, and hide himself once again.

Batu was also not able to conquer the towns of the lower Volga region. From the accounts of European travellers it is known that the Mongols attempted to take Saqsin by siege. This effort failed. Summerkent, a smaller settlement on an island in the Volga Delta, on a middle branch, also resisted the Mongols. The city had no walls, but the surrounding area was covered by water during the summer when the river rose. These events are not dated, but could have happened before or after the Bulgar campaign in 1232. Presumably Saqsin and Summerkent were allied with Bachman. The defiant Kipchak strongman and the Volga cities were, however, not lucrative targets. Eager to extend his domain in a real sense, Batu cast his eyes on the wealthy Volga Bulgars. Batu invaded Bulgar territory in 1232, advancing towards the capital Bilyar. The Mongols spent the winter inside Bulgar territory, but did not reach the capital. These few facts are known from Russian chroniclers. Perhaps the Bulgars offered to submit as Rashid al-Din says, but if so it cannot have taken Batu long to figure out this was only a ploy to gain a respite. Unable to defeat the Bulgars on his own, Batu asked Ögödei for help. He asked for Sübe'etei to return.

Ögödei agreed to support his nephew, but Batu got more than he had bargained for. Ca'adai proposed to Ögödei that each son of Genghis Khan provide two princes to support Batu. Ca'adai dispatched his grandson Buri (son of his oldest son who had passed away) and his 6th son Baidar; Ögödei his first son Güyük and his 6th son Qadan; and from Tolui's family came the oldest son Möngke and the 7th son Bochek. In addition, naturally, all sons of Joci took part. Those who are mentioned leading military operations are Batu, the 2nd oldest, Orda, the oldest, as well as Barka (number three), Shiban (number five), Tanqut (number six), and Shingqor (number nine). Kölgen, Genghis Khan's son, also took part in the expedition. This means that 14,000 soldiers from the guard took part.[2] Ca'adai's idea completely transformed the strategic context, as he knew it would. Kökö, Mogatu, and Muqur Qa'uran probably also marched with Sübe'etei. In total, the Mongols may have fielded up to 40,000 horsemen.

Sübe'etei, aged about 70, was the old man amongst youngsters. In 1236 Batu was about 41 years old, and Orda a year or so older. They had by now been on their own in the west for almost a decade and must have become quite experienced military men. Güyük was about 36. He had campaigned with Ögödei in China in 1231 and 1232 and commanded the army in Manchuria in 1233; he had also operated with Sübe'etei before in 1228. Möngke was about 34, and judging from his biography this was his first significant military command. A number of the princes were very young. Shiban, Baidar, and Qadan must have been around 30. Kölgen, Buri, and Bochek were around 20. Möngke's mother was a daughter of Jaqa Gambo, Sorghaghtani Beki. Sübe'etei may first have seen Jaqa Gambo aged 15 when To'oril, Jamuqa, and Genghis Khan made a raid on the Merkit camp. Güyük's mother was Toragana Khatun. She had been a wife of Qudu whom Sübe'etei hunted down and killed in 1219. Güyük and Möngke both later became *Great Khans*. Sübe'etei's son Uriangqadai, now aged about 35, also took part in the European expedition. He had been the tutor of Möngke.

The army assembled during summer of 1236. The monk Julian was at that point amongst the Bashkirs, a people held to be related to the Hungarians (Magars). They are described as 'most active in warfare.' They lived beyond the Volga, presumably east of the Bulgars who were surely their overlords. While with the Bashkirs, Julian met a Mongol envoy or person somehow associated with the Mongols. He said the Mongols assembled '5 days distant' (100 km?), at the moment waiting 'for another army which they sent to the destruction of the Persians.' Perhaps the Mongols were waiting for Sübe'etei who had wreaked havoc amongst the Persians 15 years before? The Mongol envoy also said the Mongols 'intend to go against Germany'.

The Mongols attacked the Volga Bulgars in autumn. The main Bulgar city was Bilyar, but there were many other fortified towns and forts. In some places they

---

2   Taking the totals from Rashid al-Din's 1227 army list. He says elsewhere that Kölgen's son Quca inherited 6,000 men, not 4,000.

even constructed fortified lines. Some faced south, presumably constructed to hold off Kipchak raiders. It seems possible that the Mongols segmented their forces into three and approached Bilyar from different directions. Presumably Batu and Sübe'etei came from the south, perhaps moving up the Volga. They could move up Bolshoy Cheremshan, perhaps taking Suar before arriving in front of Bilyar. Another column could have come from the south-east, from the region of the upper Maly Chereshan. The third column came from the north-east. It had to move through the Ural Mountains in the east, and could first have subjected the Permians, Samoyeds, and Ucor-Colon (Nocnoy-terim or Chuds). Afterwards, the Mongols may have overcome the Vodians (Poydov, Votyaki, or Udmurty), and could then move down the Kama into Bulgar territory. The Mongols occupied Juketam (Zhukotin) before also moving on Bilyar. Sübe'etei defeated Jiqu and Bayan and took Bilyar. The city was destroyed, Juvaini says as 'warning to others.' The Mongols took many other places before and after Bilyar, according to Julian, 60 fortified castles were taken in Bulgar and Saqsin territory.[3] It is, however, unlikely that the Mongols tried to take all the important strongholds of the Bulgars at this point. By early 1237 the Bulgarian western lands were also ravaged.[4] West of the Volga the Mongols, specifically perhaps the right wing, attacked the Mordvins. Rashid al-Din says that the Mongols 'conquered [… the Mordvins …] in a short time.' The Mordvins were split into two tribes: the Moksha submitted, but the Ersha fled into the forest. Julian says their leader fled to a 'highly fortified place with a few of his followers'. The Veda, who lived further to the south-east (with Burda as a major settlement) and the Merov (Maritsy) north of the Volga presumably also submitted.

Having conquered the Bulgars, in April–May Sübe'etei dispatched Möngke and Büjek and the left wing to hunt down Bachman and Qachir-Ukula, leader of the As.[5] Möngke may have taken Saqsin and Summerkent as he pushed south. The Kipchaks sought refuge in the forests on either side of the lower Volga: the Mongols tracked them down as if it was a great hunt, with their army forming a huge semi-circle on either side of the river. They had 200 barges move down the river itself. Bachman's forces were isolated on an island and defeated in a one-hour engagement after a low tide allowed the Mongols to easily reach it. Bachman and Qajir-Ukulu were captured. Bachman was ordered to kneel before the Mongol lords. Defiantly he replied: 'Do you think I am a camel?' Möngke had him executed, letting his brother Büjek kill him. Bachman had asked Möngke to kill him himself.

The Mongols rested along the Volga during the summer months. Bulgars, Mordvins, and Kipchaks were drafted into the army. Many Kipchaks had entered into Mongol service as early as 1224. Now the son of Hulusaman, called Baltuxhaq, served under

3 He mentions Veda, Maritsa, and Vodia. Saqsin was taken later.
4 This is attested by archaeology. Some places could have been destroyed by forces moving up the Volga towards Bilyar. Other places may have been taken later by the Mongol right wing crossing over the Volga after the conquest of Bilyar.
5 How an Alan (As) leader ended up with Bachman is not explained. Saqsin was said to have a part Alan population. Perhaps the Alan leader is associated with this place?

Möngke with a body of men. The news of the Mongol offensive triggered migrations further west with Kipchak tribesmen moving across the Danube.

At around this time Julian reached the Rus state of Vladimir. Yuri II, the local lord, told him that a Mongol envoy had been intercepted. The envoy carried a letter from Batu to King Bela IV of Hungary, urging him to expel the Kipchak exiles (that had been in Hungary since 1223?) or face a Mongol attack. Possibly Julian misunderstood who the letter was addressed to: a Rus state would seem a more likely recipient than Hungary. Yuri was well aware of the looming Mongol threat, telling Julian that 'day and night the Tatars deliberate upon how they may come and conquer the Christian kingdom of Hungary. For they are said to have in mind to come and conquer Rome and land beyond Rome.' Yuri was perhaps trying to stir other European powers into action and gone beyond what actual intelligence told him. Certainly he knew his own kingdom was under threat.

Sources: Wang Yun, pp.7–8; *Yuanshi* 4, p.57, 121, pp.2977–2978, 122, p.3009, 128, 3131; the *Secret History*, 270; Julian, p.104; Riccardus, p.79; William of Rubruck, in Dawson, *The Mongol Mission*, p.207; *The Tartar Relation*, pp.72–76, 80; Juvaini, pp.553–554; Rashid al-Din, 475; *The Chronicle of Novgorod*, p.87; *The Nikonian Chronicle*, vol.2, p.307; V. Minorsky, 'Caucasica III: The Alan Capital Magas and the Mongol Campaigns', pp.221–238; Benson, *Six Emperors*, pp.172, 174–175; Allsen, 'Prelude to the Western Campaigns', pp.14–15; Allsen, 'The Princes of the Left Hand', *Archivum Eurasiae Medii Aevi*, 5 (Wiesbaden: Harrassowitz, 1987), p.10 (citing Vassaf); K. A. Rudenko, 'The Mongol Conquests and Their Reflection in Material Culture of the Peoples of the Middle Volga and Kama Regions', *Golden Horde Review*, (#6, 2014) (the 13th–early 14th centuries; according to the archaeological data), pp.136–140.

47

The Conquest of Russia

Rule 1, on page 1 of the book of war, is: 'Do not march on Moscow.'

– Bernard Montgomery to the House of Lords in 1962

Properly prepared, the Rus states should have been able to field a very large army against the Mongols. If only 1 percent of the population was mobilised, they might have been able to field 70,000 men. The Rus, however, remained divided and failed to raise large forces. A large number of Rus princes had fought without success against a small Mongol army in 1223: warned by the Kipchaks in good time, the Rus united and raised a coalition force. Faced with a much larger Mongol army, Yuri II Vsevolodovich (second reign from 1218 to 1238), the Grand Duke of Vladimir–Suzdal, did not seek support from the other states. The Chronicle of Novgorod says he 'wished to make war separately' against the invaders. In the face of a stronger Mongol army than before the Rus failed to unite. Sübe'etei first targeted the states Ryazan and Vladimir–Suzdal in December 1237; the right wing struck from Bulgar territory up along the Volga. Orda and Berke may have commanded this group. The centre and left wing assembled along the Voronezh. Qadar and Buri commanded the left, and took up position in the area around Voronezh (Orgenhusen) itself, close to the Don River. Batu, Sübe'etei, Güyük, and Möngke led the centre up along the Voronezh, advancing through snow covered forest country, to approach Ryazan from the south. Ryazan was a minor state with a divided leadership. Sübe'etei thus selected a soft target. It is likely that Batu and Sübe'etei moved on Ryazan at the same time as Orda and Berke crossed into Vladimir–Suzdal territory.

Ryazan was a minor state with a divided leadership. Sübe'etei thus selected a soft target. It is likely that Batu and Sübe'etei moved on Ryazan at the same time as Orda and Berke crossed into Vladimir–Suzdal territory. Vladimir–Suzdal had over the years fought many wars against the Bulgars. Armies moved up and down the Volga transported on boats, and Yuri and his advisers would have considered it likely that the Mongols would sooner or later strike up along the Volga. An army was therefore stationed at Gordodets/

Nizhiy Novgorod with Sviatoslav as the commander.[1] The Mongol right may have been content to mask this force. In the south, the Mongol left wing was in position to threaten the Don Kipchaks, Kiev, Chernigov and the other southern Rus cities, keeping them from sending support to Ryazan or Vladimir–Suzdal. The Rus cities in the south were in the hands of Mikhail Vsevolodovich and his relatives. The two Mongol wings thus helped Sübe'etei to isolate Ryazan. When the Ryazan leaders understood that the Mongols were about to attack they sent messages to Vladimir–Suzdal, and perhaps Chernigov, asking for help. Yuri, however, concerned about the Mongol threat from the east, was not prepared to send large forces to help Ryazan.

The Mongol main body attacked and took Onuze,[2] and from here sent an embassy (the Chronicle of Novgorod says 'a sorceress and two men') to Ryazan, demanding they submit and pay tax. Yuri Ingvarevich and the other lords of Ryazan rejected the surrender demand, assembled an army at Ryazan and set out against the Mongols, evidently unaware of the actual size of the Mongol army. No numbers are reported, but Ryazan is unlikely to have fielded much more than 1,000 men and they may have faced an army more than 10 times as large. The 'Tale of the Destruction of Ryazan' certainly highlights the overwhelming force of the Mongols ('Each Ryazan warrior had to fight with 1,000 of the enemy'). On 4 or 5 December the Rus collided with the Mongol army close to the border of Ryazan, and the Rus army was, unsurprisingly, wiped out.[3] The Rus fled into Ryazan (Yuri Ingvarevich), Pronsk (Vsevolod II Ingvarevich), and Murom (David Ingvarevich). Roman Ingvarevich also escaped. It seems Kolomna lord Gleb Ingvarevich was killed in the battle.

The Mongols took Pronsk, Izjaslavl, and Belgorod before moving up the river Pronya on Ryazan. Sübe'etei built a stockade around it during the first nine days and afterwards subjected the city to a five day bombardment before successfully storming it (6 to 21 December). The city was sacked and most people killed, either as a deliberate terror act to show the Rus that to resist the Mongols was futile, or more likely because the Rus cities were made of wood and therefore burned easily. Yuri was killed. The Mongol main forces marched from Ryazan towards Kolomna, and this city was taken also. During the siege, Kölgen was killed.

Yuri sent a force – *The Chronicle of Novgorod* calls it 'a patrol' so it was a tiny force – towards Kolomna. Vsevolod Vsevolodovich and Eremei Glebovich were the leaders, and Roman Ingvarevich joined them, perhaps along with some retainers. They seem to have managed to escape from the first battle against the Mongols unless he had gone to Vladimir to solicit the help from Yuri even before they struck. The Mongols intercepted the Rus detachment before it reached Kolomna: near Nadolob they were driven back on a hill and destroyed. Again the Rus must have been heavily outnumbered.

---

1   Sviatoslav had been operating on the eastern frontier against the Bulgars in 1219 and against the Mordvins in 1227.
2   Also called Nuzia or Nukhla. Location uncertain, but following Fennell it may have been in the area where the Pol'noj meets the Lesnoj Voronez.
3   *The Nikonian Chronicle* says that an 'evil massacre ensued.'

It is reported in the 'Tale of the Destruction of Ryazan' that Eupaty Lvovich Kolovrat came back to Ryazan from Chernigov at the head of a 1,700 men strong force. According to the story, he followed the Mongols into Suzdal where he attacked their far stronger forces. The Rus fought bravely, but were overwhelmed. The Mongols reportedly used siege artillery against them. Batu admired the bravery of Eupaty and on 11 January 1238 allowed him to be buried in Ryazan. Eupaty would have to have moved quickly from Chernigov to Ryazan and Suzdal, as he had to cover more than 700 km.[4] It is hard to see even a grain of truth in this story. Perhaps Eupaty was a Ryazan lord who fell fighting the Mongols later when they ventured into the territory of Chernigov, or possibly – if the date is to be taken seriously – Eupaty fought against the Mongol left wing.

Sübe'etei advanced against Moscow from Kolomna. He thereby outflanked Vladimir, cutting off the route to Novgorod. The right wing approached Vladimir from the south. Moscow was taken in five days. The small city was situated inside a triangle formed by the Moscow and Neglinnaya Rivers: the most direct approach for the Mongols would have been to attack from the open side, though during the winter with the rivers frozen, all sides might have been vulnerable to attack.

Grand Duke Yuri decided not to remain inside Vladimir, his main city, and instead left to assemble an army at Yaroslav further north. He was probably confident that Vladimir could hold out against the Mongols, giving him time to assemble an army. Yuri called on his brothers Iaroslav and Sviatoslav to join him. Sviatoslav is likely to have camped close to Gorodets; Iaroslav was certainly in Novgorod. Forces coming from Rostov (Vasilko Konstantinovich), Pereyaslavl (Vsevolod) and Uglich (Vladimir) joined Yuri at Yaroslav. The three lords were his nephews.

Sübe'etei surrounded Vladimir, encircling the city with earthworks on 3 February 1238. He was initially uncertain if Yuri was still in the city. A Mongol group was detached from the main body to reduce Suzdal: it fell quickly on 4–5 February, so probably simply submitted. Perhaps it lacked a sufficient number of defenders. Vladimir did not hold out for long either. On 8 February the Mongols stormed the city, breaking into the western part at four different points. Additional walls protected the city centre, but the Mongols broke through these as well, and two Rus princes fell fighting there. Möngke distinguished himself during the fighting.

Having reduced Vladimir, Sübe'etei turned against the army of Yuri at Yaroslav. Sviatoslav had joined him, but not Iaroslav. From Vladimir, Sübe'etei sent a force commanded by Batu towards Novgorod to intercept any force that might arrive from this direction. Meanwhile, the Mongol right wing pushed up the Kliazma to reach the Volga, and took Gorodets and Galich Merskiy before moving on Yaroslav.[5] The Mongol centre and right wing encircled the Rus army. Yori sent an advance guard (a reported 3,000 men) south to locate the Mongols. The commander of the detachment

---

4   He had to be first informed about the Mongol attack. Allow one week for this. Next he must assemble his forces, say another week. Then he has to march to Ryazan and Suzdal during the winter. At least 30 days are needed. In total this means about seven weeks. How could he do all that before 11 January?

5   Jeremiah Curtin says they also took Kostroma. This seems quite likely.

quickly returned to report that 'the Tatars have surrounded us.' On 4 March Sübe'etei crushed the Rus army: the Chronicle of Novgorod says the Rus were attacked before they had been able to deploy in battle line. The Chronicle faults Yuri for not scouting properly.[6] Yuri fled, but the Mongols pursued him along the Sit, where he was killed. The Mongols next marched westward along the Volga, having a camp near the Sherensk Forest. Vasilko of Rostov was captured during the Yaroslav battle and executed near Kasin (Sirinskij).

Batu's forces, meanwhile, moved past Iuriev (Yuriev Pol'skiy), Pereyaslavl, Dmitrov, Volok Lamskiy to Tver. It is possible all these cities simply submitted.[7] On 11 March the Mongols started to besiege Torzhok. Evidently the people there were ready to resist. The Mongols made a breach in the wall, but an attempted storm ended in failure after the defenders fought them off with 'knives'. The Rus made a sortie, overrunning the Mongol catapults, but after a stiff fight were cut to pieces, though the defenders claimed to have killed 4,000 Mongols. Torzhok only fell after Sübe'etei arrived to personally supervise the siege, perhaps having marched due west from Sherensk. The city was taken on 25 March, three days after Sübe'etei arrived. Spring thaw may have forced him to give up any idea of moving on Novgorod. He was only 100 km from the city, close to the Seliger Lake. The two week resistance offered by Torzhok could have saved Novgorod from destruction; however it is not at all clear if the Mongols were interested in attacking Novgorod at this point.

Sübe'etei turned south, advancing on a broad front. Chernigov had now had a five month warning and must have prepared the defences of the important cities. Sübe'etei moved through the eastern parts of Chernigov from the north, Qadan and Bori probably crossing the Chernigov borders in the south-east at the same time. The garrison of Kozelsk ventured outside the city walls and claimed a success over the Mongol advance guard. The Mongols besieged the city, which held out for seven weeks before being taken and completely destroyed. Qadan and Bori arrived with the left wing three days before the city was finally taken. They may have taken Kdrachev, Boldyzh, Kromy and Domagoshch en route. The Mongol main forces may have taken Mosal'sk, Serensk and Vshchizh at the same time as Kozelsk was besieged.

The Mongols did not attack Smolensk, located as it was further to the west. A local tradition held that Mercurius, with divine assistance, defeated the Mongols: 'he came to the regiments of the evildoing emperor, defeated the enemy, gathered together the Christian prisoners and, sending them back to the city, he courageously galloped over the regiments of Batu even as an eagle soars through the air.' Mongol scouts could well have approached Smolensk and perhaps an encounter with a local force was the origin of this story?

Sübe'etei and Batu set up summer camp in the area between the lower Dnieper and the Don, the same wider region Sübe'etei and Jebe rested in during 1223. West of the Dnieper the Rus princes carried on as normal. Danilo recovered Galich, moving on the city while Mikhail and Rostislav, the masters of the city, were campaigning

---

6   *The Galician–Volynian Chronicle* also faults Yuri for not having set up sentries.
7   During the month of February, 14 cities had been taken in Vladimir–Suzdal.

against the Lithuanians. Danilo had been wounded in the battle against the Mongols along the Kalka in 1223 and understood very clearly the threat they represented. The looming threat of the Mongols must have worried him, but fighting against rival princes was still top of the agenda.

The Mongols fielded 40,000 or more cavalry under a single command. Such a large force could not operate in one place during the winter months of Russia, but though divided into separate columns, the Mongols did coordinate their operations closely. The Rus were split into seven or more major political entities fielding their own forces; united they should have been able to raise as large a force as the Mongols and certainly as many as the Mongols operated with in a single place. As it was, the various forces of Ryazan and Vladimir–Suzdal were defeated in three separate battles. In each of these battles the Mongols must have had a massive superiority in numbers. If the various Rus states had reacted faster and concentrated a strong combined force well west of Vladimir they could surely have offered some effective resistance. Failing to unite, the Rus princes found themselves united under foreign rule.

Sübe'etei used his trademark ploys, outflanking first Vladmir and next Yuri's army. The right wing outflanked the Rus much as the same wing did against Xia in 1226–1227 and Jin in 1231–1232. Sübe'etei's conquest of Russia was a smooth affair. The weather and logistical constraints did not hinder him as was later the case for Karl XII, Napoleon, and Hitler. Sübe'etei had with success broken Montgomery's dictum: 'Don't march on Moscow.' The Mongols seems to have advanced at an average rate of about 10 km per day. However, some time was used on siege operations and some spent resting, so the actual marching rate must have been higher. Even so, it seems clear that they did not move extremely fast. Of the Rus cities, only Kozelsk was destroyed completely. The other cities were sacked, but because they were made of wood they are likely to have easily burned down more-or-less completely. It is not at all evident that Sübe'etei made use of any deliberate 'terror' strategy. Some commentators say that the Mongols attacking during the winter in part to surprise the Rus, who preferred to campaign during the summer. However, the Mongols *always* attacked during the winter and rested during the summer.

Sources: Wang Yun, p.7; *Yuanshi* 121, pp.2977–2978, 122, p.3009; Rashid al-Din, 476–477; Julian, pp.101–109; *The Galician–Volynian Chronicle*, pp.45–47; *The Chronicle of Novgorod*, pp.81–83; *The Nikonian Chronicle* 2, pp.308–317, 319; Martin Dimnik, *The Dynasty of Chernigov*, 1146–1246 (Cambridge: Cambridge University Press, 2003), p.346; Jeremiah Curtin, *The Mongols in Russia* (Boston: Little Brown, 1908), p.237; George Vernadsky, *A History of Russia* (New Haven: Yale University Press, 1970), vol. 3, pp.117, 325; Serge A. Zenkovsky, *Medieval Russia's epics, chroniclers, and tales* (New York: Dutton, 1974), pp.201, 209–210; Konstantin S. Nossov, *Medieval Russian Fortresses AD 862–1480* (Oxford: Osprey, 2007).

48

Securing the Plains Around the Black Sea

During the autumn, Möngke Qan and Qadan proceeded against the Cherkes and, in the winter their king, Tuqar by name, was killed. Shiban, Bochek, and Buri proceeded against the region of Qirim and conquered Tabqara of the Kipchak people. Berke proceeded against the Kipchaks and captured Arjumal, Qura'umas and Qira, the leaders of the Makuti.

– Rashid al-Din, 477

The Mongols restarted military operations towards the end of 1238, after the usual summer break. Qadan, leading the left wing, operated against the Circassians (Cherkes or Cherkesses). He captured Tuqfas or Buqan,[1] the Circassian leader, presumably taking Matrica (T'mutorokan). Siban, Büjek, and Buri marched into Crimeria where Sudaq was sacked on 26 December. The local Kipchak Tabqara tribe submitted. Berke operated against the Kipchaks living west of the Dnieper. He fought against a group Rashid al-Din calls Mekruti, capturing leaders called Arjumal, Qura'umas, and Qiran. Kötän had fled with his people to Hungary. Before going there he corresponded with Bela IV, the king of Hungary, and agreed to become a Catholic. He claimed to have defeated the Mongols twice before, but this time he said he was surprised and unable to assemble an army in time. Kötän and the Kipchaks entered Hungary through the Radna Pass on 2 March,[2] and settled in the plains along the Tisza, Maros, and Temes. Already in 1227 a Kipchak group had accepted Hungarian overlordship, though they remained west of the Carpathians. A Hungarian force setting out from Transylvania claimed to have gained a success against the Mongols. The Voyvode of Transylvania is said to have surprised a Mongol detachment close to Meotis Marshes. It is quite possible that Hungarian and Mongol scouting detachments had an encounter.

The Mongols took Pereyaslavl on 3 March 1239, and may also have ravaged Zadesen'e, territory located along the south side of the Seym. It is not clear what

1   Rashid al-Din offers two different names.
2   According to one source Bela met Kötän in Transylvania in February 1238. If so the Kipchaks looked at entering Hungary long before the Mongols attacked (Roger, p.139, note 5).

forces were involved. The approaches to Pereyaslavl were covered by long trenches on the south side, but whether they were in use and played a role is not reported.

Mikhail of Chernigov left Kiev with his family and close associates, relocating to Kamenets. Yaroslav Vsevolodovich, new Grand Duke of Vladimir–Suzdal, succeeding his brother Yuri II (having been in Novgorod when the Mongols struck), attacked Mikhail in Kamenets. Mikhail got away, but his wife was captured. That Yaroslav could attack Kamenets seems extraordinary, given that his own territory was devastated a year before and that Kamenets is a long distance from Vladimir. Yaroslav marched via Smolensk. The Lithuanians attacked Smolensk around the same time, and Yaroslav helped drive them off.

The Mongols later sold captured Kipchaks and Circassians into slavery. Many ended up in Egypt where they became slave-soldiers. In time they formed the core of the army, which famously defeated the Mongols at Ain Jalut in 1260.

Sources: Rashid al-Din, 476, 582; Roger, pp.137–139; Allsen, 'The Mongols and North Caucasia', pp.5–40; Z. J. Kosztolnyik, *Hungary in the Thirteenth Century* (New York: distributed by Columbia University Press, 1996), p.130.

49

The Conquest of Chernigov

Güyük Khan, Möngke Qa'an, Buri, and Qadan proceeded against the town of Magas and took it in the winter.

– Rashid al-Din, 477

You pretend that you have accomplished it alone, whereas you set out under the shelter of Sübe'etei and Bujek.

– Ögödei to Batu, the *Secret History*, 276

Chernigov was along with Kiev and Novgorod one of the large Rus cities, and it was the next target of Sübe'etei. The Mongols advanced west along the north bank of the Seym and took Kursk, Ryl'sk, Glukhov, Khorobor, Sosnitsa and Snovsk before starting to besiege Chernigov itself. Mstislav Glebovich, the local lord, attempted to challenge the Mongols in the open, marching to Chernigov from his place of residence, perhaps located somewhere west of the city. He was defeated. The battle was fought close to the city walls, on 18 October 1239: using siege machinery the Rus fired stones from the walls at the Mongols,[1] but Chernigov fell after the battle. Other places in the area were also taken, including Blestovit, Novgorod Severskiy, Orgoshch, Listven, Gomiy and Lyubech. Möngke headed south, either from Chernigov or to Glukhov where a part of the Mongol army marched after the fall of Chernigov. He appeared on the east side of the Dnieper River opposite Kiev. Local lord Mikhail refused to surrender, and killed the Mongol envoys. The Mongols made treaties with Vladimir Ryurikovich of Smolensk, and Danilo; Mstislav Glebovich submitted. Kiev was isolated.

Qadan remained in the Caucasus. In October–November a Mongol scouting detachment spent 10 days close to Bab al-Qist Rija, skirmishing with local forces. Güyük, Möngke and Bori reinforced Qadan, bringing forces from the centre. They must have moved very fast and are unlikely to have brought substantial forces. Even

---

1   According to *The Hypatian Chronicle*. *The Laurentian Chronicle* has a different version of events.

so, Sübe'etei evidently judged the planned offensive against Alans to be a serious task. Mongol scouting detachments could operate far from the main army, but with a small Mongol detachment at Rija it is possible that Güyük was at this point east of Alan territory. Möngke and Güyük may therefore have been positioned to attack the Alans from two different directions.

The Alans fled into their fortified strongpoints, which the Mongols began to reduce one by one. Möngke and Güyük reduced one small fort, which was covered by 'wooden palisades.' Here Aersilan (Ajis) submitted with his faction. He supported operations against other Alan groups, but was killed fighting against a certain Sheergo; Aersilan's son Asanzhen remained in Mongol service. Finally, in December, the Mongols started to besiege Magas (perhaps Nizhne–Arkhyz along the Bolshoi Zelenchuk), the main Alan stronghold. They brought siege artillery into position and started to bombard the fortress; Zhen Xian led a small suicide squad to seize a part of the wall. He secured a section of it, making it possible for the main Mongol forces to break into the fortress, and in March 1240 Magas was taken and sacked. The Alans, it seems, had five major cities. They were perhaps all taken, but the Mongols certainly did not have time to reduce all the fortresses in the region. Armed opposition to the Mongols continued for many years.

Möngke sent a detachment to secure Derbent, and this city was taken and destroyed. At the same time, or just before, Mongol forces operated in conjunction with some Alan allies and the Qaitaqs against the Qazi Ghumigs. They attacked from two sides, the west and the east, defeating some local forces near a fort located close to Kudali Mosque. In March the Mongols and their allies killed 70 enemy fighters. Afterwards, Möngke marched back to rejoin Batu and Sübe'etei.

During the summer, Batu quarrelled with Güyük and Buri, his cousins. Messengers went to Mongolia and back. Ögödei reacted by ordering his sons to return home. Möngke also returned to Mongolia. It seems possible, in spite of this *Secret History* tale, that it was always the plan to recall the core forces after the Bulgars, Rus, and Kipchaks had been conquered.

Meanwhile, the Rus lords were – as always – occupied with their own feuds. Vladimir Ryurikovich occupied Kiev, and Danilo in turn chased him off and left a garrison to guard the city. Danilo may have assumed the Mongol offensive was over and that they were content with having the Dnieper River as the border.

Sources: the *Secret History*, 275–277; Rashid al-Din, 477, 482–483; *The Galician–Volynian Chronicle*, p.47; *The Nikonian Chronicle* 2, p.319; Allsen, 'The Mongols and North Caucasia', pp.5–40; Dimnik, *The Dynasty of Chernigov*, 1146–1246, pp.346–350.

The Invasion of Hungary and Poland

[The Russians] captured a Tatar called Tovrul from their camp and he described the [Tatar's] vast army to the Russians; [it was led by] Batyj's brothers – the strong voyvodas Urdju, Bajdar, Birjui, Kajdan, Becak, Mengu, and Kjujuk, who [had] returned home … and his chief voyvoda, the bagatyr Sebedjaj, the bagatyr Burrundaj.

– *The Hypatian Codex*

Everything we have achieved we owe to Sübe'etei.

– Batu to Sübe'etei at a banquet, *Yuanshi* 121

Ögödei had led back the forces of the centre to Mongolia soon after the battle of Sanfeng, leaving Sübe'etei with the rest of the forces to complete the conquest of Henan. The same seems to have happened now, as Güyük and Möngke must have led sizeable forces back to Mongolia. What portion of the total forces was withdrawn is a matter of guesswork. The Mongols later operated with three widely separated columns, as before in Russia. To divide the army like that presumably means that it was still large. New recruits might have almost fully balanced out the forces withdrawn, though the quality and reliability would not be the same.

Towards the end of 1240, having conquered the territory east of the Dnieper the Mongols now, struck across this river and pushed into Central Europe with the Pripet Marches on their right. In front of them was first the domain of Danilo and next, further west, the Polish principalities to the north and Hungary in the south. The Mongols aimed to conquer Hungary. Why, is not known, but it had been a favoured object of nomad tribes since early times. Further, the Hungarians hosted a large number of Kipchak refugees who had eluded the Mongols. These were not very strong reasons for making an attack, and the real driver was perhaps Sübe'etei's quest for military exploration.

Europe was politically divided, with no dominant power and with relatively weak kings. A king was invariably challenged by subject strongmen not wanting a strong overlord; he was a first amongst equals who could not even dream of having the political

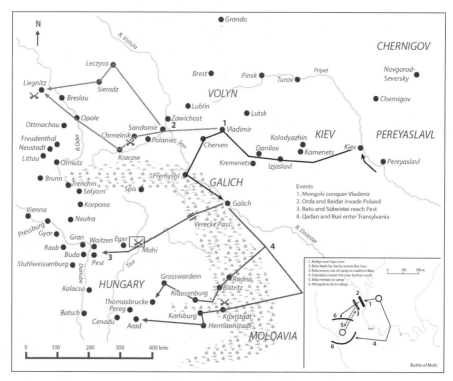

25. The invasion of Central Europe 1241.

power of Genghis Khan or Ögödei. The most significant European power of this era was the so-called Holy Roman Empire, essentially the territory now making up modern Germany, at this time ruled by Frederick II (reigned 1220–1250). Like many of his predecessors he was engaged in a bitter political and military struggle with the Pope. He was well aware that the Mongols were coming, but took no steps to deal with them. He later defended his passive stance, saying he that was distracted by the fight with the Pope and that he had expected Poland and Hungary, his eastern neighbours, to be able to stop the invaders. Poland had once been a fairly strong monarchy, but was now divided into five separate realms. The stronger (senior) lord was Henry II of Silicaa (reigned 1238–1241) whose key city was Breslau (Wrocław). The other political entities were centred on Oppeln (Opole), Kracow, Mazovia and Pomerania. None of these seem to have taken significant measures to prepare themselves against attack. If they had united their forces they could have raised a large army, but on their own they were weak, much like the Rus. Hungary was a powerful kingdom with an estimated population of more than two million people, excluding Croatia, which was a subject territory.

The Hungarians were well-informed by events in the east through travelling missionaries as well as Rus visitors and Kipchak exiles. King Bela IV (reigned 1235–1270) hosted Kötän and other Kipchak refugees. Kötän by now had significant Mongol experience and certainly provided Bela with valuable information. In addition the travelling monk Julian offered much information. Returning from one trip in 1236, he was able to tell the Hungarians that the Mongols were on the way. He returned to the eastern regions again in 1237, but stopped in Vladimir-Suzdal after learning that the Mongols had conquered the country located east of the Volga. When Julian returned to Hungary in 1238 he brought the letter to Bela from Batu, who demanded that the Kipchaks who had sought refuge in Hungary were expelled. The demand was ignored. Danilo, lord of Galich and Valich, was most exposed, but he probably thought he had a working treaty with Batu, and did nothing to prepare his defences. Perhaps unburdened by any concerns, he went to Hungary with the aim of securing a marriage alliance with Bela.

Many of the places the Mongols attacked this year have different names in different languages. Generally the German name is used. In the table at the end of the chapter, German, Hungarian, and Romanian names for the cities are given.

The conquest of Kiev, Volyn and Galich

In autumn 1240 Sübe'etei set the Mongol forces in motion again. Some forces were detached to guard the rear of the army, possibly a third of the full force along with many of the spare horses. Kotan (Toqa Temür) and Shingqor, a brother of Batu, were probably amongst the commanders left behind. The Mongols crossed the Dnieper and moved on Kiev, arriving outside the city on 26 November.[1] Strong walls protected it, but it had been taken and retaken many times during the recent decades and was hardly in a position to offer prolonged resistance. *The Galician–Volynian Chronicle* says that Mongols 'set up ... [their] ... catapults in a line parallel to the Ljadskije Vorota.' The ground closer to the city was covered by scrub. The Mongol siege artillery breached the walls in one place, and the Mongols attempted to gain entry into city through the gap. The Rus, naturally, tried to stop them. Both sides fought with lances and shields. The Rus resistance collapsed after the Mongols brought a 'barrage [of] arrows' to bear on their line. Kiev fell on 4 December and the city was sacked, but not destroyed. The Rus garrison commander was taken captive, but the Mongols 'did not kill him because of his courage.' Other places near Kiev, such as Vitichev, Vasilev, and Belgorod, were also taken. Several long trenches covered the south side of Kiev: whether the Rus tried to hold any of these is not known, though it seems unlikely.

The Mongols afterwards moved west, advancing on a broad front. Rashid al-Din says that 'they proceeded in a hunting ring, *tümen* by *tümen*, against all the towns.' They took Kolodyazhin by means of a ruse, Kamenets, where 12 catapults were deployed before the Rus surrendered, and Izjaslavl. All the cities belonged to Kiev. The Mongols continued into Vladimir. Sübe'etei bypassed Kremenets and Danilov, and marched quickly to the capital Vladimir. The city was taken in three days, probably during mid January. The Mongols also took Cherven, Galich, and other cities. Genreally they seem to have dealt brutally with the civilian populations. Danilo was away in Hungary

---

1   Possibly the Mongols passed through the trenchline south of Kiev on 19 November. If the line was defended, the sources fail to mention it.

and played no role in the defence of his principality; famed for his bravery, this was not his finest hour.

Initial raids

In January 1241 a small Mongol force raided towards Lublin and Zawichost in the region east of the middle Vistula River. Conrad, lord of Mazovia, may have thought the Mongols were about to attack him. The raid would have left him unwilling to send forces to support Kracow, Oppeln, or Breslau. A second strike was made into the territory of Boleslav IV of Kracow, and Sandomir was sacked in February. A monastery in nearby Koprzywnica was also plundered. The Mongols then advanced over Wislica and Skarbimierz towards Kracow, where Wlodzimierz assembled a force and set out against the invaders. The Mongols retreated to Polaniec on the Czarna. Following, Wlodzimierz appears to have surprised the Mongols there, but in the end it was his smaller force that had the worst of the fighting; even so, it was the Mongols who retreated. This Mongol raid alerted Boleslav, Mieczyslaw, and Henry to the danger they faced, and Henry started to assembly an army close to Breslau.

In later sources a Mongol detachment is also reported raiding into Lithuania, just east of Masovia. The Mongols plundered the area around Lutsk. A certain Shaibek crossed the Nieman north of Novogordek, and local strongman Erdvilas is credited with defeating these Mongols at a place called Sheibeklaukis (Shaibek's field). Further back, Qadan (Khadaan) led the main Mongol force up along the Nieman. He took Grondo, where Yury son of Gleb was killed. When Erdvilas moved towards him, Qadan retreated and the Lithuanians pursued. Qadan turned about and attacked and defeated Erdvilas at Ratno. Erdvilas was killed (February 1241?). As the European sources record a Lithuanian defeat, the raid may be historic. However, Qadan generally operated on the left (south) and is surely unlikely to have made a raid to Grondo and then soon afterwards attack Transylvania. Meanwhile, Bela fortified the passes on the Carpathians, using timber to block them. He inspected the Verecke Pass in person during January,[2] leaving a detachment under the command of Denes Türje to guard it. The King afterwards returned to Buda. The Hungarian lords held a council of war there some weeks later, on 17 February, but the main army had not yet been mobilised.

Sübe'etei had evidently acquired some knowledge of Central European geography and politics. He opted on this occasion not use his trademark outflanking attacks, preferring to seize and exploit a central position. This may reflect a concern that he faced strong enemies as well as a certain uncertainty about what he was dealing with. In China and Russia he had dealt with an enemy he had started to know well, but he was now moving into less familiar territory. The plan was to move directly on Buda with the main part of the army, while secondary forces struck into Poland and Transylvania to protect the flanks. The raid into Poland was certainly designed to distract, though Sübe'etei may initially have planned for this wing to swing around to the south to approach Buda from the north-west. This would be in line with his standard practice.

2   The Russian Gate.

The minor raids preceding the Polish main offensive may have been designed to lure the European powers – including Hungary – into thinking the main assault would come in the north. The objective of the southern Mongol offensive was probably to tie down local forces and perhaps also to distract the Hungarian army in Buda, which included contingents from Transylvania. Central Hungary and Poland were attacked at the same time. The southern group crossed the Carpathians two weeks later for unknown reasons. As in 1238 and 1239, Qadan commanded the southern forces, and may have spent the first two weeks operating against Hungarian targets located east of the mountains. The Mongols aimed to invade Transylvania from two separate points. It must also have taken extra time to get the two armies into position, as the southern pincer needed to cover a longer distance.

The Mongols advance to Pest and Kracow

Sübe'etei led the main Mongol force through the Verecke Pass, coming from Ladomeria, and the Mongols started to remove the barriers set up by the Hungarians. Denes Türje hurried off a messenger to Bela asking for reinforcements, and reached him c.10 March 1241. Bela at that point had not yet mobilised his forces, so was in no position to send help. In any event he was too far away for forces to arrive in time, and the Mongols quickly crushed the Hungarian border force. On 12 March the defenders were overwhelmed by archery fire. Denes Turje reached Bela at Buda 'on the 4th day' to personally inform him of the defeat. The Mongols pursued towards Pest, and were a half day's march from the Danube by 15 March. The distance from the border pass to Buda and Pest is about 290 km. The Mongols were certainly capable of moving quickly, but they could well have outflanked the Hungarian position at Verecke and started moving forward before the Hungarian border guard was overwhelmed. This was what Sübe'etei did in early 1232 when 3,000 horsemen were sent forward well before he followed after with the main body.

Meanwhile, Bela assembled his forces. Contingents came from Gran (under Matthias and Albert), Stuhlweissenburg, Raab, Hermannstadt (Nicolaus), Siebenburgen (Reynold), Kolocsa (Ugolin), Neutra (Jakob), Fünfkirchen (Bartholomew) and Batsch (Eradius). Laszlo, the *ispano* of Segesd only came later. Benedict also seems to have set out from Grosswardein somewhat late. A group of French Templar Knights joined Bela at Buda, and Coloman, Bela's brother, arrived from Croatia with additional forces. Bela asked his neighbour Frederick II of Austria to help him. Bela would eventually be able to field 10,000 men or more, and in addition the Kipchak exiles supported him and may have fielded over 4,000 armed men.[3] Bela could have planned to gather 20,000 fighting men; however he needed about two weeks to assemble the army. He sent some Kipchaks across the Danube to hold Pest, and soon followed with some Hungarian forces – those coming from Gran and Stuhlweissenburg. The Mongols stopped a half day's march from the Danube, and started to plunder the countryside. The Hungarian forces at Pest skirmished with the Mongols. Archbishop Ugolin of

3   It is said that Kötän led 40,000 warriors into Hungary. Taking this total as population and allowing for 10 percent fighting men would give 4,000 men.

Kalosca was angered by the Mongol plundering of the countryside and on 16 March moved forward, but a sham retreat drew the Hungarians to their ruin. Ugolin rushed into wet ground where his heavy armed men got stuck: the Mongols moved around, encircled the detachment, and wiped it out, though Ugolin managed to escape back to Pest. The next day the Mongols took Waitzen, storming a fortified church.

Frederick II of Austria, known as the 'Quarrelsome', it seems for good reasons, came to Pest with a group of soldiers. Roger says he had 'only a few men and unarmed.' He skirmished with some Mongol forces outside the city, where Frederick charged one Mongol with his lance. The lance broke, but the Mongol fell off his horse. When another Mongol moved forward to aid his comrade, Frederick drew his sword and cut off his arm, and afterwards the other Mongols fell back. The dismounted Mongol was brought back as a captive to Pest. Frederick started to intrigue with the Hungarian lords, and made a big story out of his skirmish with the Mongols.

Bela's lords mistrusted the Kipchaks, and a series of events led to the death of Kötän and his family. Furious, the Kipchaks decided to leave, and marched south along the west side of the Danube, passing San Martini and Segesd. Bishop Bulzo of Czanad and Nicolaus (Miklos) son of Borc (Barc) were on the way to join their fellow Hungarian lords at Buda: the Kipchaks attacked and shattered their army. They later sacked Steinamanger before crossing the Danube to enter the March, the land between the Danube and the Seva.[4] Frederick II for his part returned to Austria.

Benedict led forces, according to Roger a 'sizeable army', from Grosswardein towards Buda. He confronted a Mongol detachment near Erlau, having been tempted towards this place by a report that the Mongols were plundering the city. He had some days before gained a success over a 'minor group' and was thus encouraged. The Mongols, reports Roger, mounted dummies on spare horses to fool the Hungarians. When Benedict and his men pressed forward, closing with the Mongols at the base of the hill, the non-fighting men led the horses with the dummies around the flanks, making the Hungarians think they were about to be attacked from several sides. The Hungarians were defeated (c.20–25 March?). Benedict retreated to Grosswardein and from there made his way westward across the Danube.

Orda and Baidar, with perhaps 3,000 soldiers,[5] initiated the main attack on Poland in early March. They crossed the frozen Vistula and occupied Sandomir for a second time on 13 March. The Mongols operated with several columns: their intent may have been to give the impression of having very large forces and to throw the north into a panic by threatening at many points. One part of the army, possibly commanded by Baidar, marched towards Kracow along the Wyslicia route. The forces of Kracow and Sandomir assembled in the former place; Kracow palatin Vladimir and Sandomir palatin Pacoslav shared command. On 18 March Baidar defeated the Polish forces near Tharzek or Chmielnik just west of Kracow: the Polish combined force was weaker than the Mongols and only deployed in one line. Perhaps Baidar had 500 men ready

4   Bela could now claim that he had in fact expelled the Kipchaks as the Mongols had demanded.
5   *The Tartar Relation* says the Mongols had 10,000 men, reported as being one fifth of the forces Batu led into Hungary. Perhaps the author heard it was one tümen and assumed it was 10,000 men strong?

for combat against less than half of that for Vladimir and Pacoslav. Vladimir deployed on the left and Pacoslav on the right. The Polish forces attacked and twice drove back the first Mongol line. Then the Mongols committed the second line with their 'foremost warriors' and scored a complete victory. The two Polish commanders were killed, as were the lords Clemens and Jacobs,[6] The survivors fled westwards. Kracow's population also fled. Boleslav, the local prince, hurried with his family first towards Hungary, and later, after hearing the Mongols also invaded Hungary, to Moravia. The Mongols burned deserted Kracow on 24 March. The remains of the Polish forces retreated towards Oppeln. Sulislav, brother of the fallen Vladimir, was now in charge of the local military forces. In central Poland, the Mongols operated in the area around Leczyca, Kujawy, and Sieradz; some entered into the territory of Conrad.[7] It is likely that these were only scouting columns. The movement into central Poland must have been seen as a threat to Poznan as well as Plock, thus tying down the forces, or at least the attention, of Greater Poland and Mazovia.

In the south, Qadan and Buri crossed the Sereth, probably at Sereth, and pushed south along the east side of the Carpathians into the country of the Cuman Bishops (Terra Episcopi Cumanorum). It seems likely that they crossed into Hungarian territory at the same time as Sübe'etei and Baidar. No Hungarian force seems to have opposed them. Forces were sent from Transylvania to join Bela at Buda, but a detachment took station at Karlstadt to keep an eye on Qadan and Buri and keep them from crossing the Carpathians.

The battles of Liegnitz, Mohi and Hermannstadt

Sübe'etei must have been happy with the results achieved so far. He masked the main Hungarian army at Pest; his right was secured with Orda and Baidar holding Kracow and Qadan and Buri were in position to enter Transylvania from two different points. He thus had broken through the Carpathians with his main force with his secondary forces camped along the mountains on the right and left side. He ordered Baidar to cross the Oder and enter Silesia. Qadan was to invade Transylvania. If his initial idea was for Baidar to cross the mountains in order to enter Hungary from the north, he now changed his mind. Sübe'etei wanted Baidar to distract the Polish–German and Bohemian forces to keep them from supporting Hungary. Sübe'etei remained in position at Buda with the main forces, waiting for Bela to act. If Bela remained inactive he would find Qadan working his way around his right.

Baidar did not stay long in Kracow, as the Mongols pushed on towards the Oder. Mieczyslaw had destroyed the boats along the river, but did not actively try to defend the river line. The Mongols built a bridge at Raciborz and crossed over at this point, then set out for Breslau. Mieczyslaw, after claiming success in a skirmish, retreated

---

6   Jan Długosz is the source for the battle. The earlier Bosuchwala says nothing about it, saying the first engagement was fought at Oppeln. In the Capituary Annals of Kracow mention is made of early 'battles'.
7   Emperor Frederick II in a letter says one Mongol column operated in Prussia. Otto II of Bayern mentions an attack on Conrad in a letter to Siboto in Augsburg, and says the forces of Conrad were defeated. In Conrad's territory the Withow Monastry was hit.

from Oppeln to Liegnitz (Legnica) where he linked up with Henry. Sulislav was with him. Henry had a sizeable army, and had his own cavalry as well as that of Mieczyslaw and Sulislav. The miners from Goldberg contributed militia foot. Boleslav, a son of the Moravian margrave, commanded this contingent. The army was perhaps 2,000 men strong with a sizeable contingent of heavy cavalry.[8] Orda joined Baidar at Breslau on 2 April. The Mongol occupied Breslau city, but not the castle. A large Bohemian army, commanded by Wenceslas, was on the way to join Henry; he set out on 7 April, though from where is not certain. Eager to defeat Henry before the Bohemians arrived on the scene, Orda and Baidar gave up the siege of Breslau Castle and rode toward Liegnitz. Unwisely, Henry set out to fight them and the two sides clashed on 9 April at Liegnitz Pole or Wahlstadt. The Polish army deployed in three lines. The first, commanded Boleslav, consisted of mixed forces, many of which were not well armed; the Goldberg miners were in this line. The second line contained the two units with the heavy cavalry of Mieczyslaw (Oppeln) and Sulislav (Kracow); and Henry (Silesia) himself took up position in the third line with his own forces. Most likely the forces were deployed in a diamond shape. It is not certain how the Mongols deployed, but drawing on Długosz it may be that they deployed in two lines with two hidden detachments deployed beyond the flanks of the first line. Perhaps there were two or three units in the first line and one in the second.

The first Polish echelon, really a skirmishing line, moved forward, but could make no impression on the Mongols. Struck on the flanks by Mongol archers that may have come from a hidden position, they fell into confusion. It may be inferred from Długosz that the Mongols encircled the Polish unit. Mieczyslaw and Boleslav brought forward their forces; the cavalry was supported by crossbowmen. The Mongols engaged in close combat and Mieczyslaw decided to retreat, drawing the whole Polish line with him. Henry now committed his reserve line: he rallied the forces of Mieczyslaw and Boleslav and pushed forward with his full forces, and the Mongols fell back. This time it seems possible that the Polish foot remained behind. Suddenly the Mongol reserve fell upon the Polish cavalry, while the light horse showered them with missile fire from the flanks. The Mongol light horse spread a smoke screen between the enemy horse and foot, and the cavalry clash ended as a Mongol victory, but it was a close run thing. The Mongols told travelling monks just a few years later (as rendered by *The Tartar Relation*): 'when they [the Mongols] were themselves on the point of flight the columns of the Christians unexpectedly turned and fled.' When the Mongols had finished off the enemy cavalry they turned on the foot soldiers, and Orda and Baidar won a total victory. The Polish–German losses are not known, though the Teutonic Knights alone admitted a loss of 11 senior soldiers and 500 others.

Qadan and Buri entered Transylvania a few days before 31 March. Qadan moved on Rodna, with the silver mines. Roger says it took him three days to cross the mountains. A feigned withdrawal relaxed the defences and Qadan was able to capture the town easily on 31 May. Six hundred Saxons were drafted into the Mongol army, perhaps

---

8   Mare Cetwinski. Gerard Labuda says 7,000 to 8,000, which seems high. Boguchwala says Henry had 'many thousands of courageous warriors.'

to serve as guides. Qadan next took Bistritz on 2 April, and Klausenburg sometime after 11 April. Of the 10,000 people in Bistritz, 6,014 perished. The Mongols marched westwards and took Grosswardein, overcoming serious opposition. The Mongols had found the castle strongly held, and fell back 5–10 km and waited. When the garrison ventured outside the fortress, the Mongols made a surprise attack and overcame them, breaking down a newly-repaired wall with siege engines to gain entry to the castle. It seems a Mongol detachment passed Zilah/Zalau and Trestenburg. With the conquest of Grosswardein, Qadan was firmly in control of the Koros River region. Rashid al-Din says: 'Qadan and Buri took the field against the Sasan people and defeated them after 3 battles.' The Sasan people are evidently the Saxons of Transylvania. Perhaps the three battles refer to the fighting around Radan, Bistritz and Grosswardein.

Buri, having entered into the country of the Cuman Bishops, pushed onwards into Burzenland, crossing forests and mountains as he advanced. Zenth Leleukh (Szent Lélek) was destroyed. On 31 March the Mongols defeated Pozsa, voyvode of Transylvania, probably close to Kronstadt. Buri next seized Kumelburch on 4 April, and Hermannstadt on 11 April, but did not take the castle of the latter place. The Mongol commander subsequently pushed up the Maros, sacked the Kercel Abbey and took Karlsburg and Zalalhna.

At Buda and Pest, the Hungarian lords finally united in face of the Mongol menace. The Mongols had defeated Ugolin, Benedict, and Poza, the Kipchaks had crushed Bulcsu and Nicolaus, and Ladislas had not yet arrived. Bela, Koloman, Matthias, Albert, Gregory, James, Eradius, Bartholomew, Matthias, Nicolaus, and Reynold had provided contingents and Ugolin was still with the army and clearly still had fighting men even after the defeat he had suffered. They fielded a sizeable force. Siban 'sent word [to Batu] that they [the Hungarians] were double the size of the Mongol army.' He was clearly impressed by the heavily armed European knights as he said that each man was a *buhadur*. Juvaini says that the Hungarian army was 400,000 men strong; Rashid al-Din speaks of 40 *tümens*. Perhaps Bela really fielded 40 units, but if so these units cannot have been more than 250 men strong on average, or if so, each lord provided about 1,000 men on average.[9] It is unlikely that the Hungarian army was stronger than the Mongol army, but the Hungarian heavy cavalry was probably better armed than his Mongolian counterpart. Sübe'etei decided to fall back, aiming to lure Bela into following him. The Mongol army retired on 6 April, 24 days after arriving at Pest (c.6 April). Bela pursued the Mongols, reaching the Mohi Heath just west of Sajo River some 165 km from Buda. The Hungarians set up camp just west, or slightly south-west of modern Muhi along a small stream. Some seven kilometres north-east of the camp there was a stone bridge, providing passage over the Sajo.[10] Bela covered the camp with wagons in the traditional Magyar style. Bela is censured by the sources for packing his men too closely in the camp, meaning the Hungarians could not quickly deploy into a battle-line. In addition they failed to post sentries.

9   The Hungarian units were called 'banderias'. They were usually between 50 and 400 men strong.
10   A point made in a letter from emperor Frederick II to Henry III of England.

Sübe'etei decided to start an assault on the Hungarian position during the night of 10–11 April. He had perhaps 15,000 fighting men against 10,000 for the Hungarians. Bela made a frontal attack across the bridge to distract the Hungarian army, while Sübe'etei crossed the Sajo further south, planning to fall on the Hungarian right flank. The area east of the river was wooded and the trees and scrub masked his movements. The river was shallow close to where Batu camped, but deep where Sübe'etei had to cross, therefore Sübe'etei first had to bridge it. Though the river was fordable around the stone bridge, it was wide, and the bridge 200 metres long. Batu sent a detachment to secure it during the night. A Rus captive escaped from the Mongol camp and alerted the Hungarians about the impending assault: Coloman and Ugrin brought forces out of the camp around midnight and surprised and defeated the Mongol detachment at the bridge. Thomas of Spalato wrote: 'the Hungarians immediately charged into them and did battle with them most bravely. They cut down a great many of them and pushed the rest back over the bridge, causing them to be drowned in the river.' About 2:00 a.m. the Hungarians returned to the camp, leaving a unit to guard the bridge.

Some hours later the Mongols attacked again. They brought forward siege artillery, seven catapults, and attacked across the bridge and through the water north of it, near modern Onod. Batu and an officer called Boroldai secured the bridge and brought the Mongol forces across the river (perhaps 4:30 a.m.). Shiban might have crossed the river further north: Rashid al-Din says he 'moved out on his own.' The Hungarian bridge guard fled back to their camp, raising the alarm. The Hungarians as a whole failed to respond to the situation ('they were barely able to rouse those who were asleep there'), but Coloman, Ugrin, and 'a certain master of the Knights Templars' were ready for action and rushed towards the bridge. Bela did not move forward or even prepare the full army at this point. Coloman, Ugrin, and the Templar lord were too weak relative to the Mongol forces they now faced, and Ugrin hurried back to the camp, censuring Bela for not bringing to full army forward. By the time additional Hungarian forces moved out, Batu was ready for battle. Rashid al-Din says the Mongols 'made a massive charge in unison.' The more lightly-armed Mongols were at disadvantage in the constrained terrain, but Batu held out long enough for Sübe'etei to make his way across the Sajo and approach the Hungarian right flank. The Mongols crossed the river just south of modern Girinics and moved towards the Hungarian camp along the path where road 35 now runs. Informed about the new threat, Bela broke off battle against Batu and retreated back into his camp.

The Mongols surrounded the enemy camp ('enclosed by the enemy on all sides'). The Hungarians made sorties, but were driven back by Mongol archery fire. The Mongols bombarded the camp with incendiary devices for many hours (8:00–12:00 a.m.), again making good use of siege artillery on the battlefield. Coloman led a renewed sortie northwards, perhaps coming to close quarters with the Mongol lancers. The Mongols made an opening in their line on the opposite side, seemingly offering the Hungarians a way out ('some of the enemy made way for them and permitted them to go through'), and some Hungarians quickly made use of it. Seeing that these men made it, more people followed and soon there was a mass exodus from the camp. Too few remained to defend against Sübe'etei's attack, and those who did, including the forces of Coloman, were overwhelmed. Meanwhile Mongol light horse pursued the Hungarians, who in their flight lost all semblance of order. The Mongol horse emerged on either side of the shallow valley through which the Hungarians fled and inflicted severe losses upon them. King Bela fled with his bodyguard: a Mongol crack force attempted to intercept him, but his men held them off and saved him. Some of the Mongols fought with lances. Coloman also managed to escape, though he was badly wounded. Bishop Bartholomew (Pecs) and some of his men got away, but were pursued. Luckily they met Ladislas (Somogy) and his contingent, who drove the Mongols off. Many of the senior Hungarian lords were killed, including Matthias and Albert (Gran), Ugolin (Kolocsa), Georg (Raab), Jakob (Neutra), Eradius (Bacs), Reynold (Siebenburgen), and Nicolaus (Hermannstadt). The dead were found across a long distance along the road towards Pest. The Hungarians are said to have lost between 35,000 and 80,000 men killed. One source gives the somewhat more reasonable but still high 10,000. If the army was about 10,000-strong it really could have lost more than half.

The Mongol losses are not recorded, but they were clearly not light. According to the long Sübe'etei biography, Batu 'disputing the bridge, was taken advantage of by the enemy and lost [a] third [of his] armoured men along with the subordinate commander Bagatu.' This Bagatu should be the Boroldai known to Rashid al-Din. If Batu had half the army and 40 percent of his men were heavily armed, then he might have lost 1,000 men. Batu reportedly lost his resolve, suggesting to Sübe'etei they retreat. Perhaps this suggestion was made after, rather than during the battle? Sübe'etei refused: 'If the princes wish to go back, then they will go back alone. I shall not turn back until I reach the Tuna [Danube] City [Buda and Pest] of the Macha [Hungarians].' Batu and Sübe'etei pursued the Hungarians from Mohi to the Danube. Pest, unprepared for defence, was taken and sacked on 16 April. Reportedly 100,000 people were killed.

After the battle, Batu faulted Sübe'etei for being tardy, lamenting the loss of valiant Mongol soldiers. Sübe'etei answered him: 'When the Prince attacked he did not realise that where I crossed the water was deeper and my bridge was not ready; if he says that I was late he should remember the reason.' Later at a banquet, Batu offered Sübe'etei a cup of wine, saying: 'everything we have achieved we owe to Sübe'etei.' This was evidently common knowledge. When Ögödei wrote to Batu after the quarrel between Batu and Güyük, he said: 'As for you do not boast too much of your victories. They were gained by Sübe'etei.' Mongol pride in their achievement is probably reflected in the comments found in the text of Rashid al-Din: 'Pulu and Bashqurd is a great area difficult (to access) and they conquered it.' Thomas of Spalato, an eyewitness, observed: 'No people in the world know as much as the Mongols, especially in warfare in open country, about how to conquer an enemy either by daring or by knowledge of war.' Both he and later Carpini understood that the Mongols prevailed due to superior methods rather than overwhelming numbers.

Subsequent operations
Refusing to stay to help the defenders, the wounded Coloman fled via Pest to Segesd. Bela fled along a more northern route, through Gomor County to Neutra where he

German	Hungarian	Romanian
Batsch	Bacs	
Bistritz	Beszterce	Bistrita
Burzenland	Barcasag	Tara Barsei
Cenadu	Csanad	Cenad
Erlau	Eger	
Fünfkirchen	Pecs	
Gran	Esztergom	
Grosswardein	Nagyvarad	Oradea
Güns	Kőszeg	
Hermannstadt	Nagyszeben	Sibiu
Karlsburg	Gyulafehérvár	Alba Iulia
Klausenburg	Kolozsvár	Cluj-Napoca
Komorn	Komarom	
Kumelburch	Küküllővár	Cetatea de Baltă
Lutzmannsburg	Locsmand	
Neutra	Nyitra	
Ödenburg	Sopron	
Orod	Egres	
Martinsberg	Pannonhalma	
Pressburg	Pozsony	
Raab	Gyor	
Steinamanger	Szombately	
Stuhlweissenburg	Székesfehérvár	
Trestenburg	Tasnad	Tasnad
Thomasbrucke		Tamasda
Waitzen	Vac	
Wieselburg	Moson	

Cities of Hungary/Transylvania.

met elements of his bodyguard. He passed Pressburg into Austrian territory, where Frederick II welcomed him (perhaps in Hainburg), but Frederick quickly showed his true colours. He extracted money from Bela and forced him to hand over Wieselburg, Ödenburg, and Lutzmannsburg. Bela was then allowed to leave. He made his way south towards Zagreb in May 1241. Coloman joined him in Zagreb, but then died there. Bela went to the Adriatic coastal region.

The southern Mongol columns continued active operations. Qadan marched south from Grosswardein, took Thomasbrucke and then marched to Hermannstadt. The city was sacked for a second time, and the people fled into the castle. Qadan retreated, only to return during the night. He captured the castle in mid April. Büjek seized Cenadu sometime before Qadan took Thomasbrucke. A detachment led by an officer called Lanad joined Büjek, presumably detached by Qadan. Büjek and Lanad took Pereg – using captives to do the dirty siegework – and Egresh. The people were massacred. Arad was also taken. Roger left a livid eyewitness account of the events in the south. He fled Grosswardein for Thomasbrucke, but unwilling to be drafted into the defence there he went to an island on the Cris where people from Adea, Viovadeni, and Iermata had sought refuge. Later he went to Cenadu. When he came there he found the city already taken by another Mongol force (entering Hungary 'from the other side'). He then returned towards Thomasbrucke. By then this place had been taken. He returned to the island, but later a Mongol army arrived and made an attack on it and the defenders attempted to improvise a defence. The Mongols, says Roger, 'gave the impression of attacking the island through the water, deceiving the people of the island into shifting to defend those parts, the Tartars then pushed upon the exposed gates of the fort on the other side.' The defenders were overwhelmed. Many were captured. Perhaps Qadan made this attack after taking Hermannstadt?

In Silesia, the strategic situation was completely changed with the Mongol victory at Liegnitz. A Mongol scouting column reached Zittau (130 km east of Liegntiz). Wenceslas later camped at Königstein south of Dresden (650 km east of Liegntiz) where additional forces from Saxony and Thuringia reinforced his army. Baidar and Kadan, after failing to cow Liegnitz into submission, turned south to plunder upper Silesia, camping for two weeks at Ottmachau (21 April to 9 May). Wenceslas was therefore free to assemble a large army without interference. The Mongols next turned west to raid into Moravia during May, and sacked Freudenthal, Neustadt, and Littau. They subsequently marched via Brunn to rejoin Batu and Sübe'etei in Hungary. They marched past Trenchin, Solyom, Korpona, and Waitzen to reach the Danube at Komorn, and from here marched downriver to arrive at Pest. Wenceslas and his army only entered Morovia after the Mongols had left the region. It was perhaps the Mongol column coming from Moravia that clashed with Austrian forces close to Pressburg. In May, Frederick of Austria claimed in letters to have killed 300 or even 700 Mongols; in July he attempted without success to occupy Hungarian held Pressburg. He occupied the town and castle of Raab, but local Hungarian forces afterwards drove the Austrian garrison out. They took the castle and, says Roger, 'burnt all the Germans in it.'

Jan Długosz reports about later events in Poland: 'After their defeat of King Bela, the Tatars hurriedly sent a force through Spis to Kracow, whose inhabitants are unarmed and unprepared; the Tatars slaughter them indiscriminately. They loot the city and return through Oswiëcim to their camp in Hungary.'[11] In Masovia, Conrad had escaped the Mongol onslaught. He took advantage of the plight of his neighbours and seized Kracow soon after the Mongols had left the country. He was supported by a detachment sent by the lord of Pomerania. Boleslav returned from Moravia, backed by some German mercenaries, and tried to drive off the garrison left by Conrad in Kracow, but Conrad returned at the head of a large force and drove him off.

Conrad of Mazovia had given Danilo sanctuary in the city of Vysegorod. Danilo later returned to Vladimir where 'not one person remained alive.' Mikhail Vsevolodovich settled on an island near Kiev, and his son Rostislav went to Chernigov. Rostislav Mixajlovich and the Boloxovian princes raided into Danilo's territory, approaching Baktoa. Kuril defended the city; he probably had about 300 cavalry and 3,000 infantry and was with this force able to hold the Boloxovians off. Rostislav Mixojlovich fell back across the Dnieper, and Danilo reacted by making a counter-raid into Boloxovian territory. He took Derevich, Gubin, Kobud, Kudin, Boz'skyj, and Djad'kov. Kuril arrived to support him, and Danilo let him and his men plunder Djad'kov. Danilo treated the Boloxovians harshly because the Mongols had 'left [the Boloxovians in peace] to plant wheat and millet for them' (winter 1241–1242).

In May–July Konrad IV, the 13-year-old son of Holy Roman emperor Frederick II, was tasked to assemble an army in Nurnberg for a crusade against the Mongols, but interest was limited and it came to nothing. By then the Mongols were turning away from Poland and concentrating on Hungary.

The 1241 campaign is, along with that of 1232, the only one of the early Mongol campaigns which can be followed in part on a day-by-day basis. It is clear that Sübe'etei coordinated the movements of his columns closely. The intent was to make a diversionary attack into Poland and the neighbouring countries to keep the local lords from supporting Hungary. Sübe'etei penetrated into central Hungary before Bela had assembled his forces, but was not able to gain a decisive quick victory. Even so, Bela was unable to concentrate his full forces. On the other hand one contingent made an unauthorised attack, the Kipchaks attacked two lords, and one lord failed to arrive. Bela may finally have assembled about 10,000 men, but with better preparation he probably could have assembled 20,000. He ended up with fewer, 67 percent due to his own actions and 33 percent due to the Mongols. Sübe'etei used a feigned retreat to tempt Bela forward and then made a double attack on the weaker Hungarian army. The feigned retreat had worked against the Wild Kipchaks in 1219, Georgians in 1221, and Rus in 1223, but not against the Jin in 1232. Bela was tempted forward. He really should have known better as the example of the Rus in 1223 was there for him

---

11   Perhaps this detachment skirmished with the Olmutz garrison. Wenceslas is said to have sent Jaroslaw von Sternberg and some forces (6,000 men) to Olmutz where he earned fame by making a successful sortie on 25 July 1241. It was claimed a senior Mongol lord was killed.

to see. The ploy of giving an encircled foe a route of escape had been used before in 1220 and 1232, but not in Europe.

Mongols columns reached Kracow and Pest within 10 days of each other (respectively 24 March and 16 March). Sübe'etei next unleashed the two southern groups. These entered Transylvania at different points on the same day, 31 March. Finally the victory at Mohi, Liegnitz and Hermannstadt was gained on almost the same day (respectively 9, 10–11 and 11 August). All this is evidence that Sübe'etei and the Mongols managed to time their operations to an amazing degree. Denis Sinor held that: 'The glue that held the separate plans together was a rigid adherence to a previously agreed timetable for joining forces.' It seems more likely that the key to the Mongol operations was continued communication between the various columns. Sübe'etei may, for example, have communicated with Baidar when he was in Kracow and told him what day he planned to fight the deciding battle against the Hungarians. He had a measure of control over his columns unmatched by any other commander active before the Industrial Revolution.

The Europeans are likely to have fielded more heavy cavalry than the Mongols at both Mohi and Liegnitz, but failed to create a tactical context out of which they could get advantage out of this fact. They would have been better advised to deploy in a fortified position on a hill, fighting dismounted. The Hungarian performance at Mohi seems particularly inept as a part of the army failed to get out of the camp quickly. Again Sübe'etei did not have to fight a set-piece battle. Orda and Baidar, by contrast, seem to have fought a bloody direct battle against Henry.

Hungary, like Russia, was poorly fortified, at least east of the Danube. They did not have many stone castles, like the network constructed by the Teutonic Knights in Prussia. If they had developed a more extensive fortress network it would have been much harder for the Mongols to gain a quick victory. Food and forage would have run low before the country could have been conquered. The Teutonic Knights had in fact been headquartered in Transylvania less than two decades before, but were expelled before they were able to establish themselves. Hungary needed strong fortresses and forts along the Danube and Theiss rather than in just Transylvania. Perhaps the Teutonic Knights could have provided a start for such a process?

Paul Buell held up the 1241 campaign as the 'masterpiece' of Sübe'etei. As a commander leading an army that was 8,000 km away from his base he was certainly at the limits of what was possible, but as a military achievement it cannot be ranked above the Sanfeng campaign.

Sources: the *Secret History* 271; Wang Yun, p. 7; *Yuanshi* 121, pp. 2977–2978; 122, p. 3009; Juvaini, pp. 270–271; Rashid al-Din, 474–475, 482–484; Roger, pp. 161, 164, 169–171, 179–181, 185, 193–195, 197, 201–207; Thomas of Spalato, Hansgerd Göckenjan and James Sweeney, *Der Mongolensturm*, pp. 236–261; Epternacher Notiz, gleichzeiting, MG.S.XXIV.65 note, Letter of Abbey of Marienburg. MG.S.XXXVIII.209. (1242, 4 January), Ann. S. Pantal. Col., gliechzeitig, MG.S. XXIV; *Scriptores Rerum Hungaricarum* II, 564, 576–577, 582; *The Tartar Relation*, pp. 19, 80–82; Matthew of Paris, pp. 341–347; *The Galician–Volynian Chronicle*, pp. 48–51; Jan Długosz,

324   THE MONGOL CONQUESTS

pp.177–178; Oman, 328–331; Franz Palacky, *Der Mongolen Einfall im Jahre 1241*; G. Strakosch-Grassmann, *Der Einfall der Mongolen in Mitteleuropa in den Jahren 1241–1242*, pp.38, 42–43, 182–183; Shinobu Iwamura, 'Mongol Invasion of Poland in the Thirteenth Century', pp.103–157; Harold Lamb, *The Earth Shakers*, pp.159–169; C. A. Macartney: 'Where Was "Black Wallachia" in the Thirteenth Century?', *The Journal of the Royal Asiatic Society of Great Britain and Ireland*, No. 2 (April 1940), pp.198–200; Buell, 'Sübötei', in de Rachewiltz, *In the Service of the Khan*, p.24; Kosztolnyik, *Hungary in the Thirteenth Century*, p.138, 151–164; Benson, *Six Emperors*, pp.185, 193–195, 199–215, 212–213, 221, 237–238, 240; Nora Berend, *At the Gate of Christendom: Jews, Muslims, and 'pagans' in Medieval Hungary, c.1000–1300* (Cambridge: Cambridge University Press, 2001), pp.71–72; Július Bartl, *Slovak History: Chronology & Lexicon* (Wauconda, IL: Bolchazy-Carducci Publishers, 2002), p.191; Dimnik, *The Dynasty of Chernigov, 1146–1246*, pp.356–360; Paul Lendvai, *The Hungarians: A Thousand Years of Victory and Defeat* (Princeton: Princeton University Press, 2003), p.50; Peter Jackson, *The Mongols and the West: 1221–1410* (Taylor & Francis Ltd., 2014), p.66; Sarolta Tatar, 'Roads used by the Mongols into Hungary, 1241–1242', *Olon Ulsyn Mongolch Erdemtnii X Ikh Khural* (Ulaan Bataar 2012), pp.334–341.

51

Into the Heart of Europe?

After the death of Ögödei, a great meeting of all the princes was convoked.

– Yuanshi 121

The Mongols rested during the summer, remaining between the Danube and Tisza Rivers. Bela left a lord called Paul, the judge of his court, with some forces to guard the Danube. However, he did not have enough forces to seriously attempt to hold the river line. The Hungarians attempted to break the ice to keep the Mongols from crossing the river, but did not have enough forces to seriously attempt to defend the Danube. When on 25 December 1241 the river suddenly froze, in spite of Hungarian efforts to break the ice, the Mongols could simply cross over. Buda (Acquincum) was taken. One Mongol column took the city of Gyor (Esztergom), using 30 siege engines, but not the citadel. Simon, who was from Spain, defended the citadel with 'many crossbowmen.' The Mongols also failed to take Stuhlweissenburg, which had a strong garrison and was located in swampy terrain, Pannonhalma, and Tihany Monastery in Zala.[1] Possibly quite small Mongol forces were active. Qadan undertook the only significant operation, moving along the southern border of Tyrol and reaching Udine; he pushed onwards to the south-west in search of Bela. Sübe'etei, presumably, still kept the bulk of the Mongol forces around Pest on the east side of the Danube. If enemy armies advanced against the Mongols from Germany or Italy, Sübe'etei would be able to turn on them from the central position he had selected. It is likely that he planned to act much as during 1232–1234 or 1238–1239, when he sent out columns on various missions, but kept his main forces securely placed in a central location. It was hardly his plan to strike into Germany during this campaigning season.

Bela had fled to an island in the Adriatic, but soon left this place for Spalato. Perhaps not feeling safe there he went to Trosir (Trogir). Qadan first marched into Slovenia, destroying Zagreb en route. Learning that Bela was further south, Qadan followed and in March set up camp at Verbacz, 20 km north-east of Spalato. The

---

1 A letter was sent to the Pope from Fehervar in January explaining this.

civilian captives moving with his army were reportedly killed there. He scouted towards Spalato and Trosir: Bela left Trosir to seek safety on an island off the coast. Qadan approached Clissa, but pushed on after learning that Bela was not there. He divided his detachment, sending one part towards Spalato and leading the rest against Trosir. He attempted to take this city, but a channel covered it and the Mongols could not get across the water. Qadan plundered the open country before leaving the area, then again divided his detachment. One detachment pushed through Bosnia with Qadan in charge, and the other pushed south along the coast into Dalmatia and Albania (in Ragusa there was 'little damage'). This group took and sacked Kotor ('consumed in flames'), Drivost and Suagium (the two last places were 'depopulated'). A Croatian army claimed victory over the Mongols at Grobnik ('Field of Graves') near Rijeka. It was most likely a very minor affair that developed into a romance story only known from much later sources.

In February, more than two months after the event, the Mongols learned that Ögödei had died on 11 December the year before. Batu and Sübe'etei broke off the campaign and returned home. The captive Roger reports that Mongol forces again marched through Transylvania. Other forces marched along the north side of the Danube. Qadan was at Scutari when he was informed about the decision to evacuate Europe. He marched east along the south side of the Danube and rejoined the main Mongol forces somewhere north of the mouth of the river. Bulgaria most likely submitted to Qadan, possibly paying tribute. In June 1241 the strong Bulgarian king Ivan Asen II had just died: two minor sons succeeded him, leaving the kingdom in a difficult position. A Mongol detachment penetrated into Latin territory south of Bulgaria, ruled by Baldwin II. The Latins won an initial encounter, but lost a second. The Heiligenkreuz Annals report: 'meeting with them; he defeated them in a first encounter, but was overcome by them in a second.' Batu sent two officers with a force into Galich to look for Danilo; they must have marched along the route Batu followed when he entered Hungary. Rostislav Mixajlovich and the Boloxovian princes raided into Galicia for a second time, and approached Galich after first occupying Domamir Pecera Castle. Danilo and Vasilko hurried after them. Rostislav retreated to Scekotov, and Danilo and Vasilko headed for Bakota, Kalius, and Vladimir. Warned in Kholm by a Kipchak princess called Aktaj that two Mongols called Manman and Balaj were coming to look for him, Danilo went into hiding. The Mongols reached Volodava before returning (spring 1242). Around the same time a Mongol detachment put Rostislav 'to flight in Bork'; he fled from Chernigov to Hungary. The Mongols failed to capture Danilo, but in 1246 he went to submit to Batu in person and was accepted as a subject lord.

Many Kipchaks made their way into Bulgaria in order to evade the Mongols. Some, perhaps a group left isolated by the Mongol advance through Russia, clashed with the forces left by Sübe'etei to guard his rear (that is, the base camp and some of the spare horses). The Mongols, led by Kötän and Shingqor, defeated them. It is not said where the battle was fought, but it was perhaps somewhere close to the Dnieper or the Don. The Kipchaks fled into the Caucasus where they made their way towards the mountains. A Mongol officer called Ila'udur intercepted and defeated them near Derbent during the autumn.

The Mongols did not try to hold Hungary or any part of Poland. The Rus states, however, remained Mongol subjects. Even Novgorod, not actually attacked, later submitted.

The 1242 campaign was interrupted during the early stages, though evidently no major offensive had been planned for that year. It is curious that the Mongols did not send a detachment to hunt down Bela earlier. Genghis Khan sent Sübe'etei and Jebe to hunt down Muhammad soon after taking Samarkand. Sübe'etei only sent Qadan after Bela several months after the Mohi battle and the conquest of Pest. Heavy rainfall in Hungary may have slowed down the Mongol main forces during the first months of 1242. It is unlikely that the Mongols could have conquered significant parts of Western Europe with the forces available. They could certainly humble the main forces of the Holy Roman Empire and wreck havoc in southern Germany or northern Italy, but to take one by one all the stone fortresses and castles of Western Europe would have been beyond what Sübe'etei's forces could have managed. Centuries earlier Ostrogoths, Gepids, and other groups backed Attila and the Huns and later large numbers of Slavs backed the Avars. The Mongols had found willing recruits amongst the people living east and south of the Rus, but in Central Europe the situation might have been different. If they wanted to make a sustained effort there, they needed local fighting men willing to back them. Given the many divisions in Europe at that time, gaining local allies might have been possible, but as it was none are known to have sided with the Mongols.

Sources: Rashid al-Din, 483; Benson, *Six Emperors*, pp.245–246, 252; Kosztolnyik, *Hungary in the Thirteenth Century*, p.172; Dimnik, *The Dynasty of Chernigov, 1146–1246*, p.360; John Fine, *The Late Medieval Balkans: a critical survey from the late twelfth century to the Ottoman Conquest* (Ann Arbor: University of Michigan Press, 1994), pp.155–156; Peter Jackson, *The Mongols and the West: 1221–1410*, p.66.

52

The Mongol–Song War

In the face of the enemy's growing strength and adaptability, continued Song success at repulsing Mongol attacks suggests that Song forces, regarded even at home as no match for the Mongols, were not so weak after all. Moreover, maintaining their superior command of rivers and tributaries to the east, the Song were able to move troops and provisions with relative speed along efficient lines of communication.

– Richard L. Davis, on Song resistance to the Mongols by the late 1230s

The war against the Song continued after Sübe'etei left China during the latter part of 1234. The Mongols thus undertook the invasion of Europe, while at the same time waging war in China. Like Genghis Khan before him, Ögödei was ready to fight on two fronts. However, the Mongols repeatedly tried to negotiate a settlement with the Song to end the conflict and were evidently not at this stage committed to an all-out war to destroy the Song. The Song Court was unresponsive to the Mongol peace overtures.

Of the 'core' Mongol forces not more than 30–40 percent can have been committed in Europe, but as some were in other theatres and some guarded Mongolia, the Mongol forces in China may have been even smaller. By now, however, the locally recruited forces were substantial, drafted men rather than just volunteers. Furthermore there was the cavalry from Liaodong. In effect, it was a continuation of the Jin–Song war with the north under new management. The Mongols had more cavalry than the Jin before them, but with many rivers, mountains, and fortified cities in the south this arm was less significant that it had been in the north. The Song increased their forces from a nominal total of 400,000 to 700,000. These totals included some non-combatants, but not locally raised militia. The Mongols had 97,575 registered Han Chinese soldiers by 1241 and must have had more than 150,000 soldiers in total. Like the Song, the Mongols increased the total number of men fielded as the war progressed. In the actual combat theatres the Mongols would often have fielded the larger forces.

The Mongols operated with separate armies in Sichuan, along the Han River, and along the Huai River without much effort to devise an overall campaign plan. Unable to conquer and hold the well-fortified cities along the Yangtze, they made no progress.

In fact they suffered several defeats. The Song constructed many small strongpoints held by soldier-settlers, most famously in Sichuan. The Mongols sometimes penetrated deep into Sichuan, but they could not conquer and hold the province. Like the Mongols, the Song segmented their command into three with a senior military official in charge of the Sichuan, the Han, and Huai sectors. Ultimately reporting to a civilian, these military leaders still had great military as well as administrative powers. The most significant Song military leaders were Meng Gong, Yu Jie, and Lu Wende; all were capable of dealing with the Mongols. Operating from strong defensive positions, they attacked when and where there was an opportunity.

Ögödei did not ramp up the war effort quickly. He first sent Wang Ji to censure the Song for the 1234 attack (later the same year). Only in the second half of 1235 did the Mongols initiate offensive operations. Ögödei appointed his sons Kököcü and Kötän to senior command. Kötän was placed in the west, and was perhaps not closely involved in military operations. Tagahi Gambo was his chief commander, a Tangut who had taken service with Muqali in 1221. His subordinates included Anjur, Temür Buqa, Heima, and Zhuge, the son of Yelü Tuhua. The Önggüt Wang Shixian (1195–1243) was a newcomer, only taking service with the Mongols in 1235. He quickly emerged as a dashing and capable commander. Kököcü operated in the eastern sector. Senior officers serving under them included Caqan, Tacar, Shi Tianze, Zhang Rou, and Yen Shi.

1235

The serious operations started only after the summer, leaving a year-long lull following the summer fighting in 1234. In July–August 1235, before initiating operations, the Mongols conscripted one in 20 able-bodied men in many districts. Köden initially operated against Jin positions remaining in the western regions. Jin officer Guo Hama had escaped from Fengxiang years earlier with some followers, and later gained control over parts of Jinzhou, Lanzhou, Dingzhou, and Huizhou. In November–December Köden took Qinzhou and besieged Wang Shixian inside Gongzhou. He was not able to break into the city, but sent the Önggüt Anjur to offer amnesty to the defenders. Shixian, after first considering going over to the Song, accepted the offer.

Having secured his rear, Köden was ready to move against the Song, who guarded the passes at Wuxiu, Xianren and Qifang. Behind these passes forces were stationed in Jie, Cheng, Feng, and Tianshui. They had earlier maintained some 100,000 soldiers in the sector, but that total had by now declined to 30,000. Kötän passed Xi'an, where the Jin official in charge submitted to the Mongols, and crossed the mountains, brushing aside attempts to stop him in the passes. In January 1236 he took Mianzhou. It was clear to the Song that this fortress could not be defended, but Gia Jia refused to leave and fell fighting, having taken up position in fortified points in the hills close to Mianzhou. Jia was a Chinese Leonidas. The Song governor of Hanzhong, Zhao Yanna, occupied the Qingyen Pass; the Mongols attacked this position without being able to break through. Cao Youwan deployed some forces at Yangping under the command of Wang Jin, and some at Jiguan'ai commanded by Wang Zi and Bai Zaixing. He stationed his own unit at Xiling, closer to the former position. When some Mongol forces approached Yangping they were driven back. Youwan moved forward with his own unit to support his men. He believed that the Mongols would next turn towards Jiguan'ai, and therefore he moved towards this place with his own and the forces previously deployed at Yangping. The Mongols did indeed move on Jiguan'ai, and caught between the two Song detachments, they suffered a clear defeat.

In the centre, Kököcü, Qutuqu (a grandson of Joci Qasar), Tas, Tacar, Shi Tianze, and Zhang Rou moved towards the Han River. They took Tang in the summer of 1235. The Mongols later took Caoyang, in October–November. From Caoyang, Kököcü detached Tacar and Zhang Rou eastwards, and they took Xuzhou and Peizhou (late 1235 to early 1236). Zhang Rou then rejoined Kököcü. Meanwhile, in October–November, Kököcü had advanced up along the Han River, aiming to secure Xiangyang. Shi Tianze won a victory at Xiao Shidan (a river battle). Aided by a defection the Mongols afterwards took Xiangyang, and then Deng. The Song commanders failed to deploy their forces effectively against the Mongols and offered little effective resistance. The Mongols captured a lot of supplies in Xiangyang.

1236

Kököcü followed up the success achieved in 1235 by taking Yingzhou in March–April 1236. The Song garrisons in Sui, Jingmen, and Ying (commanded by a certain Qiao Shishou) retreated in face of the Mongol advance. The Mongols afterwards took Fuzhou between Jiangling and Huanzhou. The officer in charge of the fortress fell fighting. Another part of the Mongol army took up position at Zhijiang and Jianli on the Yangtze, on either side of Jiangling. The Mongols were inside the narrow 'loop' between the Yangtze and the lower Han, and prepared to cross the former river.

Meng Gong guarded Huanzhou (Hanyang) where he had improved the defensive works and deepened the moat. He constructed houses for refugees coming from the north and helped them settle. When a Mongol column made a raid on Qizhou in February 1236, Meng Gong detached forces from Huanzhou to ward them off. Yu Jie was the officer in charge of defending Qizhou. Meng Gong was afterwards ordered to succour Jiangling. Song officer Zhang Shun arrived there first, crossing over from the south side of the river. Meng Gong moved up river from Huang, coming from the east. Zhao Wu, his brother-in-law, led the advance force. Meng Gong took measures to make his army look bigger than it really was: he spread out his forces and lit many fires at night, and placed his men so that the reflection of the fires in the water of a river made the forces look even bigger. The Mongols fell back northwards, perhaps missing an opportunity, as Meng Gong at this point seems to have been quite weak. A second Mongol advance, led by a fleet, was driven back after Meng Gong hit the vessels with incendiary arrows. The Meng Gong biography says he recovered 24 stockades and rounded up 20,000 displaced civilians.

In Shaanxi, in October, Anjur besieged Guo Xia inside Huizhou; Xia attempted to break out after running out of supplies, and was defeated outside the city gate. The Mongols broke into the city in the wake of this success, but had to engage in some furious house-to-house fighting before securing the city. Xia killed his family and took his own life rather than face capture, setting the house on fire. A maid brought his infant son to the Mongols, asking them to take care of him, then walked back into the fire to perish with the others. Anjur took pity on the child and ordered that he should be taken care of. That was the end of the last Jin loyalist.

In September the Mongols again drafted fairly aggressively in territory they controlled. Kötän again attacked the Song during the late summer. Cao Youwan at this point guarded the Xianren Pass, but the Mongols struck further east, sizing Xingyuan. Turning west they collided with Youwan at Jiguan'ai. The Song army was some 10,000 men strong (or large). The Song attacked at night with plenty of crossbows, and the Mongol advance guard was defeated. Youwan rashly pursued for more than 10 km; faced with the main Mongol body, his forces were quickly surrounded and overwhelmed and he fell fighting on 4 August. Anjur led a separate detachment further west where he seized Jiezhou and Wenzhou. He was with the help of local guides able to work his way over the mountains into Sichuan, like Deng Ae in 263. In October–November another Mongol army entered Sichuan through the usual route (Guangyuan), and the Mongols quickly seized and sacked Chengdu, a very large city as Beijing or Kaifeng had been. They failed, however, to take any other significant place, and did not attempt to hold Chengdu for long either, deciding to evacuate Sichuan. This was raid rather than conquest. Hanzhong, however, remained in Mongol hands. The Song nominally had 80,000 soldiers in Hanzhong and Sichuan, a substantial force even if the effective total was lower, and there were sizeable forces holding other places in Sichuan, such as Lu, Guo, and He, making a quick conquest impossible.

The Mongols again attacked in the central sector after the summer. Kököcü opted to push south-east instead to attempt to conquer territory south of the Han, and in August–September he took and sacked De'an. In November he fell ill and died, and Temetai took over command.

1237

The death of Kököcü caused the Mongols to halt major operations in the west and centre, only resuming attacks towards the end of 1237. Zhang Rou set out for Caowu (Kaoyu). He headed into the Jiuli Pass, aware that he was likely to encounter Song forces. A Song detachment emerged from a hidden position, but Rou drove them off. He took up position at Zhangfengling, just north of Caowu, and was able to secure 20 Song forts in the hilly country around Caowu. The Mongols finally took Caowu itself. From here Rou headed north, storming Hongshanzhai, a small place in the same general region.

Temetai led a Mongol army into Hanyang. On his left, Kwenpuhua entered Huaidian with a second Mongol army. The Song detachments guarding Chi and Sui panicked and fell back. In August Kwenpuhua started to besiege Shouchun (Anfeng) on the Huai, but Du Gao defended the fortress effectively and when in October Yu Jie and other Song officers led reinforcements forward the Mongols retreated. Kwenpuhua, turning westwards, besieged Guangzhou and Temetai, Zhang Rou, Keng Yen-hui, and Shi Tianze marched to support him. Caqan also served with this army. Kwenpuhua besieged Guangzhou for some time before finally taking the city in October–November. He could not, however, take Huanzhou. The biography of Meng Gong says of this:

Then [the Mongol Army], reinforced by the forces, grains and weapons from these three states, attacked Wang Jian, head of Huanzhou, and Wan Wensheng, commander of the navy. The fight was unfavourable.[1] Then Meng Gong came into the city.[2] Both the soldiers and civilians were so happy and said, 'Now our father has come.' [Meng Gong] set up his commanding camp at the city gate tower to manage the defence battle. Finally, the entire city was saved. He killed 49 captives before the public to warn the Mongols. The emperor sent him a letter of praise in his own handwriting, awarding the army per their battle achievements.

Tas attacked the Beixia Pass, overcoming Wang Dongjii, who surrendered. From October 1237 to spring 1238 he raided into Sichuan.

1238

Zhang Rou left the central army with 200 men and joined Caqan and the army in the east. Caqan attacked Tiancheng, Chuzhou, and Shouzhou.

Tagai, Anjur, and Wang Shixian again struck into Sichuan after the summer, passing Jinping and Da'an. Wang Shixian pushed ahead with some cavalry to make an attack on Song officer Yang Zhuman. The Song had prepared an ambush and struck from two sides, but Wang Shixian defeated both attacks. The Mongols entered Sichuan and in August–September took several places, defeated the Song outside Chengdu, and sacked Chengdu for a second time. A second Mongol detachment supported this offensive. Attacking from Xi'an, it took Jinzhou and from there entered Sichuan. It took Ta and Wan on the Yangtze River, then the Mongols pushed eastward from Wanzhou. Song forces camped on the south side of the Yangtze; Wang Shixian crossed the river further up and defeated them. He pursued them to Gui Canyon and Wushan where he again defeated them. The Mongols then took Guizhou.

After the summer, in September–October 1238, Caqan besieged Luzhou, planning to operate with a fleet on the Zhaoho. Du Gao rushed forward with forces, defeating the Mongols. Caqan then turned against Chuzhou. Yu Jie, leading crack forces forward, also gained a victory over the Mongols. Caqan again retreated: the water-dominated terrain was not the kind of fighting environment he was used to. Had Genghis Khan directed operations, he might have returned to the scene of his defeats and explained what he did wrong. Now there were was no such leader.

1239

In January–February the Mongols prepared to raid down the Han River; however Meng Gong learned about this in advance and made a spoiling attack. He feinted at different points and sent a force against Dengzhou to destroy Mongol depots and timber stock for building boats. His biography says his officer 'Liu Quan fought at Jiongtou, then Fancheng, then Langshenshan, (gaining) victory after victory … Cao Wenyong recovered Xinyang, (and) Liu Quan Fanchen. Afterwards was recovered …

---

1   Part of the Mongol forces marched to Zhangjia and Wujia where they started to assemble a fleet.
2   Meng Gong hurried to Huang from Ozhou.

Liu Quan sent Tan Shen to recover Guanghua. Xizhou and Caizhou surrendered.' Xiangyang fell into Song after deputy officer Lui Yi rebelled inside the fortress. The Mongols gave up the planned offensive.

As the Song struck northward in the centre, the Mongols moved forward in the west and then turned against the Song in the centre, pushing down along the Yangtze and entering Guizhou. In January a detachment took and sacked Shizhou; regrouping, Meng Gong placed 2,000 men at Xiazhou and another 1,000 in Guizhou. Jin De led his private army from Guanghua to join the Song. Meng Gong welcomed him and made use of his forces. He sent his brother Meng Ying to Songzi to provide back up to Guizhou with 5,000 'picked troops'. Furthermore, Yu Dexing was sent to take up station at Wanhugu, a pass located just west of Guizhou. He also sent Wu Sizhi with 1,000 men to take up position in Shizhou. Meng Gong was at this point distracted by a Mongol attack in the east, when a force struck from Suizhou into Lingjiang. Meng Gong ordered Liu Quan to deal with this threat from Xiangyang. The main threat, however, came from the west. The *Songshi* says the Mongols on this side had 800,000 men, which can at least be taken to mean they had a large force. The Song forces were not concentrated in one place, but all detachments occupied strong defensive positions. Meng Gong's biography says: 'Meng Gong built more camps and stockades, distributed the warships, and sent Zhang Rou to arrive at Runzhou via a bypath.' The last movement must have been an attempt to threaten the Mongol line of communications. Meng Gong also made sure he had plenty of grain to supply his men. In the end there was not much fighting:

> The Mongol army ferried across Wanzhou Lake. [People in] Shizhou and Guizhou were terrified. Meng Jing, elder brother of Gong, then administrator of Xiazhou … sent an urgent letter [to Gong], requesting to be ready for defence. Gong … ordered his forces westwards. Meng Jing sent Jin Duo with his force to resist [the Mongols] at Yayazhai in Guizhou. Liu Yi won the battle at Qingping Village, Mabadong County. Meng Zhang, Gong's younger brother, sent 2,000 picked troops to camp at Lizhou to watch out for enemies from Shizhou and Guizhou.

In February–March 1239 the Mongols retreated: they were probably running out of steam well before encountering Song resistance in Guizhou. Meng Gong knew the Mongols lacked logistical capabilities to sustain the offensive and therefore opted to fight a delaying war.

The Mongols made a sudden attack in the central sector during the summer of 1239, seizing Chongqing. The Song were surprised because the Mongols mounted a major attack during the traditional off season, but the Mongols did not attempt to hold the city.

240 and later

In early 1240 the Song rejected a Mongol peace offer.[3] The Mongols, again ordered forward by Ögödei, mounted raids to keep the Song occupied, but did not attempt to take any major cities. The intensity level of the conflict dropped.

Meng Gong improved the defences of Sichuan, after taking command there during the spring of 1240. He turned Chongqing into the central strongpoint, connecting it with Hezhou, Luzhou, and Jiading. He also constructed mountain fortresses in places such as Rongshancheng in Hejiang, Sanjiangqicheng in Jiang'an, Anleshancheng in Hejiang, Chi'niu cheng in Liangshan, and Diaoyucheng in Hezhou. Twenty garrisons were set up along the Yangtze River. Meng Gong tasked garrisons to farm, and increased local agricultural output. The improved defences were needed, as there were now only 50,000 soldiers in the sector compared to 80,000 some years before; again, these are paper totals.

In the east, Mongol forces raided across the Huai. Zhang Rou and others led seven *myriarchs* across the river.

The low-intensity fighting continued in 1241. Caqan attacked Shouchun; Liu Jie, leading a fleet forward, engaged the Mongols in combat over a 40 day period. Finally, in autumn, the Mongols retreated.

The improved Song defences in Sichuan did not deter the Mongols from attacking again. Led by Anjur and Wang Shixian, they took Chengdu after some protracted fighting, and a Song defector helping them gain entry into the city. Commanding officer Zhen Lungzhi was captured. His subordinate Wang Gui held Hanzhou. The Mongols told Zhen Lungzhi to induce Wang Gui to surrender, but instead the captured commander urged his subordinate to continue fighting and Wang Gui moved forward with 3,000 men. The Mongols crushed this force, surrounded Wang Gui and the survivors inside Hanzhou, and began to besiege the city. Wang Gui managed to escape at night, covering his departure with 'fire-oxen' sent towards the Mongol positions. Wang Gui adopted the stratagem of Tian Dan, but to cover a retreat rather than secure a great victory. The Mongols quickly took Hanzhou, massacring the population, and 20 other cities in the area. After the Mongols retreated, the Song recovered some ground in late 1241.

Kötän sent Dorta with a small army into Tibet, where he sacked rGyal Lha Khang and Rva-sgreng, two monasteries. Two others were not sacked. A fog covered Stag-lung and so kept it hidden from the Mongols and a miraculous stone shower saved Bri-gung. Evidently the narrative as given has a religious bias. Tibet was at this time a country with no strong central authority; a little later it submitted to the Mongols.

In 1242 the Mongols continued to give priority to the Sichuan theatre – somewhat oddly as it was hardly ideal cavalry country – and they took Suining. Yu Jie took over command from Meng Gong in Sichuan. He continued to set up new fortified points, adding another 20, and linked various strongpoints with waterways. Transferred from Sichuan to Jiangling, Meng Gong found the defences in a sorry state, repaired the

---

3   The Song were unwilling to pay tribute to the Mongols as they had done before to the Jin.

fortifications and extended the waterways to connect the many forts around the city in a network. In the east, in July, Zhang Rou made a raid: he crossed the Huai at Wugogou and raided into Yangzhou and Hozhou along the lower Yangtze River.

The Mongols started to fortify the border area in the Huai River sector in 1243. Zhang Rou set up his own headquarters in Ji, fortifying the place, and in January–February established a 3,000-man military colony in Xiangcheng. He also appears to have set up colonies in Ji and Bozhou. Anjur raided into Sichuan.

In 1244 the Mongols took some places in the western Huai River sector.

The Song had initially been on the defensive, but as the conflict continued their armed forces improved in quality, as did their logistics and defensive arrangements. They won some major defensive victories and launched some smaller offensives to recover lost ground. Meng Gong prepared well and was able to ward off one attack after another. The Song relied on Meng Gong and some other individuals rather than an institutional infrastructure.

The Mongols operated with skill, but without the step-by-step determined conquest approach of Genghis Khan, or an overall coordinated plan that characterised the operations of Sübe'etei. The raid up along the Yangtze in 1238–1239 was a spectacular effort. Surely with better high command this could have been a war winning effort? Wang Shixian was an enterprising commander: his offensive strategy seems more impressive that anything shown by other non-Mongol commanders.

Sources: *Jinshi* 124, pp.2710–2711; *Yuanshi* 2, 119, 2937–3940, 120, pp.2955–2957, 147, pp.3471–3475, 155, p.3649, 155, pp.3657–3663; *Songshi* 449, pp.13230–13233; Luciano Petech, 'Tibetan relations with Sung China and with the Mongols', in Rossabi (ed.), *China Among Equals*, p.181; Hsiao, 'Shih T'ien-tse', 'Chang Jou', in de Rachewiltz, *In the Service of the Khan*, pp.30–31, 53–54; Herbert Franke, *Sung biographies* (Wiesbaden: Steiner, 1976), pp.781–786; K'uan-chung Huang: 'Mountain fortress defense', translated by David Wright, *Warfare in Chinese history*, pp.222–251; Sawyer, *Fire and Water*, p.119; Davis, 'The Reign of Li-tsung (1224–1264)', pp.863–868; Atwood, 'The first Mongol contacts with the Tibetans', pp.31–38.

53

Again Against the Song

Thereafter he assigned and dispatched armies in every direction, sending Subedei Ba'atur and Caqan Noyan with a large army into Khitai.

– Rashid al-Din, 570

Güyük sent Sübe'etei to China, perhaps during the 1245–46 campaigning season.[1] Sübe'etei operated with Caqan. It is recorded in the *Yuanshi* that Caqan and Zhang Rou with 30,000 horsemen pushed across the Huai and made a raid towards the lower Yangtze. They took Shouzhou (Shouchun) and threatened Sizhou, Xuyi (located east of Shouzhou), and Yangzhou. Zhao Kui, the Song regional commander in chief, asked for a truce in autumn 1245. Zhang Rou went to Mongolia to see Güyük early the next year (January–February 1246) so the operations must have ended quite early (October or November 1245).

The next campaign season saw Shi Quan, the son of Shi Tianni, operate in Huainan where he took Hutouguan. In late winter 1246 the Mongols then marched on Huanzhou. In spring the next year Zhang Rou attacked Sizhou; Tacar and Tehchi led another raid into Sichuan. The Song defences proved to be more effective than before.

Meng Gong retired in 1246. He said: 'For 30 years I have laboured to capture the hearts of the people of the Central Plain, but I can no longer muster the will power to continue.' He was during the final years of his life increasingly disillusioned because of the poor Song grand strategic management. It is said he advocated setting up extensive defensive lines in the upper Yangtze region to strengthen the Song left flank, but this was only partially done. He died in 1248, the same year Sübe'etei passed away. Meng Gong was evidently a great military organiser, though as a commander in action he never won a really significant victory. He never faced Sübe'etei, but was more than capable of defeating the Mongols' thrusts towards the Yangtze no matter

---

1   Rashid al-Din dates the campaign to 1246–1247. The *Yuanshi* says Caqan campaigned in China during 1245–1246. The Mongol–Chinese sources seem to make more errors than usual in connecting events around the time when new rulers took over. Buell places the campaign after the coronation. If Sübe'etei and Caqan were in China in 1246–1247 then the campaign must have been uneventful.

who commanded the force. Meng Gong must rank amongst the best Han Chinese commanders of the 13th century. His enthusiasm for agriculture recalls Cao Cao, Zhuge Liang, and the other leading commanders of the Three Kingdom era.

On 24 August 1246, after a long delay of more than five years after Ögödei died, Güyük was set up as *Great Khan*. By then Sübe'etei was back in Mongolia. Giovanni da Pian del Carpini was at the Mongol Court during the coronation, and listed Sübe'etei amongst the people he saw. Carpini wrote that he was: 'an old man who is known among them as "the knight." ' Sübe'etei had returned to the land of his childhood, living along the Tuul River; he died in 1248. Güyük passed away in April the same year. He was then near Samarkand with a large army, intent on confronting Batu. Possibly they would have worked out their differences without any fighting. Batu remained de facto independent, and backed by Batu, Möngke was chosen to succeed Güyük. The lineage of Tolui replaced that of Ögödei on the throne. The family of Sübe'etei were closely associated with the family of Tolui and descendants held senior posts in the Yuan establishment.

The Mongols put a complex plan in operation against the Song in 1258. It is possible, perhaps even likely, that it was Sübe'etei who had developed the plan a decade earlier. The Mongols outflanked the Song and then attacked them at different points with four separate armies. The plan certainly had the audacity, sweeping scale, and complexity that were typical of Sübe'etei. Kököcü and Uriangqadai, his sons, played key roles in the offensive. Kököcü was with Möngke and the main Mongol army in Sichuan[2] and Uriyangqadai led the Mongol outflanking force, setting out in 1253 from the area where Sübe'etei had operated in 1227–28. He attacked the weak spot identified by Meng Gong. Events proved, however, that the plan itself had certain weak points and the Mongol attack was not really successful. The Mongols did secure Yunnan and so created a base in the south-west, but the main attack in Sichuan bogged down. The outflanking force failed to seriously distract the Song, though it could have proved more useful had the offensive into Sichuan not ended in failure. Sichuan was a restricted theatre of war, strongly fortified by the Song, and it was hardly an appropriate *schwerpunkt* for the Mongol main army. In the centre the Mongols made their way over the Yangtze, something they had rarely done before. Uriangqadai, having been as far away as North Vietnam, arrived from the south having moved through the entire Song territory, overcoming one Song army after the other. This expedition was even more remarkable than the raid of Samuqa and mark Uriangqadai as a truly outstanding commander.

The Mongols were subsequently distracted by civil war. Only years later, in 1267, was the war against the Song resumed in earnest. Song resisted fiercely, but was finally conquered. The Mongol strategy was then more straightforward. They conquered the fortresses guarding the Han River, notably stubbornly defended Xiangyang, and pushed up the Yangtze. The Mongol army was by then different in nature than before, with large Chinese contingents and a powerful fleet. The Song was conquered by

2   Rashid al-Din, 602: 'On the right was Mongka Qan and Subatai's son Kokchu with 10 tümens.'

means of traditional Chinese strategy rather than the trademark ploys and old style army of Genghis Khan or Sübe'etei. The key tactical commander of the Mongol army was then Aju, Sübe'etei's grandson. The Mongol army had evolved, but the Sübe'etei family still played a key part. Sübe'etei, Uriangqadai, and Aju easily rank amongst most outstanding military commanders of the 13th century. No other family known to history can make such a claim.

The Mongols' 1259 offensive ended as a failure, but if Sübe'etei had been in command he might have found a way to prevail. He never allowed his forces to get bogged down by a secondary objective and was unwilling to engage in protracted siege operations against major targets. In Sübe'etei's hand, the Mongol forces in Sichuan could very quickly have struck across the Yangtze and moved eastward along that river. Even as it was, the Mongols might have been more successful had Möngke not died suddenly.

Sources: *Yuanshi* 2, p.136; Rashid al-Din, 570; *Songshi* 412, pp.12369–12380; Carpini, p.65; Buell, 'Sübötei', in de Rachewiltz, *In the Service of the Khan*, p.25.

54

Conclusions

'Did strategy … exist before 1800? The question will probably come as a surprise to some military historians, bent as they are on quarrying their examples from every campaign from Marathon onward … I argue, however, that strategy in the sense that Napoleon, Jomini, and Clausewitz made classic hardly existed before their time, and this was due above all to the fact that strategic command was all but impossible to exercise.

– Martin van Creveld[1]

Unless history can teach us how to look at the future, the history of war is but a bloody romance.

– J. F. C. Fuller[2]

In the course of 40-odd campaigns, Genghis Khan and Sübe'etei had conquered much of the known world. Initially only leading a small family band, Genghis Khan created a huge empire which continued to expand long after his passing. At its peak it dwarfed in size any previous empire, be it that of the Persians, Macedonians, Han, Romans, Tang, Umayyids, or Abbasids. It was comparable in size to the later British Empire. Remarkably, Genghis Khan proved equally adept as a minor lord, a major tribal leader, and a first class warlord. Temür *Lenks* matched him in this regard, but there are not many leaders in history that have been able to handle so well so many different types of challenges.

When Genghis Khan was a young man, Inanca Bilge, To'oril, and perhaps Zuxu were the most notable Inner Asian tribal leaders. Jamuqa and Toqto'a were other influential leaders closer to the Mongol pasture grounds. Genghis Khan killed the two sons of Inanca Bilge, Buyiruq and Bai Buqa, as well as his grandson Küclüg; To'oril was killed fleeing from a crushing defeat and his son Senggüm died in exile; and Zuxu supporter Mägüdjin-säültü and his sons Alaq Udur and Caqun were defeated and

---

1   Martin van Creveld, *Command in War* (Cambridge, Mass.: Harvard University Press, 1987), p.18.
2   J. F. C. Fuller, *British Light Infantry in the Eighteenth Century* (London: Hutchinson & Co., 1925), p.224.

probably all killed as well. Jamuqa was captured and executed, and Toqto'a was killed in battle. All rivals in Mongolia were crushed and wiped out. The sedentary leaders fared no better. Xia, West Liao, and Khwarezm were all crushed, its rulers killed or hunted to death. Jin was driven south of the Huang River, losing its ancestral home and North China. Ruling emperor *Aizong* was destined to be the last real ruler. The Song was south of the Yangtze River, further from the Mongols, though they had already clashed with Mongol armies during the lifetime of Genghis Khan. Korea had seen Mongol armies strike across the Yalu River and the Mongol impact had also been felt in Europe where the finest warriors of the Rus had been wiped out in battle. The triumph of Genghis Khan was complete and the reach of his armies was ominous for states located far, far away from his birthplace.

Apart from Muhammad II, all of the foes Genghis Khan had been at most 1,500 km from his earliest grazing grounds and most were much closer. Almost all of the foes of Sübe'etei were at least 1,500 km from old Mongol territory and most were much further away. Sübe'etei dealt with Qudu and finally *Aizong*, but spent most of his campaigns against leaders the early Mongols had never heard about. He crushed the Kipchaks Inazu, Yuri, Daniel, Kötän, and Bachman, the Kangli Khotosy, the Georgian Georgi III, the Rus Mstislav Mstislavich, Romanovich, Yuri, Oleg, Yaroslav, Roman, Yuri II Vsevolodovich, Mstislav Glebovich, and Daniel, the Bulgars Jiqu and Bazan, and the Hungarian Bela IV. In addition he defeated a large number of Song officers.

Genghis Khan ended up with a vast empire, but it seems clear he had no grand plan of conquest. Much of his early effort was directed against the hated Tatars and the divided Tayici'uts. When To'oril turned against him, he crushed him. The Naimans, used to be more powerful than the Kereyits, could not tolerate the dominant position Genghis Khan had secured. Genghis Khan crushed them as well. He had grown up in the shadow of the Jin and was determined to prove that he, with a united Mongolia behind him, was now the strongest. His desire, however, was to prove his power, not to conquer China. In his place, Alexander III would have pushed deep into China and could have ended up deep inside India. The great expedition against Khwarezm was brought about by the insult of Muhammad II. Muhammad was the only foe Genghis Khan fought against whom he would not have known about when growing up. In contrast to his master, Sübe'etei did have an agenda of conquest, having an urge to move into distant regions: he was an explorer with an army.

Genghis Khan had a winning personality and attracted able men into his service, much like Seleucus (of the *Diadochi*), Lio Bang (founder of the Han), or Ieyasu (master of Japan). Like them, Genghis Khan established an enduring dynasty. The first Inner Asian warlord to do so was Modo. Like Genghis Khan, he defeated rival tribes and set up a house that ruler over Inner Asia for centuries. However, Modo's realm did not extend far beyond the Altai and he did not win great victories over the Han Chinese. He was finally killed in an ambush by rivals, evidently not having as good control over the tribes as Genghis Khan had. Genghis Khan's power left a big imprint on the region. Centuries later, even the powerful Temür *Lenks* had a figurehead descendent of Genghis Khan as nominal ruler.

Geographic reach

Genghis Khan made step-by-step conquests, taking on the next foe in sight. He was a methodical conqueror. He was also methodical on the operational level. Against Khwarezm he first targeted the cities along the Syr Darya and took Samarkand; reaching the Syr Amu, he segmented his forces. One force was sent to pursue Muhammad II, another to take the enemy capital, and a third to secure Khorasan. Once the two latter tasks were achieved, he sent forces into the plains north-east of the Aral Lake and struck into Afghanistan with his main forces.

Sübe'etei moved with incredible mobility. He struck the Merkits along the Chu River in 1217; two years later he was close to the Ural River. Sent into pursuit of Muhammad II in 1220, he reached Azerbaijan before the year was out. In 1223 he operated along the Dnieper and Volga. Against Xia he opened a new front by attacking from the west and he opened up the Jin defences in Henen by striking through Hanzhong. Returning to Europe, he struck across the Volga in 1237 and reached the Danube by 1241. Compared to Genghis Khan, Sübe'etei moved much quicker into the middle of enemy territory. Having crushed their main forces, he spread out his own forces and reduced areas still holding out. He could then be patient, playing an attrition game.

In 335 BC Alexander dispersed Illyrian tribesmen in what is now Albania, and by 326 BC struck across the Sindhu River, 6,000 km away. Temür *Lenks* later had a slightly smaller span, operating between Smyrna (Izmir) in Turkey and New Delhi in India. Napoleon was in Madrid in 1808 and in Moscow four years later, having covered more than 4,000 km. Genghis Khan was almost 5,000 km from home when he reached the Sindhu River, going somewhat further than earlier nomad warlords had managed. Sübe'etei besieged Kaifeng in 1232 and approached Vienna in 1242, having covered more than 8,000 km. His territorial reach dwarfs that of any other pre-industrial warlord on land.

Campaign odds

The number of fighting men fielded by the Mongols increased from fewer than 10,000 to 200,000 men by the end of the period covered. Perhaps leader of 15,000 men by 1192, Temüjin had more than 100,000 by 1205 and more than 170,000 by the time he died. Based on the assumed increase of numbers over the years, an estimate can be made on the forces he and his allies fielded. The numbers of those he opposed are even harder to quantify. In the table below an attempt is made.

	1194	1196	1196-7	1198	1199	1200	1201	1202	
Mongols	30,000	40,000?	40,000?	20,000?	20,000?	70,000?	40,000?	50,000?	
Foe	30,000	smaller	smaller	smaller	even	even	larger	smaller	
	1203	1204	1206	1207	1208				
Mongols	20-40,000	65,000	50,000?	60,000?	70,000?				
Foe	40-20,000	even	smaller	smaller	smaller				
	1209	1211	1212	1213	1220	1221	1222	1226	1227
Mongols	60,000?	70,000?	80,000?	80,000?	60,000?	50,000?	50,000?	70,000?	70,000?
Foe	even	even	even	even	even	smaller	smaller	even	smaller

Genghis Khan was probably only seriously outnumbered in 1201, 1202, and early 1203. In China his foes may have fielded large forces, but most were infantry of little value in open country. In the context of odds faced, his most successful conduct was perhaps in 1201 and 1202.

Sübe'etei commanded small forces during his first campaigns, but later had very large forces at his disposal:

	1217	1219	1220	1221	1222	1223	1224	
Mongols	6,000	14,000	10,000	15,000?	15,000?	18,000?	12,500?	
Foe	smaller	larger	smaller	even	larger	larger	even	
	1226	1227	1228	1229-30	1230-31	1231-32	1233-34	1234
Mongols	70,000?	70,000?	70,000?	30,000?	120,000	120,000	30,000	30,000
Foe	even	even	smaller	smaller	even	larger	smaller	larger
	1236-37	1237-38	1239	1240-41	1242	1246-47		
Mongols	40,000?	40,000?	40,000?	30,000?	30,000	30,000?		
Foe	smaller	even	smaller	larger	smaller	even		

Sübe'etei was probably outnumbered in 1219, 1222, 1223, 1231–32, 1234 and 1241. His raid around the Caspian Sea, campaigns in Central China, and expedition into Europe all rank amongst the most impressive achievements found in the annals of war.

Though the campaign odds on average were fairly good for the Mongols, they moved against foes in sequence and overcame very large forces with small ones. After they had united Mongolia and without including the Song, the 100,000 Mongol horsemen must have overcome forces outnumbering their own by more than five times.

Manoeuvre

Napoleon complained that Swedish king Gustav II Adolf did not manoeuvre:

There is your great Gustavus! In 18 months, he wins one battle, loses another, and is killed in a third. A cheaply earned reputation if there ever was one! ... Tilly and Wallenstein were better generals than Gustavus Adolphus. There is not a single scientific manoeuvre this prince is known to have made. He evacuated Bavaria because Tilly[3] outmanoeuvred him, and he allowed Magdeburg to be taken right under his eyes. A fine reputation![4]

Napoleon did not really understand how Gustav II Adolf manoeuvred, how he operated. He too, like Napoleon, had some favoured ploys. Napoleon liked when outnumbered to operate from a central position and to outflank and block (or master) the enemy line of communications when he was stronger. Gustav Adolf used attrition strategy when he was weak and quick surprise advance when he wanted to attack. What were the favoured manoeuvres of Genghis Khan and Sübe'etei?

Genghis Khan was usually ready to accept battle, though he sometimes tried to gain early advantage by means of a quick surprise advance. If unable to gain victory in battle, he could wage evasive war or attempt to crush enemy forces in detail. Sübe'etei lacked Genghis Khan's enthusiasm for set-piece battle, preferring first to manoeuvre the enemy into a position of weakness. His favoured strategic battle plan was more complex than anything attempted by Genghis Khan. He operated with several armies. While diversionary attacks pinned down enemy forces in secondary sectors, the main attack could come from the rear or from the front. Facing a strong enemy army, he could wage delaying war, feigned retreat, or deception to trick the enemy into some unwise decision.

The willingness of Genghis Khan to force a decision through large-scale battles was an innovation in Mongolia as well as in China. How he came to adopt this approach is not explained, but he seems to have had this focus from early on. Evidently he was confident of his ability to better organise and manage an army and to operate more effectively than his rival as a battlefield commander. His ruthless pursuit of advantage gained was also an innovation. His ability to deal with enemy groups in detail in 1201–1202 and to hold off a large enemy army by means of attrition in 1202 showed he also had real skills in strategic manoeuvring.

Sübe'etei's approach to battle was more in line with traditional nomad thinking. He attacked only when and where the situation was favourable. His innovation was in the field of strategic movement and control. Dividing his forces, he feinted at many points before concentrating his forces against an isolated target. To make the timing work, he would fight evasive warfare or used a feigned retreat. Against a stronger foe he sought to divide and defeat in detail. His outflanking attacks in 1222, 1226, and 1232 are amongst the most remarkable such initiatives known to history.

Genghis Khan was confident in his army and his ability to command it on the battlefield. Sübe'etei was confident in his superior understanding of geography and the strategic military situation. He managed and controlled a large theatre of war in a

3   In fact Wallenstein.
4   Conversation 1817.

way no commander managed to do until modern times. No commander matched him in this regard until Napoleon.

Genghis Khan
Surprise advance, quick advance/unexpected path Jeje'er Heights (1203), Ulugh Taq (1206), Buqdurma (1208), Wulahai (1209)
Mass for battle, gain decisive battlefield victory Onon River (1200); Naqu (1204), Yelü Ling (1211), Weichuan (1213), Beijing (1214), Lingzhou (1226)
Pursuit, exploit advantage gained Ulengüt Turas (1200), Jin interior (1214), Persian Iraq (1220), Sindhu (1221–1222)
Resort to stratagem, when unable to defeat enemy or enemy refuse battle Qailar (1201), Köyiten (1202), Keyimen (1209), Wuhu Mountains (1213)

Sübe'etei
Divide and defeat enemy in detail, by means of central position, feigned retreat, bait, or divide and conquer diplomacy Irghiz River (1219), Georgia (1221), Terek River (1222), Don River (1223), Kalka River (1223)
Converging attack, exploit superior numbers by attacking from several sides Rayy (1220), Don River (1222), Liangzhou (1226), Sanfeng (1232), Bulgar (1236), Yaroslav (1238), Mohi (1241)
Attrition, delay and wear down enemy Sanfeng road (1232), Henan (1232–1233), Luoyang (1234)

Battles

A detailed list of the battles of the period covered is given in Appendix 2.

In 30 known battles Genghis Khan was defeated three or four times. Jamuqa fought against him perhaps three times, winning twice. He was probably the most able foe Temüjin ever faced even if he failed to translate his operational brilliance into tangible strategic results. He can be credited with making ambitious outflanking attacks in 1191, 1194, 1199, and 1203. It seems fair to assume he did it on other occasions not captured in the sources. The spotlight is on Genghis Khan, not Jamuqa. For example, what Jamuqa did between 1194 and 1199 is not known. Genghis Khan may also have been defeated in 1200 and was defeated in 1209, though that reverse was not serious.

Little is known about the grand tactics of Genghis Khan. At Naqu, Weichuan, and Sindi he outflanked and made use of reserves. It seems likely he had a battle scheme a little like the 'strategic battle' of Napoleon; outflanking forces brought pressure to bear on the enemy flanks and finally reserves were committed at a key point to secure victory. In general, Genghis Khan was quite ready to engage enemy forces in close quarter fighting. He was confident in the fighting capabilities of his men.

In about 35 battles, Sübe'etei lost twice. In both cases he returned to finally crush those who defeated him, though in the case of the first defeat against the Bulgars he only got revenge 13 years later. Jin commanders Wanyan Heda, Yila Pua, and Wanyan Hochen Heshang offered probably the best opposition Sübe'etei ever faced. Taken as a team, they could claim to have won victories or gained advantage in 1228, 1229, and 1230–1231. Muqali defeated Heda in 1221, but gained limited advantage out of the victory. Sübe'etei confronted Heda and his colleagues in 1230–1231 and 1231–1232. Though he suffered a defeat during the first campaign, the strategic results were on balance positive. During the second campaign he won a crushing victory. Song officer Meng Gong and some of his colleagues were probably even better commanders than the Jin trio, but they never collided with Sübe'etei directly. Meng Gong was close to Sübe'etei, even joining Mongol forces during the siege of Cai, but it seems the two never met.

Sübe'etei had a better win ratio than Genghis Khan, in part because he only fought battles after having manoeuvred the enemy into a position of weakness. He did engage in desperate battles when surprised by the enemy as happened along the Irghiz River in 1219, perhaps in 1222 after passing Derbent Pass, and both times he was defeated (though in both of these he may have retreated quickly). Of his battles, 5–10 percent were desperate affairs. Genghis Khan engaged in furious battles at Dalan Baljut, Ulengüt Turas, Buyira, Qalaqaljit Sands, and Naqu. None of the later battles in China seems to have been difficult for him. At least 15–20 percent of the battles were hard-fought.

The doctrine of war

Many commentators and historians use their understanding of the Mongol campaigns to draw general conclusions about the Mongols and their army. According to Harold Lamb '[the army] of Genghis Khan followed a fixed plan in invading a hostile country.' Timothy May agrees with this: 'The Mongols had a set method of invasion, which varied only slightly from campaign to campaign. First the Mongol army would invade in several columns. Often it was three-pronged attack, consisting of an army of the center and then two flanking forces. Flanking forces in some cases went into neighboring territories before rendezvousing with the army of the center.' To illustrate or prove this system of conquest, the Khwarezm (1219–1223) or European campaigns (1236–1242) are often used as examples. However, when Sübe'etei led an army into Europe, other Mongol armies battled against the Song. It is in these campaigns hard to see any higher strategy and the Mongols suffered plenty of reverses. If there was a system of conquest, why was it applied in Europe and not against the Song? Nor do the Mongol operations in Korea fit with a standard system of conquest, and when the Mongols finally conquered all of China during the 1270s they used traditional Chinese strategy, essentially using the same methods as the Jin (3rd century), Sui (6th century) or Tang (7th century) used centuries before. Zeng Guofang used the same general strategy against the Taiping rebels in 1861. He said: 'since ancient times the strategy for pacifying the lower Yangtze has been to establish a strong position in the upper region and then press down-stream.'

Genghis Khan had his own style and Sübe'etei his. Muqali also operated in his own way, though cast in the mould of Genghis Khan. There was, however, no articulated Mongol doctrine of war to define high strategic methods. This is hardly surprising. For example, the generals of Napoleon did not use his style when he was not present in person. Even when he offered a plan to Moreau in 1800, Moreau failed to make use of it. On the somewhat lower level, it may be that Mongols liked to reduce smaller places before turning on the bigger ones. Genghis Khan, Sübe'etei, Muqali, and other officers did this at different times in different theatres of war. This, however, cannot be seen, as 'system' of conquest and it was also the practice of the Khitans before the Mongols. The detailed military methods of the Mongols were almost completely the same as the Liao/Khitans. They were probably the first Inner Asian tribe to adopt these methods, though West Liao must have used them as well. The Khitans used these methods for a long time and with Inner Asian forces serving in their army and Liao armies often operating in Mongolia it is not surprising to see a diffusion of ideas.

Mongol siege capabilities

The Mongols were quick to recruit Khitan and Han Chinese siege engineers and to build siege equipment. They adopted the Liao methods for dealing with fortresses, but found it hard to take first-rate fortresses. Neither Genghis Khan nor Sübe'etei are noted for their abilities to take fortified cities. Alexander III, Caesar and Temür were in their eras far more effective. Genghis Khan failed to take Zhongxing in 1209–1210 and Datong in 1212. Beijing was only taken after a long blockade, and Genghis Khan did not lead the operation in person. Samarkand and Bokhara fell quickly, but hardly offered effective resistance. When the Mongols invaded Xia in 1226 they proved better at reducing cities, though Zhongxing held out for some time. Sübe'etei was no more successful than Genghis Khan, though he was perhaps more interested in the details of siege operations. He took many cities in Persia, Russia, and Central Europe. In China, he took small cities; bigger ones were a different matter, and the attempts to take Luoyang, Kaifeng, and Guide all ended in failure in 1232. Eventually he secured all these cities, but it was by means of attrition rather than active siege operations. The smaller Caizhou was taken, but here the allied Song played a major role. The Mongol brilliance at siege warfare is a myth.

Mongol terror strategy

The Mongols are famous for using terror to overawe their enemies and this view dominates most treatments of Mongol history. Almost all commentators and historians see the terror strategy as a key component of the Mongol conquests. Hugh Kennedy estimated: 'without the use of terror, it is unlikely that even Subetai's military genius would have been able to make the conquests he did.'[5] John Keegan wrote: 'the Mongols preferred terror, counting on the word of their approach to dissolve resistance.'[6] David Morgan says 'Chingiz's principle seems to have been much the same as President Truman over Hiroshima and Nagasaki. The apparent rationale was that if the population of one city was subjected to a frightful massacre, the next city would

5   Hugh Kennedy, *Mongols, Huns, and Vikings: Nomads at War* (London: Cassell, 2002), p.144.
6   John Keegan, *Intelligence in War: knowledge of the enemy from Napoleon to al-Quaeda* (London: Hutchinson, 2003), p.9.

be more likely to surrender without resistance, thus avoiding unnecessary Mongol casualties. The morality of this approach to warfare is no doubt open to discussion, but there can be disputing that it worked.'[7] If what they say is true, then the Mongols should quickly destroy a few towns that had resisted, discouraging other cities from trying to oppose them. It is not how the Mongols operated.

Consider the operations of Genghis Khan against Khwarezm. Juvaini goes into detail how the cities taken were treated in 1220, 1221 and 1222:

Fanakat	Soldiers killed, young men drafted into levy
Khojend	Citadel defended, town occupied
Tashkent	Captured, *shahna* left
Jand	Lives spared
Otrar	People driven out, city looted
Bokhara	Part of city destroyed by fire, men drafted into levy
Samarkand	Some men into levy, craftsmen taken; rest back to city
Urganj	Slavery, execution
Bamian	All killed
Talaqan	Destroyed
Balkh	Destroyed
Termez	Destroyed

The only cities destroyed where the enemy capital, cities that revolted, and the city where a relative of Genghis Khan was killed during the siege. There was no initial deliberate city sacking to scare other cities into submitting quickly. Otrar, Khojend, Bokhara and Samarkand were not destroyed. Balkh, Merv, Heart, Nishapur, and Ghazni were destroyed only later on. In China, Beijing was sacked in 1215, but not completely destroyed. No major Jin city was destroyed. Kaifeng was after offering some protracted resistance only lightly plundered in 1233. The Xia capital was destroyed in 1227. Like Urganj, it earned the special wrath of Genghis Khan because its lord had wronged him.

The Chinese registered population shrank from Jin and Song times to Yuan (Mongol) times. Song China is credited with a population of 119 million around 1120 and Yuan China is estimated to have 70 million people around 1290. Many people no doubt died directly or indirectly because of the long wars, but the fall in the registered population cannot be accepted as a measure of the drop of the actual population size. A similar drop occurred from Sui to Tang times and reflected the need to re-establish central authority and again collect taxes from the whole population. China suffered during the decades of war after the Mongols first attacked in 1211, much like Germany was devastated during the Thirty Years' War from 1618 to 1648. Then the German population dropped by more than two thirds in the worst affected regions (like Pfalz and Mecklenburg) and between one third and two thirds in all the other favoured theatres of war.[8] The armies of the Mongol period were probably as

---

7   David Morgan, *The Mongols* (Oxford: Blackwell, 1986), p.93.
8   Georg Westermann, *Grosser Atlas zur Weltgeschichte* (Braunschweig: G. Westermann, 1976), p.107, map II.

brutal as the armies of that later war in Europe, but did not have an articulated terror strategy or agenda of genocide. The Mongol general Bayan did make use of terror in 1275 to break the Song will to resist.[9] This, however, was a single incident that had no link back to a previous Mongol practice. If anything, the strategy of Bayan fits better into the Chinese tradition of war than the practice of Genghis Khan and Sübe'etei. A deliberate act of terror was very much an articulated ploy in the tradition of Sun Tzu and the other Chinese military commentators.

Even without an articulated terror strategy, the Mongols did operate with great brutality. Civilian captives rounded up for siege and other work seem to have routinely butchered when no longer needed. Populations judged to be faithless by Genghis Khan were butchered without sentiment, as were entire tribes in Mongolia.

Why were the Mongols successful?

Genghis Khan gained a measure of control over Inner Asia like no other leader before or after him. This was a political and administrative achievement as much as a military achievement. The political power of Genghis Khan as well as his organisational skills allowed him to effectively field and control very large forces. It is instructive to compare Genghis Khan with Aboaji, the founder of the Khitan state. He created a military machine similar to that of Genghis Khan, but he was much less successful as a battlefield commander and as a conqueror. Why is that? As master of Liaodong, Aboaji had only 20,000 to 30,000 horsemen, three or four times fewer than the Mongols. In addition Aboaji had trouble at home, repeatedly having to deal with revolts by family members. With smaller forces and less securely in control at home, Aboaji was able to achieve much less as a conqueror than Genghis Khan. In addition, Genghis Khan was probably a more effective ruler in general and a better military leader.

Genghis Khan was skilled at winning over allies and was an active diplomat. He was in Mongolia often warned by friends in the enemy camp about impeding attacks; he supported a revolt by the Khitans against the Jin; and sent envoys to Khwarezm to pacify Muhammad II before he sent an army to invade West Liang. By contrast, the foes of the Mongols failed to remain united. Already faced with a far stronger army, the enemies on many occasions made it easier for the Mongols by not being politically united. Examples include Jin and Song – who fought each other rather than unite against the Mongols – the divided Rus princes, or the feuding leaders of Hungary. The Jin probably had a real chance to defeat the Mongols early on if they had reacted quickly and with energy. However, in 1211 they did not commit large forces; in 1212 when they did field a large army they should have remained in the defensive and waged a delaying war; and in 1213 internal strife distracted them. They lost North China, but established themselves strongly further south. From 1215 to 1231 they held off the Mongols and could perhaps have continued to do so for some time. Even in 1232 they could perhaps have prevailed had they avoided mistakes. Sending the main army to the south and having no proper guard on the Huang River were key mistakes.

9   David Curtis Wright, 'Mongol general Bayan and the massacre of Changzhou in 1275', *Calgary Papers Military and Strategic Studies*, vol. 12, pp.105–116.

The Song initiated all-out war against the Mongols in 1234. They were poorly prepared and led and easily lost. Step by step the border became better fortified and the armies improved with training and combat experience. From 1237 onwards the Mongols made no progress. Major offensives during the 1250s produced some spectacular victories, but no decisive breakthrough. It was only during the 1270s that the Mongols finally destroyed the Song. By then the Mongol army had plenty of effective Han units and a strong fleet. This was a 'Chinese' victory rather than a 'Mongol' one.

The Song held off the Mongols in Sichuan by means of many fortified points backed by a fleet on the rivers and waterways. Surely Hungary could have been defended in the same manner? Perhaps even Transoxiana and Henan could have been held in this way as well. It required, however, investments in field engineering, adequate logistical arrangements, and other steps only an organised state could put in place. Bela IV, Muhammad II, and even *Aizong* were weak rulers unable to unite the people and drive through the needed actions. If they had been better organised there was probably a number of different ways to hold off the Mongols. Jin, Xia, Song, West Liao, Khwarezm, the Rus, Poland, and Hungary were all politically weak or divided. Later in Egypt, Baibars seized power and took measures to field a strong army and prepare the defences and in India, in Delhi, Balban did the same. These states were admittedly at the edge of the Mongol Empire and were never confronted by very large Mongol forces, but they were well managed and fairly easily held off the attacks the Mongols did make. The Mamluks had a very strong heavy cavalry force that was probably stronger man for man than anything the Mongols could field. This was another way to defend against the Mongols that worked. The Mongols suffered tactical defeats against other enemies as well: Jalal al-Din prevailed in open country by means of a defensive–offensive stance in 1221, the Bulgars surprised the Mongols in 1224, and the Jin used high technology weapons to wipe out a Mongol detachment in 1233. The Jin won a sequence of defensive successes before 1232 and later the Song won even greater victories while holding off Mongol attacks. Apart from the Song, none of the victors managed to create a strategic context that would allow them to hold off the Mongols. That was only achieved by Mamluk Egypt, the Delhi Sultanate, and for a while the Song.

Sun Tzu explained how to predict victory in the beginning of *The Art of War*:

Which of the two sovereigns is imbued with the Moral law (The moral law causes the people to be in complete accord with their ruler, so that they will follow him regardless of their lives, undismayed by any danger)? Which of the two generals has most ability? With whom lie the advantages derived from Heaven (signifies night and day, cold and heat, times and seasons) and Earth (comprises distances, great and small; danger and security; open ground and narrow passes; the chances of life and death)? On which side is discipline most rigorously enforced? Which army is stronger? On which side are officers and men more highly trained? In which army is there the greater constancy both in reward and punishment? By means of these seven considerations I can forecast victory or defeat.

None of the leaders opposing Genghis Khan matched him as a ruler; he enforced discipline strictly, his men were highly trained, and his rewards and punishments were consistent. And in time he fielded large forces. This, more than the specific military doctrine of the Mongols, was the foundation of their victories.

In addition, Genghis Khan and Sübe'etei – supported by their teams – were certainly outstanding military leaders. As seen in the beginning of this book, Napoleon admired Alexander III, Hannibal, Caesar, Turenne, and Frederick II of Prussia for the military impact they had. Certainly he could have added both Genghis Khan and Sübe'etei to his list of Great Captains. With two outstanding leaders, the Mongols had a double impact: 'It was not the Mongol horsemen that reached the Yangtze, Sindhu, and Danube; it was Genghis Khan and Sübe'etei.'

Appendix I

The Breakdown of the Mongol army

The *Secret History* provides details on the Mongol officers and the forces they commanded c.1206 (202–208, 242–243). Rashid al-Din gives a similar breakdown for the army c.1227 (399–417). In 1206 the total was said to add up to 105,000 men. However, the total included the 5,000 Önggüts who only submitted in 1207 or a little later. The Oyirats are not included; they submitted in 1208 and were credited with having 4,000 men. The Juyins submitted in 1207, bringing 3,000. That would bring the early total by 1211 up to 112,000 men. By 1227 the army total had increased to 129,000. The total given by Rashid al-Din for 1227 included 10,000 Khitans and 10,000 Jurchens. Excluding these, there were 109,000 men. The total therefore hardly changed. The 'Mongol' total shows a decline of some 3,000 men. Units stationed in the Near East could be missing in the count of Rashid al-Din.

In 1204 Genghis Khan had 65 minghan commanders outside the guard, a total increased to 90 without the Öngüts by 1206. At the end of the 1206 list are Cigü with 3,000 Onggirads, Alci with another 3,000 Onggirads, and Butu with 2,000 Ikires. They are unlikely to have been post-1204 additions and may have been placed last because they had larger contingents. Further they were sons-in-law of Genghis Khan as were four other late listed commanders who would also have been early appointments.[1] If the sons-in-law are simply a special group placed at the end, those added after 1203 may have been 58 to 79.

Around 1227, Rashid al-Din says the right wing had 38,000 men. There were 23 units so several commanders commanded more than one minghan. The left wing was stronger with 62,000 men, but Khitans and Jurchens supplied 20,000. There were therefore 42,000 'Mongols', also in 23 units.

Genghis Khan originally had a small guard. It was increased to 1,000 men in 1206 and had reached 29,000 by 1227. The guard was in 1227 split as follows:

---

1   Five if Kingqiyadai should be included in that group.

Family member	Size	Known commanders	Comments
Börte	3,000	2	
Genghis Khan	1,000	1	
Joci Qasar	1,000	1	
Otcigin	5,000	3	4,000 Jalayirs, 1,000 of Kilungghut of Oronar
Alcidai	3,000	1	
Joci	4,000	4	Later expanded to 10,000 and more
Ca'adai	4,000	4	
Ögödei	4,000	3	
Kölgen	4,000	2	Kölgen's son Quca inherited 6,000 men

Of the 29 units in the guard, the commanders of 9 are not known. Ögödei formed a new 3,000 men strong guard unit for his son Kötän in 1229.

Commander	Joined	1206	1227	Comments
Right wing				
Bo'orcu Noyan (博尔术), followed by his son Boroldai (孛栾台)	Early	2	1 right	Arulats
Boroqul Noyan (博尔忽), followed by his son Jubukur Qubilai (脱欢袭职)	Early	15	2 right	Hushin
Jetei Noyan	1193	23	3 right	Mangqut, tasked to guard Tolui
Kingqiyadai	1193	80?	4 right	Olqunu'ut
Tolon, son of Mönglik	1194	12	5 right	Qongqotan, had guard service
Söyiketü, son of Mönglik	1193	31	6 right	Qongqotan, had guard service
Bala (八剌)	1193	35	7 right	Jalayir, tasked to guard Tolui
Arqai Qasar (阿兒海哈撒兒), brother of Bala	1193	Guard 8	8 right	Jalayir
To'oril, a son of Cülgetei?		14?	9 right	Suldus, related to Sodon Noyan
Cila'un (赤老温), the son of Sorqan Sira, later Cila'un's son Sodon took over the unit	Early	27	10 right	Suldus

Sigi Qutuqu (忽都忽)		16	11 right	
Tobsaqa, associated with Doqsin?		72?	12 right	Dörben
Mangqal Türkän, brother of Qorci	1193?	25 or 84?	13 right	Ba'arin
Quduqa	1208		14 right	Oyirat
Qubilai Qorci, perhaps with Taqai and Asiq	1193	4, 5, 84?	15 right	Ba'arin, had 2,000 or 3,000 men
Buluqan Qalja		28	16 right	Barulas (Olqunu'ut)
Taicu *Guregan* (Sa'ur Secan), son of Olar[2]	Early	79	17 right	
Muqur Qa'uran	1203[3]	70	18 right	Hadargin, settled in Russia
Yesun Toa Taraqi, Jelme's son		Guard 2	19 right	
Qada'an	1193	63	20 right	Sönit or Tarqut
Father Mönglik (滅里)	1194	1	21 right	Qongqotan
Alaqus (阿剌兀)	<1211	91–95	22 right	4,000 Önggüts
Kökö (阔阔) and Megetü		47, 62	23 right	Oyirats; credited with having 10,000 men
Left wing				
Muqali (木华黎), followed by his son Bol (孛鲁) and next grandson Tas (塔思)	1196	3	1 left	Jürkin
Yedu Buqa Taishi, a son of Jelme Uha, perhaps took over from Toqucar who could be Aqutai		9?	2 left	Uriangqadai
Jürcedei (术赤台), followed by his sons Ketei Noyan (怯台) and Buqa (不花)	1194	6, 58, 81?	3 left	4,000 Uru'uds
Butu (孛徒) Guregan, followed by his son Uludai	1193	89–90	4 left	2,000 Ikires
Yeke Qutuqu(t) Noyan		86–87	5 left	Genghis Khan's brother-in-law

2   Genghis Khan's uncle.
3   Early follower, but defected 1202 to 1203.

Alci Noyan (按察兒), brother of Genghis Khan's first wife Huqutu Noyan, Qata, Butu, Tagudar, and Singqor	1203	21	6 left	
Quyildar Sachan (畏答兒), son Möngkö Qalja	1194	21	7 left	Mangqut
Naya'a, a Ba'arin	1200	32, 26?	8 left	3,000 Ba'arin
Sutu	1194		9 left	Qongqotan
Jalayirtai Yisa'ur			10 left	
Önggur (雍古兒), followed by Boroqul	1193	13	11 left	Baya'ut
Uqai Qalja and Guchu (Qarachu)		54?	12 left	Jalayirs; there is a Qurcaqus in the 1206 army list
Sübe'etei Ba'atur (速不台), son follow	1193	52	13 left	Uriangqadai
Doqolqu Cerbi (槊直腦鲁华), his brother Tacar (塔察兒) probably replaced him in 1233	1193	Guard 6	14 left	Arulat
Udutai		49	15 left	Forest Uriangqadai, guarded the tomb of Genghis Khan
Belgutai (別里古台), Genghis Khan's half-brother, followed by his son Kuwen Butu (口温不花)	Early		16 left	
Cigü Güregen	1203	85	17 left	Onggirad, Rashid al-Din says he had 4,000 men and that he settled in Tibet
Ukar Qalja and Quduz Qalja		43?	18 left	Ba'arins. There is a Qudus in the 1206 army list
Ogolen Cerbi	1193	Guard 3	19 left	The Secret History: Aralut (brother of Bo'orcu), Rashid al-Din: Sönit
Tamudar Noyan			20 left	Sönit
Daisun (帶孙),[4] Muqali's brother	1196		21 left	Jürkin, 2,000 men

---

4   Same name as Tas.

Qashaul and Jusuq	1207		22 left	Qoshaquns, a borderline Mongol unit
Möngkö Qalja (木哥汉札)	1194	53	23 left	Mangqut
Uyer (吾也而)			24 left	A Mongol, commanding Khitans
Yelü Tuhua (耶律秃花)	1196		25 left	A Khitan, commanding Jurchens
Guard				
Gücü		17	Börte	Adopted Merkit
Kököcu		18	Börte	Adopted Qorolas
Caqan (察罕) succeeding Yeke Ne'urin?		Guard 1	Genghis Khan	Adopted Tangut
Jebke		45	Joci Qasar	Jalayir, later fled to hide in the mountains
Uru'ud		33	Otcigin	Noyakin
Qorqasun		19	Otcigin	
Gücugür		34?	Otcigin	
Ca'urqai, the brother of Sübe'etei	1193	59	Alcidai	Uriangqadai
Qunan	1193	7	Joci	Kinggut
Möngke'ür		40	Joci	Tayici'ut
Kete		51	Joci	
Bedai?		56	Joci	Hushin
Qaracar, cousin of Buluqan[5]		29	Ca'adai	Barulas
Muge		39	Ca'adai	Jalayir
Idoqudai		66	Ca'adai	
Kökö Cos		60	Ca'adai	
Ilüge		5	Ögödei	Jalayir
Degei	1193	11	Ögödei	
Dayir		37	Ögödei	Besüt

5   Ancestor of Temür *Lenks*.

| Qubilai | 1193 | 8 | Kölgen | Qongqotan, the Dayir in the Near East must be a different person |
| To'oril, son of Caqa'an Qo'a | 1193 | 25 | Kölgen | Ne'us |

From the 1206 list officers missing include Tüge (10), perhaps Cülgetei (14), Siluqai (22), Oronartai (36), Bogen (42), Maral (44), Yuruqan (46), Udutai (49), Kete (51), Geügi (55), and Kisliliq (57), Toqon Temür (62), Moroqa (64), and Dori Buqu (65), Siraqul (67), Da'un (68), Tamaci (69), Alci (71), perhaps Tobsaqa (72), Tungquidai (73), Tobuqa (74), Ajnai (75), Tüyideger (76), Sece'ür (77), Jeder (78), Quril (82), perhaps Buqa (81), Asiq (83), and Qadai (84). Some could be the unnamed guard units, others inside groups in the 1227 list, and finally some under new management.

Muqali had in China important commanders called Seunidei (肖乃台), Bolot Beiluo (孛罗), Burqai Ba'atur (不里海拔都兒), and Kökö Buqa (阔阔不花). Possibly they were sub-commanders in his and his brother Daisun's units. Zhao Hong says that an older brother of Muqali, he calls him Gi-li-go-no, commanded a unit of 1,000 in 1221. This could be Güyigünek who is mentioned in 1211 and 1231–1232.

The Sönit Canmaqan led three tümens to the Near East in 1230. One was newly raised west of the Altai, and Malik Khan commanded the unit. The Besüt Baiju and the Qorolas Yeke Yisa'ur led two other units coming from Mongol core territory. The latter two are not in the list of Rashid al-Din. Baiju was a relative of Jebe and could have commanded Jebe's old unit (48). More likely this unit was with Jebe's son Suqursun who is not mentioned in the list of Rashid al-Din.

The non-Mongol forces
Rashid al-Din listed, as shown above, Uyer and Yelü Tuhua, each with a *myriarch* ('10,000'). In 1229, Ögödei recognised three myriarch commanders, namely Heima, Jalar, and Shi Tianze. The first two were perhaps under the authority of Yelü Tuhua, but he never commanded in the field (he died in 1231). By then Uyer had retired. Zhang Rou and Yan Shi also commanded sizeable forces. They were recognised as myriarch commanders by 1232, but clearly played a prominent independent role before that. According to Peng Daya, the key the commanders were Yen Shi based on Yunzhou, Shi Tianze based on Zhending, Zhang Rou based on Mancheng, and Liu Heima based on Tiancheng.[6] In addition there were other commanders based in Liaodong. Jalar was one of these. A few year later additional Chinese myriarch commanders were appointed. In 1229 it was said there were 36 *chiliarchs* or about 36,000 men. A census in 1241 counted 97,000 Chinese and Khitan soldiers. By then the protracted war with the Song had started. Significant additional numbers of Chinese forces were raised in 1232 and during the second half of the 1230s.

Jalar, Heima, Shi Tianze, Zhang Rou, and Yan Shi must have commanded the bulk of the 36,000 or so non-Mongol soldiers in China in 1229. This means they had

6   Peng Daya, p.202.

on average at most 7,000 men.[7] A part of the forces must have been tasked to guard the various cities so an average field army must have been smaller. Jalar led 3,000 horsemen on campaign in 1232. If this was a typical-sized contigent, the total was 15,000. That could represent the total number of horsemen.

7   Yen Shi had 8,000 men in 1234.

Appendix II

Battles of the Mongols and their allies

Battle	Time	Mongol leader	Opponent	Outcome
Bu'ura	Late winter 1191?	To'oril, Jamuqa, and Temüjin	Toqto'a and Dayir Usun	Kereyit victory
Dalan Baljut	Early 1194?	Temüjin	Jamuqa	Mongol defeat
Naratu Sitü'en and Qusutu Sitü'en	Summer 1996	To'oril and Temüjin	Mägüdjin-säültü	Kereyit–Mongol victory
Dolon Boldau	Late 1196	Temüjin	Saca Beki and Taicu	Mongol victory
Upper Kerulen River	Early 1197	Temüjin and Jaqa Gambo	Toqto'a	Mongol victory
Telegetü Pass	Late 1197	Temüjin and To'oril	Saca Beki and Taicu	Mongol victory
Mürüce Se'ul	Late 1198	Temüjin	Toqto'a	Mongol victory
Bu'ura	Early 1199	To'oril	Toqto'a	Kereyit victory
Kizil Bas	Late 1199	To'oril, Temüjin and Jamuqa	Buyiruq	Kereyit–Mongol success
Telegetü	Late 1199	Kökse'ü Sabraq	Senggüm and Jaqa Gambo	Naiman victory
Hulaan Qud	Late 1199	Senggüm and Bo'orcu	Kökse'ü Sabraq	Kereyit–Mongol victory?

Onon River	Spring 1200	To'oril and Temüjin	A'ucu Ba'atur, Quril and Qudu'udar	Kereyit–Mongol victory
Ulengüt Turas	Spring 1200	Temüjin	Qudu'udar and Tarqutai Kiriltuq	Mongol victory
Buyira	Late 1200	To'oril and Temüjin	Cirgidai and Buq Coroqi?	Kereyit–Mongol defeat?
Dalan Nemürges	Early 1201?	Temüjin	Alaq Udur and Caqun	Mongol victory
Qailar	Late 1201?	Temüjin	Jamuqa?	Mongol victory
Bijan I	Summer 1202	Temüjin	Jalin Buqa?	Mongol victory
Bijan II	Summer 1202	Temüjin	Yeke Čeren	Mongol victory
Köyiten	Winter 1202–1203	To'oril and Temüjin	Buyiruq	Kereyit–Mongol success
Qara'un Jidun	Summer 1203	To'oril and Jamuqa	Joci Qasar	Mongol defeat
Qalaqaljit Sands	Summer 1203	To'oril and Jamuqa	Temüjin	Mongol defeat
Near Jeje'er Heights?	Autumn 1203	To'oril	Jamuqa	Kereyit success
Near Baljuna	Autumn 1203	Sübe'etei and Ca'urqan	Bandita	Mongol victory
Jeje'er Heights	Autumn 1203	Temüjin	To'oril	Mongol victory
Naqu	Summer 1204	Temüjin	Bai Buqa	Mongol victory
Tamir River	Summer 1204	Temüjin	Küclüg	Mongol victory
Qaradal Source	Autumn 1204	Temüjin	Toqto'a	Mongol success
Ulugh Taq	Late 1206	Genghis Khan	Buyiruq	Mongol success
Buqdurma River	Late 1208	Genghis Khan	Toqto'a and Küclüg	Mongol victory
Wulahai	May 1209	Genghis Khan	Li Cunxiang	Mongol victory

Keyimen I	October 1209	Genghis Khan	Weiming	Mongol defeat
Keyimen II	November 1209	Genghis Khan	Weiming	Mongol victory
Yehu Ling	September 1211	Genghis Khan	Doji Qian Zhong	Mongol victory
Huiho Bao	September 1211	Genghis Khan	Cheng Yu	Mongol victory
Ding'an	October 1211	Jebe?	Hu Shahu	Mongol victory
Migukou Valley	Late 1212	Genghis Khan	Aodun Xiang	Mongol victory
Dijinawuer	June 1213	Yelü, Liuge, Alci, and Butu	Wanyan Husha	Mongol victory
Weichuan	September 1213	Genghis Khan	Wanyan Gang	Mongol victory
Wuhui Mountains	November 1213	Genghis Khan	Wu Huiling?	Mongol victory?
Gao Qiao	2–30 November 1213	Ketei and Buqa?	Hu Shahu and Zhuhu Gaoqi	Indecisive
Lugou Bridge	August 1214	Jalar and Bisier	Wanyan Fuxing	Rebel Khitan victory
Hote	March 1215	Muqali	Ao Denxiang	Mongol victory
Yongding River	May 1215	Shansa and Shimo Mingan	Li Ying	Mongol victory
Xuanfengzhai	May 1215	Shansa and Shimo Mingan	Wanyan Hezhu and Ahsing Songe	Mongol victory
Xianping	May 1215	Yelü Liuge	Puxian Wannu	Mongol defeat
Huizhou	Summer 1215	Uyer and Shi Tianxiang	Dalu	Mongol victory
Xingzhou	Summer 1215	Uyer and Shi Tianxiang	Zhao Shouyu	Mongol victory
Lungshan	July 1215	Uyer and Shi Tianxiang	Dalu	Mongol victory
Shenshui	September 1215	Muqali	Zhang Zhi	Mongol victory

Chu River	November 1216?	Sübe'etei	Qudu	Mongol victory
Balasagun	Early 1217?	Jebe and Sübe'etei?	Küclüg	Mongol victory
Zima River	Early 1217?	Boroqul	Tumeds	
Beijing	Summer 1217	Uyer and Shi Tianxiang	Jin rebels	Mongol victory
Che River	Summer 1217	Uyer and Shi Tianxiang	Jin rebels	Mongol victory
Zima River?	Late 1217	Dörbei Doqsin	Tumeds	Mongol victory
Sariq Qun	Early 1219?	Jebe	Küclüg	Mongol victory (2 battles)
Mancheng	Spring 1219	Zhang Rou	Wu Xian	Mongol victory
Yuyu	April 1219?	Sübe'etei, Jebe, and Joci	Inazu and Qudu	Mongol victory
Irghiz River	April 1219?	Sübe'etei, Jebe, and Joci	Muhammad II	Indecisive
Zhongshan	Summer 1219	Zhang Rou	Ge Tieqian	Mongol victory
Chiyang	Summer 1219	Zhang Rou and Dong Run	Wu Xian	Mongol victory
Bokhara	February 1220	Sübe'etei?	Inanch Khan	Mongol victory
Samarkand	March 1220	Genghis Khan	Alpär Khan, Shaykh Khan, Balan Khan	Mongol victory
Nishapur	24 May 1220	Sübe'etei and Jebe	Sharaf al-Din's guard	Mongol victory
Sijus	July 1220?	Sübe'etei and Jebe	Beg Tegin Silahdar and Kuch-Bugha Khan	Mongol victory
Taizhou	September 1220	Möngkö Qalja	Jin?	Mongol victory
Tus	September 1220?	Qush Temür	Siraj al-Din	Mongol victory
Huanglinggang	November 1220	Muqali	Wusulun Shihu	Mongol victory

Ustuva	January 1221	Mongols?	Jalal al-Din	Mongol defeat
Ustuva	January 1221	Mongols?	Ozlagh and Aq	Mongol victory
Bagh-i-Khurram	January 1221?	Ca'adai and Ögödei's advance guard	Khumar-tagin	Mongol victory
Nisa	February 1221?	Mongols?	Shaikh Khan and Inanch Khan	Mongol defeat
Dastajird	24 February 1221	Tolui	Ikhtiyar al-Din	Mongol victory
Sagan River	February 1221	Sübe'etei and Jebe	Georgi III Lasha	Mongol victory
Waliyan	Spring 1221	Taqacaq and Mulgar	Jalal al-Din	Mongol defeat
Parwan	Summer 1221	Sigi Qutuqu	Jalal al-Din	Mongol defeat
Peizhou	22 June 1221	Jirwadai, Heima, and Yan Shi	Meng Gugang	Mongol victory
Djerdin	August 1221?	Caqan?	Jalal al-Din	Mongol defeat
Near Sindhu River	September 1221?	Caqan?	Orkhan	Mongol victory
Hamadan	September 1221	Jebe	Jamal-ud-Din	Mongol victory
Sindhu River	September 1221	Genghis Khan	Jalal al-Din	Mongol victory
Angai	19 November 1221	Yebu Gambo	Wanyan Heda	Mongol defeat
Yan'an	8 December 1221	Muqali	Wanyan Heda	Mongol victory
Terek River?	Early 1222?	Sübe'etei and Jebe	Alans and Derbent Kipchaks	Final Mongol victory (2 or 3 battles)
Don River	Late 1222?	Sübe'etei	Jurij Koncakovic and Daniilo Kobiakovich	Mongol victory (2 battles)

Kalka River	31 May 1223?	Sübe'etei and Jebe	Mstislav Mstislavich and Mstislav III Romanovich	Mongol victory
Penze	Early 1224	Sübe'etei and Jebe	Volga Bulgars?	Mongol defeat
Jurjan	February 1224	Mongols?	Inanch Khan	Mongol victory
Bozebali	Summer 1224	Sübe'etei and Jebe	Khotosy	Mongol victory
Yinzhou	September 1224	Bol	Taga Gambo	Mongol victory
Zhongshan	June 1225	Seunidei and Shi Tianze	Ge Diaqiang	Mongol victory
Canhuang	August 1225	Daisun	Peng Yibin and Wu Xian	Mongol victory
Zhengding	December 1225	Shi Tianze	Wu Xian	Mongol victory
Hei-Shui	March 1226	Genghis Khan	Xia?	Mongol victory
Lingzhou	6 December 1225	Genghis Khan	Weiming *Linggong*	Mongol victory
Zhi River	May 1227	Shi Tianze, Bol, and Uyer	Li Quan	Mongol victory
Shanzhou	December 1227	Alcidai, Güyük, and Sübe'etei	Aotun Alibu and Wanyan Zhongde	Mongol victory
Xihezhou	Early 1228?	Anjur	Qiang Jun	Mongol victory
He Marsh	Early 1228?	Alcidai, Güyük, and Sübe'etei	Zheng Xin	Mongol victory
Dachangyuan	Early 1228?	Tangut Ba'atur	Wanyan Chen Heshang	Mongol defeat
Caspian Sea	Late 1229?	Sübe'etei	Bachman	Mongol victory
Qingyang	January 1230	Cila'un?	Yiua Pau	Mongol failure
Luzhou	October 1230	Tas	Wu Xian	Mongol defeat
Luzhou	October 1230	Eljigidei and Tas	Wu Xian	Mongol victory

Weizhou	November 1230	Shi Tianze	Wanyan Chen Heshang	Indecisive
Daohui Valley	7 February 1231	Sübe'etei	Wanyan Heda	Mongol defeat
Yangzhou	18 February 1231	Li Chuan	Zhao Guai and Zhao Fan	Mongol defeat
Huazhou	April 1231	Ögödei, Tolui, and Sübe'etei	Wanyan Heda	Mongol victory
Xingyuan	9 June 1231	Sübe'etei?	Guo Zhengsun	Mongol victory
Tongson	October 1231	Mongol advance guard	Yi Chasong	Mongol defeat
Anbuk	November 1231	Satai	Yi Chasong	Mongol victory
Da'an	19+ November 1231	Sübe'etei?	He Jin	Mongol victory
Yushan	17 January 1232	Tolui and Sübe'etei	Wanyan Heda	Indecisive
Xiancheng	25 January 1232	Mongols?	Wanyan Lou Shi and Wanyan Lou Shi	Mongol victory
Near Angao	1 February 1232	Jalar	Wanyan Heda	Mongol defeat
Sanfeng	9 February 1232	Tolui and Sübe'etei	Wanyan Heda	Mongol victory
Xuzhou	12–13 February 1232	Alci and Zhang Rong	Tudan Yidu	Mongol victory
Yangyi	24 February 1232	Seunidei	Wanyan Qing Shannu	Mongol victory
Tieling	1 March 1232	Huluhanzhi?	Tushan Wudian	Mongol victory
Mixian	20 August 1232	Sübe'etei	Neizu Silie	Mongol victory
Yuzhou	January 1233	Huang Guisanhe?	Wu Xian	Mongol victory
Huanglinggang	12–13 February 1233	Sübe'etei	He Duxi	Mongol victory
Baigong Temple or Oumagang Mountain	23 February 1233	Doqolqu Cerbi, Shi Tianze, and others	Baisa	Mongol victory

Huaizhou	February 1233?	Ismail	Wang You	Mongol victory
Xiaoxian	April 1233	Wang Zhen	Zhang Yuange and Miao Xiuchang	Mongol victory
Guanghua	May 1233	Meng Gong	Wu Tianxi	Song victory
Shunyang	June 1233	Meng Gong	Wu Xian	Song defeat
Wangjiasi	12 July 1233	Doqolqu Cerbi	Pucha Guannu	Mongol defeat
Madeng	16 to 23 August 1233	Meng Gong	Wu Xian	Song victory
Tangzhou	September 1233?	Meng Gong	Wulinda Hutu	Song victory
Maxindian	4 October 1233	Song?	Pucha Heda	Song victory
Pei	Start 1234?	Zhang Rong	Suo E	Mongol victory
Xuzhou	February 1234	Zhang Rong	Guo Yongan	Mongol victory
Longmen	25 August 1234	Tacar?	Yang Yi	Mongol victory
Luoshui River	30 August 1234	Tacar?	Xu Minzi	Indecisive
Jiguan'ai	Early winter 1235	Mongols?	Cao Youwan	Mongol defeat
Jiguan'ai	4 August 1236	Kötän	Cao Youwan	Mongol victory
Bilyar	Late 1236?	Sübe'etei	Jiqu and Bazan	Mongol victory
Ryazan	4–5 December 1237	Sübe'etei and Batu	Yuri, Oleg, Yaroslav	Mongol victory
Nadolob	December 1237	Sübe'etei and Batu	Roman	Mongol victory
Yaroslav	February 1238	Sübe'etei	Yuri II Vsevolodivich	Mongol victory
Luzhou	September 1238	Caqan	Du Gao	Mongol defeat
Chernigov	18 October 1239	Sübe'etei and Batu	Mstislav Glebovich	Mongol victory

Czarna	February 1241	Mongols?	Wlodzimierz	Indecisive
Sheibeklaukis	February 1241?	Sheibek	Erdvilas	Mongol defeat
Ratno	February 1241?	Qadan?	Erdvilas	Mongol victory
Verecke Pass	12 March 1241	Sübe'etei and Batu	Nador Denes	Mongol victory
Waitzen	16 March 1241	Mongols?	Ugolin	Mongol victory
Chmielnik	18 March 1241	Baidar	Vladimir and Pacoslav	Mongol victory
Erlau	20–25 March 1241?	Mongols?	Benedict	Mongol victory
Kronstadt	31 March 1241	Buri	Pozsa	Mongol victory
Liegnitz Pole	9 April 1241	Baidar and Orda	Henry II	Mongol victory
Mohi Heath	April 1241	Sübe'etei and Batu	Bela IV	Mongol victory
Grobnik	Early 1242?	Mongols?	Croatians	Mongol defeat?
Bulgaria	Early 1242?	Mongols?	Bulgarians?	Mongol defeat and victory
Dnieper/Don River?	Autumn 1242	Kötän and Shingqor	Kipchaks?	Mongol victory
Derbent	Autumn 1242	Ila'udur	Kipchaks?	Mongol victory

Bibliography

Mongol and Chinese primary sources

Abramowski, Waltraut, 'Die Chinesischen Annalen von Ögödei und Güyük', *Zentral Asiatische Studien* 10 (Wiesbaden, 1976)

Babelstone, 'Two Tangut Families', http://babelstone.blogspot.ch/2015/01/two-tangut-families-part-1.html, last accessed 31/12/2015

Buell, Paul, 'Readings on Central Asian History', https://www.academia.edu/245639/Readings_on_Central_Asian_History, last accessed 31/12/2015

Chan, Hok-lam, *The Fall of the Jurchen Chin: Wang E's memoir on Ts'ai-chou under Mongol siege* (Stuttgart: F. Steiner, 1973)

Cleaves, Francis W., 'The Biography of Bayan', *Harvard Journal of Asiatic Studies*, 19 3/4 (Cambridge, 1956), pp.185–303

Cleaves, Francis W., *The Secret History of the Mongols* (Cambridge, Mass.: Harvard University Press, 1982)

de Harlez, C., *Histoire de l'Empire de Kin; Ou, Empire d'Or Aisin Gurun-I Suduri Bithe* (Louvain: Typ de C. Peeters, 1887)

de Rachewiltz, Igor, *The Secret History of the Mongols: A Mongolian Epic Chronicle of the Thirteenth Century* (Leiden: Brill, 2004)

Emerson, John, 'Sheng Wu Jin Cheng Lu: Partial translation, comments and notes', http://www.johnjemerson.com/shengwu.htm, last accessed 31/12/2012

Gaubil, Antony, *Histoire de Gentchiscan et toute la dynastie des Mongous ... tirée de l'histoire chinoise* (Paris: Briasson, 1739)

Haenisch, Erich (translator), 'Die letzen Feldzuge Cinggis Hans und sein Tod', *Asia Minor* 9 (1933), pp.503–551

Haenisch, Erich, *Die Ehreninschrift für den Rebellengeneral Ts'ui Lih* (Berlin: Verlag der Akademie der Wissenschaften, 1944)

Haenisch, Erich, *Zum Untergang zweier Reiche; Berichte von Augenzeugen sus den Jahren 1232–33 und 1360–1370* (Wiesbaden: F. Steiner, 1969)

Hsiao, Ch'i-ch'ing, *The Military Establishment of the Yuan Dynasty* (Cambridge, Mass.: Harvard University Press, 1978)

Krause, F. E. A., *Cingis Han: Die Geschichte seines Lebens nach den chinesischen Reichannalen* (Heidelberg: C. Winter, 1922)

Olbricht, P. and Pinks, E., *Meng-Ta Pei-Lu und Hei-ta Shih-Lüeh: chinesische Gesandtenberichte über die frühen Mongolen 1221 und 1237* (Wiesbaden 1980)

Onon, Urgunge, *The Secret History of the Mongols: The Life and Times of Chinggis Khan* (Richmond, Surrey: Curzon, 2001)

Pelliot, Paul and Hambis, Louis, *Histoire des campagnes de Gengis Khan: Cheng-wou ts'in-tcheng lou* (Leiden: Brill, 1951)

Pelliot, Paul, *Histoire Secrète des Mongols: restitution du texte mongol et francaise des chapitres I à VI* (Paris: Librairie d'Amérique et d'Orient, 1949)

Remusat, A., 'Souboutai', *Nouveaux melagnes asiatiques*, volume 2, (Paris, 1829), pp.89–97

Tuotuo, *Jinshi* (Taipei, 1970, Beijing, 1975)

Tuotuo, *Songshi* (Beijing, 1977)

Tzu, Sun, *The Art of War*, translated by Samuel B. Griffith (New York: Oxford University Press, 1963), p.78.

Waley, Arthur, *The Travels of an Alchemist: the journey of the Taoist, Ch'ang-ch'un, from China to the Hindukush at the summons of Chingiz Khan, recorded by his disciple, Li Chih-ch'ang* (London: Routledge, 1931)

Wang, Guowei, *Meng-ku shih liao ssu chung* (Taipei, 1970)

Wang, Yun, Wuliang shi xian miao bei ming 兀良氏先庙碑铭, Qiuqian xiansheng daquan wenji 秋涧先生大全文集 (Sibu congkan ed.)

Zhou, Mi 周密, Qidong yeyu 齐东野语 (Beijing, 1983), pp.77–80

Arab, Persian, and Near Eastern primary sources

Aboul Ghazi Bahadour Khan, *Histoire des Moguls et des Tatares*, translated by Le Baron Desmaisons (St Petersburg, 1874)

Al-Umari, *Das Mongolische Weltreich*, translated by Klaus Lech (Wiesbaden: Harrassowitz, 1968)

Bar Hebraeus, *Chronography of Bar Hebraeus*, translated by W. Budge (Oxford: Oxford University Press, 1932)

Grigor Aknerc'i, 'History of the Nation of the Archers', translated by Robert P. Blake and R. N. Frye, *Harvard Journal of Asiatic Studies*, 3–4 (1949), p.269–443

Ibn al-Athir, *The Chronicle of Ibn al-Athir for the Crusading Period from al-Kamil fi'il-ta'rikh*, part 3, translated by D. S. Richards (Aldershot: Ashgate, 2008)

Juvaini, *The History of the World-Conqueror*, translated and commented by John Andrew Boyle (Manchester: Manchester University Press, 1958)

Juzjani, *Tabakat-i-Nasiri*, translated and commented by H. G. Raverty (Calcutta, 1895)

Kirakos Ganjakec'i, *History of the Armenians*, Robert Bedrosian (1986), http://rbedrosian.com/kg1.htm, last accessed 31/12/2015

Khwandamir, *Habibu's-Siyar Tome Three: The Reign of the Mongol and the Turk*, translated by W. M. Thackston (Cambridge, Mass.: Harvard University, 1994)

Munis, Munis, and Muhammad Riza Mirab Agahi, *History of Khorezm*, translated by Yuri Bregel (Leiden: Brill, 1999)

Nasawi, *Histoire du sultan Djelal ed-Din Mankobirti prince du Kharezm par Mohammed en-Nesawi*, translated by O. Houdas (Paris: E. Leroux, 1895)

Rashid al-Din, *Rashiduddin Fazlullah's Jami'u't-tawarikh* (Compendium of Chronicles), translated by W. M. Thackston, 3 volumes (Cambridge, Mass.: Harvard University Press, 1998–99).

Rashid al-Din, *The Successors of Genghis Khan*, translated and commented by John Andrew Boyle (New York: Columbia University Press, 1971)

Ulug Big, *The Shajrat ul Atrak of Muhammad Taragay ibn Šahruh*, translated by Col. Miles (London: W. H. Allen and Co., 1838)

Vardan Arewelc'I, *Compilation of History*, translated by Robert Bedrosian 2007, http://rbedrosian.com/vaint.htm, last accessed 31/12/2015

European primary sources

da Pian del Carpini, Giovanni, *The story of the Mongols whom we call Tartars*, translated by Erik Hildinger (Boston: Branden Publishing Company, 1996)

The Chronicle of Novgorod: 1046–1471, translated by R. Mitchell and N. Forbes (London: Camden Society, 1914)

Dawson, Christopher, *The Mongol Mission: Narratives and letters of the Franciscan missionaries in Mongolia and China in the thirteenth and fourteenth centuries. Transl. by a nun of Stanbrook Abbey* (London: Sheed and Ward, 1955)

Długos, Jan, *The Annals of Jan Dlugosz: A History of Eastern Europe 965 to 1480*, translated by Maurice Michael and Paul Smith (Charlton, West Sussex: IM Publications, 1997)

Göckenjan, Hansgerd and Sweeney, James, *Der Mongolensturm: Berichte von Augenzeugen und Zeitgenossen, 1235–1250* (Graz: Styria, 1985)

Herodotus, *The Histories* (London: Penguin, 1972)

The Hypatian Chronicle: The Galician–Volynian Chronicle, translated by George A. Perfecky (München: W. Fink, 1973)

Iwamura, Shinobu, 'Mongol invasion of Poland in the Thirteenth Century', *Memoirs of the Research Department of the Toyo Bunko* (Tokyo 1938), pp.103–157

Mathew of Paris, *Matthew Paris's English History. From the Year 1235 to 1273* (London: H. G. Bohn, 1859–89)

Roger, *Anonymus and Master Roger*, translated by János M. Bak and Martin Rady (Budapest, 2010)

Monumenta Germaniae Historica (Hanover & Berlin, 1826+)

The Nikonion Chronicle, translated by Serge A. Zenkovsky and Betty Jean Zenkovsky, vols. 2–3 (Princeton: Kingston Press, 1984–89)

The Vinland Map and the Tartar relation, translated by R. A. Skelton and others (New Haven: Yale University Press, 1965)

Secondary sources

Ai, Gong Wei, 'Consolidation of southern Sung China under Hsiao-Tsung's reign', Denis Twitchett and Paul Jakov Smith (eds.), *The Cambridge History of China*, vol. 5 part 1 (Cambridge: Cambridge University Press, 2009)

Akerly, J., *Military Maxims of Napoleon* (New York: Wiley and Putnam, 1845)

Allsen, T. T., 'Prelude to the Western Campaigns', *Archivum Eurasiae Medii Aevi*, 3 (Wiesbaden: Harrassowitz, 1983), pp.5–24

Allsen, T. T., 'The Mongols and North Caucasia', *Archivum Eurosiae Medii Aevi*, 7 (Wiesbaden: Harrassowitz, 1991), pp.5–40

Allsen, T. T., 'The Circulation of Military Technology in the Mongolian Empire', *Warfare in Inner Asian History* (Leiden, 2002), pp.265–293

Allsen, T. T., 'The Princes of the Left Hand', *Archivum Eurasiae Medii Aevi*, 5 (Wiesbaden: Harrassowitz, 1987), pp.5–40

Allsen, T. T., 'The rise of the Mongolian empire and Mongolian rule in north China', in Herbert Franke and Denis Twitchett (eds.), *The Cambridge History of China*, vol 6 (Cambridge: Cambridge University Press, 1994), pp.321–413

Amitai-Press, Reuven, *Mongols and Mamluks: The Mamluk-Ilkhanid war 1260–1281* (Cambridge: Cambridge University Press, 1995)

Arnold, James, *Crisis on the Danube: Napoleon's Austrian Campaign of 1809* (New York: Paragon 1990)

Atwood, C. P., 'The date of the "Secret History of the Mongols" reconsidered', *Journal of Song Yuan Studies*, vol. 37 (2007) p.1–48

Atwood, C. P., 'The first Mongol contacts with the Tibetans', *Revue d'Etudes Tibétaines* (2015), pp.21–45

Atwood, C. P., 'Historiography and transformation of ethnic identity in the Mongol Empire: the Öng'üt case', *Asian Ethnicity* (Indiana, 2014), pp.514–534

Atwood, C. P., *Commentary of Shenwu qinzhenglu*, http://cces.snu.ac.kr/com/18swqe.pdf, last accessed 31/12/2012

Atwood, C. P., *Encyclopedia of Mongolia and the Mongol Empire* (New York: Facts on File, 2004)

Aubin, Françoise, 'The Rebirth of Chinese Rule in Times of Trouble', S. Schram, *Foundations and limits of State Power in China* (Hong Kong: Chinese University Press, 1987), pp.113–146

Avery, Julie J., *A Record of the Defense of Xiangyang's City Wall, 1206–1207* (Ph. D., Massachusetts, 2009)

Barfield, Thomas, *The Perilous Frontier: nomadic empires and China* (Cambridge, Mass.: B. Blackwell, 1989)

Barthold, V. V., *Turkestan down to the Mongol invasion*, translated by H. A. R. Gibb (London: Luzac and Co., 1968)

Bartl, Július, *Slovak History: Chronology & Lexicon* (Wauconda, IL: Bolchazy-Carducci Publishers, 2002)

Bedrosian, R., *The Turco-Mongol Invasions and the Lords of Armenia in the 13–14th Centuries* (Ph. D., Columbia University, 1979)

Benson, D. S., *Six Emperors: Mongolian aggression in the thirteenth century* (Chicago, Ill: The Author, 1995)

Berend, Nora, *At the Gate of Christendom: Jews, Muslims, and 'pagans' in Medieval Hungary, c.1000–1300* (Cambridge: Cambridge University Press, 2001)

Bieler, Samuel, 'Private Armies in the Early Korean Military Tradition (850–1598)', *Penn History Review*, Vol. 19, Iss. 1, Article 4.

Biran, Michal, *The Empire of the Qara Khitai in Eurasian History: between China and the Islamic World* (Cambridge: Cambridge University Press, 2005)

Bonaparte, Napoleon, *Memoirs ecrits a Sainte-Helene* (Paris, 1847)

Boyle, J. A., 'The summer and winter camping grounds of the Kereit', *Central Asiatic Journal*, vol. 17, No. 2/4 (1973), pp.108–110

Bregel, Yuri, *An Historical Atlas Of Central Asia* (Leiden: Brill, 2003)

Bretschneider, E., *Medieval Researches from Eastern Asiatic Sources; fragments towards the knowledge of the geography and history of central and western Asia from the 13th to the 17th century* (Ludgate, 1888)

Buell, Paul D., 'Early Mongol Expansion in Western Siberia and Turkestan', *Central Asiatic Journal*, 36 (1992), pp.1–32

Buell, Paul D., *Tribe, Qan and Ulus in early Mongol China: some prolegomena to Yüan history* (Ph. D., University of Washington, 1977)

Buell, Paul D., *Historical Dictionary of the Mongol World Empire* (Oxford: The Scarecrow Press, Inc., 2003)

Buniyatov, Z. M., *A History of the Khorezmian state under the Anushtedginids 1097–1231* (Samarkand: IICAS, 2015)

Candy, Christopher, *An Exercise in Frustration: The Scottish Campaign of Edward I, 1300* (Unpublished M.A. dissertation, University of Durham, 1999)

Caraway, William M., *Korea in the Eye of the Tiger*, http://www.koreanhistoryproject.org/Ket/C04/E0403.htm, last accessed 31/12/2012

Chan, Hok-lam, *The Historiography of the Chin Dynasty: three studies* (Wiesbaden: Steiner, 1970)

Chen, Dezhi, 'The Kerait Kingdom up to the Thirteenth Century', in Luo, Xin, *Chinese Scholars on Inner Asia* (Bloomington, 2012), pp.411–662

Chandler, David, *Atlas of Military Strategy* (London: Arms & Armour Press, 1980)

Cleaves, Francis W., 'The Historicity of The Baljuna Covenant', *Harvard Journal of Asiatic Studies*, vol.18, no.3/4 (1955), pp.357–421

van Crefeld, Martin, *Command in War* (Cambridge, Mass.: Harvard University Press, 1987)

Curtin, Jeremiah, *The Mongols in Russia* (Boston: Little Brown, 1908)

Curtin, Jeremiah, *The Mongols: A History* (Conshohocken, Pa.: Combined Books 1996)

Dambyn, Bazargür & Dambyn, Enkhbayar: *Chinggis Khaan: A historic-geographic atlas* (Mongolia, 1996)

Davis, Richard L., 'The Reigns of Kuang-tsung (1189–1194) and Ning-tsung (1194–1224)', 'The Reign of Li-tsung (1224–1264)', 'The Reign of Tu-tsung (1264–1274) and His Successors to 1279', in Frederick W. Mote and Denis Twitchett (eds.), *The Cambridge History of China*, vol. 7 (Cambridge: Cambridge University Press, 2009), pp.756–838, 839–912, 913–962

Dennis, George, *Maurice's Strategikon: handbook of Byzantine military strategy* (Pennsylvania: University of Pennsylvania Press, 1984)

Di Cosmo, Nicola, *Warfare in Inner Asian History: 500–1800* (Leiden: Brill, 2002)

Dien, Albert E., 'The Stirrup and its effect on Chinese Military History', *Ars Orientalis*, 16 (Michigan, 1976)

Dimnik, Martin, *The Dynasty of Chernigov, 1146–1246* (Cambridge: Cambridge University Press, 2003)

Dimnik, Martin, *Mikhail, Prince of Chernigov and Grand Prince of Kiev 1224–1246* (Toronto: Pontifical Institute of Mediaeval Studies, 1981)

Dunnell, Ruth, *Tanguts and the Tangut State of Ta Hsia* (Ph. D., Princeton University, 1983)

Dunnell, Ruth, 'The Fall of the Xia Empire', in G. Seaman and D. Marks, *Rulers from the Steppe: state formation on the Eurasian periphery* (Los Angeles: Ethnographics Press, 1991), pp.158–185

Dunnell, Ruth, 'Locating the Tangut Military Establishment', *Monumenta Serica XL* (1992), pp.219–234

Dunnell, Ruth, 'The Hsi Hsia', in Herbert Franke and Denis Twitchett (eds.), *The Cambridge History of China*, vol. 6 (Cambridge: Cambridge University Press, 1994), pp.154–214

Dupuy, Trevor, *Numbers, Predictions, and War: using history to evaluate combat factors and predict the outcome of battles* (Indianapolis: Bobbs-Merrill, 1979)

Fang, Cheng-Hua, 'Military Families and the Southern Song Court – The Lü case', in Peter A. Lorge, *Warfare in China to 1600* (Aldershot: Ashgate, 2005), pp.441–463

Fennell, J., 'The Tatar Invasion of 1223: Source Problems', *Forschungen zur Osteuropaischen Geschichte* (Berlin, 1980), pp.18–31

Fennell, J., 'The Tale of Batu's Invasion of North-East Rus', *Osteuropa in Geschichte und Gegenwart* (Vienna, 1977), pp.34–46

Fennell, J., *The Crisis of Medieval Russia, 1200–1304* (New York: Longman, 1983)

Fine, John, *The Late Medieval Balkans: a critical survey from the late twelfth century to the Ottoman Conquest* (Ann Arbor: University of Michigan Press, 1994)

Françoise, Aubin, 'The Rebirth of Chinese Rule in Times of Trouble', *Foundations and limits of State Power in China* (Hong Kong 1987), pp.113–146

Frank, Allen J., *Islamic Historiography and 'Bulghar' identity among the Tatars and Bashkirs of Russia* (Leiden: Brill, 1998)

Franke, Herbert, *Sung Biographies*, 3 volumes (Wiesbaden: Steiner, 1976)

Franke, Herbert, *Studien und Texte zur Kriegsgeschichte der südlichen Sungzeit* (Wiesbaden: Harrassowitz, 1987)

Franke, Herbert, 'The Chin dynasty', Herbert Franke and Denis Twitchett (eds.), *The Cambridge History of China*, vol. 6 (Cambridge: Cambridge University Press, 1994), pp.215–320

Franke, Herbert, 'The Military System of the Chin Dynasty' in *Krieg und Krieger im chinesischen Mittelalter* (12. bis 14. Jahrhundert): drei studien (Stuttgart: Steiner, 2003), pp.215–245

Franke, Herbert: 'Siege and Defense of Towns in Medieval China', Edward L. Dreyer, Frank A. Kierman and John K. Fairbank, *Chinese Ways in Warfare* (Cambridge, Mass.: Harvard University Press, 1974), pp.151–201

Fuller, J. F. C., *British Light Infantry in the Eighteenth Century* (London: Hutchinson & Co., 1925)

Fuller, J. F. C., *The Generalship of Alexander the Great* (New Brunswick: Rutgers University Press, 1960)

Gibbon, Edward, *The history of the decline and fall of the Roman Empire* (London, 1829)

Golden, Peter, 'Cumanica I: The Qipcaqs in Georgia', *Archivum Eurosiae Medii Aevi*, 4 (Wiesbaden: Harrassowitz, 1984)

Golden, Peter, 'Cumanica II, The Ölberli', *Archivum Eurasiae Medii Aevi*, 6 (Wiesbaden: Harrassowitz, 1986), pp.5–29

Golden, Peter: 'Cumanica IV: The Tribes of the Cuman-Qipcaqs', *Archivum Eurasiae Medii Aevi*, 9 (Wiesbaden: Harrassowitz, 1995–1997), pp.99–122

Golijenkov, *Battle on Kalka, 31 May 1223* (Moscow, 1994)

Grousset, René, *Empire of the Steppes: a history of Central Asia* (New Brunswick: Rutgers, 1988)

Haenisch, Erich, 'Die letzten Feldzüge Cinggis Han's und sein Tod', *Asia Major 9* (1933): pp.503–551

Haenisch, Erich, 'Kulturbilder aus Chinas Mongolenzeit', *Historische Zeitschrift*, number 164 (München: Oldenbourg, 1941)

Hamdani, Agha Hussain, *The Frontier Policy of the Delhi Sultans* (Islamabad: National Institute of Historical and Cultural Research, 1986)

Han, Rulin, 'The Kirghiz and neighboring tribes in the Yuan Dynasty', in Luo, Xin, *Chinese Scholars on Inner Asia* (Bloomington: Sinor Research Institute for Inner Asian Studies, Indiana University, 2012), pp.353–410

Heath, Ian, *Armies and Enemies of the Crusades 1096–1291: organization, tactics, dress and weapons* (Goring-by-Sea: Wargames Research Group, 1978)

Heissig, W., 'A new Version of the "Battle with the Tayičighut"', *Central Asiatic Journal*, vol. 31, no. 3–4 (1987), pp.209–223

Henthorn, William, *Korea: The Mongol Invasions* (Leiden: Brill, 1963)

Hoàng, Michel, *Genghis Khan* (London: Saqi Books, 2001)

Howorth, Henry H., *History of the Mongols from the 9th to the 19th Century* (New York: Cosimo, 2008)

Huang, K'uan-chung, 'Mountain fortress defense: the Experience of the Southern Song and Korea in Resisting the Mongol Invasions', translated by David Wright, in Hans van de Ven (ed.), *Warfare in Chinese history* (Leiden: Brill, 2000), p.222–251

Jackson, Peter, 'Jalal al-Din, the Mongols, and the Khwarazmian conquest of the Panjab and Sind', *Journal of the British Institute of Persian Studies*, 28 (London, 1990), pp.45–54

Jackson, Peter, *Studies on the Mongol Empire and Early Muslim India* (Farnham: Ashgate Publishing, 2009)

Jackson, Peter, *The Mongols and the West: 1221–1410* (Taylor & Francis Ltd., 2014)

Kaplan, Edward Harold, *Yueh Fei and the founding of the Southern Sung* (Ph. D., University of Iowa, 1970)

Kazuaki, Tsutsumi, 'The Subetei Family and the Establishment of Khubilai's Political Power', *The Journal of Oriental Researches*, 48(1)(1989), pp.120–147

Kazuaki, Tsutsumi, *Two prominent Mongol families as administrative leaders of South China under the Dai-On ulus Dynasty* (Osaka, 2000), pp.193–218

Keegan, John, *The Face of Battle* (Harmondsworth: Penguin, 1983)

Klein, Kenneth D., *The Contributions of the Fourth Century Xianbei States to the Reunification of the Chinese Empire* (Los Angeles: University of California, 1980)

Korobeinikov, Dimitri, 'A broken mirror: The Kipcak world in the Thirteenth Century', Florin Cuta and Roman Kovalev, *The other Europe in the Middle Ages: Avars, Bulgars, Khazars, and Cumans* (Leiden: Brill, 2008), pp.379–412

Kosztolnyik, Z. J., *Hungary in the Thirteeth Century* (New York: distributed by Columbia University, 1996)

Kovacs, Szilvia, 'Brotz, a Cuman chief in the 13th century', *Acta Orientalia Academiae Scientiarum Hungaricae* (vol. 58 #3, 2005), pp.255–266

Ledyard, Gari, 'Two documents from the Koryo-sa', *Journal of the American Oriental Society*, vol. 83, no 2 (1963), pp.225–239

Liddell Hart, B. H., *Scipio Africanus: Greater than Napoleon* (New York: Da Capo Press, 1994)

Long, Gavin, *MacArthur as military commander* (London: Batsford, 1969)

Macartney, C. A., 'Where Was "Black Wallachia" in the Thirteenth Century?', *The Journal of the Royal Asiatic Society of Great Britain and Ireland*, No. 2 (April 1940), pp.198–200

Macartney, C. A., T*he Magyars in the Ninth Century* (Cambridge: Cambridge University Press, 2008)

Marquart, J., 'Über das Volkstum der Komanen', *Osttürkische Dialektstudien* (Berlin, 1914)

Martin, Desmond, *The Rise of Chingis Khan and his Conquest of North China* (Baltimore: John Hopkins Press, 1950)

Martin, Desmond, 'Chinghiz Khan's First invasion of the Jin Empire', *Journal of the Royal Asiatic Society* (1943)

Martin, Desmond, 'The Mongol wars with Hsi Hsia 1205 to 1227', *Journal of the Royal Asiatic Society* (1942)

May, Timothy, *The Mongol Art of War* (Barnsley: Pen & Sword Military, 2007)

McCreight, Richard, *The Mongol Warrior Epic: Masters of Thirteenth Century Maneuver Warfare* (Master's thesis, Washington, 1971)

McDaniel, Ryan James, *The Mongol invasions of the Near East* (dissertation; San Jose 2005)

Minorsky, V., 'Caucasica III: The Alan Capital Megas and the Mongol Campaigns', *Bulletin of the School of Oriental and African Studies* 14/2 (1952), pp.221–238

Morgan, David, *The Mongols* (Oxford: Blackwell, 1986)

Mote, Frederick, *Imperial China 900–1800* (Cambridge, Mass.: Harvard University Press, 2003)

Needham, Joseph, *The Science and Civilisation in China* (Cambridge: Cambridge University Press, 1959), vol. 5, parts 6 and 7

Nicolle, David, *Lake Peipus 1242: Battle of the Ice* (Oxford: Osprey Military, 1996)

Nicolle, David, *Armies of Medieval Russia 750–1250* (Oxford: Osprey Military, 1999)

Nicolle, David & Shpakovsky, V., Kalka River 1223: *Genghiz Khan's Mongols invade Russia* (Oxford: Osprey, 2001)

Nicolle, David & Shpakovsky, V., *Armies of the Volga Bulgars & Khanate of Kazan* (Oxford: Osprey, 2013)

Nossov, Konstantin S., *Medieval Russian Fortresses AD 862–1480* (Oxford: Osprey, 2007)

Qu, Dafeng, 'A study of Jebe's expedition to Tung Ching', *Acta Orientalia Academiae Scientiarum Hungaricae*, vol. 51, No. 1/2 (1998), pp.171–177

Qu, Dafeng, 'On the Qusiqul Army and the Tamaci Army', *Central Asiatic Journal*, vol. 45, no.2 (2001), pp.266–272

Palacky, Franz, *Der Mongolen Einfall im Jahre 1241* (Prag, 1842)

Pecchia, Vito, *Geography of 'the Secret History of the Mongols': Location of C13th Mongol Place Names and Topographical Features in NE Mongolia* (paper; 2010)

Pelliot, Paul, *Notes sur l'histoire de la Horde d'Or* (Paris: Adrien-Maisonneuve, 1949)

Pelliot, Paul, *Notes on Marco Polo*, 3 vols. (Paris, 1959, 1963, and 1973)

Pétis de la Croix, François, *History of Genghizcan the Great* (London, 1722)

Pritsak, O., 'The Polovcians and Rus', *Archivum Eurosiae Medii Aevi*, 2 (Wiesbaden: Harrassowitz, 1982), pp.320–380

Pylypchuk, Y., *Монгольское завоевание владений восточных кыпчаков и Волжской Булгарии* (Казань 2011), pp.143–156

Pylypchuk, Y., *Первое вторжение монголов в Восточную Европу (1222 г.)* (Донецк 2012), pp.325–336

de Rachewiltz, Igor, *In the Service of the Khan: Eminent personalities of the early Mongol-Yuan period* (1200–1300) (Wiesbaden: Harrassowitz, 1992)

Ratchnevsky, Paul, *Genghis Khan: His Life and Legacy* (Oxford: Blackwell, 1991)

Ratchnevsky, Paul, 'Sigi-Qutuqu, ein mongolischer Gefolgsman', *Central Asiatic Journal*, volume 10 (Wiesbaden, 1965)

Rossabi, Morris (ed.), *China Among Equals: the Middle Kingdom and its Neighbours, 10th–14th Centuries* (Berkeley: University of California Press, 1983)

Royle, Trevor, *A Dictionary of Military Quotations* (London: Routledge 1990)

Rudenko, K. A., 'The Mongol Conquests and Their Reflection in Material Culture of the Peoples of the Middle Volga and Kama Regions', *Golden Horde Review* (#6, 2014), pp.136–140

Sawyer, Ralph, *The Art of War* (Boulder, Colo.: Westview Press, 1994)

Sawyer, Ralph, *Fire and Water = Huo zhan yu shui gong: the art of incendiary and aquatic warfare in China* (Boulder, Colo.: Westview Press, 2004)

Schram, Stuart R., *Foundations and limits of State Power in China* (Hong Kong: Chinese University Press, 1987)

Selby, Stephen, *Chinese Archery* (Hong Kong: Hong Kong University Press, 2000)

Sinor, Denis, 'On Mongol Strategy', in Cheih-hsien Ch'en (ed.), *Proceedings of the fourth East Asian Altaistic conference* (Tainan: National Ch'engkung University, 1975), pp.238–249

Sinor, Denis, 'The Mongols in the West', *Journal of Asian History*, v.33 n.1 (1999)

Smith, John Masson, 'Mongol Manpower and Persian Population', *Journal of the Economic and Social History of the Orient*, 18 no 3 (1975), p.271–299

Spinei, Victor, *The Romanians and the Turkic Nomads North of the Danube Delta from the Tenth to the Mid-Thirteenth Century* (Leiden: Brill, 2009)

Strakosch-Grassmann, G., *Der Einfall der Mongolen in Mitteleuropa in den Jahren 1241 und 1242* (Innsbruck: Wagner, 1893)

Swietoslawski, Witold, *Arms and armour of the nomads of the great steppe in the times of the Mongol expansion* (Łódź: Oficyna Naukova MS, 1999)

Tan, Qixiang, *The Historical Atlas of China*, volume VI (Cartographic Publishing House, 1982)

Tao, Jing-Shen, 'The Move to the South and the Reign of Kao-tsung (1127–1162)', Denis Twitchett and Paul Jakov Smith (eds.), *The Cambridge History of China*, vol. 5 part 1 (Cambridge: Cambridge University Press, 2009)

Tatar, Sarolta, 'Roads used by the Mongols into Hungary, 1241–1242', *Olon Ulsyn Mongolch Erdemtnii X Ikh Khural* (Ulaan Bataar, 2012), pp.334–340

Tennant, Roger, *A History of Korea* (London: Kegan Paul International, 1996)

Thorau, Peter, *The Lion of Egypt: Sultan Baybars I and the Near East in the Thirteenth Century* (London: Longman, 1987)

Togan, Isenbeke, *Flexibility & Limitation in Steppe Formations, The Kerait Khanate & Chinggis Khan* (Leiden: Brill, 1998)

Togan, Isenbeke, 'The Qongrat in History', *History and Historiography of Post-Mongol Central Asia and the Middle East* (Wiesbaden, 2006), pp.61–83

Torrens-Spence, Johnny, *Historic battlefields of Pakistan* (Karachi: Oxford University Press, 2006)

Tsang, Shi-lung, *War and peace in Northern Sung China: Violence and Strategy in Flux 960–1104* (Arizona: University of Arizona, 1997)

Tsurtsumia, Mamuka, 'Couched Lance and Mounted Shock Combat in the East: The Georgian Experience', *Journal of Medieval Military History*, XII (2014)

Twitchett, Denis & Tietze, Klaus-Peter, The Liao, in Herbert Franke and Denis Twitchett (eds.), *The Cambridge History of China*, vol. 6 (Cambridge 1994), pp.321–413

Vernadsky, G., *Kievan Russia*, vol. 2 (New Haven: Yale University Press, 1948)

Vernadsky, G., *The Mongols and Russia*, vol. 3 (New Haven: Yale University Press, 1953)

Vernadsky, G., *A History of Russia*, vol. 3, (New Haven: Yale University Press, 1970)

Verbruggen, J. F., *The Art of Warfare in Western Europe during the Middle Ages: from the eighth century to 1340* (Woodbridge: Boydell Press, 1997)

Waldron, Arthur, *The Great Wall of China: from history to myth* (Cambridge: Cambridge University Press, 1990)

Walker, C. C., *Jenghiz Khan* (London: J. Darby, 1939)

Wang, Xueliang, *Ideal versus reality: Han Shizhong and the founding of the Southern Song 1127–1142* (University of Arizona, 2000)

Westermann, Georg, *Grosser Atlas zur Weltgeschichte* (Braunschweig: G. Westermann, 1976)

Wittfogel, Karl A. & Feng, Chia-Sheng, *History of Chinese Society: Liao 907–1125* (Philadelphia: American Philosophical Society, 1949)

Wright, David C., 'Mongol general Bayan and the massacre of Changzhou in 1275', *Calgary Papers Military and Strategic Studies*, 12 (2008), pp.105–116

Wu, Pei-Yi, 'Yang Miaozhen: A woman warrior in thirteenth-century China', *NAN NÜ* (vol. 4, #2, 2002), pp.137–169

Zenkovsky, S. A. (ed.), *Medieval Russia's epics, chronicles, and tales* (New York: Dutton, 1974)

Zhongsan, Xue and Yi, *Ouyang: A Sino-Western calendar for two thousand years 1–2000 A.D.* (Taipei, 1970)

Zhou, Qingshu, 'A critical examination of the year of birth of Chinggis Khan', in Luo, Xin, *Chinese Scholars on Inner Asia* (Bloomington: Indiana University, 2012), pp.331–352

Zimonyi, Istvan, 'The First Mongol Raid Against the Volga-Bulgars', *Altaistic studies* (Stockholm, 1985), pp.197–203

Mongols as military supermen

Cahun, Leon, *Introduction al'histoire de l'Asie; Turcs et Mongols, des origins a 1405* (Paris, 1896)

Chambers, James, *The Devil's Horsemen, The Mongol Invasion of Europe* (London: Cassell, 1988)

Dupuy, Trevor N., *The Military Life of Genghis: Khan of Khans* (London, 1969)

Dupuy, Richard E. & Dupuy Trevor N., *The Encyclopedia of Military History: from 3500 B.C. to the Present* (New York: Harper & Row, 1986)

Gabriel, Richard A., *Subotai the Valiant: Genghis Khan's Greatest General* (Westport, Conn.: Praeger, 2004)

de Hartog, Leo, *Genghis Khan, Conqueror of the World* (London: I. B. Tauris & Co. Ltd., 1989)

de Hartog, Leo, *Russia and the Mongol Yoke: the history of the Russian principalities and the Golden Horde, 1221–1502* (New York: British Academic Press, 1996)

Keegan, John, *Intelligence in War: knowledge of the enemy from Napoleon to al-Qaeda* (London: Hutchinson, 2003)

Hugh Kennedy, Hugh, *Mongols, Huns, and Vikings: Nomads at War* (London: Cassell, 2002)

Lamb, Harold, *Genghis Khan, The Emperor of All Men* (New York: R. M. McBride and Co., 1927)

Lamb, Harold, *The March of the Barbarians* (New York: Doubleday, Doran & Co., 1940)

Lamb, Harold, *The Earth Shakers* (Garden City, New York: Doubleday & Company Inc., 1949)

Liddell Hart, B. H., 'Two Great Captains: Jenghiz Khan and Sabutai', *Blackwood's Magazine*, vol. 215 (W. Blackwood, 1924), p.646

Liddell Hart, B. H., *Great Captains Unveiled*, chapter 1: Jenghiz Khan and Sabotai (Salem: Ayer Co. Publishing Inc., 1928, reprinted 1984)

Liddell Hart, B. H., *Strategy* (New York: Praeger, 1967)

Marshall, Robert, *Storm from the East: from Genghis Khan to Khubilai Khan* (London: BBC Books, 1993)

Prawdin, Michael, *Tschingis-Chan und seine Erben* (Stuttgart/Berlin, 1938)

Reid, Robert W., *A brief political and military chronology of the Medieval Mongols, from the birth of Chinggis Qan to the death of Qubilai Qaghan* (Bloomington: The Mongolia Society, 2002)

Turnbull, Stephen, *The Mongols* (Oxford: Osprey, 1980)

Turnbull, Stephen, *Genghis Khan & the Mongol Conquests, 1190–1400* (Oxford, 2003)

Index

INDEX OF PLACES

INDEX OF PEOPLE

INDEX OF GENERAL TERMS

CHRONICLES & HISTORIES